A HISTORY OF ZIONISM

A HISTORY OF
ZIONISM

Walter Laqueur

With a new preface by the author

SCHOCKEN BOOKS, NEW YORK

All rights reserved under International and Pan-American
Copyright Conventions. Published in the United States by
Schocken Books, a division of Random House, Inc., New York,
and simultaneously in Canada by Random House
of Canada, Limited, Toronto. Distributed by Pantheon Books,
a division of Random House, Inc., New York. Originally published in
hardcover in the United Kingdom by Weidenfeld & Nicolson, Ltd.,
London, and in the United States by Holt, Rinehart and Winston,
New York, in 1972. Originally published in paperback in the
United States by Schocken Books, Inc., in 1976.

Library of Congress Cataloging in Publication Data
Laqueur, Walter Ze'ev, 1921–
A history of Zionism.
Bibliography: p.
Includes index.
ISBN 0-8052-1149-7
1. Zionism—History. I. Title.
[DS149.L256 1976]   956.94'001   75-36491

Printed in the United States of America
8 ['03] 9 7

To the memory of my parents

CONTENTS

MAPS

Illustrations between pages 312 and 313

ACKNOWLEDGMENTS

We would like to thank the following for permitting us to use photographs from their archives: Bassano and Vandyk Studies and William Gordon Davis, figure 15; Imperial War Museum, figure 16; The Jewish Agency, Jerusalem, figures 1, 2, 4, 5, 6, 7, 8, 9, 10, 11, 12, 17, 20, 22, 23, 24, 25, 26, 27; The Jewish Agency, London, figures 3, 13, 18, 21; *Radio Times* Hulton Picture Library, figures 14, 19.

Maps 1, 2, 3, 5, and 6 are reproduced from *Jewish History Atlas* by Martin Gilbert (cartography by Arthur Banks). Map 4 is drawn by Arthur Banks from *United Palestine Appeal 1941 Yearbook*, New York, 1941.

GLOSSARY

Agudat Israel religious-orthodox, non-Zionist political movement, founded 1912.

Ahdut Ha'avoda (Labour unity) Jewish workers' party, 1919–30.

Aliya immigration to Israel.

Betar (Brit Trumpeldor) Revisionist youth organisation, founded 1923.

Brit Shalom (Peace Covenant) Jewish association advocating Jewish-Arab rapprochement, *c.* 1925–33.

Endziel the final aim (of the Zionist movement).

Galut diaspora.

Gdud Avoda Labour Legion (1920–7).

Gegenwartsarbeit Zionist work in the diaspora.

Hagana (defence) Jewish defence organisation.

Halukka distribution of alms from abroad among the orthodox community in Jerusalem.

Halutz pioneer.

Hapoel Hatzair (The Young Worker) Jewish workers' party (1905–30).

Hashomer (The Watchman) Jewish watchmen organisation before the First World War.

Hashomer Hatzair (The Young Watchman) left-wing socialist movement, founded as a youth movement in 1913.

Haskala enlightenment.

Hassidim mystical-religious trend in east European Jewry.

Hatiqva (hope) Zionist and Israeli national anthem.

Heder primary religious school.

Histadrut the Israeli General Federation of Trade Unions, established 1920.

Hoveve Zion (The Lovers of Zion) pre-Herzlian Zionist organisation.

Irgun Zvai Leumi (IZL) national military organisation (Revisionist), 1931–48.

Kibbush Avoda Conquest of (Jewish) Labour.

Kibbutz collective agricultural settlement.

Kvutza collective agricultural settlement.

Lehi Fighters for the Freedom of Israel (Stern group), 1940–8.

Mapai Labour party, founded 1930.

Maskil supporter of the *Haskala*.

Mizrahi Zionist religious party, founded 1902.

Moshav Ovdim cooperative agricultural settlement.

Poale Zion (The Workers of Zion) Socialist party, established 1903.

Shekel ancient coin, annual membership fee providing the right to vote for the Zionist Congress.

Va'ad Leumi National Council (of Palestinian Jewry), 1920–48.

Yishuv (settlement) the Jewish population of Palestine.

Zohar the Revisionist Party, founded 1925.

A note on spelling

Zionist leaders of East European origin have used at different stages of their life various spellings of their names in their publications. An attempt to unify the spelling has been made, but it has been impossible to achieve full consistency; the same applies to the transliteration of Hebrew names.

PREFACE

to the 2003 Edition

Theodor Herzl has entered political history as the author of two small books: a political pamphlet titled *Der Judenstaat* (The Jewish State) and a work of political science fiction he called *Altneuland* (Old New Land). *Altneuland*, published in 1902, describes the visit to Palestine, after an absence of many years, of two Europeans sympathetic to the Zionist cause. Confronting a Jewish state for the first time, they are awestruck by the enormous achievements that have been made, over and above what even the most enthusiastic visitors could reasonably have expected. Had they postponed their visit a bit longer, their amazement would have been even greater. Even those who knew Palestine in 1948, the year the Jewish state actually came into being, would not recognize it today. The number of Jews living in Palestine in 1948 was about half a million; it has increased tenfold since. Palestine was a tiny community at that time; Israel today is more populous than half a dozen European countries, including Norway and Finland. It absorbed during its first years of statehood a population of immigrants three times larger than the population already living in the country, a feat unique in the annals of mankind. Many hundreds of new cities, towns, and suburbs came into being. While for years Israel depended on outside financial help, it gradually became economically independent. Its standard of living is comparable to that of many European countries, it has a vibrant cultural life, with many universities, theaters, and symphony orchestras, and its scientific institutions are second to none (as indeed Herzl had envisaged). In reports produced by international organizations that measure various types of economic and social progress, Israel usually appears among the first ten or twenty countries. But the quality of its domestic political life is far from ideal. There are too many political parties, and there has been corruption at even the highest levels of government; minorities have not always been treated fairly. But elections are still free, and the judiciary is still independent. The media enjoy almost complete freedom. It is the only democracy in a part of the world in which democracies are conspicuously absent.

Militarily, Israel does not depend on outside help but has armed forces capable in every respect of defending itself. And yet the Jewish state finds itself in serious trouble during the sixth decade of its existence. Contemporary visitors to *Altneuland,* having been duly impressed by the extraordinary achievements, are bound to ask whether the society that came into being still corresponds in any significant way to the dreams of Herzl and the other early leaders of the Zionist movement.

Let us be realistic: *Altneuland* was, of course, a utopia, and utopias are seldom realized. In the inevitable collision between dreams and realties, realities inevitably prove stronger. Herzl and his contemporaries did not really expect the Jewish state to be somehow superior, more highly accomplished, more ethically motivated than other countries; they were primarily looking for a refuge for the persecuted Jewish people and were aware of how difficult it would be simply to build a country like all others. If Israel has not lived up to expectations, it is certainly true that many of the countries that came into being after World War II have been disappointments to those who envisioned them and fought to bring them into being. Some of the basic reasons for such disappointments are rooted in history, and it would be pointless to put the blame on human shortcomings. It was the historical tragedy of Zionism (as I note in the last chapter of this book) that it appeared very late on the international scene, but it could not have appeared earlier on. The great majority of Jews did not want a state of their own before the twentieth century, and when storm clouds appeared on the horizon (and it is the historical merit of Zionism that it recognized this earlier than all others), when it became increasingly urgent to find a refuge for the Jews of Europe, the gates of Palestine were virtually closed. Nor was there sufficient willingness on the part of European and American Jewry to invest energy and financial resources in building a Jewish national home.

When the war began, a few hundred thousand Jews had found refuge in Palestine, but millions more eventually perished. At the end of the war the great reservoir of European Jewry that the Zionists had hoped would build the Jewish state had disappeared. The Jews of Palestine wanted a state of their own because there was no realistic political alternative. To almost everyone's surprise they resisted the onslaught of the armies of the neighboring Arab countries that resulted when they declared their independence. But it was also clear that the demographic base necessary for a viable state was far too small, and so the "ingathering of the exiles" became the commandment of the hour. This led to a profound social and cultural change in the composition of the population of the new country. Zionism had been a European Jewish movement. Among the Jews in the Oriental countries there was a messianic religious belief in the ultimate return to Zion—or at least a feeling of historical attachment to it—but there was no overwhelming urge to move to Palestine. Zionist organizations in those countries were very small or nonexistent.

There was, however, an increase in anti-Semitism in the Middle East and North Africa during World War II and during the years leading up to it, and there was also a rise in those countries of a xenophobic nationalism. Foreigners were expelled from Egypt, and there were pogroms in Iraq, Libya, and elsewhere. The majority of Jews in these countries would have had to leave anyway, and for a considerable number of them (not, however, the well-to-do and the intelligentsia) Israel was the obvious haven. It is doubtful in retrospect whether this was true with regard to Moroccan Jews; they were the largest of the Jewish communities of the Middle East and North Africa and lived (as many of them later argued) more or less in peace with their neighbors. By urging this community to move to Israel, the enthusiastic Zionist emissaries created problems which, in all probability, they could not have predicted. North African immigrants complained about discrimination and exploitation. This was certainly not true on the political level—presidents of Israel came from among their ranks, as well as foreign and defense ministers, army chiefs of staff, etc. But a great many of the Sephardic immigrants were unhappy in their new homeland, complaining about their inferior social status and their dismal living conditions. They were not Zionist pioneers, as the early settlers from Eastern and Central Europe had been, and their expectations were high. They were unwilling to put up with the living conditions in the hastily constructed development towns to which they had been sent. They expected the state to take better care of their social and economic needs, but the state was not financially able to do so. And even if the state had done more, they would still have had legitimate complaints about European paternalism and a lack of national respect for their culture and traditions. By and large, Sephardic feelings of solidarity with their Ashkenazic coreligionists were strictly limited. Eventually they established their own political party to defend their interests, a party that while anti-Arab was not classically Zionist in character.

In the wake of the collapse of the Soviet Union in 1991, approximately one million Soviet Jews arrived in Israel. Few had expected this, and I had certainly not imagined that a Russian translation of this book would appear in Moscow in my lifetime. The great majority of former Soviet citizens who arrived in Israel in the 1990s (in contrast to the Soviet Jews who had arrived in the preceding two decades) were not Zionists; a significant percentage were not even Jewish (the spouses, children, or grandchildren of Jews, they were eligible for Israeli citizenship under Israel's Law of Return). They came simply in the hope of creating a better life for themselves and their families. Yet their economic absorption into Israel proceeded more smoothly than most had envisioned, most likely because they were better educated than the Sephardic Jews who had arrived decades earlier. The difficulties with the absorption of Soviet Jews into Israeli society exist on a different level: many of them proudly maintain their own cultural traditions, and they show little interest in shedding them to become part of a homogeneous Israeli society.

"We are a people. One people," Herzl had declared to thunderous acclaim in a famous speech at one of the early Zionist congresses. But was this still true? There certainly had been a single, united Jewish people at one time, but Zionism had probably come too late to reunite it. Over the centuries of exile its various branches had gone their own ways. Jews throughout the world still shared some common beliefs and traditions, and they felt a degree of responsibility for one another during times of crisis. But most of them no longer believed in the biblical notion of redemption and in the ancient prophets' promised rebuilding of the Israelite Kingdom.

The Jewish community in Palestine in 1948 consisted largely of a Labor Zionist cultural and political elite; massive influxes of new immigrants, most of them not Socialists and/or Zionists in the classic political sense, have led to societal polarization. The pre-state Zionists had succeeded in creating one of the world's most egalitarian societies; today Israel rivals only the United States among developed nations as the country with the most pronounced disparities between the wealthy and the poor in income and economic status. This trend has been accompanied by an equally unfortunate ideological polarization. In every democracy there is a political left wing and a political right wing; often there are also extreme left-wing and extreme right-wing fringe elements. Although the issues at stake in Israel no longer involve capitalism versus socialism (in fact, the wealthy suburbs vote overwhelmingly for the Labor party, while the economically disadvantaged development towns opt for the right-wing parties), the growing influence of both left-wing and right-wing extremists portend a national crisis.

Over the past thirty years a belief has gained ground among the right wing that the entire historical Palestine is "ours by divine right." This has resulted, among other things, in the mushrooming of settlements in areas of the West Bank and Gaza that have been occupied by Israel since the Six-Day War in 1967. Most of them do not make sense either economically or militarily, and defending and guarding them ties down a considerable part of Israel's army. They are also a major obstacle on the road to some form of peaceful coexistence with the Palestinians. The pseudo-religious mysticism that rationalizes their existence would have been wholly alien to earlier generations of Zionist thinkers who, while giving all due deference to traditional religious practices, were profoundly secular in outlook and would have regarded with abhorrence the intrusion of religion into politics. If the lack of governmental planning in advance of the "ingathering of the exiles" in the 1950s was a serious mistake, the failure of the State of Israel in those years to adopt a written constitution that provided for a division between religion and state was another.

This new manifestation of right-wing nationalism is not, as Herzl's Zionism had been, a product of the Enlightenment; it is not connected with the struggle for political liberty and a free society. It fears alien influences, is antagonistic to strangers, and does not count individual freedom among its primary concerns. As one of the ideologues of this new creed put it, "This Zionism does not seek to solve the problem of the Jews by setting up a Jewish state, but it is an instrument in the hands of the Almighty which prepared the people of Israel for their Redemption." Pre-state Zionism had not been based on religious zealotry and chauvinism. And even the religious Zionism of that era had stressed the international, universal message of Torah and redemption, rather than national egotism. To the Revisionist Zionist leader Vladimir Jabotinsky, a nationalist in the liberal nineteenth-century mold, the anti-Western, isolationist character of today's right-wing Zionism would have been incomprehensible and repugnant.

What caused such changes to the character of post-independence Zionism? Probably it was the *annus mirabilis* of 1967, which culminated in a nationwide abandonment of a sense of reality regarding the newly acquired land. The rise of worldwide fundamentalism might also have played a part, as well as a decline in the quality of national leadership. Pre-state Zionism had attracted formidable intellects and visionary leaders. In recent decades there has been a notable decline in the quality of national leadership; those who could and should have been leaders were put off by the rough-and-tumble of Israeli politics and looked instead for fulfillment in other fields of endeavor. Such a decline in the quality of leadership has taken place in countries throughout the world. But a newly created and embattled country such as Israel, a country by no means universally accepted, needs an enlightened and farsighted leadership more than any other.

And as if this were not enough, post-independence Zionism has been afflicted by two other plagues, essentially not new but appearing in new guises. One is the ultra-Orthodox, or *haredi*, camp, which in Eastern Europe had rejected and fought Zionism tooth and nail from the very beginnings of the movement. In Palestine, too, there had long been a small anti-Zionist ultra-Orthodox community in Jerusalem's Mea She'arim neighborhood and in a few other areas as well, which kept strictly apart from the Jewish community and its organizations. But since 1948 ultra-Orthodox neighborhoods have greatly expanded (due in part to the high birth rate in ultra-Orthodox families). The numbers of adult men attending yeshivot (religious seminaries) has increased dramatically between 1948 and the present day. All this would have mattered little if, as in the pre-state days, the *haredim* would have essentially kept to themselves. But they have instead become increasingly involved in the Israeli government and have used their increased numbers to compel the state to support their institutions and to finance their way of life. (They refuse to serve in the army and many of them are not gainfully employed.) In recent years they have begun to impose their religious restrictions on the rest of the Israeli population, causing bitter conflicts and something akin to a *Kulturkampf* in Jerusalem and in other cities.

On a certain level, Zionism had been founded as an expression of opposition to the way of life of the Eastern European ghetto, and one of its main missions in Israel was to create a productive society in contrast to the parasitical life so commonly associated with the *shtetl*. Yet the ghetto and its mentality proved to be resilient, and it has come back to haunt the Zionists in the country they had created. Given the fragmentation of Israeli political life, the ultra-Orthodox have achieved a degree of influence, in the Israeli Knesset and in municipalities, that is out of proportion with their numbers. They have also succeeded in extending their influence beyond the Ashkenazic community and into some sections of the Sephardic Jewish community, even as they disdained the latter's ancient religious and cultural practices.

Zionism's other long-time antagonist is also an old acquaintance that now appears in a new guise and has been renamed post-Zionism. In the early years of the twentieth century, Communists, Trotskyites, and related political groups waged ideological war against Zionism (including left-wing Zionism) because of what they termed its reactionary, imperialist, and colonialist character. The Jews, they believed, had no right to a state of their own because this could be achieved only by expelling another people who were already living on the land they claimed as their own. Zionists were either being dishonest or deluding themselves when they described Palestine as a "land without people." But the Zionists had never sincerely argued this, and Arabs do appear in Herzl's *Altneuland*. When Herzl convened the first Zionist Congress in 1897 the inhabitants of Palestine numbered approximately 500,000 and included, in addition to Jews (approximately eight percent of the population) and Muslims, Christian Arabs, Greeks, Armenians, and members of other ethnic and religious groups. Perhaps Herzl might be forgiven for assuming that the presence of a few hundred thousand people did not present an insurmountable obstacle to his plans. The 1896 edition of Baedeker's *Guide to Vienna* gives the number of the inhabitants of the city in which Herzl lived as 1,364,500; in other words, the non-Jewish residents of Palestine totaled a little more than one-third of the population of the Austrian capital. The next sentence in Baedeker's guide helps to explain why the idea of Zionism occurred to Herzl in the first place. The stated population figures, it says, "includ[e] 118,000 Jews and 22,651 soldiers." There lived in Vienna at the time tens of thousands of Poles, Czechs, Croats, Hungarians, Italians, and Slovenians, among numerous other national groups. But only the Jews received special mention; perhaps they were thought to be transients, like the soldiers mentioned along with them.

Marxism went out of intellectual fashion in the last quarter of the twentieth century, but the impulses underlying it did not. Hence the appearance of new socio-political concepts, such as post-colonialism, of which post-Zionism is an offshoot. (The actual term "post-Zionism" is, of course, value free; it appears on the first page of the preface to the first edition of this book, which was published well before contemporary Israeli post-Zionists arrived on the scene.) The contemporary post-Zionists belong to a generation of Israeli academics that has never personally experienced anti-Semitism, for whom the Holocaust is not a real historical experience, who did not have to face the danger of destruction and to flee Europe to save their lives. Their rejection of Zionism (and frequently also of Israel) is, nevertheless, psychologically understandable as a rebellion against their parents' and grandparents' generations.

The post-Zionists' deconstruction of Zionist ideology resulted in a number of discoveries that they considered to be of great importance. They found that many of the stories taught in school and based on the Old Testament were not rooted in fact but in mythology. It was not a certainty that the Israelites had ever lived in Egypt or crossed the Red Sea, and Joshua's trumpet had in all probability not caused the crumbling of the walls of Jericho. King David's kingdom had not been a major nation but was most likely a small principality; and there was even some doubt as to whether or not King David had ever really existed. In their enthusiasm, these post-Zionists tended to forget that the origins of every religion—indeed, of any nation from ancient Greece and Rome onward—is not grounded in historical fact but, rather, is shrouded in myth. Testing their theories against more recent historical events, they now doubt whether the mortally wounded Yosef Trumpeldor ever said at Tel Hai that it was good to die for one's country. Sometimes their arguments were inconsistent: on the one hand they maintain that the Zionists should never have settled in Palestine in the first place, but at the same time they blame them for not having done enough to save

European Jewry during World War II. According to them, Zionists persuaded Jewish displaced persons to move on to Palestine after World War II even though the refugees were reluctant to do so. During Israel's War of Independence, Zionists had not treated Palestinian Arabs with sufficient humanity but, instead, either directly or indirectly engineered the expulsion of hundreds of thousands of them from their villages and then either occupied or destroyed their homes.

Academicians engaging in post-colonial studies were not many in number, but they influenced Israeli society and educational policy to the extent that the latest crop of Israeli schoolbooks included a picture of Gamal Abdul Nasser but not one of David Ben Gurion. The problem with post-Zionism was not that its premises were incorrect, but that what was correct was not new, and what was new was not correct. Post-Zionists seemed to be unwilling to acknowledge the fact (and here they deviated from Marxists, who were far more realistic in this respect) that no nation has ever come into being by friendly persuasion or through a legal contract. Nation-states are rarely born without violence. They have from time immemorial produced innocent victims, and there is no reason to assume that the birth of an Israeli nation would be any different in this respect.

This book is a history of Zionism, not of the State of Israel and even less of the ongoing Israeli-Arab conflict. But the conflict cannot be ignored, for it has had a considerable effect on both pre- and post-1948 Zionist ideology. Palestinian Arabs were deprived of a country of their own as a result of the establishment of Israel, but many Israelis found it difficult to look at the situation from their point of view: Did they not live better than before? Was their lot not preferable to that of Arabs in Israel's neighboring countries? The Palestinian Arabs, on the other hand, failed to understand that their misfortune was at least in part of their own doing, since they had rejected the initial idea of establishing a single bi-national state in Mandatory Palestine, and then went on to reject all other suggested two-state compromises.

It was the misfortune of Zionism that its ancient homeland should be located in the middle of a particularly troubled part of the world, one that has shown in modern times a particular ineptitude in establishing democratic societies and in making social and economic progress. The travails, the frustrations, the resentments of the people of the Muslim and Arab world are well known and need not be discussed in detail here. The very existence of a Jewish state within this world is seen by these people as a provocation, and it is not surprising that Israel has borne the brunt of much of their rage and frustration.

It is more than doubtful that a conflict between Israelis and Palestinians could have been prevented, given the fact that two peoples were claiming the same land. But far from trying to defuse the conflict and prevent its spread, Israeli policy has often added fuel to it, thus increasing the dangers confronting the state. Prior to 1967 there was nothing for Israel to discuss with its Arab neighbors because they rejected the very existence of Israel. But after the Six-Day War Israel was in a position to make concessions; it waited for Arab initiatives that never came. But why should it have surrendered the occupied territories in the West Bank and Gaza if the Arabs were still unwilling to make peace? For the simple reason that Israel could not indefinitely impose its rule over so many people who did not want to live in a Jewish state and at the same time maintain the democratic character of the country. Establishing Jewish settlements in the middle of a hostile Arab population was not an answer; on the contrary, it aggravated the problem. Sooner or later the settlements would have to be given up, and the longer this was delayed, the more painful it was going to be. The second sin of omission concerned the Arab citizens of Israel. There is no certainty that they would have become Israeli patriots if they had been given full equality, or even if preferential treatment had been given to them. But only a halfhearted attempt was made to integrate them into Israeli society, and there were too many promises that were not fulfilled.

The question of Jerusalem illustrates best the enormous difference between historical Zionism and the ideology that has replaced it. Jerusalem contains the holy places of three world religions, and elementary prudence if not basic tolerance should have prevented declarations according to which Jerusalem was to remain forever undivided under Israeli rule. It was in any case an empty declaration, for in actual fact Jerusalem is of course a divided city. When Herzl first visited Jerusalem he saw only the musty deposits of two thousand years of inhumanity, intolerance, and impurity; he perceived superstition and fanaticism on all sides. It was not surprising that he suggested Haifa as the capital of the new Jewish state. But it was not only Herzl, the assimilated Jew, who reacted in this unsentimental manner. Chaim Weizmann always feared becoming involved in the Jerusalem imbroglio. And because their emotional attachment to the city was not overwhelming, David Ben Gurion and other leaders of the second aliya did not visit Jerusalem for the first time until two or three years after their arrival in the country. For many years not a single pre-state Zionist leader chose to live in Jerusalem. For them, Jerusalem symbolized the negative past of Jewish history, that part of the tradition from which they wanted to disassociate themselves. The idea that Jerusalem was the beginning and the end of Zionism, that Israel could not exist without having full sovereignty over the entire city, emerged only after 1967 and with the growth of a religious fanaticism and aggressive nationalism that had more in common with the ideology of the Muslim Brotherhood than the founding fathers of Zionism.

And so, guarding the holy sites has become a nightmare and Jerusalem itself has become a dangerous flashpoint. The insanity of a few religious fanatics—Jewish, Muslim, or Christian—has the potential for transforming a local conflict into a religious war with incalculable consequences.

International opposition to Zionism reached a new climax in June 1975 with United Nations Resolution 3379, which equated Zionism with racism. This resolution was revoked after a decade, but the attitude underlying it did not change. At the United Nations World Conference Against Racism, which was held in Durban, South Africa, in the fall of 2001, Zionism was placed at the top of the list of obstacles to human rights. Israel's occupation and settlement of the West Bank and Gaza plays into the hands of those who are opposed to the very existence of a Jewish state, and it is used by them not only to delegitimize the State of Israel, but for other, more nefarious purposes. If in the decades after World War II blatant anti-Semitism has gone out of fashion, anti-Zionism has become an acceptable, politically correct outlet for it. Within Israel the temptation is great to blame all its woes on an anti-Semitic world that has never been in favor of its existence. But, to a considerable extent, the fault lies within Israel itself: the mistakes it has made, its shortsightedness, its failure to accept the fact that it is a small nation that must make compromises to survive in a region full of hostile, powerful neighbors. The Jewish genius has manifested itself over the centuries in many areas, but political wisdom has not been among them. This is perhaps the inevitable result of having been deprived for two thousand years of the experience and the responsibility of political statehood, but it is vitally needed now, as Israel and, indeed, the world as a whole face a new period of unprecedented danger.

Walter Laqueur
Washington, D.C.,
January 2003

PREFACE

The term Zionism was first used publicly by Nathan Birnbaum at a discussion meeting in Vienna on the evening of 23 January 1892.* The history of political Zionism begins with the publication of Herzl's *Judenstaat* four years later and the first Zionist congress. But the Zionist idea antedates the name and the organisation. Herzl had precursors in Germany, Russia, and in other countries, whose writings reflected the longing for the ancient homeland, the anomaly of Jewish existence in central and eastern Europe, and the need to find a solution to the 'Jewish question'.

The emergence of Zionism in the 1880s and 1890s can be understood only against the general background of European and Jewish history since the French Revolution on one hand, and the spread of modern antisemitism on the other. The present book starts with a discussion of the European background of Zionism, covers the prehistory of the movement and five decades of Zionist activities, and ends with the establishment of the state in May 1948, the turning-point in the history of the movement. It is debatable whether there is a history of Zionism beyond 1948, and not only because many of its functions have been taken over by the state of Israel. Before the word 'Zionism' became generally accepted, the term *Palestinofilstvo (Hibat Zion)* was widely used in Russia. A similar term, Philisraelism, may well provide an accurate definition of the present, post-Zionist, phase. Even if my assumption should be wrong – periodisation being a risky business – a good case can still be made, I think, for ending this history of Zionism in 1948.

Long as this book is, I was aware from the beginning that a full, detailed history of Zionism was not only beyond my capacity but also, most probably, beyond the tolerance of the non-specialist reader, not

* Strictly speaking the term had already appeared in print on a few occasions in 1890/1 without, however, any clear political connotation.

to mention the publisher. Zionism, a worldwide movement, consisted of dozens of federations and political parties. To do justice even to the more important among them an entire library of monographs would be needed. The abundance of published and unpublished material does not make the task of the historian any easier. The shelves of the Zionist Archives in Jerusalem extend for two miles; for every Zionist past or present there is a book, or at least an article in a periodical, or several issues of a newspaper. The present writer had to be selective in his approach and concentrate on what he considered the main lines of development.

This volume, with all its limitations and imperfections, is the first comprehensive history in English on a comparable scale. Of the two major histories written previously, Sokolow's comes only to the end of the First World War and is devoted largely to the precursors of political Zionism, while Böhm's *Zionistische Bewegung*, to which every work on the subject is greatly indebted, stops in the mid-1920s (it has never been translated). These books, as well as some others much briefer (such as Israel Cohen's surveys), were written by leading Zionists. They bear witness to the commitment of the writers; their very involvement is their main source of strength. A history of Zionism written now must be more than a labour of love; it should not proselytise but must ask searching questions if it is to be faithful to the truth of history.

In some respects it is easier now to write with detachment of past quarrels, and there are always the benefits of hindsight. But there are also difficulties which my predecessors did not have to face. Some of them are of a methodological character: up to 1917 the history of the Zionist movement presents no particular problems; it is the story of a somewhat eccentric movement of young idealists who met every other year at a congress and espoused various political, financial, cultural, and colonising activities. But after the Balfour Declaration at the latest, the issue becomes much more confusing: there was still the Zionist movement, more widespread and influential than before, but there was also the Jewish community of Palestine growing in numbers and strength. It may be possible to write the story of Palestine in the Mandatory era without constant reference to the Zionist movement, but it is quite impossible to do the reverse. Within Zionism, too, the situation became more complicated with each year after 1917, as new parties and factions appeared, and some of them broke away from the world movement. Up to the Balfour Declaration the most useful approach is the chronological; after that date this becomes difficult, sometimes impossible. I have tried to deal with these difficulties in my own way. There may be other and better methods, but I could not think of one. Most of this book is based on material published by, about, or against the Zionist movement in the various *linguae francae* in which these discussions were conducted: German, Russian, Yiddish, Hebrew, and English. The Zionists were a talkative tribe; no secret could be kept for long – all of them can be found somewhere in the books and journals. Through the last decade of events described in this volume I lived in Palestine, watching events and sometimes the *dramatis personae* from a close angle. This provided a certain perspective and, I believe, understanding: which is difficult to acquire from the study of archives alone. This personal element should be mentioned, for without it I probably would have lacked the incentive to write this book in the first place. I had the opportunity to discuss some of the events described here with veterans of the Zionist movement; to all of them I am grateful; one of them in particular, Robert Weltsch, has been of great help throughout. These discussions did not yield many startling new revelations, but they made for a better understanding of the metapolitics of a movement that had many facets to its character, in addition to the purely political one. I have on a few occasions made reference to unpublished material, with regard to some aspects of Zionist history which have not yet been adequately studied. But this hardly affects the general picture as it can be pieced together from generally accessible sources.

A preface is not the ideal place for the author's credo; my thoughts on the subject emerge from the following pages. The question whether Zionism was a good or a bad idea is discussed in this book, but it is not the only nor indeed the central question which has preoccupied me; it is of undoubted historical interest, and on a philosophical level the debate may well continue for a long time. This study is not, however, an exercise in the philosophy of history; it deals with the fate of a sorely tried people and their attempt to normalise their status, to escape persecution, and to regain dignity in their own eyes and in the eyes of the world. Perhaps they were wrong in pursuing this aim; perhaps their efforts were bound to create new and intractable problems. However, several decades ago Zionism moved out of the realm of the history of ideas, good, bad, or indifferent, into the field of action. It has resulted in the birth of a nation, to the joy of some and the distress of others.

It was my intention to provide a truthful account of the origins and development of one of the most embattled movements in recent history. Since I do not believe that historical truth is likely to be located somewhere in the middle between two extremes, I have not tried to disguise my own position and am aware that others may not necessarily share my views. It is, I believe, a truthful account, in the sense that I have not knowingly suppressed historical evidence and that I have tried to discuss dispassionately views which are not my own and actions which I deplore.

The apologetic character of Jewish historiography has traditionally been one of its main weaknesses. Zionism has been instrumental in changing this. Some of the most critical comments on Jewish history have emanated from Zionist ranks and, on the other hand, some of the most bitter attacks on Zionism have come from Jewish critics. I did not feel particularly self-conscious in writing this book; I did not take as my motto 'Tell it not in Gath, publish it not in the streets of Askelon'. On the other hand, I make no claim to Olympian impartiality. When Acton launched the *Cambridge Modern History*, he told his contributors that 'our Waterloo must satisfy French and English, German and Dutch alike'. Few critics would agree that this aim has been achieved, and I suspect that such a history of Zionism will be written, if ever, only when the subject has ceased to be of topical interest.

I would like to express my thanks to the Deutsche Forschungsgemein-schaft for a research grant to study the history of German Zionism, to Mr Meyer Weisgal and to the John Simon Guggenheim Memorial Foundation for a fellowship. Dr Benjamin Eliav guided me along the highways and byways of the history of revisionism but the views expressed on this as on other issues are, for better or worse, my own. Mrs Jane Degras, old friend and stern critic, read the manuscript, and I have benefited, as so often before, from her editorial skill and experience.

London–Jerusalem
1971

PART ONE

OUT OF THE GHETTO

In the history of modern Europe the French Revolution is the great divide; together with all the other changes and movements it ushered in, it also marks the beginning of a new era in the life of the Jews. After centuries of massacres, of persecution, of social ostracism, a new and more humane approach towards the Jews began to prevail with the spread of the ideas of the Enlightenment. But it needed the shock of revolution to give official sanction to the principle of equality before the law. The time would come, Herder predicted, when no one in Europe would again ask whether someone was Jewish or Christian, 'because the Jews, too, will live according to European laws and contribute their share to the common good'. In the French National Assembly of 1789 Clermont Tonnerre demanded that the Jews as individuals should be denied no rights. Emancipation spread rapidly: the Rome ghetto was opened and even in Germany, where the improvement in the status of the Jews had been discussed inconclusively for many years, there were at long last substantial changes. Between 1808 and 1812 the groundwork was laid for their full legal emancipation in Prussia, the leading German state.

They had waited for the day with impatience and they responded with enthusiasm. When the Prussian king called his subjects to the colours to fight Napoleon, the patriotic response of the Jews was second to none: 'Oh, what a heavenly feeling to possess a fatherland!' one of their manifestos proclaimed; 'Oh what a rapturous idea to call a spot, a place, a nook one's own upon this lovely earth.' Until a few years before they had been treated like pariahs. Ludwig Börne, the greatest publicist of the age, has given a graphic description of their position in his native Frankfurt when he was young. They enjoyed, as he put it, the loving care of the authorities: they were forbidden to leave their street on Sundays, so that the drunks should not molest them; they were not permitted to marry before the age of twenty-five, so that their offspring

3

should be strong and healthy; on holidays they could leave their homes only at six in the evening, so that the great heat should not cause them any harm; the public gardens and promenades outside the city were closed to them and they had to walk in the fields – to awaken their interest in agriculture; if a Jew crossed the street and a Christian citizen shouted, 'Pay your respects, Jud', the Jew had to remove his hat, no doubt the intention of this wise measure being to strengthen the feelings of love and respect between Christians and Jews.

European Jewry suffered setbacks on the road towards full legal emancipation: Napoleon revoked some of the rights the revolution had bestowed on them, and the Prussian king and the German princes reimposed in 1815 many of the old restrictions. Many professions were still barred to them: only one Jewish officer was retained in the Prussian army, and with the exception of a postman in the city of Breslau there were no Jewish civil servants. A decree issued in the 1820s prohibited them from acting as executioners if any of them had felt the inclination to do so. The veterans of the patriotic war, some of them bearers of the Iron Cross, complained bitterly that they were treated like step-children by their new fatherland. And yet, despite these disappointments, there was little doubt among German Jewry that these setbacks were only temporary. They firmly believed that full citizenship would soon be theirs by right and not on sufferance, and that reason and humanism would eventually prevail in the counsels of their government. The new Jewish establishment that had emerged was confident that they had already joined the mainstream of European civilisation.

At the beginning of the nineteenth century the number of Jews in the world was about two and a half million; almost 90 per cent of them lived in Europe. There were roughly two hundred thousand in Germany, one-quarter of them concentrated in Posen, the eastern district recently acquired by Prussia as a result of the partition of Poland. Most of them still lived in the countryside; few had been permitted to reside in the big cities. Berlin, for instance, counted barely three thousand in 1815. The bürger, and especially the city guilds, were strongly opposed to Jews settling in their midst. During the Middle Ages many had engaged in usury and other base forms of trade. During the eighteenth century their occupational range gradually widened but most of them were still small traders, middlemen between the cities and the villages. They frequented the fairs, bought and sold meat, wool, and spirits; in Hesse they traded

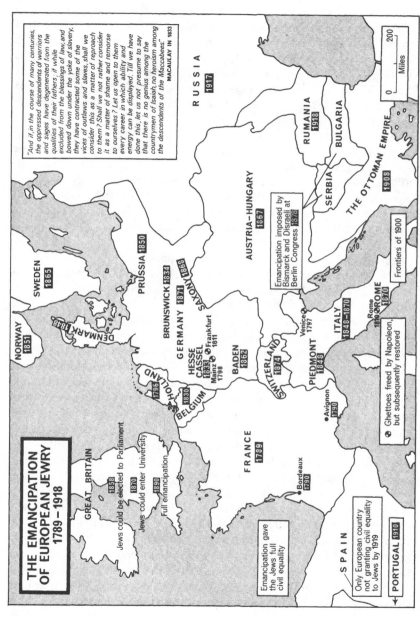

THE EMANCIPATION
OF EUROPEAN JEWRY
1789–1918

GREAT BRITAIN
1858 Jews could be elected to Parliament
1870 Jews could enter University
1830 Full emancipation

Emancipation gave the Jews full civil equality

NORWAY 1851
SWEDEN 1865
DENMARK 1848

HOLLAND 1796
BELGIUM 1830

PRUSSIA 1850

BRUNSWICK 1834
SAXONY 1868
GERMANY
HESSE CASSEL 1833
Mainz 1798 ● Frankfurt 1811
BADEN 1862

FRANCE 1789

Bordeaux 1790
● Avignon 1790

SWITZERLAND 1874

PIEDMONT 1848

ITALY 1848–1870
Venice 1797
Rome 1810 ● ROME 1870

● Ghettoes freed by Napoleon, but subsequently restored

Frontiers of 1900

SPAIN

Only European country not granting civil equality to Jews by 1919

◄ PORTUGAL 1910

AUSTRIA–HUNGARY 1867

RUSSIA 1917

RUMANIA 1918

SERBIA

BULGARIA 1908

THE OTTOMAN EMPIRE

Emancipation imposed by Bismarck and Disraeli at Berlin Congress 1878

0   200
Miles

"And if, in the course of many centuries, the oppressed descendents of warriors and sages have degenerated from the qualities of their fathers; if, while excluded from the blessings of law, and bowed down under the yoke of slavery, they have contracted some of the vices of outlaws and slaves, shall we consider this as a matter of reproach to them? Shall we not rather consider it as a matter of shame and remorse to ourselves? Let us open to them every career in which ability and energy can be displayed. Till we have done this, let us not presume to say that there is no genius among the countrymen of Isaiah, no heroism among the descendents of the Maccabees."

MACAULAY IN 1833

Map 1

in cattle, in Alsace they acquired a strong position in the wine trade. In the formerly Polish territories there were many Jewish artisans but their existence was precarious; their position was as remote from the wealth and status of the members of the city guilds as that of the little Jewish hawkers from the 'royal merchants' of Hamburg or Lübeck. As a Jew, Moses Mendelssohn wrote to a friend, my son can become only a physician, a trader, or a beggar. True, a few Jewish bankers had become very rich, such as the Eichtals, the Speiers, the Seligmans, Oppenheims, Hirschs, and above all the Rothschilds. There were more Jewish than non-Jewish banking establishments in Berlin in 1807, and it has been said that without them no European government would have been able to float a loan during the first half of the nineteenth century. To quote but one example: more than 80 per cent of the state loans of the Bavarian government during the first decade of the century were provided by Jewish bankers. But this new aristocracy of money was numerically small; a Jewish middle class was just beginning to emerge, while the great majority were living in extreme poverty. Substantial changes in the occupational structure of German Jewry took place only in the following decades with the great influx of young Jews into the professions, wholesale and retail trade, and industry.

The beginnings of social and cultural assimilation date back to the early eighteenth century. The notion (prevalent for a long time) that the emancipation of German Jews started when Moses Mendelssohn played chess with Lessing does not stand up to investigation. Many Jews spoke and wrote in German in the first half of the eighteenth century; their common language (Yiddish, Jargon), though written in Hebrew letters, became closer and closer to the colloquial German spoken at the time. Many also had a working knowledge of other languages. While Frankfurt and other cities still kept their Jews penned together like cattle in dark overcrowded ghettoes, elsewhere they were not confined to special living quarters and social intercourse with their Christian neighbours was not uncommon. Even in their outward appearance many of them were hardly distinguishable from their neighbours: they shaved their beards and wore periwigs, while young ladies adopted the crinoline and other such fashionable garments. The rabbis complained bitterly about the new freedom in relations between the sexes and other manifestations of moral decline, but their authority and everything they stood for was rapidly declining. The knowledge of Hebrew among their congregations was usually limited to the recital (by rote) of a few prayers; observance of the religious law was, to say the least, imperfect, and the more pessimistic rabbis already lamented the impending end of traditional Judaism.

What gave Moses Mendelssohn his importance was not that he was a great philosopher, major essayist, or revolutionary theologian. His philosophical writings were quickly forgotten and his attempts to prove the existence of God were neither original nor did they have a lasting impact. His main achievement was to show, by his own example, that despite all adversity a Jew could have a thorough knowledge of modern culture and converse on equal terms with the shining lights of contemporary Europe. Born in Dessau in 1729 in abject poverty, he earned his livelihood as a private tutor and later as an accountant. Devouring the libraries to which he had access, his efforts to educate himself attracted the attention of non-Jewish well-wishers; within a few years he had published weighty studies on Leibniz's philosophy and the problem of evidence in the metaphysical sciences. A hunchback of fascinating ugliness, he stoically bore all the chicanery and degradations to which Jews in his time were still exposed, including, for instance, the famous head tax imposed on Jews and cattle moving from town to town. In his private life – as the letters to his bride bear witness – Mendelssohn was a man of angelic patience and high idealism, a living contradiction of the clichés about the depravity, fanaticism and ignorance of Jews. His name figured prominently in the arguments of those late eighteenth-century reformers who favoured the abolition of the laws and regulations keeping the Jews in a state of semi-servitude.

Mendelssohn's translation of the Bible into German was welcomed by many Jews in his day as a liberating act, and denounced as an act of betrayal by others. For nineteenth-century liberal Jewry he was the greatest Jew of modern times, whereas later generations have been more critical in their appraisal of his work. A typical son of the Enlightenment, Mendelssohn taught that Judaism was a *Vernunftsreligion*, that there was no contradiction between religious belief and critical reason. This was sweet music to the ears of all the educated Jews who were open or secret admirers of the French Enlightenment; it is said that Voltaire had more supporters in Jewish homes in Germany at the time than anywhere else. At the same time Mendelssohn's teaching was anathema to many orthodox rabbis who suspected, not altogether wrongly, that his reforms were a half-way house on the road to apostasy. In contrast to the liberal reformers, they believed that in order to survive, Judaism needed the exclusivity of the ghetto. Admired by many, bitterly denounced by others, Moses Mendelssohn became a landmark in modern

Jewish history, not so much because of what he did, as for what he was: the very symbol of Jewish emancipation.

Despite the reimposition of restrictive laws, social assimilation made rapid progress during the early decades of the nineteenth century. Many Jews moved from the villages into larger towns, where they could find better living quarters; they sent their children to non-Jewish schools and modernised their religious service. Among the intellectuals there was a growing conviction that the new Judaism, purged of medieval obscurantism, was an intermediate stage towards enlightened Christianity. They argued that the Jews were not a people; Jewish nationhood had ceased to exist two thousand years before, and now lived on only in memories. Dead bones could not be exhumed and restored to life. Jewish spokesmen claimed full equality as German citizens; they were neither strangers nor recent arrivals; they had been born in the country and had no fatherland but Germany. The messianic and national elements in Jewish religion were dropped in this rapid and radical *aggiornamento*. Towards the middle of the nineteenth century Gabriel Riesser, the most eloquent and courageous advocate of emancipation, suggested that a Jew who preferred a nonexistent state and nation (Israel) to Germany ought to be put under police protection not because his views were dangerous but because he was obviously insane. About the depth of patriotic feeling and of commitment of men like Riesser there could be no doubt: 'Whoever disputes my claim to the German fatherland', he said on one occasion, 'disputes my right to my thoughts and feelings, to the language that I speak, the air that I breathe. He deprives me of my very right to existence and therefore I must defend myself against him as I would against a murderer.' On another occasion he declared that the 'forceful sounds of the German language, the poems of German writers have kindled in our breast the holy fire of freedom. We want to adhere to the German people, we shall adhere to it everywhere.' Riesser summarised his philosophy, the spiritual marriage of Judaism and Germany, in a rhymed device: *Einen Vater in den Höhen, eine Mutter haben wir, Gott ihn, aller Wesen Vater, Deutschland unsere Mutter hier.* (We have one father in heaven and one mother – God the father of all beings, Germany our mother on earth.) He was by no means in favour of abandoning Judaism as he understood it; on the contrary, he never for a moment considered baptism, the easy way out chosen by so many of his contemporaries, and this despite the many bitter disappointments he suffered as a Jew. Riesser had to leave Altona because he was not permitted to pursue his professional work as a lawyer in his native town.

He was refused a teaching position in Heidelberg, and in Hesse, where he went next, he was even refused citizenship. But like many other of Germany's step-children he did not give up the struggle; the inner alliance of the liberal Jew with German civilisation (as one historian has put it) had become so firmly rooted within a few years that his instinctive answer to any setback, to him individually, or to the community, was to seek deeper and closer assimilation.

But why should Jews have wanted to remain Jews? During this second stage of transformation Judaism became a religion of universal ethics and it was not readily obvious why they should be so reluctant to give up what divided them from their Christian neighbours. Jewish spokesmen provided various explanations: some argued, in the true spirit of the Enlightenment, that religion was the individual's private affair. Others, like Riesser, maintained that Christianity as well as Judaism was in urgent need of reform and purification; Christianity's record in recent centuries had not exactly been that of a religion of love. It had 'throttled generations and drowned centuries in blood'; by what moral right could it demand the baptism of the Jews? But a critique of Christianity did not necessarily involve an attachment to Judaism. Freethinking attitudes spread among those who came after Mendelssohn, and the third generation was even more remote from established religion. A leading orthodox rabbi wrote in 1848 about the young Jews of his time, that nine-tenths of them were ashamed of their faith. Statements like these abound; they were perhaps not meant to be taken literally but they indicated a general trend. Of Mendelssohn's children all but one changed their faith, and many of his pupils, too, converted. David Friedlaender, the most important among this group, enquired in a public manifesto published anonymously about the possibility of a mass conversion of leading Berlin Jews and their families. This overture was rejected, for Friedlaender had some mental reservations ('Christianity without Jesus', his critics claimed); subsequently he retreated with some of his friends into Reform Judaism. Others, less scrupulous, discarded their reservations and embraced Christianity. For baptism, as Heine said, was the entrance ticket to European civilisation, and who would let a mere formality stand between him and European civilisation?

The dilemma facing that generation of Jewish intellectuals is highlighted in the life stories of the ladies who established the great literary salons in Berlin and Vienna: Rahel Varnhagen, Henriette Herz, Dorothea Schlegel, Fanny Arnstein – to name the most prominent hostesses of the age. They entertained statesmen and generals, princes and poets, theologians and philosophers. Some of these noblemen were of doubtful provenance, and the character of some of the ladies did not always conform to the standards of the age. But the happenings in their salons were on the whole highly respectable: the aristocracy found in their houses luxury, intelligent conversation, a lively cultural interest, and above all a social and intellectual freedom unknown at the time among the German middle class. The aesthetic tea parties arranged by these ladies played an important part in German cultural history; they certainly helped to make Berlin, better known in the past for its soldiers than its poets, a cultural metropolis. There was hardly a figure of cultural eminence who did not frequent these salons at one time or another. Some talked about these occasions with derision, others wrote with genuine appreciation about the role played by the daughters of the Cohens, the Itzigs and the Efraims, who promoted the cult of Goethe and Jean Paul at a time when most Germans were still immersed in *Rinaldo Rinaldini* and Kotzebue. Their intellectual interests were wide-ranging: Henriette Herz studied Sanskrit, Malay and Turkish, and exchanged love letters with Wilhelm von Humboldt written in the Hebrew alphabet. The emphasis was, however, on the soul rather than the intellect. There was a great deal of affectation in the exalted conversation and in the letters exchanged, an artificial ardour, a sensibility that did not always ring true. Their libertinism struck their contemporaries and the succeeding generation as very wicked; Graetz refers to these goings-on in almost apoplectic terms. Today it all seems naïve and tedious, but at that time whoever did not possess the depth of feeling demanded by contemporary fashion tried at least to go through the right motions of sentimentality and emotional ecstasy. The platonic and not so platonic affairs of these ladies, usually with much younger men, were slightly ridiculous. There was an element of madness in the general malaise of the Romantic Age but there was nothing specifically Jewish about it.

All the great Berlin hostesses eventually became Christians. Dorothea, Mendelssohn's daughter, converted first to Protestantism and then, following the Romantic fashion, to Catholicism. Some of them became very religious indeed; Heine poked fun at the new converts who over-adapted themselves, lifting their eyes in church higher to heaven than all others and twisting their faces into the most pious grimaces. The best thing Henriette Herz found to say of her own father, Moses Mendelssohn, and the men of their generation, was that they had possessed the virtues of Christian love and tenderness. It is easy to cast doubt on the genuineness of these conversions, but there were mitigating circumstances: they had received little Jewish education, and what they knew they loathed. Judaism as a religion was in their eyes very inferior to Christianity and made no appeal to their imagination. Such was the state of Judaism that even a good and faithful Jew like Lazarus Ben David, who was deeply saddened by the mass exodus, found it not at all surprising. How could one blame these people (he once wrote) if they preferred the joyous, well-frequented church to the sad and desolate synagogue? For Rahel Varnhagen, the most formidable of the Berlin ladies, the fact that she was born a Jewess was the great tragedy of her life; it was 'as if a dagger had penetrated my heart at the moment of birth'. She was also the only one who had second thoughts later on; in her old age she wrote that she would not now forswear what she had once regarded as the greatest disgrace of her life, the harshest suffering and misfortune, namely to have been born a Jewess.

Latter-day Jewish thinkers have treated these apostates with contempt, but can one really betray what one does not believe in? Many of them genuinely needed a 'religion of the heart', something which Judaism obviously could not offer. The position of the Jewish *avant-garde* in the early decades of the nineteenth century was more difficult than it had been in Moses Mendelssohn's time. Enlightenment preached a spirit of tolerance and implied a growing belief in *Vernunftsreligion*. But intellectual fashions had changed: Enlightenment had almost become a dirty word, and from reason and tolerance the emphasis had shifted to sentiment and tradition. Rationalism was out of date; it had become far more important to be a patriot and a gentleman than a good citizen of the world. The Romantic Age put heavy emphasis on faith and mystery and the *Volksgeist*; how could one belong to the German people without sharing also its religious experience?

The number of educated Jews in Germany was increasing by leaps and bounds; despite all the restrictions, Jews succeeded in entering many professions that had been closed to them before. Some became booksellers, and since bookselling and publishing were closely linked in those days, they also entered journalism in force and thus, through the backdoor, politics. German Jews could still not be judges, army officers or university professors unless they adopted Christianity. But they no longer lived in a social ghetto and this created problems which had not existed before. A hundred years earlier there had been a great deal of fraternising with the non-Jewish world at the top of the social pyramid, among the court Jews, and at the bottom, among the beggars and the underworld. Now, with the rise of a substantial Jewish middle class, the attitude towards its surroundings became a major issue. Jettchen Gebert in Georg Hermann's novel of that name provides an illuminating account of the way of life, the beliefs and the behaviour of this new Jewish bourgeoisie in the Berlin of the 1820s and 1830s. There was still a seemingly insurmountable wall between the beautiful young heroine and her non-Jewish lover (the fact that he belonged to the bohème was an additional complication). 'It was bound to come', is the constant refrain: Jettchen, the family decided, had to marry the good provider, the crude, unromantic 'typically Jewish' cousin from the small town in Posen with whom she was not at all in love. But as the family saw it, traditional ties and social conventions had to be respected. Jason, Jettchen's favourite uncle, is a free-thinker who does not have the courage of his convictions and who, with all his irony and criticism, does not break away from the family.

Others were less timid; this was the beginning of the period of inter-marriage as a mass phenomenon, of which Fontane wrote in 1899 that few people now remember it, because it was regarded as a perfectly natural thing – no one made any fuss about it. The Jasons of 1825 were all Hegelians, at least for a while; they were influenced by the master's views; Judaism, Hegel wrote, was the world of the wretched, of mis-fortune and ugliness, a world lacking inner unity and harmony. These Jews were ashamed of their origins: a cousin wrote to Rahel Varnhagen that he liked to study in Jena because there were so few Jews around. Börne, in a letter to Henriette Herz (with whom he was in love), reported from his university that a few Jews of good family were studying there, but that it was remarkable how anxious they were to hide their origins: 'One never sees two Jews walking together, or even just con-versing.' One of the Jewish periodicals of the day (*Orient*) wrote that the Berlin Jew was blissfully happy if he was told that there was nothing 'specifically Jewish' about him. With the growing social and cultural differentiation inside the community, the more educated were often ashamed of their less fortunate co-religionists who were less assimilated than themselves but with whom they were nevertheless identified in the public mind. 'They are a miserable lot,' Heine wrote about the Ham-burg Jews, 'you must be careful not to look at them if you want to take an interest in them.' Lassalle, the future Socialist leader, who belonged to a still younger generation, put it in even stronger terms: he loathed the Jews, 'the degenerate descendants of a great tradition who had acquired the mentality of slaves during centuries of servitude'. True, from time to time Lassalle, like the young Disraeli, had visions of grandeur, of leading the Jews towards a great future. But, unlike Disraeli, who thought that the Jews should be given full civic rights not on sufferance but because they were a *superior* race, Lassalle felt that they had deteriorated beyond redemption: 'Cowardly people, you don't deserve a better lot, you were born to be servants.'

Börne was baptised after having prepared for the Frankfurt Jewish community a long and detailed memorandum about the discrimination to which his co-religionists in his native city were subjected; Heine converted after writing to one of his closest friends that it was beneath his honour and dignity to become a Christian just in order to enter the state service in Prussia. Times are bad, he added ominously – honest men have to become scoundrels. A few weeks after his baptism he wrote to the same friend: 'I am now hated by Christian and Jew alike; I very much regret my baptism, nothing but misfortune has occurred to me since.' And he was at his most sarcastic in a pun about those shame-facedly embracing Christianity:

> Und Du bist zu Kreuz gekrochen
> Zu dem Kreuz, das Du verachtest
> Das Du noch vor wenigen Wochen
> In den Staub zu treten dachtest!

> (So you have repented,
>   crawling towards the very
> cross which you derided
> only a few weeks ago!)

Heine's conversion has remained something of a mystery. Only a little while before he had written to another friend, Moritz Embden, that he was indifferent in matters of religion and that his attachment to Judaism had its roots in his deep antipathy to Christianity.

Heine made a great many contradictory statements about Judaism, as he did about Germany and the future of Socialism; it is rarely profitable to search for ideological consistency in the work of a poet, nor is its presence necessarily a virtue. Börne, his contemporary, was more of a politician, and his strength too was the literary essay, not politico-economic analysis. But precisely because Börne and Heine, unlike Marx, did not try to develop a scientific *Weltanschauung*, they were better able to understand the essence of the Jewish question; they felt in their bones that there was no breaking out of what Börne once called the 'magic Jewish circle'. Everyone spoke about the Jews; he had experienced this a thousand times and yet it remained forever new: 'Some accuse me of being a Jew, others forgive me for being a Jew, still others even praise me for it. But all of them reflect on it.' Both Börne and Heine were more concerned with Jewish topics after their conversion than before; Heine announced towards the end of his life that he felt no need to return to Judaism because he had never really left it. Börne, too, took a more positive view in his later years. The Jews had more spirit than the non-Jews, he noted; they had passions – but only great ones (which recalls Heine's saying that the Greeks had always been no more than handsome youths, whereas the Jews were always men). Börne defended the Jews against their detractors in the same way as he used his pen on behalf of other just causes; like Heine he felt no link with any positive religion. Judaism had no deeper meaning for the modern Jew of which these two writers were the first perfect specimens. It was the family disease that had followed them for thousands of years, the plague that had been carried forth from Pharaonic days, as Heine wrote in a poem dedicated to the new Jewish hospital in Hamburg; it was an incurable illness – no steam bath, modern drugs, or other appliances or medicines could heal it. Would it disappear, perhaps, in that future, better, world order, the vision of which intrigued Heine in his more optimistic moments? Was there any point in reflecting about the future of Judaism and the Jews? The narrow limits of intellectual analysis were acutely stated in a private letter of Moritz Abraham Stern, a mathematician and one of the first Jewish professors in Germany, to his friend Gabriel Riesser:

I am as remote from Judaism as from Christianity. What binds me to Judaism is a feeling of duty, of reverence. I am tied to this religious party in the same way as I am bound to my mother, my family, my fatherland. Such feelings should not be dissected with the anatomical knife; one should not trace the deeper underlying motives, it does not help us to become better men.

There are no exact statistics about Jewish conversions; Rahel's statement in 1819 that half of the Berlin community had converted during the last three decades was no doubt exaggerated.* But equally there is no doubt that in Germany at the time, the most gifted in every walk of

---

* According to the available evidence there were in fact fewer Jewish conversions during the nineteenth century in Germany than in England, and much fewer than in Russia and Austria-Hungary. De la Roi, *Judentaufen im 19. Jahrhundert*, Berlin, 1900.

life, and above all the leaders, were affected: the intelligentsia in fact, those who had attained social, economic or political status and prominence. In some communities almost all the leading families converted; frequently the parents hesitated to take the fateful step but had their children baptised at birth. It was not a totally unprecedented phenomenon in Jewish history; it had happened before in Spain in the Middle Ages, and Jewish communities in some countries had vanished altogether. With the disappearance of the intellectual elite and social establishment it seemed that only the downtrodden and uneducated, the backward elements in the community, would remain. The theologian Schleiermacher, Rahel's friend, announced that Judaism was dead; von Schroetter, the Prussian minister, took a more cautious view: he gave it another twenty years. Few Jewish intellectuals of that generation did not on one occasion or another play with the idea of baptism. They established sundry cultural and social circles 'to search after truth, to love beauty, to do good'. But what was specifically Jewish in this praiseworthy endeavour? All of them wanted to Europeanise Judaism, to purge it of its archaisms; 'Away from Asia' was one of their main slogans. There were suggestions to ban Hebrew and the Talmud. The introduction of the German language into the synagogue became fairly general. Ben Seev, one of Mendelssohn's pupils and close collaborators, complained of the gradual disappearance of Hebrew and put equal blame on enlightened parents and conservative rabbis. The parents wanted their children to learn only subjects that would assist them in their professional career: languages, mathematics, the sciences. The orthodox rabbis on the other hand banned worldly subjects altogether, opposing religion to science. Thus different sections of the Jewish people were gradually drifting apart; some were still devoting their best years to the study of Hebrew, but Hebrew for them was mainly a tool for the study of the Talmud. David Friedlaender, another of Mendelssohn's pupils, came out squarely against traditional Jewish education. Writing to his brother-in-law, in a little Silesian town, who had asked for advice concerning the education of his son, he stated flatly that there was no room for half measures and compromise. The son would become a *yeshiva bocher*, convinced of the exclusivity of the Jewish people and of the great superiority of his studies over all other kinds of human endeavour. He would not touch any book in German but he would know the answers to all sorts of questions – whether, for instance, the daughter of a high priest who had been whoring should be stoned or burned. A compromise was not possible – a man wearing on one foot a riding boot and on the other a dancing shoe would be able neither to dance nor to ride.

In Mendelssohn's days Jews were still Jews and everyone referred to a Jewish nation. But in 1810 *Sulamit*, the leading German-Jewish periodical, changed its subtitle to *Israelit*, and a few years later many Jews began to refer to themselves as of the 'Mosaic confession'. By the 1830s the *Me'assef*, the Hebrew journal established by Mendelssohn's pupils, had ceased to appear. The knowledge of Hebrew among the general public was by then restricted to a few prayers and some colloquial phrases; even the Jewish scholars used the language only sparingly. Luzzatto, the great Italian-Jewish thinker, said in a letter to Graetz, the historian of the Jewish people, that he regretted very much that neither Graetz nor Zacharias Frankel (the director of the leading Jewish theological seminary) liked to write Hebrew: 'What will your pupils do, where will the language find a home after the demise of the present generation?' The complaint was all the more poignant since Graetz and Frankel were fervently opposed to attempts to de-Judaise Judaism.

The religious reform movement gathered momentum throughout the first half of the century; prayers were translated and abridged, those of national rather than religious content or referring to the coming of the Messiah were deleted. Organs and mixed choirs appeared in the synagogues (or 'temples', as they were now called). Girls as well as boys went through the ritual of confirmation. The reform rabbis, to the horror of their orthodox colleagues, dropped the provision for the ritual bath and the elaborate mourning and funeral rites; some even introduced religious services on Sunday and left it to the discretion of the parents whether their new-born sons should be circumcised. The curriculum of the Jewish schools changed out of recognition, and it was alleged that in some of them children were singing Christian hymns such as 'Ein feste Burg ist unser Gott'; they were lighting the candles of both the *menora* (the Chanukka candelabra) and the Christmas tree.

A powerful impetus to reform Judaism had been given by Moses Mendelssohn, who saw no contradiction between the essentials of a Jewish religion and his own moral maxims such as 'Love truth, love peace' (*Jerusalem*). At the same time the scientific study of Judaism (*Wissenschaft des Judentums*) began to prosper, reawakening interest in the Jewish poetry of the Middle Ages, and retracing the development of Jewish prayers and ritual customs. But even those who were deeply convinced of the values of Judaism, its tradition and its contribution to civilisation, regarded it more as an impressive fossil than a living faith.

When towards the end of the nineteenth century Steinschneider, a leader of this school, was told by one of his students about early Zionist activities, he looked longingly and sadly at his great collection of Jewish books and said : 'My dear fellow, it is too late. All that remains for us to do is to provide a decent funeral.'

The German-Jewish *Haskala* (enlightenment) led many Jews away from Judaism and it has come in for bitter attacks from both the orthodox and the latter-day Jewish national movement. Mendelssohn and his pupils had paved the way for de-Judaisation, the argument ran, for the apostasy of individuals, and ultimately for the disappearance of the faith altogether. But such attacks ignore the historical context and therefore usually miss the point. The great decline in faith had set in well before the turn of the century. Judaism had been undermined from inside; the Haskala was not the cause of this crisis but its consequence. Orthodox Jews naturally expressed their horror at the progressive Christianisation of the synagogue, for this, not to mince words, is what it amounted to. But the reform movement was only the reaction to the chaotic state of religious life. The Haskala did not kill religious piety; on the contrary it tried, even if not successfully, to restore dignity to rabbis and synagogues, whose prestige, according to eighteenth-century witnesses, had fallen to an all-time low. Prayers, mechanically recited, were interrupted by social conversation, the exchange of business information, and even occasional brawls and fisticuffs. Such a religion had little attraction for a new generation of educated men and women.

Those who left Judaism have been harshly judged by later generations for the lack of dignity they displayed and their craving for recognition by the outside world; they were dying to become the monkeys of European civilisation (as Luzzatto put it), aping all the intellectual fashions of a rotten age. The resentment is only too intelligible; deserters from a fortress under siege – and the Jews were still subject to discrimination and even persecution – are never looked upon with favour. Of those at the time who chose baptism, many did so no doubt in the hope of material gain or social recognition; others simply grew away. But it is doubtful whether those who accepted Christianity did so only for material advantage. The sad truth which most defenders of traditional Judaism have always been reluctant to face was that it had become meaningless for many people. This was the age of the decline of traditional religion; with the disappearance of this common tie many educated Jews no longer felt any obligation, moral or other, to their community. These lapsed Jews admitted to a common ancestry and tradition. But what did this tradition amount to when compared with the overwhelming attractions of European civilisation, the Enlightenment, the classic and Romantic Movement, the unprecedented flowering of philosophy and literature, music and the arts? The crisis of religion was less acutely felt in the non-Jewish world, for both Catholicism and Protestantism showed themselves far more adaptable than orthodox Judaism to the winds of change. Even if a German ceased to believe in Christian dogma he still remained a German, whereas a non-believing Jew had no such anchor. It was not just that Judaism had nothing to put against the powerful influence of the Encyclopedists, of Kant and Hegel, Goethe and Beethoven. These, it could be argued, belonged to all mankind. The real problem was that Judaism as a religion (and few at the time regarded it as anything else) had little if any attraction for western-educated people. The last movement that had stirred the Jewish world, the messianism of Shabtai Zvi and his pupils, had long ago petered out; some of its offshoots, such as the Dönmeh in Turkey and the Frankists in Galicia, had ended up by adopting Islam and Christianity respectively. Throughout the eighteenth century the leading German rabbis had been engaged in perpetual internal strife, suspecting each other of various heresies. Rabbi Emden of Altona claimed that the amulets sold by Rabbi Eybeschütz of Hamburg to pregnant women (they were supposed to have a magic effect) included a reference to Shabtai Zvi; this was the great confrontation shaking central European Judaism for many years. With the keepers of the faith engaged in disputations of this kind, was it surprising that the Jewish readers of Voltaire had little but derision for what they regarded as the forces of obscurantism? Much of the influence of the Enlightenment was shallow and its fallacies were demonstrated only too clearly in subsequent decades. But in the clash between secularism and an ossified religion based largely on a senseless collection of prohibitions and equally inexplicable customs elaborated by various rabbis in the distant past, there was not the slightest doubt which would prevail. It was a conflict between a modern philosophy and a moribund religion.

Both the apostates and the advocates of assimilation were later accused of seeking to emancipate themselves as individuals instead of fighting for the emancipation of their people. German Jews in particular have been severely criticised for their pusillanimity. But those who opted out (it cannot be emphasised too often) did not feel themselves at all members of a people; at most they sensed that they were members of a community of fate whose destiny had been fulfilled. Nor was assimilation confined to Germany; the idea that the Jews were no longer a people had been given official sanction by the Sanhedrin convened by Napoleon in 1807. What happened in Germany during the first half of the nineteenth century was by no means unique; it simply predated developments elsewhere in Europe by several decades.

And yet, of those who opted for conversion, some took the decision with a heavy heart. They had ceased to believe in Judaism but they still felt that open dissociation from the ancestral faith was a cowardly act. Shortly after he was baptised Heine wrote to a close friend referring to the members of their own circle – the Association for Culture and Science among the Jews – that no one should be called an honest man before his death: 'I am glad that Friedlaender and Ben David are now old, and they at least are safe, and no one will reproach our age that we did not have a single one among us who was without blame.'

For the majority of Jews there was less temptation. The orthodox, the many small-town Jews, and those who did not have constant professional or social contact with the gentile world, were held together by tradition and inertia. Their family ties had always been closer than was customary among the surrounding gentile world. They were distinguished by certain common traits of mentality and character, often but not always by their looks, by a certain affinity they felt for each other, by memories and traditions which went far back. They were not always aware of these common traits; the outside world frequently saw them much more clearly. Marx felt himself anything but a Jew; so did Lassalle whom he loathed. Marx's exchange of letters with Engels is replete with references to the 'Jewish Nigger' Lassalle, his lack of tact, his vanity, impatience, and other 'typically Jewish' traits of character. But to the outside world men like Marx and Lassalle remained Jews, however ostentatiously they dissociated themselves from Judaism, however much they felt themselves Germans or citizens of the world. Well-wishers saw in Marx a descendant of the Jewish prophets and commented on the messianic element in Marxism; enemies dwelt upon the Talmudic craftiness of the Red Rabbi; there was no getting out of Börne's 'magic circle'. It was above all this hostility on the part of the outside world, and in particular Christian opposition to emancipation and later on the antisemitic movement, that prevented the total disintegration of the Jews as a group.

The demand for emancipation had been first advanced by a few humanists; the majority were either indifferent or actively hostile. Contemporary sources relate that peasants who had killed a Jew near

Elmsbeck were most indignant when arrested and brought to trial; after all the victim was only a Jew. The inhabitants of Sachsenhausen (a suburb of Frankfurt) threatened revolt when one of them who had killed a Jew was about to be executed. Many leading spirits of the age were anything but philosemites. Goethe said the Jews could not be given a part in a civilisation whose very origins they negated. Fichte was against making Jews fully fledged citizens because they constituted a state within the state, and because they were permeated with burning hatred of all other people. He would much rather have them sent back to Palestine or, as he once wrote, cut off their heads overnight and replace them with non-Jewish heads. According to official Christian theology, Jews as individuals could be redeemed if they wholeheartedly embraced Christianity, shedding their superstitions and improving themselves morally and culturally. But in practice this positive approach was by no means generally accepted, whether by the state or even within the Church. It was argued both that the Jews had sunk so low that they were incapable of moral improvement, and that while cultural assimilation was possible it was by no means desirable. *Sulamit*, the leading Jewish journal, wrote in 1807 that even the more sympathetic gentile preferred the 'real Jew' to the westernised Jew whom he loathed: 'the average Christian prefers the dirtiest orthodox to the cultured man'. Grattenauer, a leading antisemitic pamphleteer, jeered in 1803 at those Jews who, to demonstrate their cultural level, publicly ate pork on the Sabbath, promenading noisily in the city streets, reciting aloud Kiesewetter's 'Logic' and singing arias from 'Herodias before Bethlehem' (a contemporary opera). Grattenauer much regretted that honest Christians were no longer permitted to kill Jews; Hundt-Radowski, his most widely read successor, argued in 1816 that the murder of Jews was neither a sin nor a crime but at most a disturbance of public order. Since, however, public order was not to be disturbed, he proposed the castration of all male Jews, the sale of females to bordellos, and the disposal of the rest as slaves to the British for work in their overseas plantations.

These were extreme voices but they were by no means uninfluential, and some of these pamphlets were frequently reprinted. A slightly more moderate form of antisemitism found expression in the writings of university professors such as Rühs and Fries. They argued that Judaism was *odium generis humani*, a pest that should be exterminated though not necessarily by fire and sword; it was not just a confession but a nation and a state within the state. Jews should not be given equal rights; on the contrary, they should be compelled to wear certain distinguishing marks so that the unsuspecting gentile would be able to recognise the enemy without difficulty. These writers usually struck a note of alarm: half of the wealth of Frankfurt was already in Jewish hands; in another forty years the children of the leading Christian families would be reduced to the status of servants in Jewish houses unless drastic measures were taken in time.

These attacks created deep consternation among German Jewry and produced a sizable counter-literature. The Jews had been oppressed for many centuries, the apologists argued; but given a few decades of unfettered development they would be indistinguishable from the rest of the people – honest, industrious, good citizens making their full contribution to society. They explained that the antisemitic pamphleteers were wholly ignorant of the facts of Jewish history; Spain had not been ruined by the Jews, but on the contrary by their expulsion. They also stressed that the recent antisemitic writings were simply a rehash of the literature of bygone centuries which had been frequently and conclusively refuted. Such well-meaning defence of Judaism and the Jews was bound to be ineffective because it ignored the irrational origin of the attacks. Rational arguments, however logically marshalled, were bound to make no impact in these conditions. How could Fries be refuted when he said: 'Go out and ask anyone, peasants as well as townspeople, whether they do not hate the Jews who take away their livelihood and corrupt the German people'. With all the exaggeration in statements of this kind there was this kernel of truth: Jews were disliked. Individual Jews could pass and were occasionally accepted and respected, but there was a deep-seated feeling that as a whole they were undesirable, a danger to the German people and its development.

On the intellectual level this backlash against the Enlightenment has to be viewed in the general context of the times. The Romantic Movement rediscovered the beauty of the Middle Ages and preached the ideal of a Christian-German state; the war against Napoleon produced a wave of xenophobia and gave a powerful impetus to Teutomania (*Teutschtümelei*). The new patriotism, the precursor of the *völkisch*-racial movement of the latter part of the century, was a reaction to the humanitarian-cosmopolitan movement of the century before; it stressed national exclusivity and was soon to insist on the inferiority of other races.

The Romantic fashion passed but it was not followed by a return to the ideals of Lessing. Antisemitic attacks did not cease, and they came from the left as well as the right: Bruno Bauer's pamphlet on the Jewish question is now remembered mainly because it provoked Marx's reply. Jewry could not be fully emancipated, Bauer maintained, if it refused to be liberated from its ancient particularism. Jews could be free and equal partners only in a purely secular society; all traditional religion had therefore to be abandoned. Marx's answer moved on an even higher level of abstraction; he was not really interested in the Jewish question as such but in the social order in general which had to be overthrown; Judaism symbolised the profit motive, egoism. Marx's *aperçus*, too, would hardly be remembered today but for the person of the author. There was often an extra edge of animosity in the comments of the philosophers that cannot be explained by the general aversion to religion that was fashionable in the age of the Young Hegelians and Feuerbach. Even a radical change in the political outlook of an author did not necessarily affect his attitude towards the Jews. Bruno Bauer's essay in the 1840s was written from a left-wing position; twenty years later he had turned into a pillar of the conservative right, but his views on the Jews became even more extreme. They were the white Negroes (he wrote), lacking only the crude and uncouth nature and the capacity for physical labour of their black brethren. Some of these attacks were not devoid of real insight into the Jewish problem and the difficulties of assimilation. Constantin Frantz, writing in 1844 from a religious-conservative point of view, compared the Jewish people with the eternal Jew of the medieval folk tale: dispersed over the whole globe, they found no peace anywhere. They wanted to mingle with the people and to surrender their own national character (*Volkstum*), but were unable to do so; only with the coming of the Messiah would full integration be possible.

During the 1840s there was a temporary decline in antisemitism, but the revolution of 1848 was accompanied by a fresh wave of attacks all over central Europe; in some villages in south Germany the local Jews were so intimidated that they actually relinquished their newly won political rights, afraid that this would create even more ill-feeling.

The Jews were puzzled by these outbreaks of antisemitism; they regarded them as a mysterious atavism, a ghost from the Middle Ages which, with the spread of education, would gradually be laid to rest. They believed that by being exemplary citizens they would convince the antisemites of the erroneousness of their views. If they had weaknesses these were the residue of centuries of oppression and economic constraints. They angrily rejected the argument that social ostracism and persecution had left ineradicable traces in their national character. Given fifty years of educational effort and peaceful development, they would show the world how well they fitted into civil society. Heine indeed predicted that their contribution to civilisation might be greater than that of other people. Jews were indignant when an antisemite like Rühs argued that they still constituted one nation ('they are somehow one nation from Brody to Tripoli'). They and their ancestors had been born in Germany, and they emphasised on every occasion their attachment to the country that continued to treat them like step-children. Only a few expressed doubts about the future relationship of Jews and Germans. A Jewish writer in *Orient* who argued in 1840 that 'we are neither Germans nor Slavs nor French', and that the southern Semitic original tribe (*Urstamm*) could never merge with the racial descendants of the north, was looked upon as an oddity. The lightning-rod theory of antisemitism was the one most commonly accepted: the Germans, being latecomers among the nations of Europe, still lacked a true national consciousness; they had to prove their patriotism by persecuting others and they blamed the Jews for the misfortune besetting them.

Börne thought that Judaeophobia was originally economic and social in character. His conclusions were pessimistic; it was pointless to try to refute antisemitism logically. All the arguments had been known for fifty years; reason apparently did not count. From the very beginning of the modern antisemitic movement Jews were in two minds whether it was wiser to reply to the attacks or to ignore them. Some Jewish periodicals decided to play down the extent and significance of the anti-Jewish riots of 1819 and again of 1848: 'Occasional stupidities of the German Michel against the Jews must be regarded from broader vistas', Berthold Auerbach, the novelist, wrote to a friend in 1848. Jewish apologetic literature was curiously restricted in its arguments; it defended the Jews, but counter-attacks were considered in bad taste. Saul Ascher, almost the only one who made no secret of his feelings about Teutomania, did not have the blessing of his fellows. Years later Jewish spokesmen dissociated themselves from Börne and Heine, the emigrés who had shown excessive zeal in their struggle against the ultra-nationalists. It seems unduly timid, but a good case can be made in retrospect in justification of those who counselled caution. Attacks on the incipient *völkisch* nationalism could not have had the slightest impact; they would have been bound to strengthen the Teutomans in their belief that Jews were the enemies of the German people. If a man was convinced that Jewish influence was corrupting, nothing a Jew said or wrote would shake him in his belief; there was no room for a dialogue, not even for polemics. Much of the apologetic literature concentrated on refuting antisemitic attacks on the Jewish religion, but in this respect the Jewish liberals were on shakier ground than they realised. The antisemites rediscovered the Talmud and the Shulkhan Arukh, whereas the Jews had just about managed to forget them. Educated Jews of that generation genuinely believed that 'their religion had always taught universalist ethics' (Y. Katz), and the general Jewish public was genuinely astonished and outraged when it realised that this just was not so and that the Talmud included sayings and injunctions which made strange reading in the modern context.

The anti-Jewish attacks came as a shock, but most Jews were still convinced that these were a rearguard action on the part of the forces of darkness. Despite all the restrictions still in force, between 1815 and 1848 they entered a great many professions hitherto closed to them and some of them rose to positions of prominence; the chosen people suddenly seemed omnipresent.

> *Wohin ihr fasst, Ihr werdet Juden fassen,*
> *all ueberall das Lieblingsvolk des Herrn*

wrote the poet Franz Dingelstedt in 1842 in his 'Songs of a cosmopolitan night-watchman'. The Jews were reluctant to ponder the social and political implications of these changes; other than the struggle for emancipation, they seemed no longer to have common interests. True, the ritual-murder case in Damascus in 1840 gave a fresh impetus to feelings of solidarity, but it did not last; those who had shed their religious beliefs did not feel much in common with the orthodox, and the educated were ashamed of the masses in their semi-barbaric backwardness. From time to time there were complaints about the lack of Jewish dignity; even Rothschild, it was reported, had given three hundred thaler for the completion of Cologne Cathedral but only ten for the reconstruction of the Leipzig synagogue. Was this not typical of the lack of Jewish self-esteem?

With the revolution of 1848 a new era opened in the history of central European Jewry, bringing with it a wave of enthusiasm among them, both because of the revolution's democratic character, and in connection with the great surge of the movement for German unity. The revolution was accompanied by antisemitic excesses and the constitutional achievements (such as the abolition of all discrimination on religious grounds) were again whittled down once the reactionary forces won the upper hand. Jews could still not be judges or burgomasters, for this involved administering the Christian formula of the oath. But the gains greatly outweighed the setbacks. For the Jews the 1850s and 1860s were a happy period. They attained full civil equality in Germany and Austria-Hungary, in Italy and in Scandinavia. In 1858 the first British Jew entered Parliament, and after 1870 Jews could attend English universities. On the continent there was little public antisemitism, and the spirit prevailing in the Jewish communities was one of genuine optimism. They shared in the general prosperity, and some amassed great riches. But much more significant was the emergence of a strong middle class; from hawking and other forms of small trade the Jews streamed into more substantial forms of business, industry, and banking, and above all into the free professions. In Berlin they constituted in 1905 less than 5 per cent of the population but provided 30 per cent of the municipal tax revenue; in Frankfurt on Main 63 per cent of all Jews had in 1900 an income of more than 3,000 marks; only 25 per cent of the Protestants and no more than 16 per cent of the Catholics reached that level. Jewish urbanisation continued at a rapid pace. The Berlin Jewish community, which had numbered about 3,000 in 1816, rose to 54,000 in 1854 and in 1910 to 144,000. The growth of the Vienna community was even more striking: from 6,000 in 1857 it increased to 99,000 in 1890; during the next twenty years it again almost doubled, rising to 175,000. In absolute terms the communities continued to grow almost everywhere, but relative to the general population their percentage decreased in Germany from 1·25 in 1871 to 0·9 in 1925; with growing prosperity the birth-rate declined. The number of conversions reached an all-time low in the 1870s; the outside pressure, the drawbacks and inducements which had previously driven Jews to embrace Christianity, were much weaker now. Mixed marriages on the other hand became more frequent; they occurred most often in the upper-middle class, but were also a common practice in all sections of the Jewish population. On the eve of the First World War there was one mixed marriage for every two among Jewish partners in Berlin and Hamburg; in 1915 (admittedly not a typical year) there were actually more mixed marriages in Germany than marriages between two Jewish partners. Similar trends were apparent all over central Europe; in Hungary, where mixed marriages had been officially banned up to 1895, their rate subsequently rose to almost one-third. In Copenhagen it reached 56 per cent in the 1880s and in Amsterdam 70 per cent in the 1930s. The decline and probable disappearance of west and central European Jewry figured prominently in the writings of the sociologists well before 1914.

The history of the Jews in central and western Europe during the second third of the nineteenth century was thus one of continuous political and social progress. Two Jews, Crémieux and Goudchaux, were members of the French Republican government of 1848; Achille Fould became Louis Napoleon's minister of finance. The Frankfurt Constituent Assembly counted five Jewish deputies and several more who were of Jewish origin. Individual Jews attained cabinet rank in Holland in 1860 and in Italy in 1870; Disraeli was baptised while a youth but in the eyes of the public he remained a Jew. Jewish politicians and voters alike gravitated to the liberal, left-of-centre parties because these had led the struggle for full equality before the law. Some, however, found their field of action among the Conservatives and not a few joined the emergent Socialist parties.

More significant even than the appearance of Jews on the political scene was their great cultural advance. There was a major invasion of secondary schools and universities, and within a few years the proportion of Jews in these institutions exceeded by far their proportion in the population. Out of a hundred Christian boys in Germany only three went to a gymnasium, the grammar school which was the stepping-stone to the university, but twenty-six out of a hundred Jewish boys went to these schools. This in turn resulted in a great influx of Jews into the free professions. In Prussia after the First World War every fourth lawyer and every sixth physician was a Jew; in the big centres such as Berlin and Vienna the percentage was higher still. Before 1850 few had attained any prominence in science; now, out of the sons and grandsons of the hawkers and street-traders there emerged a galaxy of chemists and physicists, mathematicians and physicians, who inscribed their names in golden letters in the annals of science. Some, such as the bacteriologist Paul Ehrlich, had almost instant success; others, such as Freud or Einstein, whose work involved a revolution in scientific thought, had to wait years for recognition. Even the antisemites grudgingly admitted that in the field of science Jews were making a contribution out of all proportion to their numbers. From the early years of the century they had shown a strong proclivity for journalism and the stage; later on they also appeared in professions that had been considered quite 'un-Jewish' before. Emil Rathenau became one of the pioneers of Germany's electrical industry; Albert Ballin was head of Germany's leading shipping company; Max Liebermann was thought to be Germany's greatest living painter; and German musical life was unthinkable without the part played by Jews. Even the phenomenal success of Wagner would have been impossible without the support he received at every stage of his career from Jewish audiences, despite the fact that he had asserted in a famous pamphlet that the Jews lacked all creative talent.

In Germany and in France, in Holland and in Britain, Jews came to feel that they had at last found a secure haven and were accepted. Even Heinrich Graetz thought so, although his life-long study of the history of the Jewish people was not exactly conducive to optimism. When Graetz in 1870 wrote the preface to the eleventh and last volume of his great work, he noted with satisfaction that, 'happier than any of my predecessors', he could conclude his history with the 'joyous feeling that in the civilised world the Jewish tribe had found at last not only justice and freedom but also a certain recognition. Now at long last it had unlimited freedom to develop its talents, not as an act of mercy but as a right acquired through thousandfold sufferings.'

The new self-confidence and prosperity were reflected in the life and activities of the communities. The newly established synagogues were substantial and impressive buildings without being ostentatious. The extreme reform movement had made little further progress, but the religious services had been streamlined and shortened, and the sermons were in German. The synagogues became much more dignified, in contrast to the noise and disorder which had characterised the traditional 'schul'. Those who aspired to become rabbis went to study Judaism scientifically in academic seminaries; the traditional *yeshivot* went out of fashion and ultimately out of existence. But the gain in dignity was accompanied by a further decline in religious belief. One went to the synagogue because this was part of the Jewish way of life as much as the family reunions on Sunday afternoon or particular dishes at weddings.

The ties between the communities were no longer close. According to antisemitic folklore, the *Alliance Israélite Universelle*, founded in Paris in 1860, was the secret Jewish world-government; in fact its main task was the establishment of schools in Morocco and the Balkans. The task of the Anglo-Jewish Association, established in 1870, was also largely educational, while the assignment of the German *Hilfsverein* (1901), the Russian ORT (1899), and the Jewish Colonial Association, established in Paris in 1891, was to help the immigrants from eastern Europe on their way to a new life in America and other parts of the world. A

'Jewish International' existed only in the imagination of paranoid anti-semites. The newly acquired patriotism of the Jews in western Europe made any closer link between the different communities impossible, nor was there any need felt for a supra-national organisation. It was a cause of great satisfaction to German Jews that the delegation which offered the German crown to the King of Prussia in Versailles in 1871 was headed by Heinrich von Simson, a politician of Jewish origin, and that the group of young maidens (*Ehrenjungfrauen*) who welcomed the emperor upon his return to Berlin was led by a rabbi's daughter. German Jews who emigrated to the New World maintained not only their customs but their language and cultural links with the old country; they still read Schiller and sang Schubert's *lieder*; for what had America to offer that was remotely comparable? They were annoyed by the remaining anti-Jewish restrictions, but compared with their position only a few decades earlier the progress made seemed colossal. 'Friedenthal is a Prussian minister', Berthold Auerbach wrote to a close friend. 'Who would have anticipated a generation earlier that a man of Jewish origin would become a minister?' That this was nothing out of the ordinary was in Auerbach's view 'perhaps the most fabulous aspect'. These feelings of satisfaction were sometimes of short duration. 'I have lived and worked in vain', Auerbach wrote six years later, commenting on the new antisemitic wave. 'It is a terrible fact that such brutality, mendacity and hatred are still possible.' The swing of the pendulum between such extremes of hope and despair was typical of the state of mind of German Jewry during the last quarter of the century. After the great boom of the early 1870s there was a major financial crisis, and individual Jews who had played a prominent part in speculation were made responsible for it. The attack on them (the '*Gründerschwindel*'), culminating in a new antisemitic wave, was part of the general onslaught on liberalism, which had never taken deep root in Germany. The anti-Jewish campaign proceeded on various levels: agitation by street-corner rabble-rousers, petitions to limit Jewish influence in public life, the appearance of fresh revelations on the Talmud, the exclusion of Jews from student organisations. Treitschke, one of the leading German historians of the day, coined the phrase which was to gain wide currency: 'the Jews are our misfortune'. He maintained that only the most radical assimilation would solve the Jewish question; there was no room for two nationalities on German soil. Stöcker, chaplain to the Imperial Court, admonished the Jews to desist both from attacks on Christianity and from their aspirations to amass great fortunes. Wilhelm Marr, who was the first to use the term antisemitism, argued that the penetration of Jewish influence had already gone too far and too deep; the Jews had made the Germans slaves and had become the dictators of the new empire. Marr concluded his observations on a pessimistic note: 'Let us bow to the inevitable and let us say: *Finis Germaniae*'. Others preached activism and demanded a variety of measures ranging from excluding the Jews from certain professions to their wholesale expulsion from Germany. Various antisemitic leagues and parties were founded, and in 1893 in the elections to the Reichstag, sixteen deputies were elected on a specifically antisemitic platform.

The German Jews were not only deeply shocked but genuinely baffled by these events. The poison they had thought dead was in fact still very much alive, and they looked desperately for an explanation. Could it be that modern antisemitism was a socio-economic phenomenon? There is, no doubt, some connection between the ups and downs of the business cycle in the German economy and the antisemitic movement, from the commercial and agrarian crisis of the post-1815 period, through the boom of the 1870s and the depression of the 1880s, to the world economic crisis and the rise of Nazism in the 1920s. Sometimes the coincidence seems striking: antisemitism sharply increased with the slump of 1873, and it fell almost equally dramatically after 1895 with the opening of a new boom. But such explanations leave many question marks, for while certain anti-Jewish attacks were triggered off by economic crises, others were of different origin; nor does this theory explain the occurrence of antisemitism in pre- and post-capitalist societies. The competitive character of capitalism provided, no doubt, an excellent breeding ground for collective dissatisfaction and insecurity, but why was it that the Jews were singled out for attack? Perhaps they were more exposed than other minorities; perhaps their influence had grown too fast? Whatever the explanation, there were two ominous aspects to the new antisemitism. While the government behaved on the whole correctly, its attitude *vis-à-vis* the Jews was one of icy coldness; it certainly did nothing to denounce or combat antisemitism. Very few non-Jews spoke up for their Jewish fellow citizens; there was no new Lessing to preach humanity and tolerance. More dangerous yet was the changing character of Judaeophobia, the transition from religious to racial antisemitism. Racial theories had existed in an inchoate form since the beginning of the nineteenth century, and had acquired respectability with the spread, from France, of the new, quasi-scientific doctrine of Gobineau and his disciples. In earlier times the enemies of the Jews had put the blame on their religion and on the ritual law which, they claimed, had caused the corruption of the Jewish people. Racial antisemitism rejected these arguments as irrelevant, maintaining that it had discovered the real reasons underlying the 'Jewish danger'. The antisemitism of Stöcker was a half-way house between the old and the new antisemitism; the Jewish question, he maintained, was not only religious in character; but as a prominent churchman he could not very well accept the materialist concepts of pure racialists such as Dühring, and he referred therefore to the 'cultural-historical aspects' of the problem. The transition from religious to racial antisemitism was not as abrupt, and the ties between the old and the new anti-semite doctrine not as tenuous, as they subsequently appeared to be. The changing argumentation merely reflected the climate of opinion of the new post-religious phase and the growth of anti-liberal and anti-humanist ideologies in general. Racial antisemitism could spread only among peoples indoctrinated for many centuries with religious anti-semitism who had been taught that the Jews had killed Christ and rejected his mission.

For the German Jews the 1880s thus constituted a turning point, even though only a few realised it at the time. Carried to its logical conclusion, the new antisemitism meant the end of assimilation, the total rejection of the Jew. The magic circle was replaced by a new ghetto whose walls could no longer be scaled. For racial characteristics, according to the new doctrine, were unchangeable; a change of religion and the rejection of his own heritage did not make a Jew into a German, any more than a dog could transform itself into a cat. The antisemitism of the last quarter of the nineteenth century did not weaken the move-ment for assimilation among the Jews, but its limits became much clearer and even its extreme protagonists admitted that within the foreseeable future Jews would remain distinct from Germans.

Full legal emancipation had been achieved in 1869; no more than a decade later it could have been seen that assimilation would not work. To those who argued on these lines, a national revival among the Jews should have taken place there and then. But the great majority of German Jews did not see it that way, and in retrospect one can see many good reasons for not giving in to the forces of unreason. The *rapprochement* with German civilisation had come a long way; Ludwig Bamberger, the liberal politician, in a book published in the year of crisis stressed that the symbiosis, the identification of the Jews with the Germans, had been closer than with any other people. They had been thoroughly Germanicised well beyond Germany's borders; through the medium of language they had accepted German culture, and through culture, the German national spirit. He and his friends thought there was obviously some affinity in the national character which attracted Jews so strongly to Germany and to the German spirit*. Raphael Loewenfels, in a pamphlet published in 1893, put the case in even blunter terms: were educated Jews not nearer to enlightened Protestants than to the fanatics who believed in the wisdom of the Talmud? Were they not closer to German Catholics than to French Jewry? Whoever still used in his prayers the old formula 'Next year in Jerusalem', Loewenfels maintained, should go where his heart drew him. But no educated Jew would be willing to leave his beloved fatherland for a country where in time immemorial his forefathers had lived. This was not just the belief of an individual; it expressed the convictions of a great many Jews. In the year this pamphlet was published, the Central Association (Zentralverein) of German Citizens of Jewish Persuasion was founded, to become later on by far the strongest organisation of German Jewry. The first point in its programme stressed its attachment to Germany: the ties between them and Jews abroad were similar to those between German Catholics and Protestants and their co-religionists in other countries. The Zentralverein stressed the need for Jewish pride and consciousness and rejected the extreme and undignified forms of assimilationism which had proved both ineffective and dangerous, while asserting that for German Jews there was no future but on German soil; in the modern world there were few if any totally homogeneous nations; everywhere different religions and nationalities existed side by side.

---

* A statement like this makes strange reading in the light of the Hitlerian experience. Yet for all that it was essentially correct. The affinity between Germanism and Judaism was felt and expressed not only by assimilationists but also by many ardent Zionists. 'No culture had such a decisive impact on the Jews as the German', Nahum Goldmann wrote in 1916, in a pamphlet in which he maintained that in many ways the Zionists were much closer to the German national spirit than the assimilationists, who had received their inspiration from the liberal thinkers of Britain and France. 'The young national Jewish movement, on the other hand, had made the national idea the central concept of its philosophy: Fichte, Hegel, Lagarde (*sic*) and the other leading spirits of the German national idea – they were also our teachers. It was no accident that Theodor Herzl, the genius who founded modern political Zionism, came from German culture to the Jewish national idea.' (Nahum Goldmann: *Von der weltkulturellen Bedeutung und Aufgabe des Judentums*, Munich, 1916.) Writing in the middle of the First World War, Goldmann, in a series of propaganda leaflets, overstated his case, and it is not difficult to misconstrue statements of this kind. But there is no denying that German philosophy of the nineteenth century was a source of inspiration to modern political ideologies from the extreme left to the extreme right all over Europe, and Zionism was no exception.

Despite the particularities setting them apart from the rest, the Zentralverein thought that there was every reason to believe that there would be an honourable place for Jews in the broader framework of the German nation. It is tempting in retrospect to dismiss all this as so much wishful thinking. But the spirit of the age was still basically optimistic, and it was commonly assumed that the appeal of anti-semitism was bound to be restricted to the backward sections of society, in particular to those who had suffered from the consequences of industrialisation. The reaction against the Enlightenment and liberalism, the new cult of violence, and anti-humanism, were thought to be transient cultural maladies. Growing prosperity would help to restore both sanity and social stability. There were more than a few straws in the wind which seemed to justify such optimism: the antisemites, divided into several factions, lost much of their political influence after 1895, though they continued to exist as small sects bitterly fighting each other. The emergence of the new antisemitism had shown that there were grave problems and strains that had been ignored, or at any rate underrated, but there seemed to be no good reason to give up hope.

Nor was there any reason why German and Austrian Jews should regard their own position with special concern. In Russia and Rumania the situation was incomparably worse; from 1881 on eastern Europe was plagued by a series of pogroms. Even in France, which had a smaller Jewish community than Germany, their position was far more precarious. The French antisemitic movement predated Marr, Stöcker, and Dühring; it was more articulate and its influence more widespread. It was, in fact, the pioneer of modern anti-Jewish ideology; the German and Russian antisemites frequently imported their ideas from Paris. Later on, during the Dreyfus affair, antisemitism in France became a nation-wide issue to a far greater extent than in contemporary Germany.

The main attack on assimilation came from within the Jewish camp, from those who maintained that the perfect synthesis between Judaism and western civilisation had nowhere materialised. The assimilated German Jew, as his eastern co-religionists saw it, had lost his Jewish spontaneity and warmth and his inner peace; he had invested a great deal of effort in being like the others but had not achieved the recognition he so much desired, and as a result he was an unhappy being, suffering from a peculiarly painful and apparently incurable form of schizophrenia. This, for instance, was the impression young Chaim

Weizmann gained when he came to Germany as a young teacher in the 1890s. German Jews, he found, did not believe in the existence of a Jewish people; they had no real understanding of the nature of anti-semitism; there was no real Jewish life – it was all stuffy, unreal, divorced from the people, lacking warmth, gaiety, colour, and intimacy. In one of his essays (*Avdut betoch Herut* – Slavery in the Midst of Freedom), Ahad Ha'am maintained that western Jews knew in their innermost heart that they were unfree because they lacked a national culture. To justify their existence they had to dispute the view that every people had an individual character and assignment.

Such criticism contained much that was true, but it was not very helpful since it ignored the essential differences between Jews in eastern Europe and their co-religionists in the west. The issue was exceedingly complex. What Weizmann wrote about German Jews is sometimes almost textually identical with the views expressed by Herzen and the Slavophiles a generation earlier about the lifeless, Philistine Germans. Could it be that Russian Jews and German Jews had been infected by the disdain their respective host nations felt for each other? Ahad Ha'am played a central role in the history of the Jewish cultural renaissance, but in his case, too, the ideas he popularised were by no means part of the Jewish tradition but had their roots in the west. Jews in eastern Europe were able to retain their national identity because there were so many of them and it was therefore much easier to preserve their way of life and a folklore of their own. Nor was there a strong temptation to accept Russian, Rumanian, or Galician culture, whereas western Jews, much fewer in numbers, had been strongly attracted by German, French or English civilisation simply because it was so much superior. We cannot and do not want to retreat from emancipation, a Zionist (F. Oppenheimer) wrote; if we analyse ourselves we find that 95 per cent of our culture is composed of western European elements. The Jewish nationalists from eastern Europe had a more acute perception of antisemitism and the limits of assimilation, but they failed to understand the problems facing Jews living in a milieu so unlike their own. Western Jewry, rootless and relatively few in numbers, could not help but be absorbed. History had shown that even big countries have found it impossible to shut themselves off from more advanced cultures and more modern ways of life. Latter-day critics have said that the process of assimilation went too fast and too far: 'What had begun as furtive glances soon turned into a passionate involvement' (G. Scholem). This resulted both in a great deal of newly awakened creativity and in deep insecurity. Many Jews, it was further argued, enriched German economics, philosophy, science, literature and the arts, whereas only a very few made a corresponding contribution in the Jewish field. But there was no Jewish science, philosophy, or economics, and it is more than doubtful whether there was room for a specifically Jewish literature or art in western Europe. By and large the love affair between Jews and Germans remained one-sided and unreciprocated; the Jews showed more enthusiasm and understanding for what was best in German culture than most Germans. Regrettably, no one showed much gratitude to the Jews. But assimilation was a natural process, and it was in no way limited to German Jewry.

Elsewhere in western Europe assimilation began later but went further than in Germany. The integration of Italian Jewry was more complete than in Germany, where the constant influx of Jews from the east provided a blood-transfusion – or an irritant, according to the way one saw it. The situation in Britain differed from that in the rest of Europe. There was more intermarriage, in particular with the aristocracy, than anywhere else. Emancipation came to England in the traditional way such issues are resolved in that country – piecemeal, on an empirical basis, not as the result of ideological, abstract debates. After the king had visited a London synagogue one Friday evening in 1809, following an invitation by the Goldsmid brothers, social contacts with Jews became respectable. It took until 1867 for a Jewish Member of Parliament, duly elected, to be permitted to take his seat. Lionel de Rothschild, the first Jewish Member of Parliament, did not make a notable contribution to British politics; in fact he never spoke in a debate. But the ice was broken, and a few years later a Jew became solicitor-general and the last disabilities were removed. There was no danger that Jews would reach a position of cultural pre-eminence in Britain as they had in Germany; their numbers were smaller and their contribution to cultural life much less significant. Moreover, the British did not suffer from feelings of insecurity; there was no fear of 'racial pollution'. Full assimilation, on the other hand, was not even considered desirable. While Jews had of course to conform to the British way of life, they were at the same time expected to keep some aspects of their individuality. They were considered a race apart, and a country accustomed to ruling an empire saw in this an enrichment rather than a danger to its national existence, provided, of course, Jews did not get too numerous and powerful.

The parallels between assimilation in Germany and France are much closer. Almost everything that has been said about both the achievements and the shortcomings of the assimilation of the Jews in Germany applies also to France. If Mendelssohn's children converted to Christianity, so did the children of Crémieux, the great fighter for the rights of French Jews. It was often said that Jews felt closer to the Germans than to any other European people, and that they became more deeply rooted there than anywhere else. Yet those who made such claims usually did so without much knowledge of the state of affairs of France. During the nineteenth century French Jews were integrated in the social life of their country. The younger ones, whether conservative or radical, an observer noted towards the end of the century, were totally absorbed in their non-Jewish surroundings; they had no philosophy other than that of the camp to which they belonged. To raise the Jewish question would have been considered tactless. Judaism for this generation was no longer a religious, social, or political concept (Tchernoff). Jews were second to none in their French patriotism; many of them left Strasbourg and Colmar and moved to France when these provinces became part of Germany after the defeat of 1870. The hesitancy of French Jews to take collective action during the Dreyfus trial showed that they wanted to believe that the affair had no specifically Jewish aspect. Bernard Lazare, an ardent Socialist who was in favour of full assimilation and of the eventual disappearance of the Jews as a separate people, later on became a Zionist. But he was a rare exception. On the whole the Zionist movement struck few roots in France; the great majority of French Jews always stressed their attachment to the French nation, denying that their feelings differed from those of other Frenchmen. Many a Frenchman of Jewish extraction has described how as a child he wept over French defeats and rejoiced at French victories; Jewish history and traditions had no meaning for him. It was not a question of hiding his Judaism or being ashamed of it. Marc Bloch, the great historian, was anything but a coward or a hypocrite; but he belonged to a generation for which Judaism had lost all meaning. Ahad Ha'am's strictures against the slavery of western Jews he would have angrily rejected as the misguided, artificial construction of a man who had the misfortune to live under tsarist despotism, and who in his parochialism could not conceive how Jews elsewhere felt. 'I have felt myself during my whole life above all and very simply – French', he wrote. 'I have been tied to my fatherland by a long family tradition; nourished by its spiritual heritage and its history, unable in truth to conceive of any other country where I could

35

breathe at ease, I have loved it very much and served it with all my strength.' 'Being a stranger to all confessional formalism and to all racial solidarity', Bloch requested before his execution by the Nazis that Hebrew prayers should not be said at his grave. Sometimes Judaism was projected on men of this generation from the outside, and their inner harmony and security was disturbed, but this made them at most Jews *par point d'honneur*; only seldom did it mean a return to 'positive Judaism'. Raymond Aron wrote: 'I think of myself as a Jew because the world around me wants it that way, but I do not feel that this is really a part of my existence.' A great deal has been written about the self-hatred of individual German Jews; it is not at all difficult to find it in France; there was no case in the annals of German Jewry as strange and pathological as that of Maurice Sachs.*

The east European critics of assimilation usually forgot that there was a time when in eastern Europe, too, assimilation had been regarded as the wave of the future. It had strong support among Russian Jews during the 1860s and 1870s, and this despite the fact that the prospects for assimilation were, for obvious demographic, social, and economic reasons, far worse than in the west. The editor of the first Jewish journal in Russian, Osip Rabinovich, complained bitterly that the Jews were clinging to their poor, ugly-sounding and corrupt dialect instead of making the 'wonderful Russian language' their own: 'Russia is our fatherland, and its air, its language, too, should be ours.' The leading Jewish publicist of the period, I. Orzhansky, appealed for the full absorption of the Jews in the Russian nation, and said that they were striving with great energy to acquire the Russian national spirit, the Russian way of life, to become Russian in every respect. These views were shared by leading writers such as A. L. Gordon, who thought that Hebrew ought to be used only so long as the majority of the Jews did not have a full mastery of Russian. Lev Levanda called on Russian Jewry to 'awake under the sceptre of Alexander II'; Emanuel Soloveichik wrote in 1869 that the fusion of Russian and Jew, the submerging of the Jews in the Russian people, was the new messianic movement awaited by educated Russian Jews with great impatience. After the pogroms of the early 1880s these hopes vanished; there was no longer any reason to assume that the tsarist régime would favour a movement

---

* Working for the Germans during the Second World War, this *homme de lettres* wrote to a friend from Hamburg in September 1943 that he 'adored this country and its national character. . . . The people here have a smile on their faces the like of which one does not see anywhere else in the west.'

for cultural or social assimilation. Political rights seemed as distant as ever; nor was there much optimism about the attitude of the Russian and Ukrainian people towards the Jews living in their midst. But a new form of assimilation appeared among the many Jews who joined the left-wing movement. For a young revolutionary such as Trotsky his Jewish origin meant nothing; his place was in the ranks of the vanguard of the Russian proletariat fighting for world revolution. There were thousands like him.

Assimilation, then, was a general problem, a historical phenomenon not confined to countries where Jews constituted a marginal group. True, it made more rapid progress the smaller and the more prosperous the Jewish minority, the higher the culture of the host country, and the closer the economic ties between Jews and non-Jews. Arthur Ruppin, who was the first to study the sociology of the Jews, noted well before the First World War that assimilation was a general process; during the Middle Ages their particular economic and social position had made assimilation well-nigh impossible, but the tremendous changes which had taken place since had weakened the ties between Jew and Jew in every respect. If some viewed this process with unease, Ruppin himself regarded it as a grave danger. Others saw it as an inevitable development to which moral and emotional judgments could not and should not be applied. The orthodox found it easier to resist because most of them were sheltered from close contact with the outside, non-Jewish world. But it was not at all unusual to see the transformation within a very short time, of an orthodox Jew who had ventured outside the ghetto, from Talmudism and strict observance to extreme assimilation. Samuel Holdheim and Moritz Lazarus, leaders of the Reform movement among German Jewry, belonged to this category. Others viewed the gradual disappearance of the Jews as regrettable but inevitable, and some even thought that the vocation of Israel was not self-realisation but self-surrender for the sake of a higher, trans-historical goal. Many liberals and Socialists felt that national distinctions were losing their importance all over the world, and that the Jews, because they had no national home, would be in the vanguard of this movement towards one global culture, one way of life. They did not share the belief that God had created peoples to exist forever and that each of them had an eternal mission. One of the heroes in Gottfried Keller's *Fähnlein der sieben Aufrechten*, a stalwart Swiss patriot, raised the question in discussion with his friends:

Just as a man in the middle of his life and at the height of his strength will think of death, so he should consider in a quiet hour that his fatherland will vanish one day . . . because everything in this world is subject to change . . . is it not true that greater nations than ours have perished? Or do you want to continue existing like the Eternal Jew who cannot die, who has buried Egypt, Greece, and Rome and is still serving the newly emerged peoples?

If even a staunch Swiss patriot could doubt the mission of his people, was it not natural that many Jews, lacking most of the attributes usually marking members of one nation, should have given up the belief in the exclusive character of their group.

This, in briefest outline, was the position of Jews in central and western Europe before the national revival took place; the situation in eastern Europe, on which more below, was totally different. European Jewry west of the tsarist empire and Rumania had made tremendous progress since the beginning of the nineteenth century. The social and economic anomalies of their existence had been reduced, though they had not altogether disappeared. At the beginning of the nineteenth century there were a few very rich families while the great majority were desperately poor; three generations later the Rothschilds and the other banking families were no longer pre-eminent; the great national banks which had come into existence in Germany, France, and elsewhere dwarfed even the biggest private banking houses. Many poor Jews had risen on the social ladder and now constituted a substantial middle class. They had also produced a new elite, replacing the old Jewish establishment, which in its majority had abandoned Judaism. They entered a great many professions that had been closed to them before. Very few had taken to agriculture, and not many were employed in industry. But even so their social structure had become much more variegated than in the previous century. As a social problem the Jewish question was far less acute in 1880 than it had been generations earlier; but political and cultural tensions persisted and were the source of the new antisemitism. Zionist critics like Ahad Ha'am argued that assimilation had been pursued too quickly and too relentlessly. England in this respect was a notable exception; there emancipation had been gradual, never too far in advance of public opinion. But such criticism was largely academic. Once the walls of the spiritual ghetto had come down there was no holding back the thousands of eager young men and women who wanted to be submerged in the mainstream of European culture. Assimilation was not a conscious act; it was the inevitable fate of a people without a homeland which had been for a long time in a state of cultural decay and which to a great extent had lost its national consciousness.

The optimism of the early emancipation period had petered out by 1880 as unforeseen tensions and conflicts appeared, causing occasional pessimism and heart-searching. But only very few Jews accepted the argument of the racial antisemites that they could never be assimilated and had therefore to be ejected from the body politic of the host people. No one anticipated a relapse into barbarism, and most Jews continued their struggle for full civic rights as patriotic citizens of their respective countries of birth. A retreat from assimilation seemed altogether unthinkable, though perhaps its ultimate goals had to be redefined, perhaps the process of integration would take much longer than had been commonly believed. The rebirth of nationalist and racialist doctrines in Europe after 1870 should have been a warning, but there were a great many problems and conflicts besetting the European nations at that time and the Jewish question seemed by no means the most intricate or the least tractable. As far as western Jewry was concerned, assimilation had proceeded very far and an alternative solution seemed to most of them neither desirable nor, indeed, possible.

THE FORERUNNERS

Zionism, according to a recent encyclopaedia, is a worldwide political movement launched by Theodor Herzl in 1897. Equally it might be said that Socialism was founded in 1848 by Karl Marx. It is clearly difficult to do justice to the origins of a movement of any consequence in a one-sentence definition. The Jewish national revival which took place in the nineteenth century, culminating in political Zionism, was preceded by a great many activities and publications, by countless projects, declarations and meetings; thousands of Jews had in fact settled in Palestine before Herzl ever thought of a Jewish state. These activities took place in various countries and on different levels; it is difficult to classify them and almost impossible to find a common denominator for them. They include projects of British and French statesmen to establish a Jewish state; manifestos issued by obscure east European rabbis; the publication of romantic novels by non-Jewish writers; associations to promote settlement in Palestine, and to spread Jewish culture and national consciousness. The term Zionism appeared only in the 1890s,* but the cause, the concept of Zion, has been present throughout Jewish history.

A survey of the origins of Zionism must take as its starting point the central place of Zion in the thoughts, the prayers, and the dreams of the Jews in their dispersion. The blessing 'Next year in Jerusalem' is part of the Jewish ritual and many generations of practising Jews have turned towards the east when saying the *Shemone Essre*, the central prayer in the Jewish liturgy. The longing for Zion manifested itself in the appearance of many messiahs, from David Alroy in the twelfth century to Shabtai Zvi in the seventeenth, in the poems of Yehuda Halevy, in the meditations of generations of mystics. Physical contact

---

* For a full discussion of the earliest uses of the term Zionism (*Zionismus, Zionisten*), see Alex Bein, 'Von der Zionssehnsucht, etc.', in *Robert Weltsch zum 70. Geburstag*, Tel Aviv, 1961, p. 33 *et seq.*

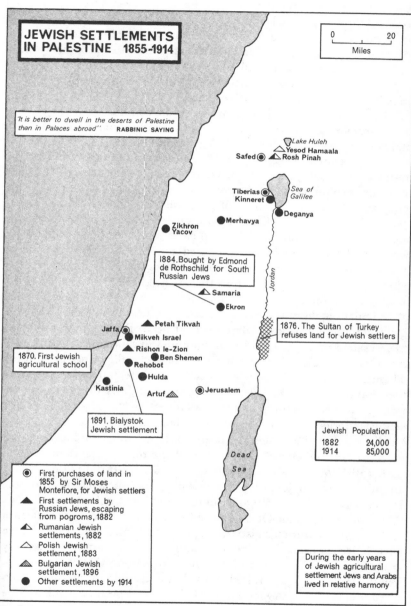

JEWISH SETTLEMENTS IN PALESTINE 1855-1914

0 — 20
Miles

"It is better to dwell in the deserts of Palestine than in Palaces abroad" **RABBINIC SAYING**

Lake Huleh
Yesod Hamaala
Safed ◉ ▲ Rosh Pinah

Tiberias ◉ — Sea of Galilee
Kinneret ●
● Deganya

● Merhavya

● Zikhron Yacov

1884. Bought by Edmond de Rothschild for South Russian Jews

▲ Samaria

● Ekron

1876. The Sultan of Turkey refuses land for Jewish settlers

▲ Petah Tikvah
Jaffa ◉
● Mikveh Israel
▲ Rishon le-Zion
● Ben Shemen
● Rehobot

1870. First Jewish agricultural school

● Hulda
● Kastinia
Artuf ▲
◉ Jerusalem

Jordan

1891. Bialystok Jewish settlement

Jewish Population
1882   24,000
1914   85,000

Dead Sea

◉ First purchases of land in 1855 by Sir Moses Montefiore, for Jewish settlers
▲ First settlements by Russian Jews, escaping from pogroms, 1882
▲ Rumanian Jewish settlements, 1882
△ Polish Jewish settlement, 1883
▲ Bulgarian Jewish settlement, 1896
● Other settlements by 1914

During the early years of Jewish agricultural settlement Jews and Arabs lived in relative harmony

Map 2

between the Jews and their former homeland was never completely broken; throughout the Middle Ages sizable Jewish communities existed in Jerusalem and Safed, and smaller ones in Nablus and Hebron. Attempts by Don Yosef Nasi, Duke of Naxos, to promote Jewish colonisation near Tiberias failed, but individual migration to Palestine never ceased; it reached a new height with the arrival of groups of Hassidim in the late eighteenth century.

Memoranda and pamphlets proposing the restoration of the Jews to their ancient homeland abounded in England in the eighteenth and nineteenth centuries. During his Egyptian campaign Napoleon published a proclamation calling the Jews of Asia and Africa to join him in restoring the old Jerusalem. Colonel Pestel, the leader of the first Russian revolutionary movement, the Decembrists, suggested in his programme the establishment of a Jewish state in Asia Minor. Even earlier, in 1797, Prince Charles de Ligne developed the same idea in a private memorandum, and Manuel Noah, an American-Jewish judge, writer and former diplomat, proposed the establishment of a token Jewish state (Ararat) on Grand Island near Buffalo. Beginning with the 1840s, Jewish newspapers frequently discussed the return to Palestine as a laudable though obviously impractical scheme; with the progress of assimilation there seemed to be less readiness to entertain projects for which there was obviously no urgent need. Elderly Jews still went to Jerusalem to die, the Jewish communities in Palestine still sent their emissaries on yearly begging tours to their co-religionists in Europe. These missions never failed to evoke some response, but at the same time they impressed only too clearly on European Jews the depth of the misery and degradation of their brethren in the Holy Land. For centuries under Turkish rule, later on a bone of contention between the khedives of Egypt and the sultan in Constantinople, administered – to use a blatant euphemism – by often cruel and mostly inefficient Turkish pashas, the country was in a state of utter decay. It did not even have an administrative identity, for Palestine had become part of the Damascus district. The situation in the Holy Land reflected the decline that had overtaken the Ottoman empire since its heyday in the fifteenth and sixteenth centuries. This desolate province seemed an unlikely haven for Jews from Europe, however poor and backward. But it was precisely as a result of the weakness of the Ottoman empire that the issue of a Jewish state was again raised towards the middle of the nineteenth century. The Eastern Question, the sickness and possible demise of the Ottoman empire, was widely discussed in the chanceries of Europe.

Between 1839 and 1854, as interest in Palestine grew, all the major European powers and the United States established consulates in Jerusalem. In 1839 the London *Globe* published a series of articles advocating the establishment of an independent state in Syria and Palestine, envisaging the mass settlement of Jews. The *Globe* was a mouthpiece of the Foreign Office and the project was known to have Palmerston's support. The author of this series, as another writer in *The Times* pointed out (17 August 1840), did not assume that the masses of European Jews would immediately migrate to Syria, but he thought that a concentration of oriental Jews in Palestine was by no means an unreal vision: the European Jews had the money to buy (or lease) the country from the sultan, and the five big powers would provide a guarantee for the new state. Some of these policy planners were in favour of an independent monarchy, others of a republic, but all were convinced that with England taking the initiative in returning the Jews to Palestine, like Cyrus in antiquity, a sufficient number of them would settle to make the project a going concern. The fact that a Jewish state would constitute a buffer between the Turks and the Egyptians and enhance British influence in the Levant was a consideration which no doubt played its part, but political, military, and economic interests alone hardly suffice to explain the strong support given by many public figures for the idea of a Jewish state. England had other opportunities in the Near East and the Jewish option was by no means the most obvious or promising. The enthusiasm of Colonel Henry Churchill, a former consul in Damascus, and other ardent protagonists of the idea, can be understood only against the background of the deep-rooted biblical tradition in Britain, and the belief that it was Britian's historical mission to lead the suffering Jews back to their homeland.

There was a strong romantic element in all these visions, a mood which also found expression in some of Disraeli's novels. 'You ask me what I wish', he wrote in *Alroy*; 'my answer is "Jerusalem, all we have forfeited, all we have yearned after, all for which we have fought".' In *Coningsby* and *Tancred*, the story of the son of a duke who goes to Palestine to study the 'Asiatic problem', Disraeli returned to the same topic. The vicissitudes of history found their explanation in the fact that 'all is race'; the Jews were essentially a strong, a superior race; given the right leadership there was nothing they would not be able to achieve. Disraeli's novels, published in the 1840s and 1850s, were full of mysterious hints, lacking a clear focus. George Eliot's *Daniel Deronda*, on the other hand, which appeared in 1876, was a novel with a specific

Zionist programme. Daniel Deronda (the 'most irresistible man in the literature of fiction' according to Henry James) decides to devote his life to the cause of a national centre for the Jews. The figure of Mordechai Cohen, Deronda's mentor, is there to show that Judaism is still alive, that it is on as high a level as Christianity, and that the Jews still have a mission to fulfil – the repossession of Palestine.

The Jewish reaction to these noble visions by well-meaning non-Jews and lapsed Jews was on the whole lukewarm. Ludwig Philippson, the editor of the leading periodical of German Jewry, wrote* that it was only too easy to understand that some young Jews, having to face antisemitism everywhere, were tired of the fruitless struggle and wanted a little place on the earth all their own, where they could find complete recognition as human beings. But Palestine was an unlikely and un-promising place for any such endeavour; a Jewish state dependent on the mercy of an oriental potentate and the protection of remote powers would be the plaything of stronger forces. There was a real danger that it would perish – many other states situated on these dangerous cross-roads of Europe, Asia, and Africa had been destroyed throughout history. What kind of freedom, what level of material existence could Jews expect in that forsaken land? What had a movement of this kind in common with their messianic hopes? Anglo-Jewry did not engage in open polemics against the visions of these well-meaning but obviously eccentric compatriots; its members acknowledged them gratefully, promised support if someone else would take the initiative, and shelved the whole idea. Nor did east European Jewry at the time take much notice.

The British had no monopoly of blueprints of this kind; several Jewish writers on the continent were also advancing similar projects at the same time. They usually entered into surprising detail but it was no doubt in anticipation of a hostile reception that most of them were published anonymously. One of these projects, *Neujudäa*,† published in Berlin in 1840, accepted the idea of a Jewish state but for practical reasons rejected Palestine, which 'had been the cradle of the Jewish people but could not be its permanent home'. It suggested the American middle west, Arkansas or Oregon; ten million dollars would be sufficient to induce the American Government to put at the disposal of the Jews an area the size of France. There was every reason to hurry with the

---

* *Allgemeine Zeitung des Judentums*, 1840, p. 542 *et seq.*

† *Neujudäa. Entwurf zum Wiederaufbau eines selbständigen jüdischen Staates von C.L.K.* New edition by Heinrich Löwe, Berlin, 1903.

realisation of the plan, for in the near future the Americas and even Australia would be settled by newcomers and then it would be too late. The unknown author believed that such an opportunity should not be allowed to pass: antisemitism was endemic in Europe, it would not diminish, and the Jews were condemned to lead a parasitic existence among peoples who hated them. In America, on the other hand, they had the opportunity to demonstrate their real ability. An agency on the pattern of the East Indian Company should be founded to establish an 'aristocratic' republic in which only Jews would be citizens. In brief, America, as far as a Jewish state was concerned, as in other respects, was the country of unlimited possibilities.

Another anonymous project published a few months later is remarkable because of its acute analysis of the sources of the Jewish problem: the writer was convinced that emancipation had by no means solved the Jewish question: Jews were at best suffered, nowhere were they welcome or loved. For the Jews *were* strangers; there was a world of difference in body and soul between the semitic *Urstamm* and those whose ancestors lived in northern Europe. The Jews were neither Germans nor Slavs, neither French nor Greek, but the children of Israel, related to the Arabs. The writer called for an early return to Palestine; the sultan and Mehemet Ali could be persuaded to protect the Jews; the main obstacle was the passivity of the Jews themselves. The Serbs and the Greeks had won a great deal of outside support in their struggle for national liberation. It should not be impossible to find a major government to support the establishment of a base of humanism and progress in anarchy-torn Syria.* This project had a mixed reception; its supporters argued that a neutral Jewish state between the Nile, Euphrates, and Taurus could restore equilibrium among the powers in the east; it would help Turkey against Mehemet Ali. Elsewhere there was scepticism with regard to the intentions of the European powers; would they really want to play the role of a Messiah, or was it not more likely that they were simply pursuing their great-power ambitions? Was not hostility towards Catholicism and France the main motive behind the plan in favour of a Jewish state recently submitted to the Protestant monarchs, rather than a genuine humanitarian desire to help the Jews? It was generally acknowledged that there was in Britain sincere sympathy for the restoration of Israel, and that this coincided with its imperial interests, but as one of the leaders of German Jewry

---

* *Orient*, 27 June 1840. The discussion triggered off by this project is reviewed in Gelber, *Vorgeschichte des Zionismus*, Vienna, 1927, chapter XI.

declared: for us Germans the orient is simply too remote; perhaps our British co-religionists are cleverer than we are.

The projects of the 1840s showed a great deal of ingenuity, acute analysis, and sometimes a remarkable gift of prophecy. But in the last resort they were all romantic and artificial constructions suspended in mid-air; they did not provide an answer to one all-important question: who would carry out these projects, who would lead the Jews in their return to their homeland? The anonymity of the authors made it clear that they were not volunteering for this mission.

The spate of projects at this time was a direct outcome of the acute crisis in the Near East, the beginning of the dissolution of the Ottoman empire. But they did not coincide with any marked rise in Jewish national awareness. Despite all the setbacks on the road to emancipation, the overwhelming majority of western Jews were by no means willing to abandon that goal. The idea of settling in an uncivilised, backward country, subject to the whims of arbitrary and cruel Turkish pashas, was unlikely to appeal to them. The various plans were not devoid of political vision, but the link between the dream and its realisation was missing, and for that reason, in the last resort, they were bound to have no effect. They were premature, just as the ideas of the Utopian Socialists had no lasting impact because they were propagated in a vacuum, without reference to the political and social forces which could provide leadership in the struggle for their realisation. Even Moses Hess' *Rome and Jerusalem*, the most important by far of these appeals, belongs to this genre. Published in 1862, it had no immediate effect. Isaiah Berlin, who compared it to a bombshell, exaggerated its impact; 160 copies of the book had been sold one year after publication and soon after that the publisher suggested that Hess ought to buy back the remainder at a reduced price. When Herzl wrote his *Judenstaat* more than thirty years later, he had not even heard of it. And yet *Rome and Jerusalem* stands out in the literature of the time for reasons that will be immediately obvious.

Moses Hess

Moses Hess, born in Bonn in 1812, was known in his lifetime chiefly for his activities as a Socialist. He was prominent in the theoretical exchanges between the Young Hegelians during the 1830s and 1840s, collaborated for a while with Marx and Engels, had to flee from Germany, and spent many years in political exile in France. He was one of the main representatives of what Marx contemptuously referred to as the 'true Socialists', castigated in the *Communist Manifesto* as those who merely translated French ideas into German: 'speculative cobwebs, embroidered with flowers of rhetoric, steeped in the dew of sickly sentiment, a Philistine, foul and enervating literature'.

Shorn of invective, the difference between Hess and Marx was the insistence of the founder of 'scientific Socialism' on the study of the laws of social development which were making for the emergence of a Socialist society. Hess on the other hand put the stress on Socialism as a moral necessity; for him the conscious will, the decision in favour of Socialism rather than the 'objective forces of history', was the decisive factor. As a theoretician and original thinker, Hess, abstract and unsystematic, was not in Marx's class; latter-day historians relegated him to what seemed well-deserved obscurity. It took more than a century and the emergence of Communist movements totally unlike Marx's expectations to reawaken interest in the ideas of Hess and other early apostles of Socialism outside the Marxist tradition.

Hess was forever bursting with childlike idealism; he thought with his heart rather than his head. Amateur fashion, he dabbled in many subjects with which he was clearly not equipped to deal. Yet on the Jewish question his analysis was, as subsequent events proved, more realistic and less abstract than Marx's. Hess retired in 1852 from active politics and devoted himself to the study of natural sciences. Then in 1862, quite unexpectedly, he published a book which was to have been entitled *The Revival of Israel* but became known under the somewhat misleading title *Rome and Jerusalem, the last nationality question*. It opens with a moving personal confession:

After twenty years of estrangement I have returned to my people. Once again I am sharing in its festivals of joy and days of sorrow, in its hopes and memories. I am taking part in the spiritual and intellectual struggles of our day, both within the House of Israel and between our people and the gentile world. . . . A sentiment which I believed I had suppressed beyond recall is alive once again. It is the thought of my nationality, which is inseparably connected with my ancestral heritage, with the Holy Land and Eternal City, the birthplace of the belief in the divine unity of life and of the hope for the ultimate brotherhood of all men.*

Hess was born into a family in which, unlike Marx's, the Jewish religious tradition was still alive. When his parents moved to Cologne he was left in the home of his grandparents because Cologne was not

---

* Quoted from A. Hertzberg, *The Zionist Idea*, New York, 1959, based on an earlier translation by Meyer Waxman.

thought to offer sufficient opportunities for a Jewish education. But like almost all his contemporaries, Hess turned his back on religion; the Mosaic religion (as he wrote in his diary) was dead, its historical role was finished and could no longer be revived. If a religion had to be chosen, Christianity was obviously better fitted for the present time.* Hess did not undergo conversion, but he was not opposed in principle to baptism. In his first book (*The Sacred History of Mankind*) he said that the people chosen by their God must disappear forever, that out of their death might spring a new, more precious life. Later on, in *Jugement dernier du vieux monde social*, published in 1851, he mentioned the two 'horrible examples of unfortunate peoples' who had been punished for still identifying themselves with their dead institutions – the Chinese, 'a body without a soul, and the Jews, a soul without a body, wandering like a ghost through the centuries'.† True, under the impact of the Damascus affair in 1840, Hess had pondered the anomaly of Jewish existence; perhaps the Jews would remain strangers forever. He also wrote on one occasion that the Jew who denied his nationality was a contemptible creature. In 1840 Hess was painfully reminded (he wrote twenty years later) that he belonged to an unfortunate, maligned, despised and dispersed people, but one that the world had not succeeded in destroying: 'I wanted to cry out in anguish in expression of my Jewish patriotism, but this emotion was immediately superseded by the greater pain which was evoked in me by the suffering of the proletariat of Europe.' He thought there was no point in taking a lead in the struggle for the revival of the Jewish nation, if only because the Jews themselves were sure neither of themselves nor of their cause.

What, two decades later, brought about the profound change in Hess's thought and in his priorities? The position of the Jews in western society was certainly not critical; on the contrary, it had immensely improved during those years. Within their communities there were hardly any traces left of national spirit and enthusiasm. Two books published shortly before – Laharanne's *La nouvelle question d'Orient*, and J.Salvador's *Paris, Rome, Jerusalem, ou la question réligieuse au XIXe siècle* (Paris, 1860) had dealt with the prospects of a Jewish national revival, but it is doubtful whether they exerted a powerful influence on him.‡

* Edmund Silberner, *Moses Hess. Die Geschichte seines Lebens*, Leiden, 1966, pp. 23–4.
† Quoted in Theodor Zlocisti, *Moses Hess*, Berlin, 1921, p. 257.
‡ Laharanne, a young non-Jewish official in the French government, thought highly of the Jews and their historical mission: 'Yours is a mighty genius. You were strong in the days of antiquity, and strong in the Middle Ages. You have paid a heavy tax of eighteen centuries of persecution.' But those who remained were still strong enough to erect anew

In the course of his scientific studies he had become interested in the question of racial antagonism, to which he now attributed far greater importance than before. But in the last resort Hess's reconversion to Judaism was emotional, and fairly sudden at that; only a few years before he was still expressing opinions very much in contrast to those put forward in *Rome and Jerusalem*.

The most striking feature of that book is the startling, revolutionary and deeply pessimistic analysis of antisemitism. Almost all Hess's contemporaries on the Left were firmly convinced that antisemitism reflected the dying convulsions of the old order, that it was reactionary, and politically of little consequence. Hess did not share their confidence. Writing well before modern racial antisemitism became a major political force, he had already realised its dangerous potential: the racial antagonism of the Germans towards the Jews was a deep, instinctive force, far more powerful than any rational argument. Reform and assimilation, eradicating the signs of their Jewishness and denying their race, would not save them:

But even an act of conversion cannot relieve the Jew of the enormous pressure of German antisemitism. The Germans hate the religion of the Jews less than they hate their race – they hate the peculiar faith of the Jews less than their peculiar noses. Reform, conversion, education and emancipation – none of these opens the gates of society to the German Jew; hence his desire to deny his racial origin.

But noses could not be reshaped nor could black, wavy hair become blond and straightened by constant combing. There simply was no way out of the dilemma: the modern Jew could not hide behind geographical and philosophical abstractions; he could mask himself a thousand times over, change his name and religion and character, he

---

the gates of Jerusalem. Joseph Salvador, a philosopher of Jewish origin on his father's side, who belonged to a famous Sefardi family in the south of France, was preoccupied with the idea of Judaism, with its enduring elements rather than with its present difficulties. His philosophy, developed in a series of books beginning with *Loi de Moïse et du peuple hébreu*, was that the basic ideas of Judaism were, on the one hand, the unity of the human race, its equality and fraternity, and, on the other, a new and higher messianism, called upon to establish a new order replacing Caesars and Popes. To that end he advocated the establishment of a new state between orient and occident, on the coast of Galilee and Canaan. According to Salvador, there were only two races in Asia Minor capable of civilisation and progress, the Greeks and the Jews, and notwithstanding their deep degradation the Jews were still capable of infusing new life into the mountains of Judea. Salvador's writings, permeated with deep belief in the future of the Jewish nation, were very much in the tradition of mid-nineteenth-century speculative philosophy of history, concerned with the destiny of the European nations, Russia and America.

would still be recognised as a Jew. The Jew might become a naturalised citizen, Hess argued, but he would never convince the gentile of his total separation from the gentile's own nationality. For the nations of Europe had always regarded the existence of Jews in their midst as an anomaly:

> We shall always remain strangers among the nations. They may even be moved by a sense of humanity and justice to emancipate us, but they will never respect us, so long as we make *ubi bene ibi patria* our guiding principle, indeed almost a religion, and place it above our own great national memories. Religious fanaticism may cease to cause hatred of the Jews in the more culturally advanced countries; but despite enlightenment and education, the Jew in exile who denies his nationality will never earn the respect of the nations among whom he dwells.*

The racial issue, Hess thought, was particularly acute in Germany because many Germans were deeply prejudiced in this respect without even being aware of it; humanism had not yet become part and parcel of their national character to the extent it had in the public mind of the Roman peoples. For Jews, homelessness was the heart of the problem. Like other peoples they needed a normal national life: 'Without soil a man sinks to the status of a parasite, feeding on others.' Hess's definition of Jews ('a race, a brotherhood, a nation') and Judaism was somewhat vague, but it is clear that he felt acutely that the liberal assumptions and definitions of the day were simply untrue. He maintained that if emancipation was not compatible with adherence to the Jewish nation, Jews ought to give up the former for the latter. They were not a religious group, but a separate nation, a special race, and the modern Jew who denied this was not only an apostate, a religious renegade, but a traitor to his people, his tribe, his race.

The main danger to Judaism did not come from the pious old Jew who would rather have his tongue cut out than misuse it by denying his nationality. It came from the religious reformers who with their newly invented ceremonies and empty eloquence had sucked the marrow out of Judaism and left only a shadowy skeleton of this most magnificent of all historical phenomena. This kind of reform had no basis in either the general situation in the modern world or the essential national character of Judaism, for which the reformers had not the slightest respect: they were at great pains to erase every echo and memory of it from their creed and worship. The reformers tried to make Judaism, which was

---

* Quoted in Hertzberg, *The Zionist Idea*, p. 121.

both national and universal, into a second version of Christianity cut on a rationalist pattern, and this at a time 'when the original was already mortally sick'. Hess ridiculed those reformers who claimed that the Jews, representing pure theism, had a mission in the diaspora to teach intolerant Christianity the principles of humanitarianism, to work for a new synthesis of morality and life, which had become divorced from each other in the Christian world. Such a mission could be achieved only by a nation which was politically organised, which could embody this unity of morality and life in its own social institutions. Hess also made some scathing observations about the Jewish obscurantists who buried their heads in the sand, denouncing all science and every aspect of modern secular life.

Could a bridge be built between the nihilism of the Reform rabbis and the conservativism of the orthodox who had forgotten nothing? Hess thought the answer was the return to the land, a Jewish state in Palestine. The hope of a political rebirth of the Jewish people should be kept alive, until political conditions in the orient were ripe for the founding of Jewish colonies. He had no doubt that conditions were rapidly improving with the digging of the Suez Canal and the building of a railroad to connect Europe and Asia. France, he believed, would undoubtedly help them to establish their colonies, which might one day extend from Suez to Jerusalem and from the banks of the Jordan to the shores of the Mediterranean. At this stage Hess drew heavily on Laharanne's analysis of the Eastern Question: what European power would oppose a plan for the Jews, united in a congress, to buy back their ancient fatherland? Who would object if they flung a handful of gold to decrepit old Turkey and said: 'Give us back our old home and use this money to consolidate the other parts of your tottering old empire.'*

Hess had definite ideas about the character of the future Jewish state. He did not doubt that the majority of Jews in the civilised west would remain where they lived. The nobler natures among them would again interest themselves in the Jewish people, of whom they knew little, but, having achieved the breakthrough to western culture and society they

* Laharanne, it should be added in parenthesis, also envisaged the emergence of a big Arab state which would include Syria and Mesopotamia as well as Anatolia. The sultan was to be left only with his European possessions to prevent their falling into Russian hands. As for the inhabitants of the New Judea, a great calling was reserved for them: they would be the bearers of civilisation to peoples as yet inexperienced, the mediators between Europe and Asia. They would come to the land of their fathers wearing the crown of age-long martyrdom, and there at last would be healed of their ills.

would not lightly give up their newly won civic position; such a sacrifice of a recently acquired prize was contrary to human nature. But Hess did not doubt that many thousands of east European Jews would emigrate. In this context he mentioned Hassidism, of which he knew enough to realise that it was one of the few living forces in contemporary Judaism; few western Jews had so much as heard of Hassidism at the time. Hess argued that in the last resort, given modern means of communication, it did not really matter how many of the Jewish race would dwell within the borders of a Jewish state and how many outside. The state was needed both as a spiritual centre, and, as Hess said in a later essay, as a base for political action. In this state the existence of a Jewish identity would have neither to be demonstrated nor to be hidden.

The state was to be basically Socialist in character. Hess envisaged the establishment of voluntary cooperative societies (associations on the pattern developed by Louis Blanc) which would operate with the help of state credits on the basis of 'Mosaic, i.e. Socialist principles'. The land would be owned not by individuals but wholly or largely by the nation. For Hess, a Jewish state was not an end in itself but a means towards the just social order to which all peoples aspired.

Rome and Jerusalem suffers from grave weaknesses. Its very form, twelve letters and ten notes written to a fictional lady, was neither a happy nor an effective medium for a work which its author hoped would bring about a radical revolution in Judaism. It is difficult to imagine the authors of the *Communist Manifesto* presenting their ideas in this fashion. The style, as Isaiah Berlin has noted, is by turns sentimental and rhetorical and at times merely flat; there are far too many digressions and irrelevancies. The substance of the book, too, is open to serious criticism. The analysis of antisemitism and of the drawbacks of assimilation is far more convincing than the rest of the argument. The idea that Turkey could be induced to part with Palestine for a handful of gold betrays, to put it kindly, a lack of realism on the part of one who had been preoccupied for several decades with political issues. Hess's reliance on French help for the venture was, as some of his friends in Paris told him, clearly over-optimistic. Weakest of all are the sections dealing with the Jewish religion; Hess felt that so long as a Jewish state did not exist, this was the great preservative and nothing ought to be done to undermine or dilute the Jewish religion, of which in *Rome and Jerusalem* he spoke with the greatest admiration; hence his fierce attacks on the 'nihilism' of Reform Judaism. Old customs should not be abolished, he argued, nor holidays cut down. Judaism was just and equitable, the true source of all the noble aspirations of mankind.

It is not easy to reconcile such views, the unctuous approach and the frequent genuflexions before established religion, with his earlier writings. Only three years before writing *Rome and Jerusalem* he had opposed all religion, explaining it as the symptom of a pathological state of mind; that the history of religions was the history of human error.* Did Hess suddenly 'see the light'? There remain doubts as to how genuine his conversion really was. While preaching the virtues of religious observance to his people, Hess himself did not adhere to his own prescription. Having convinced himself intellectually that religion was for the time being essential to prevent the total disintegration of the Jewish people, he could not in his private life muster sufficient enthusiasm to live up to his new discovery. He had found in himself the feeling of solidarity with his people and a belief in its future, but religious belief could not be reproduced at will. Nor is the religious element in *Rome and Jerusalem* altogether essential to the main theme; its introduction strikes an inharmonious note. Hess was no doubt aware of the dilemma of the post-religious Jew, but he preferred not to dwell on it. And yet, with all its lapses and shortcomings, the book is more than a powerful and moving plea; it is in part a work of prophetic genius. His analysis of the problems facing the Jew in modern European society was incomparably superior to that of any of his contemporaries, including far more sophisticated thinkers than himself. Later Zionist writings, even the most influential among them, such as Pinsker's *Autoemanzipation* and Herzl's *Judenstaat*, only gave concise expression to issues that had been discussed for years; their basic ideas had been in the air. Hess on the other hand was a genuine pioneer, breaking fresh ground. When Herzl read Hess for the first time, soon after completing his *Judenstaat*, he noted in his diary: 'Everything we tried is already there in his book.'†

Hess was bound to make little impact precisely because he was so far ahead of his time. The *Kulturjuden*, as he called them, bitterly attacked him. Abraham Geiger, the leader of Reform Judaism, referred to him contemptuously as a virtual outsider who 'after bankruptcy as a Socialist and all kinds of swindles wants to make a hit with nationalism. Along with Czech and Montenegrin nationality, he wants to restore Jewish nationality.' Most Socialists and liberals knew nothing of the book, while those who read it rejected it as a romantic-reactionary chimera,

---

* *Das Jahrhundert*, 1857, p. 363, quoted in Silberner, *Moses Hess*, p. 420.
† *Tagebücher*, Berlin, 1923, vol. 2, p. 599.

on the same level as the antisemitic rantings of Bruno Bauer. A very few Jewish writers welcomed it, the most prominent among them being the historian Heinrich Graetz. As for a broader public, *Rome and Jerusalem* was rediscovered only forty years after its publication. While Hess regarded it as essentially philosophical in character, it was of course a political book. But in the 1860s its basic ideas seemed altogether impractical.

Hess continued to take part rather half-heartedly in Jewish activities in Paris. After 1862 he again devoted his main attention to the Socialist movement, as a leader in Lassalle's new party and a member of the First International. His views on things Jewish did not change, but the problem lost some of its urgency. He was neither a leader nor a prophet, and felt no call to take the initiative. Or perhaps he simply realised that the time was not ripe for his plans? During his last years he returned to the study of natural science, and died, a forgotten man, in Paris in April 1875. A few newspapers published short and incorrect obituaries; no representative of any Jewish organisation spoke at his funeral.

Few east European Jews at the time had heard of *Rome and Jerusalem*, which was translated into Hebrew and Yiddish only many years after the death of its author. Yet by a curious coincidence a little pamphlet in Hebrew, entitled *Drishat Zion* (Seeking Zion) was published in the same year (1862) in a small town in the extreme north-east of Germany. Based on totally different ideological premises, it advocated a doctrine and political solutions remarkably similar to those outlined by Hess. Hirsch Kalischer, its author, was a rabbi in Thorn, a town in the province of Posen. A man in his sixties, he wrote in the classical and somewhat clumsy Hebrew then used by orthodox rabbis; his book opened with statements by several renowned religious scholars certifying that the reverend author, illuminated throughout his life by the study of the holy Torah, could be trusted even when venturing outside his own field of specialisation – that of Talmudic legalism.

On every page of his short pamphlet Kalischer refers to the Bible, the Mishna and the Talmud. But shorn of its ritualistic invocations, and with all its lack of philosophical sophistication, it is a modern, almost existentialist piece of writing, with a message that could not be more outspoken: the Redemption of Israel will not come as a sudden miracle, the Messiah will not be sent from heaven to sound a blast on his great trumpet and cause all people to tremble. Nor will he surround the Holy City with a wall of fire or cause the Holy Temple to descend from heaven. Only stupid people could believe such nonsense; wise men knew that redemption would be achieved only gradually and, above all, would come about only as the result of the Jews' own efforts. If the Almighty were to work a miracle, what fool would not be willing to go to Palestine? But to renounce home and fortune for the sake of Zion before the days of the Messiah – that was the real test and challenge. Kalischer maintained that from a religious point of view it was highly meritorious to live in Palestine. There were a great many Jews in Europe with political and economic influence; it was up to them to take the necessary first steps towards the resettlement of the Holy Land. Time and circumstance favoured such an endeavour. Kalischer refers to the Italian Risorgimento, the national struggle of the Poles and Hungarians, and asks: why do these people sacrifice their lives for the land of their fathers while we, like men bereft of strength and courage, do nothing? Are we inferior to other peoples who disregard life and fortune when it is a question of their land and nation?

Kalischer was primarily concerned with the principle of the return to Zion. (It should be noted at least in passing that another rabbi, Yehuda Alkalay, writing in Serbia twenty years earlier, had already drawn up a practical programme towards the same end, suggesting the establishment of an association on the lines of a railroad company to ask the sultan to give the Jews their land at an annual rent.*) Nor was Kalischer an impractical man. Towards the end of his book he discusses some of the arguments likely to be used against his scheme. Would not the property of the Jews in Palestine be insecure? Would not rapacious Arabs rob the Jewish peasants of their harvest? This is probably the first time the Arab question is mentioned in Zionist literature. But the danger, Kalischer says, is remote, for 'the present pasha is a just man severely punishing robbery and theft'.

The impact of *Drishat Zion* on east European Jewry was as limited as that of *Rome and Jerusalem* on Jews in the west. The only practical outcome was the establishment of an agricultural school in Mikve Israel, on the outskirts of Jaffa, by the Paris *Alliance Israélite*, largely owing to the untiring efforts of Kalischer. But this remained an isolated initiative. It gave no fresh impetus to immigration into Palestine or to any major political effort. On the contrary, the pious Jews of Jerusalem protested against the profane and dangerous enterprise of teaching young Jews how to earn a living and thus deflecting them from the study of the holy scriptures. The time was clearly not yet ripe for the realisation of the dreams of these early prophets of Zionism.

* *Kitve Rabbi Yehuda Alkalay*, Jerusalem, 1954, vol. 1.

Eastern European Jewry

Mention has been made so far almost exclusively of the Jews of Germany and western Europe, the challenges and problems facing them, their thinkers and leaders. But the great majority of the Jewish people were to be found in the towns and villages of Lithuania, White Russia, Poland, Galicia and Rumania. More than five million lived in Russia at the end of the nineteenth century, about ten times as many as in Germany. They were concentrated in the western areas of the tsarist empire, which they were not permitted to leave. Only about two hundred thousand of them, well-to-do merchants, university graduates, veterans (with twenty-five years of army service) and some others were permitted to live in places like St Petersburg, Moscow or Kiev, and other towns outside the so-called pale of settlement. Jews accounted for about 16–18 per cent of the inhabitants of the Warsaw, Grodno, and Minsk administrative districts, and 24–8 per cent in the Jassy, Cracow, and Lemberg areas. But since they were not allowed to live in villages, the urban percentage was far larger; cities like Vilna, Brest Litovsk, Bialystok, Zhitomir, Berdichev or Vitebsk were predominantly Jewish. At the turn of the century Warsaw, with 220,000 Jews, had the biggest Jewish community in Europe, followed by Odessa with 140,000. Under a law promulgated in 1858, they were not allowed to live within forty miles of the frontier, and according to other regulations they had no right to reside in several important cities within the pale, such as Kiev, Sevastopol or Yalta – the last perhaps because the tsar did not want to see too many of them from his palace.

Their economic situation was bad and after 1880 continued to deteriorate. True, a few Jewish millionaires such as the Ginzburgs and Poliakovs were prominent in banking and later on in the development of railways. The sugar and textile industries were largely Jewish, as were the grain and timber trades, and, to a lesser extent, the milling, brewing, tobacco and leather industries. There were many artisans in the Jewish ghettoes but they were gradually being squeezed out of business as modern industry spread, just as coachmen were being displaced by the railways. Few Jews lived from the soil; efforts were made to increase the number in agriculture, and this did indeed rise from 80,000 to 180,000 between 1860 and 1897. But the majority in the pale of settlement were men without a definite occupation, living from hand to mouth, 'Luft-menschen' without roots and without hope. Each morning they congregated in the market place or in front of the synagogue, waiting for any job, however degrading, however badly paid, to come their way. Many professions were closed to them; they were virtually barred from entering government service, except as physicians, but few had the opportunity to study medicine; there was a *numerus clausus* for Jews in the universities – 10 per cent in the pale, 5 per cent outside it, and 3 per cent in Moscow and St Petersburg.

The government saw to it, however, that they were fully represented in one not very popular field of service: they accounted for 4 per cent of the total population but provided 6 per cent of all army recruits. The heart-rending scenes accompanying the call-up of Jewish boys, often no more than twelve or fourteen years old, were frequently described in contemporary literature:

It was one of the most awful sights I have ever beheld [Alexander Herzen wrote]. The boys of twelve and thirteen might somehow have survived it but infants of eight and ten. . . . No brush, however black, could portray such horror on canvas. And these sick children, without attention, without a caress, exposed to the icy wind which blows unhindered from the Arctic Ocean, were going to their graves.*

The state of health in the ghettoes being what it was, they were ill-prepared for the rigours of military life. They could be away from home for up to twenty-five years and they were not, of course, able to observe the commandments and prohibitions of their religion while in the army. In the early 1890s the American government sent two emissaries to Europe to investigate the reasons for the sudden rise in immigration to the United States. Messrs Weber and Kempster were not professional do-gooders but hard-boiled immigration officers; in their report, published in 1892, they declared flatly that they had never seen such incredible conditions of poverty and misery in their lives, nor did they ever hope to witness them again.† The majority of Russian Jews lived in conditions even worse than the poorest of Russian peasants and workers. Many families were crammed into one small house, infant mortality was high, and labour productivity low. If the bread-winner fell ill this usually spelt doom for the whole family. Even antisemitic Russian newspapers admitted that the bulk of Russian Jewry was exposed to slow death by starvation.

The tsars and their advisers had no clear idea how to solve the Jewish

---

* A. Herzen, *Byloe i Dumy*, vol. 1, p. 189.

† *Reports of the commissioners of immigration upon the causes which incite immigration to the United States*, Washington, 1892.

question, and throughout the nineteenth century often changed course. Many of the laws restricting freedom of movement and choice of profession dated back to the late eighteenth century. Alexander I, on the other hand, pursued a relatively liberal policy: Jewish children were permitted to attend public schools, Jews could buy land and settle on it. Nicholas I entered Jewish history as a second Haman, whereas the reign of Alexander II, who abolished serfdom, was considered the golden age of Russian Jewry. Under his comparatively enlightened rule the restrictive laws were reviewed and some modest efforts made towards the political and social integration of the Jews. Most of the restrictive laws were not in fact abolished, but with the new spirit of toleration hope prevailed that at some future date they would receive full civil rights, at any rate to the extent that such rights were compatible with tsarist autocracy. In a popular song expressing the spirit of the period, Alexander II was apostrophised as an angel of God who found the flower of Judah soiled by dirt and trampled in the dust; the good tsar rescued it, reviving it with live water, and planted it in his garden where it would flourish once more.

With the murder of Alexander II and the accession to the throne of Alexander III, the situation deteriorated rapidly. As a result of the 'provisional laws' of May 1882 (most of which remained in force up to the downfall of the tsarist régime) tens of thousands of Jews were expelled from the villages in which they had settled and also from cities outside the pale of settlement. Official chicanery and persecution had disastrous consequences, but there were even more ominous events; beginning with 1881, pogroms became an almost permanent feature of the Russian scene. There had been minor anti-Jewish excesses before, as in Odessa in 1859 and 1871, but no particular significance had been attached to these events at the time since they seemed no different in character from the clashes between other nationalities which had occurred from time to time in the empire of the tsars. But the attacks which occurred in April-June 1881 shortly after the murder of Alexander II were more widespread and far more vicious in character. They took place mainly in southern Russia, in cities such as Elizavetgrad, Kiev and Odessa, where Jews had been slightly better off than in Poland and White Russia. These pogroms (from the Russian verb *pogromit*, to destroy) continued in 1883 and 1884 in Rostov, Yekaterinoslav, Yalta and other cities. In all these places Jews were killed and injured by a fanatical mob and much of their property destroyed. According to rumours which gained wide currency among the illiterate masses, they had killed the good tsar, and his successor had issued an order to plunder the Jewish quarters. The government did little to provide protection. Indeed, in some cases the attackers were abetted by the local administration and the police. These attacks ceased in 1884, but after an interval of about twenty years of relative quiet a fresh wave of pogroms on a much larger scale broke out.

In the Kishinev riots of April 1903, forty-five Jews were killed and many more wounded. Similar attacks followed in Gomel and Zhitomir. The outbreak reached its climax in October 1905 when in the course of twelve days 810 Jews were killed in riots all over western and southern Russia. The number of victims was small in comparison with the catastrophe that befell the Jewish people in Europe forty years later, but the particular brutality of the attacks, the inactivity of the central government, and the positive incitement by many of its local representatives aroused a storm of protest in western Europe and the United States. This was in many respects a more civilised age than our own. Unashamed cynicism on the part of governments and individuals in the face of acts of barbarism had not yet become an accepted fashion. Some populist groups had played a certain part in stirring up anti-Jewish sentiments during the early phase of these attacks, on the mistaken assumption that riots against 'Jewish parasites' would eventually turn into a revolutionary movement directed against the government, the landowners and capitalists. The main instigators, especially during the later period, were the 'Black Hundred' and other movements of the extreme Right, which preached a mixture of extreme nationalism and religious obscurantism.

The tsarist government was rightly accused of aiding and abetting the pogromists in the hope of diverting popular dissatisfaction. But antisemitism was not manufactured by the administration or forced upon an unwilling or indifferent population. It had deep roots among at least part of the population, and not much encouragement on the part of the authorities was needed to kindle the flame of race hatred. This mood was not restricted to one specific section of the people. It was found among the peasants and the aristocracy, the middle classes and even the intelligentsia, some of whose members firmly believed that the Jews were an alien body which could not and should not be assimilated. Some of the accusations against them, such as wholesale exploitation, were ludicrous; in their overwhelming majority they were penniless; the Jews of Mogilev, who constituted 94 per cent of the town's population, could not have made a living by exploiting the remaining 6 per cent in that city. They were also accused of harbouring subversive sentiments, and it was certainly true that there was little love lost among them for a government that cruelly oppressed them. While the number who took an active part in the revolutionary movement in the 1880s and 1890s was small, more and more young Jews joined in the following years the one movement which held out the promise of a better future in Russia.

As already mentioned, the government had no clear and consistent policy. From time to time half-hearted measures were contemplated to further cultural assimilation, promote agricultural employment, open the gates of the pale of settlement, and allow the Jews to disperse over the vast territories of the empire. But few of these projects ever got beyond the planning stage, and those which did were tackled without much conviction. What other possible solutions existed? With all their oriental ferocity, the rulers of Russia were neither cruel nor systematic enough to contemplate the physical extermination of the Jews. They did not expect much from encouraging or enforcing mass baptism. There were simply too many of them. Emigration was the last resort; and in despair the Jews began to flee the country of their birth in thousands. Mass emigration, mainly to America, and to a much lesser extent to Britain, South Africa, and western Europe, followed the May Laws and the pogroms of 1882. It is estimated that between that year and 1914 about two and a half million Jews left eastern Europe, including Austria, Poland and Rumania. During the fifteen years before the outbreak of the First World War, 1·3 million Jews emigrated from Russia. The wave reached its peak in 1903-6, the years of the worst pogroms, when four hundred thousand Jews left Russia for the United States.

Thus a new, major chapter opened in the long history of Jewish migration. This is not the place for a detailed analysis of the mass exodus, nor for an account of the hardships and privations they had to endure. But it was not a tale of unmitigated woe. Their sufferings hardened them. The fight for survival brought out some of the qualities which explain their success in the country of their adoption. The challenges facing them generated an enormous fund of resilience, inventiveness and intelligence. Those who stayed behind drew closer together. A western observer, Harold Frederic, visiting Russia in the 1880s noted the 'remarkable solidarity, at once so pathetic and prejudicial', which marked the Russian Jews:

Once you cross the Russian frontier, you can tell the Jews at railway stations or on the street almost as easily as in America you can distinguish the Negroes. This is more a matter of dress – of hair and beard and cap and caftan – than of physiognomy. But even more still is it a matter of demeanour. They seem never for an instant to lose the consciousness that they are a race apart. It is in their walk, in their sidelong glance, in the carriage of their sloping shoulders, in the curious gesture with the uplifted palm. Nicholas [the First] . . . solidified [the Jews] into a dense, hardbaked and endlessly resistant mass.*

Frederic expressed astonishment that any religion and any rudimentary notion whatever of honesty survived in these terrible conditions.

The great bulk remained simple and devout people, clinging doggedly to their despised faith, helping one another where they could, keeping up virtues of temperance and family affection which their Russian taskmasters hardly knew by name.†

With all this, life in the ghetto was dismal, even if its inhabitants were not always aware of the full extent of their degradation. True, from Mendele Mocher Sfarim (*In those days*) onwards, there has been a tendency to grow sentimental about the ghetto, to describe it in a rosy, almost idyllic way. Life in the pale had its bright sides and not a few of those who grew up in the ghettoes of eastern Europe later on stressed the vitality, the warmth, the solidarity, the we-are-the-people aspect which was so sadly absent among later generations. But the darker aspects of life in the pale were of course far more striking and provided much bitter comment among contemporaries. A.D.Gordon wrote about the 'parasitism of fundamentally useless people', Frischmann about the disgust generally evoked by Jewish life. Berdichevsky said that the Jews in the pale were 'not a nation, not a people, not human', and Joseph Chaim Brenner, the most radical critic of all, used such epithets as 'gypsies and filthy dogs'. The anomalies of Jewish life were bound to find expression in the search for radical solutions to the general misery, the *Judennot* which was not just political and economic, but increasingly also psychological in character.

Intellectual Life

The mood of east European Jewry was reflected in changing religious fashions and intellectual currents. Hassidism had developed partly under the impact of the Khmelnitsky massacres in 1648, and had a strong hold in the Ukraine, Podolia, and eastern Galicia. It was not a philosophical

* Harold Frederic, *The New Exodus*, London, 1892, pp. 79–80.
† *Ibid.*, p. 32.

movement but anti-rationalist, based on religious emotion and with strong elements of Messianism. For the Hassidim, God was not an abstract concept; they saw his presence in every particle of the world, inherent in all creatures, animals and plants; the relationship between man and God was immediate. In this and other respects Hassidism resembled other mystical movements and the pantheism of previous centuries. It tried to combine mutually exclusive elements; its leaders argued that divine providence was omnipotent and omnipresent, that the Creator was present in every act of man, that divinity (*shechina*) manifested itself in all human activity, even in sin. If so, what was left of the traditional Jewish idea of the freedom of the individual and, incidentally, of the concept of sin? Such philosophical contradictions did not trouble the leaders and followers of Hassidism. It was a folk religion, with a tremendous appeal for the common people precisely because it stressed qualities of real piety in contrast to the rabbinical tradition with its emphasis on external performance, on the observance of all the commandments and taboos of the Torah. Hassidism preached not asceticism but the enjoyment of life, considering such enjoyment a form of worship. It took a poor view of the leading rabbis and their arid style of learning and scholarship, stressing instead contemplative understanding of religion. The Hassidic prayer was not a mechanical duty but an act of direct communion with God. The right kind of prayer could cure the sick, make the poor rich, avert all kinds of evil. All depended on the intensity of prayer; the ecstasy of the Hassidim at the time of prayer, their wild bodily contortions and their dances were the most dramatic characteristics of the movement.

By the middle of the nineteenth century the original impetus of Hassidism had largely petered out. Instead a cult of *Zadikim* had spread, the cult of saint-leaders; they were the real mediators between God and the world, inscribing amulets, providing special prayers (in Yiddish) and incantations for their followers. On a lower level the *Magidim*, the itinerant preachers and miracle men, became very popular. Hassidism had given birth to a great religious revival, but there were many who had watched its manifestations with serious misgivings because of its 'cult of the personality', its unbridled emotionalism, and other features utterly opposed to Jewish tradition. A thirty-year war between Hassidism and its opponents split east European Jewry right down the middle; the two camps physically attacked and outlawed each other, and even denounced the other side to the Russian authorities, asking for their intervention against the hated enemy.

Hassidism appealed to the masses; it was unlikely to satisfy the more sophisticated elements who were witnesses to the great material and intellectual changes in the world around them. Such men were likely to find their place in the *Haskala*, the movement of enlightenment, which from the early years of the nineteenth century tried to combine some elements of Jewish tradition with modern secular thought. In Germany and western Europe the Haskala led towards cultural and political assimilation; in eastern Europe, with its millions of Jews, it was bound after similar beginnings to take a different course. The early centres of the east European Haskala were Odessa and to a lesser extent Vilna. Some of the leaders of this school regarded it as their main task to bring about a revival of Hebrew literature – in contrast to the Yiddish vernacular. Others felt that a purely literary movement would fail to make any substantial impact on Jewish life, and consequently emphasised the need to guide the Jewish masses towards a more normal and productive life. Their activities were followed with suspicion and active opposition not only by the orthodox rabbis but by the great majority of simple Jews, distrustful of western education, western attire, and the western way of life in general. The life of the early small-town *Maskil*, described in countless contemporary autobiographies and novels, was not enviable; divided by an abyss from the mass of fellow Jews, his call for reform all too often fell on stony ground. Socially isolated, deeply hurt by the open hostility facing them, some of the early Maskilim despaired of their people who, they thought, were bound to remain forever ignorant and backward. Others, more optimistically inclined, collaborated with the Russian authorities who during the 1850s and 1860s favoured the reform movement. The appeal of Russian culture was considerable, and there seemed to be a real prospect that cultural assimilation would bring about a radical change in the entire position of the Jews.

Thus the new age of reason finally reached the ghettoes of eastern Europe. A new world was arising as the forces of darkness were receding; the moral and intellectual regeneration of the Jewish people seemed only a question of time. 'Awake! Israel and Judah arise! Shake off the dust, open wide thine eyes', Abram Ber Gottlober wrote; and Yehuda Leib Gordon: 'Arise my people, 'tis time for waking! lo, the night is o'er, the day is breaking!'* This was the keynote of the period. The poetry was not beyond reproach but the message was clear. The spread of secular education was no longer to be stopped. When Rabbi Israel

* Quoted in Jacob S. Raisin, *The Haskalah Movement in Russia*, New York, 1913, pp. 231–2.

Salanter learned that his son had gone to Berlin to study medicine, he removed his shoes and sat down on the floor of his house to observe the traditional seven days of mourning for the death of a beloved relative. Such uncompromising attitudes towards the winds of change sweeping the ghettoes became rarer during the 1860s and 1870s. 'Let there be light' was the motto chosen in 1860 for the first Jewish newspaper in the Russian language. The general trend was towards Russification; even those who wrote in Hebrew were not at all certain whether the language and the culture had a future: Who knows, Gordon asked in a famous poem, whether I am not the last of the writers of Zion – and you the last readers? Our children, the same poet lamented on another occasion, have become strangers to our nation. The conflict between fathers and sons, described in Turgenev's famous novel, had its parallel in the Jewish quarters. The Jewish Bazarovs, too, 'believed in nothing', to quote one of Turgenev's Russian heroes. They took to radical ideas like thirsty men to water; populism and early Socialist ideas found enthusiastic followers in this generation of young Jews, among them quite a few such as Eliezer Ben Yehuda, Yehuda Leib Levin, and Yehiel Chlenov, who were later to become Zionist leaders.

The pogroms of the early 1880s and the anti-Jewish policy of Alexander III were a shattering blow to the hopes of these men and women for a gradual integration into Russian society. More young Jews joined revolutionary groups, others turned to the new movement calling for a national revival of the Jewish people. The beginning of this movement dates back several decades, more precisely to some early writers of the Haskala, who were the leading advocates of the national revival. Abraham Mapu and Yehuda Leib Gordon were contemporaries of Tolstoy and Dostoievsky (which is not to say that their contribution to world literature was of equal significance). They were above all mentors and educators and only incidentally writers; this much they had in common with the Russian radical writers of the period such as Nekrasov (who was much admired by Y.L.Gordon), Pisarev, and Chernyshevsky (who strongly influenced Lilienblum). They regarded their poems, their essays and their novels as the most suitable vehicle for their message. Their writings are of considerable interest, reflecting various social and cultural facets of Jewish life at the time. Even the most ambitious novels, such as Smolenskin's *Hatoeh bedarke hehayim* (*The Wanderer on the Path of Life*) are weak judged by purely literary criteria. Shrill, verbose, lacking psychological refinement, oblivious of nature, these Jewish *Bildungsromane* all describe the difficulties faced by small-town Maskilim. The young heretics are usually expelled from their parental home (or the *Yeshiva*); they make their way to Odessa or some other centre of the Haskala. They are invariably poor but honest – in glaring contrast to the leaders of the community. Their material problems are often solved by sudden legacies from rich uncles in America. The villains (such as Rabbi Zadok in Mapu's *Ayit Zavua*, or Menasse in Smolenskin's novel) are criminals or at best boors and imposters who, posing as pious people, somehow manage to dominate their communities and use their influence to oppress the weak and poor Maskilim. At their best these novels describe the great Hassidic rabbis holding court, the exploits of the itinerant miracle men, the forerunners of both Barnum and modern revivalism. Jewish society as it emerges from these novels is engrossed in unending internal strife, engulfed in obscurantism and prejudice, stubbornly resisting any reform. True, there are redeeming features, such as the traditional respect for learning; but the traditional subjects are criticised for their total irrelevance to the modern world. The Yeshiva student thus ceases to be the glamour boy of Jewish life. He is not even any longer the ideal husband. More than once the Haskala novel deals with the conflict arising from the unwillingness of an educated Jewish girl to marry the Yeshiva student picked for her by her parents.

The writers of that age are now remembered for their role as social critics and prophets of a national revival. To this extent their impact on Jewish circles is comparable to that of Belinsky and Chernyshevsky, and there was a certain similarity with regard to the problems facing them. The Jews, like the Russians, had their 'westernisers' and their 'Slavophiles' in the 1860s and 1870s. The westernisers (assimilationists) had many supporters; later on the majority turned to the ideal of a national revival. The slogan of the Slavophiles, 'pora domoi' (literally: it is time to go home), had its equivalent among the Jews of eastern Europe.

One of the first to attack cultural assimilation in the name of the Jewish cultural idea was Peretz Smolenskin, born near Mogilev in 1842. At the age of twenty-five he settled in Vienna where he edited *Hashachar* (The Dawn), the most influential Hebrew newspaper of the time. He was also its main contributor, proof reader, distributor, and sometimes even typesetter. In a series of long articles he attacked the Berlin Haskala and, in particular, Mendelssohn (whom he called 'Ben Menahem') for having assumed that the Jewish nation was irrevocably dead and for preaching an 'artificial cosmopolitanism'. The Jews, Smolenskin emphasised time and time again, were a people, a nation.

They never ceased to be a people even after their kingdom was destroyed. They were a spiritual nation (*Am Haruach*); the Torah was the foundation of its statehood. It was the unforgivable sin of the German Haskala to have made the love of their own people unfashionable among Jews. Then they had proceeded to destroy the other pillar of Judaism – its religion – and as a result the house of Israel had completely collapsed.

The accusations were of course one-sided; Smolenskin, moreover, tended to forget that his own nationalism was by no means part of the Jewish tradition but stemmed from other spiritual sources, and that he too had advocated religious reform in his earlier years. He frequently quoted the evil precedent of the German Haskala in his struggle against both Russification and cosmopolitanism. He preached Jewish nationalism when it was not yet fashionable to do so and he was also one of the few to predict antisemitic outbreaks well before the riots of 1881. The source of antisemitism, Smolenskin maintained, was not primarily economic rivalry – though this too played a part – but the Jewish lack of self-respect and national honour, their low position among the nations. In a series of verbose essays (some running to several hundred pages)* which constantly digressed from his main theme, he developed his ideas – unsystematically, and, on the whole, not on a high level of intellectual sophistication. His criticism was often quite effective, his constructive proposals much weaker. Smolenskin believed that without Hebrew there was no Torah, and without the Torah, no Jewish people. For that reason he opposed all religious reforms, which could only further divide the Jewish people. The main task was to establish schools for teachers and rabbis who were to infuse new life into the young generation, to teach it Hebrew, and thus to promote national consciousness and loyalty to its people. Smolenskin had little hope that Hebrew would again become a spoken language, and up to 1881 he advocated a national revival in the diaspora rather than in Palestine. Only in his last essays did he express the idea that it would be best for the Jews to leave Russia, to migrate to Eretz Israel, to set up agricultural colonies there and thus to 're-establish the real unity of the Jewish people'.

Smolenskin's writings, antiquated as they now appear, had a great impact on many young Jews. Groups of students in Moscow and St Petersburg gave him an enthusiastic welcome when he went back for a visit. Others were not so captivated by a religious romanticism which

---

* *Am Haruach* (The Nation of the Spirit); *Et Lata'at* (It Is Time to Plant); *Et La'assot* (It Is Time for Action).

appealed almost exclusively to the emotions. A younger generation of intellectuals refused to take Jewish values and traditions for granted. Micah Joseph Berdichevsky, subjecting this heritage to searching criticism, complained about the narrowness of traditional Jewish life and its bondage to a system of outdated laws. He demanded a Nietzschean 'transvaluation of values'.* Shaul Hurwitz (who translated Moses Hess into Russian) maintained that Judaism could not satisfy the modern Jew who had become estranged from the ghetto.† Hurwitz and Berdichevsky were twenty years younger than Smolenskin. The issue was put with even more brutal frankness by a representative of an even younger generation, Joseph Chaim Brenner. Smolenskin once referred to the verse in Ecclesiastes about living dogs and dead lions. Brenner took up the comparison: true, the live dog was better off, but what was the worth of a 'living people' whose members had no power except to moan and hide until the storm blew over? Existence was pleasant, Brenner countered, but it was not a virtue in itself. It was not necessarily the noblest who survived: 'Caravans come and go, as Mendele Mocher Sfarim put it, but the *Luftmenschen* of Kislon and Kabtziel go on forever.' Jewish survival was indeed a mystery, but the quality of Jewish existence was not a source of great pride. Masses of them continued to live in a biological sense, but there was no longer a living people in a sociological sense, as a social entity: 'We have no inheritance. No generation gives anything of its own to its successor. And what is transmitted – the rabbinical literature – were better never handed down to us.'‡

Such an attitude would have been anathema to Smolenskin, with his fiery appeals for a national revival. During the 1860s and early 1870s he was very much a voice in the wilderness, but towards the end of the 1870s, and particularly after the riots of 1881, he was no longer fighting the battle alone. Among those who joined him was Yehuda Leib Gordon (Yalag), the greatest Hebrew poet of the time. He had been in favour of cultural assimilation. His saying 'Be a human being outside and a Jew at home', had been often and widely quoted. Moses Leib Lilienblum, the leading essayist of the period, had been in his earlier years one of the sharpest critics of the Talmud, and an advocate of Socialist ideas. He too now became a confirmed nationalist; so did Eliezer Perlman, better known under the pen-name Ben Yehuda, formerly a convinced *Narodnik*

---

* *Nemushot* and *Erakhim*, 1899, *passim* (Berdichevsky).

† *Hashiloach*, VII, 1904 (Hurwitz).

‡ *Revivim*, v, Jerusalem, 1914, p. 111, quoted in A. Hertzberg, *The Zionist Idea*, New York, 1959, p. 307.

who had fully identified himself with the national aspirations of the Russian people and the southern Slavs.

By the late 1870s, Gordon no longer believed in cultural and political integration. In an anonymously published pamphlet he suggested the establishment of a Jewish state in Palestine under British suzerainty.* For Lilienblum, the rise of modern antisemitism in the west, and the riots of 1881, were a shattering blow, and he too became one of the main spokesman of early Russian Zionism. 'We need a corner of our own,' he wrote in 1881. 'We need Palestine.'† Ben Yehuda, under the impact of the Bulgarians and Montenegrins, reached the conclusion that the Jewish people, too, had to become again a living nation. The revival of Hebrew was to become his life work, but he realised very early that there was no future for the language in the diaspora; it could flourish only if the nation was revived and returned to its homeland.

The riots of 1881 put an end to many illusions and gave rise to much heart-searching among Russian Jewry. Was there a future for them in the empire of the tsars? If not, where should they turn? What were the causes of antisemitism? Lilienblum, in a remarkably astute analysis of antisemitism, had reached the pessimistic conclusion that 'aliens we are and aliens we shall remain'. The progress of civilisation would not eliminate anti-Jewish persecution based on nationalism rather than on religious prejudice. The trend all over Europe was towards nationalism. Perhaps it was a progressive development but as far as the Jews were concerned it was the very soil on which antisemitism was flourishing. Nor should their hope be put in Socialism and the proletariat, as Lilienblum himself had done in earlier years. If the workers came to power they would regard the Jews as rivals who deprived them of their livelihood: 'We will be regarded as capitalists and as usual we will fill the role of the scapegoat and the lightning rod.' Antisemitism, Lilienblum maintained, was not a transient phenomenon, not an anachronism. A return to the Middle Ages seemed inconceivable to many Jews, but Lilienblum was less optimistic. The Jewish question could be solved only if the Jews were transferred to a country where they constituted the majority, where they would no longer be strangers but able to lead a normal life. Such a possibility did not exist in Spain‡ nor in Latin America nor even in the United States, but only in Palestine. It was

* *Die jüdische Frage in der orientalischen Frage*, Vienna, 1877. The pamphlet was for a long time thought to have been written by Disraeli. More recently historians have come to attribute it to Yalag. See Alkoshi, in *Kiryat Sefer*, Jerusalem, 1959.

† *Rassvet*, 1881, pp. 41-2.

‡ King Alfons XII had offered asylum to some of the victims of the Russian riots.

pointless to wait for an initiative on the part of the Jewish plutocrats; the impetus could come only from the ranks of the people.*

The question whether to emigrate and where to turn agitated Russian Jewry for many years. Smolenskin became a Zionist after the riots of 1881 and in his writings listed the advantages of Palestine over the countries of North and South America. He noted that only a few years earlier the very word Eretz Israel had been derided by almost all Jews except those who wished to be buried there. Now there was talk about establishing agricultural settlements; this in fact was becoming the chief topic of conversation among all those who loved their people. Other publicists were less sanguine about Palestine. These included Dr Zamenhof, the inventor of Esperanto; Dubnow, then a young historian; and even Sokolow, one of the future leaders of Zionism. They had serious doubts about the feasibility of establishing a Jewish state in Palestine. Was it not above all a practical question? Jews could migrate to America, whereas substantial numbers could not for the time being settle in Palestine. Palestine was not a solution for the acute problems facing Russian Jewry; moreover, they would not be safe or free there, but exposed to the unpredictable whims of the sultan and his local representatives. Yalag, on the other hand, who knew his rabbis, was more afraid of theocracy in a Jewish state than of the arbitrary rule of the sultan. The idea of a Jewish state in America was aired only to be dismissed. The Jew could not compete with the Yankee and there was no guarantee that European antisemitism would not ultimately infect America as well. Ignatiev, the Russian minister responsible for the May Laws, expressed a preference for Palestine because there, he told Jewish visitors, the Jews would be able to work on the land and could also preserve their national identity, which they could not do in America.

The Russian-educated Maskilim of Odessa and southern Russia, strongly affected by Russian culture, tended on the whole to choose America, whereas the more traditional Jews of Lithuania and White Russia were more attracted by the idea of a Jewish revival in Palestine.† But it is also true that with a few exceptions the initiative for the establishment of a pro-Palestine committee also came from south Russia (Odessa, Kiev, Kharkov, Elizavetgrad). On the whole, the America vs. Palestine debate was not one of fundamental principles. Those who

* On Lilienblum's writings after the riots of 1881, see *Baderekh Teshuva*, Warsaw, 1889, *passim*.

† See the summary of the discussions in Israel Klausner, *Behitorer Am*, Jerusalem, 1962, pp. 104–17.

preferred America did so not from any aversion to Palestine, but because emigration to Palestine was in the given circumstances not a practical proposition. The tired, poor and huddled masses of Russian Jews ('the wretched refuse of your teeming shores'), the hundreds of thousands who left during the 1880s and 1890s, could not wait.

Leo Pinsker

There existed in Odessa in the 1870s a society for spreading enlightenment among the Jews; its main assignment was the teaching of the Russian language and of secular subjects to the younger generation. At a meeting of this group in the summer of 1881 one of its oldest and most respected members announced in great agitation that he was resigning on the spot; it was pointless to discuss whether this or the other deserving student should be given a stipend at a time when the whole Jewish people was under attack and when what was needed was leadership and initiative to save the nation, rather than the chance for a few individuals to improve themselves. Leo Pinsker, who provoked this showdown, was then sixty years of age, a physician who had in the past been one of the leading advocates of cultural assimilation.* The son of a distinguished Hebrew scholar, Pinsker had graduated from Moscow University. For his services in the Crimean War he had been rewarded by the government. The Odessa riots of 1871 had first sown doubts in his mind about the future prospects of the Jews in Russia, and the attacks of 1881 finally convinced him that his life-work, propagating cultural assimilation, had been in vain. Out of this recognition grew a pamphlet which, published anonymously in German in Berlin, became a milestone in the development of Zionist thought.†

Some of the basic ideas in Pinsker's *Autoemanzipation* were not altogether novel, but never before had they been developed systematically, with such clarity and logic. Never before had it been said with such passionate conviction that unless the Jews helped themselves, no one else would. Before Pinsker it had been the rule among the Jews in both west and east Europe to explain antisemitism solely as the result of the backwardness of a given country and the evil character of its inhabitants. A dispassionate analysis, taking account of the anomaly of Jewish existence, had not been attempted before, with the sole exception of

* The scene was described years later by M.Lilienblum, in *Voskhod*, 6, 1902.
† *Autoemanzipation, ein Mahnruf an seine Stammesgenossen, von einem russischen Juden*, Berlin, 1882.

Hess's forgotten book. Perhaps it was Pinsker's training as a physician that made it easier for him than for so many of his contemporaries to face unpleasant truths. He was not satisfied to interpret antisemitism solely in terms of jealousy or obscurantism. He, too, regarded Judaeophobia as a psychic aberration, but in his view it was hereditary. Transmitted as a disease for two thousand years, it was incurable, at least so long as its cause was not removed. To combat this hatred by way of polemics he regarded as a waste of time and energy: 'Against superstition even the gods fight in vain.' Prejudice, subconscious notions, could not be removed by reasoning, however forceful and clear.

This was a revolutionary thesis. For several generations Jewish assimilationist spokesmen all over Europe had maintained precisely the opposite. They had argued that antisemitism could be reduced or even eradicated altogether by patient reasoning and argument, by explaining time and time again that Jews did not commit ritual murder, that they were willing to accept civic responsibilities and were capable of making positive contributions to the economic, social and cultural life of their countries. This had been the basic belief of the various leagues and associations for combating antisemitism which came into being during the last quarter of the nineteenth century. It was also shared, with some slight modifications, by most Jewish Socialists. Writing about anti-semitism in the 1890s, Bernard Lazare, a fervent Socialist, one of the main figures in the campaign to rehabilitate Dreyfus and later on a Zionist, still maintained that mankind was moving from national egotism towards a spirit of brotherhood. Under Socialism, even during the transition towards Socialism, the Jews were bound to lose some or all of their own particular characteristics. Antisemitism was in the last resort a revolutionary agent, working towards its own ruin, for it paved the way for Socialism and Communism, and so for the elimination of the economic, religious and ethnic causes which had engendered antisemitism.*

Pinsker did not share the optimism of the liberals and Socialists. The anomaly of Jewish existence, he claimed, was such that the disease could be cured only by getting at its roots. Having lost their indepen-dence and fatherland, the Jews had become a spiritual nation. The world had come to see in them the frightening spectre of the dead walking among the living. Everywhere they were guests, nowhere at home. Thanks to their adaptability they had usually acquired the alien traits of the people among whom they dwelt. They had absorbed certain

* Bernard Lazare, *Antisemitism. Its History and Causes*, New York, 1903, pp. 373-5.

cosmopolitan tendencies and lost their own traditional individuality. They had deliberately renounced their own nationality, but nowhere had they succeeded in obtaining recognition from their neighbours as citizens of equal rank. All this was no mere accident or misfortune. There was a certain logic in it. No people, Pinsker wrote, has any predilection for foreigners. But the Jew was subject to this general law to an even greater degree than other foreigners precisely because he had no country of his own, because he was the stranger *par excellence*. Other foreigners had no need to be, or to seem to be patriots. They could claim hospitality and repay it in the same coin in their own country. The Jew, having no country, could make no claim to hospitality. He was a beggar rather than a guest.

Relentlessly Pinsker went on to destroy illusions in which only a few years before he had shared: that Jews had lived in a certain country for many generations did not change the fact that they remained aliens. True, they were, or would be, legally emancipated and accorded civil rights, but they would not be socially emancipated and accepted as equals. Emancipation was always the fruit of a rational cast of mind and enlightened self-interest, never the spontaneous expression of the feeling of the people. Therefore the stigma attached to the Jews could not be removed even by legislative emancipation imposed from above 'as long as it is the nature of this people to produce vagrant nomads, as long as they cannot give a satisfactory account of whence they come and whither they go, as long as the Jews themselves prefer not to speak in Aryan society of their Semitic descent and prefer not to be reminded of it – as long as they are persecuted, tolerated, protected, emancipated'. Pinsker concluded his analysis of antisemitism with a definition of the image of the Jew:

For the living, the Jew is a dead man; for the natives an alien and a vagrant; for property holders a beggar; for the poor an exploiter and a millionaire; for patriots a man without a country; for all classes, a hated rival.

Having described the etiology of the disease, Pinsker went on to discuss possible treatments – if not total cure. Jews were foolish to appeal to eternal justice and to expect of human nature something which had always been in short supply – humanity. What they needed was self-respect. They had waged a long and often heroic war for survival, but for survival not as a nation with a fatherland, but as individuals; in this struggle they had been forced to adopt all kinds of dubious tactics detrimental to their moral dignity, sinking even further in the eyes of their opponents. What they lacked was not genius but self-respect and dignity.

Nor were they justified in making the outside world responsible for their misfortunes. They had no providential mission among the nations, but should seek their own salvation in the struggle for independence and national unity. They were a sick people, for many of them did not even feel the need for an independent national existence, in the same way as a man affected by disease did not feel the desire for food and drink. But there was no other way out. The Russian Jews would have to emigrate unless they wanted to remain parasites and thus exposed to constant pressure and persecution. But since no other country was likely to open its gates to a mass immigration, they needed a home of their own. They were now passing through an important historical moment which might not recur. The consciousness of the people was awake, the time was ripe for decisive action – if only they were willing to help themselves. The Jewish societies already in existence, Pinsker suggested in conclusion, should call a national congress to purchase a territory for the settlement of several millions of Jews. At the same time the support of the powers should be obtained to ensure the perpetual existence of such a refuge. He did not expect that the entire people would emigrate to the new state; western Jews would probably remain where they were. But there was a saturation point in every country beyond which the number of Jews could not increase without exposing them to persecution, which might recur not only in Russia but also in other countries. Only in this way would it be possible to secure the future of the Jewish people, now everywhere endangered. He implored his fellow-Jews not to allow the great moment to pass. Self-liberation was the commandment of the hour: help yourselves and God will help you!

Pinsker's appeal received wide notice from Jewish writers in Russia but hardly any attention from the people for whom it had been intended and from whom he expected leadership, namely western, and more particularly German, Jewry. When he discussed his views with Jellinek, the chief rabbi of Vienna, he was advised to take a rest in Italy to restore his obviously shattered nerves.* Most Russian-Jewish writers commented that there was little new in *Autoemanzipation*; similar ideas had been propagated in the Russian-Jewish Press for a number of years. A little patronisingly, Smolenskin wrote that *Autoemanzipation* could perhaps fulfil a useful function among German Jews, for whom such views were

* Later on Jellinek came to take a more positive view of Pinsker's ideas.

novel. Others criticised Pinsker for his ambiguous attitude towards Palestine. In his pamphlet he had stated that they should 'above all not dream of restoring ancient Judaea. . . . The goal of our present endeavours must be not the "Holy Land" but a land of our own.' Elsewhere he mentioned a territory in North America or a sovereign *pashalik* in Asiatic Turkey as alternative possibilities. He was preoccupied with the immediate political problem facing Russian Jewry. The religious-national longing for Palestine was for him, as for Herzl fifteen years later, not the primary concern. When he wrote his pamphlet he was a territorialist, not a Zionist. Only later, under the influence of Lilienblum, Max Mandelstam (an ophthalmologist from Kiev), and Professor Herman Shapira (a mathematician at Heidelberg, of Russian origin), was he converted to the Zionist cause. During his last years – he died in 1898 – he took a leading role in the 'Lovers of Zion' (Hoveve Zion), the forerunners of political Zionism. Like Herzl after him, he has been criticised for largely ignoring what others before him had written and done about a Jewish state. This criticism is justified. When Pinsker wrote *Autoemanzipation* he was not aware of Moses Hess and Kalischer, nor even of the proto-Zionist groups that had sprouted a few years earlier in various Russian cities. Herzl in his turn was not aware of Pinsker and other predecessors of Zionism when he wrote the *Judenstaat*. But it is doubtful whether a knowledge of these various activities on behalf of Palestine would have induced Pinsker to modify his basic beliefs, that the leadership of the new national movement had to come from central and west European Jewry. He did not have a very high opinion of the political and organisational ability of his fellow Russian Jews, and his scepticism was, as subsequent events were to show, not unfounded. By the time Pinsker died the Lovers of Zion had failed in most of their endeavours, and with the rise of political Zionism the centre of gravity moved to Vienna and Berlin, to Cologne, and subsequently to London.

When Pinsker wrote *Autoemanzipation* he was past sixty, and much as Zionism became the centre of his life, he lacked the dynamism of youth, and also the ambition and vanity which were so characteristic of Herzl. The time was ripe, but he could not and would not be the new Moses. 'History', he once wrote, 'does not grant a people such guides repeatedly.' Pinsker's name figures larger in the history of ideas than in the history of Jewish politics. The immediate political impact of his work was limited; not many were converted to Zionism as the result of reading *Autoemanzipation*, but those few constituted the nucleus of the Zionist movements in eastern Europe in the 1890s. Without their support it is doubtful whether Herzl and Nordau would have been able to accomplish what they did.

The Lovers of Zion

Associations for the promotion of Jewish emigration to Palestine were founded during 1881–2 independently of each other in a number of Russian cities. The first was set up in Suvalki near the Polish-Lithuanian border, another in Kremenchug, while Rabbi Mohilever of Radom was instrumental in establishing several such associations in Poland. They were a mixed lot. Some consisted mainly of orthodox Jews, others of radical students who got their inspirations largely from the then fashionable *narodnichestvo* (populism). Some took the question of emigration very seriously, preparing themselves for immediate departure, while others were mainly philanthropic in character, collecting money for the support of the few Jewish colonies already in existence. At first there was hardly any coordination among them; the various groups sent emissaries to Palestine to find out about conditions there. Those who went on behalf of the Suvalki group had instructions to get the answers to no fewer than twelve hundred queries. The most active group was that founded by high-school and university students in Kharkov in 1881; it called itself Bilu (*Bet Yaakov lechu ve nelcha* – 'O house of Jacob, come ye, and let us go', Isaiah 11, 5). They decided upon immediate emigration and some of them left for Odessa on their way to Constantinople and the Holy Land. The history of the Jewish colonisation of Palestine usually dates from their arrival – the first *aliya* (immigration wave). Their subsequent fate is typical of the whole movement. Out of three hundred members, a third set out for Odessa, but only forty reached Constantinople. About sixteen ultimately arrived in Palestine. They first established a working group on Socialist lines, predating the efforts of the Kibbutzim and Kvutzot. For a start they went to work at Miqve Israel, the agricultural school which had been established a decade earlier. Later they established Gedera, an agricultural settlement south of Jaffa which still exists, though it ceased to be run on Socialist lines a long time ago.

The enthusiasm of the Biluim was matched only by their lack of preparedness. They knew nothing about agriculture, and found the work in unaccustomed climatic conditions almost unbearable. Above all, they had no money to buy land and equipment, and there were no funds for the construction of houses. Since, according to a contemporary account, they had neither horses nor oxen nor agricultural implements, they had to work the stony land with their bare hands. The orthodox Jews of Jerusalem were far from enthusiastic about these new arrivals, in whom they saw both dangerous subversive elements and also rivals for the distribution of the money sent each year by Jewish communities abroad for use in Palestine (*Halukka*). Occasionally they showed open hostility towards the Bilu, informing on them to the Turkish authorities. There was not a single pair of *Tefilin* (phylacteries) in the whole colony, the rabbis complained. Young men and women were dancing together: 'It would be preferable that the land of our forefathers should be again an abode of jackals than become a den of iniquity.' This was how the orthodox for many years viewed the activities of the 'Russian anarchists'.

The Turks too were suspicious of the newcomers, in whom they saw potential agents of a power threatening the very existence of their country. The Bilu members, who had set up a central office in Constantinople, waited therefore in vain for a *firman* (official permit) to establish a series of settlements in Palestine which would create the basis for mass immigration. The Turkish government put many obstacles in their way, and in 1893 banned altogether the immigration of Russian Jews into Palestine and the purchase of land. These orders were frequently circumvented by registering the land that was bought in the name of Jews from western Europe and by distributing baksheesh among the local administration. In this way a few settlements were established, but these were hardly the conditions envisaged by Pinsker for mass immigration, let alone the establishment of a Jewish state.

Among the first agricultural settlements established during that period were Zikhron Ya'akov, south of Haifa, and Rosh Pina, built by new immigrants from Rumania. Petah Tiqva, north of Jaffa, had been founded as early as 1878 by young Jews from Jerusalem, but they had to leave because most of them were affected by malaria. They returned after a year and in 1883 Yessod Hama'ala, and in 1884 Mishmar Hayarden, were founded, both in Galilee. Other colonies organised before the turn of the century included Rehovot (1890), Moza and Hadera (1891), Metulla and Har Tuv (1896). Everywhere the new colonists faced harrowing trials and not a few perished of exhaustion or disease; malaria claimed the heaviest toll at Hadera. Only after the draining of the swamps was it possible to envisage normal agricultural work. In Russia, meanwhile, attempts were being made to coordinate the activities of the various local Lovers of Zion groups. At a conference in Kattowitz in Upper Silesia in 1884, a central organisation was established. Pinsker was elected president, and stressed in his opening address the importance of a 'return to the soil'. The conference decided to establish two main committees, one in Warsaw, the other in Odessa, as executive bodies of the movement. The former soon ceased to exist but the latter remained up to the outbreak of the First World War the main centre of Zionist activity in Russia.

The Kattowitz conference has entered the annals of Zionist history as one of its most important milestones. In fact it was a very modest beginning. The thirty-six delegates were in general agreement that something ought to be done for Palestine, but there was no real attempt to define clearly the scope and purpose of the new organisation, let alone to consider ways and means of carrying out practical plans. Rich Russian Jews were reluctant to support Zionist initiatives and as a result the new organisation had hardly any funds at its disposal. The discussions at Kattowitz were taken up by such questions as whether one or two emissaries should be sent to Palestine and how much money should be allocated to the individual colonies.* This and subsequent conferences of the Lovers of Zion clearly showed that it was basically a philanthropic, not a political association, and not a very effective one at that – they collected a mere 15–20,000 roubles a year. Some of its members emigrated to Palestine, but the great majority consisted merely of well-wishers and sympathisers. A movement of this kind could not make a substantial contribution towards solving the most burning issue facing Russian Jewry – that of emigration. About twenty thousand Jews left Russia in 1881–2, but only a few hundred went to Palestine, and in later years the disproportion became even more marked. When Pinsker wrote *Autoemanzipation*, and when Smolenskin and Lilienblum issued their manifestos and appeals, they had thought of more ambitious projects than the creation of a few tiny settlements in the Mutessariflik of Jerusalem and the districts of Nablus and Acre. The movement was torn by internal strife. The rabbis, led by Mohilever, tried to get rid of the 'free-thinkers', and Pinsker was gradually squeezed out of the leadership. These internal squabbles consumed much time and energy and temporarily paralysed the movement.

In the meantime the news from the colonies became more and more alarming. The lack of agricultural experience was taking a heavy toll, and there were no funds to see the settlers through their early setbacks. The land which had been acquired by the emissaries of Russian and

* M.Gelber (ed.), *Die Kattowitzer Konferenz 1884. Protokolle*, Vienna, 1919, p. 24.

Rumanian Jewry was stony or marshy and infested with malaria. They did not know that the planting of eucalyptus trees was indicated in conditions such as those obtaining at Hadera, and they would not have been able to carry out afforestation, for lack of means, even had they known this. Generally speaking, they had no idea what to grow or how or when to grow it. They lived in caves and wretched hovels, exposed to an unfamiliar and usually inclement climate. The original enthusiasm could not sustain them forever. Within a few years many of them had reached breaking point. Some returned to Russia, others went on to America. A few moved on to Jerusalem, assisted by Christian missions, since they failed to obtain the support of the local Jewish community. The whole venture seemed doomed. To save the colonies, Rabbi Mohilever and an English Christian Friend of Zion, Laurence Oliphant,* enlisted the help of Baron Edmond de Rothschild and Baron Maurice de Hirsch, another noted Jewish philanthropist. Hirsch made his cooperation conditional on a contribution of 50,000 roubles on the part of Russian Jewry, and when this did not materialise he decided to concentrate his efforts on Jewish colonialisation in the Argentine. Rothschild was ready to help, and it was only owing to his support that Rishon, Zikhron, Rosh Pina and the other colonies survived. He also assisted in the establishment of two new colonies, Ekron and Metulla. With the arrival of another small wave of immigration in 1890–1 following the expulsion of Jews from Moscow, some more land was bought and two major colonies, Rehovot, south of Rishon le Zion, and Hadera, midway between Jaffa and Haifa, came into being. Altogether twenty-one agricultural settlements existed by the end of the century, with about 4,500 inhabitants, of whom two-thirds were employed in agriculture.

Rothschild did not trust the abilities of the colonists and insisted on direct supervision and control by his agents. A paternalistic régime was established, which was not at all to the liking of the Hoveve Zion. For Rothschild this was just another philanthropic scheme. Initially it caused much resentment among the recipients, but without his help the colonists would not have survived. It is estimated that during the 1880s the Baron spent about $5 million on supporting the settlements, whereas the Hoveve Zion were able to provide only about 5 per cent of that sum. Its support was limited in fact to Gedera, the original Bilu settlement. Under the supervision of Rothschild's representatives vineyards were planted in Rishon and Zikhron; elsewhere the cultivation of wheat and

* Author of *Land of Gilead*, 1879; Oliphant settled in Haifa.

of silkworms and the manufacture of rose oil was initiated. All these early trials were costly and some unsuccessful. The colonies became going concerns only during the first decade of the twentieth century when they began growing citrus fruits. The dependence of the colonists on Rothschild's generosity had some negative consequences. At first there were many complaints about the interference of the baron's agents in all their activities, but gradually the settlers came to take this for granted. They lost all initiative and became accustomed to turning to Paris whenever they encountered difficulties. Of their pioneering enthusiasm little was left when, after three decades, they had overcome their early troubles. The Zionist-Socialist convictions of the early settlers had given way to very different attitudes. By 1910 the settlers were owners of plantations employing mainly Arab workers. Their own children were sent for education to France, and a fairly high proportion of them did not choose agriculture or did not even return to Palestine. When a new wave of immigrants began to reach Palestine in 1905–6, the newcomers found it exceedingly difficult to obtain employment in these settlements, which preferred the cheaper and more experienced Arab labour. After this long philanthropic interlude the Zionist initiative thus became a strictly commercial venture. This was no doubt preferable to the degrading and unproductive existence of the old Jewish community in Jerusalem, which made organised begging a way of life, but it was hardly what the Lovers of Zion had dreamed about.

The decline of the movement was hastened by the insistence of the orthodox on certain biblical injunctions, such as the one which forbade the working of land each seventh year. The orthodox rabbis of Russia and Jerusalem insisted on strict observance of the Sabbatical year. But how could modern agriculture be combined with such outdated customs? The orthodox rabbis, meanwhile, were involved in a bitter quarrel with their ultra-orthodox colleagues as to whether the ethrogim (apples of Paradise needed for the ritual observance of the Feast of Tabernacles) should be imported from Corfu (as the latter demanded) or from Palestine, according to the wishes of the former. It is not surprising that a subsequent generation of Russian Zionists, which was to include Weizmann, was most reluctant to collaborate with the rabbis in their Zionist enterprises.

Pinsker and Lilienblum had been concerned with the future of the Jewish people, its national revival, the issue of mass immigration. Now, as leaders of the Odessa committee, they found themselves preoccupied with the livestock at Gedera and the question whether attacks by the inhabitants of Masmich, the neighbouring Arab village, constituted a serious danger to the Jewish settlement. This was not what they had envisaged, and the conviction grew among them that their early approach to the problem had been mistaken. In 1891 and again in 1893 one of the leading younger members of the Odessa committee, Asher Ginzberg (Ahad Ha'am), was sent to Palestine, and in a series of articles entitled 'The Truth from Eretz Israel', he sharply criticised the methods pursued by the Lovers of Zion. Colonisation could be successful, he maintained, only if undertaken not in a hurry, but with practical sense and on an adequate scale. All these factors were missing in Palestine, which could not absorb the Jewish masses; it should be a cultural and spiritual centre but not the political or economic basis of the Jewish people.

In 1890 the Lovers of Zion were at last permitted by the Russian government to register as an association; previously they had had to pursue their activities in conditions of semi-legality. Now they founded an association for the promotion of farming and manufacture in Palestine and Syria, but the fact that the organisation was now legal did not give a fresh spur to its activities. The leaders of the Hoveve Zion, with their many sterling qualities, had neither the vision, the genius and ambition of leadership, nor the relentless energy needed to make a success of their movement. Internal dissensions further weakened it: Pinsker and Lilienblum, the secularists, were opposed by the rabbis and their followers. Only a few rabbis had been interested in the movement for a national revival, among them Ruelf of Memel, Pinsker's close friend, Zadok Kahn of Paris, and Israel Hildesheimer, one of the leaders of German-Jewish orthodoxy. Later on, a great many were willing to support it, but only on condition that the movement would be religious in character. Lastly there were Ahad Ha'am's disciples preaching cultural Zionism. According to their views the majority of the Jewish people were to stay in the diaspora and only a small, select group was to settle in Palestine. Such ideas were unlikely to serve as the basis of a political mass movement.

Organisationally and politically the Hoveve Zion was a failure, but although its visions did not materialise, thousands of its members and sympathisers continued to believe that one day their dreams would come true. These men and women were found not only in Russia and Poland; there were also small groups in Vienna and Berlin. Nathan Birnbaum, with a few friends of Jewish-Polish and Rumanian background, founded a national students organisation which, following a suggestion by Peretz Smolenskin, adopted the name *Kadima*, meaning both 'forward' and 'eastward'. Birnbaum was a man of sharp critical intelligence and great ambition. His early essays reveal an original, sometimes prophetic frame of mind.* He was a Zionist well before Herzl. Indeed, the movement owes its very name to him. Better than the Lovers of Zion he understood the importance of political Zionism. It was not sufficient to establish a few colonies whose economic and political existence was by no means secure. Zionism had to gain the confidence of the Turkish government. Birnbaum's analysis of anti-semitism was more sophisticated than Pinsker's and Herzl's. As a Socialist he did not deny the importance of economic factors in history, nor did he believe that national hatreds (including antisemitism) would last forever. But he also realised that antisemitism was not primarily an economic phenomenon, that a revolution in the social structure would not by itself affect it, and that, lastly, it might take a thousand years to eradicate it. During this interim period Socialism simply did not have an answer to the Jewish question.

Birnbaum was isolated and desperately poor. His mother sold her little shop to finance her son's literary efforts, which covered the publication of *Selbst-Emanzipation*, a Zionist fortnightly, in which, anticipating Herzl, he developed a plan for the establishment of a Jewish state in Palestine, discussing in detail all the implications and refuting possible counter-arguments. Birnbaum had every reason to expect to be among the leaders of the Zionist movement when, following Herzl's initiative, it received a new lease of life. But for a variety of reasons (partly through his own fault) he never found his place in the new movement. Soon he left it altogether and drifted from Zionism and Socialism to preaching an active, national Jewish policy in the diaspora, which only a few years earlier he had declared *a priori* impossible. The former Hebraist became a fervent advocate of Yiddish, the popular language which was ana-thema to most Zionists. The free-thinker joined the ultra-orthodox Agudat Israel, of which he eventually became a leading official. At every stage of his erratic intellectual development he defended his current views with great conviction. He lacked neither intellectual depth nor honesty but his instability disqualified him as a political leader.

Small groups of Lovers of Zion existed in many parts of the world. Newspapers and periodicals taking a special interest in the Jewish colonisation of Palestine were published from Bucharest (*Hayoez*) to

* See, for instance, 'Die Jüdische Moderne', in Nathan Birnbaum's *Ausgewählte Schriften*, Czernowitz, 1910.

Boston (*Hapisga*) and Baltimore. In Jerusalem there was a Zionist periodical, Ben Yehuda's *Ha'or*. Max Bodenheimer, a German-Jewish lawyer, published a brochure in 1891 (*What to do with the Russian Jews*), followed two years later by another (*Syria and Palestine as a haven for Russian Jews*), in which he developed Zionist ideas quite independently of the Lovers of Zion or any other Jewish organisation. In 1896 the young engineer Menahem Ussishkin, brusque and opinionated but business-like and dynamic, took over the leadership of the Odessa committee. Ahad Ha'am established a little semi-conspiratorial *corps d'élite*, called *Bnei Moshe*. These men shared Ahad Ha'am's views about the central importance of a cultural renaissance of the Jewish people; many of the later leaders of Russian Zionism belonged at one time or another to this group. Its immediate political importance was not very great, nor was it meant to be. Ahad Ha'am's biographer says that Milton's 'They also serve who only stand and wait' could well have been its motto.*

In Berlin a *Verein* of Jewish students from Russia had been founded in 1889. In this (the Russian-Jewish Scientific Association) young nationalists like Leo Motzkin, Nahman Syrkin and Shmaryahu Levin were active. Later on Chaim Weizmann became one of its members. They were desperately poor but full of ideas and enthusiasm. They met at the Hotel Zentrum on the Alexanderplatz where (as Weizmann recalls) they could get beer and sausages on credit.

I think with something like a shudder of the amount of talking we did. We never dispersed before the small hours of the morning. We talked of everything, of history, wars, revolutions, the rebuilding of society. But chiefly we talked of the Jewish problem and Palestine. We sang, we celebrated such Jewish festivals as we did not go home for, we debated with the assimi-lationists, and we made vast plans for the redemption of our people. It was all very youthful and naïve and jolly and exciting; but it was not without a deeper meaning.†

The *Verein* existed 'outside time and space'. It had no connection with German Jewry; only a few young students such as Heinrich Loewe were to attend its meetings and become converts. The gap between these Russian students and German Jewry seemed unbridgeable, but Loewe was not easily discouraged. He helped to establish a student's association with a Jewish national orientation. In his little magazine *Zion* he reported on his study trip to Palestine in 1896, and the handful of

* Leon Simon, *Ahad Ha'am*, Philadelphia, 1960, p. 81.
† Chaim Weizmann, *Trial and Error*, New York, 1966, p. 37.

Zionists were greatly encouraged by the fact that in the same year Berlin Jews were given their first taste of Rishon wine. Still, all these activities were on a small scale and quite ineffectual. In 1896 no one but half a dozen rabbis, a few young people in Berlin and Cologne, and some older intellectuals and businessmen hailing from Russia, even knew about the idea of Zionism.*

The religious-national longing for Zion in eastern Europe had deep emotional roots and constituted a great potential reservoir for a political movement. But no mass movement had arisen during the fifteen years since the publication of Pinsker's *Autoemanzipation.* Only a few Lovers of Zion groups engaged in cultural and philanthropic work, and some small newspapers kept alive the visions and dreams of a national revival and a return to the homeland. The twenty-odd colonies founded in Palestine since 1881 had survived, but as the century drew to its close it was only too clear that they could not serve as a base for mass immigration. The old mythical and messianic Zionism was a source of edification, but it had proved incapable of inspiring a political mass movement. If its history had ended in 1897 it would now be remembered as one of the less important sectarian-Utopian movements which sprouted during the second half of the nineteenth century, an unsuccessful attempt at a Jewish *risorgimento*, trying to graft the ideas of the Enlightenment on to the Jewish-religious tradition.

Zionism, in brief, was comatose when in 1896 Theodor Herzl appeared. Within a few years he was to transform it into a mass movement and a political force.

* Richard Lichtheim, *Die Geschichte des deutschen Zionismus*, Jerusalem, 1954, p. 122.

3

THEODOR HERZL

In mid-February 1896 Breitenstein, the Viennese booksellers, offered in their display window a small new booklet entitled *Der Judenstaat* (*The Jewish State: An Attempt at a Modern Solution of the Jewish Question* in English translation). Its author was a journalist and playwright well known in the Austrian capital, Theodor Herzl. An entry in Herzl's diary dated 14 February reads: 'My five hundred copies came this evening. When I had the bundle carted to my room, I was terribly shaken. This package of pamphlets constitutes the decision in tangible form. My life may now take a new turn.' And on the following day: 'Meanwhile, the pamphlet has appeared in the bookshops. For me, the die is cast.'* When the pamphlet appeared Herzl was thirty-six years old. He had published a dozen plays and innumerable essays, had been a foreign correspondent for many years, and was a man with a considerable reputation in his field. His fears and expectations were not those of a novice for whom the publication of his first book is an event of world-shaking importance. This new book was very different in character from those he had previously written, and Herzl was not far off the mark when he expressed the view that the ideas he had formulated in his little book could bring about a change in the history of the Jewish people. Modern political Zionism begins with the publication of *Der Judenstaat*.

Herzl disclaimed having made any sensational new discovery. On the contrary, as he said in the very first sentence: 'The idea which I have developed in this pamphlet is an ancient one. It is the restoration of the Jewish state. . . . I have discovered neither the Jewish situation as it has crystallised in history, nor the means to remedy it.' The *Judenstaat* came as a surprise and shock to Herzl's friends and colleagues, who knew him as an able journalist and gifted essayist capable of providing at short notice interesting travelogues on London, Breslau, or a Spanish village, a man who could write with equal ease about Anatole France and *The*

* M. Lowenthal (ed.), *The Diaries of Theodor Herzl*, New York, 1956, pp. 96–7.

84

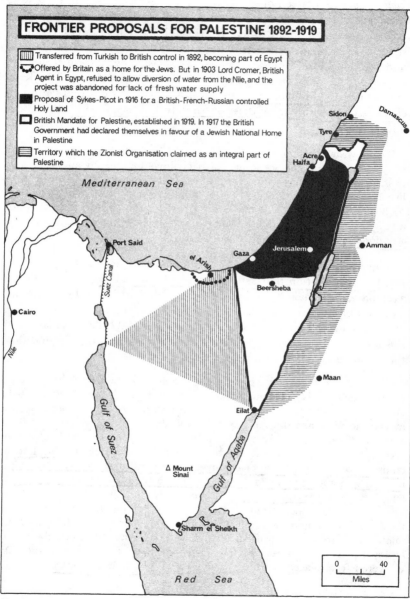

FRONTIER PROPOSALS FOR PALESTINE 1892-1919

Transferred from Turkish to British control in 1892, becoming part of Egypt

Offered by Britain as a home for the Jews. But in 1903 Lord Cromer, British Agent in Egypt, refused to allow diversion of water from the Nile, and the project was abandoned for lack of fresh water supply

Proposal of Sykes-Picot in 1916 for a British-French-Russian controlled Holy Land

British Mandate for Palestine, established in 1919. In 1917 the British Government had declared themselves in favour of a Jewish National Home in Palestine

Territory which the Zionist Organisation claimed as an integral part of Palestine

Mediterranean Sea

Sidon
Damascus
Tyre
Acre
Haifa
Port Said
el Arish
Gaza
Jerusalem
Amman
Beersheba
Cairo
Suez Canal
Nile
Maan
Gulf of Suez
Eilat
Gulf of Aqaba
△ Mount Sinai
Sharm el Sheikh
Red Sea

0   40
Miles

Map 3

Jungle Book, a coffee-house litterateur *par excellence* – but hardly an ideologist. His new book did not just deal with a topic he had not touched before; it was in a totally different style, as if written by another man, in short, clear, powerful sentences wholly unlike the involved, elegant, tired, and half-ironical style of the fashionable essayist. The following examples convey the flavour: 'In this pamphlet I will offer no defence of the Jews. It would be useless. Everything that reason and everything that sentiment can possibly say in their defence already has been said.' Or, about antisemitism:

The Jewish question still exists. It would be foolish to deny it. It is a misplaced piece of medievalism which civilised nations do not seem able to shake off, try as they will. . . . The Jewish question persists wherever Jews live in appreciable numbers. Wherever it does not exist, it is brought in by Jewish immigrants. . . . I consider the Jewish question neither a social nor a religious one, even though it sometimes takes these and other forms. It is a national question.

What scandalised most of Herzl's contemporaries in this pamphlet was his flat assertion that assimilation had not worked. How could an assimilated Jew make such a patently absurd claim? Herzl was after all an editor of the *Neue Freie Presse*, one of Europe's leading newspapers. He was living in Vienna, not in one of the ghettoes of the east. Yet Herzl, in this merciless analysis of the situation of the Jews in Europe, found that the dilemma facing them was basically everywhere the same:

We have sincerely tried everywhere to merge with the national communities in which we live, seeking only to preserve the faith of our fathers. It is not permitted to us. In vain are we loyal patriots, sometimes super-loyal; in vain do we make the same sacrifices of life and property as our fellow citizens; in vain do we strive to enhance the fame of our native land in the arts and sciences, or her wealth by trade and commerce. In our native lands where we have lived for centuries we are still decried as aliens, often by men whose ancestors had not yet come at a time when Jewish sighs had long been heard in the country. The majority decides who the 'alien' is; this, and all else in the relations between peoples, is a matter of power. . . . In the world as it now is and will probably remain, for an indefinite period, might takes precedence over right. It is without avail, therefore, for us to be loyal patriots, as were the Huguenots, who were forced to emigrate. If we were left in peace. . . . But I think we shall not be left in peace.*

---

* *Der Judenstaat*, quoted here from the translation in Arthur Hertzberg, *The Zionist Idea*, New York, 1959, p. 209, which is based on the first English translation by Sylvie d'Avigdor.

Such fears had been voiced by other writers before, but of this Herzl was quite unaware when he was writing. According to an entry in his diary dated 10 February 1896, he had just been reading Pinsker's *Autoemanzipation*, and discovered an 'astounding correspondence' in the critical part: 'A pity I did not read this work before my own pamphlet was printed. On the other hand, it is a good thing that I didn't know it – or perhaps I would have abandoned my own undertaking.'*

Theodor (Benjamin Ze'ev) Herzl was born in Budapest in 1860. His father was in the clothing business. There was still a certain amount of Jewish religious tradition in the family, but culturally it was fully assimilated, as were most Jews of similar social and cultural background. Young Herzl received a conventional education at a local high school. He was interested in literature and, needless to say, in the 'last questions' concerning the purpose of life. His student years in Vienna were uneventful. He enrolled in 1878 in the faculty of law, specialised in Roman Law, and in 1884 received his doctorate and was admitted to the Vienna bar. He read a great deal during those years, and wrote several short plays and many essays. Most of his friends were Jews. He witnessed the emergence of the antisemitic movement in the Austrian capital, and in 1883 resigned from Albia, the student fraternity to which he belonged, because it was about to embrace antisemitism. But these events did not constitute a turning-point in his life. The Jewish question was not Herzl's main preoccupation at the time. His great ambition was to be accepted as a German writer and playwright. His friends thought of him as a gifted young man, of great literary promise, but they were not unaware of his shortcomings. Heinrich Kana, his closest friend, wrote that Herzl was 'intolerant, inhumane in his judgment of people, domineering and hyper-egoistic'.†

After a not too enthusiastic start in law Herzl turned to writing, first freelancing for a leading Berlin newspaper, and from 1887 on a more permanent basis for Viennese journals. Though widely acclaimed as a feuilletonist, he did not fare too well in the theatre. His comedies were neither better nor worse than most of the run-of-the-mill productions of those years. They were trivial and not really very funny, and this at a time when the burning social and philosophical questions of the day were beginning to dominate literature and the stage. Herzl's plays were in the tradition and style of a bygone period. Of this he was quite unaware. He remained genuinely convinced that his real gifts were

---

* R.Patai (ed.), *The Complete Diaries of Theodor Herzl*, vol. I, New York, 1960, p. 299.
† Alex Bein, *Theodor Herzl*, Philadelphia, 1945, p. 50.

literary and that he had been misjudged and ignored. Years later, when his name had already become a legend, when he was (in his own words) an ageing and celebrated man, he noted in his diary that he had become world famous in a sphere where he had accomplished 'next to nothing intellectually', but had merely displayed a mediocre political skill: 'But as an author, particularly as a playwright, I am held to be nothing, less than nothing. . . . And yet I feel, I know, that I am by instinct a great writer, or was one, who failed to yield his full harvest only because he became nauseated and discouraged.'*

In October 1891 the *Neue Freie Presse* appointed him its correspondent in Paris. He was to stay there for a number of years and these turned out to be the decisive period in his life. Paris was then the centre of the civilised world, the focus of all new political and cultural movements. The Paris years gave him an insight into the workings of French affairs and European politics, and he came to know many of the leading spirits of the age, acquiring a new sophistication and self-confidence. It was in Paris, too, that he was again confronted with the Jewish question. For these were the years of the Panama scandal and the beginning of the Dreyfus affair. Jews were prominently implicated and there was a resurgence of antisemitism in France as well as in other European countries. Jewish topics began to preoccupy Herzl and appeared more and more frequently in his writings. He did not claim that the charges of the antisemites were altogether unjust: the ghetto, which had not been of their making, had bred in them certain asocial qualities; the Jews had come to embody the characteristics of men who had served long prison terms unjustly. Emancipation had been based on the illusion that men are made free when their rights are guaranteed on paper. The Jews had been liberated from the ghetto but basically, in their mental make-up, they had remained ghetto Jews. What then was the answer to the Jewish question? Perhaps the radical dissolution of world Jewry, as he said in conversation with the editor of his paper? On one occasion, in 1893, he suggested that half a dozen duels would do a great deal to improve the situation of Jews in society. Herzl was always inclined to think in terms of radical solutions; there was a strong romantic element in his ideas and also a belief in the virtues of grand gestures, demonstrations and showmanship. At one stage, again in 1893, he envisaged the general baptism of Jewish children, because the Jews must submerge themselves in the people. He wanted to appeal to the Pope: help us against antisemitism and I in return will lead a great movement amongst the Jews for volun-

---

* *Complete Diaries*, vol. 4, p. 1283.

tary and honourable conversion to Christianity. He envisaged a solemn festive procession to St Stephen's Cathedral at noon on a Sunday, accompanied by the ringing of bells. The adult leaders of the community would be at the head of the procession, and would proceed to the threshold of the church. Though the leaders would stay outside, the others would embrace Christianity. These were just fantasies. It was pointed out to Herzl that, all other considerations apart, the Pope would never receive him.

He abandoned the plan, but the Jewish problem continued to preoccupy him. Then, within a few months, he suddenly came up with a new solution, apparently no less Utopian: 'It bears the aspect of a mighty dream', he wrote in the very first entry in his Zionist diary. He decided to approach Baron von Hirsch, one of the leading Jewish philanthropists of the age, and in a meeting in June 1895 he developed his new plan. He already saw himself as the leader of the Jews: 'You are the great money Jew, I am the Jew of the spirit'. In the conversation Herzl sharply criticised the methods used by the baron to help the Jews. Philanthropy was of no use. On the contrary, it could only do harm because it debased the character of the people. 'You breed beggars,' he told the astonished baron. What of Herzl's own solution? Some of his proposals might seem too simple, he said, others too fantastic, 'but it is the simple and fantastic which leads men'. At this point the baron grew impatient and began to doubt the sanity of his visitor. Where would he get the money for his fantastically ambitious schemes? Rothschild would probably donate five hundred francs. For the rich Jews, Hirsch said, were bad; they took no interest in the sufferings of the poor.

Herzl sadly concluded that the baron clearly did not understand what fantasy meant, or grasp the importance of imponderabilia floating high in the air. On the same day, following this conversation, Herzl wrote to the baron that he would launch a Jewish national loan to finance migration to the Promised Land. It would be a national, not a philanthropic movement: a flag, his interlocutor might ask mockingly, what was a flag? A stick with a rag at the end of it. No, Herzl replied, a flag was a great deal more. 'With a flag people are led – perhaps even to the Promised Land. For a flag men live and die.' But although the attempt to win over the baron was clearly a failure, Herzl did not give up. If the conversation had not been a success it had helped Herzl to clarify his own ideas. Within the next three weeks he wrote a long memorandum which contained all the basic ideas subsequently developed in *Der Judenstaat*. He wanted to address the family council of the Rothschilds;

Herzl had still not given up the idea of winning over the 'money Jews'.

These were for Herzl weeks of profound emotional tension. 'During these weeks I was more than once afraid that I was going out of my mind', he wrote in his diary. He no longer doubted the greatness of his mission; he would be named among the great benefactors of mankind. Perhaps he was solving not just the Jewish question, but a general social problem as well? His move from Vienna to Paris was a 'historical necessity'. The Jewish state was a world need: 'I believe for me life has ended and world history begun.' Then again doubts: would the Jews be able to appreciate his mission? Would those timid, helpless creatures understand the call to freedom and manhood? One day he would feel sanguine about his mission, the next day depressed. 'I have given up the whole thing. There is no helping the Jews for the time being. If someone were to show them the way out of their misery they would treat him with contempt. They are disintegrated ghetto natures.' But Herzl persevered. The despair, the black moods were confided only to his diary. To the outside world he radiated assurance and confidence. Years later, when Zionist fortunes had reached a low ebb, he was to tell his closest friends: 'I am not better nor more clever than any of you. But I remain undaunted and that is why the leadership belongs to me.'

For the time being, however, Herzl was not leading anyone; only a few friends knew about the manifesto he had been writing. One of them thought Herzl's mind had become unhinged as the result of overwork. He advised rest and medical treatment. Others were moved by his sincerity and the moral force of his ideas but believed that an appeal to the Rothschilds would be quite fruitless. Perhaps Herzl should publish his views in the form of a novel? Herzl accepted the challenge. Having been slighted or ignored by the 'money Jews', he might as well appeal to the general public. And so, in an edition of three thousand copies, *Der Judenstaat* was published by Breitenstein in February 1896.

The basic ideas can be briefly summarised: the world needed the Jewish state, Herzl wrote in the introduction, therefore it would arise. It was not a Utopia for the simple reason that the Jews were impelled, by their plight, to find a solution. It might well be that he was ahead of the time, that the sufferings were not yet acute enough, that the Jewish state still remained for the moment a political romance. But even if the present generation was too dull to understand it, a future and finer generation would rise to the historical mission. Herzl saw antisemitism, 'the Jewish question', as did most of his assimilationist contemporaries, as an anachronism, a remnant of the Middle Ages. But his prognosis was not optimistic: man was steadily advancing on the ethical level, but his progress was fearfully slow: 'Should we wait for the average man to become as generous-minded as was Lessing . . . we would have to wait beyond our lifetime, beyond the lifetimes of our children, of our grandchildren and our great grandchildren.'* And until then? Fortunately, technical progress had made it possible to solve problems that had been intractable only a few generations earlier. Herzl then went on to discuss his ideas for a Jewish state. He did not want to compel anyone to join the exodus. If any or all of French Jewry protested against his scheme because they were already assimilated, well and good; the scheme would not affect them. On the contrary, they would only benefit, because they, like the Christians, would be freed of the disquieting and inescapable competition of a Jewish proletariat, and antisemitism would cease to exist. Herzl tried to anticipate and refute yet another argument: the exodus would not lead from civilisation into the desert. It would be carried out entirely in the framework of civilisation: 'We shall not revert to a lower stage but rise to a higher one. We shall not dwell in mud huts; we shall build new, more beautiful, and more modern houses, and possess them in safety.'

But was the exodus really necessary? Herzl surveyed the varieties of persecution to which Jews were subjected. Everywhere they were attacked, in parliaments, in assemblies, in the street, from the pulpit. Attempts were made to thrust them out of business ('Don't buy from Jews'). The Jewish middle classes were threatened, the position of doctors, lawyers, teachers was becoming daily more intolerable, the passions of the mob were incited against the wealthy. Princes and governments could not protect them; they would only incur popular hatred by showing them too much favour: 'The nations in whose midst Jews live are all covertly or openly antisemitic.' Such statements sounded exaggerated, alarmist, almost hysterical in 1896, and when Herzl derided the belief in the unlimited perfectibility of man as so much sentimental drivel he was, of course, attacked as an obscurantist. Yet he was in some respects still too optimistic, as subsequent European history was to show. He maintained that where Jews had received equal rights these could not be rescinded, for this would be contrary to the spirit of the age and would also drive all Jews into the ranks of the revolutionary party.† Their

---

* *A Jewish State*, London, 1896 (first English translation), p. 3. ⟵ how wrong he'd be

† Nordau, his colleague, likewise rejected the possibility of a holocaust. In a speech at one of the first Zionist congresses he said that he did not believe the dreadful persecution of

expropriation could not be effected without causing a major economic crisis and was therefore quite impractical. But if their enemies could not get rid of the Jews, this was bound to deepen their hatred of them. Antisemitism was growing day by day and hour by hour. And it would continue to increase because its causes still existed and were ineradicable. The Jews could perhaps vanish without a trace into the surrounding peoples if they were left in peace for just two generations: 'But they will not let us be. After brief periods of toleration, their hostility erupts again and again.' Whether the Jews wanted it or not, they were one people, a group whom affliction bound together; their enemies were making them one people, whatever their own wishes.

Efforts had been made in the past to solve the Jewish question, but the attempt to turn Jews into peasants in their countries of origin was quite artificial. The peasant was a creature of the past, a type on the way to extinction. Assimilation was no panacea, as historical experience had shown. There remained the new, obvious, simple solution – to create a Jewish state, to give the Jews sovereignty over a portion of the globe adequate to meet their national requirements. The exodus and the building of the state would not be a sudden act, but a gradual process lasting decades. The poorest Jews, those in immediate need, would go first, cultivate the soil, construct roads, build bridges and railways, regulate rivers and provide themselves with homesteads. They would be followed by those of the next grade, the intellectual mediocrities, 'whom we produce so abundantly and who are oppressed everywhere'.

Herzl envisaged the establishment of two agencies to initiate and supervise the building up of the country: the 'Society of Jews', which would provide a scientific plan and political guidance, and the 'Jewish Company', modelled on the lines of the great trading associations, which would carry them out, wind up the affairs of the emigrants, and organise trade and commerce in the new country. The Jewish Company would be a joint stock company, framed according to English law, with its principal centre in London and a capital of approximately £50 million. At the very

---

the past would recur, though recent events had shown that the murder of a whole people was possible even in modern times. It was unlikely that tens of thousands of Jews would be killed and the rest expelled from a country. 'There is now a European conscience, a world conscience which (even if it is not yet broad enough) prescribes certain outward forms and does not easily tolerate mass crimes' (Max Nordau, *Zionistische Schriften*, p. 83). But he added: 'On the other hand I am convinced that our ice age will still last a long time. . . . People are knifed and die at the stake, but he who freezes to death is also no longer alive.' It should be noted that earlier Russian Zionists like Lilienblum and Smolenskin had on occasion been more pessimistic and had not ruled out the physical destruction of the Jews in the diaspora.

beginning of his book Herzl stated that he did not intend to depict another agreeable Utopia, but that he was interested in the central idea of a Jewish state which he wanted to submit to discussion. He did not want to prepare (as other writers of Utopias had done) a complicated scheme with many cogs and wheels. Yet by necessity the *Judenstaat* is not free of such detailed proposals. Herzl's training as a lawyer clearly emerges and his views on social problems as they took shape during his Paris years are aired in his pamphlet. He discusses, for instance, the seven-hour working day, the type of buildings in the new state, the means of raising money, the organisation of immigration.

He preferred a democratic monarchy, or an aristocratic republic. Nations were not yet fit for unlimited democracy, and in this respect Jews were no better than the rest of mankind. The political issues facing the new state would not be of the simple kind, to be settled by Ayes and Noes. Politics would have to take shape in the upper strata of the new society and work downwards. But no member of the Jewish state would be discriminated against. Herzl was opposed to any form of theocracy. The priests would receive the highest honours but should not be allowed to interfere in the administration of the state. They would be kept within their temples, as the army would be kept within barracks. (Herzl envisaged the formation of a relatively small army, since the state he conceived was to be neutral in world politics.) Every man and woman in the Jewish state would be free and undisturbed in his faith (or disbelief) as in his nationality. Everyone, regardless of creed and nationality, would have equality before the law. 'We have learnt toleration in Europe', he wrote; adding as an afterthought, 'This is not said sarcastically'. *

The Jewish state obviously needed a banner, and Herzl suggested a white field (symbolising the pure new life) with seven golden stars (the seven golden hours of the working day). Having promised to deal only with the general idea of a Jewish state, he time and again involved himself in the discussion of technical detail, much of it quite unnecessary. But this was perhaps inevitable. A blueprint restricted to generalities would not have carried much conviction. Other contemporary Utopias went into far greater detail. Menahem Eisler's *Ein Zukunftsbild*, published in Vienna in 1885, which also envisaged the establishment of a Jewish state, supplied a ready-made constitution of fifteen hundred separate clauses and provisions.* As he was working on the *Judenstaat*, Herzl, a

---

* See G. Kressel (ed.), *Hisione Medina*, Tel Aviv, 1954, p. 64 *et seq.* It also predicted an attack by its neighbours on Jehuda (as the new state was to be called) from which the Jewish state would emerge victorious.

man of colossal imagination, jotted down many more ideas to be realised in the future society: a labour exchange, a clearance office for capital, the nationalisation of banking, railroads, insurance, and shipping, a standing army (strength: one-tenth of the male population), and even foreign copyright agreements. Education would make use of patriotic songs, the Maccabean tradition, religion, heroic plays, etc. But the Jewish love of luxury was also exploited. After a visit to the Paris Opera Herzl wrote: 'We too shall have such resplendent lobbies – the men in full dress, the women altogether sumptuous.' And on another occasion: 'Circuses [games] as soon as possible: German theatre, international theatre, opera, musical comedy, café-concerts, cafés, Champs Elysées'. But games of chance were not to be tolerated: 'Old men may play cards, but not for money.'

The high priests in the Jewish state would wear impressive robes, the cavalry would wear yellow trousers and white tunics, the officers silver breast-plates. Herzl wanted at all costs to prevent the emergence of a crop of professional politicians; as stipends for 'my brave warriors, aspiring artists, and faithful, talented officials' he would use the dowries of 'our wealthy girls'. He was much concerned with the blueprints and techniques of building. He suggested bright, airy halls, borne on columns. Construction should be decorative and of light materials, in exposition style. Three years later, during his visit to Jerusalem, Herzl wrote: 'If Jerusalem is ever ours, I would begin by cleaning it up, clearing out everything that was not sacred, building an airy, comfortable, properly sewered, brand new city around the holy places.' In his Utopian novel *Altneuland*, published a few years later, Herzl included many other detailed suggestions.

This all seemed a little premature, for the two basic questions were as yet unresolved: how was statehood to be achieved and where was the state to be located? Herzl noted that significant experiments in colonisation had been made but they were all based on the mistaken principle of infiltration. This could not work, for sooner or later the moment would come when the government in question, under pressure from the native populace, would put a stop to the further influx of Jews. Immigration in the form of infiltration was futile unless based on guaranteed autonomy. In this respect his plan differed radically from earlier Zionist proposals. Shortly after the publication of the *Judenstaat* he told a friend that if infiltration continued unchecked, land would increase in value and it would become progressively harder for the Jews to buy it. The idea of a Declaration of Independence, 'as soon as the Jews were strong enough over there', was also impractical, for the great powers would not recognise it. Infiltration, in brief, should be stopped and all efforts concentrated upon a charter, the internationally sanctioned acquisition of Palestine. 'To achieve this we require diplomatic negotiations . . . and propaganda on the largest scale.'*

In May 1896, when this conversation took place, Herzl's thoughts were already focused on Palestine. In the *Judenstaat*, written the year before, he had still left open the question whether it was to be Palestine or Argentina. Argentina, he wrote, was one of the most fertile countries in the world, sparsely populated and with a temperate climate; it would be in the highest interest of the Republic of Argentina to cede to the Jews a portion of its territory. Palestine, on the other hand, was the unforgettable historic homeland, its very name a rallying cry. If the sultan were to give Palestine to the Jews, they could in return undertake the management of Turkey's finances and save the sultan from chronic bankruptcy. The Jewish state, neutral in character, would form part of a defensive wall for Europe in Asia, an outpost of civilisation against barbarism. Europe would guarantee its existence, and the Holy Places would be put under some form of extra-territoriality. The Jews could in fact mount a guard of honour about these Holy Places and this would symbolise the solution of the Jewish question.

In conclusion, Herzl dealt with some of the main objections likely to be raised. He did not think that he was providing 'weapons for the anti-semites'. Some critics might claim that the venture was hopeless because even if the Jews were to obtain the land and sovereignty over it, only the poor would emigrate. But this was hardly a valid argument: 'It is precisely they whom we need first! Only desperate men make good conquerors.' Others were likely to argue that if the scheme were feasible it would have been tried long before. But no, Herzl countered, it had not been possible in the past. Only with technical progress, with man's growing domination over nature, had the scheme become a practical possibility. True, the establishment of the state might be a long-drawn-out affair. Even in the most favourable circumstances many years would elapse. But he expected immediate relief. Once the Jews began to execute their plan, antisemitism would cease and everywhere the Jewish intellectuals would find an outlet for their energies in the preparation of the great work. The Jews who willed it, he wrote, would achieve their state: 'A wondrous breed of Jews will spring up from the earth. The Maccabees

---

* Conversation with Bodenheimer, *Complete Diaries*, vol. 1, p. 335.

will rise again. We shall live at last as free men on our own soil, and in our own homes peacefully die.'

Herzl was not totally unprepared for the book's reception. He had expected to be ridiculed as a mad visionary, and his expectations were amply fulfilled. Some simply refused to take his ideas seriously; perhaps the whole thing was an elaborate joke? Herzl was known as an accomplished feuilletonist and satirist. He had as yet never aspired to be a prophet or shown particular interest in the fate of his people. Those who did take the *Judenstaat* seriously were deeply divided. The majority thought it was a chimera, a revival of medieval messianism. Güdemann, Vienna's chief rabbi, who had been close to Herzl, sharply attacked his ideas in a pamphlet in which he protested against the '*Kuckucksei* of Jewish nationalism', maintaining that Jews were not a nation, that they had in common only their belief in God, and that Zionism was incompatible with the teachings of Judaism.* The same arguments were to be voiced in one form or another against the Zionist movement for years to come.

But even among Zionists the reaction was at best lukewarm. No one had ever heard of Herzl in Jewish-national circles. Did he suddenly wish to arrogate to himself the leadership of a movement? Why had he not mentioned in his pamphlet the existence of Jewish colonies in Palestine, the activities of the Lovers of Zion in various countries, the fact that his analysis of antisemitism as well as many of his constructive proposals were by no means novel? The obvious explanation, that Herzl simply was not aware of these things, did not occur to anyone. There was severe criticism to come particularly from the cultural Zionists such as Ahad Ha'am: was there anything specifically Jewish about a Jewish state as Herzl envisaged it? Herzl was not a Hebrew language enthusiast: 'Who among us would be capable of buying a railway ticket in Hebrew?' he asked. The pamphlet was of course anathema to the east European Zionists for whom the cultural renaissance was a central issue in their doctrine.

Given the lack of response on the one hand, the ridicule and hostility on the other, it would not have been surprising had Herzl dropped the whole idea then and there, as he had indeed intimated in his pamphlet, for his original intention had been only to restart the discussion. But had he done this, the judgment of many of his Viennese contemporaries would have been justified, namely that Herzl was a mere litterateur, a feuilletonist playing with ideas and concepts, considering and then

* Moritz Güdemann, *Nationaljudentum*, Leipzig and Vienna, 1897, p. 42.

dropping them once he got bored, the familiar syndrome of the Viennese *fin-de-siècle* intelligentsia. But these contemporaries misjudged Herzl just as twenty years later they were to misjudge the Russian revolutionaries whom they had known in the coffee houses and whom no one expected to start and lead a revolution. For Herzl was serious. Once the idea had taken hold of him he was like a man possessed. The transformation of a dandy and man of letters into a leader and man of action was nothing short of miraculous but it was very real. He sacrificed everything to his idea and to the movement – his marriage (which admittedly had been on the rocks for a number of years), his money, and his health. From now on every free minute was to be devoted to Zionism. This transformation was a complex process, coinciding with a personal crisis in his life, and it is no doubt correct, as has been argued, that the narcissistic streak in his character played a great part in it.* Herzl relished the role of the Messiah-King which he was to assume during the years to come. But only a man truly possessed would have taken on the leadership of a cause which seemed doomed to fail. He had no illusions in this respect; a year later, when the Zionist movement was advancing, he wrote in his diary: 'I have only an army of *schnorrers*. I stand in command of a mass of youth, beggars and jackasses.'

Herzl lived for eight years after the publication of *Der Judenstaat*. These were hectic years of diplomatic and organisational activity. The foremost task was of course to create a mass basis, to build up a strong movement. His idea of winning the 'money Jews' first and carrying out a 'revolution from above' had to be given up. But he also knew that he would not succeed in getting a strong following among his own people unless he had some successes to show in the diplomatic field. No one was likely to listen to his message unless there was real hope of obtaining a charter from the sultan. And so he hurried from one European capital to another, trying to establish connections with the mighty of this world, seeking audiences with the sultan and the German emperor, with the Pope and King Victor Emmanuel, with Joseph Chamberlain and Lord Cromer, with Plehve and Witte – the key figures in tsarist Russia. In between, almost single-handed, he organised the first Zionist world congresses, established the central Zionist newspaper (*Die Welt*), and ran the day-to-day affairs of the growing movement. He also wrote for his newspaper, *Die Neue Freie Presse* – for this, and not the leadership of the Zionist movement, was his pass-key in the chancelleries of Europe. He had to attend

---

* Carl E. Schorske, 'Politics in a New Key: An Austrian Triptych', in *Journal of Modern History*, December 1967, p. 343 *et seq.*

personally to even the smallest details. When he first went to Constantinople he had not only to think up convincing arguments to sell Zionism
to the sultan, but had also to buy strawberries, peaches, and bundles of
asparagus for the sultan's flunkeys, their wives and ganymedes at the
Hotel Sacher.

Herzl was an imposing figure and his bearing became almost regal as
he assumed the leadership of the movement. One of the delegates at the
first Zionist congress, Ben Ami, gave the following account:

> This is no longer the elegant Dr Herzl of Vienna; it is a royal descendant
> of David arisen from the grave who appears before us in the grandeur and
> beauty with which legend has surrounded him. Everyone is gripped as if a
> historical miracle had occurred . . . it was as if the Messiah, son of David,
> stood before us. A powerful desire seized me to shout through this tem-
> pestuous sea of joy: *Jechi Hamelech*, Long live the King.

Zangwill, the Anglo-Jewish writer, was a more sophisticated man, less
given to sudden enthusiasm, but he too was deeply impressed: 'A majestic
oriental figure, not so tall as it appears when he draws himself up and
stands dominating the assembly with eyes that brood and glow – you
would say one of the Assyrian kings whose sculptured heads adorn our
museums.' Herzl was in some respects the ideal diplomat. He could exude
great charm, his manners were impeccable, he had great self-possession;
the years in Paris had made him a man of the world. But the kings and
their ministers, unlike the delegates to a Zionist congress, were not
swayed by moral pathos and romantic visions. Their first question was
always: whom does he represent? And of what possible benefit can he
be to us?

What could Herzl say in reply? In the early phases of his activity he
represented no one but himself, and later on a dedicated but uninfluential minority among the Jewish communities. It was most doubtful
moreover, whether this small group of visionaries could be of assistance
to anyone, even to weak and impoverished Turkey, which held the key
to all of his schemes. In the circumstances it was miraculous that he
even gained access to dukes and ambassadors, and later to kings and
ministers. His two chief aides in the diplomatic field, both non-Jews,
were, to put it mildly, highly unconventional people. William Hechler,
chaplain at the British Embassy in Vienna, believed that according to
the prophets Palestine was to be restored to the Jews, and he was firmly
resolved to do his share towards the fulfilment of this biblical prophecy.
He had been tutor to the son of the Grand Duke of Baden, and knew

the German emperor, and could thus provide useful introductions in Berlin.

Philip Michael Nevlinsky, an impoverished nobleman, had been a minor Austrian official in Turkey until he incurred debts which compelled him to leave the diplomatic service. He then established a newspaper, *Correspondance de l'Est*, devoted to Turkish and Near Eastern affairs. He knew a great many people in the Turkish capital, and once on Herzl's payroll could provide useful contacts. Herzl was already in two minds about his two closest diplomatic advisers: Hechler ('an impecunious clergyman with a taste for travel') he thought a naïve enthusiast with a streak of collector's mania – an incredible figure when looked at with the quizzical eyes of a Viennese Jewish journalist – 'but I have to imagine that people altogether different from us see him quite differently'. Perhaps he was after all a suitable instrument for Herzl's purposes? Nevlinsky was an even greater riddle: far better educated than most noblemen, he was both payable and proud, wily and sincere. He was, as Herzl wrote in June 1896, the most interesting figure he had met since taking up the Jewish cause. Herzl had merely wanted to use him as an instrument, but had come to love and respect him. One year later he was less certain; both Hechler and Nevlinsky were to attend the first Zionist congress: 'It will be one of my tasks to keep them from seeing too much of each other.'

When Nevlinsky died in April 1899 it transpired that his newspaper had been a swindle: 'A dozen subscribers, and blackmail did the rest'. A Turkish diplomat told Herzl that the late-lamented secret agent had cheated Herzl, had never brought his ideas to the knowledge of the sultan and his advisers, but on the contrary had volunteered to spy on him for the Turks. Nevlinsky took most of his secrets with him to the grave. He was, as Herzl wrote, 'never presentable', and those who made use of him always took care to conceal the fact. He had cost Herzl a great deal of money, but then he could have done the Zionists a great deal of harm. Herzl concluded that it was impossible to establish whether 'he had done anything for us with the sultan or even if he was in a position to do so'. And yet Nevlinsky had shown courage and concern: 'He seems in my eyes, after his death, to loom head and shoulders above the whole scum – to sink to whose company was the tragic blunder of his life.'*

A small circle of young Zionists rallied to Herzl's side after the publication of the *Judenstaat*, mainly members of the Vienna Jewish students organisations. There were also encouraging letters from Galicia and

* *The Diaries*, pp. 304–10.

Bulgaria. Two early converts were David Wolffsohn and Max Nordau. The former, born in Lithuania, became a timber merchant in Cologne and was one of the leaders of the German Lovers of Zion. An eminently practical man, he was rooted to a far greater degree than Herzl in Jewish tradition and was the first to explain to Herzl that without the active help of the Jewish masses in eastern Europe his whole scheme would remain no more than an abstract construction. Max Nordau, like Herzl born in Budapest, was Herzl's senior by eleven years. When Herzl came to know him in Paris he was already one of Europe's best known literary essayists. In fact his *Conventional Lies* and *Degeneration* were the best-sellers of the 1880s and 1890s. He was to play a leading role in the Zionist movement up to the outbreak of the first world war, even though he lacked that ultimate measure of devotion and self-sacrifice which Herzl brought to the movement.

These then were Herzl's earliest supporters and sympathisers. There was no Zionist organisation, not even the nucleus of one when he set out on his first self-imposed diplomatic mission. The Grand Duke of Baden, one of the more sympathetic of the German princes, with whom he had a long conversation, was impressed by Herzl's personality and promised to intervene with the German emperor on his behalf. But the key to success or failure was in Constantinople, and Herzl decided to go there before trying his luck in the European capitals. He saw the grand vizir, the secretary-general of the Foreign Ministry, and a great many other officials, but he did not succeed in meeting the sultan, who in running the government often ignored even his closest advisers. It was Herzl's intention on this as on his subsequent visits to explain to the Turkish officials that the Jews could help them to reassert their independence *vis-à-vis* foreign powers by providing major loans. On more than one occasion he referred to the story of Androcles and the lion. The thorn to be removed by the Jews was of course the Turkish debt. In return he asked that the Jews should be given Palestine as a vassal state.

But the sultan and most of his advisers had no intention of giving away any part of the Ottoman empire. They were willing to consider Jewish immigration into Asia Minor, but the newcomers would have to adopt Turkish citizenship and their colonies would have to be scattered, not concentrated in one area. The Turks also had doubts about Herzl's real influence. On whose behalf was he speaking, and did he really have the necessary money at his disposal? Herzl was of course bluffing. He had as yet no organisational support behind him, and the leading Jewish communities and the great banking families wanted nothing to do with his schemes. He simply hoped that he would be able to raise both political and financial support on the strength of a promise from the sultan. The Turks probably realised this but did not want to turn him down altogether; perhaps his presence in Constantinople would act as a spur to other, more substantial, financial offers from other quarters.

Herzl returned from Constantinople with the *Medjidje* order and some vague promises. He had made no tangible progress at all, but at least he had been received and listened to. The news about his mission spread through the Jewish world and sparked off many exaggerated hopes. At Sofia railway station masses of Jews were waiting for him, their spokesman kissed his hand, he was hailed in speeches as the Leader, the Heart of Israel. Herzl was dumbfounded, embarrassed, and profoundly moved. So far he had appealed to the rich and powerful, who had rejected him; his confrontation with the French Rothschilds still lay ahead, but the outcome was to be as negative as other such meetings in the past. The idea of appealing directly to the Jewish masses must have occurred to him just before he went to London, almost immediately after his trip to Turkey. He had been to England the previous year, to try out his Jewish state concept with the Maccabeans, a group of Anglo-Jewish professional men who had given him a sympathetic hearing. Zangwill had expressed support, and in Cardiff a colonel commanding a Welsh regiment had told him: 'I am Daniel Deronda'. Born a Christian of baptised Jewish parents, he had found his way back to the Jewish people. His daughters, Rahel and Carmela, were learning Hebrew and he, Colonel Goldsmid, wanted to devote his life to the Jewish people.

The second London visit was not a success. Some supporters excused themselves; Colonel Goldsmid had to inspect one of his battalions; Sir Samuel Montagu the banker (on whom Herzl had counted to raise at least £200,000 for a pilot loan to impress the Turks) said that Edmond de Rothschild had to be won over. Herzl's English publisher told him that he had sold altogether 160 copies of *The Jewish State*. The Maccabean dinner was a flop, and Herzl was to refer to them henceforth as the Pickwickians. He had genuinely believed that this dining and debating club could be transformed into a militant action committee. But many thousands of poor Jews came to a mass meeting at the Working Man's Club in the East End, where in a fearful heat Herzl spoke extemporaneously for one hour. He later wrote in his notebook:

As I sat on the platform . . . I underwent a curious experience. I saw and heard my legend being made. The people are sentimental; the masses do not see clearly. . . . But even if they no longer see my features distinctly, they still sense that I mean truly well by them and that I am the little people's man.*

After the unsuccessful London trip, and a disastrous meeting with Rothschild in Paris ('I consider the house of Rothschild a national misfortune for the Jews', he wrote to Zadok Kahn, the French chief rabbi), his mind was made up. The rich Jews were all against him. He would now appeal directly to the masses. An organisation with branches all over the world would be set up. Above all he would get the support of the enthusiastic young generation. So far he had engaged in secret diplomacy, but the inactivity and hesitations of his followers compelled him to become a popular leader. There were moments of despair. On 13 October 1896 he wrote in his diary:

I must frankly admit to myself: I am demoralised. From no side, help, from every side, attacks. Nordau writes to me that nobody stirs any longer in Paris. The Maccabeans in London are more Pickwickian than ever. . . . In Germany I have only opponents. The Russians look on sympathetically while I slave away, but none of them lends a hand. In Austria, especially Vienna, I have a few adherents. Those who are not self-seekers do absolutely nothing; the others, the active ones, want to 'get a boost' in their career.

But nine days later Herzl was invited to a gala reunion of the Jewish students' union and he notes: 'A series of ovations . . . All the speakers referred to me. *On ne parle que de moi là dedans.*'†

Visitors and letters began to arrive from all parts of the world. Zionism, Herzl realised, was gradually winning the esteem of ordinary men in all sorts of countries, people 'are beginning to take us seriously'. But one million florins was needed to put the movement squarely on its feet. Unless he could overcome these initial difficulties 'we shall have to go to sleep, although it is full daylight'. Meanwhile, as a Zionist friend wrote from London, everybody was waiting to see how the cat would jump. If he succeeded they would join. If not, he would be ridiculed and forgotten. And so Herzl laboured on, unaided and singlehanded. He still believed (as he wrote the year before) that gravity (and inertia) could be overcome by movement, the dynamic element was all: 'Great things need no firm foundation. An apple must be placed on a table to keep it from falling. The earth hovers in the air. Thus I can perhaps found and secure a Jewish state without a firm anchorage. The secret lies in movement. Hence I believe that somewhere a guidable aircraft will be discovered.'

* *Ibid.*, p. 182.
† *Ibid.*, pp. 198–9.

During the early months of 1897 he needed all the faith he could muster. On 4 June the first issue of *Die Welt* was published. It was to remain the central organ of the world Zionist movement up to the First World War. Herzl had not only to provide the money and attend to all the technical details. He had also at first to supply much of the contents. He worked himself to utter exhaustion, while the outcome of the venture seemed highly doubtful. Ten days before the publication of the first issue only two subscriptions had come in, and this despite a considerable promotion campaign. (Ten months later it had 280 subscribers in Vienna among a Jewish population of about 100,000.) A little later Herzl convened a small committee in Vienna which decided to call a Zionist congress in Basle. It was first scheduled to take place in Munich because the Russian delegates were wary of Switzerland and the German city had kosher restaurants. But the leaders of the Munich Jewish community did not want to act as hosts to the congress. This resistance was typical of the attitude of many Jewish institutions and individuals towards Zionism. They claimed that there was no Jewish question, certainly not in central and western Europe. Why stir up trouble and supply ammunition to the antisemites who had argued all along that the Jews constituted a nation apart with their own secret government, that they were not and could not be loyal citizens? Herzl was not disheartened by the wave of protests and the great disunity in his own ranks. The Lovers of Zion in Britain and France, and some of the Russians, decided to boycott the meeting. Some of his early German supporters also tried to sabotage the plan from within. Several Viennese Zionists attended, but only to try to oust him from the leadership. Herzl remained firm: 'The congress will take place.' As a result of his unceasing efforts, pleadings, and his willingness to make constant financial sacrifices, the first Zionist congress was opened on 29 August 1897.

Despite the preparatory talks, there was a great deal of confusion. No one knew exactly what the congress was to decide and who was going to attend. Herzl, as a participant later wrote, was the only one who knew what he wanted. He had few illusions about the strength of his movement. On the eve of the congress he again noted in his diary: 'I stand in command of striplings, beggars and sensation mongers . . . some of them exploit me. Others are already jealous or disloyal. Still others desert me as soon as any little career gives them an opening. Only a few are unselfish enthusiasts. Nevertheless, even this army would do the job if success were in sight.'

The task of the congress, as he formulated it in his first speech, was 'to lay the foundation stone of the house which is to shelter the Jewish nation'.* For Herzl this was a most delicate operation – an 'egg dance, with the eggs invisible'. He could not offend the rabbis or the modernists; he had to accommodate the Austrian patriots and not arouse the suspicions of the Turks. Nothing disagreeable could be said about the Russian government for fear that it might outlaw altogether the semi-legal Zionist movement. But how could the situation of the Jews in Russia be passed over in any survey of the situation of world Jewry? The question of the Holy Places was a major egg, and so was the Rothschild family, which could not openly be criticised because of the help they gave to the Palestinian settlers. Herzl attached tremendous importance to the solemnity of the occasion. One of his local followers had hired a large hall with a gaudy vaudeville stage, but Herzl immediately decided to move to more dignified quarters. When Nordau appeared in a frock coat Herzl implored him to change into full dress (swallow-tails and white tie for the opening session). Everything was to be in the grand style, impressive and solemn. These elaborate preparations came as a surprise to the 197 delegates attending the congress; for most it was their first encounter with Herzl.

The congress was opened by Dr Lippe, an old Lover of Zion who recited the prayer *Shehekheyanu*: 'Blessed art Thou o Lord our God, King of the Universe, who hast kept us alive and brought us to witness this day.' He was to have spoken for ten minutes, but instead went rambling on, with well-meaning platitudes, making, as Herzl saw it, one embarrassing slip after another. Herzl sent word to him four times, and finally ordered him to stop. He concluded his speech by proposing an address of thanks and devotion to the sultan. The two speeches which followed, by Herzl and Nordau, were the highlights of the congress. There was nothing startling or novel in Herzl's message: the feeling of union, of solidarity among the Jews, had been fading when modern antisemitism broke on them. But now 'we have returned home. Zionism is the return of Judaism even before their return to the Jewish land.' The world again recognised that the Jews were a people. They needed a strong organisation. They had nothing to hide since they would engage in no conspiratorial activities. They wanted to revive and cherish the Jewish national consciousness and to improve the material conditions of the Jewish people. The eyes of hundreds of thousands of Jews were fixed on them in hope and expectation. The merits of sporadic colonisation were not to be ignored, but the old, slow methods, without any basis of legal recognition, would

* *Protokoll des ersten Zionisten Kongresses in Basel* (reprint), Prague, 1911, p. 15.

not help to solve the Jewish problem. Only recognised right should be the future basis, not sufferance and toleration. The movement would have to become far greater, much more ambitious and powerful if it was to achieve any of its aims: 'A people can be helped only by itself; and if it cannot do that, then it cannot be helped.'*

Herzl was greeted with tremendous applause lasting fifteen minutes. ('I remained altogether calm and deliberately refrained from bowing so as to keep the business at the outset from turning into a cheap performance', he noted in his diary.) He was followed by Nordau, who presented a brilliant survey of the situation of the Jews in various parts of the world, its material and moral aspects and implications. Nine-tenths of world Jewry were literally starving, fighting for their bare existence. Western Jewry was no longer subject to legal discrimination but it had been emancipated well before their host peoples had been emotionally prepared to give them equal rights. The emancipated Jew had given up his old Jewish characteristics but he had not become a German or Frenchman. He was deserting his own people because antisemitism had made him loathe it, but his French and German compatriots were rejecting him. He had lost the home of the ghetto without obtaining a new home.

This was the moral *Judennot* which was even more difficult to endure than material suffering, because it affected sensitive and proud people. The emancipated Jew was uncertain of himself and of other people, fearful, lacking equilibrium, suspicious of the secret feelings even of his friends. Some Jews, new Marranos, were trying to escape the danger by conversion, but the new racial antisemitism did not recognise this easy way out. Still others were joining the revolutionary movement, hoping that with the destruction of the old order, antisemitism too would disappear. Lastly there were the Zionists. It was the task of the first Zionist congress to consider ways and means of tackling the acute emergency facing the Jewish people. Nordau spoke freely, almost without notes. Always a superb orator, he rose to new heights at this congress. Herzl noted in his diary: 'He spoke gloriously. His address is and will continue to be a monument of our age. When he returned to our table I went over to him and said: *Monumentum aere perennius* – a monument more lasting than bronze.'

Subsequent speakers dealt in detail with the situation of the Jews in eastern and western Europe, and there were comments on the historical and economic justification of Zionism, and on colonisation in Palestine. One of Herzl's close collaborators suggested that no more Jews should

* *Ibid.*, p. 17.

emigrate to Palestine until there was an internationally recognised legal basis for their settlement. This was in accordance with the official programme of the movement adopted at a previous session:

Zionism seeks to secure for the Jewish people a publicly recognised, legally secured home in Palestine for the Jewish people. For the achievement of its purpose the congress envisages the following methods:
1 The programmatic encouragement of the settlement of Palestine with Jewish agricultural workers, labourers and those pursuing other trades.
2 The unification and organisation of all Jewry into local and wider groups in accordance with the laws of their respective countries.
3 The strengthening of Jewish self-awareness and national consciousness.
4 Preparatory steps to obtain the consent of the various governments necessary for the fulfilment of the aims of Zionism.

The preamble was adopted after a lengthy debate. The original draft had mentioned only a legally secured home (or homestead), but some of the younger delegates, like Schach from Cologne, and Leo Motzkin, argued that Zionism had nothing to hide. Its aim should be to win over the sultan for its aspiration to gain autonomy in Palestine. Without international legal guarantees there was no future and no security for the Jewish people. To the argument that such youthful impetuosity could harm the already existing colonies, Motzkin replied that 'the old style colonisation will lead to nothing anyway'. A few thousand Jewish peasants had been settled in Palestine in fifteen years, but this had not aroused much interest among other Jews and the original impetus had petered out.* After these interventions the weaker formula was discarded and the definition originally used by Herzl, 'publicly recognised, legally secured' (*öffentlich-rechtlich*), reinstated. The congress also dealt with organisational questions. How was Zionism to be transformed from an inchoate movement into an effective, powerful organisation? It was decided that the Zionist congress should become the supreme organ of the movement and that for dealing with current political questions an action committee of twenty-three members was to be elected. All those over the age of eighteen accepting the Basle programme and paying a shekel (one shilling or 25 cents) had the right to vote in elections to the congresses.

In the discussions a great many ideas and suggestions which were in later years to play a large role in Zionist activities were first aired. Bodenheimer, a close friend of Wolffsohn in Cologne, outlined a plan

* *Ibid.*, pp. 131–4.

for the establishment of a Zionist bank and central fund. Herman Shapira, a Russian-born professor of mathematics at Heidelberg, suggested that a Hebrew university should be opened in Palestine. As the third day of deliberations drew to its close, Max Mandelstam, one of the oldest Lovers of Zion, asked for the floor and in a tremulous voice expressed his and the other delegates' gratitude to 'that courageous man who was primarily responsible for the gathering of Jews from all countries taking counsel on the future of our people'.* Amid shouts of thanks and loyalty and tumultuous applause, the first Zionist congress came to an end.

It was a milestone in modern Jewish history. In contrast to the Kattowitz conference fifteen years earlier, it was not a small meeting of a few notables, receiving no publicity and leaving no traces. Acclaimed with fervent enthusiasm by some, attacked with equal intensity by others, the first Zionist congress achieved exactly the aim which Herzl had set himself: to reopen public discussion on Zionism. Jewish and non-Jewish newspapers all over the world reported the congress and reflected on its significance. For Herzl the foundation of a Zionist organisation was of tremendous importance. In his diplomatic activities he would now have the official backing of a new, dynamic movement. No longer was he simply Dr Herzl of the *Neue Freie Presse*, but the head of a world-wide organisation. Of great importance for the future of the movement was his meeting with the representatives of Russian Jewry, who with seventy delegates had constituted the strongest contingent in Basle. Herzl was impressed by the calibre of these men, of whose existence, with very few exceptions, he had been only dimly aware.

The Russian Jews, on the other hand, accepted Herzl as their leader, though not without reservations. Weizmann, who came to know Herzl only at the second congress, wrote: 'I cannot pretend that I was swept off my feet.' He was impressed by the man's deep sincerity and great gifts, but he also felt that Herzl had undertaken a task of immense magnitude without adequate preparation. Herzl, as Weizmann saw it, was naïve, not a man of the people, and his leaning towards clericalism (or rather his excessive respect for the rabbis) distressed him. Weizmann's teacher, Ahad Ha'am, who had been present in Basle, took an even more negative, in fact almost apocalyptic view: the Zionist congress had destroyed more than it had built up, Ahad Ha'am argued. Who knew whether this was not the last sigh of a dying people? Herzl seemed to him little better than a well-meaning confidence trickster. Be careful, he admonished his

* Alex Bein, *Theodor Herzl*, p. 242.

readers, 'the salvation of Israel will come through prophets, not diplomats'. But Herzl was more than satisfied, and in the immediate post-congress euphoria he noted in his diary that Zionism had now entered into the stream of history: 'If I were to sum up the congress in a word – which I shall take care not to publish – it would be this: At Basle I founded the Jewish state. If I said this out loudly today I would be greeted by universal laughter. In five years, perhaps, and certainly in fifty years, everyone will perceive it.' On various occasions Herzl and his friends discussed how long it would take to realise the Zionist dream. Nordau thought it might take three hundred years to carry out a task of such magnitude; Herzl's prediction was nearer the mark: fifty years and nine months after he made this entry in his diary the Jewish state was proclaimed in Tel Aviv.

The euphoria of Basle did not last long. Herzl had not revealed to the delegates that his first mission to Constantinople had ended in virtual failure. The sultan had stated, if Nevlinsky was to be trusted, that he could not dispose of any part of the Ottoman empire, for it belonged not to him but to the Turkish people. The Jews might as well save their money. And he had added, prophetically: 'When my empire is divided, perhaps they will get Palestine for nothing. But only our corpse can be divided. I will never consent to vivisection.' Herzl did not give up hope, but persuaded his followers that the success or failure of any future approach to the sultan depended on whether the Zionists would be able to raise the money needed for a loan. But the collection of money for the Colonial Bank (its official name was The Jewish Colonial Trust), the share capital of which was to be £2 million, did not go at all well. Subscriptions came in slowly, the Rothschilds had decided to stay out, the rich Berlin Jews were lukewarm, and the Russian Jewish millionaires, although they made substantial promises, did not follow them up.

Much of Herzl's energies during the next few years were devoted to fund-raising, a task for which he was not suited and which he loathed. How often he was to complain of the absence of a 'lousy million' which made it impossible for him to conduct large-scale propaganda and give him freedom of manœuvre in his negotiations in Constantinople. The Zionist organisation was so poor, the income from subscriptions so small, that the executive kept its finances secret for years in order to avoid ridicule.

The second Zionist congress, which took place a year after the first, reflected the growth of the movement. The number of delegates doubled (four hundred), and it was announced that whereas before the first congress 117 Zionist groups had been in existence, their number had now risen to 913. Nordau again gave a brilliant survey of the state of world Jewry; Herzl in his address demanded the capture of the Jewish communities; and the Zionist left wing, the Socialists under Nahman Syrkin, made its first appearance. Herzl showed himself a little more conciliatory towards the Hoveve Zion. One of their leading representatives, Mandelstam, suggested a synthesis between Herzlian (political) Zionism and the principles of Ahad Ha'am, aiming at gradual colonising work as a result of which Palestine would become a cultural centre.

The first congress had aroused great expectations. How much progress could Herzl report in good faith one year later? He knew best that there were no tangible successes, and with one notable exception – the mass meeting in London in 1898 when he hinted that the time was not far off when their dreams would come true – he carefully refrained from raising false hopes. What if his diplomatic attempts in Turkey were to fail altogether? In that case the Jews would have to wait until the general eastern crisis came to a head. As he noted in his diary, 'A people can wait.' But there were already occasional signs of impatience. Even before the second congress he considered whether the movement should not be given a nearer territorial goal, such as Cyprus, reserving Zion as the final aim. Or perhaps an eye should be kept on South Africa or America until Turkey disintegrated? For mass emigration from eastern Europe continued. The poor Jewish masses needed immediate help and Turkey was not yet so desperate as to accede to Zionist wishes.*

Herzl engaged in unceasing diplomatic efforts to make fresh converts to his cause. He met Philip Eulenburg, one of the closest friends of Wilhelm II, on several occasions, and he also tried to reach the German emperor through the Archduke of Baden. But the kaiser's entourage, including Bülow the foreign minister, was hostile, and in any case Herzl tended to overrate the kaiser's interest in middle eastern affairs. (He also overrated the kaiser's strength of character and general intelligence: 'He has truly imperial eyes – I have never seen such eyes. A remarkable, bold, inquisitive soul shows in them.') In his memoranda Herzl played on the fear of the kaiser and his collaborators of revolutionary Socialism: Jews would continue to supply the revolutionary parties with leaders and lieutenants unless a remedy was found for their plight. At one stage Herzl took it for granted that the kaiser would intervene on his behalf with the sultan and support the Zionist demand for a German protectorate under the suzerainty of the Porte. To live under the protection

* *Complete Diaries*, vol. 2, p. 644.

of this strong, great, moral, splendidly governed, tightly organised Germany, Herzl wrote in his diary, could only have the most salutary effect on the Jewish national character. He had a great talent for being carried away by his own frequently changing ideas; six weeks later, when his efforts had failed, he concluded that the fact that the kaiser did not accept the protectorate was of course an advantage for the future of the Zionist cause, because 'we would have had to pay the most usurious interest for this protectorate'.*

Between these two diary entries the German emperor had visited Palestine, and Herzl had followed him to Constantinople and Jerusalem with a small group of supporters. This was Herzl's first visit to the Holy Land but he was not overwhelmed. The landing at Jaffa was uncomfortable. He was struck by the confusion in the streets and in the hotel – poverty, heat and 'misery in gay colours'. Even much praised Rishon-Lezion, the nearby Jewish colony, struck him as a very poor place. There was thick dust on the roads, and again great poverty; plank beds and squalor in the houses of the Jewish labourers. The railway trip to Jerusalem in cramped, crowded and hot compartments was sheer torture, the countryside looked dismal and desolate, and Herzl was running a fever.

Jerusalem he found magnificently situated, a beautiful city even in its decay, but the 'musty deposits of two thousand years of inhumanity, intolerance, and uncleanliness lying in the foul-smelling little streets' made a terrible impression. In a Jewish hospital he found misery and dirt, but for appearance's sake he had to testify in the visitor's book to its cleanliness: 'This is how lies originate.' The local Jewish leaders and rabbis were afraid of meeting him for they were worried about the reaction of the Turkish authorities. Herzl was favourably impressed, on the other hand, by the cavalcade of twenty young and daring Jewish horsemen who, singing Hebrew songs, welcomed him in Rehovot. They reminded him of the cowboys of the American west: 'I had tears in my eyes . . .'. It showed into what the young trouser-salesmen could be transformed.

Herzl and his friends were received by the emperor in Jerusalem on 2 November 1898. 'That brief reception will live on forever in Jewish history, and possibly may entail world consequences', he noted in his diary. The date is of interest, but for a different reason. On the same day, nineteen years later, Balfour wrote his famous letter to Lord Rothschild. Herzl and his colleagues were so excited on the eve of the meeting that

* *Ibid.*, p. 769.

Dr Schnirer, his friend and also a member of the Inner Action Committee, wanted to prescribe a bromide. But Herzl refused. 'I wouldn't want it for the sake of history.' The audience came as an anti-climax. The kaiser replied, to Herzl's appeal for a German protectorate, that further investigation of the whole problem was necessary. 'He said neither yes nor no', Herzl commented, and this, in the circumstances, was not good enough.

The official German communiqué simply stated that the emperor had expressed benevolent interest in the efforts directed towards the improvement of agriculture in Palestine as long as these accorded with the welfare of the Turkish empire and fully respected the sovereignty of the sultan. Wilhelm II, who at one time had shown some interest in Zionist projects, had obviously lost his earlier enthusiasm. The German ambassador to Turkey, and some of the emperor's advisers, notably in the Foreign Ministry, had reservations, foreseeing strong opposition on the part of the sultan. It was also thought that what the kaiser saw of the sorry state of the Jerusalem Jews had not made him any better disposed towards the Zionist cause and its prospects. Be that as it may, the critics within the Jewish camp seemed to be vindicated: the Zionist goal was a chimera. Despondency reigned in the circle of Herzl's friends, for this was the end of one of the leader's fondest dreams. For once Herzl had no illusions: 'We shall not achieve our Zionist goal under a German protectorate', he wrote to the Grand Duke of Baden. 'I am sorrier than I can tell you.'*

The Zionist movement desperately needed a tangible achievement if it was to maintain its original impetus and dynamic character. One of Herzl's chief fears was that a decline would set in once the novelty had worn off unless it could show some striking success. It was at moments like this, when all seemed lost, that he showed his greatness. He was very tired, the symptoms of heart disease were increasing. He went through moments of black despair. On 1 May 1900 he entered in his diary: 'I have thought of an appropriate epitaph for myself: "He had too good an opinion of the Jews".'† Nevlinsky's death was a further blow. But Herzl carried on as if success were within reach, liberally distributing baksheesh from the limited funds of the Action Committee among the flunkeys surrounding the sultan. He enlisted Arminius Vambery, the legendary traveller and a friend of Abdul Hamid, orientalist and free-wheeling political agent, of Hungarian-Jewish

---

* *The Diaries*, p. 302.
† *Ibid.*, p. 325.

origin, who had in the course of a long life professed five religions, two of them as a priest. Vambery advised Herzl that the sultan was both mad and an arch liar and explained that nothing could be achieved in Constantinople by way of frontal assault. Vambery helped to arrange an interview between Herzl and the sultan in May 1901, but in addition the initiative of a great power was needed. Herzl no longer expected active German support, and as his Palestinian mission had failed his eyes turned to England as the power most likely to help. Lord Salisbury, then prime minister, was preoccupied with the Boer War and displayed little interest, but Herzl was not discouraged. The fourth Zionist congress was held in London in August 1900, for 'we had outgrown Basle'. England, Herzl said, was the only country in which God's old people was not confronted with antisemitism: 'England, free and mighty England, whose vision embraces the seven seas, will understand us and our aspirations. It is from here that the Zionist movement, we may be sure, will soar to further and greater heights.'*

Herzl had decided that a world Zionist congress should be convened every year. He feared that the movement would lose momentum if there were too long an interval between these meetings. The third congress had taken place in Basle in August 1899, the fourth exactly one year later in London, the fifth again in Basle in December 1901, the sixth, the last in which he took part, also in Basle in August 1903. The first congress, small and improvised as it was, had stirred profound emotions. The subsequent meetings attracted many more participants but as organisational routine developed their character began to change; they became less exciting and more businesslike. The congresses were always opened by Herzl (always greatly acclaimed) with relatively short programmatic speeches. He was followed by Nordau, who would present a masterly survey of the situation of world Jewry. These were brilliant and deeply moving speeches, but essentially they were variations on the same theme: the material deprivations of the Jews in eastern Europe and their moral and spiritual plight in the west. Nordau reported the reappearance of the old murder charges, and fresh anti-Jewish persecutions, which made it all the more imperative that a haven should be found for the victims. The reports of the Inner Action Committee contained impressive figures on the organisational growth of the movement. Between the third and fourth congresses, for example, the number of local Zionist organisations rose in Russia from 877 to 1,034 (with 100,000 paying the shekel), and from 103 to 135 in

* *Ibid.*, p. 330.

the United States. At the fifth congress it was reported that Zionism had spread to Chile and India, to New Zealand and Siberia, in fact to the furthest corners of the globe.

There was less optimism in the financial reports: at the fourth congress it was announced with regret that it had not yet been possible to establish the Colonial Trust which Herzl regarded as the essential prerequisite for any future political and economic action. Instead of the £250,000 needed, only about half that sum had been collected, and that only after enormous efforts. The rich Jews were obviously not putting their money on the Zionist horse. There were lectures about the physical degeneration of east European Jewry (Professor Mandelstam at the fourth congress, and Nordau – a physician by training – at the fifth), and the urgent necessity to do something about it. But all agreed that little could be done in the given circumstances; physical and spiritual recovery would follow economic and national normalisation, but this would happen only in their own country. East European Jewish spokesmen such as Sokolow put a great deal of stress on the discussion of cultural issues, in contrast to Herzl and his Viennese friends. The speeches and debates on the 'cultural question' dominated entire sessions of the early Zionist congresses and even provoked violent clashes. For the kind of spiritual renaissance advocated by Sokolow, Motzkin and Weizmann (partly under the influence of Ahad Ha'am) was not what the pro-Zionist rabbis had in mind. Weizmann tried to convince Herzl that the importance of the rabbis to the Jewish public and their potential support for the Zionist movement was much less than Herzl assumed. Motzkin provoked a minor storm when he said that the rabbis had not been present at the first congress and that their attempt to join the bandwaggon and impose their views on the whole movement should be resisted.* Herzl agreed that religion was a private affair, but his policy all along was to preserve the unity of the movement and to eliminate factors making for dissension. The young Russians, however, resented both the autocratic way he stage-managed the congresses and the way he ran the movement in between. The smaller Action Committee in Vienna was made up of his cronies: Marmorek, Schnirer and other well-meaning mediocrities.

The minutes still reported long applause and stormy ovations when Herzl appeared at the congress, but he was no longer a figure beyond reproach. Motzkin criticised him at the third congress for having

* *Stenographisches Protokoll der Verhandlungen des IV. Zionisten Kongresses in London.* Vienna. 1900, p. 100.

promised too much, arousing false hopes. The Zionist students from Russia organised a 'democratic fraction' which appeared as a pressure group at the congresses. Under the leadership of Syrkin and others there also emerged, much to Herzl's dismay, a Socialist-Zionist party demanding the establishment of a Socialist state in Palestine and the neighbouring territories. Syrkin bitterly attacked the domination of the Zionist movement by the bourgeois and religious-orthodox elements, as well as the 'rotten intellectuals' who wanted the movement to dissociate itself from the high ideals of progressive mankind. Such heretical views pained not only Herzl, who had never shown much interest or sympathy for the Socialist movement; they were even more strongly resented by young Weizmann, who in his Russian environment had acquired a fairly close knowledge of it. Commenting on one of the early Zionist-Socialist pamphlets, he wrote to his future wife: 'A red cap with a blue and white ribbon, a national group hailing internationalism with childish yells, dancing around great names; self-worship and Jewish impudence. What an outrageous mixture of meaningless phrases and sheer stupidity.' Weizmann was to become more friendly towards Socialist Zionism in later years, but at this time he clearly regarded it as a 'kind of pestilence'.*

Herzl was disappointed by the lack of progress and aggrieved by the attacks on him. By 1899 he had spent the larger part of his fortune and that of his wife on the movement, which made him more than ever dependent on his journalistic activities. On his forty-first birthday he wrote in his diary that it was almost six years since he had started on this movement, six years which had made him old, tired and poor. What sacrifices had been made by the penniless young Zionists from the east who were always so quick to criticise him at the congresses? He was equally dissatisfied with his close collaborators. Herzl was not a good judge of character, and utterly lacked business experience, and he quarrelled with his nearest and most devoted friends such as Wolffsohn. They in turn reproached him for his inability to suffer around him men with opinions of their own and to delegate authority.

Spells of dejection were followed by bouts of hyperactivity. In February 1901 the new Turkish restrictions on immigration came into force, which in some ways hit Herzl less hard than the Russian Zionists, for unlike them he had always believed in a charter, not in

* *The Letters and Papers of Chaim Weizmann*, vol. 1, London 1968, p. 137; Dr I.Klausner, *Oppositzia leHerzl*, Jerusalem, 1958, p. 80; Ben Elieser, *Die Judenfrage und der sozialistische Judenstaat*, Berne, 1898; *Manifesto to Jewish Youth*, London, 1901, p. 16.

'infiltration'. Shortly after, in May 1901, Vambery informed him that the sultan would at last receive him, not as a Zionist but 'as a chief of the Jews and an influential journalist'. Vambery warned him: 'You mustn't talk to him about Zionism. That is a phantasmagoria. Jerusalem is as holy to him as Mecca. Nevertheless Zionism is good [as far as the sultan is concerned] against Christianity. I want to keep Zionism alive and that is why I have secured the audience for you as otherwise you would not be able to face your congress. You must gain time and carry on Zionism somehow.'* It is interesting that Herzl's Turkish advisers had also advocated the strategy of indirect approach: 'There are questions which must not be tackled head-on,' Nuri had told him years earlier. 'Take Aleppo, buy land around Beirut and then keep spreading out. When the time comes that things go badly [in Turkey] and your services are needed, you step forward and ask for Palestine.'

On 17 June, Herzl was called to an audience in the royal palace. He was made to sit in the shade (a rare favour) and watched the long procession of soldiers, eunuchs, pashas, diplomats and other dignitaries. An official suddenly appeared to offer him the Order of the Medjidie, second class. After politely refusing it, the Grand Cordon of the same order was bestowed on him. Then the formal audience began. Herzl described the sultan as a small, thin man with a great hooked nose, full, dyed beard and a weak, quavering voice; he was sitting on a divan with his sword between his knees. He introduced himself as a constant reader of Herzl's newspaper, the *Neue Freie Presse*, a somewhat surprising statement since he knew no German. Herzl began with his favourite analogy, that of Androcles and the lion: the Jews would help Turkey to repay its foreign debt, the thorn in its side, so that it would be able to gather fresh strength. The great powers wanted to keep Turkey weak, to prevent its recovery, but Herzl could enlist the help of world Jewry and promote the country's industrialisation. And unlike the Europeans, the Jews would not enrich themselves quickly and then hurry away with their spoils. Palestine was not mentioned, but the sultan stressed that he was a great friend of the Jews, that he would make a public pro-Jewish announcement and give them lasting protection if they sought refuge in his lands.

The negotiations with the sultan's aides continued for a few more days. Herzl had made a good impression on Abdul Hamid: 'That Herzl looks like a prophet, like a leader of his people', the sultan told Vambery a few years later. Herzl received a present, a diamond scarf

* *The Diaries*, p. 333.

pin, but this was, as he sadly noted in his diary, about all he had achieved that day. He had distributed some fifty thousand francs among the various agents who maintained that they had been instrumental in arranging the audience, and there was no one who did not stake such a claim. Even Vambery was no exception, although when he first met Herzl he had said that he was a rich man, with a quarter of a million to his name.

The sultan's advisers formulated a number of conditions which were altogether unacceptable to Herzl: the Jews would establish a syndicate with £30 million to help liquidate the Turkish debt; they would be permitted to settle in Turkey, but would have to become Turkish citizens; above all there could be no concentrated mass immigration but only scattered settlement – five families here and five there. Herzl countered by proposing the establishment of a land company to take over uncultivated Turkish property in Palestine. Before his departure he was given to understand that the sultan expected definite financial proposals within a month. Herzl left Constantinople in a cautiously optimistic mood. He had been received by the sultan and had talked to him for almost two hours, something of which few ambassadors could boast. He had been impressed by the sultan as a 'weak, craven, but thoroughly good-natured man' surrounded by a criminal gang.* He had kept the dialogue going and had actually entered upon nego-tiations for the charter, something which Vambery had thought quite impossible. Herzl realised that he had not yet achieved anything tangible, but he felt confident that it now needed 'only luck, skill and money, to put through everything I had planned'. For years to come he was to claim that he could have got Palestine for the Jews on that occasion if only the money had been available. At the same time he was not unaware that the Turks were merely using him as a pawn to get a loan from a more substantial financial consortium headed by the Frenchman Rouvier. Herzl's attempts to win the support of the moneyed Jews whom he invoked so often in his negotiations were quite unsuccess-ful, but he continued to act as if it was within his powers to relieve the sultan of the Turkish debt, estimated at a nominal £85 million, and that as a result he would at last receive his charter.

In February 1902 the sultan (who had been given the code name Cohn in Herzl's private correspondence), again called him to the Turkish capital. He complained that nothing concrete had so far emerged from the talks. Herzl had made a few friendly declarations in public,

* *Ibid.*, p. 350.

but that was all. The sultan was prepared to open his empire to Jewish refugees on condition that they would become Ottoman subjects and that they could establish themselves in all provinces except – at first – Palestine. He suggested that in return Herzl was to form a syndicate for the consolidation of the Ottoman public debt and he was also to take over the concession for the exploitation of all mines in Turkey. This was a charter at long last, but since it excluded Palestine and unlimited immigration it was unacceptable. When Herzl continued to insist on Palestine, his Turkish interlocutors explained that the sultan could not agree to sponsor a scheme which would be so unpopular among his subjects. Cohn, as Herzl wrote Vambery, offered far too little and demanded too much.

Negotiations did not however break down. In July 1902 Herzl was again summoned to Constantinople to what was to be the final showdown. Again the old, by now familiar picture: 'Dirt, dust, noise, red fezzes, blue waters'; the baksheesh snatchers at the palace entrance greet Herzl with their familiar grin. He suggested that his friends could greatly improve on the rival French scheme if the charter for colonisation in Mesopotamia offered to him a few months before were to include the Haifa region. He pointed out that the Jews likely to immigrate were neither a dangerous nor a troublesome element, but on the contrary sober, industrious and loyal, 'bound to the Moslems by racial kinship and religious affinity'.*

Yet it was all to no avail. The Turkish officials were like sea foam, Herzl noted in his diary. Only their expressions were serious, not their intentions. He indicated that he would always remain a friend of Turkey and its pro-Jewish sultan, but the misery of the Jewish people in eastern Europe was such that he could not wait any longer. He would have to ask the British, with whom contact had already been established, for a Jewish colony in Africa.

This was to all intents and purposes the break, the end of a chapter in Zionist diplomacy. Yet even then Herzl did not despair altogether. They had grown accustomed in Constantinople to look upon him as someone interested in the vilayet of Beirut. One day perhaps, when reduced to beggary, they would send for him and throw the thing in his lap. But these were distant hopes. Having returned from Turkey empty-handed it was pointless to make any further advances, and Herzl knew he had to concentrate his efforts on London with, perhaps, some manoeuvring in Rome and Berlin.

* *Complete Diaries*, vol. 4, p. 1321.

Herzl's negotiations in Constantinople had been an educational experience but the price paid was high. 'So here I am, escaped again from the murderers' den and the robbers' country', he wrote after his final visit. He had been compelled to sweat for hours in anterooms, to distribute a small fortune among lackeys, to put a great many dignitaries on his payroll, to 'die of boredom listening to the childish claptrap of the various ministers'. He had had to eat with exclamations of delight countless 'loathsome meals of those innumerable barbaric dishes – veritable snake food'. He had had to praise the lofty wisdom of the sultan and to stress his own unalterable devotion in countless epistles, all in the end to no purpose. Worse still, he had had to intimate time and time again that he could be of help to the sultan against his enemies, which had been understood as a proposal to make the *Neue Freie Presse* a channel for Turkish propaganda. But the editors of the paper would not have cooperated, nor had Herzl had the slightest intention of prostituting his pen (though proud and independent as he was, his attitude on some issues he considered marginal was not above suspicion; he was ready to use his influence to play down the anti-Armenian persecutions which provoked the ire of some of his collaborators, among them Bernard Lazare).

Herzl with his restless and inventive mind had made constant suggestions and offers to the sultan to ingratiate himself and to show that his movement could be of great help. It was embarrassing, even degrading, but had there been any other way to attain his aim? In May 1902, for instance, he had suggested the establishment of a Jewish university in Jerusalem. To make it more palatable to the sultan he had explained that such an enterprise would be of the greatest service to the Ottoman empire. It would help to eradicate any 'unhealthy spirit'; the Turks would no longer have to send their young people abroad for higher education where they became infected by dangerous, revolutionary ideas.

Herzl had been forced to adapt himself to the Byzantine atmosphere, the mendacity and duplicity prevailing in Yildiz Kiosk. His diary is full of anecdotes revealing his horror at the kind of people with whom he had to associate. He was carried away more than once into making suggestions and proposals of whose full implications he was probably not aware. Fortunately for him and for his place in history they were not taken up. His intimates were aware only of a small part of his activities, but even what they knew stirred deep misgivings among them. What was the point of all this secret diplomacy? Would it not deeply compromise the Zionist movement? Herzl in this respect was unscrupulous. He was firmly convinced (as he told his nearest confidants) that there was simply no other way by means of which a small, impecunious group of intellectuals, with no political or military backing at their disposal, could attain their aims. This attitude was in line with his views about propaganda and public relations. At the very outset of his Zionist career one of his friends had expressed doubts about the wisdom and efficacy of making so much noise. Noise, Herzl replied in anger, was everything. World history was nothing but noise – noise of arms and advancing ideas: 'Men must put noise to use – and still despise it.'* And this precisely was his attitude towards secret diplomacy.

In 1902, after the failure of his Turkish ventures, the centre of Zionist diplomatic activities shifted to London. Although, as noted earlier, Lord Salisbury showed no interest, there was one issue which came to the fore. Public opinion in Britain was becoming concerned about Jewish immigration from eastern Europe, and the consequent growing threat of cheap labour. A royal commission was appointed to investigate the question and this gave Herzl an opportunity to propagate his schemes in the British capital. The British Zionists managed to have him invited as a witness, much to the dismay of Nathaniel Meyer Lord Rothschild, who was a member of the commission. Despite his early disappointments, Herzl had not given up hope of gaining the support of the Rothschild family, and while in London it was again impressed on him that he would find it very difficult to make any headway with the British government without at least their tacit support. So yet another attempt was made to win over the leading Jewish family. The 'Lord of Banking Hosts' told Herzl that he did not believe in Zionism, that the Jews would never get Palestine, and that in contrast to France there would never be appreciable antisemitism in England. Herzl's appearance before the commission, Rothschild argued, could only have two effects: the antisemites would be able to say that Dr Herzl, the expert, maintained that a Jew could never become an Englishman; and if Herzl harped on the bad situation of the Jews in eastern Europe and their need to emigrate this would lead to restrictive legislation.

There was a heated exchange, another Rothschild brother was called in, and at last Herzl had a chance to discuss his own plans:

I moved my chair round to the side of his better ear, and said: 'I want to ask the British government for a colonisation charter.' 'Don't say "charter". This word has a bad sound', Rothschild replied. 'Call it what you please,' I replied. 'I want to found a Jewish colony in a British possession.' Rothschild said: 'Why not take Uganda?' 'No,' I answered, 'I can only use – and as there were other people in the room I wrote on a slip of paper: Sinai peninsula, Egyptian Palestine, Cyprus. And I added, 'Are you for it?' He thought it over, chuckling, and said: 'Very much.' This was victory.*

The next day Herzl mentioned his plan to Lord James of Hereford, chairman of the Aliens Commission, who thought he might be able to carry out his Sinai-Cyprus project with the help of the Rothschilds. Herzl's appearance before the commission was in his own view less than successful. He wanted to propagate Zionism and to win new adherents, without, however, saying anything which could be used as an argument for restricting immigration into Britain, for however grandiose its vision, there was nothing the Zionist movement could do at that moment to alleviate the fate of east European Jewry. Herzl could not, as he said in a letter to Rothschild, refuse to consider any scheme for emigration and settlement. He claimed that he had drawn up a plan for the organisation of a Jewish Eastern Company because the Rothschilds ('the most effective force our people has possessed since our dispersion') had declared themselves opposed to Palestine. Yet the idea of Jewish territory, if not a Jewish state, in a country other than Palestine had occurred to him more than once before. Back in 1898 he had noted in his diary that the Jewish masses needed immediate help and could not wait until Turkey was so desperate as to give the Zionists what they wanted.

How to set an immediatly accessible goal without yielding any historical rights? After the third Zionist congress, when the position of Rumanian Jewry was deteriorating, he thought the Cyprus plan might be a possible alternative to be submitted to the British government if no progress were made with Turkey over Palestine: 'I . . . shall have the congress decide to go to Cyprus next.' But whereas some of Herzl's collaborators, such as Davis Trietsch, had been strong supporters of the Cyprus project for years, the great majority, above all the Russian Hoveve Zion, would not hear about it, and Herzl had to move cautiously even in regard to his own closest collaborators.

In October 1902 he was received by Joseph Chamberlain, the colonial secretary, that famous 'master figure of England'. The moment

* *Ibid.*, p. 367.

was well chosen: British public opinion felt that something should be done for east European Jewry if they were to be barred from entering England. Chamberlain did not reject in principle the idea of founding a self-governing Jewish colony in the south-eastern corner of the Mediterranean. Herzl described his negotiations with the sultan:

You know what Turkish negotiations are. If you want to buy a carpet, first you must drink half a dozen cups of coffee and smoke a hundred cigarettes; then you discuss family stories, and from time to time you speak again a few words about the carpet. Now I have time to negotiate, but my people have not. They are starving in the Pale. I must bring them help.*

Chamberlain made on Herzl the impression of a competent business-man; not a man of imagination but with a clear and unclouded head. He could talk to Herzl only about Cyprus – Herzl would have to take up the El Arish and Sinai project with Lord Lansdowne, the foreign secretary. As for Cyprus, Britain would not evict the Greeks and Muslims for the sake of newcomers.

Chamberlain was in favour of the idea of Jewish settlement in the Brook of Egypt (Wadi el Arish) if Lord Cromer, the viceroy, accepted it. As for Egypt itself, briefly mentioned by Chamberlain, Herzl immediately retorted: 'We will not go to Egypt – we have been there.' But he did mention his Haifa hinterland idea; he was hoping to induce the Turks to lease the Haifa district at a lower rate once the Jews turned up at El Arish and showed that Zionism meant business.

Next day Herzl again briefly saw Chamberlain and, at greater length, Lord Lansdowne, whose attitude was on the whole sympathetic. He asked for a written memorandum for the cabinet and promised to write to Cromer about it. Herzl dispatched to Cairo Leopold Greenberg, an English Zionist who was later to become editor of the *Jewish Chronicle*. Greenberg met both Cromer and the Egyptian prime minister, who mentioned various difficulties, such as Turkish claims on the territory in question and the failure of a previous attempt to establish a Jewish colony in the region of ancient Median. Cromer suggested the dispatch of a commission of experts. Herzl accepted the idea, emphasising that since the Jews had no alternative they would accept land considered unsuitable by others. It did not take him long to realise that Cromer was all important; the British government would go as far as Cromer, no farther.

The expedition was dispatched and Greenberg continued his talks

* *Ibid.*, p. 374.

in Cairo, but Herzl, who felt left out and feared that things were not proceeding as smoothly and rapidly as he wanted, also decided to go to Cairo. His meeting with Cromer ('the most disagreeable Englishman I have met') was not a success. The viceroy told Herzl that he need not bother about the Turkish representative in the Egyptian capital. But the question of water supplies was of vital importance. Water for irrigating land could come only from the Nile, and Herzl would have to wait for an expert report. With this Herzl was dismissed. 'A bit too much arrogance', he noted in his diary; 'a touch of tropical madness and unlimited vice-regalism.' After meeting Cromer he felt sympathy for Egyptian nationalism. He had been struck by the intelligent-looking young Egyptians whom he had met at a lecture: 'They are the coming masters. It is a wonder that the English don't see this. They think they are going to deal with fellahin forever.'* Herzl stayed in Egypt only a few days, but the negotiations dragged on for many months. In the end there was yet another failure. The Egyptian government turned the El Arish project down because their irrigation expert had reached the conclusion that five times as much water as originally thought would be needed to make the scheme a success. The diversion of so much water from the Nile was thought to be impossible. On 12 May 1903 Herzl received a cable that the plan had definitely been rejected. Four days later he noted in his diary that he had thought the Sinai scheme so certain that he no longer wanted to buy a family vault in the Doebling cemetery where his father had been provisionally laid to rest: 'Now I consider the matter so utterly shattered that I have been to the borough court and have acquired vault 28.'†

Herzl did not give up. In London a month earlier a new project had been mentioned. Chamberlain, who had meanwhile been on a tour of Africa, told Herzl that he had seen Uganda and had thought: 'There's a land for Dr Herzl – but of course he only wants to go to Palestine or its neighbourhood.' Uganda, Chamberlain reported, was hot on the coast, but the climate in the interior was excellent for Europeans. Sugar and cotton could be raised there. Herzl brushed the idea aside. The Jewish base would have to be near Palestine. Later on the Jews could also settle in Uganda, for there were great masses of them ready to emigrate. But one month later, after the failure of the El Arish project and after a further meeting between Greenberg and Chamberlain, Herzl was more inclined to consider the East African scheme. The

* *Complete Diaries*, vol. 4, p. 1449.
† *The Diaries*, p. 385.

political significance of the offer seemed considerable. Perhaps it could be used as a training ground for the Jewish national forces? On 30 May he wrote Rothschild: 'I am not discouraged. I already have another plan, and a very powerful man is ready to help me.'* Thus began yet another fateful chapter in Herzl's desperate efforts to find a country for the people without a land, and it was to involve the Zionist movement in the deepest crisis it had so far faced.

Before the discussions on Uganda reached a decisive stage Herzl was to engage in yet another political mission which aroused deep misgivings and bitter criticism within the ranks of his own movement. In August 1903 he went to St Petersburg to discuss with leading members of the tsarist government various possibilities to speed up the emigration of Russian Jews. How could Herzl talk to Plehve, the arch reactionary, who as minister of the interior had to bear responsibility for the terrible wave of pogroms which had swept Russia only a few months before, the man 'whose hands were stained with the blood of thousands of Jewish victims'? (Weizmann). Only a few months earlier, between 6 and 8 April, a pogrom had taken place in Kishinev in the course of which about fifty Jews had been killed, many more wounded, and many Jewish women raped. The feeling in the Jewish community was one of horror, but also of terrible shame that Jews had been beaten and killed like sheep without offering resistance. 'Great is the sorrow and great is the shame', Bialik wrote after the massacre; 'and which of the two is greater, answer thou, o son of Man.' 'The grandsons of the Maccabeans – they ran like mice, they hid themselves like bedbugs and died the death of dogs wherever found.'

Kishinev was a turning point in the history of the Jews in eastern Europe, the beginning of Jewish self-defence. The Russian pogroms of 1903 had produced a wave of indignation in western Europe, and Herzl assumed, not incorrectly, that the tsarist government, eager to refurbish its image, might be willing to make certain concessions. Plehve had given instructions in June to take energetic measures against Zionist propaganda which, he asserted, had deviated from its original aim, namely the emigration of Jews to Palestine, and was directed instead to strengthening national consciousness among the Jews and the organisation of closed societies. Above all, the sale of shares in the Jewish Colonial Trust had been banned, as well as collections for the Jewish National Fund, and this constituted a real danger for the Zionist movement.

* *Complete Diaries*, vol. 4, p. 1501.

Herzl hoped that the tsarist government, eager to get rid of at least some of its Jews, could be induced to exert pressure on Turkey to absorb some of them. This idea was more than a little fanciful, for Turkey was in any case concerned about encroachments of its powerful northern neighbour, and Russian Jews were in Turkish eyes potential Muscovite agents. Herzl had introductions to both Plehve and to Witte, the minister of finance. Plehve, who had been described to him as a brute, made a far better impression on him than Witte, who had the reputation of a liberal and even friend of the Jews. Plehve spoke with cynical frankness: the Jews lived in a ghetto and their economic situation was bad; the benefits of higher education were extended to a few only, 'as otherwise we should soon have no positions left to give to the Christians'. Of late their situation had grown worse because so many of them had joined the revolutionary parties. Herzl suggested Russian intervention with the sultan to secure a charter, the removal of the restrictions on Zionist work in Russia, and Russian financial aid for emigration. Plehve showed himself astonishingly well-informed about the affairs of the Russian Zionist movement. He claimed that since the Minsk conference (in September 1902) it had been more interested in promoting cultural and political work than in its original aim, emigration, and anyway, its leaders with a few exceptions were up in arms against Herzl. Herzl countered by comparing his situation with that of Christopher Columbus: a revolt of the sailors against the captain, as week followed week with no land in sight: 'Help us faster to land and the revolt will end. So will defection to the socialist ranks.'

When Herzl saw Plehve again a week later, the tsar had been informed about his proposals and it was agreed that the Zionist movement should receive moral and material assistance with respect to measures which would lead to a diminution of the Jewish population in Russia, but there was also a warning that Zionism would be suppressed if it were to lead to any intensification of Jewish nationalism. The tsar announced that he had been hurt at the thought that anyone should have dared to assert that the Russian government had abetted the pogroms. Did not the tsar, in his great and well-known kindness, extend his goodwill to all his subjects? He was therefore particularly grieved at even being thought capable of the slightest inhumanity. Plehve, a more honest man than his master, again admitted that the situation of the Jews was unhappy: 'If I were a Jew I too should probably be an enemy of the government.' But there were too many Jews and the tsarist government was unable to change its policy. It

wanted to keep those of superior intelligence, able to assimilate themselves, but had to get rid of the rest, and for that reason favoured the
establishment of an independent Jewish state capable of absorbing
several millions of them.

Herzl's meeting with Witte was less of a success. According to
Herzl's report, Witte said that the Jews were arrogant, poor, dirty,
repulsive, and engaged in the vilest pursuits, such as pimping and
usury. Witte was opposed to making their lot even more miserable,
but there was no way out – they would have to continue to endure the
present state of affairs. The ideas of Zionism seemed to him not un-
attractive but on the whole impractical. When Herzl left Witte he
wondered how the minister of finance had ever acquired a reputation
for being a friend of the Jews when he had done less than nothing to
help them during his thirteen or fourteen years in government. Perhaps
Witte merely wanted to capitalise on Plehve's troubles over the
Kishinev affair, in the hope that it would lead to the downfall of his
rival? The results of Herzl's mission to Russia have been bitterly
disputed. Herzl related that Plehve told him that but for his (Herzl's)
intervention Zionism would have been banned in Russia. But Plehve
was killed by a terrorist the following year, and there were more
pogroms, often with the tacit approval of the government, which was
far too preoccupied with other problems to take any constructive
initiative on the Jewish problem. Herzl's critics maintained that his
negotiations were indefensible, that he had made a deal with Plehve
promising that the Jewish Socialists would no longer attack the tsarist
government, and that he had tried to influence the Poale Zion, the
left-wing Zionists, in this direction. Herzl did in fact declare at the
sixth Zionist congress that the Russian government would put no
obstacles in the way of the Zionist movement if its activities remained
within a legal framework.*

This statement provoked indignation, not only among the Left.
Weizmann thought that Herzl's talks in Russia had been utterly
pointless: he was overwhelmed by the calamities of Russian Jewry,
foresaw further persecution, and wanted a quick solution. But his
assumption that men like Plehve would be of any help was totally
unreal: 'Antisemites are incapable of aiding in the creation of a Jewish
homeland; their attitude forbids them to do anything which might
really help the Jewish people. Pogroms, yes; repressions, yes; emigration, yes; but nothing that might be conducive to the freedom of

* Boehm, *Die Zionistische Bewegung*, vol. 1, p. 256; *Protokolle des Sechsten Kongresses*, p. 82.

Jews'.* It was a dilemma which faced Zionist leaders from Herzl onwards and caused them much heart searching. Thirty years later Weizmann was to be received in audience by Mussolini. Should they have restricted their diplomatic activities to liberal and democratic statesmen? To have refrained from meeting dictators and antisemites would have saved them a great many moral conflicts. But it would have severely limited their freedom of action and might have hampered their efforts to save Jewish lives.

Whatever the scruples of Zionist leaders and militants, the Jewish masses prepared a welcome for Herzl such as had never been accorded to any Jewish leader. Tens of thousands shouted 'Hedad' (Hail) as he passed. About the reception in Vilna, Herzl wrote in his diary that the day would remain engraved forever in his memory. It was the first time that he had come face to face with the Jewish masses in eastern Europe. The unhappiness of these oppressed people was only too genuine: 'There was a note in their greetings which moved me to a point where nothing but the thought of the newspaper reports was able to restrain my tears.'† He had been warned of the bitter opposition of the Bundists – the anti-Zionist Jewish Socialists – and he watched with some misgivings the approach of some young working men, with hard, determined expressions on their faces, whom he took to belong to that party. Much to his amazement one of them came forward and proposed a toast to the day when 'Melech Herzl' (King Herzl) would reign. Such was the fathomless despair of the Jewish masses, such – to quote Weizmann again – the great surge of blind hope, baseless, elemental, instinctive and hysterical, attending his visit.

One week after his Russian trip Herzl was in Basle for the sixth Zionist congress. He reported to the Action Committee on his negotiations in St Petersburg and was amazed and embittered by the ingratitude of the Russian Zionists: 'It didn't occur to a single one of them that for my unprecedented labour I deserved so much as a smile, let alone a word of gratitude.' All he got was a shower of reproaches. The next day he informed his colleagues of a message just received by Greenberg from Sir Clement Hill, chief of the Protectorate Department in the Colonial Office, in which the Zionist movement was told that the British government was 'interested in any well considered scheme aimed at the amelioration of the position of the Jewish race'. As for the talks with Dr Herzl about the establishment of a Jewish settlement in Africa,

---

* *Trial and Error*, p. 82.
† *The Diaries*, p. 404.

time had been too short to go into the details of the plan and it was therefore impossible to pronounce any definite opinion. But the British government was willing to give every facility to a Zionist study commission which should go there to ascertain personally whether there were any suitable vacant lands. If the result were positive, and the scheme commended itself to the government, there would be a good chance of a Jewish colony or settlement being established under a Jewish official as chief of the local administration in which the members would be able to observe their national customs.*

The letter, formulated in the usual cautious diplomatic language, created a profound impression. Chlenov, the Russian Zionist leader, broke spontaneously into the *Shehekheyanu* – the ritual blessing upon receiving good news. This was both a recognition of the Jewish people as such by a major power and the expression of its willingness to help. Others were more sceptical. But to all the scheme came as a surprise. Herzl himself was not entirely happy about it. Greenberg had written that Joseph Chamberlain was considering a region between Nairobi and the Nan escarpment. Herzl was not certain whether this area was suitable for European colonisation, nor was it clear whether the British government was willing to give the colonists the independence he envisaged. Lastly, he knew of course that any such scheme could be realised only with a great deal of enthusiasm to overcome the many initial difficulties. And even Herzl, with his immense prestige and great hold over the movement, must have doubted whether he would be able to induce the Zionists to follow him to Uganda.

At first all seemed plain sailing. When the congress was told about the British message there was a storm of applause. Shmaryahu Levin, one of the secretaries, saw on the faces of the delegates 'amazement, admiration – but not a sign of protest. . . . The first effect of the magnanimity of the British offer was to eclipse all other considerations.'† Yet when the various factions and caucuses withdrew to consider the scheme in detail there was much opposition, and this despite the fact that the congress was not even asked to decide between Uganda and Palestine but merely to give support to the dispatch of an investigation commission to East Africa. Herzl made it clear in his opening speech that Uganda was not, and could never become Zion. It was envisaged as an emergency measure, to help those Jews forced to emigrate immediately, to prevent their scattering all over the world, and to

---

* The letter was first published in *Die Welt*, 29 August, 1903.
† Quoted in Bein, *Theodor Herzl*, p. 455.

promote colonisation on a national and state basis. Nordau, who had considerable misgivings, used the phrase *Nachtasyl* – a temporary shelter for the hundreds of thousands of Jews who could not as yet enter Palestine, a shelter which would provide a political training ground for the greater task ahead. The Jews owed it to England to subject the Uganda project to thorough examination, but Zion would always remain the final aim. There was yet another consideration: with each year Jewish immigrants would find it more difficult to enter other countries. The presence of little more than a hundred thousand Jews in Britain had sufficed to provoke restrictions. How much longer would the gates of America remain open?

Nordau was not at his most persuasive, and the fact that a great many west European delegates supported him did not help. Most Russian Jews were instinctively against Uganda and it was from eastern Europe that the immigrants were expected to come. As one of them put it, while they were enthusiastically promoting the Palestine idea they were now suddenly told by their leaders that they had been dreamers, that they had been wasting their time building castles in the air. Zion was the great ideal, but it could not be attained, redemption would come only from Uganda. This was quite unacceptable, and how could the leaders negotiate with the British government without even consulting the Jewish people, the Sovereign, on whose behalf they were acting? Practical arguments were also used: East Africa was quite unsuitable for mass immigration; both the man power and the funds at the disposal of the Zionist movement were strictly limited, and any diversion of either would have fatal consequences. Herzl and Nordau had recommended Uganda in order to find a palliative for the steadily growing *Judennot*. But the Jews had waited for Palestine so long that they could wait a little longer. Was it not symbolic that the delegates from Kishinev, the town which had suffered the worst pogrom, were unwilling to go anywhere except Palestine? As Weizmann said in a speech to his fellow delegates: 'If the British government and people are what I think they are, they will make us a better offer.'

Everyone realised that the movement faced the most important decision in its history. Tempers were running short and excitement mounted hourly. An eye-witness described the scene at the end of one critical session:

For about half an hour people were shouting; some were singing Russian songs, others climbing on chairs, throwing leaflets from the galleries into the hall, banging the chairs on the floor. There was a tremendous noise in the galleries; some twenty girls had entered the hall through a side door and were adding to the clamour. Zangwill and Greenberg left the platform in an attempt to calm the public but the demonstrators just carried them shoulder high and the turmoil did not cease even after the lights had been turned off. . . . The tumultuous scenes continued into the small hours of the morning; the casino where the congress took place was besieged by masses of excited people. Only a very few could think of sleep that night.*

Herzl's tremendous prestige sufficed to push the resolution through. By 295 votes to 178 it was decided to send a commission to East Africa. But there could be no mistake: the east European Jews would not go to East Africa. Herzl was called a traitor to his face, and a short time after the congress a Zionist student tried to kill Nordau.

There was a real danger that the movement would split. The opposition, which had already walked out, returned and declared that their action had not been a political demonstration against the leadership but the spontaneous expression of a profound spiritual shock. Herzl in his closing speech said that hope for Palestine was not lost, since the Russian government had promised its help. There was to be no break, no alteration in the Basle programme. With his right hand uplifted he said: '*Im eshkakhekh Yerushalayim*'. . . . If I forget thee, O Jerusalem, may my right hand wither.†

Outward unity was restored, but Herzl was profoundly depressed and so were most of the delegates. When, after the final session, he left the congress completely worn out, he told his closest friends what he would say at the seventh congress if he was still alive. He would have either obtained Palestine by then or have realised the complete futility of his efforts. In the latter case he would say: 'It was not possible. The ultimate goal has not been reached and cannot be reached within a foreseeable time.' But since there was a land in which the suffering masses could meanwhile settle on a national basis, the movement was not entitled to withhold this relief for the sake of a beautiful dream. This choice would lead to a decisive rupture, and since the rift would centre on his own person he would step down. Two executive bodies would come into existence, one for Palestine, the other for East Africa, but he, Herzl, would serve on neither.

Herzl's health deteriorated during 1903. The excitement of the sixth congress had been an additional, intolerable strain. There were frequent forebodings of death in his diaries. But for him there was no long rest

---

* *Jüdische Rundschau*, no. 33, 1903, p. 412.
† *Stenographisches Protokoll der Verhandlungen des VI. Zionistenkongresses*, Vienna, 1903, p. 340.

cure, and soon he was setting off on yet another diplomatic mission. In Rome he met Victor Emanuel III, the young king who had succeeded to the throne a few years earlier, as well as Pius X, the new pope. The king, who had been to Palestine, noted that the country was already largely Jewish and would no doubt one day belong to the Jews. When Herzl remarked that they were no longer allowed to enter, the king replied: 'Nonsense, everything can be done with baksheesh.'* The pope was less helpful: 'We are unable to favour this movement', he told Herzl. 'We cannot prevent the Jews from going to Jerusalem, but we could never sanction it.'

Herzl's last months were embittered by the quarrel with the Russian Zionists. Ussishkin, their most aggressive leader, who had been in Palestine at the time of the congress, published a letter after his return accepting his election to the Action Committee while stressing that he did not feel bound by the Uganda resolution. This was open rebellion, and Herzl in his answer sharply attacked Ussishkin and the policies advocated by the Russian Hoveve Zion whom he represented. What was the purpose of private land purchases in Palestine? Ussishkin could buy up every plot in his native Yekaterinoslav but it would still remain part of Russia. The Russian Zionists at their conference in Kharkov passed a resolution to the effect that Herzl had violated the Basle programme, and appointed three of their number to meet him, to demand in categorical terms that he drop his autocratic methods and in future submit all his projects to the supreme elected body, the Action Committee. He was also to promise in writing that he would not ask the support of the congress for any territorial projects other than those concerned with Palestine and Syria. The ultimatum greatly offended Herzl and caused much resentment within the Zionist movement outside Russia. It was regarded as an attempt to overthrow the leader. Herzl refused to meet the committee but saw the emissaries individually, and at the meeting of the Action Committee in April 1904 made a successful effort at reconciliation. He said he would not go to Uganda, nor would he exert any pressure in favour of East Africa. He wanted the Jewish people to decide on the basis of the facts. But he insisted on the primacy of political Zionism over the old Hoveve Zion approach. The Russians were always telling him that they had already been Zionists for twenty or twenty-five years, but what had they achieved without political Zionism? They had met in their small groups and had collected a little money. The Russians accepted Herzl's

* *The Diaries*, p. 424.

argument that the Action Committee had done all it could for Palestine and would continue to do so, and gave Herzl a vote of confidence. The Uganda scheme receded into the background. Conflicting reports came from London about whether the British government still supported it. There had been adverse comments by experts and the white settlers in East Africa had protested against an influx of Jews.

Herzl did not live to see the seventh Zionist congress officially bury the scheme. His condition rapidly worsened, and he died on 3 July 1904 at the age of forty-four. The severity of his disease had not been known even to his nearest friends, and his death came as a tremendous shock to the movement. For hundreds of thousands of Jews in eastern Europe this was the saddest day of their life. Herzl had created the Zionist movement almost singlehanded. He symbolised their dearest hopes and their longing for a better future. He had been the new Moses who would lead them out of the house of bondage to the promised land. There was a great deal of hero worship, even among his central European followers. One of them relates how on the day the message about Herzl's death was received he wanted to bow when he saw Herzl's small son and to pay respects to him as crown prince.* Herzl had stipulated in his will that he should be buried like the poorest of the poor. But many thousands came to pay their last respects and the Herzl cult became even more intense. Such adulation appeared strange and inexplicable to his critics, for Herzl was a failure, not only in their view but also in his own eyes. All his hectic diplomatic activity had been in vain. When he died, the Zionists were further away than ever from receiving Palestine. The German and the Russian governments were neither willing nor able to do anything on their behalf, and others were even less friendly. They had turned down Uganda and there was no reason to believe that the British would make a better offer. Herzl's diplomatic activity had largely been *Schaumschlaegerei*, a public relations operation. The dramatisation of the Jewish problem was all he had managed to achieve. Governments and peoples in Europe had at last become interested in the Jewish problem and had heard about a possible way to solve it.

Herzl had a burning ambition to achieve fame as a writer and dramatist, yet in these fields he had no outstanding talent. He was very much taken by the bearing and the way of life of the non-Jewish aristocracy. He despised journalists and mediocre Jewish intellectuals, though he was himself very much one of them. Fame but not success

* Dr E.M.Zweig, in *Theodor Herzl Jahrbuch*, Vienna, 1937, p. 283.

came to him as a man of action during the last years of his life. There was a strong narcissistic streak in him; he was totally singleminded and demanded from his followers blind obedience. The psychological pattern must be seen in the light of the devotion which was lavished on him, their only son, by his parents, their boundless indulgence, their immense admiration (especially his mother's), which hampered his maturing and crippled his judgment both of the world and of himself.* He was closely attached to his mother, who had the highest ambitions for him. As far as the origins of political Zionism are concerned, such explanations are of course quite irrelevant. Nor is it very helpful to interpret Herzl's ideological development in terms of the general breakdown of liberalism which he witnessed during his Paris years. Herzl was not an original political thinker. His analysis of the Jewish question did not go any deeper than Pinsker's, written two decades earlier. True, he despaired of liberalism inasmuch as the solution of the Jewish question was concerned. This has induced some to see him as part of the same tradition which gave rise to nationalist movements all over Europe towards the end of the century. He realised that assimilation did not work, and he sensed that the Jews faced great dangers in eastern and central Europe.† But in all other respects he was very much a son of the liberal age; certainly he was not a narrow-minded nationalist. His desire to find some solution to the Jewish question preceded his wish to see a Jewish state established in Palestine.

There was, as Herzl's east European critics often pointed out, very little that was specifically Jewish in Herzl. This emerges perhaps most clearly in his vision of the Jewish state, *Altneuland*, a novel published in 1902. Half political fantasy, half early science fiction à la Jules Verne, it describes the visit of the two narrators to Palestine which by 1923 has become a modern Jewish state. The exodus of European Jewry having been accomplished, Palestine has flourished and with the help of modern technology and modern methods of irrigation has become a prosperous and modern country. A new, progressive society has come into being based on cooperative effort, not Socialist in the orthodox Marxist sense but located somewhere between individualist capitalism and collectivism. Land does not belong to individuals. The open air factories are models of their kind. Women are fully emancipated, education is free, criminals are not punished but re-educated. There is

* Ludwig Lewisohn, in *Herzl Yearbook*, vol. 3, New York, 1960, p. 274.
† Henry J. Cohn, 'Theodor Herzl's conversion to Zionism,' in *Jewish Social Studies*, April 1970, p. 101 *et seq.*

132

a clear division between religion and state and full freedom of conscience. Tolerance is the supreme principle on which the new state is based. 'The stranger must feel at home with us' are the last words of the dying president of the state, who is modelled on Professor Mandelstam, the veteran Russian Zionist. The Arab problem has been solved without any difficulty: Reshid Bey, one of the closest friends of the hero, asks: 'Why should we have anything against the Jews? They have enriched us, they live with us like brothers.'

Herzl's vision of the future state is that of a typical liberal, permeated with optimism and enlightened ideals, a model society on a progressive pattern. *Altneuland* thus refutes any attempt to regard the breakdown of liberalism as the key to Herzl's political thought. He had despaired of Jews finding a place in European society, but his vision of the future state was in fact so tolerant and cosmopolitan that it was bound to provoke resentment among cultural Zionists like Ahad Ha'am. What was specifically Jewish in the new state, Ahad Ha'am asked. The very name Zion did not once appear, its inhabitants did not speak Hebrew, and there was little if any mention of Jewish culture. It was just another modern, secular state, and Ahad Ha'am resented what he regarded as one more manifestation of assimilationism. If African Negroes managed one day to build a state of their own, he argued, it might well be very similar in character to Herzl's vision. Such criticism was justified inasmuch as Herzl envisaged a modern, technologically advanced and enlightened state inhabited by Jews, not a specifically Jewish state. Ahad Ha'am looked in vain for some specific Jewish qualities in Herzl's vision, or, as Nordau put it, maliciously and somewhat crudely but not altogether without justification, he could not or would not leave his ghetto.

Herzl's vision and his policies have been criticised on many counts. His ideas on social policy were primitive and he underrated the importance of the Socialist movement. Nor did he foresee the clash with the Arabs, but those who criticise him in this respect tend to forget that the total number of Arabs in Palestine at the time was little over half a million and a Palestinian Arab national movement did not yet exist. In his negotiations in the world's capitals he used questionable arguments and methods, but then being a general without an army, he was not exactly negotiating from strength. His autocratic style and his fondness for secret diplomacy were justly criticised on occasion, but no other form of diplomacy would have yielded results, and no one but an autocrat could have brought a minimum of discipline into that unruly band of followers, each of whom was a politician in his own right. Herzl was in some respects astonishingly blind, but this may well be a prerequisite for the man of action. Only total singlemindedness was likely to make any impact on friend and foe alike. Mass movements are not created by men who fail to exude confidence, who are not utterly sure of themselves. In his innermost heart Herzl may have lacked the conviction that he would ever attain his aim. Certainly there were many moments of despair. But this did not for a moment affect his outward behaviour, proud, utterly sure of himself and the success of his cause. He never relaxed his efforts, knowing only too well that without some tangible results in the not too distant future, the movement he was leading would disintegrate and the hopes he had raised would give way to despair.

When Herzl died there was no longer any real hope that the Zionist movement would gain a firm foothold in Palestine before the disintegration of the Ottoman empire. The political Zionism which he had preached seemed bankrupt, and a few years after his death the leadership of the movement passed more or less by default into the hands of the 'practical Zionists', those who had claimed all along that there would be no sudden miracle, that only as a result of steady and necessarily slow colonisation would the bases be created in Palestine for political action at some future date. And yet Herzl's work was not in vain. But for him Zionism would have remained a movement of fairly narrow appeal, aiming at a cultural renaissance which incidentally also engaged in philanthropic-colonising activities. Herzl transformed a mood into a political movement and put it on the European map as one of the national movements aspiring to what in a later age was to be called 'national liberation'. Through his efforts a tremendous uplift was given to the self-confidence of hundreds of thousands of Jews in eastern Europe who could not be integrated into their countries of origin, and to many in the west who acutely felt the problematic, marginal character of their whole existence in a non-Jewish society. Lastly, Herzl laid the foundations for the subsequent achievements of the Zionist movement, and he can be called with some justification the architect of the Balfour Declaration.

A detailed study of Herzl's motives, his mental and emotional make-up, lies beyond the scope of this history of the Zionist movement. For his friends and followers he was a messianic figure selflessly working for the redemption of his people, for whom in the end, saint-like, he sacrificed himself. Later historians, outside the spell of his political ideas and his personal magnetism, have stressed the complicated character of his personality, the deeper reasons of his conversion to Zionism, the sources of his behaviour.* That men and women enter politics for a great many reasons, usually involved and complicated ones, goes without saying: vanity, the search for self-fulfilment, a sense of mission, must all play a part, as well as a great many other factors. To disentangle them is a fascinating but usually not very rewarding task, for on the substance of the subject's ideas it throws little light. It would not be difficult to point to many similarities in the characters and thoughts of Herzl and Lassalle: their dreams about leading the Jews out of servitude, the romantic elements in their thought, their fascination with the aristocratic tradition, showmanship and duels, their unsuccessful literary ambitions, and so on. They were about equally estranged from Judaism, but the one despaired altogether of the Jews whereas the other made a Jewish national revival the central idea of his life.

As far as history is concerned all that matters is that in the 1890s a Jewish journalist named Theodor Herzl expressed in a famous pamphlet the mood of a growing number of his contemporaries, and that subsequently he provided leadership for the movement that developed among them. His inspiration was basically romantic, his ideas inconsistent and often muddleheaded. He compares unfavourably with the more sophisticated political thinkers of his age. Yet on one issue, the central one in his life, he was right: he sensed the anomaly of Jewish life in Europe and the dangers that would face the Jews during the years to come, and he was looking desperately for a solution before it was too late. Perhaps those of his critics were right who argued that antisemitism was a transient phenomenon and not even a very important one *sub specie aeternitatis*. But these critics were concerned with mankind in general not with the fate of the Jews: Herzl felt – and in this respect the *fin-de-siècle* Austro-Hungarian background is of importance – that the Jews could simply not wait. He was a prophet in a hurry.

---

* 'Disappointed in marriage, bereft of his dearest friends, Herzl's emotional life in the Paris years was thus more than usually impoverished. It may help to explain his readiness to abandon his aloofness from the social world, to identify himself heart and soul with a wider cause. The Jewish body social became a collective love object to him as he returned to a fostering mother he had never adequately recognised.' Thus Professor Schorske, following the inspiration of Norman O.Brown (*Journal of Modern History*, December 1967, p. 375). The same writer maintains that Herzl sketched out his dream of the Jewish secession from Europe after attending a performance of *Tannhaeuser*, 'exalted, in a fever of enthusiasm akin to possession', with Wagner as the 'vindicator of the heart against the head' (*ibid.*, pp. 377–8).

4

THE INTERREGNUM

After Herzl's death it was widely thought that the Zionist movement was at the end of its tether. The movement was his creation; what united its members was above all loyalty to the leader. He had been both president and prophet, and there was no leader in sight able to inspire similar enthusiasm and confidence. If even Herzl's position had been somewhat shaky during the last two years of his life, if there had been many attacks and bitter criticism, how much less likely was another leader to succeed in holding the movement together. At the time of his death it was only too transparent that his policy, the diplomatic approaches in Constantinople and various European capitals, had failed. The Uganda debate was still unresolved; moreover caucuses, factions, even separate parties, were gradually emerging within the Zionist movement. It was perhaps an inevitable process, but it made the position of the president, who no longer had a secure basis of support, almost impossible. If a second Herzl were to arise, one of his closest collaborators wrote a year after his death, he would be crushed in the struggle between the various factions.*

Above all there was the problem of Russian Zionism. The Russians admittedly had contributed more to the movement than any other federation, but under the tsarist régime Zionism was only semi-legal. Russian Jews had no influence whatever on their own, let alone on other governments, nor had they international connections or diplomatic experience. The leadership of the movement had to be in the hands of western Jews, however deeply these were distrusted by the Russian Zionists. But central and west European Zionists were at a loss as to the future direction of the movement. Until then Herzl had provided most of the ideas, but even his closest collaborators had little doubt that the revered leader had been a failure, despite his genius, energy and

* H. York Steiner, in L. Schoen, (ed.), *Die Stimme der Wahrheit*, Würzburg, 1905, p. 57.

136

devotion. When the question of publishing Herzl's diaries came up not long after his death, Nordau spoke out against it in the most emphatic terms: You will ruin Herzl's name if you publish his diaries. Whoever reads them is bound to believe that he was a fool and a swindler.* The seventh Zionist congress, held in Basle in late July 1905, had to take a decision about the Uganda project. It was, not unexpectedly, rejected, which led to tumultuous scenes and to the exodus of the Territorialists under Zangwill, as also of some east European left-wing groups, including leading Zionists such as Syrkin. The congress also had to elect a new leader. This was not just a question of finding a suitable personality; there was widespread demand for a policy reorientation. The Russian Zionists under Ussishkin, but also some others, had argued for a number of years that Herzl's secret diplomacy had led nowhere and that until political conditions for a charter were ripe the main emphasis should be on practical work, on establishing new agricultural settlements, and, in general, on strengthening the Jewish presence in Palestine. Herzl had opposed this approach of the Lovers of Zion for more than two decades without any marked success. He envisaged the colonisation of Palestine on a grand scale, but this was quite impossible without prior political agreement with the Turks. The investment of money and manpower in small-scale colonisation meant not only squandering the scanty resources of the movement: it left the Jewish settlers defenceless, hostages in the hands of the Turks.

Herzl was adamant on this: 'Not a single man, not a single penny for this country, until the minimum of privileges, of guarantees, has been granted.'† Nordau, Bodenheimer, Marmorek and other members of Herzl's inner circle shared this view. The movement had to wait until a political constellation arose inside Turkey in which negotiations for a charter would be more promising. Until then all the projects for large-scale colonisation would have to be postponed. But there were many others favouring practical work (*Gegenwartsarbeit*) as an alternative. This slogan encompassed both small-scale settlement in Palestine and the strengthening of the movement in the diaspora. The 'practicians' were not in principle opposed to diplomacy, but they anticipated that gradual concessions were more likely to be won than a comprehensive charter; the stronger the Jewish presence, the easier it would be to obtain concessions.

* P.A.Alsberg, *Mediniut hahanhala hazionit memoto shel Herzl ve'ad milkhemet haolam harishona*, Doctoral dissertation, Jerusalem.

† A.Böhm, *Die zionistische Bewegung*, vol. i, Berlin, 1935, pp. 3, 35.

A compromise resolution was eventually passed by the seventh congress to the effect that while rejecting philanthropic, small-scale colonisation, lacking plan and system, the Zionist movement was to work for strengthening the Jewish position in Palestine in agriculture and industry ('in as democratic a spirit as possible'). A new executive was elected, consisting of three advocates of practical Zionism (Professor Warburg, Ussishkin, and Kogan-Bernstein), as well as three political Zionists (Leopold Greenberg, Jacobus Kann, and Alexander Marmorek). The president of this body, of the Inner Action Committee and of the movement, was David Wolffsohn, who declared somewhat prematurely in his concluding speech that the crisis was over.*

Wolffsohn and his Critics

David Wolffsohn was forty-nine when he took up the post, an old man in a movement consisting predominantly of young people. Born in Lithuania, not far from the German border, he had received a traditional Jewish education, entered the timber trade, and made a huge success of the firm which he established in Cologne. A Lover of Zion since his youth, his interest in things Jewish had never flagged, and he had been one of Herzl's earliest supporters. Herzl had called him 'the best', the one practical man among hundreds of dilettanti, had regarded him as his successor, and had asked him in his testament to take care of his family. Herzl's way of transacting business had frequently driven Wolffsohn to despair, and it was generally expected that Wolffsohn's past and experience would make him gravitate towards 'practical Zionism'. But it was precisely his business acumen and, of course, his loyalty to Herzl which made him continue the tradition of political Zionism. The same was true of Jacobus Kann, the other businessman in the new executive. As he saw it, large-scale investment without political guarantees was a doubtful proposition.

Wolffsohn genuinely did not want to be the new leader. He went to Paris to persuade Nordau to accept the succession, and when he was called by his interlocutor the 'only possible choice', he countered by saying that surely Nordau was out of his mind.† He accepted the nomination only under general pressure, with even the Russian Zionists supporting him. He knew of course that there would be a great deal of opposition. The Russians thought him well-meaning and devoted, generous and hard-working, but 'without personality or vision – he did

* *Stenographisches Protokoll, VII. Kongress*, Berlin, 1905, p. 316.
† E.B.Cohn, *David Wolffsohn*, Amsterdam, 1939, p. 167.

his best to imitate his ideal, Herzl, but he had neither Herzl's personality
nor his organising ability'.* 'All our European visitors had the same
story to tell about Wolffsohn', Louis Lipsky relates: he was said to be a
man of ordinary education, without ability, without judgment, lacking
dynamism and the capacity for leadership, who did not understand the
Herzlian ideal of which he professed to be a disciple.†

Such criticism was grossly unfair; Wolffsohn was by no means an
amiable half-wit. As an organiser at any rate he was superior to Herzl.
He was certainly not an intellectual, and he had no grand design, no
major new ideas to offer. But his common-sense provided on many
occasions a necessary counterweight to the fantasies of other early
Zionists. David Frischman, the Hebrew writer who was present as an
observer at the ninth Zionist congress, wrote that Wolffsohn behaved
like the only adult person in an unruly kindergarten. ‡ The obstruction
tactics of the Russian Zionists would have made more sense if they had
had an alternative candidate for the leadership. But Ussishkin did not
get along with Chlenov, Weizmann did not think highly of Motzkin,
and Sokolow, a Polish Jew, had little support among his colleagues
from further east. If no political successes were achieved during the
years after Herzl's death, it was simply because of adverse circumstances:
'Even a cleverer man would have achieved nothing.' § Herzl had established the organisational framework, he had given fresh hope to hundreds
of thousands of Jews, and he had put Zionism on the European political
map. But the public relations aspect apart, however important that may
have been, there was no tangible achievement. Herzl had failed to
persuade the Turks or to win decisive support among the powers. There
was little his successor could do other than strengthen the movement
and wait for a more favourable international constellation.

Wolffsohn did not neglect the contacts established by Herzl. He
visited Rothschild in Paris and was slightly more successful than his
predecessor in gaining at least some measure of platonic support. He
met Vambery, and in 1908 decided to send Victor Jacobson, a Russian
Zionist and Ussishkin's brother-in-law, to act as the permanent representative of the executive in the Turkish capital. Wolffsohn went twice
to Constantinople. The intention of the first visit was to induce the
Turkish authorities to revoke the ban on Jewish immigration and to

* C.Weizmann, *Trial and Error*, New York, 1966, p. 112.
† L.Lipsky, *A Gallery of Zionist Profiles*, New York, 1956, p. 28.
‡ D.Frischman, in *Parzufim*, quoted in A.Robinsohn, op. cit., p. 91.
§ R.Lichtheim, *Rückkehr*, Stuttgart, 1970, p. 116.

establish a combined Turkish-Jewish immigration committee. His visit in October 1907 coincided with a new Turkish financial crisis. Wolffsohn was, in fact, half invited by the government.

A plan was submitted to the Turks under which fifty thousand Jewish families were to settle in Palestine, but not in Jerusalem. They were to become Ottoman subjects and serve in the army, but would be exempt from taxation for twenty-five years. Land would be acquired by the Zionist executive and remain its property.* The Turks wanted a loan of £26 million to consolidate their debt. Wolffsohn countered with an offer of £2 million, but this too was a somewhat foolhardy gesture, apparently not expected to be taken up, for the annual budget of the executive at the time was £4,000, about as much as a wealthy British or German Jew would spend yearly on the upkeep of his family. Wolffsohn was faced by insistent demands from Herzl's old agents, like Izzet Bey for instance, who asked for one million francs for services rendered, such as the revocation of the ban on immigration. Wolffsohn distrusted them even more than had Herzl. When the Turkish authorities intimated that a gesture of goodwill on their part could be expected only after the Zionists had made the first move, Wolffsohn countered by saying that he could do nothing unless the Turks took the initiative. While the bargaining was still going on, the Young Turks staged their revolution and the sultan was deposed.

The changes in Turkey aroused enthusiasm among the Zionists. 'If Herzl had lived to this day', Nordau said at a meeting in Paris, 'he would have been overjoyed and said: "This is my charter!"'† The overthrow of the absolutist régime and the democratic manifestos issued by the Young Turks, the fact that they appeared in some degree willing to meet the demands of the minorities in the Ottoman empire, were interpreted as the opening of a new era. Many Zionists were over-optimistic in this respect. Whatever declarations about decentralisation were made in the first flush of excitement, the Young Turks had not the slightest intention to liquidate the empire. They were more, not less nationalistic than Abdul Hamid, and the chances of obtaining a charter were in fact worse than before. It was therefore quite mistaken to argue (as some Zionists did) that their leaders were missing a great opportunity in not showing more initiative in the Turkish capital.

Wolffsohn was doubtful from the very beginning whether it was worthwhile to negotiate with the Young Turks. This was also

---

* Alsberg, *Mediniut hahanhala hazionit...*, p. 24.
† *Die Welt*, 1, 1909.

Jacobson's appraisal of the situation: 'There is no one to talk to.'* In March 1909 a new coup took place in the Turkish capital which strengthened Wolffsohn in his belief that his original assessment of the political situation had been correct. In June 1909 he discussed Zionist aims with Husain Hilmi Pasha, the grand vizir, but there was no progress. Colonisation in Palestine on a large scale was ruled out by the Turks, and the ban on immigration, which meanwhile had been reimposed, would not be lifted. Nordau had returned from Constantinople with misgivings a little earlier, but this was even worse. Stalemate was complete and negotiations with the Turks ceased for the next two years.

In the circumstances Wolffsohn was reluctant to put any concrete suggestions on paper, since he was fairly sure that they would be rejected. But he had not given up all hope. Like Jacobson, he was still basically a 'Turkey-firster', believing that Constantinople held the key. Jacobson once said that even a very weak Turkey was much stronger than the Jews in Palestine and the Zionist movement backing them. At the same time Wolffsohn was reluctant to invest too much in political work in the Turkish capital. The idea of financing a daily newspaper (*Jeune Turc*) did not at first appeal to him, and the project was carried out mainly through the support of the Russian Zionists, who better realised its potential importance.†

Jacobson was worried by the lack of coordination among the Jewish organisations active in Constantinople. Not only the Zionists negotiated with the Turks, but also the Alliance Israélite; and later on Dr Nossig became a frequent visitor. Nossig, an early Zionist, had left the movement when his schemes for Jewish colonisation in the Ottoman empire – outside Palestine – had been rejected. A gifted but erratic man, he was at one and the same time writer, sculptor, political scientist, historian, statistician, philosopher, and playwright. Some thought him a well-meaning dilettante, others a dangerous charlatan.‡ Born in Galicia, he became a German patriot and apparently worked for German intelligence during the First World War. Thereafter he was a leading pacifist. He was executed, at the age of almost eighty, by the Jewish resistance in the Warsaw ghetto on the suspicion, possibly mistaken, that he was a Gestapo agent.

Jacobson, who had the thankless task of explaining to the Turkish

---

* Alsberg, *Mediniut hahanhala hazionit . . .*, p. 32.
† *Ibid.*, p. 34.
‡ Lichtheim, *Rückkehr*, p. 119.

authorities that Nossig represented no one but himself, was the first Jewish diplomat of modern times, a highly cultured though somewhat inarticulate man. Facing much opposition, he nevertheless succeeded in making many friends in the Turkish capital. He thought it pointless to emphasise the political aims of Zionism and concentrated instead on immigration, stressing at the same time the importance of Palestine as a cultural centre for the Jewish people. After his election to the Zionist executive in 1913, he could no longer spend much time in Turkey, and his place was taken by Richard Lichtheim, his former assistant.

Lichtheim was one of a group of young German Zionists (he was only in his twenties at the time) from assimilated families who, having rediscovered their Jewish background, became active as speakers and writers on behalf of the Zionist movement. A man of independent means, he found the work in the Turkish capital of absorbing interest and revealed considerable political acumen in his analysis of the international situation and in his contacts with Turks and foreign diplomats. Unlike Jacobson, he doubted whether the Ottoman empire was likely to last much longer, and expected that if it were to disintegrate – either as the result of an armed conflict or in some other way – England was likely to play a major role in the future of Palestine. But Lichtheim agreed with Jacobson that whatever the long-term prospects, a great deal of work remained to be done in the Turkish capital. But for the lack of enthusiasm on the part of Jewish *haute finance*, the Zionist movement could have acquired various economic concessions which were for sale in and around Palestine, and whose validity, incidentally, was later recognised by the British mandate. Yet such was the state of Zionist finances, even after the improvement which had taken place under Wolffsohn's management, that all the executive could or would contribute towards the building of the Hedjaz railway was £500.

The Turkish-Italian war in 1911 gave a fresh impetus to Zionist activities. The Turkish government emerged weakened from this conflict and from the Balkan wars, and there was as a consequence greater willingness to listen to the Zionist request. The restrictions on immigration were partly lifted and it was made easier for foreign citizens to buy land in Palestine. By that time, however, the central government no longer had complete control, and the local Turkish representatives had a great deal of freedom in their interpretation of the directives emanating from Constantinople. It was not at all easy for the executive to steer a safe course in these turbulent years. When *Jeune Turc* attacked Italy, there was a storm of protest from European

Zionist circles. But how could a Turkish newspaper refrain from attacking the enemy at a time of war?

The idea of mobilising Palestinian Jewish youth for the war against Italy was discussed and dismissed. In any case few would have enlisted of their own free will. It was decided instead to dispatch a team of Jewish physicians, and there were declarations of sympathy, albeit somewhat vague, in Zionist newspapers and in the European press. The Zionists had to tread warily because too many conflicting interests were involved, and they had to be equally cautious with regard to Turkish domestic policy. Prudently, they did not take a stand in the conflict between the Young Turks and the opposition Union Party (the *Entente Libérale*). Within the narrow limits imposed by circumstances Zionist diplomacy in Constantinople was not unsuccessful; and but for its lack of resources it would have achieved even more. Not that a basic change in Turkish policy could have been effected, however much money had been invested: Palestine was not for sale. The main task of the Zionist representatives in Constantinople was to protect the yishuv in times of peace and war. Considering that they were operating not exactly from a position of strength, they accomplished this remarkably well.

Zionism had no clear foreign political orientation during the years before the outbreak of the First World War. It tried to win friends wherever it could. Herzl had believed that he could gain the support of the kaiser, but this illusion quickly faded: Germany was not interested. German Zionist leaders such as Bodenheimer and Friedmann did on a few occasions meet German Foreign Ministry officials, but on the whole the links with Germany were weaker than with the other big powers. The language conflict in 1913 did not make the position of the German Zionists *vis-à-vis* the Berlin authorities any easier : the *Hilfsverein*, a Jewish non-Zionist organisation, had helped to establish a technical high school in Haifa on condition that German was to be the medium of instruction. This caused much resentment among Palestinian Jewry, which insisted on the priority of Hebrew. There were demonstrations and the Turkish police had to intervene.

The weakness of the Zionist position in Germany did not, however, fool the London *Times*. As far as the most influential of British newspapers was concerned, Zionism was merely a tool of the German Foreign Ministry. The seat of the movement was after all in Germany, and most of its leaders and members were 'Yiddish-speaking Jews all of whom understood German'.* Britain, *The Times* warned, would have

* *The Times*, 28 November 1911.

to be very careful in its relations with this movement, not only because of its 'German character', but also in view of Britain's interests in Muslim powers. Isolated attempts were, however, made by the Zionist executive to influence British policy. Weizmann met Balfour first in 1906. Sokolow came to London in 1912 on an official mission and talked to a few politicians. There were no tangible results, but the feelers were symptomatic of a gradual (and partial) reorientation on the part of some Zionist leaders towards England. Even though there was no immediate success, these initial meetings were to be of some importance later on in the context of Zionist diplomacy during the war.

Little was done to attract French support. Pichon, head of the French Foreign Ministry, expressed sympathy in a conversation with Nordau, who was perhaps the first to foresee the coming struggle between London and Paris for spheres of influence in the Levant.* Wolffsohn's own diplomatic efforts were mainly directed to alleviating the pressure on the Zionist movement in eastern Europe. He met Andrassy, the Austro-Hungarian statesman, following rumours that the Zionist movement might be banned in Hungary. This proved to be a false alarm, but the situation in Russia was going from bad to worse: leading Zionists were being arrested, their offices searched, their newspapers suspended. In March 1908, Wolffsohn sent a memorandum to Stolypin, the Russian prime minister, and in July of that year he was received by him and also by Izvolsky, the foreign minister, and by Makarov, the deputy minister of the interior.† The Russians were willing in principle to recognise the Zionist movement on condition that it ceased to concern itself with Russian domestic affairs and dealt exclusively with issues related to emigration. After Wolffsohn's departure, Chlenov, the Russian Zionist leader, maintained these contacts, without however achieving any substantial results. In 1910 several Zionist officials were again arrested, and the offices of the movement were closed on the charge of illegally collecting money.

During all these years Russian Zionism faced the question whether or not to take an active part in domestic politics. Before 1905 there had been little enthusiasm, but after the first revolution and the greater intensity of political life, the Zionists found it impossible to stay aloof – it would have meant leaving the field to the anti-Zionists. They participated in the elections to the first Duma, and eight of the fourteen Jewish candidates successful at the first stage were Zionists. But such was

---

* Alsberg, *Mediniut hahanhala hazionit...*, p. 105.

† Y.Gruenbaum, *Hatnua hazionit*, vol. 3. Jerusalem, 1957, p. 146.

the complexity of the electoral system (and the inbuilt discrimination against the Jewish electors) that only five managed eventually to win seats in the Duma. The debate on the aims of Zionism was resumed after the revolution in Turkey. There was to be no retreat from the Basle programme, though Wolffsohn on at least one occasion offered an interpretation in which the idea of a Jewish state, which earlier on had been left deliberately vague, was described as something quite unreal. In his opening speech to the ninth congress, Nordau announced that in view of the overthrow of the autocratic régime in Turkey the time had come to drop the idea of a charter, one of Herzl's central concepts, to which however there had been no reference in the Basle programme.* The executive also dissociated itself from the slogan of a homestead to be guaranteed by the big powers. This had always been a thorny issue in relations with Turkey, for the Turks naturally resented any scheme likely to perpetuate and legalise the intervention of foreign powers. But these were tactical changes, shifts in emphasis rather than in the basic attitude of the movement.

The Wolffsohn era officially began in July 1905, when the seventh congress elected a small action committee of seven members. The president resided in Cologne, the other members were located in London (Greenberg), the Hague (Kann), Paris (Marmorek), Berlin (Warburg), Odessa (Kogan-Bernstein), and Yekaterinoslav (Ussishkin). This of course was an impossible arrangement, for the executive could not be convened at short notice. It meant in fact that Wolffsohn had to run the movement single-handed. The transfer of the central office of the movement to Cologne, where Wolffsohn lived, was not an ideal choice either. At the next congress at the Hague, a small steering committee of three was elected, upon Wolffsohn's request – Wolffsohn himself, Kann, a Dutch banker and protagonist of the political trend, and Professor Warburg, a leading advocate of practical Zionism. The vote for Wolffsohn as president was 135 to 59. When there were loud protests from his opponents, Wolffsohn said he hoped he would have won their confidence too by the time of the next congress.

Far from achieving this, at the next congress in Hamburg in late December 1909, Wolffsohn faced an even stronger and more determined opposition. The very choice of the place and the date provoked the anger of his critics. He was accused of having made his selection in such a way as to guarantee that attendance would be low. The opposition criticised Wolffsohn for running the movement like a despot, of behaviour more

* *Stenographisches Protokoll, IX. Kongress,* Cologne and Leipzig, 1910, p. 20 *et seq.*

autocratic than Herzl's but without Herzl's inspiration, political genius and iron will. All the leadership had achieved, the critics maintained, was the movement of its offices from Karolinger Ring 6 (Wolffsohn's home) in Cologne, to number 31 in the same street. Wolffsohn's diplomatic missions were regarded as failures. Professor Warburg was the only member of the executive to find favour in the eyes of the opposition because he understood the commandment of the hour, colonisation in Palestine. But he was said to have been hampered by his two colleagues who had more or less sabotaged his various initiatives.*

Wolffsohn's rebuttal was quite effective: he had no difficulty in showing that those who now wanted his resignation had attacked Herzl on the same grounds. He ridiculed the demand for a broader, more democratic leadership. When there had been a broader executive, he pointed out, many of its members had not attended its sessions or had not even bothered to reply to his letters. And the Russian faction always had five presidents not because it was a paragon of democracy but because it could never agree on the choice of any one leader. This surely was not the way to lead the Zionist movement. Wolffsohn praised Professor Warburg for his initiatives, but implied that many of them were impractical. He pointed out also that the financial situation of the movement had greatly improved. Despite the fact that the Russian Zionists had sabotaged the central leadership by not remitting the money collected locally, this was the first time that the movement was not in debt. Wolffsohn also announced that he was no longer willing to carry the burden of leadership. He had sacrificed his time and his health, and throughout these years there had not been one word of encouragement, let alone of praise. He could not lead the movement against the desire of a considerable and vocal minority.

It was an effective speech which disarmed the opposition without convincing it. Weizmann led the counter-attack: Wolffsohn had referred to the Russian Zionists in the terms a German chancellor would use of nihilist Russian students. He was forever stressing his business experience, and everyone trusted his ability in this respect. But why would he not see that the movement simply could not be run on the same principles as a sound business enterprise? Why was it so difficult to understand that the political challenges could not be met, nor the cultural and colonising tasks accomplished, by one or two people living in Cologne, far from the mainstream of Jewish life?† But hard as it tried, the opposition to

---

* *Stenographisches Protokoll* . . . , p. 38 *et seq.* (Pasmanik.)
† *Ibid.*, pp. 102–3.

146

Wolffsohn found it impossible to agree on an alternative leader, and in the end the outgoing president was asked to stay in office. Wolffsohn complied without particular joy. He was no longer in good health and had to spend long periods away from his desk convalescing. Nothing had been resolved; the final showdown had merely been postponed.

The leaders of the Russian faction regarded the Hamburg congress as a major disaster and were more determined than ever to oust Wolffsohn at the next (tenth) congress, which took place in Basle in August 1911. One of the first speakers, Adolf Böhm, the historian of Zionism, said that he did not wish to attack Wolffsohn, since the president was obviously ailing. Never you mind, Wolffsohn interjected, I am ill here (pointing to his heart), not here (pointing to his head).* Wolffsohn was still in fighting spirit in his rebuttal of the attacks against him, but he had decided to resign well before the congress opened. A new executive was elected consisting of two Germans, Dr Hantke and Professor Warburg (who was to be the president of the Inner Action Committee), and three veteran Russian Zionists: Victor Jacobson, Shmaryahu Levin and Nahum Sokolow. Berlin was to be the seat of the new executive. Since Wolffsohn had stepped down of his own free will, the congress ended on a note of reconciliation: Chlenov praised the outgoing president and Ussishkin called him the real hero of the gathering. Thus a new, and, it was hoped, happier period was ushered in.

Wolffsohn had accepted the leadership with great misgivings, which in the event proved only too justified. Zionists, Harry Sacher wrote, are not notoriously generous to their leaders, and Wolffsohn was the least appreciated of all. In those who fought against him he excited at best a depreciatory shrug – a mediocrity, a timber merchant. When he resigned, his health was shattered, and he died within two years. But the possibilities that opened up to the movement with the First World War could not have been used by a Zionist leader resident in Germany. Posterity has dealt with Wolffsohn less harshly than his contemporaries: 'The role of successor is not dramatic: it calls for the prosaic rather than the heroic qualities. But when without salvage there will be a complete wreck, the tug master who brings the storm-battered ship home to port does a notable service. That service Wolffsohn rendered to Zionism, and no other could in the time and the circumstances have done it as well.'†

The struggle between political and 'synthetic' Zionism (first formulated by Weizmann in a speech at the eighth congress) was over. With

---

* *Stenographisches Protokoll, X. Zionisten Kongress*, Berlin-Leipzig, 1911, p. 65.

† H.Sacher, *Zionist Portraits and Other Essays*, London, 1959, pp. 34–5.

Wolffsohn went Nordau. The keynote speech of the eleventh congress, the last before the war, had been given by Sokolow, since Nordau refused to come. Kann had dropped out even earlier. So had Alexander Marmorek and other members of Herzl's inner circle. Representatives of east European Jewry now took over the leadership. It had been a fierce conflict, yet it seems in retrospect that its origins are to be sought at least as much in personal animosities and differences in style as in basic differences on policy. For the old leadership, despite its caution, had not altogether neglected practical work in Palestine; the new executive was not able to do much more. No one had been more critical of the diplomatic approach than Weizmann, but the opponent of political Zionism became the chief Zionist diplomatist only a few years later, and obtained the 'charter' of which Herzl and Nordau had dreamed. It was one of the many ironies in the history of the Zionist movement.

The new leadership was presided over by Professor Otto Warburg, a botanist of world renown and member of a well-known Hamburg banking family. A gentleman through and through, he was one of the very few leaders who did not have a single enemy in the movement. His interest was directed almost solely to colonisation and its problems. Politics he found boring and he was only too happy to leave this field to his colleagues.* He came from an assimilated background and his interest in Palestine and the Zionist movement had been awakened by his wife's family. He was habitually criticised by Wolffsohn, and even more sharply by Kann (who administered the property of the Dutch royal family), for engaging in costly experiments in Palestine which the movement could ill afford. These complaints were by no means unjustified. Yet how could agricultural settlement be encouraged without taking certain risks and suffering setbacks and disappointments? But for Warburg's infectious enthusiasm and occasional foolhardiness, not much progress would have been made in agricultural settlement in Palestine between 1905 and the outbreak of the war.

Almost equally remote from practical politics was Shmaryahu Levin, the most effective propagandist of the movement, 'teacher of a whole generation of Jewish educators and Zionist officials'. A native of Russia, he had been one of those in the Duma who signed the manifesto protesting against its dissolution. As a result he had to leave his native country in 1906. Like Weizmann, Motzkin and Victor Jacobson, he had studied in Berlin in the 1890s and had been among the founders of the Russian Scientific Association, whose members came to play leading

* Lichtheim, *Rückkehr*, p. 198.

roles in the Zionist movement. A restless man, forever agitated and agitating others, steeped in Jewish and western culture, he retired altogether from politics in later years as his interests shifted to cultural problems and education.

If Levin was the most effective orator of the movement, Nahum Sokolow was its most prolific and influential writer. He wrote gracefully and at great length on many subjects in several languages. His essays were not always models of profound thought, but he did a great deal to introduce western culture to east European Jewry. While Levin regarded himself as a disciple of Weizmann (although actually his senior), for Sokolow (born 1859) Weizmann (born 1874) always remained the upstart young man, talented but hardly capable of engaging in serious diplomatic conversation with leading statesmen. Sokolow was a man of impeccable manners. Sporting spats and a monocle, he 'enjoyed life best when he moved in an atmosphere of diplomatic deportment. The born diplomat, he was at his best when dealing with the French and Italian diplomats.'* Sokolow wanted to be president of the movement, but in fact he held this position only late in life and for but a short time. He was unfitted for leadership; temperamentally he was a cautious man, incapable of quick decision and inclined to stay above the battle. At the fateful Uganda debate he abstained from voting.

Mention has been made of Victor Jacobson, the first representative of the Zionist movement in Constantinople. In 1913 he was replaced as vice-president by Yehiel Chlenov. A Moscow physician and one of the leaders and founders of Russian Zionism, Chlenov was preferred to Ussishkin, his south Russian rival, because he was more conciliatory, a better diplomat and committee man. Lastly there was Dr Hantke, neither a great orator nor a prolific writer, but an ideal administrator without whose orderly mind and firm guiding hand the Berlin executive would have accomplished little.

It had been decided after Wolffsohn's resignation that the Inner Action Committee, consisting of five to seven members, should be subject to the control of the Action Committee of twenty-five members, meeting not less than four times a year. These decisions were adhered to until, with the outbreak of war, Zionist activities were interrupted and international meetings on a large scale became virtually impossible. The Russian Zionist Federation no longer held back the funds it had collected; 127,000 Zionists throughout the world paid the shekel in

* Lipsky, *A Gallery of Zionist Profiles*, p. 66.

1912–13, more than ever before, even though collections in Russia fell that year as a result of police chicanery. The rise in revenue was badly needed, for the executive had to meet ever increasing expenses – £15,000 for salaries and office costs, for instance, in 1912–13.

The struggle for power had ended but the polemics between the political Zionists and the 'practicians' continued. The executive sent Professor Auhagen, an agricultural expert, to Palestine to report on the state of Jewish settlement and the progress of Warburg's and Ruppin's schemes. The official report sounded reassuring, but when Wolffsohn met Auhagen in private a less rosy picture emerged.* In Wolffsohn's eyes it was a tale of woe, of bad planning and mismanagement. He was proud to have put the movement on a financially sound basis. Unlike Herzl he had succeeded in accumulating funds that would serve as a substantial lever once a charter had been obtained, whereas the advocates of 'synthetic Zionism', as he saw it, wanted to squander the money, maintaining that what had been collected ought to be invested immediately in new plantations or settlements. For when the great day of the charter came, even the three or four million pounds of the Colonisation Bank would be altogether insufficient.

The political Zionists criticised the new leaders for lack of initiative in their foreign policy, for missed opportunities to press Zionist claims – such as the peace conferences after the Balkan wars in 1912–13 – and above all for the one-sidedly pro-Turkish inclination of the executive. Such criticism was however largely academic, for as long as Turkey ruled Palestine, there simply was no political alternative.

The last congress before the war was on the whole less turbulent than the previous meetings, but there was still plenty of tension and conflict. Wolffsohn was slighted by the new leaders. According to custom, the presidency at the eleventh Zionist congress in September 1913 should have been offered to him. When the executive suggested that there should be two presidents, Wolffsohn and Chlenov, the former declined. Eventually the executive retreated and offered the presidency to Wolffsohn to prevent a split. The 'practicians' did not have it all their own way. Jean Fischer, a Belgian Zionist leader, demanded in an impassioned speech the appointment of a special political committee to engage in diplomatic activities. He warned his audience that the preoccupation with small-scale colonisation schemes would turn the Zionist movement into a poor man's J.C.A. – the non-Zionist Colonisation Association.

* Cohn, *David Wolffsohn*, pp. 304–5.

Ruppin defended himself against his critics in a long speech in which he stressed that deficits were inevitable in any form of experimental colonisation. He was worried about the pitifully small scale of Zionist activities: 'It is essential that our beginnings shall not be too small and the foundations not too narrow, for it is the beginning which sets and determines the possibilities of expansion in the future.' Ruppin, who first went to Palestine in 1907 and settled there the following year, provided a detailed survey of the work that had been done under his supervision and upon his initiative. He admitted that he had been mistaken in expecting the newly founded farms to show a profit at the end of the first year. There had been too many unforeseen and unproductive expenditures. There was a basic difference between the yardsticks applied in private business and in a large-scale enterprise of national importance. Only those petrified in a purely business attitude would insist on immediate cash profits. Paying big dividends could not be the sole criterion. 'I can say with absolute certainty: those enterprises in Palestine which are most profit-bearing for the businessman are almost the least profitable for our national effort; and per contra, many enterprises which are least profitable for the businessman are of high national value.' If the transformation of city-dwellers into land-workers was to be guided by considerations of dividends, was it not equally sensible to demand that schools should be run on a profit basis?

The training of workers was an obvious case in point; it certainly would not show any profits in the ledger at the end of the year, but who would deny that it was an enterprise of essential national importance? Towards the end of his speech Ruppin made yet another point in justification of 'practical Zionism' which had never been made so clearly: 'For a long time to come our progress in Palestine will depend entirely on the progress of our movement in the diaspora.'* This was a far cry from the early visions of Herzl and Nordau, the idea that there would be a wave of mass migration resulting in the establishment of a Jewish state, and that thereafter the state would be in a position to solve the Jewish question.

Ruppin was not a great orator, but his case was forceful and convincing and he got a big ovation. Compared to other Zionist leaders his background was unconventional. Born in eastern Germany, he had worked his way up against heavy odds. The extreme poverty of his boyhood was movingly described many years later in his autobiography.†

* A.Ruppin, *Building Israel*, New York, 1949, pp. 47–9, 65.
† A.Ruppin, *Pirke Khayai*, Tel Aviv, 1944, vol. 1.

Forced to leave high school at the age of fifteen, he was apprenticed to a firm of grain merchants, but he had already decided that he would reach the top of the ladder within a few years, earning enough money to finance the continuation of his studies. Having graduated from university in economics, philosophy and law – and having incidentally won a major prize for a study on genetics – he entered the legal profession. Later on he became interested in the sociology and demography of the Jews, a field little cultivated at the time. After some preliminary research he published a number of studies which remained standard works for many years. This was the man who at the age of thirty-one had been picked by the executive to be its representative in Palestine – hardly a dreamer, a visionary, an impractical intellectual. It was in some ways an unlikely choice: Ruppin was not even a committed Zionist at the time of the appointment. Yet no better man could have been selected. For more than three decades he showed an astonishing measure of foresight, initiative and humanity in all his actions. He was never in the limelight, but Jewish settlement in Palestine owes more to him than to anyone else.

At the congress which witnessed his first appearance there was also a long debate on cultural problems. Weizmann reported on the preparations for the establishment of a Jewish university in Jerusalem, following a resolution that had been passed in Herzl's days by the fifth congress. For some Zionists this was an issue of paramount importance. Ahad Ha'am had declared at the first conference of Russian Zionists that one university was as important as a hundred settlements. A plot on Mount Scopus was acquired in 1913, a national library had been started in Jerusalem, and it was now proposed to establish a special commission to pursue the project. This aroused much enthusiasm: Bialik spoke of the great vista of the cultural revival. It was a relatively calm, unhurried congress after the storms of the previous years. Those present looked forward to years of steady, peaceful, constructive work in Palestine. 'See you again at the next congress', Wolffsohn said in his concluding address. But the following summer the war broke out, and the leaders of world Zionism were not in fact to see each other again for eight years, and when they next met the charter in which they had lost belief had become an established fact. Wolffsohn did not live to see that day; the second president of the Zionist movement died in September 1914, shortly after the outbreak of war.

'What can be done in Palestine?' Dr Ruppin asked after his first visit, and at once answered his question: 'We must liquidate the *Halukka* system, which still provides most of the Jews with the largest part of their income, by the substitution of work.'* The second big immigration wave began the year Herzl died. Between 1905 and 1914 tens of thousands of new immigrants entered the country. In the year between the Vienna congress and the outbreak of war six thousand new arrivals were counted. As a result substantial changes took place in the social composition of the Jewish population, and a new impetus was given to economic and political development. It was only in 1908, with the establishment of the Palestine Office in Jaffa under Dr Ruppin, that the Zionist movement had begun to adopt a systematic colonisation policy. Until then plots had been acquired haphazardly by the Jewish National Fund (near Tiberias, Lydda, and along the Jerusalem-Jaffa railway). On the whole, Zionism had been preoccupied with criticising previous methods of settlement, mainly those of Baron Hirsch's JCA rather than pointing to a clear alternative.

The means at the disposal of the Jewish National Fund were still extremely limited – about £50,000 in 1907 – but Ruppin was firmly resolved that a beginning had to be made to extend landholdings, establish new settlements, and consolidate those already existing. He decided to concentrate his efforts in areas not too far from the urban centres in which Jews already constituted a sizable proportion of the population, in Lower Galilee and Judaea.† For this purpose the Palestine Land Development Company (PLDC) was founded in 1908, to train Jewish workers for settling on land which was to be purchased in co-operation with the Jewish National Fund and JCA. The PLDC was instrumental in founding the various cooperative and communal settlements, whose early history is reviewed elsewhere in the present study. Between 1908 and 1913, some 50,000 dunam were bought in various parts of the country. On the day war was declared the Palestine Office was on the point of buying 140,000 dunam of the most fertile land in the Jesreel Valley, but the events of August 1914 prevented this and other major acquisitions.‡

Urban land was acquired on the slopes of Mount Carmel and north of Jaffa, where Tel Aviv was built, and by 1914 this new centre counted fifteen hundred inhabitants. Attempts to enlist private initiative were not particularly successful, but a number of small- and medium-scale enterprises were founded during the last prewar years, including a

---

* Ruppin, *Building Israel*, p. 10.
† Alex Bein, *The Return to the Soil*, Jerusalem, 1952, p. 47.
‡ *Bericht des Aktion Komitees der Zionistischen Organisation an den 11. Zionisten Kongress*, n.p., 1913, p. 111; *Palestine during the War*, London, 1921, p. 7.

cement and brick factory, the cultivation and processing of sugar beet, and an engineering workshop. One of the biggest enterprises was launched by *Bezalel*, the arts school, specialising in the manufacture of carpets, wood carvings and similar articles. A Hebrew high school was founded in Jaffa and a teachers' training college in Jerusalem, in addition to the technical high school and other institutions maintained by the German *Hilfsverein*. The foundations were laid for a network of purely Hebrew schools sponsored by the Zionist Organisation. Jerusalem had two daily newspapers in Hebrew, a National Library, several publishing houses, a sports association, a theatre club. The teachers' association founded by Ussishkin counted 150 members. In public life Hebrew was used. Ahad Ha'am, professional pessimist though he was, admitted that a miracle had taken place, which he had thought impossible at the time of his first visit almost two decades earlier. For him and other cultural Zionists the emergence of a cultural centre was the most important development of all. Political activities and economic expansion were mere prerequisites, not ends in themselves. To all Zionists the resurrection of the Hebrew language was a major achievement, for a common language was obviously essential to any normal corporate national life.*

Despite the late start of organised economic and cultural activities in Palestine, the Zionist movement by 1914 had to its credit several important achievements. Jews in Palestine constituted a higher percentage of the total population than in any other country, and more of them were engaged in productive occupations than anywhere else. They had demonstrated that Jews could be farmers, and in the collective settlements they had developed new and highly original forms of communal life. The revival of the Hebrew language was a historical fact. It was no doubt premature to state, as Shmaryahu Levin did, that a new 'totally Jewish type' of man had already emerged.† But the experience of the second immigration wave had shown that there were enough Jews who wanted to settle in Palestine, despite the hardships and sacrifices entailed, and that, given a period of peaceful development and the goodwill of the Turkish authorities, there was every chance that the new Jewish community would grow in strength and one distant day attain greater political importance. But the whole enterprise was still on a diminutive scale, highly vulnerable, and almost totally dependent on the world Zionist movement and the Jewish communities abroad.

* S.Brodetzky, in H.Sacher (ed.), *Zionism and the Jewish Future*, London, 1916, p. 171 *et seq.*
† Böhm, *Die Zionistische Bewegung*, vol. i, p. 478.

Although their numbers were growing quickly, the Arab population was also increasing, so that the absolute numerical difference was becoming greater. Jewish Palestine was a tender plant; the achievements of the last prewar decade could easily be undone by the deportation of a few thousand people, and this almost happened during the war. The 'political Zionists' were not altogether wrong. It is doubtful whether, but for the war, Zionism would ever have attained any degree of autonomy. But they were wrong inasmuch as they tended to neglect opportunities to strengthen the Jewish position in Palestine. In the event every dunam worked by Jews counted when, after the war, the British mandate came into force. Jewish settlement was not only an important economic factor; it counted heavily in the political balance.

Zionism – East and West

With the spread of the movement the local federations began to play a greater part in Zionist politics. The Russian Federation was the strongest by far, Russia and Poland being the heartland of Zionism, for this was where the Jewish question was most acute. But while Russian Zionism had constituted the main opposition to Herzl and Wolffsohn, it did not play a constructive role commensurate with its numerical strength in the movement. It was labouring under various handicaps: its legal status was disputed, it was under almost constant attack from the authorities, and it lost by emigration to Palestine and other countries many of its most capable members. After 1905, the Russian Zionists became involved, inevitably perhaps, in Russian and Russian-Jewish politics, which absorbed much of their energies. In the Helsingfors programme their leaders voiced the demand for full national equality and the democratisation of Russian political life.

In elections to the Duma they cooperated with other Jewish groups in the effort to attain these aims – without any conspicuous success. There were thirteen Jewish representatives in the first Duma, six in the second, and two in the third. The authorities did not find it difficult to manipulate the results of the elections, as the Jews had to compete against both Russian voters and those of other nationalities. The electoral struggle in Poland brought them into conflict with the Polish national movement. When faced with the choice between a Polish nationalist with antisemitic leanings and a Polish Social Democrat, they opted for the latter. This in turn caused great resentment in Polish national circles and Jewish shops were boycotted. The revolutionary disturbances of 1905–6 were followed by years of repression, which strongly affected Zionist activities.

In Germany Zionism faced no such obstacles. Founded in Cologne in May 1897 shortly before the first congress, it was headed at first by Wolffsohn and Bodenheimer. Since they had no press of their own, German Zionists found it difficult to make their existence known to the wider public. The situation changed only with the acquisition of the *Jüdische Rundschau* in 1902. The number of shekel payers rose from 1,300 in 1901 to over 8,000 in 1914. (It was third in size after the United States and Russia, whose Jewish communities were much larger than the German.)[*] The members were dedicated men and women, some of them *Ostjuden*, recent arrivals from eastern Europe, others from assimilated families who felt acutely the anomaly of Jewish existence even in the relatively mild antisemitic climate of Wilhelmian Germany.

Among its leaders, apart from those already mentioned, there was Kurt Blumenfeld, a highly cultured man and a persuasive speaker, who was instrumental in gaining the support of eminent people outside the orbit of Zionism, such as Albert Einstein.[†] Blumenfeld was secretary of the German Federation from 1909 to 1911, later secretary of the world organisation, and from 1924 president of the German branch. Zionist attempts to establish positions of strength in the Jewish communal organisations were not at first successful. In the internal disputes shaking world Zionism the Germans at first tended to support Wolffsohn and the political trend, but the younger generation was gradually won over to practical Zionism by Weizmann and the Russian leaders, and after the ninth (Hamburg) congress their influence became predominant in the German Federation.

How to explain the fact that only a comparatively small minority of Jews joined the movement in Germany and that the majority was actively opposed? It has been said that German Jews, smitten by blindness and unaware of the precariousness of their situation, pursued an ostrich-like policy. Such *post hoc* rationalisations are of little help in understanding their situation at the time, which was anything but desperate. Even if some careers were barred to Jews, the majority were reasonably content and felt themselves at home in Germany. There was less antisemitism there than in France or Austria, not to mention eastern Europe. Despite certain unlovely features in its political system, Germany was a *Rechtsstaat*. It was unthinkable that any citizen could be

---

[*] R.Lichtheim, *Die Geschichte des deutschen Zionismus*, Jerusalem, 1954, p. 152.

[†] K.Blumenfeld, *Erlebte Judenfrage*, Stuttgart, 1962, pp. 162–7.

arrested without due process of law. The state was sufficiently liberal to tolerate even a minority which proclaimed its allegiance to another state as yet to be established. When Kurt Blumenfeld propagated a radical programme, calling all Zionists to prepare themselves for emigration to Palestine, he was accused of trying to uproot German Jews artificially. His argument that they were in fact uprooted was by no means generally accepted even within Zionist circles.* It needed a world war and the general dislocation in its wake, and eventually the rise of Nazism, to attract wider sections to the Zionist idea.

Herzl had always attached particular importance to Britain and was much encouraged by the moral support he found among Anglo-Jewry. He first gave public expression to his ideas about the Jewish state at a meeting of the Maccabeans, a small association of Jewish professional people in London, in September 1895. The great assembly in Whitechapel in July 1896 was his first encounter with the Jewish masses. These early expectations later gave way to disappointment. Neither the Rothschilds nor the Anglo-Jewish establishment were willing to embrace the new faith. But Herzl's followers did not give up and with the outbreak of war British Zionism became a factor of decisive importance. The Lovers of Zion had been active in Britain even before Herzl. Among the oldest and most respected families, such as the Montefiores, the Montagues, and the D'Avigdors, there was a great deal of traditional, albeit platonic sympathy for the resettlement of Jews in Palestine. Herbert Bentwich and Israel Zangwill were among the organisers of the 'Maccabean Pilgrimage' to Palestine in 1897. In the following year the Clerkenwell conference, with Colonel Albert Edward Goldsmid as its chairman, laid the foundation for the establishment of a British Zionist Federation.† Most of the supporters of the movement were recent arrivals from eastern Europe, but there were also some from old-established families. Sir Francis Montefiore gave his name and some of his time to the movement. And Joseph Cowen (also English-born) and Leopold Greenberg were warm supporters of Herzl and, after his death, of political Zionism.

The majority of the community were, however, as in Germany, indifferent or even actively hostile. The secession of Zangwill and the 'territorialists' after the Uganda congress weakened the movement. Territorialism had the support of Lord Rothschild, the lay leader of

* Ibid., p. 85 et seq.
† For the early history of Zionism in Britain, see P.Goodman, Zionism in England 1899–1949, London, n.d., passim.

Anglo-Jewry, and Lucien Wolf, its most influential ideologist, not, needless to say, because they contemplated transferring their own activities to Uganda, but because they thought the scheme likely to take the wind out of the Zionist sails. The movement suffered from the conflict between Herzlian and practical Zionists, and there was also much personal antagonism among the leaders. The crisis came to a head in 1909–10, when no one could be found to act as chairman of the federation.

For a while its very existence was in the balance. Eventually Joseph Cowen was prevailed upon to accept the thankless task. He was succeeded by Leopold Kessler, who had led the El Arish expedition. After 1912, with the appearance on the scene of a new generation of young Zionists, such as Leon Simon, Norman Bentwich, Harry Sacher, Israel Sieff and Simon Marks, there was a new expansion of activities. Together with Weizmann, who had settled in Manchester in 1904, they constituted the backbone of a revived movement. This was the 'Manchester school of Zionism', defined by one of its members as a fellowship of friends, brought together by a common cause and sharing a common approach under an unofficial leadership: 'The old controversy between "politicals" and "practicals" had ebbed away as far as the younger generation was concerned for lack of combatants and a battleground . . . they were Zionists first and sectarians (if at all) a long way after.'*

By 1914 the Zionist Federation of Great Britain had some fifty branches and during the war it gained many new adherents. A resolution in 1915 in favour of the establishment of a publicly recognised, legally secured home for the Jewish people in Palestine was signed by 77,000 members of the community.

Herzl's summons to the first Zionist congress aroused little enthusiasm in America but a great deal of criticism, beginning with warnings that the weather in Palestine was inclement and ending with a reaffirmation of Israel's mission among the *goyim* to promote peace, justice and love.†
A few outsiders joined political Zionism, including a group of recent Russian immigrants in Chicago, who later became known as the Knights of Zion, and two rabbis of German-Jewish origin in their seventies – Gustav Gottheil and Bernhard Felsenthal, who welcomed Herzl's call. American Zionism in the early days was anything but a strong force though on paper its federation, founded in New York in

---

* Sacher, *Zionist Portraits*, pp. 18–19.
† J.Tabachnik, 'American-Jewish Reaction to the First Zionist Congress', in R.Patai (ed.), *Herzl Year Book*, v, New York, 1963, p. 57 *et seq.*

July 1898, looked impressive enough. It consisted of about a hundred societies with a membership of five thousand in New York alone. But this was a loose organisation consisting mainly of members of Hebrew-speaking clubs, Jewish educational societies, synagogue organisations, and fraternal lodges which had joined the federation corporatively.* Only in 1917 did the Zionist Organisation of America (ZOA) come into being; it substituted individual for group membership. American Zionists met at their yearly conventions, assured each other of their devotion to the cause, passed resolutions, sent delegations to the Zionist congresses, and a few bought land in Palestine. But despite the events in eastern Europe and the wave of pogroms which seemed to bear out Zionist analyses and predictions only too accurately, the impact of the movement was hardly felt in American life. Europe, after all, was far away and the situation of American Jewry and its prospects gave no cause for concern.

The movement was basically 'East Side' in character. It lacked money, prestige and political influence. Its leaders, on the other hand, were assimilated Jews such as Rabbi Stephen Wise, who at the age of twenty-four became secretary of the federation; Judah Magnes, another liberal rabbi, one of the few American Zionist leaders eventually to settle in Palestine; and Richard Gottheil – Rabbi Gottheil's son – a distinguished orientalist, who was head of the federation from the beginning to 1904. He was replaced by Harry Friedenwald, a well-known physician, who held the post until 1912. But despite Stephen Wise's effective oratory, Magnes' boundless energy, and Lipsky's excellent editorials (all three were at the time in their twenties), despite sustained organisational and educational work, the movement remained a sect. The breakthrough came during the early years of the war in Europe, when Brandeis became its leader. Brandeis was one of the most respected American lawyers, later a Justice of the Supreme Court. He was won over by Jacob de Haas, a British Zionist and close associate of Herzl, who had settled in America in 1901. Brandeis, in the words of another Zionist leader, was unrelated to any form of Jewish life, unread in its literature and unfamiliar with its tradition; he had to rediscover the Jewish people.† But once his imagination had been captured by the Zionist ideal he devoted much of his time and energy to the movement,

* R.Learsi, *Fulfillment*, New York, 1951, p. 145; H.Parzen, 'The Federation of American Zionists (1897–1914)', in I.S.Meyer (ed.), *Early History of Zionism in America*, New York, 1958, p. 245 *et seq.* The most detailed account of early Zionism in America is Avyatar Friesel, *Hatnua hazionit bearazot habrit*, Tel Aviv, 1970.

† Lipsky, *A Gallery of Zionist Profiles*, pp. 154–5.

whose president he was from 1914 until his appointment to the Supreme Court. It was the identification of Louis Brandeis with the movement more than any other single event which made Zionism a political force. To be a Zionist had suddenly become respectable.

But it was not Brandeis single-handed who made American Zionism what it was after the First World War. The movement grew steadily. The year before Brandeis took over, at the last Zionist congress before the war, the Americans were already represented by forty of their leading members – one of the strongest delegations. Shmaryahu Levin, who had been to America in 1906, returned there in 1913 and did a great deal to promote Zionist educational work. During the decade before the world war Zionist youth organisations were set up: the 'Doctor Herzl Zion Clubs' and 'Young Judaea'; among the early members were Abba Hillel Silver, Emanuel Neumann, and other future leaders of American Zionism. In 1912 *Hadassa*, the Zionist women's organisation, was founded with the declared aim of 'promoting Jewish institutions and enterprises in Palestine and fostering Zionist ideals in America'. Over the years it became the largest and one of the most buoyant and active branches of the American movement.

Hadassa was led for many years by Henrietta Szold, a lady of uncommon talents and character, very much rooted in American life and at the same time a Zionist even before Herzl. She became famous later when, at the age of seventy-three, she took over the direction of Youth Aliya, the organisation which brought children from Nazi-occupied Europe to Palestine. A warm and sympathetic personality, 'the captive of a cause' up to the day of her death in 1945 at the age of eighty-five, she was remembered for what she did for thousands of men, women and children.* Thus American Zionism developed within a decade and a half from uncertain beginnings, the small meetings of *Landsmannschaften* in which the *Hatiqva* was sung and money collected, into a movement of considerable strength and influence. When war broke out it was able to shoulder the great political tasks suddenly facing it.

When the first South African Zionist conference took place in Johannesburg in July 1905, the Jewish community in that country, barely two decades old, numbered about forty thousand, but the Zionist movement was already deeply rooted, with about sixty local societies dispersed over a wide area. It had penetrated every town, village and dorp: 'It had even reached the British protectorate of Bechuanaland . . . there were solitary Jewish traders living far out in the

* *Ibid.*, p. 142.

back veld, removed from every contact with Jewish life, but who still made efforts – desperate and pathetic efforts – to follow events in the Zionist world.'* South African Zionism was unique inasmuch as it encountered hardly any resistance in the community except on the part of a small group of Bundists. The South Africans were the most loyal supporters of Herzl, and later on of Wolffsohn; Wolffsohn, a Lithuanian Jew by origin like the majority of South African Jews, was given a royal welcome at the time of his visit in 1906. It was not just flattery when he told his audiences that the South African was the best organised of all Zionist federations. There was a period of decline in its activities between 1911 and the war, but recovery was rapid and South Africa remained one of the pillars of world Zionism.

Efforts to gain friends outside the Jewish community were not unsuccessful and proved in later years of great value, though hardly anyone would have anticipated it at the time. Milner became a sympathiser when he was high commissioner for South Africa, and General Smuts was also won over. He made a promise early in 1917 that he would do all he could to help the Zionist cause. A few months later he found himself, like Milner, a member of the inner circle of the British government at the very moment that the future of Palestine was at stake. Smuts had the reputation of a philo-semite, though in fact he had no special love for the Jews, who, he once wrote, did not warm the heart by graceful subjection: 'They make demands. They are a bitter, recalcitrant little people like the Boers, impatient of leadership and ruinously quarrelsome among themselves.' Smuts became a Zionist because it was a cause in which fundamental human principles were involved. Like Balfour and Lloyd George he saw in Zionism the redressing of a great historic wrong.†

Zionism was still a minority movement in the Jewish world, but its message had spread all over the globe. The report of the executive to the eleventh congress, the last before the war, mentions active Zionist associations not only in Cairo and Alexandria but also in most other Egyptian cities: 'The six Jews who live in Mineh have all bought the shekel'.‡ Zionist activities were reported from the island of Rhodes and from Bulgaria, and even in the Fiji Islands there was a Zionist representative. In Italy, according to this account, the rabbis supported Zionism almost without exception. The two Jewish newspapers in Canada (which

---

* M.Gitlin, *The Vision Amazing*, Johannesburg, 1950, p. 119.
† *Ibid.*, p. 96.
‡ *Bericht des Aktion Komitees . . .* , p. 32.

boasted thirty-three Zionist associations) were friendly. Progress was reported from Tunis. The percentage of shekel payers in Switzerland was among the highest in the world. In the Bukovina there were four Hebrew schools. Richard Lichtheim's pamphlet on the aims of Zionism had been translated into Croat, and Elias Auerbach's on Palestine into Dutch. In more than a hundred thousand Jewish homes all over the world the little blue cash box of the Jewish National Fund could be found. On a per capita basis South Africa, Belgium and Canada headed the list of contributors. It was a far cry from the beginnings of political Zionism only fifteen years earlier, when Herzl had run the whole movement from his apartment in Vienna, without, at first, even the help of a secretary. Zionism had become highly organised, a major force in the Jewish world. And yet despite the collections, the cultural and propagandist work, the enthusiasm of the rank and file, and the perseverance of the leaders, the realisation of its aims seemed in 1914 as remote as ever.

Cultural Zionism

The history of Zionism before the First World War is reflected not only in the balance sheets of the Jewish National Fund and the minutes of the Zionist congresses. Any survey of its development would be incomplete without reference, however cursory, to the ideological debates that went on. The pamphlets of Pinsker and Herzl, however effective, had not exhausted the essence of Zionism; they provoked inside the movement occasional dissent and there were different interpretations of the aims and significance of the national revival. After Herzl's death and the failure of political Zionism, the debate about the future of the movement entered a new stage of soul-searching and the reexamination of hitherto accepted truths. These discussions affected only small groups of young intellectuals. The great majority were 'instinctive Zionists' who needed no sophisticated ideological justification. This is not to say that the ideologists had no impact at all. Ahad Ha'am, for instance, influenced two generations of east European Jewish leaders, including Chaim Weizmann.

Ahad Ha'am (Asher Ginzberg) was born in 1856 in Skvira near Kiev; received a traditional Jewish education, which left him unsatisfied; studied in Berlin, Vienna and Brussels; then moved first to Odessa and later to London, where he represented Visotsky, the leading Russian tea merchant. He settled in Tel Aviv in 1922 and died there five years later. Ahad Ha'am shied away from politics and speech-making; his strength was as a writer and teacher. He was for six years editor of *Hashiloah*, the leading Hebrew cultural periodical of the time. He wrote on a variety of topics: his essays on religion, on ethics and on general philosophical themes lie outside the scope of the present study. He was a Zionist well before Herzl, even though the essay which made him famous, 'The Wrong Way' (*lo seh haderech*), published in 1889, was a sharp critique of Zionism as practised at that time. In it he claimed that immigration to Palestine and settlement there as organised by the Lovers of Zion had been a failure. Those involved had been ill-prepared for their assignment, professionally as well as in a deeper sense. The first and foremost task of the Jewish national movement was to inspire its followers with a deeper attachment to national life and a more ardent desire for national well-being. This was a difficult aim, which could not be accomplished in a year or a decade.*

Ahad Ha'am was equally critical of Herzl and political Zionism; it pretended to bring the Jewish people back to Judaism, but in fact ignored all the basic questions of Jewish culture, of its language and literature, of education and the diffusion of Jewish knowledge. Political Zionism was a flash in the pan. It was bound to fail because the majority of Jews would not and could not emigrate to Palestine. It would not put an end to the Jewish problem, nor could it help to reduce antisemitism. The only gain of Herzlian Zionism would be the increasing respect on the part of other nations and, perhaps, the creation of a healthy body for the Jewish national spirit. But Ahad Ha'am doubted whether Jewish national consciousness and self-esteem were sufficiently strong for an assignment of this magnitude. Would this motive alone, unalloyed by any consideration of individual advantage, be sufficient to spur the Jews on to so vast and difficult a task? Ahad Ha'am doubted it. Western political Zionism could be a good thing for the western Jews who had forgotten all about their traditions. The idea of a state would induce them to devote their energies to the service of their nation. But in eastern Europe the political tendency could only do harm to the moral ideal of spiritual Zionism which Ahad Ha'am advocated throughout his life.†

In 1912, after another visit to Palestine, he felt somewhat more optimistic about the future of the country. He was confident that a

---

* L. Simon (ed.), *Ten Essays on Zionism and Judaism by Ahad Ha'am*, London, 1922, p. 12.

† See his articles 'The Jewish State and the Jewish Problem' (1897) and 'Pinsker and Political Zionism' (1902), in *Nationalism and the Jewish Ethic*, New York, 1962.

national spiritual centre of Judaism was now in the making. Twenty years earlier it had seemed at best doubtful whether there would ever emerge a centre of study, or literature and learning, 'a true miniature of the people of Israel as it ought to be which will bind all Jews together'. He still saw many defects wherever he looked. He did not, for instance, believe there would ever be substantial Jewish agriculture in Palestine. But he saw in Palestine in 1912 the beginnings of a national life unparalleled in the diaspora.* Political Zionism was on the way out. Practical Zionism, embracing both colonisation and cultural activity, had prevailed all the way along the line after Herzl's death. This, he said, was not an abandonment of the national ideal, but on the contrary the healthy reaction of people who, unlike the leaders of political Zionism, were ruled unconsciously by the instinct of national self-preservation, for whom Judaism was the very centre of their being. A state such as Herzl had envisaged, bound together only by attacks on the part of the common enemy, would be at best a state of the Jews, not a Jewish state, for its citizens would not be imbued with a genuine Jewish national consciousness or a common cultural tradition.

It should be noted in passing that Ahad Ha'am's nationalism was by no means religious in inspiration. He was an agnostic; to him religion was merely one form of the national culture. While Judaism, the national creative power, had expressed itself in the past mainly in a religious framework, it was by no means certain that this would necessarily be so in the future.† Ahad Ha'am's attitude towards the future of the diaspora was somewhat ambiguous. He argued against Dubnow and others who expected a Jewish national revival outside Palestine, but he himself held that a spiritual centre would transform the scattered atoms of Jewry into a single entity with a definite character of its own, that it would accentuate their Jewishness, involving both an extension of the area of their personal lives within which the differences between them and their non-Jewish neighbours had significance, and a heightened sense of belonging to the Jewish people.‡

Ahad Ha'am repeated his warnings about political Zionism even after it had achieved success with the Balfour Declaration: 'Do not press on too quickly to the goal!' But such exhortations apart, it is not easy to point to any concrete programme in his teachings. He was concerned not with the political crisis facing the Jews but with the cultural crisis

---

* 'Summa Summarum', *ibid.*, p. 148.
† L.Simon, *Ahad Ha'am*, Philadelphia, 1960, p. 229.
‡ *Ibid.*, p. 296.

of the Jewish people in the diaspora. He admitted that he had no panacea for the salvation of the Jews as individuals, but was preoccupied with the rescue of Judaism as a spiritual entity. Many contemporaries, Zionists and non-Zionists alike, drew the conclusion that for Ahad Ha'am the existence of a Jewish majority in Eretz Israel was not an essential condition for the creation of such a centre.* 'Ahad Ha'amism', a Jewish Vatican, was adopted by some as an alternative to the idea of a Jewish state. This was not apparently what he had meant. In a letter written in 1903, Ahad Ha'am stated *expressis verbis*: 'Palestine will become our spiritual centre only when the Jews are a majority of the population and own most of the land.'† But such statements were infrequent in his published writings, and if Ahad Ha'am has been misunderstood in this respect it was above all his own fault. His sole interest was the cultural centre. The rest he took for granted and did not bother to make it clear how the political and economic infrastructure of this centre was to be created.

There were other weaknesses and inconsistencies in Ahad Ha'am's thought. He was not the Herder of Jewish nationalism as his disciples believed. His spiritual ideals and the uniqueness of the Jewish culture which he invoked so frequently were not clearly presented. He took it more or less for granted that Jewish culture and Hebrew had to be revived. While pointing to the spiritual poverty of western Jews, his own concepts of nation and nationalism were not in the Jewish tradition, but shaped by western philosophical and political thought. He based his postulate of national existence on a somewhat nebulous concept and wrote about the future of Jewish culture in isolation from political, social, and economic factors – as if it were possible to build (or revive) a culture in a vacuum. He was right in his assumption that only a relatively small part of the diaspora would find shelter in the Jewish state. More Jews eventually settled in Palestine than Ahad Ha'am had anticipated, and yet it was not at all clear whether the state would ever be the spiritual centre of world Jewry. The new cultural life did not, on the whole, harmonise with Ahad Ha'am's hopes. His doctrine was based in part on a Darwinian notion of the will to survive of the national ego, and in part on Jewish ethics. His concept of Jewish ethics made him oppose political Zionism and power politics in general. He did not realise that in a world in which the situation of the Jews was rapidly deteriorating, these two strands in his thought were bound to clash, and that the Jews

---

* I. Kolat, 'Theories on Israeli Nationalism', in *In the Dispersion*, 7, 1967.
† L. Simon (ed.), *Ahad Ha'am: Essays, Letters, Memoirs*, Oxford, 1946, p. 282.

who wanted to survive as a group had no alternative but to engage in power politics.

The chief philosophical influences on Ahad Ha'am were the positivist thinkers of the last century: Spencer, John Stuart Mill, Renan, and the Jewish *Haskala*. With Martin Buber, his junior by almost twenty years, we move from the tradition of rationalism into the realm of neo-romanticism. Whereas Ahad Ha'am exerted a powerful influence on sections of the east European Jewish intelligentsia but remained almost totally unknown in the west, Buber's influence in Jewish circles was limited to intellectuals in Prague, Vienna and Berlin, and to sections of the German-Jewish youth movement. He had no impact on east European Jewry, whereas in German and, later on, in American intellectual life his name was one to conjure with.

Born in Vienna of a family of well-known Galician rabbis, Martin Buber spent his adult life in central Europe, and emigrated to Jerusalem in 1938, where he taught at the Hebrew University. A man of wide erudition, he developed an original if somewhat intangible philosophical-theological system which, although it advocated a return to the origins of Judaism, was rejected by most of his contemporaries as un-Jewish. The main formative influences on Buber during his early years were the two great German mystics of the Middle Ages, Meister Eckhart and Jakob Böhme. From them Buber derived his concept of pantheism, the need for a deeper link with the outside world, the unity of all living matter in God. There was a God-given harmony in the world. Man had become alienated from this harmony, but could return to it by listening to the voice of inner experience, to intuition. Later on Buber discovered in the ecstasy of the Hassidic sects of eastern Europe the genuine mystical experience which led to unity with God and the world.* He introduced the forgotten Hassidic legends to western Europe, and in a series of speeches on Judaism and the future of the Jewish people provided a new *Weltanschauung* for the young intellectuals joining the Zionist movement.†

Buber had been an early Zionist. He was also among the first who together with Berthold Feiwel (and in opposition to Herzl) stressed the necessity of immediate practical work instead of waiting for that distant day when the elusive charter would be won. He had been an admirer of Ahad Ha'am but soon went his own way in his search for a new

---

* M.Buber, *Mein Weg zum Chassidismus*, Frankfurt, 1918.

† See M.Buber, *Die jüdische Bewegung* (2 vols.), Berlin, 1920; H.Kohn, *Martin Buber: Sein Werk und seine Zeit*, Hellerau, 1930.

philosophy. By accepting the then fashionable antimony between myth and intellect, organism and mechanism, *Gemeinschaft* (i.e. the organically living, genuine community) and *Gesellschaft* (the mechanical, artificial aggregate of conflicting interests), he moved dangerously close to the neighbourhood of the irrational, anti-liberal doctrines which infested European intellectual life during the decades before 1914. This impression of ideological proximity was further deepened by Buber's frequent references to the 'community of blood', by the central place of *Volk* and *völkisch* in his early thought. It is only fair to add that for Buber these were spiritual concepts which had nothing in common with the outpourings of the predecessors of German racialism.*

Far from being an aggressive nationalist, Buber sympathised with pacifism and within the Zionist movement belonged to the minimalist trend, advocating a bi-national state. The vocation of Israel as the elect of God was not Jewish nationalism, with national egoism as the highest goal, but humanism, a truly supernatural task. Israel was predestined to play such a role because it was a nation unlike any other. Since its earliest beginnings it had been both a nation and a religious community. 'Blood' for Buber was not a biological factor but the concept of the continuity of a people, experience inherited from the past, the creative mystery transmitted from one generation to the next.

His main preoccupation in later years was the search for identity on the part of the individual. Unlike the political, 'instinctive' Zionists, he did not take Jewish identity for granted, and antisemitism as a unifying factor did not satisfy him. Buber was concerned (to use the words of Moritz Heimann) with the spiritual problems of a Jew alone on a desert island. In his search to give deeper moral and religious (not in the orthodox sense) significance to the national idea he accepted Fichte's dictum that nationalism was to fulfil in modern times the function once held by religion, to infuse the eternal element, the constant values into daily life. Like Ahad Ha'am, Buber rejected the diaspora, as responsible for the degeneration of the Jewish creative urge: Judaism as a result of the diaspora had become spiritually barren.

He believed in a great mission for the Jewish, the holy people, which by returning to Eretz Israel would unite organic nature with the divine mission. In their life as a nation the Jews had the great opportunity to make a reality of (*verwirklichen*, one of the key words in Buber's philosophy) truth and justice in an organic unity. To them uniquely was it open to build a new society, a way of life and faith united by

* G. Mosse, *Germans and Jews*, New York, 1969, pp. 85-9.

dialogue (another of Buber's key concepts), mutual influence, reciprocal relations, by common land and labour. Unkind spirits have dismissed Buber's philosophy as irrelevant to Zionism, the abstruse ideas of a highly erudite aesthete. What Ahad Ha'am said about political Zionism certainly applied to Buber's philosophy: east European Jewry did not need it; at best it could be of benefit to the assimilated Jews in the west at a time of spiritual crisis. East European Jewry had little use for Buber's emphasis on the Asian character of Judaism, contrasting 'oriental boundlessness' with the European intellectual tradition, the claim that Zionism was to act as mediator between Asian and European culture myths and the *élan vital*. An activist movement by its very nature, Zionism did not need a philosophy of spirit and action as provided by Buber.

Buber early on withdrew from active politics, and only late in life made a comeback as an advocate of Jewish-Arab cooperation. He continued on occasion to provide philosophical comment on world affairs, to the joy of his admirers and the bewilderment of the rest. Thus, he interpreted the First World War as a great 'Asian crisis', which would enable the people of central Europe to participate in public life, revitalise Russia, and save the Near East for a Semitic renaissance. If this sounds not very precise, it is a fairly typical example of what irritated many of Buber's contemporaries: the dark hints, the mysterious phrases concerning subjects which above all needed precision and clarity. Buber's appearances at Zionist congresses did not have a great impact. Weizmann, whose own tendency was towards simplicity, referred to him, perhaps a little unfairly, as a rather odd and exotic figure, a good friend who often irritated him by his stilted talk, full of forced expressions and elaborate similes without clarity or beauty.

Buber found disciples among the Jewish students in central Europe who believed with him that Zionism was not yet the national revival, but was merely preparing the way for it. They shared his belief in the need to resuscitate the Jewish souls crippled by arid rationalism. The search for the creative force of the spirit was a Jewish manifestation of the neo-romantic *Zeitgeist*, with Buber as its most effective prophet. It was, in the words of Hans Kohn, a youth movement directed against the old, the tired, the lazy who could no longer be moved by enthusiasm. Zionism thus interpreted could not be argued about: 'It is not knowledge but life.'* It is easy to dismiss the anti-intellectual fashions of the pre-war period, but this does not help us to understand the spirit of the

* *Vom Judentum. Ein Sammelbuch*, Leipzig, 1914, p. viii.

young generation. For Zion, after all, was a myth, and Zionism, like all other national movements, was essentially romantic in character. No one could prove rationally that Zionism was justified and that it had a future. What attracted even young Marxists to Palestine was not scientific analysis, but romantic idealism and a myth. Buber's attempt to provide a new sense of direction was certainly not unnatural in the context of the times.

Buber formulated the aim of the young generation as 'to become human and in a Jewish way' (*Mensch werden und es jüdisch werden*). Berdichevsky (Micha bin Gurion), who came from a distinguished family of rabbis and did not have to re-acquaint himself with Hassidism, disagreed. He did not see any discrepancy between humanity and Judaism. The source of the evil was that the living Jews had become secondary to abstract Judaism, an anomaly which had led to total decay. The Jewish revival could not just be a spiritual revival (at this point he was bound to clash with Ahad Ha'am); it would have to encompass both inner and outer life. Jewish tradition, scholarship and religion could no longer be the basic values. A total overturn, a 'transvaluation of all values' (shades of Nietzsche!) was needed.* The Jews no longer had a living culture, nor could such a culture be artificially grafted on them from without. Every culture was the end of a process, not a fresh beginning induced from without. As one of his interpreters put it: the Jews needed Jerusalem, the living, not Javne, the spiritual centre.†

The balance sheet of diaspora history had been totally negative: a rebirth of the Jewish people was the commandment of the hour. But this could be achieved only by a deliberate severance from tradition, or at any rate from much of it. The present generation was called upon not to be the last Jews, but the first of a new nation, the Hebrews, men and women with a new relation to nature and life. Berdichevsky's thought had a certain impact on Labour Zionism, and in particular the kibbutz movement, but it also led well beyond Zionism. For in his view Zionism had not been radical enough in its rejection of the past. It had not realised that the whole of Jewish history in the diaspora had been a mistake. Instead it had tried to connect old and new ideas, getting caught in the process in some form of religious romanticism. Berdichevsky's iconoclasm did not have a wide appeal when it was first voiced around the turn of the century. But half a century later, as a new nation was born in Israel, different in many respects from the Jewish people in the diaspora,

* M.J.Berdichevsky, *Baderekh*, Warsaw, 1922, vol. I, *passim*.
† H.Bergmann, *Jawne und Jerusalem*, Berlin, 1919, p. 34.

the issues first raised by Berdichevsky assumed a new meaning and urgency.

Other critics of spiritual Zionism shared the view that Zionism was not radical enough, since it did not envisage the total liquidation of the diaspora. Reinterpreting Jewish history, Yecheskel Kaufman, a professor at the Hebrew University in Jerusalem, accused the Jewish national movement of being deflected from its purpose by attributing (like religious Jewry) a special sense to Jewish existence in the diaspora. What was needed was not the revival of Hebrew culture, or the social regeneration of a minority, but a solution for the existence of the Jewish people. This, for historical and sociological reasons, could not be found in the diaspora, and for that reason the resettlement of the great majority of the Jewish people was needed.

Even more radical in his approach was Jacob Klatzkin. Born in Russia, he lived for many years in Germany, where his most important essays were published, and later on moved to America. He saw the originality of Zionism in its emphasis on form, not content; without a national territory and a national language nationalism in the diaspora had no meaning, and assimilation was the logical way out for the modern Jew. As for Zionism, the longing for a return to the homeland was an end in itself. The wish to create a base for the spiritual values of Judaism was a secondary consideration: 'The content of our life will be national when its form becomes national.' A new, secular definition of Jewish identity was needed, instead of philosophising about the essence of Judaism, with its definitions of the Jewish spirit in abstract terms, its references to messianic ideas and the ideal of social justice. Klatzkin felt that the spirit of Judaism could not guarantee the survival of Judaism. Its survival in the diaspora was no guarantee against its disappearance in the near future.

Total assimilation was in Klatzkin's view not only possible, it might even be inevitable.* This was not necessarily a matter of great regret, for the Judaism of the diaspora was not worthy of survival. The diaspora could only prolong the disgrace of the Jewish people, disfigured in both body and soul.† It was no accident that Zionism arose in the west, not in the east. It was not the Jew, but the man in Herzl which brought him back to his people; not Jewish, but universal national consciousness. The east viewed Zionism as a mere continuation of Jewish tradition, not a world-destroying and world-building movement. Eastern Europe did

---

* J.Klatzkin, *Krisis und Entscheidung im Judentum*, Berlin, 1921, p. 35 *et seq.*
† Klatzkin, *Techumim*. I have used A.Hertzberg's translation, p. 522.

not have to the same extent the universal human elements, the feeling for liberty and honour, the quest for human dignity, truth and integrity which were required for a national renaissance.* Klatzkin conceded that the diaspora, even if it was an abnormality, would have to be preserved for the sake of the revival in Palestine. But once Palestine had been established as a national centre two Jewish nations would gradually emerge – the one in the diaspora, and the Hebrew nation in Israel; and as time went on they would have less and less in common.† He was at his most effective in his critique of Ahad Ha'am and Buber, the advocates of diaspora nationalism and the apostles of a spiritual mission. His direct impact during his lifetime (he died in 1948) was limited, despite the original and provocative character of his analysis of the Jewish predicament.

Like Ahad Ha'am, Klatzkin did not bother to point to political alternatives. The apostle of radical Zionism and rejection of the diaspora by no means approved of the activities of political Zionism. He had grave doubts about Britain and the effects of the Balfour Declaration. But if he saw any alternative way of building the national home he kept the secret to himself. Perhaps he saw himself in the role of a consultant physician who was essentially a diagnostician. The telling phrases about the crippling effects of the diaspora were written not in Jerusalem, but in Murnau, a pleasant little village in Bavaria, Klatzkin's retreat, and in Heidelberg. Klatzkin did not settle in Palestine, and he was to die in Switzerland. The unity of theory and practice cannot be found in his life, nor in that of most of the other ideologists and leaders of Zionism of that generation. For that reason, if for no other, there was always an element of unreality in the passionate debates that went on for so many years about a spiritual centre, the rejection of the diaspora, and the mission – if any – of a regenerated Jewish people. The debates usually revealed a profound disregard for realities, and the real world, not surprisingly, retaliated by ignoring the philosophers.

Zionism in the First World War

When the First World War broke out, two of the members of the Zionist executive, then located at 8 Sächsische Strasse, Berlin, were German citizens, three were Russians, and one (Levin) a Russian who had just acquired Austrian citizenship. World Zionism, needless to say, was no

---

* *Ibid.*

† Klatzkin, *Krisis und Entscheidung*, p. 83.

more prepared than any other international organisation to function in wartime. That the world movement was to stay out of the conflict and remain neutral went without saying, but this was easier said than done. For the Zionist leaders throughout Europe, with the obvious exception of Russia, felt it their duty to support their respective fatherlands to the best of their ability. This conflict of loyalties apart, there was the question of protecting Palestinian Jewry. Above all, there was the issue of the postwar settlement. Some Zionist leaders realised early on that what their movement had failed to attain in time of peace it might well achieve during or after a war which was bound to lead to a re-examination of many unresolved international issues.

German Zionists shared the general patriotic enthusiasm of August 1914. Their federation announced that it expected all its young members to volunteer for military service. Germany was fighting for truth, law, freedom and world civilisation against darkest tyranny, bloodiest cruelty, and blackest reaction, as represented by tsarist despotism. By allying themselves with Russia, France and Britain had become its accessories in crime. Franz Oppenheimer said that for Germany the war 'was holy, just self-defence', and Ludwig Strauss wrote that the national Jews were no worse patriots than national Germans. 'We do know that our interest is exclusively on the side of Germany', ran an editorial in the official Zionist weekly; Germany was strong and would liberate the oppressed.* Zionist publications wholeheartedly supported the war effort. It would be invidious to single out any Zionist leader for special mention because almost all were equally affected, at least during the first months of the war.† In Austria, Hugo Zuckermann, a Zionist, wrote a popular war poem in which he said that death on the field of battle held no terror for him if only before dying he could see the Austrian banner waving in the wind over Belgrade. Zuckermann was killed soon after. Elias Auerbach, the Zionist physician who had settled in Haifa, decided immediately on the outbreak of war to return to Germany to do his duty in the army medical corps.

The patriotic enthusiasm of the German and Austrian Zionists seems in retrospect singularly misguided, but it is only fair to add that the war against Russia was equally popular in eastern Europe and the United States, the two biggest Jewish concentrations. Upon receiving the news about Russian defeats Morris Rosenfeld, the most popular Yiddish

---

* *Jüdische Rundschau*, 7, 28 August, 16 October, 1914.
† *Jüdische Rundschau*, throughout August-November 1914; N.Goldmann, *Der Geist des Militarismus*, Stuttgart, 1915.

writer of the day, wrote a poem which ended with the words: 'Hurrah for Germany! Long live the kaiser!' Tsarist Russia was the country of pogroms, of Kishinev and Homel, of institutionalised oppression. The fact that after the outbreak of war the persecution of Jews in western Russia became even more intense, and that hundreds of thousands of them had been deported, did not make that country any more popular. Most leaders of Russian and Polish Jewry believed in the inevitability of a German victory. For them, as Weizmann wrote, the west ended at the Rhine. They knew Germany, spoke German, and were greatly impressed by German achievements.* And they were influenced by the painful history of the Jews in Russia. A Russian victory would perpetuate and perhaps intensify the persecution of east European Jewry, whereas the defeat of Russia was bound to open the gates to their liberation.

There were exceptions, such as Weizmann and Ahad Ha'am, Jabotinsky and Rutenberg. Nordau, too, warned against a one-sided pro-German orientation, despite the fact that the French had given him every reason to feel aggrieved; having lived in Paris for decades, he was deported to Spain as an enemy national and remained there throughout the war. But the greater part of the world Zionist movement was pro-German, even though it became more reserved after the first flush of excitement. Historical sympathies and antipathies quite apart, a strong case could be made for the importance of Berlin to Zionists. Effective political and economic aid to the hard-pressed Palestinian Jewish community could be extended only from the German capital during the first three years of the war. During this time the German armies advanced far into western Russia and the bulk of Polish and Lithuanian Jewry came under German rule. Whichever way one looked at it, Berlin was the pivot as far as Zionist politics were concerned.

A few days after the outbreak of war Dr Bodenheimer, a former president of the German Zionist Federation and still one of its leading members, approached the German Foreign Ministry and suggested the establishment of a German 'Committee for the Liberation of Russian Jewry'. Set up in August 1914, this body later on changed its name to the somewhat less provocative 'Committee for the East'. The committee was dominated at first by the Zionists – Professor Oppenheimer was its chairman, Motzkin and Hantke took part in its work, and Sokolow wrote the editorial for the first issue of its Hebrew-language journal *Kol hamevaser*.† Its aim was to promote the aspirations of east European Jewry

---

* Weizmann, *Trial and Error*, p. 15.

† M.Bodenheimer, *So wurde Israel*, Frankfurt, 1958, p. 187.

towards national freedom and autonomy, and the underlying expectation was that Germany would, in the course of the war, occupy western Russia, where most of the Jews lived. This was done with the blessing of the German authorities, who had a somewhat exaggerated notion of the extent of Zionist influence in the east, one of their advisers comparing the internal discipline of the Zionists to that of the Jesuits.*

These 'Jewish operations' were part of a general scheme to revolutionise the oppressed minorities of the tsarist empire. But German military rule did not altogether fulfil the expectations of east European Jewry, which had been called upon to rise against Russian oppression. The demand for political and cultural autonomy was largely ignored because it clashed with the aims of the Polish and Baltic national movements. The Poles in particular became more and more openly antisemitic during the war, and at its end engaged in widespread pogroms. The tsarist anti-Jewish legislation was abolished only in the northern section (*Ober-Ost*) of the occupied territory. The constitution of the committee changed during the war and representatives of non-Zionist German Jews were co-opted.

The existence of the committee became a bone of contention among the world Zionist leaders and forced them to reconsider their orientation as between the two camps. Bodenheimer at first had the support of the executive, although his activities were in clear violation of Zionist neutrality. The critics of the one-sided pro-German orientation argued that, all other considerations apart, such close cooperation with German political warfare jeopardised millions of east European Jews, for the activities of the committee, needless to say, remained no secret, and served as a justification for the anti-Jewish measures taken by the Russian government in 1914–15. Bodenheimer was compelled by his colleagues to resign as chairman of the Jewish National Fund.

To keep the world movement neutral, a meeting of the Larger Action Committee in Copenhagen in December 1914 (the first after the outbreak of war) decided to open a clearing-house there under Motzkin, and later under Victor Jacobson, to maintain contact with Zionist organisations in both camps, and as far as possible to coordinate their efforts. Weizmann's demand that the executive, still located in Berlin under the management of Warburg and Hantke, should cease to function and that the conduct of Zionist affairs should be transferred to America during the war was rejected, on the ground that it might endanger the position of Palestinian Jewry. As a compromise it was decided to transfer

* E.Zechlin, *Die deutsche Politik und die Juden im ersten Weltkrieg*, Goettingen, 1969, p. 119.

Sokolow from Berlin to London and to send Chlenov on a mission to America and Britain, from where he returned to his native Russia.* The dispersal of the members of the executive was inevitable, given the necessity to pursue political activities in several capitals at one and the same time, but it paralysed the executive. Who was now authorised to take decisions or even make declarations on its behalf? It was understood that the Berlin members had the authority to speak for the whole body, but they were a minority and disagreements were bound to arise sooner or later. It was also decided that the executive could not be party to any negotiations with the government of any country at war with Turkey. Weizmann, who was as pro-British as the German Zionists were pro-German, was not in sympathy with this resolution. Two months earlier he had written to Shmaryahu Levin that 'as soon as the situation is somewhat cleared up, we could talk plainly to England and France with regard to the abnormal situation of the Jews. . . . It is in the interest of peoples now fighting for the small nationalities to secure for the Jewish nation the right of existence. Now is the time when the peoples of Great Britain, France and America will understand us. . . . The moral force of our claims will prove irresistible; the political conditions will be favourable to the realisation of our ideal.'† Unknown to Weizmann, his optimism was shared by Herbert Samuel, an influential politician of whom it had not even been known that he sympathised with Zionist aspirations. Samuel was a member of Asquith's Liberal cabinet, and he submitted a memorandum to his colleagues in which he argued the case for a national home for the Jews in Palestine. While this bore no fruit – Asquith was totally uninterested – it was a first step in preparing the ground for the dramatic developments of 1917.

During the early phases of the war, however, Berlin remained the centre of Zionist political activities. It was the task of the executive located there to safeguard the interests of east European Jewry as large sections of it passed under German rule, and to protect the Zionist settlements in Palestine.‡ It was Weizmann's historical achievement that, in the event, Britain's victory became also a Zionist triumph. His efforts were crowned with success precisely because he held no official position in the world Zionist movement. It is easy to imagine how Turkey,

---

* Procès-verbal of Copenhagen meeting (3–6 December 1914); Lichtheim: *Rückkehr*, p. 255.
† Quoted in L.Stein, *The Balfour Declaration*, London, 1961, p. 99.
‡ Lichtheim: *Rückkehr*, p. 259; see also N.M.Gelber, *Hazharat Balfour vetoldoteha*, Jerusalem, 1939, p. 160 *et seq.*

forever suspicious of Zionist activities, would have reacted if the executive had followed Weizmann's line and shown itself in 1914 in favour of an Allied victory.

Official German attitude to Zionism was distant but not altogether unfriendly. Herzl's attempts to gain the support of the Kaiser had been unsuccessful, and up to 1914 Germany took no steps to intervene on behalf of the Zionist movement. With the outbreak of war the attitude became somewhat more positive. The German leaders did not want to antagonise the Zionists because of their influence among east European Jewry and in the United States. Bethmann Hollweg, the chancellor, and Wangenheim, the German ambassador in Constantinople, tried on various occasions to impress Talaat, then minister of the interior at the Porte, to refrain from actions which would provoke world Jewry. Between 1914 and 1917 German diplomatic representatives frequently interceded, albeit only informally, with the Turkish authorities on behalf of Palestinian Jewry.* Most of these interventions concerned Djemal Pasha, the Turkish commander in Palestine, who was determined to deport all Jews of Russian nationality, i.e. the majority of the Jewish population.

He made the first attempt in December 1914, shortly after Turkey's entry into the war, and it was successfully thwarted, but not in time to save six hundred Jews who had already been deported. There were further sporadic arrests and other forms of chicanery, and it was not until March 1915 that the central authorities succeeded in persuading their representative in Jerusalem to leave the Jews in peace. Eventually Djemal took notice, at least for a time. Then, after a few months, he began to reassert himself and compelled Ruppin, head of the Palestine Office and a German national, to move from Jaffa to the Turkish capital. But by and large the years 1915-16 were relatively quiet years for Palestinian Jewry, owing mainly to the activities of the German Zionist representatives in Constantinople and the support they had in Berlin.

The executive was less successful in realising its more ambitious schemes. It gained the support of several influential publicists who wrote in the German press about the increasing importance of Zionism as a factor in world politics. In November 1915, on Zionist prodding, a confidential instruction was sent to all German consular representatives in the Ottoman empire to the effect that the German imperial govern-

---

* Zechlin: *Die deutsche Politik* . . . , p. 318. The most authoritative account of German-Zionist relations during the First World War is a hitherto unpublished study by Isaiah Friedman, sections of which the author kindly put at my disposal.

ment was well disposed towards Jewish aspirations in Palestine.* But it proved impossible to induce Berlin to make an official declaration in support of Zionism, despite the fact that a non-committal statement was recommended not only by Jewish circles but also by various German diplomats.† A pro-Palestine committee consisting of well-known public figures was set up in 1917 to influence public opinion and to exert pressure on the German government. At the same time the news about the contacts between Dr Weizmann and British statesmen, and the increasing measure of favourable attention paid to Zionism in British and French publications, were brought to the attention of the German government. But Berlin was not willing to bring even greater pressure on its Turkish allies, and would probably have failed if the attempt had been made.

When Djemal Pasha visited Berlin in August 1917, he told Hantke and Lichtheim that he was still hostile to the idea of a Jewish Palestine, since he had to take into account the feelings of the Arab population. He might reconsider his views one day but there would be no change in Turkish policy while the war was on.‡ In a conversation with the German ambassador shortly before the Balfour Declaration, Djemal said he would be willing to concede a national home to the Jews, but for what purpose, since the Arabs would only kill them.§ The Turks would have greatly preferred not to make any concessions at all, but there was no doubt that if hard-pressed they would opt for the Arabs. This must have been clear to the Germans, who reached the conclusion that the goodwill of the Zionists was not worth a major crisis in their relations with the Turks.

Zionist policy in Germany thus failed to reach its objective. But ironically enough, the efforts to enlist German help had considerable indirect repercussions. The news about the talks between the German representatives and the Zionists was noted in London and Paris; so were the pro-Zionist articles in the German press. While Hantke, Blumenfeld and Lichtheim impressed on their Berlin contacts that England was about to make an important pro-Zionist declaration, Weizmann used the reverse argument in his dealings with the British cabinet and the Foreign Office: unless the British hurried the central powers would come out first and secure an important advantage. It is impossible to establish with absolute certainty whether Weizmann was misinformed or whether

---

* Lichtheim: *Rückkehr*, p. 333.
† E. Zechlin: *Die deutsche Politik* ..., p. 366 *et seq.*
‡ *Ibid.*, p. 370.
§ J. H. Bernstorff, *Erinnerungen und Briefe*, Zürich, 1936, p. 148.

he deliberately exaggerated the threat of a German Balfour Declaration, knowing full well that it would not be forthcoming.* Believers in the conspiracy theory of history will no doubt be inclined to search for the hidden hand, a Machiavellian plot between the Zionists in London and Berlin. But there was in fact no coordination. On the contrary, Weizmann kept his talks with British statesmen very much to himself. Frequently he did not inform even close friends, let alone the Copenhagen Bureau or Berlin. The German Zionists had made less headway, but they too had not reported to Weizmann about their moves. Each side, in brief, was in the dark in 1917 about the achievements and failures of the other.

The British government, at any rate, took the news seriously, and when the talks in the war cabinet dragged on, Balfour announced on 4 October 1917 that a decision had to be taken soon since the German government was making great efforts to gain the support of the Zionist movement.†

With the publication of the Balfour Declaration, London became the centre of the world Zionist movement even though parts of Palestine remained in Turkish hands until well into 1918. The Berlin executive fully realised that the initiative had now passed to the other side. It did not grudge Weizmann his success and welcomed the Declaration as an event of immense historical importance.‡ It continued to press the German and Turkish governments for a statement similar to the Declaration which would open the gates of Palestine to large-scale immigration and provide political and cultural autonomy. Towards the end of the war the German Zionists won the support of the leading non-Zionist Jewish organisation for a scheme which provided less than a national home but which was more than any of them had dared to hope in 1914. But this was in 1918 and the whole issue had become academic, for Jerusalem, Jaffa, and the whole of southern Palestine were by that time in British hands. The occupation of the rest of the country was merely a question of time. If the German Zionists nevertheless continued to press their demands it was no doubt with an eye to the coming peace conference. Now that the Balfour Declaration had received the blessing of the other allied powers, their intention was to gain the support of the central powers as well so that there would be unanimity with regard to Palestine's future.

The First World War was the watershed for America's involvement in

* Zechlin: *Die deutsche Politik* . . . , p. 399.
† Public Record Office, London, Cab. 23–4, 245, quoted in Zechlin, *ibid.*
‡ *Jüdische Rundschau*, 16 November 1917.

world affairs. It was also the breakthrough which made American Jewry the decisive factor in the councils of world Jewry. American Jews had taken an interest in the fate of their less fortunate co-religionists in Russia and Rumania even before 1914, but it was only during the war that, owing to America's new might, the financial position of the Jewish community, and, during the early years of the war, America's neutrality, that the Jews there assumed the leading role. During the war years Zionism made a spectacular advance. There had been only twelve thousand organised Zionists in America in 1914. They gained a mass following during the following years as the conviction grew that the war would bring in its wake a solution of the Jewish question and perhaps even result in the establishment of a Jewish state. Individuals as well as groups began to join the organisation, and there was a movement afoot to organise the entire Jewish community in support of Zionist demands.

Shortly after the outbreak of war the suggestion was made to establish a body to represent the whole of American Jewry, to represent its interests, with special reference to eastern Europe, and to state the Jewish cause at the peace conference. The proposal was strongly resisted by the American-Jewish establishment, united in the American Jewish Committee. Other anti-Zionist groups, such as the Bund, tried to take over the movement from the Zionists. But the response on the part of the masses was enormous and, fearing isolation, the opponents too eventually came to join the drive. Public opinion veered more and more towards Zionism. Leading members of the establishment, like Louis Marshall and Jacob Schiff, who only a few years earlier had dissociated themselves from Zionism, came to adopt a more positive attitude. A preparatory conference was held in 1916, and it became the declared policy of all American Jewish organisations not only to press for equal rights for east European Jewry but also to secure Jewish rights in Palestine.*

Brandeis, who was to play a decisive part in these activities, had appeared for the first time on a Zionist platform one year before the outbreak of war. After it started, he was elected chairman of the Provisional Executive Committee for General Zionist Affairs. It was at first expected that the executive would be transferred to the United States, but even though this did not take place, the new body was to play a role of considerable importance. The provisional committee helped to co-ordinate the rescue efforts for Palestinian Jewry, which, cut off from Europe, was facing economic ruin. America's diplomatic representatives in Turkey – Jews by unwritten tradition – such as Morgenthau and

* O. Janowsky, *The Jews and Minority Rights*, New York, 1933, p. 184.

Elkus – played a role second only to the Germans as protectors of the yishuv. They intervened countless times with the Porte against the deportation orders issued in Jerusalem and Jaffa.

Brandeis was almost sixty when he undertook his new role as Jewish statesman. He had been remote from Jewish affairs and he never failed to emphasise that he had come to Zionism wholly as an American. He saw no problem of divided loyalties. In the same way as every Irish-American who supported Home Rule was a better man and a better American for the sacrifice involved, he once wrote, every American Jew who helped to advance Jewish settlement in Palestine would likewise be a better man and a better American for doing so.* Brandeis was the first leader of American Zionism who was at the same time a figure of national prominence. An eminently successful and popular lawyer, a friend and consultant of leading politicians, he was in line for a leading position in the government when Woodrow Wilson formed his first administration in 1913, although the president encountered resistance because Brandeis, 'the people's attorney', had made many enemies among the rich, and there was also still much anti-Jewish feeling. Wilson instead nominated him to the Supreme Court. After the nomination had gone through, he wrote to Morgenthau that he never signed any commission with such satisfaction.†

Brandeis' prestige, his reputation as one of President Wilson's close advisers, was an asset of which 'full use was made by the Zionist leaders in London in their dealings with the British government'. London closely followed developments on the American domestic scene. Its aim was to induce America to join the war against the central powers as soon as possible. The British were aware that while most of the leaders of American Jewry were pro-British (with few exceptions, such as Magnes and Shmaryahu Levin), the Jewish masses were anti-Russian and welcomed Russian defeats while not necessarily rejoicing at German victories. A change in this respect began to set in only in 1916–17. The Jews of German descent who had supported the kaiser were antagonised by such events as the German sinking of the *Lusitania*, whereas the immigrants from eastern Europe were greatly cheered by the revolution of March 1917, which gave equal rights to Russian Jewry.

Balfour met Brandeis twice during his visit to Washington in April 1917, and American Jewry's interest in Palestine was impressed on him.

* J. de Haas, *Louis Dembitz Brandeis*, New York, 1929, *passim*.
† R. S. Baker, *Woodrow Wilson*, London, 1937, VI, p. 116, quoted in Stein, *The Balfour Declaration*, p. 196.

In September 1917 the war cabinet decided to find out whether President Wilson thought it advisable to issue a declaration of sympathy with the Zionist movement. Much to Weizmann's surprise and chagrin, Wilson, acting apparently on the advice of Colonel House, answered that the time was not opportune for any definite statement, other than one of sympathy, and this only on condition that it could be made without implying any real commitment.* Wilson may have been uneasy about an exclusive British declaration, but on the other hand he had no intention of committing America. Colonel House had told him that the English 'naturally want the road to Egypt and India blocked and Lloyd George is not above using us to further his plan'.† From the Zionist point of view this response was a disaster. Weizmann immediately mobilised his American friends, and after further discussion with Colonel House Brandeis could reassure him that the president could be relied upon to support a pro-Zionist declaration. By mid-October Wiseman, head of British intelligence in the United States, had informed the Foreign Office that Wilson had approved the formula decided upon by the British war cabinet. The Zionists had surmounted yet another major hurdle owing to the help received from American Jewry.

Weizmann and the Balfour Declaration

The main battleground, however, was London, not Washington, and it is to Zionist policy in the British capital that we must turn next. Weizmann had believed in a British victory since the beginning of the war, and the German victories during the early stages had not shaken him in his belief. While he detested the tsarist régime as much as any of his colleagues, unlike most of them he did not think much of Germany either. His own experiences as a student in Germany had been unfortunate. He seems to have been a confirmed Anglophile from the age of ten when he wrote to his teacher: 'All have decided: the Jew must die, but England will nevertheless have mercy upon us.'‡ Weizmann thought the decision to leave the executive in Berlin a grave mistake, and when his suggestion to move it to Holland (or the United States) was rejected, he ceased to correspond with his colleagues outside the *entente* countries and the United States. His activities from that moment on were as much in

---

* Stein, *The Balfour Declaration*, pp. 504–8; see also Gelber, *Hazharat Balfour vetoldoteha*, Jerusalem, 1939, p. 135 *et seq.*
† Quoted in Stein, *The Balfour Declaration*, p. 529.
‡ L.Stein (ed.), *Letters and Papers of Chaim Weizmann*, London, 1968, vol. i, p. 37.

violation of the principle of Zionist neutrality as the policies of the German Zionists. But, unlike them, Weizmann was successful in the end. When war broke out, Weizmann was on holiday with his family in Switzerland. He returned immediately to England, and talked to his friends of the great possibilities that had suddenly opened up even if there were no concrete plans at this stage: 'There was an atmosphere of uncertainty and I went about with my hopes, waiting for my chances.'* Two months later he was introduced to C.P.Scott, editor of the *Manchester Guardian*. Scott was won over to Zionism by Weizmann, who told him about the Jewish tragedy in eastern Europe and the messianic dreams for Palestine. Scott, a Bible-reading man who at one time had wanted to become a Unitarian minister, was attracted by the passionate religion of Zionism, its deep sense of continuity.† He suggested a meeting with Lloyd George, chancellor of the exchequer, who in turn suggested a meeting with Herbert Samuel first. Weizmann went to the meeting with some trepidation. 'For God's sake, Mr Scott, let's have nothing to do with that man', he had exclaimed when the name was first mentioned. He thought that Samuel, like other leaders of Anglo-Jewry, was hostile to Zionism, and he was therefore dumbfounded when Samuel told him that his (Weizmann's) demands were much too modest. Samuel advised him to 'think big', adding that the aims of Zionism were very much in the mind of his cabinet colleagues. Weizmann answered that if he were a religious Jew he would have thought that the time of the Messiah was near.‡

In January 1915 Weizmann met Lloyd George, who had first come in contact with Zionism in Herzl's days, when he had been consulted about El Arish and Uganda in his capacity as a lawyer. He had not gone on record during the intervening years with any statement in favour of Zionism, but he told Herbert Samuel a few days after Turkey's declaration of war (November 1914) that he was very keen to see a Jewish state established in Palestine. Asquith said of him that he did not give a damn for the Jews, their past or their future. But this was a misinterpretation of the man and his motives: 'His elusive spirit never became enchained to Zionism but he knew it far better than his colleagues and he liked it very much.'§ Lloyd George had an instinctive sympathy for small nations, to one of which he himself belonged. He was, as Weizmann

---

* Weizmann, *Trial and Error*, p. 148.
† C.Sykes, *Two Studies in Virtue*, London, 1953, p. 170.
‡ Stein, *The Balfour Declaration*, p. 138.
§ Sykes, *Two Studies in Virtue*, p. 190.

wrote, deeply religious. To him and to others of his contemporaries the return of the Jewish people to Palestine was not a dream, since they believed in the Bible, and Zionism represented to them a tradition for which they had enormous respect.*

His motives, needless to say, were not wholly idealistic. His active interest in Zionism cannot be accounted for, as Stein says, by emotion and sentiment alone. Before exerting himself for the Zionist cause, he made sure that such a policy accorded with British interests as he conceived them.† This refers above all to the place of Palestine in imperial defence in the postwar world, a concept that had been first developed by Herbert Sidebotham, the *Manchester Guardian*'s military correspondent and another convert to Zionism. This consideration had not escaped Weizmann's mind. His plans were based on the assumption that the Allies would win, as he wrote Zangwill even before Turkey had entered the war. In this case Palestine was bound to fall within the sphere of British influence. If developed, it would constitute a barrier separating the Suez Canal from the Black Sea and any hostility which might come from that direction. If a million Jews were moved into Palestine within the next fifty or sixty years it could become an Asian Belgium. The reference to Belgium after the German invasion of 1914 was not one of Weizmann's happier historical parallels but what he meant was clear: 'England would have an effective barrier and we would have a country'.‡

Herbert Samuel played the most important role in these early behind-the-scene activities: 'He guided us constantly', Weizmann wrote, 'and gave us occasional indications of the way things were likely to shape. He was discreet, tactful and insistent.' After his meeting with Weizmann, Samuel prepared a long memorandum for Asquith, the prime minister, in which he suggested a British protectorate over Palestine after the war, since a French protectorate was undesirable and the internationalisation of the country not feasible. Yet Samuel's assumption that there was substantial support for Zionism in the cabinet was over-optimistic. Sir Edward Grey, the foreign secretary, told him that while he personally was sympathetic, it was premature to raise the Palestine issue. Grey was reluctant to enter into any commitment and stressed the necessity to consult France before decisions were taken concerning the division of spheres of influences in the Near East.§ Grey promised Samuel that no

* Weizmann, *Trial and Error*, p. 157.
† Stein, *The Balfour Declaration*, pp. 144–5.
‡ *Ibid.*, p. 127.
§ H.Samuel, *Memoirs*, London, 1945, p. 143.

decision would be taken on the future of Syria without taking the Palestinian issue into account.

This was reassuring, but it still meant that the Zionists had not been able so far to advance their cause. For the moment Lloyd George was Samuel's only supporter. For the prime minister, Zionism had no appeal whatever. The Samuel memorandum struck him as fantastic. He could not understand how such a lyrical outburst could emanate from the 'well-ordered and methodical brain of Herbert Samuel'. By nature a cautious man, Asquith was not in the least moved by the considerations which made Zionism attractive to 'more adventurous minds and more romantic temperaments. He could see in Zionist aspirations nothing but a rather fantastic dream, and in proposals for British control of Palestine merely an invitation to Great Britain to accept an unnecessary and unwanted addition to her imperial responsibilities'.* The first initiative to persuade the cabinet to adopt the Zionist programme thus ended in failure. The government was not likely to lift a finger, and the prospect facing Weizmann and his supporters was at best that of a long and arduous uphill struggle.

Occasional meetings continued but no substantial progress was made during 1915 and the following year. The Zionists decided therefore to use the time to win stronger backing among the Jewish community. Weizmann had been joined meanwhile by Nahum Sokolow, who, unlike Weizmann, was a member of the executive and could therefore speak with greater authority on behalf of the world organisation. The Zionists knew that it was important to have the support of the Conjoint Committee, the spokesman of British Jewry, on all matters affecting Jewish communities abroad. Founded in 1878 by the Board of Deputies of British Jews (a federation of Jewish communities) and the Anglo-Jewish Association (based on individual membership), the Conjoint Committee was wholly out of sympathy with Zionist aspirations and advised the Foreign Office to ignore them.

The story of this inner Jewish battle has been told in detail and need be only briefly recapitulated here.† Weizmann's main antagonists were Claude Montefiore ('a high-minded man who considered nationalism beneath the religious level of Jews – except in their capacity as Englishmen') and Lucien Wolf, a distinguished journalist and secretary of the Conjoint Committee (who found it 'impossible to understand that English non-Jews did not look upon his anti-Zionism as the hallmark of a

---

* Stein, *The Balfour Declaration*, p. 113.
† *Ibid.*, p. 166 *et seq*; Weizmann, *Trial and Error*, p. 156 *et seq*.

superior loyalty'). The ideology of the Liberal opposition to Zionism has been discussed elsewhere in the present study. Suffice it to say in this context that Montefiore and Wolf looked upon Judaism (again to quote Weizmann) as a collection of abstract religious principles, upon east European Jewry as an object of compassion and philanthropy, and upon Zionism as, at best, the empty dream of a few misguided idealists.* The Conjoint Committee had close connections with the leading bodies of French Jewry, and given the prestige of its members and Lucien Wolf's excellent contacts with the Foreign Office, they were a formidable enemy.

Edwin Montagu, secretary of state for India, wholly shared these views and was the fiercest opponent of the Zionists in the cabinet. In some respects he even went beyond them, being genuinely convinced that all Zionists were German agents, out to promote German imperialism and to weaken British influence in Asia. About the fate of Russian Jewry he wrote in 1916: 'I regard with perfect equanimity whatever treatment the Jews receive in Russia. I am convinced that the treatment meted out to Jews in Russia will be no worse or no better than the Russian degree of general civilisation.' Shortly before the Balfour Declaration he noted in his diary that he was glad to have met in Reginald Wingate (high commissioner in Egypt) a strong opponent of Zionism, 'for this would undoubtedly bolster up German influence in Palestine, most Zionists being of German origin.'†

Weizmann and his colleagues undertook the unpromising task of searching for a compromise with the members of the Conjoint Committee. At first the outlook seemed not altogether hopeless. Sacher gained the impression in November 1914 that Wolf was anxious to find common ground with the Zionists. In conversation with Samuel in February 1915 Wolf also indicated approval of a policy based on free immigration, facilities for colonisation, and the establishment of a Hebrew university, provided the idea of a Jewish state was dropped. Weizmann too was favourably impressed when he met Wolf in December 1914, but the meeting of minds was more apparent than real, as emerged soon after at a more formal confrontation. While the Zionists (represented by Sokolow and Chlenov, who was then temporarily in Britain) stressed their demand for a Jewish commonwealth to be established after the war, the committee reiterated its view that Zionism with its 'nationalist postulates' offered no solution to the Jewish question wherever it existed.

---

* Weizmann, *Trial and Error*, p. 157.
† Quoted in Sykes, *Two Studies in Virtue*, pp. 213, 216.

The committee concluded that it would be highly inopportune to raise the question of Palestine during the war.

Thus the dialogue broke down and the committee was acting without consultation with the Zionists when Wolf in March 1916 submitted a memorandum to the Foreign Office in which the British and the other powers were asked to take account after the war of the traditional interest in Palestine of the Jewish communities. Wolf demanded the full enjoyment of civil and religious liberties for the Jews of Palestine, equal religious rights with the rest of the population, reasonable facilities for immigration and colonisation, and certain municipal privileges in the towns and colonies inhabited by Jews.* He was careful not to venture beyond these philanthropic demands, and it is of some interest to note that Grey was less cautious than Wolf in his comments on the memorandum when it was brought to the knowledge of the French and Russian governments. Grey suggested in effect that the Jews in Palestine should be given autonomy once their number equalled that of the Arabs.

The attempts made by well-meaning Jewish personalities to restart the dialogue between the Zionists and the Conjoint Committee were in vain. Weizmann and his colleagues were convinced that the assimilationists were not open to persuasion, and their attitude became less conciliatory than it had been earlier. They felt that the committee did not represent the views of the community. Early in the war Weizmann had written to Harry Sacher and Leon Simon that 'the gentlemen of the type of Lucien Wolf have to be told the candid truth and made to realise that we and not they are the masters of the situation'.† The Zionists realised that it would greatly facilitate their task if they had the blessing of the Anglo-Jewish establishment, but they were not willing to make far-reaching concessions in return. The Conjoint Committee on the other hand resented the fact that upstart east European Jews only recently arrived in Britain had established direct contacts with the government, bypassing the leading bodies of Anglo-Jewry. They were genuinely afraid that the establishment of a Jewish state in Palestine, based on the recognition that the Jews were a people, would fatally affect the position of the Jews in the diaspora and jeopardise the rights they had won in a hard struggle over many years. The committee repeatedly asserted that they were not opposed in principle to Jewish aspirations in Palestine. In a conversation with Balfour in January 1917 Wolf said that he and his friends would have no objection if the Jewish community of Palestine

---

* Stein, *The Balfour Declaration*, p. 222.
† Weizmann, *Trial and Error*, p. 150.

developed into a local Jewish nation and a Jewish state, provided it did not claim the allegiance of the Jews of western Europe and did not imperil their status and rights.* Even before, in December 1915, in a memorandum to Grey, Balfour's predecessor, Wolf had stated that while he deplored the Jewish national movement, facts could not be ignored: since Zionism in America had become so powerful in recent months, this movement could not be overlooked by the allied governments in any bid for Jewish sympathies.

Among the men most prominently involved in the activities which led to the Balfour Declaration there was, of course, above all Chaim Weizmann, who had moved from Manchester to London to work for the Ministry of Munitions. According to Lloyd George's memoirs, published many years later, the Declaration was given to Weizmann as a reward for the important work he had done in producing acetone. 'I almost wish that it had been as simple as that', Weizmann commented in his autobiography, 'and that I had never known the heartbreaks, the drudgery and the uncertainties which preceded the Declaration. But history does not deal in Aladdin Lamps.'†

The British government, to recapitulate, was divided in its attitude. One group of politicians and high officials was opposed to the idea of a Jewish Palestine, which it considered absurd, impractical and of no possible value to Britain. Others were on the whole favourably inclined but shied away from the obligations and commitment involved in the project of a British protectorate. They suggested instead a co-dominion together with France, or perhaps the United States. They saw certain advantages in an alliance with Zionism but were also aware of the drawbacks, and they were not altogether sure whether the whole scheme was worthwhile. The issue had not been given much study, and even some of those favourably inclined asked themselves whether Palestine was not too small, whether the Jews were capable of building up the country, and whether, above all, they would in any case go to Palestine if it was given to them. Another group of leading British politicians was firmly committed to the scheme, and it was owing to their resolution that it was accepted. It has been said that the Foreign Office and military experts regarded Palestine as a territory 'of the utmost importance to the future security and well-being of the British empire'.‡ Various committees were

* Stein, *The Balfour Declaration*, p. 144.

† Weizmann, *Trial and Error*, p. 150.

‡ D.Z.Gillon, 'The Antecedents of the Balfour Declaration', *Middle Eastern Studies*, May 1969, pp. 132-3; see also, Aaron S.Klieman, 'Britain's War Aims in the Middle East in 1915', *Journal of Contemporary History*, July 1968, p. 237 *et seq.*

set up during the war to define British desiderata in Turkey-in-Asia, but their reports were never officially endorsed. In any case, the future of Palestine and Zionism were two distinct issues. The fact that a certain British statesman attributed considerable political or strategic importance to Palestine did not necessarily make him a supporter of Dr Weizmann's projects – it could well have, as in Curzon's case, the opposite effect.

Lloyd George has already been mentioned as one of the chief supporters of the pro-Zionist policy. Balfour was another. Weizmann had met him first in Manchester in 1905 and again the year after, and gives the following account of their conversation: discussing the Uganda scheme Weizmann said:

'Mr Balfour, supposing I were to offer you Paris instead of London, would you take it?' He sat up, looked at me and answered: 'But Dr Weizmann we have London.' 'That is true', I said, 'but we had Jerusalem when London was a marsh.' He leaned back, continued to stare at me and said two things which I remember vividly. The first was: 'Are there many Jews who think like you?' I answered: 'I believe I speak the mind of millions of Jews whom you will never see and who cannot speak for themselves.' . . . To this he said: 'If that is so you will one day be a force.'*

Balfour was impressed by Weizmann's personality and the case for Zionism. More than twenty years later he wrote to his niece that it was this talk with Weizmann which brought home to him the uniqueness of Jewish patriotism: 'Their love of their country refused to be satisfied by the Uganda scheme. It was Weizmann's absolute refusal even to look at it that impressed me.'†

Weizmann met Balfour again in 1915–16 when he was first lord of the Admiralty, and incidentally Weizmann's chief, as the Zionist leader had meanwhile become scientific adviser to the Admiralty. Balfour's personality has remained something of a mystery. Some of those who knew him closely speak of his 'heart of stone' and his 'innate cynicism'. Yet he seems to have been firmly convinced that the Jews were the most gifted race produced by mankind since the Greeks; exiled, scattered, and persecuted, Christendom owed them an 'immeasurable debt'.‡ Weizmann always thought that Britain could be induced by a combination of idealism and self-interest to sponsor the building-up of a Jewish national home. But Balfour, the alleged cynic, was not particularly interested in

* Weizmann, *Trial and Error*, p. 111.
† Stein, *The Balfour Declaration*, p. 152.
‡ *Ibid.*, p. 157.

strategic considerations and the effect on America of a pro-Zionist declaration was not for him the decisive factor either. By nature inclined towards compromise, he was not willing to listen to arguments against Zionism; on this subject his mind was shut. As Lord Vansittart later wrote, Balfour cared for one thing only – Zionism.*

Some supported Zionism because it was a cause in the tradition of philhellenism and the Risorgimento, which had so powerfully attracted previous generations of Englishmen. There was also the religious factor. For Balfour, as for Lloyd George and Smuts and not a few of their contemporaries, the Bible was a living reality. Lloyd George once told Mrs Rothschild that the biblical names brought up in his meetings with Dr Weizmann were much more familiar to him than the towns and villages in the communiqués from the western front. The concept of the return, Weizmann later wrote, appealed to the tradition and the faith of these British statesmen. Their approach to state problems differed from that of a later age: 'The so-called realism of modern politics is not realism at all, but pure opportunism, lack of moral stamina, lack of vision and the principle of living from hand to mouth.'† England believed, according to Weizmann, that she had no business in Palestine except as part of the plan for the creation of the Jewish homeland. He would not have succeeded had he based his arguments on British self-interest alone, for these considerations were not weighty enough. British statesmen had several options in the Near East. Zionism was one of them, but neither the most important nor the most promising. A British protectorate was bound to create tension with France, the Liberals were against any further extension of the empire, and by the time the Balfour Declaration was published America had joined the Allies and there was no longer any urgent need to appease American Jewry. Self-interest by itself cannot provide a satisfactory explanation for British policy on Palestine in 1917.

The Zionists were not the only ones with designs in the Near East. While Weizmann and his colleagues tried to win support for their cause in London and Washington, negotiations were proceeding unknown to them, notes were being exchanged and agreements signed, which were directly to affect the future of Palestine. Sir Henry McMahon, Kitchener's successor as high commissioner in Egypt, came to an agreement with Sherif Hussain of Mecca: the sherif (to put a complex issue very briefly) undertook to expel the Turks from the Arab area and in

---

* Sykes, *Two Studies in Virtue*, p. 193; Stein, *The Balfour Declaration*, p. 158.
† Weizmann, *Trial and Error*, p. 178.

return the British were to recognise Arab independence. The question that matters in the present context is whether Palestine was included in the promise made to Hussain.

The debate about this point has continued for fifty years. Arab spokesmen have maintained that Palestine was to be part of independent Arabia, whereas McMahon and the English statesmen deny this.* Be that as it may, the British could always argue that they were not really bound by the deal, for the sherif had not fulfilled his part of the bargain; a general Arab insurrection was planned but never took place. Lloyd George put it somewhat harshly: 'The Arabs of Palestine, who might have been helpful in many ways, were quiescent and cowering . . . they were fighting against us.'

More important, and potentially more dangerous from the Zionist point of view, was the Sykes-Picot agreement. Sir Mark Sykes, representing the British Foreign Office, and Charles Georges Picot, on behalf of the French Foreign Ministry, prepared a draft agreement in 1915 concerning the postwar division of the Near East. It was approved in principle by Russia, provisionally signed in January 1916, and ratified (in the form of an exchange of notes between Sir Edward Grey and Paul Cambon) in May 1916. Under this agreement Palestine was to be part of the British sphere of influence, with the exception of a section of the country north of a line from Acre to the northern end of Lake Tiberias, which was to belong to the French zone. In addition, vague provisions were made for an international zone including the Holy Places (the Jerusalem enclave).† The Sykes-Picot agreement was of importance, because it bound the hands of the British government in its negotiations with the Zionists.

Weizmann learned of its existence only a year later. The British representative, Sykes, secretary to the war cabinet, became one of the most ardent supporters of the Zionist cause, so much so that he began to suspect all anti-Zionist Jews of harbouring secret pro-German leanings.‡ But Sykes' conversion took place only after the agreement with the French had been provisionally signed, and he found himself in the uncomfortable position of not being able to reveal its existence to his new friends. It has been argued that by 1917 Sykes had second thoughts about

---

* The debate is analysed in I.Friedman, 'The McMahon-Hussain Correspondence and the Question of Palestine', *Journal of Contemporary History*, April 1970. See also Arnold Toynbee's reply, *ibid.*, October 1970.

† On the making of the Sykes-Picot agreement, see E.Kedourie, *England and the Middle East*, London, 1956, pp. 29–66.

‡ Stein, *The Balfour Declaration*, p. 276.

the wisdom of the agreement with the French, and regarded the Zionist demand for a British protectorate as a 'golden opportunity to wriggle out of the 1916 agreement'.* But this is to ascribe to Sykes an undue measure of Machiavellianism and to underrate his genuine enthusiasm for the Zionist cause. He was a generous and warm-hearted man, as Weizmann described him, a colourful and romantic figure, not very consistent or logical in his thinking. His advice to the Zionists was invaluable. He helped them to keep up the pressure on the government when the issue was temporarily shelved and (again to quote Weizmann) prevented them from committing dangerous blunders. Sykes was equally fervent in his support for the Arab and Armenian national movements and envisaged close collaboration between them and Zionism.†

Despite the sympathy in high places, the memoranda and meetings, Zionism had not made any marked progress by the second and third years of the war. The British cabinet was preoccupied with problems infinitely more urgent than Palestine. The war was going on, and it was not going too well. France showed no enthusiasm for a Jewish commonwealth in Palestine under British rule, and the Americans had not yet made their influence felt. It was against this background that the cabinet crisis of December 1916 took place which led to Asquith's resignation. Lloyd George became prime minister, Balfour foreign secretary, and Milner a member of the war cabinet. These three sympathised with Zionism, and Lord Robert Cecil, assistant foreign secretary, was also a warm supporter. On the other hand, the Zionists lost in Herbert Samuel their closest ally, and Edwin Montagu, a bitter opponent, returned to the government after a short interval.

The change of government coincided with a military offensive in the Near East. The Sinai peninsula had been occupied by an expeditionary corps from Egypt in late 1916. An assault on Gaza in March 1917 ended in failure, but the war cabinet decided nevertheless on 2 April in favour of the invasion of Palestine. Sykes advised his Zionist friends as early as January to be prepared to have men on the spot when the British entered Jerusalem.‡

In February 1917 the first full-dress conference took place which led to the Balfour Declaration. Sykes and Samuel were present, as well as the leading Zionists and two members of the Rothschild family. The

---

* Gillon, 'The Antecedents of the Balfour Declaration', p. 133; see also B.Halpern, *The Idea of the Jewish State*, Cambridge, 1961, p. 276.
† Kedourie, *England and the Middle East*, p. 86.
‡ Stein, *The Balfour Declaration*, p. 331.

meeting decided against a co-dominion or the internationalisation of Palestine in favour of a British protectorate.* Sykes impressed on the gathering the importance of the rising Arab national movement and said that France was the main obstacle to the realisation of Zionist aims. It was decided to send Sokolow to Paris and Rome to induce the French and the Italians to soften their opposition, and, if at all possible, to extract a declaration of sympathy. The mission was a qualified success inasmuch as Sokolow received a letter from Cambon expressing sympathy for the renaissance of the 'Jewish nationality in that land from which the people of Israel were exiled so many years ago'.†

In Paris Sokolow was treading on thin ice because he knew from Picot that France wanted Palestine for herself and was not willing to consider co-dominion with Britain, or, worse yet, with the United States.‡ Weizmann, on the other hand, was most anxious that Sokolow should not leave any doubt in Paris that the Zionist executive preferred Britain, and he was critical of Sokolow, who apparently had not said so *expressis verbis* in his meetings with French diplomats. Weizmann feared to arouse suspicion in the Foreign Office, whereas Sykes was much less sensitive in this respect. He assumed, correctly as it appeared, that any French declaration, however vague, in favour of Zionist aspirations would strengthen the Zionist case in the Foreign Office.

Sokolow subsequently received similar assurances in Rome and the Vatican. He was told that he could count on the sympathy of the Church provided the Church received assurances about the Holy Places. Cardinal Gasparri, papal secretary of state, said in conversation that he envisaged 'reserved areas', to include not only Jerusalem and Bethlehem, but also Nazareth and its surroundings, Tiberias and even Jericho. Sokolow was dejected, for not much would have remained for a Jewish national home, but Sykes, a devout Catholic, again felt happy about the outcome of the meeting. What counted at this stage was that His Holiness had declared: 'Si, io credo che noi saremo buoni vicini' (I believe we shall be good neighbours).§

Sokolow returned to London in the middle of June 1917. His conversations had advanced the Zionist cause, but there were still certain doubts in the Foreign Office as to whether it was wise to aim at a British protectorate. Would it not be more feasible for the country to be

* N.Gelber, *Hazharat Balfour vetoldoteha*, Jerusalem, 1939, pp. 59–61.

† N.Sokolow, *Geschichte des Zionismus*, Berlin, 1921, vol. 2, p. 386.

‡ Stein, *The Balfour Declaration*, p. 399.

§ Sykes, *Two Studies in Virtue*, p. 202; see also Gelber, *Hazharat Balfour vetoldoteha* p. 85 *et seq.*

administered under an international mandate after the war? Weizmann had meanwhile learned about the Sykes-Picot agreement and had protested vigorously to the Foreign Office, claiming that it would be preferable to leave Palestine to Turkey rather than internationalise it.* But he was still optimistic that his plan for a British protectorate would eventually materialise, and in a speech in London on 20 May 1917 he said he knew that the British government was prepared to support the Zionist plans. It is not quite clear whether he was entitled to make such a statement or whether he wanted to force the hands of the Foreign Office.

Weizmann had been prepared to leave London for Egypt following Sykes' advice, which was based on the assumption that British troops from Egypt would occupy Palestine during the spring or early summer. But there was no spring or summer offensive. General Murray showed little initiative, and for the chief of the imperial general staff the Palestine theatre did not have high priority. Lloyd George saw the situation in a very different light. On the conduct of the war he was a confirmed 'easterner', remarking on one occasion that the Palestinian front was the only one he found interesting. Allenby, newly appointed, was told that the war cabinet expected the capture of Jerusalem before Christmas 1917.†

Weizmann had met both Lloyd George and Balfour in March and April 1917 and gained the impression that the statesmen who really mattered were unshaken in their support for a British protectorate over Palestine. During the summer of 1917 there was a palpable change in the political climate, reflected *inter alia* in the friendly comments of *The Times* on the idea of a Jewish national home. The Conjoint Committee was more dismayed than ever by this turn of events and its leaders decided to pass over to the offensive: Wolf had seen Balfour in January 1917, shortly after the new government had come to power, and had restated the opposition of his association to Zionist aspirations. Balfour promised that the committee would be consulted on Jewish affairs, but also suggested that Wolf and his friends should refrain from polemics against the Zionists.

The anti-Zionists, annoyed by Weizmann's speech of 20 May, in which he had referred to them as a 'small minority', decided to ignore Balfour's advice. Four days later a letter signed by David Alexander and Claude Montefiore, the presidents of the Board of Deputies and the Anglo-Jewish Association, appeared in *The Times* under the heading

* Stein, *The Balfour Declaration*, pp. 391-2.
† D.Lloyd George, *War Memoirs*, London, 1936, vol. 4, p. 1835.

'Palestine and Zionism – Views of Anglo-Jewry'. They reiterated their protest against the Zionist theory of a homeless nationality, which, if generally accepted, would have the effect everywhere of stamping Jews as strangers in their native lands. A Jewish political nationality was an anachronism; religion was the only certain criterion. The signatories also said that it would be a calamity if Jewish settlers in Palestine were to get special rights in the way of political privileges or economic preferences. This was in contradiction to the principle of equal rights for all. It would compromise the Jews wherever they had secured equal rights and would involve the Palestinian Jews in the bitterest feuds with their neighbours of other races.*

The opening of the press campaign backfired. The fact that the leaders of the Conjoint Committee had thought it right to air an internal Jewish quarrel in *The Times* made a bad impression in the community. In a reply the chief rabbi, Lord Walter Rothschild, and other prominent Jewish leaders dissociated themselves from the Alexander-Montefiore statement.† Less than a month later the Board of Deputies passed a vote of no-confidence in the Conjoint Committee. This resulted in the resignation of the president of the board, and in September 1917, in the dissolution of the committee. The ordinary Jews – Leonard Stein writes – were in growing numbers gravitating towards Zionism. They were none too clear in their minds what they wanted or expected to see in Palestine, 'they had simply an instinctive feeling that the Zionists were moving in the right direction and ought not to be obstructed. Moreover, the battle between Zionists and anti-Zionists was mixed up with a struggle for power inside Anglo-Jewry.' The affairs of the community were still managed by representatives of a few rich, socially eminent families. Their 'benevolent oligarchical régime' was out of touch with the new forces which were emerging in the community and insisting on playing their part in the inner circles of Anglo-Jewish representation.‡

In mid-May 1917, Morgenthau, a former American ambassador to Constantinople, had been commissioned by President Wilson to explore the possibilities of a separate peace with Turkey. This caused some concern in the Foreign Office and even more among the Zionists because the mission, if successful, might have left Palestine part of the Ottoman empire. Weizmann was sent to Gibraltar to meet the American emissary and to try to dissuade him from pursuing his mission, without unduly

* *The Times*, 24 May 1917.
† Sokolow, *Geschichte des Zionismus*, vol. 2, pp. 391–8.
‡ Stein, *The Balfour Declaration*, pp. 446–8.

offending Morgenthau or President Wilson. In fact, the whole idea of a separate peace with Turkey had not been well thought out or prepared. The scope of the venture was not clear and Weizmann did not find it too difficult to persuade Morgenthau to desist.

The mobilisation of Jewish public opinion in the *entente* countries in support of Zionist aspirations played an important part in the prehistory of the Balfour Declaration. Brandeis was all in favour of the plan for a British protectorate, being fully aware that the American government would be averse to the idea of a co-dominion or protectorate. Surprisingly, Weizmann and Sokolow found the going much more difficult in Russia. According to Chlenov, the provisional government which had replaced the tsar was well-disposed towards the Zionist movement, but Palestine did not figure high among its priorities, and the Russian Zionists were less happy than Weizmann about the whole scheme; their earlier admiration for Britain had been deeply affected by its support for the tsarist régime. Moreover, it was well known that the British ambassador and some leading British journalists in Petrograd were not at all friendly towards Russian Jewry. There were doubts whether Weizmann's total identification with British war aims was not imprudent. Britain had yet to make a clear promise with regard to Palestine's future. The Russian Zionists were unwilling to press in Petrograd for support for a scheme which the British had themselves not yet endorsed. Was it certain that Britain was going to pursue the Palestine campaign? And what if it did not succeed in liberating Palestine from the Turks?* Chlenov would have preferred a Jewish national home recognised by all the powers to one exclusively oriented towards Britain. Weizmann was exasperated. There was talk about dispatching Sokolow to Russia, but in the end the London Zionists had to manage without a clear statement of Russian support.

In his meetings with Balfour and Lloyd George in March and April 1917 Weizmann had gained the impression (to recapitulate) that the prime minister and his foreign secretary were committed to the idea of a Jewish Palestine under a British protectorate. But the decisive issue was how to translate the intention into practical politics. In June and July, while Weizmann was in Gibraltar, the other Zionist leaders in London drafted for consideration by the cabinet the text of a letter of support to be issued by the British government. According to the draft, prepared by Sacher, Britain was to declare that the reconstitution of Palestine as a Jewish state was one of its essential war aims. Sokolow thought this was

* *Ibid.*, p. 441.

too ambitious: 'If we ask for too much we shall get nothing.' On the other hand, he was certain that once a sympathetic declaration was issued, the Zionists would gradually get more and more.* His caution seems to have been justified, for when the Foreign Office began its own drafting, it employed terms such as 'asylum' and 'refuge' and the establishment of a 'sanctuary' for Jewish victims of persecution. This, needless to say, was rejected by the Zionists, who insisted that the declaration would have no value at all unless the principle of recognising Palestine as the National Home of the Jewish People was affirmed. Eventually, on 18 July, Rothschild submitted a compromise formula to Balfour. It mentioned not a Jewish state but a National Home, and proposed that the British government should discuss with the Zionist organisation ways and means of achieving this object. Two days before Rothschild dispatched his letter, it was reported that Edwin Montagu had rejoined the cabinet. Rothschild said he was afraid that as a result the Zionist cause had suffered a major, perhaps a fatal setback. Weizmann was less pessimistic, but he too considered the situation disturbing and wrote later: 'There cannot be the slightest doubt that without outside interference – entirely from Jews – the draft would have been accepted early in August substantially as we submitted it.'†

The Rothschild draft was submitted to the war cabinet for the first time in early August 1917, but its discussion was postponed. It reappeared on the agenda on 3 September. Both Lloyd George and Balfour were absent on this occasion, and Montagu vehemently opposed the scheme. To gain time, it was decided to ask President Wilson for advice. This came as a cold douche for the Zionists, and Wilson's first, non-committal comment aggravated the situation even further. But Weizmann and his colleagues did not accept defeat. They saw Balfour and prepared a new memorandum for the next cabinet meeting on 4 October. This time the pro-Zionist forces (with the exception of Smuts) were present in full strength. They included the prime minister, the foreign secretary, and Milner.

Montagu was aware that he was fighting a losing battle, but persisted in his opposition. He made a long, forceful, emotional appeal to his colleagues: how could he represent the British government during his forthcoming mission to India if the same government declared that his (Montagu's) national home was on Turkish territory? He was supported by Curzon, who raised a number of practical issues: Palestine was

* *Ibid.*, p. 466.
† Weizmann, *Trial and Error*, p. 204.

not big enough to absorb large-scale immigration; and how was the Arab problem to be settled? The cabinet resolved to consult President Wilson once again, but this time there was an element of urgency in Balfour's arguments. He announced that the German government was making great efforts to woo the Zionists, who had the backing of the majority of Jews. The American attitude, he added, was extremely favourable.*

A decision was clearly about to be taken despite Montagu's rearguard action. The main danger from the Zionist point of view was that it would be watered down. A little comedy of errors was enacted while the cabinet was in session. Weizmann was so agitated that he found it impossible to continue to work in his laboratory. He went to Philip Kerr, Lloyd George's secretary, and enquired whether he should be available in case the cabinet wished to question him. He was told that a private person had never been admitted to one of its sessions. He still found it impossible to return to his laboratory and went instead to the nearby office of Ormsby Gore. Then, immediately after Montagu's speech, the cabinet decided to call in Dr Weizmann and messengers were sent for him. 'They looked for me high and low – and I happened to be a few doors away.'†
At first he feared that he had missed a great opportunity, but many years later realised that he might have been carried away on that occasion and made matters worse.

The campaign now reached its climax. Wilson's answer this time was one of unequivocal support. As the anti-Zionists in the Jewish community mobilised their sympathisers, Weizmann countered with a list of 350 Jewish communities which supported the Rothschild draft. But at the next meeting of the war cabinet on 25 October again no final decision was taken, because Curzon announced that he was about to submit a memorandum on the question.‡ The Zionists and the Foreign Office regarded this as mere obstruction. They expected, rightly as it appeared a few days later, no new arguments. Curzon contended that the land was too poor, the climate inclement, the people dependent on the export of agricultural products. In brief, Palestine would not do as a national home for the Jews. He was all in favour of increased Jewish immigration from eastern Europe and giving the Jews the same civic and religious rights as the other inhabitants. But this was of course not what the Zionists

---

* War cabinet meeting, 4 October 1917: PRO London, cab. 23–4, 245. Quoted in Zechlin, *Die deutsche Politik* . . . , p. 407.

† Weizmann, *Trial and Error*, p. 206.

‡ PRO, 25 October 1917, cab. 23–4. Quoted in Zechlin, *Die deutsche Politik* . . . , p. 409.

wanted.* At the next cabinet meeting on 31 October Curzon gave in. Leopold Amery had been commissioned earlier by Balfour to prepare a draft for a declaration which would take into account both the aims of the Zionists and, to a certain extent, the objections of their critics. This accounts for the absence of any reference to a Jewish state in the Balfour Declaration. Zionist leaders themselves had made it known that the argument that the Jews wanted a state was 'wholly fallacious', that it was not in fact part of the Zionist programme.†

The Amery draft was circulated to various Jewish personalities, and the chief rabbi gave an assurance that the proposed declaration would be approved by the overwhelming majority of Jews. Other correspondents were less sanguine. At the decisive cabinet meeting of 31 October, Balfour left open the question whether the national home would take the form of a British or an American protectorate, or whether there would be some other arrangement. At the end of the debate he was authorised to write to Lord Rothschild the following letter with the request to bring it to the knowledge of the Zionist Federation:

Dear Lord Rothschild,

I have much pleasure in conveying to you, on behalf of His Majesty's government, the following declaration of sympathy with Jewish Zionist aspirations, which has been submitted to, and approved by, the cabinet.

'His Majesty's government views with favour the establishment in Palestine of a national home for the Jewish people, and will use their best endeavours to facilitate the achievement of this object, it being clearly understood that nothing shall be done which may prejudice the civil and religious rights of existing non-Jewish communities in Palestine, or the rights and political status enjoyed by Jews in any other country.'

While the cabinet was in session, approving the final text, Weizmann was again waiting outside, this time within call. Sykes brought the document out and exclaimed: 'Dr Weizmann, it's a boy!' Weizmann says he did not like the boy, he was not the one he had expected. But he knew that the new formula, however emasculated, was a tremendous event in Jewish history, a new departure.‡

The news of the Declaration was published in the British press on 8 November 1917, appearing side by side with reports from Petrograd about the Bolshevik revolution. The newspapers took it for granted that

---

* D. Lloyd George, *The Truth about the Peace Treaties*, London, 1938, vol. 2, p. 1123 *et seq.*
† N. Sokolow, *History of Zionism*, London, 1919, vol. 1, p. xxv.
‡ Weizmann, *Trial and Error*, pp. 207–8.

this 'epoch-making' event was to pave the way for a Jewish state: the *Daily Express* carried a headline 'A State for the Jews'; *The Times* and the *Morning Post* chose 'Palestine for the Jews'. The *Observer* wrote that there could not have been at this juncture a stroke of statesmanship more just and more wise.* The Jewish community was jubilant, and the enthusiasm of American and Russian Jewry was expressed in hundreds of resolutions. Henri Bergson, George Brandes and other public figures, alienated from Judaism and Jewish affairs, expressed their satisfaction and willingness to help in the building of the new Palestine.

Even the leaders of German Zionism, despite their precarious position – they could not of course associate themselves with the war aims of the British government – welcomed the Declaration as an event of world-historical importance, the longest step by far on the road towards the realisation of the Basle programme.† They redoubled their efforts to obtain a declaration from Germany and Turkey showing equal sympathy with Zionist aspirations. On 12 November the text of the Balfour Declaration was officially communicated to the German Foreign Ministry, and a meeting was requested with the state secretary. But Herr von Kühlmann was very busy; he could not see the Zionist leaders. His reply reflected the reluctance of the German government to come to the aid of the Zionists. On the other hand, Count Czernin, the Austrian foreign minister, received a Zionist delegation in November 1917 and promised support.‡ The Zionist executive made full use of the announcement, which was, however, of doubtful value. Austria could not dispose of Palestine, and, weakened as it was, now counted for little in world politics.§

When the Turkish ambassador in Berlin complained that the executive had welcomed the Balfour Declaration, Professor Warburg, still its titular head, replied that, on the contrary, he himself had been guilty of deviating from the principle of Zionist neutralism: Zionism was an international movement, but he had regarded it as his duty, both as a Zionist and a German, to remain at its helm, believing in the identity of interests between Germany, Turkey and Zionism. Or did the Turks want the transfer of the headquarters of the Zionist movement to a country hostile to Turkey?‖

---

* Stein, *The Balfour Declaration*, pp. 560–2.
† *Jüdische Rundschau*, 16 November 1917.
‡ Zechlin, *Die deutsche Politik . . .*, p. 420.
§ *Jüdische Rundschau*, 30 November 1917.
‖ Zechlin, *Die deutsche Politik . . .*, p. 422.

Neither side in the war had strictly adhered to the declared principle of Zionist neutrality. Both were genuinely convinced that the Zionist cause would best be served by the victory of their side. This went so far that on occasion the Jews on one side attacked their co-religionists on the other, as when a prominent British Jew, Sir Stuart Samuel, president of the Board of Deputies, suggested to the British government in 1917 that German and Austrian Jews should be excluded from Palestine for twenty years as a punishment. Kurt Blumenfeld realised to his astonishment at the first postwar meeting of Zionist leaders that the '*entente*' Zionists regarded the 'central power' Zionists, too, as the losers.

Neither the French nor the Italians reacted favourably to the Balfour Declaration. In a statement after the fall of Jerusalem, the Quai d'Orsay, ignoring the Balfour Declaration, announced that Palestine was to be internationalised. Two months later, following instructions from Clemenceau, Pichon stated that there was complete agreement between Britain and France on matters concerning *un Etablissement Juif* in Palestine.* But for both men the whole issue was of no great consequence, a mere public-relations gesture, and French diplomacy retreated subsequently from this profession of goodwill. The Italian Foreign Ministry would have preferred an international régime in Palestine to a British protectorate. It took Sokolow six months to extract a statement mentioning the establishment in Palestine of a Hebrew national centre while leaving open the question of the protectorate.

President Wilson had informally expressed support for the Balfour Declaration, but he was under pressure from Lansing, his secretary of state, not to commit himself publicly. Lansing pointed out that America was not at war with Turkey, that the Jews themselves were divided about the merits of Zionism, and that the other traditional interests in the Holy Land could not be ignored.† It was ten months before, prodded by Stephen Wise, Wilson made another statement assuring the Zionists of his support. There was, needless to say, little enthusiasm on the part of the new Bolshevik government in Petrograd. Lenin and Trotsky had only just seized power; Palestine was remote and unimportant. Later, when they came to reflect on the Balfour Declaration, they concluded that it was an imperialist intrigue, part of an overall network of anti-Soviet schemes, arranged to strengthen British imperialist interests against the world revolution.

We have retraced in broad outline the developments that eventually

* Stein, *The Balfour Declaration*, p. 590.
† *Ibid.*, p. 593.

led to the Balfour Declaration. The main milestones on this road are not in dispute, but the causes, as usual, are. Why did the British government decide to make the Declaration and what did it expect from it? It may be useful to put the issue into a broader perspective: for the Zionists this was the central political problem, whereas for the British leaders (not to mention the French and the Americans) it was marginal. Neither the friends nor the enemies of the Zionist cause had the time or interest to engage in a thorough study of its various aspects. Hence the frequent inconsistencies in their attitude. There was no more enthusiastic Zionist than Sir Mark Sykes, no one less patient with anti-Zionist arguments. But Sykes was also convinced that the objects of Zionism did not involve a Jewish state, and he advised the Jews in their own interest to look at the problem through Arab eyes.* Lord Cecil, assistant foreign secretary, declared in December 1917 at a public meeting: 'Our wish is that the Arabian countries shall be for the Arabs, Armenia for the Armenians and Judaea for the Jews.' Yet only a few weeks later he informed the American ambassador that all the British government had done was to give a pledge to put the Jews in Palestine on the same footing as other nationalities and to see that there should be no discrimination against them.† Such inconsistencies do not necessarily reflect Machiavellian schemes and hidden designs. The Balfour Declaration was, as Leonard Stein has pointed out, not a legal but a political document, and a fairly vague one at that. It could be interpreted in different ways, and as the international situation was so fluid, the interpretation changed from week to week.

There is conflicting evidence as to what Balfour, Lloyd George and others expected to happen in Palestine after the war. It has been argued that there never was any intention to establish a Jewish state, but this opinion was probably coloured by subsequent developments, by the fact that after 1918 influential circles within the British government gradually dissociated themselves from the original concept. There is no reason to disbelieve Forbes Adams, the Foreign Office expert on Palestine, who wrote before this change in climate took place that the intention of the British government was to create a state in Palestine and to turn it into a Jewish state.‡ Such a transformation was expected to take years, perhaps many years. Lloyd George, two decades later, wrote that the war cabinet did not intend to set up a Jewish state immediately, but that

* *Ibid.*, p. 284.
† *Ibid.*, p. 554.
‡ *Ibid.*, p. 554.

it was contemplated that Palestine would become a Jewish common-wealth after the Jews had responded to the opportunity afforded them and become a majority of the inhabitants.

Some of the reasons which helped to induce the British government to enter into a commitment *vis-à-vis* the Zionist movement have been mentioned; they were aware that the goodwill of world Jewry was an important if intangible factor. The year 1917 was not a happy one for the Allies, and they needed all the assistance they could get. The support of American Jewry for the allied cause was no longer an issue of paramount importance, since America had entered the war. But Russia was about to leave it, and thus Russian Jewry became a factor of some significance. Sir Ronald Graham, head of the Eastern Department of the Foreign Office, wrote in a memorandum dated 24 October 1917 that the Zionists might be thrown into the arms of the Germans unless an assurance of sympathy was given to them: 'The moment this assurance is granted, the Zionist Jews are prepared to start an active pro-allied propaganda throughout the world.'*

During the autumn of 1917 the situation in Russia became more and more critical. The country was exhausted, and it seemed doubtful whether the provisional government would be able to stay in power. If Russia left the war, no great powers of prediction were needed to realise that the allied forces in the west would at once be subjected to heavier German pressure: the great offensive in France had been a failure, and the Italian army was facing a critical situation. No substantial American forces had as yet appeared in Europe. In this situation, and in view of the fact that Jews were conspicuous in the Russian revolutionary movement, allied efforts to win over Russian Jewry did not come as a surprise. But it is unlikely that any British statesmen expected immediate, dramatic returns. According to the advice the British government received from Petrograd, Russian Jews were not important politically and the less said and done about the subject the better, Ambassador Buchanan had written earlier in the war. He thought (as his colleagues in Washington did) that the weight of the Jews was usually overrated and that it was hardly worth investing great efforts to win their support.

The war cabinet did not quite share this opinion. It took a graver view of the deteriorating situation in Russia and of the spread of pacifist attitudes in both Russia and America. But this (to quote Leonard Stein again) does not answer the question why the Zionists were taken seriously enough for the British government to enter into a long-term moral

* Quoted in Gillon, 'The Antecedents of the Balfour Declaration,' p. 147.

obligation towards Zionism. Its ambassadors in Washington and Petrograd, and the other critics of Zionism were, after all, not seriously mistaken in their assessment of Zionist influence. Russian Jewry was divided in its attitude towards Zionism and a Jewish national home, and would not in any case have been able to keep Russia in the war. The Allies, on the other hand – to put it somewhat crudely – would have won the war even if no promise to the Zionists had been made. Even in the third year of the war Zionism was only a minor factor in world politics.

It is true that early in December Weizmann cabled Rozov, the Russian Zionist leader, to do all he could to strengthen pro-British sentiment in Russian Jewry and counter adverse influences. 'Remember the providential coincidence of British and Jewish interests. We rely on your doing your utmost at this critical and solemn hour. Wire what steps you propose to take.'*

But neither allied difficulties nor Zionist strength were great enough to make this explanation wholly convincing. When, at a private gathering soon after the event, Balfour was asked whether it had been his intention to make a bid for Jewish support in the war, he replied: 'Certainly not.' He and Lloyd George wanted to give the Jews their rightful place in the world. It was not right, they felt, that a great nation should be deprived of a home.† Balfour believed, as Lloyd George did, that the Jews had been wronged by Christendom for almost two thousand years and that they had a claim to reparation. The whole culture of Europe, he said in a speech in 1922, had been guilty of great crimes against the Jews, and the British had at last taken the initiative in giving them the opportunity of developing in peace the great gifts which in the past they had been able to apply only in the countries of the diaspora.‡ Balfour thus had the feeling that he was instrumental in righting a wrong of world-historical dimensions, quite irrespective of the changing world situation. There was a similar element in Lloyd George's thinking. He once told Mrs James de Rothschild about Weizmann: 'When you and I are forgotten this man will have a monument to him in Palestine.'§

Such reference to moral considerations and issues of principle have appeared naïve, if not disingenuous, to latter-day historians and have been flatly rejected by some of them. Surely there must have been more tangible interests involved? It is, of course, quite true that the British

* Jon Kimche, *The Unromantics: The Great Powers and the Balfour Declaration*, London, 1968, p. 45.
† Quoted in Stein, *The Balfour Declaration*, p. 552.
‡ *Ibid.*, p. 160.
§ Weizmann, *Trial and Error*, p. 152.

statesmen of the day were convinced that the aims of Zionism were not incompatible with those of Britain in the Near East, for otherwise no support would have been forthcoming. But having established this obvious fact, we still know very little about the deeper motives. There is a temptation to explain them in terms of the psychology of British statesmen of a later age, but such an approach ignores the profound changes resulting from five decades of imperial decline. Principles counted for more at that time, and there was wider scope for disinterested action. It was still possible for a British government to take decisions from time to time which were of no obvious political, economic or military benefit. The Balfour Declaration may well have been the 'last wholly independent imperial act of a British government done without any reference at all to pressure from any other great state or combination of states'.*

The Declaration fell short in most essential respects of Zionist aspirations. It was so cautiously worded that it left the future of Palestine wide open. It stated that Britain would 'facilitate' the establishment of a national home, but it did not commit itself to the idea of a British protectorate or mandate. It made no promise that there would be a Jewish commonwealth or state in Palestine; there was merely reference to a Jewish home, which did not exclude other national homes. There was no mention of Jewish autonomy or that the Jews would have a preponderant influence on the future of Palestine. It did not promise that the Zionist Organisation or any other Jewish body would participate in the administration of the country. Much of this may have been implicit in the thoughts of the authors of the Declaration, but these principles were not spelled out in the watered-down version. Hence the lack of enthusiasm on the part of Weizmann and his colleagues upon receiving the news that this vague formula had been accepted instead of the more concrete and stronger one suggested by them earlier on. But the spirit of elation which attended the announcement of the Declaration affected not only the Jewish masses, who did not know about the struggle behind the scenes which had preceded it – Weizmann himself was infected by it. Sokolow commented on the event in biblical terms and references: 'Mid storm and fire the people and the land seemed to be born again. The great events of the time of Zerubabel, Ezra and Nehemiah repeated themselves. The Third Temple of Jewish freedom is rising before us.'†

After the publication of Herzl's *Judenstaat* and the first Zionist congress, the Balfour Declaration was the second great turning-point in the history

* Sykes, *Two Studies in Virtue*, pp. 233-4.
† Sokolow, *History of Zionism*, vol. 2, p. 84.

of political Zionism. But it was not immediate redemption, only the beginning of a new phase in an uphill struggle, which in some respects was even more arduous than earlier ones. A leading British newspaper, commenting on the Balfour Declaration, wrote that it was no idle dream to anticipate that by the close of another generation the new Zion might be a state 'including, no doubt, only a pronounced minority of the entire Jewish race, yet numbering from a million to two million souls, forming a true national people, with its own distinctive, rural and urban civilisation, its own centres of learning and art.'* It was a remarkably acute forecast, yet it would never have materialised but for another world war, untold suffering and losses to the Jewish people, and, in the end, the abdication of the very power which had given Zionism its great chance in 1917.

* *Observer*, quoted in Sokolow, *ibid.*, p. 86.

PART TWO

5

THE UNSEEN QUESTION

Zionism and the Arab Problem

Among the Jewish workers who demonstrated in Tel Aviv on 1 May 1921, the day of international working-class solidarity, there was a small group of Communists who distributed leaflets in Arabic calling the downtrodden and exploited masses to rise against British imperialism. Expelled from the ranks of the parade, they were last seen disappearing with their leaflets into the small streets between Tel Aviv and Jaffa. A few hours later a wave of Arab attacks on Jews in Jaffa started, triggered off, the Arabs claimed, by the provocation of the godless Bolsheviks, whose propaganda had aroused great indignation among the local population. In the course of these riots and of the subsequent military operations, 95 persons were killed and 219 seriously wounded.

The disturbances of May 1921, following the riots in Jerusalem and the attacks in Galilee the previous year, shocked and confused the Zionists.* Many of them became aware for the first time of the danger of a major conflict between the two peoples. It was asserted that Zionist ignorance and ineptitude were to blame, for at the time of the Balfour Declaration the Muslims had been well disposed towards the Jews, but had not found among them understanding and a willingness to compromise. Consequently they had made common cause with the Christian Arab leaders against the 'Zionist peril'. Whatever the cause of the 1921 riots, whatever the explanations offered and accepted, from then on the Arab question began to figure increasingly in the discussions at Zionist congresses, in internal controversies, and of course in Zionist diplomacy.

Yet fifteen years later, when the Arab question had become the most important issue in Zionist politics, critics were once again to argue in almost identical terms that the movement was now paying the price for having so long ignored the existence of the Arabs, their interests and their

* Jakob Klatzkin, in *Die Araberfrage in Palästina*, Heidelberg, 1921, p. 21; Dr M.Lewite, 'Zur Orientierung in der arabischen Frage', *Jüdische Rundschau*, 5 August 1921.

national aspirations. It was also said that but for this neglect a conflict between the peoples could have been prevented. The Zionists, the critics claimed, had acted as though Palestine was an empty country: 'Herzl visits Palestine but seems to find nobody there but his fellow Jews; Arabs apparently vanish before him as in their own Arabian nights.'* 'If you look at prewar Zionist literature', Dr Weizmann said in a speech in 1931, 'you will find hardly a word about the Arabs.'† This implied that the Zionist leaders had been half aware of the existence of the Arabs but for reasons of their own had acted as if they did not exist. Or had it been a case of real, if astonishing blindness?

The issue was in fact considerably more complex. The Zionists certainly paid little attention to the first stirrings of the Arab national movement and few envisaged the possibility of a clash of national interests. But they did of course know that several hundred thousand Arabs lived in Palestine and that these constituted the majority of the local population. Even the pre-Herzlian Zionists were aware of the fact that Palestine was not quite empty. Rabbi Kalischer, who had never been anywhere near the Holy Land, wrote in 1862 about the danger of Arab banditry, anticipating the question whether Jewish settlers would be safe in such a country. The Russian Zionists in their writings in the early 1880s expressed confidence that Jews and Arabs could live together in peace. Lilienblum noted the existence of an Arab population, but said that it was small and backward, and that if a hundred thousand Jewish families were to settle over a period of twenty years, the Jews would no longer be strangers to the Arabs. Levanda argued that both Arabs and Jews would profit from Jewish settlement. When Ahad Ha'am went to Palestine in 1891 he reported that the country was not empty, that the Arabs, and above all the town dwellers among them, were quite aware of Jewish activities and desires, but pretended not to notice them so long as they seemed to constitute no real danger. But if one day the Jews were to become stronger and threaten Arab predominance, they would hardly take this quietly.‡

In Herzl's mind the Arabs certainly did not figure prominently, though he did not ignore them altogether. He met individual Arabs and corresponded with a few of them. He was aware of the rising national movement in Egypt and on various occasions stressed the close relationship between Jews and Muslims. In *Altneuland*, his Zionist Utopia, Reshid Bey,

* J.N.Jeffries, *Palestine: The Reality*, London, 1939, p. 40.
† *Jüdische Rundschau*, 27 November 1931.
‡ Truth from Eretz Israel', *Hamelitz*, June 1891.

personifying the Arabs, says that Jewish immigration had brought tremendous benefits to the Arabs: the export of oranges had increased tenfold. When asked by a non-Jewish visitor whether Jewish immigration had not ruined the Arabs and forced them to leave, he replies: 'What a question! It was a blessing for all of us', adding however that the landowners benefited more than others because they had sold land to the Jews at a great profit.* Herzl's vision seemed to Ahad Ha'am too good to be true. How could millions of Jews live in a country which barely provided a poor living for a few hundred thousand Arabs? Max Nordau replied that he and Herzl were thinking in terms of modern methods of cultivation which would make mass settlement possible without any need for the Arabs to leave. They envisaged the spread of European civilisation and the growth of an open European society in which there would be room for everyone. They were opposed, he said, counter-attacking his east European critics, to a narrow, introspective, religious nationalism concerned primarily with rebuilding the Temple of Jerusalem.† Nordau, however, was not always so optimistic about the future of Arab-Jewish relations. On at least one occasion he considered the possibility of a Turkish-Zionist alliance against the danger of an Arab separatist movement.‡ Or perhaps this was only a political move to remind the Arabs, who were then anxious to enlist Turkish assistance against Jewish immigration, that the Zionists too had some bargaining power.

From the early days of Jewish immigration there were in fact clashes, often bloody, between the new settlers and their Arab neighbours. The annals of the settlements are full of stories of theft, robbery and even murder. In a report on his trip to Palestine in 1898 Leo Motzkin stated that in recent years there had been 'countless fights between Jews and Arabs who had been incited against them'.§ But such accounts have to be viewed in the context of time and place. Clashes like these were not uncommon in other parts of the world. They occurred not only between Arabs and Jews, but equally between one Arab village and another.

Moreover, the state of security in the outlying districts of the Ottoman empire was not up to the standards of western Europe.‖ On the other hand it cannot be maintained that these incidents totally lacked political undertones, that, in other words, Jews and Arabs were living peacefully together before political Zionism appeared on the scene, and, more

---

* *Altneuland*, p. 133.

† *Die Welt*, 13 March 1903.

‡ Max Nordau, *Zionistische Schriften*, Berlin, 1909, p. 172.

§ *Stenographisches Protokoll der Verhandlungen des II. Zionisten-Kongresses*, Vienna, 1899, p. 125.

‖ H.M. Kalvarisky, in *She'ifotenu*, vol. 2, 2, p. 50.

specifically, before the Balfour Declaration confronted the Palestinian Arabs with the danger of losing their country.*

As early as 1891 a group of Arab notables from Jerusalem sent a petition to Constantinople signed by five hundred supporters complaining that the Jews were depriving the Arabs of all lands, were taking over their trade and were bringing arms to the country.† Anti-Jewish feeling was spread by the Churches in Palestine. Eliyahu Sapir wrote in 1899 that the main blame was with the Catholic Church, and in particular the Jesuits, but he also mentioned the impact of the French antisemitic publicist Drumont on certain Arab newspapers.‡ It was commonly accepted at the time that the poor Muslim sections of the population who had benefited from Jewish settlement were on the whole well disposed towards the Jews whereas the Christian Arabs were hostile. This appraisal was correct to the extent that many Arab nationalist newspapers published before the First World War were in Christian hands and that, generally speaking, the percentage of Christian Arabs among the intelligentsia, and thus among the founders of the Arab national movement in Syria and Palestine, was disproportionately high. But the attitude of the Muslim upper and middle classes was not basically different, whereas early Zionist emissaries encountered outside Palestine much more sympathy among Christian Arabs fearful of Muslim domination. Sami Hochberg, the Jewish editor of a Constantinople newspaper, was told by Lebanese Christians in 1913 that they hoped the Jews would soon become the majority in Palestine and achieve autonomous status to counterbalance Muslim power.§ The idea that the Christian Arabs were fundamentally anti-Zionist, while the Muslims were potential friends, lingered on nevertheless for a long time after the First World War, despite the fact that Ruppin and other members of the Zionist executive in Palestine frequently tried to explain to their colleagues that the real state of affairs was vastly more complicated.||

* N.Mandel, 'Turks, Arabs and Jewish Immigration into Palestine 1882–1914', in Albert Hourani (ed.), *Middle Eastern Affairs*, 4, London, 1965, pp. 84–6. See also Mandel's dissertation (same title), Oxford, 1965.

† Quoted in *Sefer Toldot Hahagana*, Tel Aviv, 1954, vol. 1, p. 66.

‡ E.Sapir, 'Hatred of Israel in Arab literature', *Hashiloah*, 1899, p. 222 *et seq.*

§ Hochberg to Jacobson, Zionist Archives, Cologne AII, quoted in P.A.Alsberg, 'The Arab Question in the Policy of the Zionist Executive before the First World War', in *Shivat Zion*, 4, p. 189. See also, N.Mandel, 'Attempts at an Arab-Zionist Entente 1913–14', *Middle Eastern Studies*, vol. 1, April 1965.

|| In a report to the Zionist executive in 1912, quoted in Yaacov Ro'i, 'Attempts of the Zionist Organisation to influence the Arab Press in Palestine between 1908–14', *Zion* 3–4, 1967, p. 205.

The total population of Palestine before the outbreak of the First World War was almost 700,000. The number of Jews had risen from 23,000 in 1882 to about 85,000 in 1914. More than one hundred thousand Jews had entered Palestine during the years between, but approximately half of them did not stay. Many moved on to America; one of these wanderers between several worlds was the author of *Hatiqva*, the Zionist national anthem.

Jaffa around 1905 was a city of about thirty thousand inhabitants, of whom two-thirds were Muslim Arabs. Haifa, with its twelve thousand residents, was hardly bigger than neighbouring Acre. Jerusalem was by far the biggest city in the country. Of its population of sixty thousand, forty thousand were Jews and the rest Muslim and Christian Arabs. A contemporary guide book reports that the situation of the Jews had somewhat improved in recent years. They were no longer concentrated in the dirty Jewish quarter in the old city, many having moved to the residential quarters outside the city wall. On the Sabbath the market was almost empty and public transport came more or less to a standstill.* The majority of the Jews still belonged to the old pre-immigration community, either taking no interest in Zionism or actively opposed to it. These were pious men and women, dependent on alms given by their co-religionists abroad. They lived in a ghetto viewed with shame and horror by the new immigrants, the very existence of which reminded them of a milieu from which they had just escaped. The living conditions of the Sefardi Jews, most of them Arabic-speaking, were quite different, as there were many merchants as well as professional men and artisans among them.

The Zionist immigrants, as distinct from the established Jewish community, numbered no more than 35,000–40,000 in 1914, of whom only one-third lived in agricultural settlements. While Arab spokesmen protested against Jewish immigration, Jewish observers noted with concern that the annual natural increase of the Arab population was about as big as the total number of Jews who had settled with so much effort and sacrifice on the land over a period of forty years. Leading Zionists used to say: 'Unless we hurry, others will take Palestine.' A German Zionist physician who had settled in Haifa around the turn of the century noted dryly: 'No one will take it, the Arabs have it and they will stay the leading force by a great margin.'† Twenty years later, Dr Auerbach wrote that it had been the most fateful mistake of Zionist policy to pay insufficient attention to the Arabs in the early days. But he was not at all

---

* Meyers Reisebücher, *Palästina und Syrien*, Leipzig, 1907, p. 128.
† Elias Auerbach, in *Die Welt*, 1910, p. 1101.

certain that more attention would have solved the problem, for 'the Arabs are hostile and will always be hostile', even if the Jews were paragons of modesty and self-denial.* Relations between the Jewish settlers and their Arab neighbours were, then, from the very beginning not untroubled. The land of the early Jewish settlements had formerly belonged to Arab villagers in the neighbourhood who had been heavily in debt and had been forced to sell. There was bitterness against the newcomers, and sporadic armed attacks, and the situation was aggravated by the refusal of the Jewish settlers to share the pasture land with the Arabs as had been the custom before.† In Galilee the problem was even more acute because the Arab peasants were poorer than in southern Palestine, as were the Jewish colonies, which could not offer employment to the Arabs who had lost their land. The Jewish settlers tried to assist the nearby Arab villages by lending out on occasion agricultural machinery, while Jewish physicians were treating Arab patients often free of charge. But not all the new settlers were willing to accept the local customs, nor was it to be expected that those who had lost their land would not feel anger and resentment against the new owners.‡

A short note in a Hebrew journal published in 1909 tells the story of an Arab woman working at Wadi Chanin, a stretch of land recently acquired by the Jews. Suddenly she started weeping, and when asked by those working with her why she was crying she answered that she had recalled that only a few years earlier this very plot had belonged to her family.§

Before the fall of Abdul Hamid in 1908 the Arab nationalist mood had found no organised political expression, since no political activity was permitted within the Ottoman empire. The sultan's representatives ruled with an iron hand, and no one dared openly to express sympathy with the ideas of Arab nationalism. A sudden and dramatic change came when the Young Turks overthrew the sultan and announced that the Ottoman empire would in future be ruled constitutionally. New Arab newspapers were founded, voicing radical demands in a language unheard before. Elections were held for the new parliament and the atmosphere was charged with political tension. With this national upsurge the struggle against Zionism became almost overnight one of the central issues in

* *Jüdische Rundschau*, 13 January 1931.
† Belkind, quoted in A. Cohen, *Israel vehaolam ha'aravi*, Merhavia, 1964, p. 68.
‡ *Ibid.*, pp. 65–9 and *Sefer Toldot hahagana*, vol. 1, pp. 73–7.
§ *Hashiloah*, 1909, p. 466.

Palestinian Arab policy. Leaflets were widely distributed calling on the Arabs not to sell any more land to the Jews, and demanding that the authorities should stop Jewish immigration altogether. The Haifa newspaper *Al Karmel* was established with the express purpose of combating Zionism. Even before, in 1905, Neguib Azoury, a Christian Arab and previously an assistant to the Turkish pasha of Jerusalem, had written that it was the fate of the Arab and the Jewish national movements to fight until one or the other prevailed.* There was a sharp increase in armed attacks on Jewish settlements and on individual Jews. The newspaper campaign, as a contemporary observer noted, reached even the fellaheen in their mud huts and the Beduin in their tents.

Christian Arabs were again said to be in the forefront of the struggle, inciting the Muslim masses to carry out a full-scale pogrom to destroy not only the whole Zionist colonisation but also the Jewish population in the cities.† These fears were exaggerated, as soon appeared, but the alarmist reports received from Jaffa and Jerusalem induced the Zionist leaders for the first time to pay more than cursory attention to the Arabs of Palestine.

What could be done to establish friendly relations with them? It was easier to pose the question than to answer it. There had been some lonely warning voices. Yitzhak Epstein, a teacher and an agriculturist, had said in a closed meeting at the time of the seventh Zionist congress (1905) that the Arab question was the most important of all the problems facing Zionism, and that Zionism should enter into an alliance with the Arabs. The Jews who returned to their country should do so not as conquerors; they should not encroach upon the rights of a proud and independent people such as the Arabs, whose hatred, once aroused, would have the most dangerous consequences. Epstein's views, and the arguments used by his critics to refute them, are of considerable interest and deserve to be carefully studied. They anticipated in almost every detail the debates which have continued since inside the Zionist movement, and between the Zionists and their critics.‡

Epstein maintained that there had been not a few cases in which Arab and Druze smallholders had lost their livelihood as the result of Zionist land purchases. In law the Jews were right, but the political and moral

* Neguib Azoury, *Le Réveil de la Nation Arabe*, Paris, 1905, p. v; *Sefer Toldot Hahagana*, p. 185. Mandel, *Middle Eastern Affairs*, p. 94.

† Professor A.S.Yehuda in a report to Professor O.Warburg of the Zionist executive, dated 31 August 1911, cited by Ro'i, 'Attempts of the Zionist Organisation . . .', p. 212.

‡ His speech was subsequently published under the title 'She'ela ne'elma', in *Hashiloah*, 1907, pp. 193–206.

aspect was more complicated and they had a clear obligation to the fellaheen. It was easy to make enemies among the Arabs and very difficult to gain friends. Every step had therefore to be carefully considered. Only such land should be bought that others were not already cultivating. At the same time the Jews had to give full support to the national aspirations of the Arabs. While Herzl had aimed at a Turkish-Zionist *entente*, Epstein envisaged a charter between Jews and Arabs ('those two old Semitic peoples') which would be of great benefit to both sides and to all mankind. The Arabs had a great many gifts, but they needed the Jews to help them to make economic and cultural progress. The Jews should enter into such an agreement with pure, altruistic motives, without any intention of subjugating the neighbouring people. There ought to be no rivalry between them; the two peoples should assist each other. Hitherto in their political activities the Zionists had not been in contact with the right people. They had talked to the Ottoman government and to everyone else who had anything to do with Palestine. But they had not spoken to the Arab people, the real owners of the country. The Zionists had behaved like a matchmaker who had consulted every member of the family with the exception of the bridegroom. Epstein concluded with several recommendations for improving relations with the Arab neighbours: the most important task was to help raise the living standard of the peasants. Jewish hospitals, schools, kindergartens and reading rooms should be open to them. The Jewish schools should move away from a narrow nationalist spirit. The intention should be not to proselytise the Arabs but to help them find their own identity. The Jews should take account of the psychological situation of the Arabs, something which had been utterly neglected in the past. Once established, high-level educational institutions would attract thousands of students from neighbouring Arab countries, and this too would strengthen the fraternal alliance between the two peoples.

Epstein's thesis provoked a reply from a colleague* who argued that the Arab peasant had been exploited not by the Jews but by Arab effendis and moneylenders. Everyone agreed that the Arab had benefited from the presence of the Jews. If nevertheless one day he were to turn against the Jews, the reason would not be Jewish land purchases but the 'eternal enmity towards a people which had been exiled from its country'. To buy the friendship of the Arabs was exceedingly difficult, as Epstein himself had admitted. Why then try so hard? History was full of examples showing that the more the Jews tried to ingratiate themselves with other

* Nehama Puchachevski, in *Hashiloah*, 1908, pp. 67-9.

peoples, the more they had been hated. Had not the time come for the Jews to concern themselves at long last with their own existence and survival? But these considerations quite apart, Epstein's suggestions were said to be quite unrealistic for the simple reason that the Jews did not have the money to carry out such grandiose projects. They were facing the gravest difficulties in establishing their own elementary school system. It was therefore absurd to dream about universities for the Arabs. They themselves hardly knew how to cultivate the soil – how could they teach others? It was all very well to talk about the blessings of modern civilisation which Zionism could bring to the Arabs, but for the time being the Jews had next to nothing to offer. The Arabs had never ceased to be a people, and unlike the Jews, everywhere hated and persecuted, they needed no national revival. It was therefore quite unconvincing to maintain that they needed Jewish friendship. Epstein had argued that what the Jews could give the Arabs they could get nowhere else, and it was at this point that his critic finally lost her temper: 'To give – always to give, to the one our body, to the other, our soul, and to yet another the remnant of the hope ever to live as a free people in its historical homeland.'

The debate I have briefly summarised contained in essence all the main arguments among Zionists on the Arab question: 'healthy national egoism' being urged on the one side and on the other the demand that Jewish settlement in Palestine should be based on the highest moral principles and proceed only in agreement with the Arabs. Epstein's criticism was justified inasmuch as quite a few European Zionists tended to ignore the presence of the Arabs. Some Zionist reference works published before the First World War characteristically do not even refer to what Epstein in a most striking and meaningful phrase called the 'hidden question'. When the German Zionists produced a propaganda brochure in 1910, Elias Auerbach, who wrote on the prospects for future development, found it necessary to stress at the very beginning of his article the obvious fact that Palestine was not an empty country and that its character was shaped by the strongest ethnic element in its population.*

Some of the new arrivals looked down on the Arabs. One observer wrote that on a few occasions he had detected an attitude towards the Arabs which reminded him of the way Europeans treated the blacks.† But no one could fairly charge with lack of political caution and moral obtuseness the men who represented the Zionist executive in Palestine

* Elias Auerbach, in *Palästina*, Cologne, 1910, p. 121.
† Hugo Bergmann, *Jawne und Jerusalem*, Prague, 1919, p. 60.

at the time, and who were responsible *inter alia* for purchasing land. It is certainly no coincidence that these very people (Arthur Ruppin, Y. Thon, R. Benyamin) were among the founding members twenty years later of the *Brit Shalom*, the highly unpopular group which regarded an Arab-Jewish *rapprochement* as the main task of the Zionist movement. Undeniably the Zionist executive in Europe is open to criticism for concentrating most of its efforts on Constantinople and the various European capitals, showing little foresight in its relations with the Arabs, though from time to time it did press resolutions stressing the importance of making efforts to gain the sympathy of Palestine's Arab population. Sokolow wrote after his visit to the Near East in 1914 that 'the question of our relations with the Arab population has become more acute'.* But there was no follow-up, no consistent policy. After the First World War no congress passed without solemn declarations stressing Zionist sympathies for the national movement in the orient and the Arab national movement in particular. But, as Ussishkin said, the Zionists had no power in Palestine, and such declarations were therefore meaningless. Nor was it quite clear to whom they should have talked. There were individual Arab notables, but there was no Arab political leadership in Palestine, certainly not before 1908. The political parties which then emerged were small, consisting of a few dozen members, and not very representative.

The Zionist leaders simply would not consider the presence of half a million non-Jews an insurmountable obstacle, formidable enough to make them give up their cherished dreams about the return of the Jewish people to their homeland. They had tried to carry out some of Epstein's ideas; they had drained swamps and irrigated desert lands. But the budget of the Zionist executive was small and those responsible for the promotion of agricultural settlement knew that restricting their purchases to poor land would doom the whole enterprise. If the Arabs believed in Herzl's hints about the many millions at his disposal, the members of the Zionist executive knew better.

Jewish workers, it was thought, should have played a decisive role in improving relations with the Arab population. But it was precisely the influx of Jewish workers into Palestine with the Second Aliya which aggravated the conflict. After a clash between Arab and Jewish workers in Jaffa in the spring of 1908, Levontin, director of the local Anglo-Palestine Bank, wrote to Wolffsohn, the head of the World Zionist executive, that the young men from the *Poale Zion* were largely responsible

---

* Quoted in Yaacov Ro'i, 'The Zionist Attitude to the Arabs, 1908–14', in *Middle Eastern Studies*, April 1968, pp. 210, 216.

for the growing tension. They had been walking around armed with big sticks and some of them with knives and rifles, behaving towards the Arabs with arrogance and contempt.* On another occasion in the same year Levontin wrote to Wolffsohn that the Zionist labour leaders were sowing hatred against Zionism in the heart of the local population by speaking and writing against giving jobs to the Arabs. Arthur Ruppin, who certainly did not lack sympathy for the Jewish workers, reported to Wolffsohn in 1911 that he too was continually trying to impress on them the need to refrain from any act of hostility in their relations with the Arabs.†

What made the 'Moskub' (as the Arabs called the pioneers from Russia) an especially disturbing factor in Arab-Jewish relations? For they were influenced by the Russian populists and by Leo Tolstoy; they did not come to Palestine as conquerors, but believed with A.D. Gordon that only a return to the soil, to productive labour, would redeem the Jewish people. But when they arrived in Palestine they realised that the great majority of those employed in the existing Jewish settlements were Arabs. This they regarded as a cancer in the body politic of the yishuv. It had not been the aim of Zionism to establish a class of landowners in Palestine whose vineyards and orchards and orange groves were worked by Arab plantation workers. From the outset the pioneers and their trade unions fought for the replacement of Arab by Jewish labour wherever feasible in the face of strong opposition from the Jewish farmers, who naturally preferred cheaper and more experienced Arab labourers. Moreover the young men and women of *Poale Zion* had left tsarist Russia with the memory of the pogroms still with them, and the issue of Jewish self-defence figured high among their priorities. They were Socialists and internationalists, and the lowliest Arab peasant had as much human dignity in their eyes as any prominent Turkish pasha. But they did not take kindly to attacks and molestations, and they were sometimes liable to over-react in their response. These members of *Poale Zion* were not like the liberals of our day – they had no feelings of guilt about the Arabs. Their Socialism was largely (though not exclusively) in the Marxist tradition. Following Marx, they regarded the spread of western ideas and techniques in the east as *a priori* progressive, needing no further ideological justification. They believed in working-class solidarity, but this extended only to workers already established in jobs

* Quoted in Alsberg, 'The Arab Question in the Policy of the Zionist Executive before the First World War', in *Shivat Zion*, 4, p. 163.
† *Ibid.*, p. 184.

in industry, not necessarily to those who were competing against organised labour. Since under the centuries of Muslim rule Palestine had remained a desolate, underdeveloped country, they had no compunction about ousting a few landowners and peasants whom they held responsible for its backwardness and neglect. There was nothing in Socialist doctrine, as they interpreted it, which dictated that east European Jewry should remain poor and unproductive and that Palestine should stay backward and infertile.*

It is one of the tragic ironies of the history of Zionism that those who wanted close relations with the Arabs contributed, albeit unwittingly, to the sharpening of the conflict. Between the two world wars no one strove more actively for a reconciliation between Jews and Arabs than Haim Margalit Kalvarisky. Born in Russia in 1868, he was trained as an agronomist and came to Palestine in 1895. For many years he worked for Baron Hirsch's colonisation society and had a great many influential Arab friends. He was firmly convinced that Arab-Jewish agreement was the *conditio sine qua non* of a successful Zionist policy. Yet it was precisely Kalvarisky's activities around the turn of the century – the land purchases in the Tiberias district – which first provoked Arab resistance on a major scale. During the years 1899–1902 about one-half of this district was acquired by Jewish land companies and it was then for the first time that the danger of denationalisation became a political slogan among the Arabs.† Under the impact of these events Nagib Nasser, later editor of the Haifa newspaper *Al Karmel*, was converted to anti-Zionism and decided to devote his efforts to the enlightenment of his fellow citizens with regard to the 'Jewish peril'.‡

Among the Jewish workers no group was more pacifist and antimilitarist in character than *Hapoel Hatzair*. A.D.Gordon, their chief ideologist, was opposed in principle to the use of violence and justified self-defence only in extreme circumstances. But he and his comrades wanted every tree and every bush in the Jewish homeland to be planted by the pioneers. It was in this group that the idea of Jewish agricultural communal settlements found its most fervent adherents. They were

---

* After the First World War they showed more awareness. At the fourteenth Zionist congress in Vienna (1925) no one was more emphatic than Ben Gurion on the necessity 'to find the way to the heart of the Arab people'. Empty phrases about peace and fraternity, he insisted, were not sufficient; what was wanted was a genuine alliance between Jewish and Arab workers. He was thereupon attacked by the revisionists as a cosmopolitan and doctrinaire Socialist theoretician.

† See Kalvarisky's own account in *Ha'olam*, 7, 1914, and in *She'ifotenu*. p. 54.

‡ Mandel, St Antony's Papers, pp. 93–4.

shocked, as has been already mentioned, when they found that the settlers of the first aliya had become plantation owners, and that among the
permanent residents of these colonies there were actually more Arabs
than Jews. According to a contemporary account, every Jewish farmer
in Zikhron Ya'akov provided for three or four Arab families, and the
situation elsewhere was hardly different.* Ahad Ha'am called Zikhron
'not a colony but a disgrace'. Few Jewish peasants engaged any longer in
manual labour. This state of affairs was not, of course, in keeping with
the original aims of Zionism, let alone of Socialism. Yet, paradoxically,
as far as Arab-Jewish relations were concerned it was a stabilising factor,
whereas the activities of the Socialists, with their fanatical insistence on
manual labour ('redemption through toil'), seemed to confirm Arab
suspicions about Jewish separatism and the displacement of Arab
peasants and workers.

General security deteriorated sharply in Palestine after the revolution
of 1908 against the sultanate. Jewish settlements in lower Galilee were
frequently attacked, and there were clashes between Jews and Arabs in
Haifa, Jaffa and Jerusalem. The situation was even more critical in
Galilee. Much of this, however, was part of the general lawlessness which
spread as a result of events in Constantinople and the general weakening
of Turkish authority. The Jews were not the only victims. The German
settlements also came in for many attacks until Berlin intervened and
dispatched a warship to Haifa.† But the way in which the Arab newspapers commented on these attacks showed that there was reason for
concern. The Zionists had at first regarded the activities of Nagib Nasser
as an isolated phenomenon. But *Al Karmel* was joined by other newspapers
of a similar character, such as *Falestin* in Jaffa (founded in 1911), and *Al
Muntada* in Jerusalem, which began to appear in 1912. Virulent
pamphlets and books were published and the Arab press outside Palestine
began to open its pages to articles about the Zionist danger.‡ Leading
Jewish citizens such as David Yellin expressed apprehension: 'Fifteen
years ago the Muslims hated the Christians, while their attitude towards
the Jews had been one of contempt. Now their attitude towards the
Christians has changed for the better and to the Jews for the worse.'
A group of leading citizens wrote to Ruppin from Haifa that 'we are
alarmed to see with what speed the poison sown by our enemies is
spreading among all layers of the population. We must fear all possible

---

* Menahem Sheinkin, quoted in *Sefer Toldot Hahagana*, vol. 1, p. 135.
† *Sefer Toldot Hahagana*, p. 191.
‡ Mandel, *Middle Eastern Affairs*, p. 97.

calamities. It would be criminal to continue preserving the attitude of placid onlookers.*

In part, the deterioration was the fault of the new immigrants, who did not know the language of the Arabs and made no effort to understand and respect their customs. There is no doubt that their communal living, their radical political and social ideas, and the ostentatious equality they observed between the sexes among the new immigrants, shocked and dismayed most Arabs. Their ways must have appeared to them indecent and immoral. There were other complaints: in their new settlements the Jews refused to employ Arab guards but tried to defend themselves against the incursions of thieves and robbers. In the past, Palestinian Jews had tried to cope with such emergencies by invoking the help of the foreign consuls, or by paying *baksheesh* to the local Turkish authorities or to the headmen of the neighbouring Arab villages. The new guardians and their association, the 'Hashomer', made many mistakes, partly because few of them had mastered the Arab language, partly because they were appalled by the cowardice of the old yishuv when it came to standing up to the Arabs. They wanted to impress on their neighbours that they belonged to a different breed: if they erred, they preferred to err on the side of toughness. They did not regard themselves as a race of supermen; they did not want to be feared; they did not despise the Arabs; they simply wished to be respected. They expressly excluded from their ranks those who claimed that 'the Arab understands only the language of the whip'.†

Relations in the cities, the real focus of Palestinian politics, were even less satisfactory. In 1908 the first elections to the Turkish parliament took place. The Arabs were in a strong position, electing about a quarter of all the deputies.‡ The Palestinian Jews tried to have a representative of their community elected but there were not enough of them, and those with Ottoman citizenship and the right to vote were even fewer. Once they realised that they had virtually no prospects, they decided to establish an alliance with Muslim Arab groups on the assumption that these would think Jewish support preferable to Christian Arab support, and that those elected would feel some obligation towards their Jewish electors. Palestinian Jews acted with local Arab dignitaries in establishing

* Quoted in Ro'i, 'The Zionist Attitude . . .', p. 227.
† *Sefer Toldot Hahagana*, p. 308. This refers to Josef Lishanski, born in Metulla, who spoke the language and knew the customs of the Arabs much better than the newcomers. He was one of the most famous *shomrim* of the early period. During the First World War he played a leading part in the *Nili* conspiracy.
‡ Mandel, Dissertation, pp. 165–8.

a Jerusalem committee of 'Union and Progress', the Ottoman State Party. However, the Arabs soon founded their own political organisations, such as the Decentralisation Party, in which there was no room for the Jewish community as such, even though a few individual Jews were permitted to join. The Arab members of the Ottoman parliament, in their speeches and in their articles in the Turkish press, frequently conjured up the Zionist danger. Demanding an end to immigration and land purchase, they accused Turkish ministers and the ruling party in general of deliberately ignoring the separatist activities of the Zionist settlers who had established para-military organisations, openly displayed their national flag, were singing their national anthem, and even maintained their own courts.* The Turkish authorities did not take the Arab complaints too seriously, but to placate them a number of anti-Zionist measures were promulgated as a result of this campaign.†

When the next elections came round in 1912, the representatives of the Zionist executive in the Turkish capital recommended the Jewish electors to abstain from voting, since there was no chance of a candidate well disposed towards the Jews being elected. Palestinian Jewish leaders, on the other hand, argued that such abdication was dangerous, and suggested instead collaboration with the ruling Turkish party, 'Unity and Progress'.‡ Similar views in favour of Zionist-Turkish cooperation were voted by Max Nordau in his speech at the seventh Zionist congress. When the Arabs realised that they might have gone too far in antagonising the Zionists they tried to reassure Dr Jacobson, half suggesting the possibility of an Arab-Jewish alliance to be directed against the Turkish overlords.

It is doubtful whether there was anything of substance in these non-committal Arab approaches. But four years later the idea of an Arab-Jewish alliance was again advanced by Arab spokesmen, this time with more conviction. The Zionists found themselves at this stage in the unaccustomed position of being wooed both by the Young Turks, who after their defeat by Italy and in the Balkan war were in desperate need of allies, and by the Arab nationalists, who were dissatisfied with the policy of the Young Turks. Salim Najar, a Syrian Arab and one of the leaders of the Decentralisation Party, wrote in a letter to Sami Hochberg that since the Turkish leading circles were out to crush the national

---

* *Sefer Toldot Hahagana*, p. 186; Cohen, *Israel vehaolam ha'aravi*, p. 84; Alsberg, 'The Arab Question...', p. 168.

† Mandel, Dissertation, chapter 6.

‡ Alsberg, 'The Arab Question...', p. 169.

ambitions of both Arabs and Jews, the moment had come for the two peoples to get together and establish a common front.*

Hochberg, who was born in Bessarabia in 1869 and went to Palestine in 1889, was one of the founders of Nes Ziona; later he worked as a teacher in Tiberias. Eventually he settled in Constantinople, where he was active among the Young Turks. He founded the newspaper *Jeune Turc* which was subsidised by the Zionist executive and helped to promote the Zionist cause in the Turkish capital.†

Hochberg reported that many Arab nationalists, while uneasy about Jewish immigration, were apparently inclined to enter into some form of alliance with the Zionists.‡ According to Hochberg's report, the Cairo committee of the Decentralisation Party was the one most likely to accept in principle Jewish immigration into Palestine and an Arab-Zionist *entente*. It was agreed between Hochberg and the leaders of the Decentralisation Party that the Arabs would tone down their attacks on Zionism, while the Zionists would publish sympathetic accounts of the Arab national movement in their own newspapers and in the European press. This agreement was regarded as the first step towards a wider and more comprehensive agreement to be reached at some future stage.

In June 1913 the first Arab congress was held in Paris. Again Hochberg, who was lobbying there on behalf of the Zionists, reported some goodwill. However, there was dissension within the Arab camp and Hochberg was given to understand that they would prefer an informal understanding since an open alliance would provoke the Turks and thus harm both the Arab and Zionist cause. Several Arab spokesmen, such as Ahmed Tabara and Ahmed Mukhtar Bayhoum, argued that there was enough room in Palestine for both Arabs and Jews, but others were more reserved in their attitude. It was argued that the Jews were not supporting the Arab national movement, and in the end the congress refrained altogether from commenting on the 'Jewish issue' in its resolutions. Following Hochberg's initiative, Jacobson met Zahravi, who had acted as president of the congress, but no agreement was reached. The Turks had meanwhile dispatched the secretary of the 'Union and Progress' Party to Paris, who promised the Arabs that most of their

---

* *Ibid.*, p. 172. For a fuller discussion of the negotiations, see N.Mandel, 'Attempts at an Arab-Zionist entente 1913–14', in *Middle Eastern Studies*, April 1965, p. 238 *et seq.*

† On Hochberg, see Cohen, *Israel vehaolam ha'aravi*, p. 95, and Lichtheim, *Rückkehr*, Stuttgart, 1970, pp. 216–17.

‡ The text of his report is published in Alsberg, 'The Arab Question . . .', p. 187 *et seq.*

demands would be fulfilled. As a direct result of this Arab interest in a pact with the Zionists dwindled rapidly.* The negotiations did not, however, break down completely. The Arabs realised after a few months that they had been unduly optimistic in their appraisal of Turkish intentions and there was a renewed interest among them in negotiations with the Zionists. Dr Jacobson, after talking to various leaders in Constantinople, summarised Arab demands under three heads: they wanted financial help for Arab schools and for public works, and guarantees against the dispossession of the fellaheen. The Jews, on the other hand, insisted on the cessation of the anti-Zionist campaign in the Arab press and of the petitions against immigration and land purchase.† But the Arab leaders in Cairo and Beirut had only limited freedom of action, for the majority of the Palestinian Arab leaders wanted a clearer and firmer stand against Jewish immigration, and were in no mood for an *entente*. Torn in opposite directions, the Egyptian and Syrian Arab leaders were considering various policies *vis-à-vis* Zionism without for the time being adopting any of them. The Zionist executive and its representatives in the Turkish capital were equally undecided. They were eager in principle to reach an agreement with the Arabs but they did not want to arouse Turkish suspicions. Nor did they have any clear idea what exactly to offer the Arabs.‡

When Nahum Sokolow visited Beirut and Damascus in 1914, he was introduced to leading local nationalists, who expressed interest in a high level conference. It was decided that such a meeting should take place in July 1914 near Beirut. The attitude of the Turkish authorities was not clear. The governor of Beirut seems at first to have favoured direct Jewish-Arab talks, but later he advised the Zionist leaders against them. Preparations were made in Palestine for the meeting. The Jewish delegation was to include Kalvarisky, Dizengoff, Shabtai Levi, David Yellin and other leading figures. But the composition of the Arab delegation discouraged the Zionists. Of the ten Arab delegates appointed, only three were thought to be in favour of an Arab-Israeli *entente*. At the same time the list included several leading anti-Zionists such as the editor of *Al Karmel*. Nor did they like the agenda suggested by the Arabs, which put the onus on the Jews to prove that their intentions were not detrimental to the Arab cause. The Jewish delegates decided in their preliminary talks in Jaffa and Haifa to postpone the meeting with the Arabs, 'but to

---

* For Hochberg's report on the Paris congress see *ibid.*, pp. 195–205.
† *Ibid.*, p. 177.
‡ *Ibid.*, p. 178.

do so in such a way as not to sever all contact with them'.* The outbreak of war a few weeks later put an end to these exchanges.

Was it lack of enthusiasm, and shortsightedness, on the part of Sokolow and the Palestinian Zionists which made them miss a great chance of reconciliation with the Arabs? The prospects for agreement were not exactly brilliant. A temporary agreement could have been reached if the Zionist leadership had been able and willing to invest substantially in the Arab national movement. The Zionists could have talked to Syrian and Egyptian leaders, but these were unable to enter any binding agreement against the desire of the Palestinian Arabs. Even if an agreement had been reached in 1914, it could not possibly have survived the storm of war. Once Turkish rule was overthrown, the struggle for Palestine would have become a free-for-all and the Arab-Zionist conflict would have reappeared with a vengeance.†

Dr Thon, one of the Zionist representatives in the 1914 negotiations, relates that an Arab contact (Nasif el Khaldi) told him at a critical juncture in their talks: 'Gardez-vous bien, Messieurs les Sionistes, un gouvernment passe, mais un peuple reste.'‡ Sound advice but not really very novel. Four years earlier, at the time of the first elections to the Turkish parliament, Dr Thon's superior, Arthur Ruppin, had received exactly the same instructions from the president of the Zionist World Organisation, David Wolffsohn, who wrote that the aspirations of the local population had to be taken into account: 'The government party in Constantinople comes and goes but the Arab population of Palestine remains and it must be our first axiom to live in peace with it.' §

It is not even certain whether Dr Ruppin needed such advice, for he was less likely than other Zionist leaders to underrate the importance of the Arab question. He had explained to the Zionist executive more than once that the goodwill of the Ottoman government was not of greater importance to Zionism than the goodwill of the local Arabs: 'We must not purchase the goodwill of the one by incurring the enmity of the other.'‖ In the presence of so much understanding, then, and even goodwill, why was it impossible to find a *modus vivendi* with the Arabs?

The conflict had various causes, although the one most frequently mentioned at the time was not in fact the most important. The number of

---

* Mandel. *Middle Eastern Studies*, p. 260; see also Cohen, *Israel vehaolam ha'aravi*, pp. 107–10.
† Mandel, *Middle Eastern Studies*, pp. 263–5.
‡ M.Medzini, *Esser Shanim shel Mediniut Eretz Yisraelit*, Tel Aviv, 1928, p. 80.
§ Wolffsohn to Ruppin, 15 September 1908, quoted in Alsberg, 'The Arab Question . . .', p. 179.
‖ Quoted in Ro'i, 'The Zionist Attitude . . .', p. 227.

fellaheen dispossessed was small. Only a tiny percentage of the land acquired by the Zionists was bought from small peasants; most of it came from the large landowners. One-quarter of all Jewish land in Palestine (the Esdraelon valley) was in fact acquired from one single absentee landlord, the Christian Arab Sursuq family which lived in Beirut. Various British committees of enquiry (such as the Shaw and Simpson committees) discovered in the 1920s that a large landless class was developing in the Arab sector and that more and more land was coming into a few hands. But this was not mainly the result of Jewish immigration. A similar tendency could also be observed in Egypt, and in other countries which were gradually coming into the orbit of the modern capitalist economy.

During the early years of Zionist settlement the Jewish land buyers showed no more concern than the Arab effendis for the fate of the fellaheen who were evicted. Only gradually did it dawn on them that, moral considerations quite apart, they were facing a potentially explosive political issue. Later on, greater care was taken to pay compensation or to find alternative employment for those who lost their land. But the effects of Jewish settlement on the Arab economy were minimal, as a statistical comparison shows: urbanisation in Palestine did not proceed at a faster rate than in the neighbouring Arab countries; Arab immigration into Palestine exceeded emigration from that country; and the birth rate rose more quickly than in the neighbouring countries, as did the living standards of the Arabs in the neighbourhood of the new Jewish settlements. These facts have frequently been quoted by Zionist authors, and they are irrefutable, as far as they go, both for the prewar period and the 1920s. If some Arabs suffered as a result of Jewish settlement, the number of those who benefited directly or indirectly was certainly greater. True, if Arab living standards improved, the Jewish settlers were still much better off, and the emergence of prosperous colonies must have caused considerable envy.

From a purely economic point of view, Arab resistance to Jewish immigration and settlement was inexplicable and unjustified. But then the economic aspect of the conflict was hardly ever of decisive importance. For that reason the Zionist hope, shared by Marxists and non-Marxists alike, that economic collaboration would act as a powerful stimulus towards political reconciliation, was quite unrealistic. The conflict was, of course, basically political in character, a clash between two national movements. The Arabs objected to Jewish immigration not so much because they feared proletarisation, as because they anticipated that the

Jews intended one day to become masters of the country and that as a result they would be reduced to the status of a minority.

Only a handful of Zionists dreamed at the time of a Jewish state. The Turks had not the slightest intention of granting even a modest measure of independence to any part of the Ottoman empire. But it is quite immaterial in this context whether Zionism at the time really had plans for conquest – perhaps the Arabs were better judges of the capacity of the Jews and their ambitions than the Zionists themselves. The idea of a Jewish state had had a few protagonists from the very beginning. Zeev Dubnow, for instance, one of the early Bilu settlers, in 1882 wrote to his more famous brother, the historian, that the final aim was to restore one day the independence of Eretz Israel. To this end settlements were to be established, the land and industry were to pass into Jewish hands, and the rising generation was to be taught the use of arms.* Michael Halpern, also, one of the early *shomrim*, used to talk occasionally about the conquest of the country by legions of Jewish soldiers. But these were flights of fancy indulged in by a few individuals, and no one took them seriously at the time.

At the other extreme, and equally unrepresentative, there were a few advocates of cultural assimilation; with their return to the east the Jews were to shed their European influences and reacquire eastern customs and mental habits. The idea of the common Semitic origin of Jews and Arabs as a basis for close collaboration between the two peoples appeared early in the history of the Zionist movement. It figures in the writings of Epstein and of R.Benyamin (who worked in Ruppin's office in Jaffa). Sokolow, in an interview with the Cairo newspaper *Al Ahram* in 1914, said that he hoped the Jews would draw near to Arab culture in every respect, to build up together a great Palestinian civilisation.† After the First World War, when the wisdom of the east was enjoying a fashionable success in Europe, M.Ben Gavriel (Eugen Hoeflich), a Viennese writer who settled in Jerusalem, propagated this same idea in a series of books and articles.‡ Even a radical Socialist such as Fritz Sternberg, who

* *Ktavim letoldot Chibat Zion*, vol. 3, p. 495.
† Ro'i, 'The Zionist Attitude . . .', pp. 217–18.
‡ Beginning with *Die Pforte des Ostens*, Vienna, 1924, in which he also advocated a binational state. Jabotinsky, on the other hand, had no patience with such theories. When he approached Nordau during the war about the establishment of a Jewish Legion which was to fight against the Turks, he was told, 'But you cannot do that, the Muslims are kin to the Jews, Ishmael was our uncle.' 'Ishmael is not our uncle,' Jabotinsky replied. 'We belong, thank God, to Europe and for two thousand years have helped to create the culture of the west.'

subsequently became better known as a Marxist theoretician, attributed decisive importance to the common Semitic origins of the two peoples and to the spiritual affinity felt by the Jews for the Arabs: 'The east European Jews are still almost orientals', he wrote.* Even after the Second World War the concept of a Semitic federation in the Middle East still had some enthusiastic supporters in Israel.

It was not readily obvious what these ideologists were trying to prove, for even if a common racial or ethnic origin could have been demonstrated, they were over-optimistic in suggesting that it would have a strong political impact. Consanguinity is not necessarily a synonym for friendship, and the bitterest quarrels are traditionally those between members of one family. Most Zionist leaders of the day subscribed to the idea of Arab-Jewish brotherhood, or at any rate paid lip service to it, but they did so more often than not, it would appear, because of their inability to find any other ideological justification or a more tangible practical approach to improve relations with the Arabs. One of the dissidents was Richard Lichtheim, a leading German Zionist, who together with Jacobson represented the Zionist executive in Constantinople. In his reports to his superiors he agreed that it was vital to make every effort to win the goodwill of the Arabs, and to organise Jewish settlement in such a way as to serve Arab interests as well. But he had no illusions about the outcome of such a policy:

The Arabs are and will remain our natural opponents. They do not care a straw for the 'joint semitic spirit'. I can only warn urgently against a historical or cultural chimera. They want orderly government, just taxes and political independence. The east of today aspires to no marvels other than American machinery and the Paris toilet. Of course the Arabs want to preserve their nation and cultivate their culture. What they need for this, however, is specifically European: money, organization, machinery. The Jew for them is a competitor who threatens their predominance in Palestine. . . . †

Writing many years later, Lichtheim stated that it had been clear to him even before 1914 that the national aspirations of the Zionists and the Palestinian Arabs were irreconcilable.‡

Ruppin, on the other hand, continued to believe in a bi-national state. He would despair of the possibility of ever realising the Zionist idea, he

* 'Die Bedeutung der Araberfrage fuer den Zionismus', in *Der Jude*, 1918, p. 150.
† Reports dated October and November 1913, quoted in Ro'i, 'The Zionist Attitude . . .', pp. 214–15.
‡ Lichtheim, *Rückkehr*, p. 228.

still declared at the Zionist congress in Vienna in 1925, if there were no possibility of doing justice to the national interests of both Jews and Arabs. But soon after doubts set in. He realised that all Palestinian Arabs were opposed to Zionism, and if any solution of the Palestinian problem were made contingent on the agreement of the Arabs it would imply the cessation of immigration and of Jewish economic development. In December 1931 he sadly wrote to Victor Jacobson, his old friend from the Constantinople days: 'What we can get today from the Arabs – we don't need. What we need – we can't get. What the Arabs are willing to give us is at most minority rights as in eastern Europe. But we have already had enough experience of the situation in eastern Europe . . .'.*

Politics apart, relations between Jews and Arabs were not too bad in pre-1914 Palestine, considering the great cultural and social differences between the communities. They were neighbours, and as among neighbours all over the world there was cooperation as well as conflict. Among the old residents, notably the Sefardi community, Arabic was for many the native language. Children grew up in the same street, Jews were in business together with Arabs, some wrote poems in Arabic or articles for the Arab press. There were even, at a limited level, social contacts. Among the new immigrants, too, there was considerable interest in things Arab. The Jewish watchmen, the *shomrim*, often adopted the Arab headgear (*kefiya*), and went out of their way to make friends in the neighbouring villages. Arab colloquialisms entered the Hebrew language, though not usually on the highest literary level. With Moshe Smilansky's *Hawadja Musa*, the Arab theme entered Hebrew literature well before the First World War. His short stories about the fellaheen and their world, written with great feeling and sympathy, often idealised their way of life. The Zionists respected the Arabs as human beings, regarding them as distant, if rather backward and ineffectual cousins. There was certainly no hatred on their part. But being totally absorbed in their own national movement, they did not recognize that their cousins, too, were undergoing a national revival, and they sometimes seemed to deny them the right to do so.

In the deliberations of the Zionist executive various aspects of the Arab question were discussed from time to time. Ruppin, in his report to the eleventh Zionist congress, noted that the Zionists had to make up for a great deal they had neglected, and to correct the errors they had committed. 'It is of course quite useless to content ourselves with merely assuring the Arabs that we are coming into the country as their friends.

* A.Ruppin, *Pirke Khayai*, Tel Aviv, 1968, vol. 3, p. 203.

We must prove this by our deeds.'* At the previous congress, Shlomo Kaplanski, one of the leaders of the Labour Zionists, had stressed the necessity of a *rapprochement* with the Arabs. He did not believe in a lasting conflict between the Zionists and the fellaheen and was confident that an understanding with the democratic forces in the Arab world – though not perhaps with the effendis – could be reached.†

But Ruppin had no recipe for making friends among the Arabs and had to resort to the old arguments: Zionist colonisation had brought great material benefits to the Arabs, they had learned modern agricultural methods from the Jews, Jewish doctors had helped to stamp out epidemics among them. Ruppin was aware that the utmost tact and caution had to be used when buying Arab land so that no harsh results would follow. At one stage, in May 1911, he suggested in a memorandum to the Zionist executive a limited population transfer. The Zionists would buy land near Aleppo and Homs in northern Syria for the resettlement of the Arab peasants who had been dispossessed in Palestine. But this was vetoed because it was bound to increase Arab suspicions about Zionist intentions.‡

Although Dr Ruppin's scheme was rejected, the idea of a population transfer preoccupied other members of the Zionist executive. In 1912 Leo Motzkin, dissenting from the views of Ahad Ha'am (who had by that time reached deeply pessimistic conclusions about the Arab attitude, based on the belief that they would never accept a Jewish majority), suggested that the Arab-Jewish problem should be considered in a wider framework: there were extensive uncultivated lands around Palestine belonging to Arabs; perhaps they would be willing to settle there with the money realised from selling their land to the Zionists?§ Again in 1914 Motzkin and Sokolow seem to have played with the idea of a population transfer. Its most consistent advocate was Israel Zangwill, the Anglo-Jewish writer, who in a series of speeches and articles during and after the First World War criticised the Zionists (with whom he had parted company at the time of the Uganda conflict) for ignoring the fact that Palestine was not empty. The concept of an 'Arab trek' to their own Arabian state played a central part in his scheme. Of course, the Arabs would not be compelled to do so, it would all be agreed upon in a friendly

* Arthur Ruppin, *Building Israel*, New York, 1949, p. 63.
† *Stenographisches Protokoll* . . . , Berlin, 1911, pp. 81–2. Wolffsohn, president of the Zionist Organisation, replied: 'Don't forget to tell this to your friends in Palestine!' *Ibid.*
‡ The correspondence is quoted in Alsberg, 'The Arab Question . . .', p. 175.
§ In his speech at the annual conference of German Zionists at Posen, *Jüdische Rundschau*, 12 July 1912.

and amicable spirit. Zangwill pointed to many such migrations which had taken place in history, including the migration of the Boers to the Transvaal: why should not the Arabs realise that it was in their best interests? They would be fully compensated by the Zionists. Zangwill later explained to a friend that he expected that in the postwar world, reconstituted on a basis of love and reason, the Arab inhabitants of Palestine, for whose kinsmen, after years of oppression, a new state would be set up in Arabia, would naturally sympathise with the ideal of the still more unfortunate nation of Israel and would be magnanimous enough to leave these few thousand square miles to the race which had preserved its dream of them for two thousand years. Zangwill foresaw two states rising side by side; 'Otherwise, he did not see that a Jewish state could arise at all, but only a state of friction.'*

But the idea of a population transfer was never official Zionist policy. Ben Gurion emphatically rejected it, saying that even if the Jews were given the right to evict the Arabs they would not make use of it.† Most thought at that time that there would be sufficient room in Palestine for both Jews and Arabs following the industrialisation of the country and the introduction of intensive methods of agriculture. Since no one before 1914 expected the disintegration of the Turkish empire in the foreseeable future, the question of political autonomy did not figure in their thoughts. They were genuinely aggrieved that the Arabs were not more grateful for the economic benefits they had come to enjoy as the result of Jewish immigration and settlement. They thought that the growth of Arab nationalism and anti-Zionist attacks were the result of the activities of individual villains, the effendis (who were annoyed because the Jews had spoiled the fellaheen by paying them higher wages), and the Christian Arabs (who had to demonstrate that they were as good patriots as their Muslim fellow citizens).

When an Arab national movement developed in Palestine after 1908, the Zionists did not at first attach much importance to it because it consisted of very few people who, moreover, were divided into several factions and parties. It is not difficult to draw up a substantial list of Zionist sins of omission and commission before 1914. They should have devoted far more attention to the Arab question, and been more cautious in land purchases. Many more should have learned Arabic and the customs of their neighbours, and they should have taken greater care not

---

* Redcliffe N. Salaman, *Palestine Reclaimed*, London, 1920, pp. 175–6.

† D. Ben Gurion, in an article published in 1918 included in *Anakhnu veshekhnenu*, Tel Aviv, 1931, p. 41.

to offend their feelings. They should have accepted Ottoman citizenship and have tried to make friends with Arabs on a personal level, following the example of Kalvarisky. There were possibilities of influencing Arab public opinion, of explaining that the Jews were not coming to dominate the Arabs. But the means put at the disposal of Dr Ruppin and his colleagues in Jaffa for this purpose were woefully insufficient. Much more publicity should have been given, for instance, to Wolffsohn's statement at the eleventh Zionist congress that the Jews were not looking for a state of their own in Palestine but merely for a *Heimstaette*. Whether this would have dispelled Arab fears is less certain, for they worried not so much about the Zionist presence as about their future plans. In this respect Arab apprehension was not unfounded. The Zionists, on the other hand, did not foresee that as a result of growing prosperity the number of Palestinian Arabs would rapidly grow. They did not face the fact that the Palestinian Arabs belonged to a people of many millions which was by no means indifferent to the future of the Holy Land.

The Palestinian Arabs who had tolerated (and despised) the local Jews* were genuinely afraid of the aggressive new immigrants who seemed to belong to an altogether different breed. They resented them for the same reasons that substantial mass immigration has always and everywhere produced tension: peasants were afraid of change, shop-keepers and professional men feared competition, religious dignitaries, whether Christian or Muslim, were anything but friendly towards the Jews for traditional, doctrinal reasons. Arab anti-Zionist propaganda after 1908 was, of course, highly exaggerated. The economic situation of the Arabs had certainly not deteriorated as a result of the influx of these strangers, and they overrated the Zionist potential. The Jews had neither the money nor the intention to buy up all the land (as Arab propaganda claimed), to dispossess and proletarianise all Arab peasants. Their political ambitions certainly did not extend to the Nile and the Euphrates.

But the Arabs were correct in the essential point, namely that the Jews wanted to establish a position of strength in Palestine, through their superior organisation and economic power, and that they intended to become eventually a majority. They sensed this logic of events more correctly than the Zionists themselves, who did not think in terms of political power and lacked the instinct for it. The early Zionists were all basically pacifists. The idea that it might be impossible to establish a

---

* Eliezer Ben Yehuda, who emigrated to Palestine from Russia in 1882, wrote in his autobiography that he found that the Arabs did not hate the Jews but despised them for their cowardice. *Kitve Ben Yehuda*, Jerusalem, 1941, p. 37.

state without bloodshed seems never to have occurred to them. The first to raise the question was a non-Zionist, the sociologist Gumplowicz, in a letter to Herzl: 'You want to found a state without bloodshed? Where did you ever see that? Without violence and without guile, simply by selling and buying shares?'*

But even the most exemplary behaviour on the part of the Zionists would not have affected the real source of the conflict, namely, that the Jews were looking in Palestine for more than a cultural centre. However effective their propaganda, however substantial the material benefits that would have accrued to the Arabs from the Jewish settlement, it would still have left unanswered the decisive question – to whom was the country eventually to belong? It was more than a little naïve to put the blame for Arab anti-Zionism on professional inciters, frustrated Arab notables, and the notorious urban riff-raff, for there was a basic clash between two national movements. Full identification on the part of the Zionists with the aims of pan-Arabism from an early date would perhaps have helped to blunt the sharpness of the conflict. But this was of course not in accordance with the aims of the Jewish national revival. Nor would it have induced the Arabs to receive the Zionist immigrants with open arms. The Arab world was already plagued by the presence of religious and ethnic minorities and the conflicts between them. Any further increase in their number and strength would have only added to its anxieties. Given the character of the Zionist movement, with its basic demands (immigration and settlement), and given also the natural fears of the Palestinian Arabs, it is impossible even with the benefit of hindsight to point with any degree of conviction to an alternative Zionist policy, even before the Balfour Declaration, which might have prevented conflict.†

Jews and Arabs During the War

All political activity ceased in Palestine with the outbreak of war in 1914. Young Jews of military age joined the Turkish army, those of enemy nationality were expelled. During the later stages of the war the inhabitants of many Jewish settlements were forcibly evacuated by the Turkish authorities. But for the intervention of the German government, Djemal Pasha, the Turkish commander, would have transferred the inhabitants of Jerusalem east of the Jordan and removed the Jews from southern Palestine altogether. The Arab national movement also suffered major setbacks with the arrest of many of its leaders and the execution of some of

* W. Cahnmann, in *Herzl Yearbook*, New York, 1958, p. 165.
† Mandel, St Antony's Papers, p. 108 and dissertation.

them, accused by the Turks of separatism and treason. The centre of the political scene, as far as both Arab and Jewish national aspirations were concerned, shifted to London during the war years. Certain British statesmen (such as Kitchener) had favoured the idea of establishing an independent Arab state even before 1914, and there had been contracts, albeit vague and inconclusive in character, between the British and Hussain Ibn Ali, the sherif of Mecca.

After the outbreak of war the eastern question again became topical and policy planners were commissioned to prepare memoranda and blueprints for a postwar settlement in the Near East. British diplomats talked to the French and Russians. The Sykes-Picot agreement envisaged a division of spheres of influence between Britain and France. Palestine under this scheme was to fall into the so-called brown zone, which was to be under international control. Specific promises to the Arabs were made by Sir Henry McMahon, the chief British representative in Egypt. In a letter in October 1915 the idea of an independent Arab state was mooted from which only the Syrian coastal area west of Damascus, Homs, Hamma and Aleppo was to be excluded. Arab spokesmen have maintained ever since that Palestine was thus promised to them, and that this promise was subsequently broken. McMahon himself denied this, as did an investigation committee appointed in 1937. The British argued that the agreement was based on the understanding that the Arabs would rise against the Turks in both the Arab peninsula and Syria, and that since the Arab revolt in Syria never materialised, they were under no obligation to carry out their part of the bargain. However, the whole deal was so vaguely defined that it was bound to give rise to disputes, in the same way that Britain's promise to the Jews, the Balfour Declaration, was open to more than one interpretation.

How did Zionism view its relationship with the Arabs in the framework of the new order likely to emerge in Palestine after the war? In a detailed memorandum for the new administration of Palestine, prepared in 1916, the Zionist leaders demanded equality of rights for all nationalities, autonomy in exclusively Jewish matters, official recognition of the Jewish population as a separate national unit, and recognition of the Hebrew language as equal and parallel to Arabic. The Zionists' main concern was to gain British support for their aspirations. Conditions, as Weizmann said in a speech in Manchester in May 1917, were not yet ripe for a Jewish state, and relations with the Arabs therefore did not figure very highly on the list of Zionist priorities. A non-Jewish supporter of Zionism, Herbert Sidebotham, defined the aim of Zionism in July

1917 as the establishment of a Jewish state, one whose dominant national character should be as Jewish as the dominant national character of England was English – a definition to be repeated by Weizmann at the Versailles Peace Conference when asked what was meant by a Jewish National Home. But Weizmann also said on the very same occasion that the Zionists could not go into the country 'like Junkers'; they could not afford to drive out other people.* The first part of his definition was frequently quoted and criticised in later years. Was he not aware of the existence of the Arabs? There is evidence that Weizmann's closest collaborators certainly realised that the Arab question would be of great importance and urgency after the war. As Harry Sacher wrote to Leon Simon in June 1917: 'At the back of my mind there is firmly fixed the recognition that even if all our political schemes turn out in the way we desire, the Arabs will turn out our most tremendous problem. I don't want us in Palestine to deal with the Arabs as the Poles deal with the Jews. . . . That kind of chauvinism might poison the whole yishuv.'†

Immediate Arab reaction to the Balfour Declaration was not one of unmitigated hostility. Like the Zionists, they were perhaps not quite aware what it would amount to in practice. In the great Zionist public meeting in Covent Garden on 2 December 1917, celebrating the Balfour Declaration, two Arab speakers brought cordial greetings on behalf of their people. Weizmann, speaking in Manchester one week later, said that if there had been misunderstandings between Arabs and Jews in the past, this was all over now. The tension had been created by the deadening hand of the Turks, playing off one part of the population against the other. The attitude of the leading Arab newspapers of Cairo, such as *Mukattam* and *Ahram*, was surprisingly friendly, the former declaring that the Arabs had nothing to fear from a Jewish state; the British government had after all only recognised a historical right of which no one could have deprived the Jews.‡

Weizmann and Faisal

King Hussain's newspaper in Mecca extended a cordial welcome to the returning exiles, 'the original sons of the country from which their Arab brethren would benefit materially as well as spiritually'.§ To cement the

---

* Weizmann, *Zionist Policy*, 21 September 1919. English Zionist Federation, London, p. 12.
† Quoted in Stein, *The Balfour Declaration*, p. 622.
‡ Quoted in *Jüdische Rundschau*, 18 August 1918.
§ Quoted in M.Perlman, 'Arab-Jewish Diplomacy 1918–22', *Jewish Social Studies*, 1944, p 131.

new Arab-Jewish friendship, Dr Weizmann went to Aqaba in May 1918 to meet Faisal, Hussain's son, who assured him of his goodwill towards Zionist aspirations. Like Weizmann, he put the blame for past misunderstanding on the Turks, whose intrigues, he said, had stirred up jealousy between the Jewish colonists and the Arab peasants. On various occasions, as at a banquet given in honour of Lord Rothschild in London, and at several meetings with Jewish leaders, Faisal claimed that he shared Weizmann's ideals, that no true Arab could be afraid of Jewish nationalism, that there should be the most cordial goodwill between the two peoples. In his agreement with Weizmann, signed on 3 January 1919, he renounced any claim to Palestine, which was to become the territory of the Jews, separate from the new Arab state. There was a postscript in which Faisal announced that this agreement would be valid only if the Arabs obtained their independence as formulated by him in an earlier memorandum directed to the British. The document was thus not a binding treaty, but it certainly showed that Faisal clearly wanted the Zionists as allies during and after the peace conferences and that he was willing to accept unlimited Jewish immigration and settlement. His attitude towards a Jewish state was contradictory: if the Jews desired to establish a state and claim sovereign rights, he wrote on one occasion, he foresaw and feared serious dangers and conflicts.* But when Felix Frankfurter, a leading member of the American Zionist delegation in Paris, asked for a clarification, Faisal reiterated that the Arabs looked with the deepest sympathy on the Zionist movement, and that they found its proposals moderate and proper. The Arabs would do their best to help them through: 'We are working together for a reformed and revived near east, and our two movements complete one another. The Jewish movement is national and not imperialist . . . and there is room in Syria for us both.' Yet a few months later Faisal retreated from his pro-Zionist stand. He was, he said, in agreement with a moderate leader such as Weizmann, that there should be a 'small infiltration' of Jews into Palestine – say fifteen hundred a year – in such a way that the Zionists would one day constitute a sub-province of the new Arab kingdom. But he did not agree at all with those Zionists who wanted a Jewish state: 'We Arabs cannot yield Palestine.' They would fight to the last ditch against Palestine being other than part of the kingdom. They would not accept Jewish supremacy in the land.†

What caused Faisal's change of heart? Arab sources, to whom needless

---

* *Jewish Chronicle*, 7 March 1919. Quoted in Perlman, 'Arab-Jewish Diplomacy . . .'.
† *Jewish Chronicle*, 3 October 1919. Quoted in Perlman, 'Arab-Jewish Diplomacy . . .'.

to say the incident was highly embarrassing, have provided various explanations. The king himself later said about the Frankfurter letter that he did not remember having written anything of the kind. Arab commentators have suggested that the documents were forged by the Zionists, or that Lawrence, who acted as interpreter on various occasions, either wilfully misled the king or did not know Arabic sufficiently well, or that the Zionists came to the meetings with prepared drafts and somehow tricked the king into signing documents whose significance he did not understand.* It seems more likely that Faisal agreed to flirt with the Zionist cause because he thought the Jews could help him to strengthen his claim on Syria. He was not well informed about the situation in Palestine, in which he took only a limited interest. The British wanted him to talk to Weizmann, and Faisal complied because he was under a heavy obligation to his protectors. His was, in the words of M. Perlman, the unenviable role of the moderate leader in a period of rising intransigence;† when he realised that inside Palestine opposition to Zionism was much more formidable than he had believed, he decided to beat a hasty retreat. Later critics of the Zionist executive have asserted that Weizmann and his friends did not try hard enough at the time to win the confidence and friendship of the Arabs. Yet an anti-Zionist source reports that King Faisal was continually pestered by Weizmann: 'What does this man want? I would do anything to get rid of him. He tires me out by his long speeches.'‡

Postwar Tensions

Zionists everywhere attached tremendous importance to Faisal's declaration and regarded it as the beginning of a new era in Arab-Jewish relations. Ruppin noted that they had tried to establish contact with the Arabs for a long time, but 'we always returned disappointed and without hope'. There had been no willingness on the other side to discuss matters of principle.§ After Faisal's solemn declaration, he expected a basic change. A few Jewish observers of the Palestinian scene dissented from this optimistic appraisal, realising that the Palestinian Arabs were not at all happy about the Balfour Declaration. When the Arabs sensed that many members of the British military administration shared their misgivings, they began to protest openly against 'that terrible injustice which

---

* A.L.Tibawi, in *Journal of the Royal Central Asian Society*, June 1969, p. 156 *et seq.*
† Perlman, 'Arab-Jewish Diplomacy...', p. 141.
‡ Jeffries, *Palestine: The Reality*, p. 257.
§ *Jüdische Rundschau*, 14 March 1918. Negouib Moussali, *Le Sionisme et la Palestine*, Geneva, 1919, *passim.*

the whole world will regret'. Early in 1919 leaflets were distributed in Jerusalem and Jaffa calling on all Arabs to resist the Zionist danger. The Jews were compared in these manifestos to poisonous snakes. No nation in the world had tolerated them and Palestinian Arabs would defend their homeland to the very end against any Zionist encroachment.* Even earlier, a small Arab terrorist organisation, the Black Hand, had been founded, and in February 1919 the first meeting took place in Jaffa of the Muslim-Christian Association which became the spearhead of anti-Zionist resistance.

In January 1919 an all-Arab Palestine conference asked for the repudiation of the promise that had been given to the Jews to establish a national home in Palestine, a demand which figured prominently in the traditional Nebi Mussa celebrations in Jerusalem in 1919 and 1920. Mussa Kassem, the Arab mayor of Jerusalem, marched at the head of an anti-Zionist demonstration in February 1920. The issue was kept alive in the deliberations and resolutions of four more Arab congresses between July 1919 and May 1921, out of which the Arab higher executive emerged. This body served up to the end of the British mandate as the supreme representative of the Arabs. An Arab delegation headed by Mussa Kassem went to London in 1921 and protested to Mr Churchill, then colonial secretary, against the 'flood of alien Jewish immigration', against the recognition of Hebrew as an official language, against the 'Zionist leanings' of Sir Herbert Samuel, the first high commissioner, against a concession given to Pinhas Rutenberg to establish an electricity company, and against a great many other alleged injustices.

Arab resistance did not come as a total surprise to the architects of the Jewish national home. Balfour wrote in 1919 that he did not think Zionism would hurt the Arabs, but that of course they would never say they wanted it. The Balfour Declaration had been imprecise in wording but the general assumption at the time was that at some future date a Jewish state would emerge in Palestine. Churchill reckoned that it would have three to four million inhabitants. The general consensus was that Syria and Arabia were to be given to the Arabs, and Palestine to the Jews, and the Palestinian Arabs would have to accept this. As Balfour noted, 'Zionism right or wrong, good or bad, is rooted in age-long traditions and in present needs and future hopes of far profounder import than the desires of 700,000 Arabs'. But those who were to carry out these policy directives in Cairo and Jerusalem were not at all in sympathy with such views. Local officials tried hard, and not without success, to whittle

* Quoted in Cohen, *Israel vehaolam ha'aravi*, p. 149.

down the Balfour Declaration. In 1922 it was first decided that Jewish immigration should never exceed the economic capacity of the country to absorb new arrivals,* and in the 1930s it became axiomatic in British policy in Palestine that the building of a Jewish national home was predicated on Arab consent, which if carried to its logical conclusion would amount to the repudiation of the Balfour Declaration.

These were the disappointments of later years. During the early period Zionists were generally optimistic about relations with the Arabs, reckoning that they would calm down after the first flush of excitement and accept the Jewish national home. One of the few exceptions was Ahad Ha'am, forever playing Cassandra. He gave warning against the premature blowing of messianic trumpets to announce the redemption. According to the prophet of cultural Zionism, the Jews in Palestine should not press on too quickly because the conditions for success were not yet ripe. They should not forget that for the Arabs, too, Palestine was a national home.† More acute were the views of Ruppin, a realist, fully aware of the abyss dividing the new immigrants and the Arabs.‡ But Ruppin saw no necessary clash of interests between the two peoples: ten million dunam of unused land were still available, twice as much as the Zionists would need for their colonisation within the next thirty years. Ruppin expected the immigration of one to two million Jews within that span of time; Weizmann thought sixty to seventy thousand would come each year; Motzkin mentioned a figure of one hundred thousand; and Sokolow, the one least involved in practical work, spoke of 'five million in twenty-five years'. In fact no more than thirty thousand Jews emigrated to Palestine during the first five years after the end of the war.

Ruppin thought that Zionism would be able to play a major part in building up the union of Arab states. He envisaged, for instance, a currency union between the new Arab countries and Palestine. With the improvement of the Arab educational system they would perhaps reach the Jewish cultural level within the next generation, which, for all one knew, would be the prelude to cultural assimilation.§ David Eder, an Anglo-Jewish psychoanalyst who had been enlisted by Weizmann to serve

* *Palestine, Correspondence with the Palestine Arab Delegation and the Zionist Delegation*, Cmd. 1700, London, 1922, p. 19.

† 'After the Balfour Declaration', in *Nationalism and the Jewish Ethic*, New York, 1962, p. 122. See also his introduction to the Berlin 1921 edition of *At the Crossroads* in which the idea of a bi-national state was implicitly formulated.

‡ 'Das Verhaeltnis der Juden zu den Arabern', in *Der Jude*, 1919, p. 453.

§ A.Ruppin, *Der Aufbau des Landes Israel*, Berlin, 1919, pp. 127–31. Ber Borokhov, the theoretician of Marxist Zionism in Russia, also believed that the Palestinian Arabs would as the first diplomatic representative of the Zionist executive in Jerusalem, was equally optimistic and foresaw an era of close cooperation leading towards the integration of the Jewish national home with the federated states of the Middle East. He formulated Zionist policy under a number of heads: Jews must not segregate themselves from the Arabs; Tel Aviv must not become a symbol of Jewish exclusiveness; Jews should deal with the Arab world as a whole and show the same respect for Arab national aspirations as they demanded for their own; and as an oriental people, they should abandon their pretensions to be Europeans.*

The riots of 1920–1 shocked the yishuv, causing a hardening of attitudes in some circles and rethinking in others. No one was willing to forgive the murder of Brenner, the noted Jewish Socialist writer, and of Trumpeldor, the hero of generations of halutzim. Appearing before the royal commission enquiring into the causes of the disturbances, Eder declared that there could be only one national home in Palestine, no equality in partnership but only Jewish predominance as soon as their numbers had increased sufficiently. Jabotinsky suggested the immediate establishment of a Jewish armed force to cope with any future emergency. But there was also greater readiness to reconsider what had gone wrong in relations with the neighbouring people. This emerged most clearly perhaps in the reports from Palestine of Chaim Arlosoroff, at the early age of twenty-two already a respected Zionist leader. Writing from Jaffa in late May 1921, he criticised those of his colleagues who put the entire blame on the British high commissioner, and who thought that a 'strong hand' was all that was needed.† They had not realised that the Arab national movement was an important force which should not be belittled even if it did

eventually be culturally absorbed. Borokhov may have got the idea from Michael Halpern, a curious, tragic, and in some ways prophetic figure. Halpern advocated the occupation of Palestine by Jewish legions many years before the First World War, and at the same time called for a brotherly alliance between Arabs and Jews (to be directed against the common enemy, Christianity). To hasten the cultural assimilation of the Arabs he proposed that there should be intermarriage on a massive scale. He left Palestine temporarily after a quarrel with Rothschild's representatives, and his accounts of Arab life and customs, their hospitality and respect for strength and courage, strongly influenced a whole generation of East European halutzim, whom he fascinated with his strange and exotic stories (see Alexander Said, 'Michael Halpern', in *Yediot ha'arkhion vehamuseon la'avoda*, vols. 3–4, 1938, pp. 76–7). As a young man in Smolensk he spent a great deal of time and energy in trying to reform the local prostitutes. He is now virtually forgotten in Israel though a few old timers still remember the incident when a circus visited Jaffa a few years before the outbreak of the First World War. In answer to a challenge by the Arabs present, and to save Jewish honour, Halpern entered the lions' cage unarmed and sang the Hatiqva – to the consternation of public and lions alike.

* J.B.Hobman (ed.), *David Eder*, London, 1945, p. 162 *et seq.*
† *Jüdische Rundschau*, 17 June 1921.

not exactly conform to European criteria of what a national movement should be. Arlosoroff saw a great danger in pursuing an ostrich-like policy. There was only one way out of the dilemma – a policy of peace and reconciliation, even though it seemed not at all easy to accept such advice while passions were still running high. Robert Weltsch, a close confidant of Weizmann and editor of the *Jüdische Rundschau*, was even more outspoken in his warnings to his fellow Zionists: if the views on the Arab question held by many of them (especially Palestinians) were to prevail, then the two nations would never meet and this would mark the burial of the movement. It had been one of the dreadful consequences of the First World War that so many people had drawn the wrong conclusions from the events of recent years, namely that one could assert oneself in the world only by violence. In the short run this was the easier way out, but it was bound to lead Zionism into an impasse.* Weltsch and a few of his friends provoked the first postwar Zionist congress by asking point blank: did the Zionist movement want war with the Arabs or not?

His criticism was rejected with indignation by the Zionist leadership. The Karlsbad congress solemnly proclaimed the desire of the Jewish people to 'live with the Arab people in friendship and mutual respect, and together with them to develop the homeland common to both into a flourishing community which would ensure to each of its peoples an undisturbed national development'.† The formula was not as sweeping as the one proposed by Buber, but in the mood prevailing after the riots of 1921 not much more could be expected. Buber had criticised Weizmann for not doing enough, for negotiating only with Faisal. The president of the Zionist Organisation replied that Faisal was the symbol of Arab independence. It would be ideal if the movement had offices in all important Arab centres to maintain contact with Arab leaders. But he knew in advance that his colleagues on the finance committee would never make the necessary allocations. So far its Arab policy had cost the Zionist movement £8,000 and it had got what it could reasonably expect for the money. (Weizmann was replying to a Dutch delegate, Nehemia de Lieme, who had asked, 'As a businessman I want to know – how much does it – the Arab policy – cost us?') At the same congress Sokolow talked in cultural-philosophical terms about the traditions and historical recollections common to Arabs and Jews and stressed how popular friendship with the Arabs was in Zionist circles.‡

* *Jüdische Rundschau*, 9 August 1921.
† *Stenographisches Protokoll, etc. XII Zionisten Kongress*, Berlin, 1922, p. 715.
‡ *Ibid.*, pp. 26, 104, 285.

The next congress (Karlsbad, 1923) reiterated the resolution adopted two years earlier, adding that the awakening of the orient was one of the most important factors in world politics, and that the Jewish people would integrate itself into this process.* Meanwhile the situation in Palestine had become much calmer. Two years later still, at the fourteenth congress in Vienna, Weizmann announced that relations with the Arabs had improved and that Palestine was now the quietest part of the Middle East. Sokolow foresaw the day when Zionists and Arabs would sit down together at one common Palestinian congress. Meanwhile, the executive would refrain from doing anything which would make co-operation between Jews and Arabs impossible (Brodetsky). Ben Gurion thought that as an oriental people the Jews ought to follow with deep sympathy the national revival of other oriental peoples. Weizmann said that the Near East should be opened to Jewish initiative, that they should be able to make their contribution to the development of the area in real friendship and collaboration with the Arabs. There was not the slightest doubt among the Zionist leaders that what they were doing in Palestine was right, fully in accordance with the Jewish sense of justice – 'otherwise we would never have undertaken it' (Sokolow).†

There were discordant notes. Most official speakers at Zionist congresses stressed the high moral and intellectual qualities of the Arabs ('moderation, diligence, purity of family life' – Ruppin), and reiterated time and time again their desire for Arab-Jewish friendship. But these statements committed no one in particular; they were declamatory and had no practical implications. The elected representatives of Palestinian Jewry, the Temporary Council, certainly showed little initiative in this respect: a contemporary observer wrote that it did nothing to create an atmosphere of mutual understanding, which would have demonstrated the political maturity of the Jewish community.‡ The Palestinian Jewish leadership was weak and ineffectual and it would no doubt have failed to achieve this aim even if it had been given far higher priority. But not all Palestinians were optimistic. Some agreed with Jabotinsky that one day perhaps the Arabs would reconcile themselves to the existence of a great and growing yishuv but there was no good reason to assume that this would happen in the near future. The Palestinians' view was expressed by Glickson when he criticised Weizmann in 1923 for having declared that the mass of the fellaheen were friendly towards the Jews: 'We long

* *Stenographischer Bericht, etc. XIII Zionisten Kongress*, London, 1924, pp. 367, 517.
† *Stenographischer Bericht, etc. XIV Zionisten Kongress*, London, 1926, pp. 54, 61, 207, 328.
‡ Medzini, *loc. cit.*, p. 80.

for that day to come – but at present these are just phrases and harmful illusions.' Even Berl Katznelson, the much respected labour leader, was much more uncompromising in this matter than the European Zionist leaders, who, far from Palestine and its cruel realities, elaborated well-meaning schemes. Many of the Palestinians felt instinctively that there was a basic clash of interests between them and the Arabs. This is not to say that they altogether despaired of living in peace with the Arabs or expected to be in a state of perpetual war with their neighbours. But they were more likely than European Zionists to believe in a policy of force, of *faits accomplis*. In their eyes the Arabs were highly volatile, easily excitable people, but once the yishuv had grown stronger and more numerous, the Arabs would gradually accept them.

Arab Grievances

Events between 1921 and 1929 seemed to justify these assumptions: the Arabs were relatively quiet, and there were regular political and social contacts between Zionist and Arab leaders in Jerusalem, Amman, Cairo and elsewhere. According to Colonel Kisch there was abundant evidence not only of persistent efforts by the Zionist executive to reach an understanding with the Arabs, but also of the existence of a large body of moderate Arab opinion ready to follow a lead from the mandatory government.*

Kisch was a British officer with a distinguished war record, sober, unemotional, less given to outbursts than his east European colleagues, less likely to accuse the mandatory government of betrayal and bad faith at the slightest provocation. His criticism of British policy, therefore, carried a great deal of conviction: 'I have no doubt whatever', he wrote, 'that had it not been for the mufti's abuse of his immense powers and the toleration of that abuse by the government over a period of fifteen years, an Arab-Jewish understanding within the framework of the mandate would long since have been reached.'† Kisch was referring to Haj Amin el Hussaini, scion of one of Palestine's leading families, who had been made mufti by Sir Herbert Samuel in 1921 despite the fact that he had been prominently involved in the first wave of anti-Jewish riots. Haj Amin remained till 1937 the spiritual leader of the Palestinian Arabs, and during most of the time had the blessing of the mandatory government, despite his extremist political activities. He bears much of the responsi-

* F.H.Kisch, *Palestine Diary*, London, 1938, p. 19.
† *Ibid.*, p. 20.

bility for the riots in 1929 and the civil war in 1936–9. But it is unduly optimistic to assume that but for the appointment of Haj Amin and his activities, Arab-Jewish relations would have followed a very different course. Sooner or later the extremist element would have prevailed in the Arab leadership, with or without the support of the British high commissioner.

The Arab list of grievances was a long one: Palestine was a small country, a sheikh from Beer Sheva told a British enquiry commission in 1929, it could not possibly hold the number of Jews brought into the country.* 'There remains nothing for the Arabs in this country except to die or leave the country.' Such alarmist declarations were not altogether novel. Similar fears had been voiced occasionally even before 1914. So long as the Turks ruled Palestine, such fears were probably not widespread or deeply rooted, but by the 1920s the situation had changed and there was general concern about the effects of Zionist settlement. There were complaints that the Zionists displaced Arab workers at the ports of Jaffa and Haifa, and from the orange groves, that the Jewish trade unions consistently followed a policy of Jewish labour only ('Conquest of Labour'). Arab spokesmen pointed to the fact that according to the constitution of the Jewish National Fund, land once acquired could never be resold to Arabs, nor could Arabs be employed on such land. The Arab had benefited neither from the import of Jewish capital nor from the extension of social services or education.

The Zionists dismissed these arguments as of no substance or consequence. It is a moot point whether there was any direct connection between Jewish immigration and settlement and the situation of the Arabs. Between 1924 and 1926 almost fifty thousand new immigrants entered the country, yet these were peaceful years in Arab Jewish relations, whereas the riots of 1929 followed a period during which the number of Jewish emigrants from Palestine had actually exceeded the number of new immigrants. But 1925–6 had been years of prosperity which were followed by the slump and the widespread unemployment of 1927–8. Arab wages were twice or three times as high in Palestine as in Syria or Iraq, but Arab workers were likely to compare their income and standard of living not with those of their compatriots in other countries, but with the considerably higher wages paid to Jewish workers. 'Together we shall rise, or go under', Ben Gurion declared in 1924, drawing attention to the discrepancy in wages and working hours between

---

* *Report of the Commission on the Palestine Disturbances of August 1929* (Shaw Report), London, 1930, p. 58.

Arab and Jewish workers. The Arabs were working ten to twelve hours a day and earned fifteen piasters; Jewish workers had won the eight-hour working day and a daily wage of thirty piasters.* Admittedly it was a complex situation. If Jewish orange grove owners refused to employ Arabs they were bound to be charged with chauvinism, but if they employed Arabs they were accused of exploiting cheap labour. When the Histadrut, the federation of Jewish trade unions, attempted to organise Arab labour it was attacked for interfering in Arab politics. When it refrained from doing so it was charged with wilfully neglecting the interests of the Arab worker. When the Histadrut Arab-language newspaper called on the Arab workers to make common cause with the Jews against western imperialism, against gunboat policy and economic exploitation, it was denounced by Arabs to the mandatory government for Communist incitement.† If it refrained from attacking imperialism this was interpreted as a sign that the Zionists were utterly dependent on British bayonets.

The 'Communist peril' was frequently invoked by Arab spokesmen in the 1920s and 1930s. Arab opposition to Zionism was said to have been aroused largely by the 'Bolshevik principles' of the Zionist immigrants. The official Palestine Arab delegation which went to London in 1922 to demand the abrogation of the Balfour declaration protested specifically against the influx of alien Jews, 'many of them of a Bolshevik revolutionary type'. M.E.T.Mogannam wrote: 'The Arabs were irritated . . . by the Bolshevik principles which the new arrivals bring with them . . . this has produced an effect on the population not by the success of its propaganda but by the genuine uneasiness which it inspired among the Arabs, especially the poorer classes'.‡ Jamal Hussaini, secretary of the Arab Higher Committee, declared in his testimony before the royal commission in 1937: 'As to the Communistic principles and ideas of Jewish immigrants, most repugnant to the religion, customs and ethical principles of this country, which are imported and disseminated, I need not dwell upon them as these ideas are well known to have been imported by the Jewish community'.§ The argument that Arab opposition to Zionism is caused by the right-wing, reactionary and imperialist character of the movement is of comparatively recent date, appearing first in the late 1950s.

* Quoted in D.Ben Gurion, *Anakhnu veshekhnenu*, Tel Aviv, 1931, p. 74.

† See *Haqiqat el Amr*, 14 July 1937, and G.Mansur, *The Arab Worker Under the Palestine Mandate*, Jerusalem, 1936, p. 40.

‡ M.E.T.Mogannam, *The Arab Woman and the Palestine Problem*, London, 1936, pp. 217–18.

§ *Minutes of the Palestine Royal Commission*, London, 1936, p. 236.

The basic Arab fears were, of course, political in character. Hence their insistent demand for representative government. But on this the Zionist movement was quite unwilling to compromise, for it would have resulted in the cessation of immigration and settlement. According to the official Zionist formula developed in the 1920s, Palestine belonged on the one hand to the Arabs living there, and on the other to the whole Jewish people, not just to that part of it resident in Palestine. Even left-wing Zionists such as Kaplanski maintained that the Arabs had not the sole right of possession. From the Socialist point of view, he wrote, the Jews also had a very good claim – the right of the only landless people of the earth, the right of the dispossessed masses.* Kaplanski and other left-wing Zionists regarded the conflict as largely artificial, for in their view the labouring Arab masses could only benefit from Jewish colonisation. Inasmuch as the Arab national movement was anti-Zionist it was simply misguided, Kaplanski maintained. The struggle of the Arab ruling class for national independence was a convenient cloak behind which they exploited the toiling Arab masses. There was no basic difference between this approach and the official view of Mapai as developed by such ideologists as Berl Katznelson: the Arab national movement was not truly anti-imperialist, it lacked deep social roots, it was basically xenophobic in inspiration, and it was rooted in the desire of the native middle class and intelligentsia to take the place of the foreigners who monopolised the leading positions in government, national economy, and society in general.

This raises an issue of wider significance: the almost constant misjudgment of the Arab national movement by most Zionist leaders. They were firmly convinced that the broad masses of the Arab population had no real interest in politics, that their main concern was to improve their standard of living. In view of their backwardness and ignorance these masses were not able to form a judgment of their own and were therefore easy prey for ambitious politicians. The Zionist leaders were forever seeing a hidden hand behind the anti-Zionist movement. French and British agents were blamed in the early 1920s, Italian and German fascism in the 1930s. The riots of 1921 and 1929 were explained in terms of religious fanaticism in the usual antisemitic tradition: was it a coincidence that the old yishuv was among the main victims of the 1929 attacks, men and women from Hebron and Safed born and brought up side by side with the Arabs and on friendly terms with them? Even the more sophisticated Zionist ideologists were usually inclined to deny that

* 'Jews and Arabs in Palestine', *Socialist Review*, March 1922.

the Arabs had been able to develop a national consciousness. Arab attacks were described as mere acts of theft and murder carried out by criminal elements among the Arab population or by a mob incited by agitators devoid of moral scruples.*

History was in a way repeating itself: European Zionism had criticised the 'assimilationists', not without justice, for their inability to analyse antisemitism objectively, referring instead to the evil character and base personal motives of its advocates. And just as the assimilationist Jews were inherently incapable of making an objective assessment of antisemitism as a political and social phenomenon, so the Zionists were unable to understand and explain Arab nationalism realistically and unemotionally. It was not uncommon for Zionist extremists to describe the Arab rioters as 'the scum from Hebron, pederasts from Nablus, bastards, hooligans and gangsters from Jaffa. The Mosque of Omar where they congregated was transformed into a murderer's den.'† There was admittedly a great deal of provocation: Palestinian Arab newspapers at the time fairly regularly reprinted the standard propaganda material from European antisemitic newspapers. *Miraat ash Shark* (to give but one example) reported that Jews were distributing poisoned sweets, chocolates and dried figs in the Arab markets to kill Arab children.‡

Among the very few Zionists who kept a relatively calm and detached outlook on the Arab national movement were A.D.Gordon, the apostle of Tolstoyan Socialism, and David Ben Gurion. Gordon saw nothing surprising in the fact that the Arab movement was headed by effendis, bourgeois and intelligentsia. These social groups had, after all, provided the leadership of national movements during their early phases almost everywhere. But did this imply that the Arab national movement lacked legitimacy? Only doctrinaire Socialists could expect that the Arab working class would eventually join Labour Zionism in the struggle against the effendis.§

In Ben Gurion's view the one decisive criterion was whether a national movement could enlist mass support. The Arab national movement did have such support and that was all that mattered.‖ Ben Gurion had for a long time given much thought to the Arab question. Mention has been made of his opposition to the concept of a population transfer: such a

* See, for instance, M.Beilinson, in *Davar*, 2 and 9 October 1929.

† A.Reubeni, in *Doar Hayom*, 6 September 1929, in a poem commenting on the events of August 1929. Quoted in Wiener, *Juden und Araber in Palästina*, Berlin, 1930, p. 24.

‡ 26 September 1929. Quoted in Wiener, p. 44.

§ *Kitve A.D.Gordon*, vol. 5, p. 123.

‖ Ben Gurion, *Anakhnu veshekhnenu*, p. 180.

course he saw as reactionary and Utopian, quite apart from the fact that it was morally reprehensible.* Paraphrasing Dostoievsky, he said that Zionism did not have the moral right to harm one single Arab child even if it could realise all its aspirations at that price.† Ben Gurion maintained that there could be no common language with the effendis, in whose eyes Labour Zionists were both the national and the class enemy. He implicitly criticised Weizmann and the Zionist leadership for having tried the 'short and easy way' to reach agreement with the effendis and the dictators. Jewish Socialists had to choose the longer and more difficult road which would lead them to the Arab workers.‡ But even Ben Gurion's attitude towards the Arab national movement lacked consistency. He acknowledged that it was a real political force even though it lacked a positive social content; each people has the national movement it deserves, he observed on one occasion.

Ben Gurion, then, thought that political agreement with its present leaders was impossible. But did he believe that an understanding would have been possible with leaders who really represented the desires and interests of the masses? Would a more progressive Arab leadership have been better disposed towards Zionism? Ben Gurion was on the whole more optimistic than most of his colleagues with regard to the prospects of an understanding with the Arabs, and his attitude did not basically change during the 1930s. When Moshe Shertok claimed in 1936 that the attempts to reach an agreement with the Arabs should continue, but that there was room for scepticism, Ben Gurion replied: 'We must not be sceptical. We ought to believe that tomorrow there will be an agreement with the Arabs – and to act accordingly.'§

The very same month (June 1936) Ben Gurion wrote in a private letter that there was perhaps only one chance in ten of reaching agreement with the Arabs; even the views of an optimist like Ben Gurion were subject to sudden and violent change. It was the official policy of the Zionist executive throughout the 1920s not to enter into political discussions with the Arabs, but as Colonel Kisch noted in his diary in 1923, to 'get a strong Arab party to work with us on the basis of economic cooperation, leaving the question of the political régime out of account'.‖ Such an Arab party did not exist, nor was it likely to emerge in the given circumstances. Most

---

* *Ibid.*, p. 41.
† *Ibid.*, p. 150 (meeting with a Russian Jewish revolutionary in Berlin).
‡ Speech in Ein Harod, 1924, *ibid.*, p. 74.
§ M.Sharett, *Yoman Medini*, Tel Aviv, 1968, p. 165.
‖ Kisch, *Palestine Diary*, p. 53.

Zionists underrated the political awareness of the Arab population. The Shaw commission was more realistic in this respect, noting that the Arab villagers and fellaheen were probably more politically minded than many of the people of Europe, and that their interest was real and personal. There were at the time no fewer than fourteen Arab newspapers, and there was someone in every village to read from the papers to the gatherings of those who were illiterate: 'During the long seasons of the year when the soil cannot be tilled, the villagers, having no alternative occupation, discuss politics, and it is not unusual for part of the address in the mosques on Friday to be devoted to political affairs.'*

The Zionists were mistaken in belittling the degree of political consciousness of the Arab national movement and its political effectiveness. Their background was European and they were accustomed to measure national movements by the standards of the *risorgimento* and Masaryk, or at the very least, Pilsudski. But there was no reason to assume that national movements in backward countries would be liberal and democratic in their political orientation. Religious fanaticism and reactionary ideologies were likely to shape their character. For all that, a movement such as the Arab Palestinian awakening and its resistance to Zionism was national in character. There were conflicting class interests between effendis and fellaheen but there was also a feeling of national solidarity which Zionism tended always to underrate.

The Zionist movement did not make great efforts throughout the 1920s to influence the Arab community. Only with much delay was an Arab department established in the Jewish Agency: the publication of Arab language leaflets was left for a long time to the Communists. But it is difficult to see, even with the benefit of hindsight, that greater efforts to enlighten the Arab public about Zionism would have done much good. There was no misunderstanding between Jews and Arabs, as Weizmann and others so often claimed. Nor was it true, as many asserted, that the tension between the two peoples was mainly the fault of the Turks, and later the British in their pursuit of a policy of *divide et impera*. The Turks and the British can be criticised on many counts, but neither their sins of commission nor those of omission were of decisive importance. Having underrated Arab resistance to the Balfour Declaration, the British authorities would have only welcomed any Zionist initiative towards integration into the Arab world.†

---

* Shaw Report, p. 129.
† Robert Weltsch, in *Jüdische Rundschau*, 19 September 1922.

Brit Shalom

The members of the *Brit Shalom* were among those most concerned about the Arab problem and its potential repercussions. This group, which had supporters outside Palestine as well, came into being in Jerusalem in late 1925, and its beginnings can be traced even further back. Among the first to sound the tocsin was Judah Magnes, the American Reform rabbi who became the first president of the Hebrew university. He had been unhappy about the Balfour Declaration from the outset. The peace conference, he said at a meeting in New York in 1919, had no right to give any land to any people. He feared that the Zionists would be regarded from now on as interlopers and invaders, and that the support they received from an imperialist power would in time be a heavy burden.*

Hans Kohn, the writer and historian, was another who maintained that the Jews had no historical right to Palestine, that their love for Zion was the only basis for their claim. As early as 1919 he denounced the 'chauvinism of the new immigrants' and their dependence on British imperialism.† Similar views were expressed in the early 1920s by Robert Weltsch, editor of the *Jüdische Rundschau*. Misgivings about the course of Zionist policy were also voiced by those who before the First World War had already been preaching the necessity for closer relations: Kalvarisky, Ruppin, Hugo Bergmann, and some members of the *Hapoel Hatzair*. Brit Shalom was originally meant to be a club for the study of Arab-Jewish relations; only a minority was in favour of political activism. The association had at no time more than a hundred members. Magnes, while supporting it, did not in fact join it. Among its members were university professors, mainly of central and west European origin. A critic of Brit Shalom, referring mockingly to 'all these Arthurs, Hugos, and Hans', called them creatures who lacked roots in Palestine.

The principal idea guiding Brit Shalom was that Palestine should be neither a Jewish nor an Arab state, but a binational state in which Jews and Arabs should enjoy equal civil, political and social rights, without distinction between majority and minority. The two peoples should each be autonomous in the administration of their respective domestic affairs, but united in their common interests.‡ Brit Shalom had no mass basis and

---

* Norman Bentwich, *For Zion's Sake, a Biography of Judah L. Magnes*, Philadelphia, 1954, p. 174.

† *Der Jude*, July 1919, p. 567.

‡ *Jewish-Arab Affairs*. Occasional papers published by the Brit Shalom Society, June 1931, p. 47.

its political impact was negligible. Western Zionism, the philosopher Hugo Bergmann wrote in retrospect, was the last flicker of the humanist-nationalist flame at the very moment when anti-humanism was triumphant over all the world.* Significantly, there were no oriental Jews among Brit Shalom, and few of east European origin. But the real reason for its failure was the total lack of response from the Arab side. 'What is the point of reaching agreement between ourselves', Ruppin wrote to Magnes, 'if there is no one on the other side?'

After the 1929 riots, Magnes demanded a reorientation of Zionist policy on pacifist lines. The Jews should re-enter Palestine not as invaders following the tradition of Joshua Ben Nun, but to conquer the country by peaceful means, hard work, sacrifice and love. Magnes was quite willing to give up the idea of a Jewish majority, let alone a Jewish state, provided only that the three basic tenets (immigration, settlement and Hebrew culture) were accepted by the Arabs.† He was writing shortly after the brutal attacks on the Jewish communities of Hebron and Safed and there was little willingness in the yishuv even to listen to him. Public disfavour, however, hardly ever deterred Magnes: 'We must face this problem', he said in a speech at the Hebrew university, 'not because of the pogroms but despite of them; not as a result of violence, but as an attempt to remove excuses for violence, not because of pressure from without but because of spiritual pressure from within ourselves.'‡ Magnes anticipated some of the arguments of his critics:

We are told that when we become the majority we shall then show how just and generous a people in power can be. That is like the man who says that he will do anything and everything to get rich, so that he may do good with the money thus accumulated. Sometimes he never grows rich – he fails. And if he does grow rich under those circumstances, his power of doing good has been atrophied from long lack of use. In other words, it is not only the end which for Israel must be desirable but, what is of equal importance, the means must be conceived and brought forth in cleanliness.§

Magnes and the members of Brit Shalom were more acutely aware of the importance of the Arab question than the official Zionist leadership. For most of them this preoccupation was moral rather than political in

---

* In Felix Weltsch (ed.), *Prague and Jerusalem*, Jerusalem, 1954. Quoted in Susan Lee Hattis' doctoral dissertation, *The Binational Idea in Palestine during Mandatory Times*, Geneva, 1970.
† *Like all the Nations?*, Jerusalem, 1930, p. 6.
‡ *Ibid.*, p. 14.
§ *Ibid.*, p. 28.

character, but their predictions about the ultimate consequences of a policy of violence were only too prophetic. Brit Shalom was bitterly attacked. Its views were said to reflect the mentality of the diaspora, and its members were called 'deep down assimilationists', men devoid of Jewish national feeling. This was grossly unfair. Their Zionism was as deeply rooted as that of their opponents. But they feared that without an agreement there would be perpetual strife between Jews and Arabs which would lead to a deterioration in Zionism and ultimately perhaps to its ruin.

Their analysis was astute, their sentiments praiseworthy, but they could not point to any practical political alternatives. An anonymous reader of their magazine wrote from Moscow:

You are in favour of a democratically elected legislative assembly. But how do you know that this assembly, with a clear Arab majority, will not spell the doom of Zionism? You are in favour of negotiations with the Arabs, but you also know that the mufti and his party are not willing to negotiate; they regard any talks on the basis of mutual concessions as an act of national treason.*

Or, as Berl Katznelson put it, this binationalism is a camouflage for an Arab state. Brit Shalom sharply rebuked Colonel Kisch and Arlosoroff (who succeeded him as the foreign secretary of the Jewish Agency) for their inactivity in the field of Arab policy, but they were quite unable to outline any alternative. There was no political force in the Arab camp willing to cooperate on the basis of the minimum conditions outlined by Magnes and his friends. The Brit Shalom ideology was open to criticism on other counts as well. Some of its members went much too far in their nebulous enthusiasm for the spirit of the renascent east, which they contrasted with 'decadent Europe'. The 'spiritual reintegration of the Jewish people in the orient' was a highly problematical proposition, which could perhaps be psychologically explained as a reaction against the horrors of the First World War. But its advocates idealised out of all proportion the 'wisdom of the east' – and this at a time when the Asian intelligentsia was rapidly adopting and absorbing European ideas.

It was the main weakness of Brit Shalom that it could not translate its diagnosis into practical politics. For that reason the unceasing efforts made by the indefatigable Magnes and Kalvarisky were all in vain. Magnes met Mussa Alami, an influential Palestinian Arab, and Philby, adviser first to Abdulla of Jordan and later to King Saud, who had himself

* *She'ifotenu*, May 1932, pp. 58–9.

become a Muslim. Kalvarisky repeatedly went to Beirut and Damascus and also had many contacts with Palestinian Arabs, but whenever encouraging sounds were made by his Arab interlocutors it soon appeared that they were not entitled to speak on behalf of any organised force in the Arab community. The Arabs, on the other hand, claimed that they always found a great deal of goodwill and understanding on the part of the Zionists when discussing general issues, but that this invariably evaporated once the discussion turned to practical politics. The Arabs were not willing to accept the formula used by both Kalvarisky and the official Zionist leadership during that period: that neither people should dominate or be dominated by the other.*

The Zionist leaders followed the activities of Magnes and Brit Shalom with misgivings, but there is no doubt that they would have felt obliged to take note of them if they had held out any promise at all. Magnes and Kalvarisky asserted on various occasions that their efforts had been sabotaged by the Jewish Agency, but there was usually a less sinister explanation. The Jewish Agency regarded the contacts established by the Brit Shalom as not substantial enough to merit serious attention. There was concern even among the 'hawks' in the Zionist leadership about relations with the Arabs. When King (then Emir) Abdulla was reported in 1922 to be willing to accept the Balfour Declaration under a national, i.e. Arab, leadership, even Jabotinsky was in favour of taking up the suggestion. Ben Gurion fully accepted the formula of 'not to dominate – not to be dominated', as did the seventeenth Zionist congress. Eliahu Golomb, one of the founders and leaders of Hagana, met Colonel Kisch in 1931 to discuss the possibility of resolving the conflict by an association of Palestine with an Arab confederation.† Weizmann's attitude towards Brit Shalom was by no means unfriendly. In July 1927 he decided to make an allocation (albeit a modest one) to its budget.‡ Shortly before the establishment of Brit Shalom, Weizmann had said in a letter to Robert Weltsch, one of its founders, that his views on the Arab question coincided with Weltsch's, 'but we both know that it will take a long period of education before the Zionists settle down to realities'.§ He had never watered down his Zionism, but he was equally convinced that present-day Zionism was to a certain extent intellectually dishonest. Nevertheless, while maintaining that he accepted binationalism, and

---

* See Kalvarisky's peace programme of 1932, *Jüdische Rundschau*, 16 December 1932.
† Kisch, *Palestine Diary*, p. 374.
‡ Hattis, Dissertation, p. 29.
§ *Ibid.*, p. 46.

differed from Brit Shalom only in approach, Weizmann criticised Weltsch after the riots of 1929 for advocating negotiations with the Arabs when such a step would be fatal: 'The Arab mind is not ripe at all for any negotiations, they are not producing arguments but tricks'.*

The riots of 1929

Brit Shalom had been founded in a relatively calm period when only a few people regarded the Arab question as the foremost in Zionist politics. The year of 1929 brought a radical change, when the problem took on a far greater urgency than ever before but the prospects for reconciliation appeared even more distant. The immediate causes of the 1929 disturbances were trivial, arising from a dispute about the respective rights of Jews and Arabs at the Wailing Wall. The quarrel was by no means new. On the Day of Atonement, 1925, seats and benches had been brought in for old and infirm Jewish worshippers, but these were promptly removed by the police in the middle of the service. This provoked a strong Jewish protest, but similar scenes occurred again on the Day of Atonement, 1928, when the Arabs complained that the Jews had fastened a screen to the pavement adjoining the wall to divide the men from the women, and that several oil lamps and a number of mats had been brought in, in violation of all tradition. On Arab insistence the screen was removed by the police, to the great indignation of the Jews, who claimed that the Wailing Wall was holy to no one but themselves. The Arabs on the other hand maintained that the site was part of the wall of Haram ash Sharif, one of the holiest Muslim places, that it belonged to the Mutawil of the Abu Madian *Waqf*, and that the Jews were there only on sufferance; they had only the right of access through an alley way 28 metres long and 3·6 metres wide.†

The Arabs categorically refused to allow the Jews under any circumstances to alter the *status quo*. Several months later they began building on and around the wall in such a way as to cause great commotion among sections of the Jewish population. *Doar Hayom*, the revisionist newspaper, summoned all Jewish patriots to 'wake up and unite', not to suffer indifferently this terrible catastrophe but 'to move heaven and earth in protest against this unprecedented and unspeakable injustice'.‡ 'The

* Weizmann archives: letter to Weltsch, 25 November 1929, quoted in Hattis, Dissertation, p. 49.

† F.F.Andrews, *The Holy Land under Mandate*, Boston, 1931, vol. 2, *passim*.

‡ *Doar Hayom*, 12 August 1929 and subsequent dates.

wall is ours' became the slogan. A few hundred young Jews marched to the wall, raised the blue and white flag, kept a two minute silence, and dispersed after singing the Hatiqva. On 15 August two thousand Arabs staged a counter-demonstration, beat up the Jewish beadle at the wall and burned a few prayer books. Two days later a quarrel broke out in the streets of Jerusalem when a Jewish football fell into an Arab tomato garden. A young Jew was stabbed and died a few days later. This was the beginning of a series of attacks. On 23 August widespread rioting started, which lasted about a week. In Hebron sixty Jews were killed, in Safed forty-five were killed or wounded. About the responsibility of the mufti and his party there was no doubt. Sir John Chancellor, the high commissioner, and not a staunch friend of Zionism, denounced in a speech on 1 September the 'ruthless and bloodthirsty evil doers' who had perpetrated crimes on 'defenceless members of the Jewish population, regardless of age and sex, accompanied as in Hebron by acts of unspeakable savagery'.

The riots of 1929 marked a turning point in Arab-Jewish relations in Palestine. Throughout the centuries there had always been clashes, sometimes bloody, in the old city of Jerusalem between members of various confessions about their respective rights to the holy sites, but the events of 1929 introduced a new element. On the Arab side religious fanaticism was deliberately fanned for political purposes. This propaganda was part of the contest between the party of the mufti and its rivals, the former trying to outbid the latter with the extremism of its slogans. There was a similar development on the other side. Among the Jews the main outcry did not come from those directly affected, the orthodox and ultra-orthodox Jews, who had always shown great circumspection in their relations with the Arabs, but from the revisionists for whom the wall was a national rather than a religious symbol.

The revisionist stand on the Arab question lacked neither a certain logic nor consistency. Jabotinsky had early on reached the conclusion that Zionism did not make sense without a Jewish majority in Palestine, for the real cause of antisemitism was that Jews were everywhere a minority. Other Zionist leaders, he argued, also knew this, but preferred not to talk about it openly, on the mistaken assumption that the Arabs could be fooled by a more moderate formulation of Zionist aims.* But the Arabs loved their country as much as the Jews did. Instinctively they understood Zionist aspirations very well, and their decision to resist them was only natural. Every people fought immigration and settlement by

* 'O zheleznoi stene', in *Rassvet*, 4 November 1923.

foreigners, however high-minded the motives for settlement. There was no misunderstanding between Jews and Arabs but a natural conflict. No agreement was possible with the Palestinian Arabs, they would accept Zionism only when they found themselves up against an 'iron wall', when they realised that they had no alternative but to accept Jewish settlement. Nor was Jabotinsky optimistic about the prospects of an agreement with the Arabs outside Palestine. The Zionists could not finance Iraq and Hedjaz, and to support the Arabs in their struggle against the European powers would be both dishonest and national suicide.

Zionism, Jabotinsky argued, was either *ab initio* moral or immoral. If the basic principle was moral, it was bound to remain so even if some people opposed it.* There were no empty spaces in the world. The Jews would have encountered the opposition of a native population even in Uganda. Jabotinsky denounced the 'cannibalist ethics' of the anti-Zionists. How could anyone, on the basis of moral criteria, deny the validity of the Zionist claim, given that the Arabs had so much land and the Jews none at all? His instinctive attitude towards the Arabs was, as he once wrote, the same as to all other nations, one of polite lack of interest. He thought that it was impossible to expel the Arabs and that Palestine would always remain a multinational state. The weakest part of Jabotinsky's doctrine was no doubt his assumption that Zionism was bound to remain morally unassailable, whatever the means applied. In their transfer to Palestine Jabotinsky's views lost much of their sophistication and moderation, and served as the ideological justification for primitive and chauvinistic slogans which helped to poison Arab-Jewish relations during the 1930s and 1940s.

The Zionist movement was gravely disturbed by the riots of 1929 but comforted itself with the thought that these attacks were not the beginning of a national revolt but had their source 'in religion and in blood'. Incited by some of their leaders, who had deliberately spread false rumours, the Arabs had come out to defend their religious honour (which had not been insulted) and to revenge Arab blood (which had not been spilled). The riots, according to the official Zionist assessment, did not have a clear political or social character, nor were they countrywide, and that once the government disabused the rioters of their belief that they had official support, the movement would collapse and probably not recur.

The first Zionist reaction was to regard the uprisings as simple pogroms, the Arab grievances as totally unfounded, and to ask for strict measures

* V. Jabotinsky, 'Etika zheleznoi steni', in *Rassvet*, 11 November 1923.

by the mandatory authorities. But suggestions were also advanced by some of the more farsighted Zionist leaders for new and greater efforts to improve Arab-Jewish relations. It had gradually dawned on them that a series of favourable articles in a leading Cairo newspaper was of greater importance than a sympathetic editorial in the Polish or Italian press. The Histadrut had decided in 1927 to organise Arab workers in joint trade unions (*Irgun meshutaf*), but the practical results had been negligible so far, apart from the establishment of a small Arab workers' club in Haifa. There was still no Arab department in the Jewish Agency or the *Va'ad Leumi*, nor was there any Arab-language newspaper. Above all, the Zionist leadership still had no clear idea about what to do, and it was therefore not surprising that the years after the 1929 uprising produced a great deal of heart-searching. While the revisionists tried to compel the Zionist movement to adopt a clear resolution about the final aim, namely a Jewish state, Weizmann reiterated his belief in the principle of parity in the coming Palestinian Constituent Assembly, which, needless to say, was rejected by the Arabs. And Ben Gurion outlined a project for parliamentary representation, to be carried out in stages over many years; a Jewish majority let alone a Jewish state, was not even mentioned.

Perhaps most revealing were the vacillations of Chaim Arlosoroff, who had been one of the first to realise the importance of the Arab national movement as a political factor. After 1929, while still maintaining the need for a political agreement with the Arabs, he asserted that the Arab national movement was dominated by the forces of social reaction and political tyranny and blamed it for not having produced leaders like Sun Yat-sen or Gandhi. Arlosoroff favoured cooperation on the municipal level, economic collaboration, the dispatch of Jewish students to Al Azhar and other Arab universities, and Zionist support for Egyptian and Iraqi independence. But he was pessimistic with regard to the chances of an understanding with the Palestinian Arabs, for the simple reason that the Arabs were still convinced that they could defeat Zionism with violence.* His pessimism deepened during the early 1930s. In a letter to Weizmann he envisaged limiting the Zionist efforts to a part of Palestine – i.e. partition or cantonisation of the country. Failing that, he considered the possibility of the Jewish minority seizing power through an organised revolutionary government.†

Such counsels of despair were the result of Arlosoroff's own negative personal experience. Earlier that year, accompanied by Moshe Shertok,

---

* *Hapoel Hatzair*, 18 October 1929.
† *Yoman Yerushalayim*, Tel Aviv, 1948, p. 341.

he had met Auni Bey Abdul Hadi, a leader of the Istiqlal Party, in an attempt to discover some common ground and to open a dialogue. But Auni Bey had told his visitors point plank that there was no use in discussions on basic problems. There were no misunderstandings between Arab and Jew. He understood Jewish nationalism only too well, but unfortunately there was a fundamental clash of interests which could not be resolved through talk.* This was not, however, the end of the affair.

By the early 1930s the Zionist leaders had reached the conclusion that of the three Arab political parties the Istiqlal, however strongly opposed to Zionism, was the most promising movement in terms both of its political prospects and of the chances of Arab-Jewish *rapprochement*. Cooperation with the mufti's party was out of the question after all that had happened. The Zionists had supported the Nashashibis on various occasions (such as the municipal elections of 1926): the quarrel between this clan and the Hussainis (to whom the mufti belonged) dominated Palestinian Arab political life for many years. But the Nashashibis were closely identified with British mandatory policies and had no intention of compromising themselves in the eyes of the Arab public by cooperating with the Jews. There remained the Istiqlal, a modern, secular, nationalist group which stood for Arab unity and had many supporters among the younger generation.

The Istiqlal Party seemed in many ways an ideal political partner for the Zionists. Ben Gurion met Auni Abdul Hadi in Dr Magnes' house in July 1934 and tried to persuade him that it might be possible after all to coordinate the ultimate aims of the Jewish and Arab national movements. What if the Jews, with their political influence and financial resources, were to join the struggle for Arab unity? Whereupon Auni, according to Ben Gurion's account, became very enthusiastic and promised that he would accept the immigration of five or six million Jews, that he himself would go out into the streets and propagate the idea among his friends in Palestine and other Arab countries.† But after a few moments Auni again cooled down: 'How do we know that we can trust your promises?' Mussa Alami, another prominent Arab figure, and a moderate in his politics, told Ben Gurion that the Arabs were not particularly eager to get Jewish money and know-how, and that he would much prefer Palestine to remain poor and desolate even for a hundred years, in which time the Arabs would be able to develop the country by their own exertions.

---

* *Ibid.*
† D.Ben Gurion, *Wir und die Nachbarn*, Tübingen, 1968, p. 41.

The accounts of such meetings between the Zionist leaders and Arab representatives, or of the talks with George Antonius, the author of the standard history of the Arab national movement, make melancholy reading. The basic positions were so far apart that any agreement was illusory from the beginning. These were the years after Hitler's rise to power, and any compromise on Jewish immigration was unthinkable for the Zionists. By June 1936, after the outbreak of the third Arab revolt, Ben Gurion wrote in a private letter that he doubted whether there was even one chance in ten of reaching agreement. Of course, they should go on talking, but there was no readiness on the Arab part to accept the yishuv, though they might eventually, in complete despair, accept the Jewish presence in Palestine after the failure of the rebellion, and above all as a result of the growth of the yishuv. It was Jabotinsky's 'iron wall' all over again. Ruppin, who had been in the forefront of the struggle for Arab-Jewish *rapprochement* both before and after the First World War, and who was a founder of Brit Shalom, reached similarly pessimistic conclusions at the same time. It was only natural that there should be sporadic outbursts if the Zionists continued their work against the desire of the Arabs: 'It is our destiny to be in a state of continual warfare with the Arabs and there is no other alternative but that lives should be lost.'

Only the indefatigable Magnes and some of his closest friends continued to believe that with a little more goodwill on the part of the Jews agreement could be reached. And occasionally even Magnes had doubts about the reliability and honesty of his Arab partners. In a note to Harold MacMichael, the British high commissioner, he wondered whether there was any point in further negotiations: 'They are no more true Arabs than I am a South Sea Islander. These people around here and Beirut are true Levantines.'*

Arab rebellion

The third and biggest wave of Arab attacks began in April 1936. It was a period of feverish political and diplomatic activity. Zionist leaders maintained their contacts with the Arabs, and a great many blueprints and memoranda were produced in an attempt to resolve the conflict. The disturbances were far more widespread than those of 1921 and 1929 and claimed a much heavier toll in life and property. They lasted with short interruptions for three years, petering out in the spring and summer of

* Magnes archives: quoted in Hattis, Dissertation, p. 200.

1939, during the months preceding the outbreak of war. A major military effort on the part of the mandatory authorities was needed to defeat the armed gangs which had established their rule in various parts of the country. Unlike the riots of 1920 and 1929, this revolt was not sparked off by an isolated incident, unless the murder of a Jew by Arab highwaymen whose motives may have been partly political is considered as such. The tension had been building up gradually. After Hitler's rise to power the number of immigrants reached a new high – 30,000 in 1933, 42,000 in the following year, and 61,000 in 1935. By the middle 1930s Jews constituted 30 per cent of the total population of Palestine.

There had been a brief wave of unrest in October 1933, instigated by the Istiqlal. It was directed mainly against the British and collapsed quickly when the call for a general Arab strike was not heeded. Three years later the response to the Arab leadership's call to arms was much greater. The international situation seemed more auspicious for the Arabs. The Berlin-Rome axis effected a marked shift in the balance of power. British influence seemed everywhere on the decline: Iraq had gained independence in 1932–3, and the movement for Arab independence had made great strides in Egypt and Syria. The Palestinian Arab leaders must have reached the conclusion that the time was ripe for the achievement of their own demands: the establishment of a national (Arab) government, and the immediate prohibition of Jewish immigration and land sales. The armed revolt did not succeed and the demand for independence was not fulfilled. But it was not a total failure either, for Jewish immigration and land purchases were severely restricted, and the White Paper of 1939 envisaged the virtual repudiation of the Balfour Declaration. Jewish immigration was to stop altogether after a number of years.

Arab guerrilla warfare confronted the yishuv with several major problems. The most agonising dilemma concerned the issue of non-retaliation (*havlaga*). During the first year of the riots it was official Zionist policy to refrain from retaliation, and even Jabotinsky's extremist paramilitary organisation adhered to this policy, albeit under protest.* The decision was not an easy one. It demonstrated the political maturity of the yishuv, and it gave the Zionists a good press in Europe, but it helped to spread despondency among the Jewish community. When the Arab revolt reached its second, more intense stage in 1937–8, the policy of non-retaliation was discontinued by both the Hagana, which engaged in

---

* Abba Achimeir, *Hazionut hamapkhanit*, Tel Aviv, 1966, pp. 101–9.

selective retaliatory action, and the revisionst IZL, which was less discriminating.

Nationalist passions were running higher than ever during those years. In view of the rapidly deteriorating situation for central and east European Jewry, all sections of the Jewish community, with the sole exception of the Communists, insisted on the gates of Palestine being kept open. There was even less belief than previously that the Arabs would respect the rights of Jews in a binational state. The murder of hundreds of Assyrians immediately after Iraq acquired independence acted as a further deterrent and was quoted in many Zionist speeches and articles at the time.

The Arab attack was a trial for the whole yishuv. For left-wing Zionism, which had traditionally advocated close Arab-Jewish cooperation, it was in addition a major ideological problem. This does not apply to the Communists, who had always rejected Zionism as a reactionary movement and a tool of world imperialism, and who since 1929 had given active support to Arab nationalism. The dilemma facing a Jewish Communist in Palestine was insoluble: 'objectively' he was bound to play a reactionary role, because he could not become an Arab. The most logical and consistent way out of the dilemma, chosen in fact by some Jewish Communists, was to emigrate to another country where they could make a more positive contribution to the struggle for world revolution. But Hashomer Hatzair and the left-wing Poale Zion were both Marxist *and* Zionist. They could not regard the Arab attacks on Jewish settlements as progressive in character. They had always envisaged a common Arab-Jewish struggle for the victory of revolutionary Socialism in Palestine, and while they had never been very successful in finding allies outside the Jewish camp, they now found themselves in total isolation. Opposed to British imperialism, they had now to accept its help in suppressing the Arab revolt. But this had been the dilemma facing all those Zionists opposed to 'British imperialism', including some who were by no means Marxists.

Jacob Klatzkin, one of the more original Zionist thinkers, wrote in 1921 that the movement had to decide between an orientation towards British imperialism, which would lead automatically to an armed conflict and pogroms, and an alliance with the exploited Arab fellaheen against Arab and Jewish effendis and eventually (though this was not spelled out at the time) against British imperialism.* The idea that Jews should come as friends and that the existence of the yishuv should not be based

---

* Klatzkin, in *Die Araberfrage in Palästina*, Heidelberg, 1921, pp. 12–13.

on British support had no doubt much to commend it. But would it have been possible to maintain immigration and settlement without British help? The Arabs would not even have permitted Magnes to settle in Jerusalem, as Ben Gurion once reminded the president of the Hebrew university. The Marxist Zionists continued to claim all along that the Jewish national movement had nothing in common with imperialism, that it was predominantly working class in character, and that they had sown the first seeds of Arab-Jewish proletarian unity. The Arab national movement, on the other hand, was reactionary because it had imposed a despotic, fascist régime on the entire community.* They argued that any restriction of Jewish immigration was fatal to the Jewish masses and at the same time objectively harmful because it impeded the growth of the only revolutionary forces capable of combating fascist tendencies in Palestine.

Poale Zion reminded its revolutionary friends abroad that various congresses of the Socialist International had reached the conclusion that any limitation on immigration was a reactionary measure from the Socialist point of view, unless the new immigrants were willing to work for lower wages, thus endangering the standard of living of the native working class – which clearly was not the case in Palestine. The Arab national movement, under feudal and clerical leadership, was being used by imperialism (and fascism); but it was also indifferent to the social and economic needs of the people, it was reactionary in character.† The Arab revolt, according to this interpretation, was provoked both by the British policy of divide and rule and by the clerico-fascist Arab exploiters who feared Jewish working-class immigration because it heralded social and economic change. The spokesmen of the Zionist left proclaimed that the Jewish revolutionary working-class movement was the only fortress of progress and Socialism in the Middle East, and promised that with its help a strong Arab proletarian movement would emerge, leading eventually to a Jewish-Arab workers' state in Palestine.

These attempts to adjust their ideology to an unforeseen political situation were neither convincing nor effective. But psychologically they were intelligible, for any justification of the Arab terror would have negated their own cause, their very existence in Palestine. It was difficult enough to provide a realistic appraisal of the Arab national movement on the basis of Zionist ideology and Marxism in this context was a source of further misinterpretations. To put the blame on British imperialism and

* M.Orenstein, *A Plea for Arab-Jewish Unity*, London, 1936, p. 20.
† Z.Abramovitch, *Whither Palestine?*, London, 1936, p. 34.

the effendis was not even a half truth. The Arab movement of 1936 had broad popular support: the 'feudal' and 'bourgeois' national leaders could never have succeeded in inciting a major revolt but for the deep resentment against Zionism among the Arab people.

Moshe Sharett (then Shertok) was more realistic and fair in his appraisal of the Arab movement than those to the left of him. On 22 July 1936 he noted in his diary that the participation of young Arab women in its activities proved that it was revolutionary in character, and that the Arab intelligentsia supported the 'gangs' in the same way the Jews sympathised with the Hagana.* As for its social character, the second stage of the rebellion (1937–8) was anything but 'feudal' and 'bourgeois'. In fact the leading Arab families left Palestine post haste, and of those who stayed many were killed. The Marxists thought, quite erroneously, that by organising joint Arab-Jewish strikes they were laying the groundwork for an understanding between the toilers of the two nations. But the Arab fellaheen and workers were in fact less inclined to cooperate with the Jews than the Arab merchants in Haifa or the Arab citrus growers in the south.† The problem facing the Zionist revolutionary Left was, very briefly, that according to their own doctrine any national revolutionary movement was *a priori* progressive, since workers and peasants could do no wrong – for any length of time at any rate. The fact that the Arab toiling masses did not accept Borokhovism and refused to behave according to the canons of proletarian internationalism (as the Zionist Left understood them) put them in a quandary from which there was no ideological way out.

Vis-à-vis the world revolutionary movement, dominated by the Communists, Hashomer Hatzair and the left-wing Poale Zion were in a weak position: the argument that the Jewish masses had to leave Europe under threat of physical extinction did not cut much ice with the Comintern. The Communists told the Jewish workers – if they had any message at all – to join the revolutionary struggle wherever they lived and wait for the world revolution which would eradicate antisemitism and solve the Jewish problem once and for all. Like the Brit Shalom, the Zionist Left realised that without Arab-Jewish understanding the yishuv would have to live in a state of permanent warfare with its neighbours. But since they were even less inclined than the Brit Shalom to compromise on the issue most vital to the Arabs – immigration and settlement – the prospects of

---

* Sharett, *Yoman Medini*, p. 225.

† M.Smilansky, 'Citrus Growers have learned to cooperate', in M.Buber (ed.), *Toward Union in Palestine*, Jerusalem, 1947, p. 57.

reaching agreement with any representative Arab circles were virtually nil. In the eyes of the Arabs, 'reactionary' and 'progressive' alike, the Zionist Left was part of the enemy camp just as much as Ben Gurion and Jabotinsky. For the Arabs, the Jews' very existence, and their insistence on further immigration, was the root of the evil; the revolutionary programme of the Zionist Left was irrelevant, a mere smoke screen.

Throughout the late 1930s meetings between individual Zionist and Arab leaders continued, and with the outbreak of the Second World War the climate again became more propitious for a *rapprochement*. Among those with whom contact was maintained were Arab leaders abroad, such as Shekib Arslan, the old Syrian national hero, Dr Shahbander (killed by political enemies in 1940), and Emir Abdulla of Jordan, as well as several Palestinian Arab leaders. Nuri Said, the Iraqi prime minister, was approached at one stage, and so once more was Philby. The Egyptians, Syrians and Jordanians were on the whole somewhat more conciliatory, and even the mufti was on one occasion reported to have hinted that he would on certain conditions permit Jewish immigration until the Jews numbered 80 per cent of the Arab population. But there was, as Magnes reluctantly concluded in 1941, 'no possibility of reaching an agreement with any responsible Arab on any other basis, for the next ten to fifteen years, except on the basis of a minority in this country.'*

When Magnes made this remark, he was speaking at a meeting of the League of Jewish-Arab *Rapprochement*, which had been established in the late 1930s and was in some ways a successor to Brit Shalom (which had ceased to exist in 1933). Its political basis was broader and its programme less specific. Those who attended the meeting faced the old familiar problems: Kalvarisky was convinced that a compromise acceptable to both sides could be worked out and that Arabs could be found to sponsor this cause. Kalvarisky, it should be added in parentheses, was a great believer in *baksheesh* – a common practice in eastern politics. Some of the money came from Kalvarisky's own pocket, most from a Jewish Agency subsidy, which was cut off when the Agency decided to discontinue some of these payments and to make others directly. On the other hand, Michael Assaf, one of the leading Mapai experts, poured cold water on any such hopes. Magnes, he said, was living in that world of liberalism and humanism which was now a thing of the past. The treatment of minorities in Arab countries was enough to deter anyone. Could one

---

* Zionist archives, S 25/8987, quoted in Hattis, *Dissertation*, p. 167.

expect the Arabs to behave any better towards their minorities than, say, the Poles? Assaf accused Kalvarisky and his friends of being at bottom contemptuous of the Arabs if they thought they could cajole them by flattery. The Arabs were not stupid; in their eyes Jabotinsky was an honest man while Weizmann was a liar. It was the old confrontation between 'idealists' and 'realists' all over again, both equally incapable of preventing further aggravation of the conflict.

A great many plans for partition and cantonisation were discussed after 1936 by the Zionist leadership, a bi-national state being no longer considered practical politics. During the Second World War the Biltmore programme, envisaging the establishment of a Jewish state, became the official aim of the movement. The case against partition found its advocates among *Ihud* (Union), which reunited some of the leading members of the old Brit Shalom and, with somewhat different argumentation, of Hashomer Hatzair. Magnes opposed partition on principle. He did not rule out the possibility that the Jews could 'lick the Arabs' in a war, but he predicted that this would create so much hatred as to put the whole Jewish future in the Middle East in question. 'Satisfactory national boundaries, if the object is to promote peace', he wrote, 'cannot be drawn. Wherever you draw those boundaries, you create an irredenta on either side of the border. An irredenta almost invariably leads to war.'* Hashomer Hatzair in its memorandum predicted that partition, and thus the establishment of a Jewish state, would not eliminate the conflict between Jews and Arabs but perpetuate it, 'project it into the future by fixing and amplifying its causes'.†

Magnes and some of his friends, much to the dismay of the official Zionist leadership, gave evidence before the Anglo-American Enquiry Commission in 1946 and before the Special United Nations Commission the year after. A great deal of courage was needed to defend bi-nationalism in the face of the hardening of attitudes among the Jewish community and the total lack of response from the Arabs. Magnes maintained to the end that establishing a state was an act prompted by despair ('Partition is going to create war'), and that a bi-national state was in the long run not only the ideal but the sole practical solution.

There was a quixotic streak in Magnes. His naïveté seemed to disqualify him from active politics altogether – Ben Gurion, not unjustly, called him a political child. Yet precisely because he was so remote from political realities he sensed some of the long-term dangers facing the yishuv more

---

* J. L. Magnes (ed.), *Divided or United?*, Jerusalem, 1947, p. 75.
† *The Case for a Bi-National Palestine* (Bentov Report), New York, 1946, p. 129.

acutely than the professional politicians. But he could not provide any answer to the problems besetting the yishuv as the Second World War came to an end. The *status quo* could not continue, the remnants of European Jewry were knocking on Palestine's doors, the whole problem had assumed a new and desperate urgency.

The attempts to find 'reasonable Arab leaders' continued. During the war a 'Committee of Five' had been established, which included some of the most respected members of the Jewish community. With the blessing of the Jewish Agency they made contact with leading Arab personalities in yet another effort to find a common language. They met and talked and prepared more blueprints, only to realise in the end that in spite of all the outward civilities there was no common ground. There were occasional rays of hope: at one stage Ihud found Fawzi Darwish Hussaini, a respected Arab personality and a cousin of the mufti, willing to sign an agreement with his Jewish friends providing for a bi-national state based on the principle of no domination of one nation over the other. He suggested the immediate establishment of political clubs and a daily newspaper to combat the influence of the Arab war party. On 11 November 1946, five members of Young Palestine, Fawzi's group, signed an agreement concerning common political action with Ihud representatives, but this promising initiative came to a sudden and tragic end. Twelve days later Fawzi was killed by Arab terrorists and his group dispersed. 'My cousin stumbled and received his proper punishment', Jamal Hussaini, one of the leaders of the extremist party, declared a few days later.* In September 1947, Sami Taha, a prominent Haifa trade union leader, was killed; his society had declared itself in favour of a Palestinian, not an Arab state, acknowledging that the Jews too had certain rights. He never pressed the point very strongly, but the mere suspicion of such lack of patriotism was sufficient to make him a target for the extremists. With these and other murders, the few hopes for a Zionist-Arab dialogue were buried and the stage set for a direct military confrontation.

The few Jews who devoted so much thought and effort to relations with their Arab neighbours were a source of bewilderment and irritation to their less self-conscious brethren. Berl Katznelson, who was both the conscience and *éminence grise* of the Zionist labour movement, relates how shocked he was to discover that the question which preoccupied German halutzim was not the plight of their brothers left behind, not the Jews facing extinction in Hitler's expanding Reich, but the problem of

* Quoted in Hattis, Dissertation, p. 220.

the Arab workers. Was it right to insist on Jewish labour, they asked, after having set foot on Palestinian soil? Such atrophy of the will to live, such negation of the right to existence of the Jewish people by its own sons and daughters, was monstrous to men like Katznelson. The men and women of the second and third aliya were less affected by such moral and intellectual scruples.* The question whether the Jewish people had a right to exist did not occur to them. Bitter experience in eastern Europe had taught them that decisive issues in the history of peoples were not resolved according to abstract principles of justice, and that as long as Jews were a minority they would always be persecuted and permanently in danger of destruction. Before 1933 the question had not arisen so acutely. It was generally believed that there was enough room in Palestine for both Jews and Arabs. But as Arab resistance grew stronger, and simultaneously the pressure of immigration increased, conviction grew among the Zionists that if the national aspirations of Arabs and Jews could not be reconciled, their own case was the stronger, if only because European Jewry was in danger of extermination. The Jews had nowhere to go but Palestine. The Arabs could be absorbed if necessary in the neighbouring countries.

This was the political and psychological background to the failure to promote Arab-Jewish *rapprochement*. Most Jews would have preferred agreement with the Arabs. The recurrent riots claimed a heavy toll in lives, and in resources, which had to be diverted from productive labour. The halutzim had come to Eretz Israel not to conquer but to build a new, just, Socialist society. Only a few realised that the Arabs would not accept *faits accomplis*, that continuing immigration and settlement would involve the yishuv in a conflict which might last for generations. The repeated attacks on Jewish settlements, and the gruesome way in which some of the massacres were carried out, brought about a gradual change in popular attitudes. The image of the honest, brave and hospitable Arab gave way to a feeling of contempt for these 'dishonest Levantines'.

A minority of Zionists and Palestinian Jews were aware from the beginning of the crucial importance of relations with the Arabs. Some of them thought that the national aspirations of the two peoples could be reconciled, while the pessimists early on reached the conclusion that conflict was basic and unavoidable. The majority of Zionists were less concerned with the Arab question. Only gradually did they face it, assuming at first that the Palestinian Arabs, finding themselves economi-

---

* B.Katznelson, quoted in M.Braslavski, *Tnuat hapoalim ha'eretz yisraelit*, Tel Aviv, 1956, vol. 3, pp. 382–3.

cally prosperous and reasonably content, would eventually accept minority status in the coming Jewish state. If this was an unjust assumption, it seemed almost insignificant in view of the need to save European Jewry.

6

BUILDING A NEW SOCIETY: THE PROGRESS OF LEFT-WING ZIONISM

When the first Zionist congress met in Basle in 1897 there was no mention of Socialism. Most of those present would have angrily rejected any attempt to adulterate Zionism with Socialist ideas. But only a few years later Zionist-Socialist parties had become an integral part of the movement for a Jewish national renaissance, and within little more than three decades Labour Zionism emerged as its strongest political force. Its growth and the impact of its ideas were of decisive importance, for it shaped the character of the Zionist movement, and subsequently of the state of Israel, to a greater extent than any other group. The same decade that witnessed the birth of political Zionism saw the spread of Socialist ideas among the Jews of eastern Europe: the Bund, by far the largest Jewish Socialist organisation, was established one month after the first Zionist congress, and Nahman Syrkin's plea for a Socialist Jewish state was published one year after Herzl's *Judenstaat*. The beginnings of a Jewish labour movement can be traced back even further. Aron Lieberman's circle in Vilna was preaching Socialist ideas in the 1870s. True, it was not at all clear at the time whether Jewish workers would establish their own independent organisations or fight alongside their Russian comrades in one united movement for the defence of their rights and the attainment of their ideals. The early Jewish Socialists were powerfully attracted by Russian Socialism and its leaders. Chernyshevsky's *What is to be done*, a novel in praise of Utopian Socialism, not only shaped the outlook of several generations of Russian and east European Socialists up to the time of Lenin and Georgi Dimitrov; it was in the eyes of many young Jews 'one of the holy works of mankind, together with the Bible and the Koran'.* It is impossible to exaggerate the impact of Russian

* Chaim Zhitlovsky, *Fun mein Leben*, New York, 1935, vol. 2, p. 20.

Socialism on the Zionist Labour movement, not only on the ideological level but above all on its very attitude towards politics. The Jewish Socialists inherited from their Russian mentors unending doctrinal squabbles as well as the axiomatic belief that it was the first commandment for any Socialist worth his salt to arrange his own life in accordance with his beliefs. The unity of theory and action was not a matter open to debate. From the Populists they took over the firm conviction that manual labour was a cure for almost all ills; the second aliya was in some ways a repeat performance of the going-to-the-people as practised by the Narodniks.

At the same time the young Jewish Socialists were antagonised by what appeared to them as gross indifference on the part of their Russian comrades to the specific needs of their people. The Russian Populists were above all interested in the fate of the peasants, while the Social Democrats concentrated their efforts on the industrial workers. Most Jews were, however, neither peasants nor workers, but just poor people, many of them without any real prospect of ever being able to find productive work. Russian Socialists sympathised with the sufferings of the poverty-stricken Jews; but from their point of view this was a marginal issue. They had no advice to offer on how to put an end to their plight before the great Socialist revolution which was to solve this together with all other problems. Above all, there was the sad fact that antisemitism had its supporters among Russian workers and peasants. When Axelrod and Deutsch, two Jewish Socialists who later rose to eminence, consulted Lavrov, the most respected radical leader of the day, on how to deal with this predicament, they were told that while anti-Jewish riots were highly regrettable, the question presented many tactical difficulties. Were they to turn against the masses, just because they were misguided enough to be antisemitic? Many young Jewish revolutionaries followed Axelrod and Deutsch in accepting Lavrov's explanation, joined the Russian Socialist parties, and took a leading part in their activities. But there were men who felt, perhaps only dimly at first, that Jewish existence as a whole in Russian society presented a basic anomaly, and that for this reason there was a need for an autonomous Jewish Labour movement. Some, such as Syrkin, went further and argued that the Jews would not be absorbed in agriculture and industry even after achieving full civic rights, but that most, if not all, would become part of the middle class and thus again find themselves on the wrong side of the social struggle.

Syrkin and Borokhov

This was the starting point of Socialist Zionist thought. The revolution would not solve the Jewish question; an even more radical approach was needed. Nahman Syrkin, its first prophet and leader, scandalised successive Zionist congresses by what struck most delegates as intemperate and radical proposals, and by his frequent interruptions and constant criticism of the 'bourgeois leadership'. A native of Mohilev and a doctor of philosophy of the University of Berlin, Syrkin, a small, bearded man, was more effective in polemics than in providing political leadership. This is not to belittle his originality or the great influence he exerted on the development of the Zionist labour movement. He was no more familiar than Ber Borokhov with Palestinian realities, but he instinctively saw many of the problems more accurately than the other chief ideologist of Labour Zionism, whose theories were more sophisticated from a Marxist point of view and who had a great influence on many of his left-wing contemporaries. Syrkin saw internationalism as the ultimate goal of mankind and had no doubt that history was gradually moving in that direction. But it was moving agonisingly slowly, and while a nation (and a nation state) was not an end in itself, an absolute moral category, neither was it a stage that could be skipped. An autonomous state was a necessary historical step on the road towards the solution of the Jewish question. Syrkin did not, however, accept the tacit assumption of the bourgeois Zionist leadership, namely that such a state would emerge as the result of rich Jews giving money. He always believed that only as the result of a genuine mass movement could the Jewish state come into being.* For that reason he demanded a more representative Zionist congress and sharply opposed cultural Zionism as advocated by Ahad Ha'am. Zionism without mass emigration and resettlement was either fraud or treason. The Socialist *Judenstaat*, as Syrkin envisaged it, betrayed strong traces of Chernyshevsky (Verochka's dream in *Chto delat?*) and Fourier's Phalansteries. The land was to be owned by the state, and giant communes, each with ten thousand members, were to be established to engage in both industrial and agricultural labour.† There were to be neither small villages nor big urban concentrations in the future Jewish state, only cultural centres. The most boring and least congenial work was to be the most highly paid. Syrkin was not a fully

---

* *Kitve Nahman Syrkin*, Tel Aviv, 1939, vol. I, p. 130.

† For a discussion of Syrkin's ideas and political activities, see Jonathan Frankel's doctoral dissertation, *Socialism and Jewish Nationalism in Russia 1892–1907*, Cambridge, 1961.

fledged Marxist but he regarded the class struggle as one of the central themes in Jewish history, reflected both in the Pentateuch and the Prophets. The history of ancient Judaism as he interpreted it was the unfolding struggle of the Jewish toiling masses for a Socialist way of life.

At first Syrkin did not have many followers; for every young Jew who joined the Socialist Zionist movement many more entered the ranks of the Bund. And this for obvious reasons. In contrast to the Bund, the Zionists had no answer to the immediate problems facing Jewish workers in eastern Europe. True, during the early years of its existence the Bund did not have a clear national programme. It was meant to be the party of the Jewish proletariat, and to defend its political and economic interests. Only gradually did it adopt a specific ideology of diaspora non-territorial nationalism, thus turning sharply against Zionism. It was the beginning of a bitter struggle, which was to last for many years. Zionism in the view of the Bund was Utopian, and Socialist Zionism all the more so. For how could one possibly build in backward Turkey a Socialist and democratic society for which conditions had not yet ripened even in Europe? The Bund was militantly anti-clerical. It ridiculed the traditional religious taboos and deliberately contravened some of them, such as the one forbidding work on the Sabbath. The Socialism of the left-wing Zionists was suspect in its eyes because they wanted to build up their country under the guidance of the rabbis and according to the prescription of the *Shulkhan Arukh*. The left-wing Zionists did not find it easy to answer these charges. Many of them, both of the older generation (such as Lilienblum) and the younger, also feared domination by clerical forces. 'You may be decent and well-meaning people', the Bund apostrophised the left-wing Zionists, 'but you cooperate with the bourgeoisie.' And the Jewish bourgeoisie was interested in the Jewish state mainly as a market and a profitable field for investment and speculation. When they were less charitably inclined, which happened not infrequently, the Bund leaders claimed that the Socialism of the left-wing Zionists was a deliberate sham, that they wore a red mask to hide their real intentions and to adjust themselves to the radical *Zeitgeist*.* The Bund propagated Yiddish, the language of the Jewish masses, and scoffed at Hebrew, the language of the rabbis and a handful of aesthetes and visionaries. Zionism, on the other hand, rejected Yiddish as a caricature of a language

---

* See for instance Ben Ehud, *Zionismus oder Sozialismus* (Yiddish), Warsaw, 1899, p. 30; A.H., *Di sozialistische Fraktsie in Zionismus* (Yiddish), Warsaw, 1906, p. 96. See also A.L. Patkin, *The Origins of the Russian-Jewish Labour Movement*, Melbourne, 1947, p. 136 *et seq.*

embodying the spirit of the ghetto. This in turn shocked the Bund and its sympathisers: 'He who scoffs at Yiddish, scoffs at the Jewish people; he is only half a Jew', one of them wrote.

The left-wing Zionists grudgingly admitted that the Bund was doing valuable educational spadework among the backward Jewish masses. The revolutionary literature of the Bund was widely read and used in left-wing Zionist circles, too. But Zionists were bitterly opposed to what they called the 'nihilist' attitude of the Bund towards the national question, the assumption that the national and social problems of Jewish labour could be solved, or at least normalised, wherever they lived. The Bund's complicated concept of political-cultural autonomy for Russian Jews was largely derived from the writings of the theorists of Austrian Socialism, such as Renner and Otto Bauer. According to this concept, individual Jews wherever they lived could claim a connection with the national collective and have the right to use their own language and develop their own education and culture. In a series of resolutions the Bund rejected both assimilation and Zionism. It claimed that in so far as Zionism envisaged the settlement of a few Jews in Palestine, it was irrelevant as a solution to the Jewish question. But in so far as its ambitions went further, aiming at the resettlement in Palestine of the whole people or a large part of it, it had to be fought as a dangerous utopia bound to deflect the masses from the struggle for political and economic rights and to weaken their class consciousness.* Each camp accused the other not only of lack of political realism but also of cowardice. The Zionists asserted that the Bund did not have the courage to draw the final conclusions from their own analysis of the anomaly of Jewish existence. The Bund accused the left-wing Zionists of misleading the masses, attempting to turn them away from the actual political struggle by invoking some nebulous ideal to be realised one distant day in a remote country.

With the first Russian revolution of 1904–5, the mass strikes, the pogroms and the elections to the Duma, the question of whether or not to participate in the political struggle became an acute major issue confronting the Zionists, causing much dissension and eventually leading to a split in their ranks. Borokhov, the founder and leading ideologist of Poale Zion, the first Socialist-Zionist mass organisation, had originally opposed active participation in Russian politics, but changed his mind after the first Russian revolution. He was born in Poltava in 1881, and his early writings are those of a typical Russian and Zionist *intelligent* of

---

* Resolutions of the fourth conference of the Bund 1901, in Sh.Eisenshtat, *Prakim betoldot tnuat hapoalim hayehudit*, Merhavia, 1944, vol. 2, pp. 14–16.

the period. Anticipating Lenin, he undertook a critical analysis of the philosophy of Avenarius and empirio-criticism. As far as Jewish politics were concerned, he was a fairly orthodox Zionist, closely cooperating with Ussishkin, the leader of the movement in southern Russia, who was anything but a Socialist. A man of considerable erudition and acute intellect, Borokhov tried to show that Zionism and Marxism were by no means incompatible, but that, on the contrary, a synthesis between the two was perfectly logical. His position was not easy, for the Zionists at the time were mostly anti-Marxist, whereas the Marxists were anti-Zionist almost without exception, so that at first his efforts did not arouse sympathy on either side.

Borokhov invested a great deal of analytical skill in justifying Zionism in Marxist terms. All other solutions he discarded by elimination: their anomalous social structure made it impossible for the masses of Jews to stay in the long run in eastern Europe. Nor would emigration to America or some other territory provide an answer because there was already no room for the Jews in the basic branches of the national economy of these rapidly developing countries, and the new immigrants would again be reduced to a marginal, and therefore highly vulnerable existence in their new home. The remedies suggested by the Bund and the Russian Social Democrats, from Plekhanov to Lenin, were woefully inadequate. The Bund proposed solving social and economic problems by applying spiritual and cultural remedies. Borokhov was convinced that by a correct Marxist analysis he had found the only practical solution: the Jewish middle class would be drawn by spontaneous forces to Palestine, and gradually build up there the means of production. Expanding industry would attract the Jewish working masses to Palestine, and the industrial proletariat, pursuing a correct policy of class struggle, would establish itself as the vanguard of the national liberation movement. Borokhov's writings are replete with references to the contradiction between the means of production and the relations of production, and to other concepts familiar to the student of orthodox Marxist economics. He was an adept in manipulating the tools of Marxist analysis, much to the chagrin of his ideological adversaries, who had been accustomed to disputations about Zionism with enthusiasts arguing in romantic-Utopian terms. When Borokhov departed in 1906 from his previous policy and decided that the supporters of proletarian Zionism should after all take an active part in the political struggles of the diaspora, his movement became even less exposed to attacks by his rivals on the Left. He left his native Russia in 1907, emigrated to America, and died shortly after his return to Russia in 1917. After his death he became the patron saint of the left-wing Socialist groups within the Zionist movement, the discoverer of the 'synthesis'.

But the 'synthesis' was not quite as unassailable as his followers wanted to believe. There were internal inconsistencies in Borokhovism, and in some vital respects it simply did not conform to realities. Borokhov was far too intelligent to try to provide a vulgar Marxist interpretation of antisemitism in purely economic terms. His analysis was remarkably like Pinsker's, for he regarded it basically as a socio-psychological phenomenon. As for the future prospects of the Jewish people, Borokhov was not quite so pessimistic as the author of *Autoemanzipation*. The Inquisition and mass expulsions, he declared, were not likely to come back. Perhaps there was, after all, progress in history. But the Jews could not passively wait and accept pogroms, the hatred and contempt of their neighbours, as something natural and inevitable. They could not rely on progress, for if the angel in man had made progress, so had the devil.* Borokhov had always belittled the romantic, mystical element in Zionism. The essence of his doctrine was that Palestine would be settled and built up quite independently of the longings and desires of the Zionists. But this was one of the weakest points in his argument: Zionism shorn of its mystical element was unthinkable, and the idea that Palestine could be built up without the enthusiasm and selfless devotion of thousands of young idealists was as remote from realities as the belief that the revolution in Russia would break out irrespective of the subjective factor, i.e. the existence of a revolutionary party. Both Borokhov and Lenin needed a *deus ex machina* to break through the orthodoxy of their own constructions. However much opposed they were in principle to romanticism, they needed a myth, and also a vanguard, for neither the Russian proletariat nor the Jewish masses were likely to produce unaided that vital measure of political consciousness required to lead them along the right path.

Borokhovism was an interesting attempt to combine and coordinate the two ideologies which, more than any others, attracted the young Jewish intelligentsia of the day. It became a kind of rationalised religion, giving spiritual comfort and confidence to thousands of young men who were uneasy about the claim of orthodox Marxists that Zionism and

* 'K voprosam teorii Zionisma', in *Evreiskaia Zhizn*, June 1905, pp. 122-3. Borokhov's collected writings have been published in three volumes in Hebrew; the first contains 'Our Platform' and 'The Class Struggle and the National Question', his most important theoretical works.

revolutionary Socialism were incompatible. In that generation it was almost *de rigueur* to be a Socialist and a revolutionary, to believe in historical materialism and the revolutionary mission of the industrial proletariat. Kautsky's writings were regarded by Russian and Jewish Social Democrats for many years with the same awe that religious believers showed for holy writ. Only a few intrepid spirits outside the Marxist camp, such as Idelson, the editor of *Rassvet*, dared to raise doubts: did Kautsky really have the answer to the national question? Would a change in the social system necessarily solve the national question, or did not such an assumption, far from being based on materialism, introduce a subjective, romantic element? Were not Kautsky's *obiter dicta* against Zionism reminiscent of the bourgeois arguments against Socialism?*

There were other weighty reasons against mechanically projecting concepts established elsewhere on to the Russian-Jewish scene. 'Proletariat', 'class struggle', and 'class consciousness' meant one thing in Bialystok and another in Berlin. Jewish industrial workers were not the sons and daughters of peasants who had moved to town. They usually hailed from lower middle class families whose economic situation had deteriorated. They took a lively interest in their work, and expected to be treated like relations – at least like poor relations – by the factory owners, who were often their co-religionists. Many of them regarded their proletarian existence as temporary. As soon as possible they would try to become independent, establishing small workshops of their own, or take some examination which would qualify them for a clerical job or even to become a teacher. They had the traditional Jewish thirst for education, and working class parents wanted their children to have a chance to improve their status in society. Jewish workers lacked neither solidarity nor militancy, but their whole mentality differed from that of the rank-and-file working men of other nations.

The Second Aliya

The young men and women who began arriving in Palestine from Russia between 1904 and 1906, and who constituted the 'second aliya' (immigration wave) were not 'natural workers' but idealists, and on occasion felt themselves for that reason very much inferior. Yet 'natural workers', interested mainly in higher wages and better working conditions, would

* 'Hamarksism veshe'elat hayehudim' and 'Karl Kautsky vehayehudim', in *Sefer Idelson*. Tel Aviv, 1946.

hardly have opted for what the critics of Zionism used to call '*dos gepeigerte Land*' – the country which had died. The new arrivals were the sons and daughters of lower middle class families from Russia and Poland, many of them in their teens, full of enthusiasm to build a new Socialist society and at the same time quite unsure of themselves. Would they be up to the great assignment awaiting them in a strange country and in difficult working conditions? Yosef Baratz, later one of the founder-members of Degania, the first of the kvutzot, relates how he wept bitter tears when as a youngster of seventeen he returned home after a hard day's work; physical labour in these conditions was so difficult, would he ever become a real worker?* The example of the Biluim who settled in Palestine in the 1880s and 1890s was not exactly encouraging. They too had come to work the land. They too had been radical in their political outlook. Ussishkin and Chlenov, who later became the leaders of Russian Zionism had not been accepted as members because of their 'bourgeois background'. But their settlements had changed out of recognition since the early romantic and heroic days. The Biluim were now small *hacienderos*, fairly well-to-do farmers by Palestinian standards. They were, as far as the newcomers were concerned, the employers, the class enemy. Before the arrival of the second wave of immigrants there had been a few short-lived workers' organisations, a few isolated strikes, but the real history of the labour movement in Palestine begins only with the arrival of the Homel group of pioneers in January 1904, the harbinger of a new period in the history of the settlement of Palestine: 1,230 new immigrants left Odessa in 1905 for Palestine, 3,459 the year after, and 1,750 in 1907. Altogether some 35–40,000 new immigrants belonging to this category arrived in Palestine between the beginning of 1904 and the outbreak of the First World War.

If a reporter or a social scientist had asked the new arrivals in the port of Jaffa the reason for their coming, he would no doubt have received a great many conflicting explanations. But there were certain common factors. These were the years of the Russo-Japanese war, the first Russian revolution, and a fresh wave of pogroms. Many thought that the revolutionary movement would bring freedom to Russia and at long last liberate the persecuted Jewish minority. But others, like the young David Grin (Ben Gurion), instinctively felt that whatever the revolution would achieve for Russia, it almost certainly did not mean the end of the Jewish people's tribulations. They came to Palestine out of despair, to quote again David Grin. They had despaired of the Jewish diaspora, of

* *Pirke Hapoel Hatzair*, vol. 3, p. 322.

Socialism, but also of Zionism as preached and practised by its official representatives in the diaspora. They regarded Eretz Israel as the end of the road, the last dwelling place.

There was a strong romantic-mystical element in the young pioneers, despite the fact that many professed a belief in historical materialism. It was a left-wing Socialist who wrote that there was a mysterious thread linking Modi'in (the home of the Maccabees) and Sejera (the new agricultural settlement in lower Galilee).* Massada, where in Roman times the Jews had fought to the last man rather than surrender, again became a great symbol. But this is not to say that apocalyptic forebodings dominated their thoughts. On the contrary, they were full of vitality and, in the beginning at least, of optimism. They were taking possession again of the homeland which had been lost to the Jewish people as a result of a series of historical misfortunes. They wanted to put down roots as quickly and as deeply as possible, and in countless excursions on horseback, or more often riding a donkey or on foot, they explored their new homeland. For many of them it was like revisiting an ancestral home of which they had so often heard.†

The second immigration was by no means a homogenous group, even though almost all were young, unmarried, and came from Russia. They did not even have a common language. The main contingent came from White Russia, eastern Poland, and Lithuania. They had all grown up in a traditional Jewish environment and spoke Yiddish, but all knew at least some Hebrew. For them the Bible and Jewish literature had been a stronger formative influence than Socialist doctrine. But there were also substantial numbers from south Russia, the sons and daughters of assimilated families, higher up on the social ladder, who knew only Russian. Their grandfathers had served in the Russian army and their families had been permitted to move to areas outside the pale of settlement. These young men and women had become Zionists as a result of the Russian revolution and the pogroms, and Jewish traditions were often alien to them. Language was at first a major barrier. In the early assemblies, translations from Hebrew into Yiddish and Russian and vice versa had to be provided. Trumpeldor, the one-armed hero of the Russo-Japanese war, did not know a word of Hebrew when he arrived in Jaffa, nor did Rahel, who was later to win renown as a poet. Berl Katznelson had some knowledge of the language, but he vowed not to

* Y.Zerubavel, in *Ahdut*, 11–2, 1912.
† Yosef Gorni, 'The romantic element in the ideology of the second aliya' (in Hebrew), *Asupot*, January 1966, p. 55 *et seq*.

use any other in conversation even if it meant weeks of silence. Ben Gurion's rise to prominence began a few days after his arrival when he made a rousing speech at a workers' meeting in fluent and powerful Hebrew – an unusual event in Poale Zion circles, where Yiddish was still widely used at the time.

There was a blatant discrepancy between what the pioneers expected and what they found upon their arrival at the guest house of Chaim Bloch in Jaffa, the first station for most of them. There were the usual difficulties facing new immigrants all over the globe. But there were other, more specific problems: for Alexander Said, who had been born in Siberia and was to become one of the most famous *shomrim* (watchmen), the trouble began while he was still aboard the ship; he had no valid entry visa and was arrested by the Turkish authorities. Fortunately he had a silver watch, the only heirloom from his father, which sufficed to buy him off.* On the day of his arrival Berl Katznelson met in Jaffa a close friend who was about to leave the country, which did not exactly help to raise his spirits. Everything was strange and unfamiliar – the people, the landscape, the whole atmosphere. Even ardent Zionists like A.D. Gordon and Moshe Smilansky later admitted that it took them years to get accustomed to their new surroundings. Deep inside they still felt a spiritual attachment to the Russian landscape, its rivers, fields and forests. They did not dislike the Palestinian scenery, they simply felt that it was not part of themselves, that they were still visitors in a strange country. Paraphrasing Yehuda Halevy, the medieval Jewish poet, they could say that their body was in Eretz Israel, but their soul in some ways was still in Russia.

Living conditions were incredibly primitive even by eastern European standards. The newcomers lived in tents or miserable huts. They had to put up with malaria, snakes, scorpions, various bugs, overseers who made work hell, and a cultural environment which was either Levantine or reminded them of the *shtetl* which they had left behind. There was not enough work, the Jewish peasants of Petah Tiqva, Rishon Lezion and Zikhron Ya'akov preferring Arab to Jewish labour, the Arab worker being cheaper, more experienced and less likely to engage in argument. Frequently the newcomers were told that they had been gravely mistaken in assuming that they were needed in Eretz Israel and would be well advised to return home as soon as possible. Was it prudent in these conditions to encourage further immigration? While Yosef Witkin, a

---

* For these and other accounts, see El.Shochat (ed.), *Sefer Ha'aliya hashniya*, Tel Aviv, 1949, p. 165.

teacher and early settler, published a call to Jewish youth in eastern Europe to come to the help of their people and to serve it, Poale Zion doubted the wisdom of such manifestos. Should one artificially stimulate immigration rather than wait patiently for the natural and inevitable processes which Borokhov had predicted and which would bring both capitalists and workers to Palestine?

The pioneers of 1905 were the strangest workers the world had ever seen. Manual labour for them was not a necessary evil but an absolute moral value, a remedy to cure the Jewish people of its social and national ills. They shared the admiration of the Russian Populists for the *muzhik*, while at the same time, with the Marxists, they regarded the class-conscious industrial worker as an ideal figure. Those who for various reasons could not do manual work felt themselves inferior to their comrades and discriminated against.* They were immensely proud of their independence. Any help from home was rejected, and even accepting an invitation to a meal from a Jewish farmer was frowned upon. When one such farmer paid his Jewish workers eight piastres instead of the seven agreed upon as their daily wage, they angrily sent their wage packet back, accepting it grudgingly only after having been assured that they were paid more not because they were Jews but because they had been doing outstanding work. They also insisted on being hired labourers. The establishment of agricultural settlements of their own was ruled out because they did not want to become farmers and in doing so turn their back on the working class. The experience of the Biluim acted as a deterrent.

The demands they made on themselves were impossibly high, and the initial enthusiasm of 1904–6 was bound to be followed by a deep crisis. The second immigration wave consisted mainly of individuals rather than groups. Not a few had come to the country by mere accident, having joined friends or relations without exactly knowing where they were going or why. Some, the 'Japanese', had joined the exodus because they preferred Palestine to service in the Russian army in wartime. There were not a few of those semi-intellectual drifters described by Brenner in his novels: the first to arrive in the country, and also the first to leave, forever restless and dissatisfied, Ahasuerus's grandchildren. Despair set in because the volume of immigration had fallen far short of expectations. The Homelites, for instance, who had been the very first to arrive in 1904, had firmly believed that they were just the vanguard of a great mass movement and that many hundreds if not thousands of

* Even Shoshan, *Toldot tnuat hapoalim be'eretz Israel*, Tel Aviv, 1963, vol. 1, pp. 80–1.

fellow Zionists from their home town would soon join them.* They felt betrayed and isolated when within a year or two they realised that the main body of the army would not follow them. The great majority, 80 per cent or even more, of those who had come in 1904–6 to build Eretz Israel left the country within a few months, returning to Russia or going on to America. But those who remained eventually became the nucleus of Labour Zionism. It was they who were to provide in later years the leadership of the Socialist parties, the Zionist movement, and the State of Israel.

The workers were organised in two rival groups, both of which came into existence during the winter of 1905: Poale Zion and Hapoel Hatzair. At the start the former had sixty members, the latter ninety.† Even five years later they had no more than about five hundred members between them. The number of workers in any large-sized factory in Europe or America exceeded that of the total membership of these two Socialist parties by a wide margin. They were clans, fraternities – large families rather than political mass movements, their periodicals little more than circular letters. Against this background, the solemn speeches and writings about the historical mission of the working class and the necessity of the class struggle make strange reading. But notwithstanding their minute size, both Poale Zion and Hapoel Hatzair regarded themselves from the first as political parties, though in addition they fulfilled a great many other functions. Trade unions did not exist at the time and there were no state-sponsored social services. The workers' associations therefore established employment exchanges as well as mutual aid organisations, cultural and social clubs, and sickness funds. It had been intended originally to found one single, united organisation, but differences of opinion emerged when it came to formulating a common ideological platform. Nor could those involved agree about the name of their organisation. Those who had belonged to Poale Zion in Russia insisted on retaining this name, mainly perhaps as a demonstration against the pro-Uganda views held by many Palestinian Zionists at the time. But the majority rejected this demand. So in October and November 1905 two separate workers' parties were founded, the one with its headquarters at Chaim Bloch's guest house in Jaffa, the other at Spektor's, a rival establishment.

The real causes of the split went considerably deeper. Jewish Socialists

---

* Berl Katznelson, 'Prakim letoldot tnuat hapoalim be 'Eretz Israel', *Kitvei* . . ., Tel Aviv, 1949, vol. II, p. 111.

† Of a total of 550 Jewish workers (*Evreiskaia Rabochaia Khronika*, 23 April 1906).

from eastern Europe were notoriously disputatious, but this alone would not necessarily have prevented 'working class unity' at this early stage. But Hapoel Hatzair was a group without a clear and well-defined doctrine by eastern European standards, whereas Poale Zion was highly ideological in character. The former was an independent body unlinked to any other Zionist or Socialist organisation, whereas the latter was a part (though not the most important part) of the world organisation of Poale Zion as well as of the Second International.* The political programme of the Palestinian Poale Zion, hammered out by fewer than a dozen of its members at a clandestine meeting in a Jewish guest house in the Arab town of Ramle in 1906, was almost an exact replica of the platform of the Russian Poale Zion. The document opened with the statement that the history of mankind was a series of class and national struggles – a slight deviation from the *Communist Manifesto*. It reiterated Borokhov's thesis that the capitalists would eventually invest their money in Palestine, and that in the wake of this process a Jewish working class would come into being. The programme adopted later on by the first party convention was a little more specific: Poale Zion wanted political independence for the Jews in Palestine and a Socialist society. The concept of the class struggle as the chief political weapon still figured prominently in their writings. But it did not take the Palestinian Poale Zion long to realise that analyses and prognoses developed in Russia were of little validity in their new surroundings. What if the Jewish capitalists would not build up Palestine? Would this be the inevitable end of their dreams or would they be entitled to modify their doctrine and take an active part in building the country? How could they possibly be militant advocates of the class struggle if the 'strategic basis of the Jewish worker' which Borokhov had envisaged did not yet exist, if the employers had no need for Jewish workers and employed them merely out of the goodness of their heart?

Hesitantly at first, but more boldly later on, the Palestinian Poale Zion under the leadership of Ben Zvi, Ben Gurion and Israel Shochat, developed an independent approach which brought them into growing conflict with their ideological teachers in Russia. The Palestinians reached the conclusion that the building up of Palestine could not be

---

* For the early history of Socialist Zionism, see Y. Ben Zvi in *Sefer Ha'aliya hashniya*, on Poale Zion, p. 585 *et seq.*; Zvi Suchovolsky, on Hapoel Hatzair, *ibid.*, p. 612 *et seq.*; Yosef Shapiro, on Hapoel Hatzair, in *Asupot*, August 1965, p. 16 *et seq.* Cf. also the doctoral dissertation by Israel Kolatt-Kopelovich, *Ideology and the impact of reality upon the Jewish Labour Movement 1905–19* (in Hebrew), Hebrew University, Jerusalem, June 1964.

left to historical accident but that they were called on to give a push to history. They followed with concern the growing preoccupation of the Russian Poale Zion with problems other than Palestine. Who needed yet another Bund? When the world association of Poale Zion, its parties embarrassed by its collaboration with the bourgeois elements, decided to leave the Zionist congress, the Palestinians did not follow suit. While the world organisation continued to hold its meetings and to publish its literature in Yiddish, the language of the 'Jewish toiling masses', the Palestinians switched to Hebrew. When the Palestinians began to found cooperative agricultural settlements, they had to face bitter resistance from sections of the world movement, who argued that according to the teaching of Marxism, workers ought to fight for their class interests, and were not called on to establish economic enterprises within the framework of the capitalist system. The Palestinian Poale Zion did not accept arguments which, however firmly anchored in ideology, were utterly divorced from Palestinian realities. They went even further, and on a few occasions adumbrated in their speeches and writings the idea of a Socialist Jewish state in Palestine. But none of them thought that this was a near prospect. For the time being most of their energies were devoted to more prosaic undertakings, such as the establishment of an organisation of Jewish watchmen (*Hashomer*), and developing contacts with workers' organisations in other parts of the Ottoman empire.

Poale Zion was a thoroughly ideological party in the pre-1914 Social Democratic tradition. In its programme it elaborated in great detail its attitude towards a number of current problems and future possibilities. Hapoel Hatzair, on the other hand, believed in pragmatism, refraining almost as a matter of principle from doctrinal disputations. The one constant factor in its orientation was the emphasis on manual labour both as a spiritual, absolute category, and for its therapeutic value in the process of the national liberation of the Jewish people. Each issue of the party's periodical featured the slogan: 'The necessary condition for the realisation of Zionism is the conquest of all occupations in the country by Jewish labour.' Hapoel Hatzair realised earlier than Poale Zion that Jewish workers in Eretz Israel were facing a situation totally different from that of any other labour movement; hence its opposition to the importation of concepts and policies from other parts of the world, although it is true that there were traces in its ideas of foreign ideologies, as for instance Russian Populism. But they were first and foremost 'constructivists' and therefore opposed the class-struggle-type slogans of

Poale Zion. In the view of Hapoel Hatzair (Jewish) nationalism was the supreme value, the all-embracing category, and the Jewish worker was destined to be the pioneer of the Jewish national renaissance. All efforts had therefore to be concentrated on realising this aim rather than emphasising class divisions. Hapoel Hatzair did not reject Socialism, but it was not regarded as an inherent part of the national movement. The idea of the 'conquest of labour' was central to Hapoel Hatzair policy: it was imperative to increase the number of Jewish workers as much and as quickly as possible and to improve their working and living conditions. It was absolutely essential, furthermore, for the new immigrants to gain a firm foothold in agriculture. The parasitism of Jewish existence in the diaspora had shocked them into embracing Zionism and they feared that any backsliding, any compromise in this respect, would fatally affect the future of the Jewish national renaissance. Yet the 'conquest of labour' as they interpreted it was not meant to harm anyone. It is difficult to imagine men and women less warlike than A.D.Gordon, Yosef Ahronowitz, Yosef Sprinzak, and the other leaders of Hapoel Hatzair. Unlike the Poale Zion, they refused to participate in the foundation of Hashomer, the defence organisation, because it smacked, however faintly, of militarism.

The pacifist orientation emerged most clearly from the philosophy of A.D.Gordon, who exerted considerable influence on the men and women of the second aliya. Gordon was born in Podolia in 1856. When he came to Eretz Israel he was almost fifty and had no experience of heavy manual work. He became an agricultural labourer, first in the Jewish colonies near Jaffa, later on at Degania, the first collective settlement. For the next eighteen years – Gordon died in 1922 – he worked during the day in the fields and citrus groves with great, almost religious devotion, writing his essays at night. Gordon did not believe that the class struggle and a Socialist revolution would produce a better and more just society. Nor did he expect that man would be greatly improved as a result of the radical overthrow of institutions. Society would not change unless the individual changed, and since man was deteriorating in the same measure that he became alienated from nature, and since the Jews had been afflicted more than any other people in this respect, Gordon concluded that a real national revival was conditional on a return to normal life, with work as the great remedy against all the evils of Jewish life in the diaspora. Man, nature, work – these were the key concepts in Gordon's thought. He also stressed the importance of agricultural work as a means for man to regain his sanity and to become one again with the cosmos of which he was a part. Gordon's impact on his contemporaries cannot be assessed solely in terms of his writings. The old man in his Russian tunic with his enormous beard influenced them as much by his personal example, his simplicity, his fanatical devotion to work, as by his theories: he carried out in his own life what Tolstoy had merely preached. The weak old man, undefeated by heavy labour, by illness and the many other afflictions accompanying the painful process of growing new roots, was a source of inspiration and encouragement to those younger in years and stronger in body in their hours of doubt and despair.

Those who had come with the second aliya were unlikely to draw similar comfort from the novels and essays of Joseph Chaim Brenner, for the most influential writer of this generation was himself given to frequent bouts of deep despair. Nor could he provide any ideological guidance; during his life he drifted from one left-wing Zionist group to another, and also belonged to some which were not Zionist at all. His importance was that of a faithful chronicler of the period, implacable in his search for truth. No other Jewish writer has ever portrayed in such cruel terms his fellow Jews, the fools and the brutes, the dirty *schnorrers*, or the decay of a people which had lost all the attributes of normal existence. The picture drawn by Mendele of Jewish life in the *shtetl*, and by Israel Zangwill of the ghettos of the west, bore no resemblance at all to Brenner's descriptions. But he was equally acid in his comments on the 'verbal Zionists' in the diaspora, and much as he identified himself with the pioneers in Eretz Israel, he was by no means certain that this last flicker of hope was strong enough or had come in time to save the people from final ruin. There was nothing of the optimism and the pathos of constructive labour in Brenner's work that might have made him the favourite writer of his generation. The situation was bad enough, and the young Zionist Socialists did not need anyone to impress on them that it was almost hopeless. And yet his very unwillingness to embellish, to compromise, endeared him to Hapoel Hatzair and Poale Zion alike, and they continued to publish him even if this provoked the ire of almost everyone else in the community.

The rivalry between the two labour parties manifested itself in various ways: Poale Zion referred to their rival as a pleasant kindergarten for the sons and daughters of lower middle class parents (not that their own social background was any different), far too much preoccupied with cultural problems for their own good, who put too great an emphasis on Zionism and the Hebrew language, and who, generally speaking, isolated themselves from the 'masses'. They criticised the unwillingness of Hapoel Hatzair to participate in celebrating May Day, the day of international proletarian solidarity. The constant harping by Hapoel Hatzair on the 'conquest of labour' they regarded as irrelevant because there were not enough Jewish workers anyway. With all these polemics, Palestinian realities made the two groups draw closer together after a few years. Poale Zion realised that orthodox Marxist concepts developed in Russia were inapplicable to Palestine, while Hapoel Hatzair shed some of its exalted idealistic notions and became more involved in politics. By 1914 the number of Jewish workers had risen to about sixteen hundred; by that time yet a third party had come into existence, the 'non-partisans' (including Berl Katznelson, Yitzhak Tabenkin, David Remes), who preferred not to join any of the existing groups. There were also several hundred workers of Yemenite origin who stayed out of the violent and to them incomprehensible quarrels of their European brothers.

On the eve of the First World War there were no longer basic differences with regard to the desirability of establishing cooperative agricultural settlements. Originally Poale Zion had rejected them, because they were out of keeping with Borokhov's doctrine; in 1909, at their second world conference, Borokhov had reiterated his opposition even though Kaplanski and some others had disagreed with the traditional point of view.[*] Doctrinal considerations apart, it was argued that the class-conscious proletariat in Palestine was as yet exceedingly weak, and that any diversion of its energies from its immediate and most important task was likely to weaken it even further. But this was not how the Palestinians saw it: two years later the Palestinian Poale Zion accepted in principle, albeit with some reservations, the idea of cooperative agricultural settlements.[†] Within Hapoel Hatzair, too, there was originally opposition to the proposal that Jewish workers should establish agricultural settlements of their own. In a dispute with Witkin, Yosef Ahronowitz contended that the conquest of labour was more urgent and more important than the conquest of the land.[‡] But little progress was made in the conquest of labour in the colonies. Yosef Wilkansky, Yosef Bussel (one of the founders of Degania), and Shmuel Dayan (Moshe Dayan's father) rejected Ahronowitz's argument that Jewish capital would somehow take care of the problem of agricultural colonisation. Events had a logic of their own. While these debates continued, some agricultural workers of both

---

* Borokhov, Collected Writings, vol. 2, p. 554.
† 'Abner' (Ben Zvi), Ahdut, no. 36, 1911.
‡ 'Kibbush Ha'avoda o Kibbush Hakarka', in Hapoel Hatzair, 12, 1908.

parties took the initiative, moved from Petah Tiqva to Galilee, and established there the first collective farming communities.

The kvutza

These sporadic and uncertain beginnings, the appearance of small working groups at Sejera and Kineret, at Degania and Merhavia, constitute the origin of the *kvutza*, the unique feature of the Jewish labour movement in Palestine and also the one which in years to come was to attract the greatest attention. The idea of communistic settlements was not of course entirely novel. It had figured prominently in the thoughts of the 'Utopian Socialists', and the settlements established on these lines by Robert Owen and his disciples in the United States had existed for a long time. But with the rise of 'scientific Socialism' such ventures had ceased to attract interest; only in Russia did the idea of the 'commune' still have a few advocates. The Russian pioneers occasionally used to live on communal lines before their emigration, sharing both their income and their expenses and of course their few belongings. But the idea of permanent settlements on the Communist pattern, dispensing with private property, was thought to be fantastic. When Manya Wilbushewitz, one of the early pioneers, talked about it to Max Nordau in Paris, she was told that she was suffering from feverish delusions and was advised to consult a psychiatrist colleague.

The first collective settlements came into being not according to any clear preconceived pattern but by trial and error. After Herzl's death, during the era of 'practical Zionism', fresh emphasis was put on buying and colonising land outside the traditional areas of Jewish settlement. But who was to work the newly acquired land? There were no funds to support individual settlers, and since the farmers of Petah Tiqva and Rishon Lezion were neither able nor willing to help in the further development of Palestinian agriculture, it was decided that the land acquired by the National Fund, while remaining the property of the nation, should be rented to workers' collectives. These were to be paid according to the group piecework system. At first managers were appointed by the Zionist organisation, but later the workers themselves assumed control. Ruppin and his supporters in the Zionist executive had been influenced by the ideas of the German-Jewish economist Franz Oppenheimer concerning the advantages of large-scale collective farming over individual enterprise in agriculture. But Oppenheimer had recommended that each member should be rewarded according to his effort and output, whereas the workers demanded equal pay for all.* Dr Ruppin's willingness to support what seemed to most of his colleagues at best an interesting experiment, coincided with the desire of a growing number of Jewish agricultural workers to escape the stifling atmosphere of Petah Tiqva and the other colonies and to tackle some truly pioneering task. Their relations with the Jewish farmers had never been very happy; there had been strikes and even fighting. In Petah Tiqva the employers had on occasion decided to boycott Jewish labour altogether, their anger having been aroused by a workers' meeting in memory of their comrades fallen during the pogroms in Russia. The fact that members of both sexes had participated was an aggravating circumstance.

In Sejera, in lower Galilee, newcomers such as Ben Gurion found a different atmosphere: less monotonous work, only Jewish workers, no small shopkeepers, agents or middlemen. Practically everyone was working in the fields. Sejera became the centre of farm workers in the area. But these idyllic conditions did not last. In Kineret the workers struck against an autocratic manager who had not permitted them to visit a comrade who was lying gravely ill in the Tiberias hospital. An urgent call went out to Dr Ruppin in Jaffa. His solomonic verdict was to dismiss both manager and workers, but it had dawned on him that the traditional system of overseers was not an ideal one for Jewish workers – they were far too independent to be ordered around. Perhaps those who claimed that they would be able to work the land more efficiently without constant interference and control should be given a chance. It was not an easy decision to take and the misgivings of Dr Ruppin and his colleagues were not without foundation. The new workers certainly lacked professional experience and there was reason to doubt whether they had the necessary self-discipline to make the venture a success.

The first such experiment in self-management took place in 1905, when five workers from Kineret signed a contract with the Palestine office in Jaffa to work the land of Um Juni on their own responsibility. In November 1910 ten men and two women settled permanently in what became Degania, the 'mother of the kvutzot'. Much depended on the outcome. Failure at this stage might have had fatal consequences for the development of settlements of this kind. Two winters passed and two summers, and it appeared that despite the exceedingly difficult climate and other adverse conditions, the new-type settlement was going to be a

* A. Ruppin, *Die landwirtschaftliche Kolonisation Palästinas*, Berlin, 1915, chapter 14.

success.* But the directors of the Jewish National Fund still had their doubts. Degania had exceeded its budget by 40 per cent, and they criticised the system of accountancy according to which the kvutza had been worked at a profit from the very beginning. But Ruppin kept his faith in the settlers even against an authority like Oppenheimer, who argued that a capitalist bank could not accept responsibility for the debts and obligations of an enterprise over whose management it had not the slightest influence. Already some of the more enterprising members of the collective were playing with the idea of moving to a new place, to start once again from the beginning, and to leave Degania to another, less experienced group, eager to work in a collective settlement. But the majority view was that they should stay on, and regard Degania as their permanent home, the first in a chain of settlements to be set up in its wake. At this stage full Communism was not yet practised in the kvutza. Every member received a monthly wage of fifty francs from the Palestine office. Some paid it all into the common cash box, while others kept some back for buying clothes and shoes and for other purposes. Shmuel Dayan's suggestion that no one should marry during the first five years was forgotten after a few weeks and the birth of the first child was the occasion of a major ideological crisis: should the mother nurse and bring up her own child or should it be in someone else's care? Should children live with their parents or in a separate hut? Should the female members of the collective work in all branches of agriculture, or was their place in the kitchen, the laundry, and the children's house? Were the children – as Yosef Bussel put it – private property, or did they belong to the commune? The members of Degania opted for a compromise. More radical solutions and the abolition of private property in the collective settlements prevailed only after the end of the First World War with the arrival of a new generation of pioneers.

The story of the success of the first communal settlement spread quickly in Palestine and among Zionist-Socialist youth movements abroad, and the call went forth to establish more communes. There was, however, a tendency to stick too closely to the example of Degania. The fact that the first group of settlers had counted twelve members had been more or less accidental, but it almost became dogma, the pattern of Degania turning into an ideological imperative: it was generally assumed that

* On the early days of the kvutza, see Berl Katznelson (ed.), *Hakibbutz vehakvutza*, Tel Aviv, 1940; *Netive hakvutza vehakibbutz* (6 vols), Tel Aviv, 1958: *Pirke Hapoel Hatzair*; Harry Viteles, *A History of the Co-operative Movement in Israel* (2 vols.), London, 1966–70; Alex Bein, *The Return to the Soil*, Jerusalem, 1952; Hermann Meier-Cronemeyer, *Kibbuzim*, Hanover, 1969.

this was the optimal, indeed the only possible pattern, and that a membership exceeding twelve or fifteen would be detrimental to the intimate atmosphere prevailing in the kvutza. This belief persisted until after 1919, when, with the arrival of many new immigrants, the idea of the large kvutza began to spread.

The first commune had been founded because a growing number of Jewish agricultural workers wanted to break away from the traditional system of managers, overseers and daily wages. As the years passed, a kvutza ideology developed: the commune was not just the way to reach a certain end but became an end in itself; it was an organic cell of the future society. With the breakdown of the family in modern society a new and more progressive pattern of human coexistence was needed, a large-scale family based not on co-sanguinity but on common spiritual attitudes and values. Not all supporters of the kvutza had such far-reaching ambitions. Some simply continued to regard it as the most rational and congenial form of agricultural settlement in Eretz Israel. But everyone agreed that the project was to be pursued on a wider scale. There was also a growing awareness that it was of relevance not only within the Palestinian context but constituted a specific Jewish Socialist contribution in the search for a new society.

While the leaders of the Socialist *groupuscules* in Palestine were talking about the mission of the masses of Jewish workers, the masses themselves were still concentrated in eastern Europe. Events in Sejera and Degania had no direct bearing on their life. Poale Zion was still overwhelmingly a Russian Jewish party, though branches had come into being in Austria (Galicia) in 1904, in the United States (1905), and in Britain (1906). The hostility of the Bund to Zionist initiatives has been mentioned; it did not mellow with time. The Zionist convictions of Poale Zion, on the other hand, were put to a severe test as it became more and more involved in Russian politics. In theory there was no dividing line between the Zionism and the Socialism of Poale Zion, but as the great majority of the members of the party remained outside Palestine, their involvement in local politics became almost inevitable after the revolutionary events and the pogroms of 1904–5. The attacks by critics such as Zhitlovsky probably played a certain part in the process of de-Zionisation. How could a party which put the rebirth of the nation on its banner display typical diaspora (*galut*) mentality and lack the courage to fight for the rights of Jews wherever they lived? But once Poale Zion decided to take a more active part in Russian politics, the Zionist idea was bound to lose its central place in its activities.

This was the time of the Uganda conflict, when the realisation of the Zionist dream seemed more remote than ever. There was considerable support for the policy of a new party, the Sejmists, who seceded in 1905 from the ranks of Zionism-Socialism.* For a while they continued to regard themselves as Zionists, and indeed the official name of the party was Zionist-Socialists. But since in their demands they put the emphasis on national political autonomy for Jews in their countries of residence, it was difficult to discover with the naked eye any fundamental difference between them and the Bund. The Sejmists still believed that in the last resort the Jewish question could not be solved in the diaspora. But since they, unlike the Zionists, could not point to a territory which would be a haven for the Jewish masses, the difference between them and the Bund seemed largely academic. For a number of years the territorialists exerted a considerable impact on Jewish Socialism. They had capable leaders such as Zhitlovsky and Nahman Syrkin (who later returned to Zionism). Borokhov's ingenious 'synthesis' failed to persuade most Jewish left-wingers: granted that the Jews needed a land of their own, how could it be proved by Marxist analysis that this country should be none other than Palestine?

The Zeire Zion, a youth movement in Russia and Poland, which had come into being before the First World War, were less vulnerable ideologically, for their Zionism was not based on a scientific theory and they did not believe that the industrial proletariat would be the vanguard of the Jewish people – if only because of its numerical weakness. Yosef Witkin's appeal (1905) to the youth to serve the Jewish people in Palestine, had made a profound impression on them and they called upon their members to undergo agricultural training to prepare themselves for the pioneering assignments awaiting them in Palestine. They felt that Zionism would not be built as the result of 'objective forces' but only if enough of them were willing to devote their life to the cause. Their ideology resembled that of Hapoel Hatzair inasmuch as it was less clearly defined than that of Poale Zion; they too were Socialists, but their Socialism was based largely on ethical considerations. Later on, it was given its theoretical foundation ('Volkssozialismus') in the writings of Chaim Arlosoroff when, at the end of the First World War, the Zeire Zion movement expanded all over eastern Europe and became one of the main reservoirs of *halutz* emigration to Palestine.

* From *Sejm*, Slavic equivalent of parliament. The main sources for the history of the Sejmists are the writings of Ch.Zhitlovski, the periodicals *Serp* and *Vozrozhdenie*, and A. Tartakower's *Toldot tnuat hapoalim hayehudit*.

When the First World War broke out the number of Jewish agricultural workers in Palestine totalled twelve hundred, while the number of those employed in various trades and industries in the cities was not much higher. The war threatened whatever progress had been achieved during the preceding three decades. The poorer sections of the Jewish population were particularly hard hit. After Turkey entered the war, the citrus fruit and the wine of Rishon Lezion and Zikhron Ya'akov could no longer be exported, building funds ran out, the Zionist bank closed down, and the price of foodstuffs and other necessities rose while wages fell as the result of mass unemployment.* Beyond the political dangers facing the yishuv, arrests and persecution by the Turkish military authorities, economic ruin and acute hunger threatened the working class community and its institutions. Stagnation was not total, however: four new collective agricultural settlements were founded, including Kfar Giladi and Ayelet Hashahar.

To cope with the wartime emergency, *Hamashbir* was established, the workers' central buying and selling cooperative which subsequently played such a vital role in the development of the trade union movement and the agricultural settlements. But the spirit of the halutzim was low, and many leaders of the workers' organisations, including Ben Gurion and Ben Zvi, were expelled from the country by the Turkish authorities. The fact that the workers of Yehuda and Galilee were one big family (literally a 'face to face community'), that everyone did in fact know everyone else, had been a source of strength and solidarity, and made it easier for them to endure the deprivations of the early years. But it now contributed to the spread of defeatism and despair. Those who had regarded themselves as the spearhead of the great cause of national and social revival now began to suffer from claustrophobia. They were eagerly looking forward to the day when at last there would be some new faces in their midst. But with the total cessation of immigration in 1914 these hopes faded. Never had it been so obvious that smallness could be a curse. The disadvantages manifested themselves on almost every level. Much had been written on the advantages of the family atmosphere and the intimacy in the kvutzot, yet – as so often – there was a wide divergence between theory and reality. The fact that the twelve or fifteen members were in each other's company for most of the day, that there was hardly any privacy at all, did not enrich their personal life (as the theorists had predicted) but, on the contrary, caused spiritual impoverishment: the hypertrophy of the collective sphere did not necessarily bring out the

* W. Preuss, loc. cit., p. 44.

293

best in the individual members of the commune. It induced not a few to turn their backs on what only a few years earlier they had considered the ideal way of life.* However promising the beginnings of the cooperative settlements, it is unlikely that they would have survived but for the arrival of new immigrants from Europe. The Russian revolution of March 1917 was the first ray of hope. Eight months later the Balfour Declaration was published, and after yet another month, in December 1917, the troops of General Allenby entered Jerusalem.

In the late afternoon of one of the days of Chanukka 1919, the ship *Ruslan* with 671 new immigrants arrived in Jaffa. It was perhaps symbolical that the newcomers had to land in heavy seas. It was with this date that a new period in the history of the Palestinian labour movement began. The third immigration wave, over the next four years, brought 37,000 new immigrants, many of them members of Zionist-Socialist youth organisations. A trickle of new immigrants had come even earlier. The very first, a group of pioneers from Bendzin in Poland, arrived less than four weeks after the armistice had been signed. They made their way over the icy roads of a continent ravaged by war and civil war and on which public transport had not yet been resumed. Most came by way of Turkey, a few via Japan.† Only five years divided these new arrivals from the latecomers of the second aliya, but there was a world of difference between their outlook and that of the previous generation of immigrants. The pioneers of the postwar period were in some ways better prepared for life in Palestine. Many of them had received some agricultural training and spoke better Hebrew than their predecessors, and they came in organised groups rather than as individuals. But they had not been prepared, as an old-timer regretfully noted, for the Palestinian realities.‡

The expectations of the immigrant of 1905 had been limited in scope: he knew that he was leaving for a far-away, backward country, and that his ideal of a Socialist Zionist community lay in the distant future. The immigrant of 1919 was the child of a revolutionary age and therefore likely to be more impatient, and the Balfour Declaration had brought the realisation of the dream much nearer. He was more radical in his approach, less inclined to compromise. He was dreaming of the transformation of Palestine into one big commune, not in the distant future but within a year or two. If he had belonged to one of the Zionist youth

* N. Benari, *Zur Geschichte der Kwuza und des Kibbuz*, Berlin, 1934, p. 38.

† The adventures of the first arrivals are described in colourful detail in Yehuda Eres (ed.), *Sefer Ha'aliya hashlishit* (2 vols.), Tel Aviv, 1964.

‡ Y. Ahronowitz, quoted in Y. Shapiro, 'Bein ha'aliya hashnia vehashlishit', in *Asupot* April 1962, p.11.

movements he thought of life in Palestine as an extension of the summer camps in Galicia or the Ukraine, with their dances, banners, bonfires and other symbols and common experiences of the European youth movements. Some of the newcomers were to join the existing kvutzot, but only a few stayed, not finding satisfaction there, too much separated as they were from the men and women of the second aliya. They wanted to pursue their own way of life rather than join the existing groups. The leap from the realm of dreams to the world of reality was sudden and the landing usually painful. The newcomers were not prepared for the political setbacks, for the Arab attacks, and least of all for the unemployment which accompanied the postwar economic depression. As the mass immigration petered out and the Russian Jewish community, hitherto Palestine's main reservoir, was effectively cut off, there was a new wave of 'great despair' such as had followed the second aliya.

The Legion of Labour

If Petah Tiqva, Sejera and Degania had been the universities of the second aliya, the 'Legion of Labour' (*Gdud Ha'avoda*), with its tents and ramshackle huts along the paths between Haifa and Nazareth, and between Zemach, Tiberias and Tabha in lower Galilee, where they were to build the highroads, were the main stations of the graduates of the third aliya. The legion was founded in 1920 at a memorial meeting for Yosef Trumpeldor, who had been killed some months earlier defending Tel-Hai against Arab attackers. It had been Trumpeldor's idea to form labour legions to do pioneering work in Palestine, paving the way for mass immigration. The legion had eighty members at first, but grew eventually to seven hundred. It existed for only six years but it was the vanguard of the pioneer movement, the first to settle in the Yesreel valley, the first to establish kibbutzim. But for its initiative, Jewish workers would not have gained a foothold in building and other trades in the towns and villages. The legion was composed largely of young men – and a few young women – many of them graduates of the Russian revolution and the civil war, full of youthful fire, ready to burn and to be burned. In its ranks there were mystics in search of God, and romantic enthusiasts in search of themselves by way of the mortification of the flesh and the spirit, grandsons of Dostoievsky and nephews of Brenner. There were among them members of youth movements on whom Martin Buber had exerted great influence, and there were also hard-bitten old-timers of the second aliya who had not opened a book for years.*

* Sh. Litvin, *Kovetz Gdud Avoda*, Tel Aviv, 1932, p. 25.

The legion was organised in small groups of twelve to fifteen members dispersed over the whole country. Their part in road-building has already been mentioned. Some worked on new buildings in Haifa, Jerusalem or Galilee, others repaired motor cars in Beersheba. There were two major concentrations: one in Migdal, which served as their main base in lower Galilee, another in Rosh Ha'ayin, where several hundred members worked on a new railroad. Almost from the outset the legion adopted the principle of full Communism. Its members received no wages or salaries, all their earnings disappearing into a common fund, and their basic needs were covered according to the principle of full equality. The legion had no clearly defined position on agricultural settlement. Some of its members favoured the establishment of big agricultural collectives. The physical conditions could hardly have been less auspicious, for what was later to become one of the most fertile stretches, the *Emeq*, was at the time largely marshland, infested with malaria. There were no roads, little vegetation, no water, no electricity. Some members of the legion were sceptical about the outcome of a venture which they thought was far beyond the strength of a group which, however eager, was ill-prepared for a task of this magnitude and also lacked professional experience. But the enthusiasts carried the day. In September 1921 the first camp of tents was set up in the valley and another followed later that year. What they lacked in professional skills they made up by devoted work; against all expectations the attempt was a modest success, or at any rate, it did not fail.

It was suggested that the legion should be transformed into one big kibbutz, or several such settlements, but this issue caused the first major split in its ranks. The urban workers' commune, some argued, had no future. It was at best a provisional arrangement. The working class movement in Palestine was to find its true function and fulfilment in agricultural settlement. The majority rejected this view, for a variety of reasons: the basic idea of the legion had been to establish consumer rather than producer collectives. It was their task to gain a foothold in all kinds of jobs in the cities as well as in the countryside. To concentrate on agricultural settlement smacked of the romanticism of the second aliya, nor was it in accordance with the principle of the class struggle. The legion split in 1923, some members joining what subsequently became Kibbutz Ein Harod, while the majority continued to work in small groups dispersed throughout the country.

Three years later the legion had more members than ever before, but the original impetus had disappeared. It had clearly failed in its endeavour to attract the majority of Jewish workers in Palestine to its ranks, and to make them accept its way of life. The growing disappointment manifested itself in a process of political radicalisation. A vocal and influential minority reached the conclusion that the class struggle was their main concern and that consequently the centre of gravity of the legion's activities should be transferred to the towns. They quarrelled bitterly with the Histadrut, the General Federation of Jewish Labour which had been founded in 1920. Some members of the legion began to dissociate themselves from Zionism altogether. Since the attempt to establish a Socialist community in a non-Socialist environment had failed, and since in their scale of priorities the world revolution weighed heavier than Zionist ideals, this anti-Zionist turn seemed only consistent. In December 1926 the legion split, mainly on political lines. The larger group later joined the existing Zionist-Socialist parties, while the minority faction dissolved itself in 1928. Several dozen of its members emigrated to the Soviet Union, where they established an agricultural settlement in the Crimea. It ceased to exist following the arrest of most of its members during the purge of the 1930s.*

Hashomer Hatzair

Among the new arrivals of 1919–20 there were the first members of the Hashomer Hatzair (Young Watchman), a group which was to play a notable part in subsequent Zionist history. This movement had emerged in Galicia during the war years. Many of its members, known as *shomrim*, came from middle class families, well-off by the standards of east European Jewry. In their majority they were quite assimilated; their education had been Polish or Austro-German, and the Yiddish folk culture in which the second aliya had been steeped was not part of their cultural experience. They had become converts to Zionism not as the result of a socio-economic analysis of the situation of the Jewish masses, but had set out on their long road from a very different starting point: they had decided that they would find cultural and spiritual fulfilment both as individuals and as a group only by joining in the building of a new society in Eretz Israel. The ideas and symbols of the German youth movement exerted a strong influence on them, as did Martin Buber who, in a famous speech in Vienna towards the end of the war, had declared that youth was the eternal good fortune (*die ewige Glückschance*) of mankind, a chance which reappeared with each new generation and which

* The main source for the history of the Gdud Ha'avoda is *Gdud Avoda al shem Yosef Trumpeldor*, Tel Aviv, 1932.

was always squandered. The shomrim believed with Wyneken, the ideologist of the German youth movement, that youth was a value in itself, that only young people, unfettered by ties of family, class, and status in society, could be revolutionaries. They believed in a specific youth culture, more genuine and harmonious than that of the world of the adults with their compromises and conventional lies.

Such an approach was not as novel, revolutionary or un-Jewish as some contemporaries believed. Zionism, and in particular its left wing, the Biluim, and the Socialist pioneers of 1905–6, had also been a youth movement of sorts. The revolt against the liberal-assimilationist establishment in the west, and the decaying, parasitic world of the shtetl in eastern Europe, had been a central factor in Zionist thought from the beginning. But Hashomer Hatzair was in many ways *sui generis*. The romantic ecstasy which engulfed the young generation all over Europe had not bypassed young middle class Jews in the east. Their intellectual mentors were Marx and Freud, Nietzsche and Buber, Gustav Landauer and Wyneken. Their early publications are filled with references to religious rites and the symbols of the youth movement: 'confession', vestal fires, redemption of the soul. Their meals were to be an act of holy communion: 'The full realisation of the erotic force in our community [one of them wrote at the time] is not in conversation, not even in our dances, but in our common meals; without an altar table there can be no real commune.'*

In the Hashomer Hatzair kibbutz in the early days the atmosphere did not differ greatly from that of the summer camps back in Poland. The work on the roads was difficult, the whole environment unfamiliar, but there were compensations: the long nights, the dances, the unending *sichot* (conversations in which the members of the whole community participated and revealed their innermost thoughts), lectures on subjects such as 'Eros and our Society'. An account of one such meeting relates how suddenly, at midnight, when everyone was already asleep, the members of the group were called to an urgent meeting. They hurried to the tent in which the group assemblies were held. One member of the kibbutz was talking solemnly, haltingly ('like a high priest in the temple') with his eyes to the ground: 'I have called this meeting because I, I mean we, comrade X and myself, have just become one family.' The chronicler

---

* *Kehiliatenu*, Haifa-Jedda, 1922, pp. 21–2. The writer, Nathan Bistritsky, is also the author of a novel, *Yamim velelot*, which faithfully reflects the atmosphere in the Hashomer Hatzair working camps at the time. See also David Horowitz, *Ha'etmol sheli*, Tel Aviv, 1970, chapter 7.

BUILDING A NEW SOCIETY

unfortunately fell asleep at this point, but he was told the next morning that the sicha had continued for a long time and that it had been one of the most beautiful ever.*

The Hashomer Hatzair concept of what a collective should be was far more radical than life in the kvutzot established by the previous generation of pioneers. The children's education was to be collective, and they were to sleep in the children's house, not with their parents. The kibbutz resolved 'to liquidate the family as a social unit, recognising it only as an expression of erotic life'. The very idea that two young people might prefer their own company to that of the collective was thought to be asocial and reactionary, a relic of petty-bourgeois society. The whole atmosphere was that of a big family: when a member of the collective decided to go on a two-week tour of the country, he would call a general meeting, announce his intention, and say how much he would miss them. The dances after work were a central part of the collective life, not just an expression of youthful joy but a manifestation of inner mystic experiences. There was little political interest during these early years. Why read the empty phrases of the newspapers (one of them wrote)? Why participate in political meetings in which demagogues were using big words devoid of any significance? The shomrim still believed in the spiritual revolution. By joining the collective, by coming to Palestine to build a new home for the Jewish people, they, the happy few, had saved their souls. Almost totally immersed in their individual problems, politics seemed neither relevant nor urgent.†

Gradually cruel reality demanded its toll. 'Where is our enthusiasm of yesteryear?' a member of one of the early kibbutzim asked in 1924. The meetings were no longer well attended. They no longer took place in semi-darkness but (symbolically, perhaps) in the bright light of paraffin lamps. The old symbols of the German youth movement now seemed out of place and were gradually discarded. The exalted romanticism, the religiosity and aestheticism faded away. The members of the kibbutzim began to realise that youth was not an eternal value, and that small groups of young people, however idealistically inclined, would not bring about the world revolution as they had believed.‡ In later years

* *Al Hamishmar*, 8 February 1952; the diary quoted refers to events in February 1922.
† For the early history of Hashomer Hatzair in Eretz Israel, see *Sefer Hashomer Hatzair*, particularly vol. 1; Shlomo Rehav, *Selected Works*, Merhavia, 1966, p. 11 *et seq.*; Elkana Margalit, 'Social and Intellectual Origins of the Hashomer Hatzair Movement', *Journal of Contemporary History*, April 1969, and the doctoral dissertation of the same author.
‡ Meir Ya'ari, 'Semalim Tlushim', in *Baderekh Aruka*, Merhavia, 1947, p. 25 *et seq.* (written in 1923).

299

they reacted with some bitterness against the gods that had failed and the baneful impact of the German youth movement. But such excessive self-criticism misses some central points: would they have decided in the first place to give up the comfort and the relative security of middle class homes in Europe but for the romantic impulse received from the *Wandervogel* and the Free German Youth? It is one of the ironies of history that the German youth movement, while producing a youth subculture, failed in its more ambitious endeavours, whereas the Jewish youth movement, by its persistence and historical good fortune, succeeded in entering the annals of history as one of the few youth groups ever to develop a new and original life style.

The process of growing up, the transition from youth movement to life in the kibbutzim, took years, and it was not an easy transition. The dream of establishing a spiritual family, nomadic in character, aiming at the redemption of the individual and preaching messianic ideas, faded. There were no new ready-made ideals to replace the old ones and the adjustment to a life of poverty took its toll. The shomrim were isolated; they were criticised for their élitism, for dissociating themselves from the working-class and its real, day-to-day problems. They were attacked, above all, for the lack of any real Jewish content in their cultural life. For their part, they found not a great deal to admire in the way of life of those who had preceded them on the road to Palestine. There was also the traditional antagonism between Russian and Polish Jewry. Initially the members of Hashomer Hatzair were drawn to the philosophy of A.D. Gordon and the ideas of Hapoel Hatzair, and Gordon, for his part, was attracted by the sincerity and idealism of the young pioneers from Galicia, and the great emphasis they put on the self-education of the individual. But from the beginning the shomrim had certain reservations and these became more pronounced in the course of time. There was for their taste too much of Tolstoy and vegetarianism in Gordon's teaching. His concept of Socialism and building a new Socialist society in Palestine seemed to them, on further reflection, about as nebulous and impractical as their own which they were in the process of discarding.

Gradually they moved away from Hapoel Hatzair, without, however, entering the orbit of another political party. After the early poetic period (as one of them put it), there came a philosophical interlude, an attempt to see themselves and the world around them in a more objective light; they were searching for a new world view without the help of an ideological compass. The first kibbutz (Bet Alfa) was founded during that period, but there were also major setbacks. Many left the movement during those years and not a few returned to Europe. Those who remained established new kibbutzim such as Mishmar Ha'emeq, Merhavia, Gan Shmuel and Ein Shemer. In 1927 the first five kibbutzim, with a total membership of less than three hundred, joined forces in a countrywide association, the Kibbutz Artzi. In their kibbutzim they developed by trial and error a specific way of life far more down to earth than the exaltation of the early days. Their educational ideas, adjusted to Palestinian realities, continued to play an important part in their activities, and the youth movement in the diaspora, out of which Hashomer Hatzair had developed, served as the reservoir from which the kibbutzim in Palestine gained fresh support every year. It was the policy of the Hashomer Hatzair to found new kibbutzim rather than concentrate on a few very big ones. The optimal size for a kibbutz was thought at the time to be fewer than one hundred members.

The radicalism which had manifested itself earlier on in the belief in a spiritual revolution found new expression in politics as the movement embraced left-wing revolutionary Socialism. Emphasising the necessity for greater militancy, they disagreed with the orientation of the other Socialist groups in Palestine towards the Second Socialist International. In 1927 the Galician Hashomer Hatzair, under the leadership of Mordehai Oren, adopted a new policy which seemed to most critics of the movement to lead it away from Zionism towards the Third Communist International. But these ideological searches and struggles belong to a later period. What emerged at this stage was that the insistence of the kibbutzim of the Hashomer Hatzair on a common political platform shared by all their members set them apart from all other settlements. Such internal unity strengthened Hashomer Hatzair, but at the same time it effectively prevented close collaboration with other kibbutz movements, for the other collective settlements did not concern themselves with the personal views of their members. In later years Hashomer Hatzair became a political party, but its politics were neither unique nor particularly successful. In retrospect its main achievement remained the collective settlements and their specific structure and style. Out of the small nucleus of enthusiasts in upper Betania, with their dreams of self-realisation and a spiritual revolution, there developed within five decades a network of more than seventy kibbutzim with more than thirty thousand men, women and children, communities different in some important respects from all other known societies.

As the First World War ended, the Jewish working class, and its political parties concentrated in eastern Europe, faced new problems and challenges. The revolutions of 1917, the emergence of independent Poland and other new states, and the demands for national-cultural autonomy, created a new situation. While the Bolsheviks were opposed in principle to Zionism in every shape and form, as well as to the existence of Jewish non-Zionist left-wing groups, however close to them ideologically, the 'Jewish question' was not one of their most urgent preoccupations, either during the civil war or the years of NEP. Poale Zion in Russia, which had always been more orthodox Marxist in inspiration than its sister parties elsewhere, faced a difficult dilemma: its members were eager to be part of the great wave of the future and to join the Third Communist International, and were quite willing to dissociate themselves publicly from the World Zionist Organisation. Borokhov, after all, had for many years advocated a boycott of the Zionist congress, even though he regarded himself as a Zionist and continued to pay the shekel. But this would not have been enough for the Communists. Poale Zion was expected to reject the Balfour Declaration as well, issued after all by one of the major imperialist powers. Ultimately they would have had to disavow Zionism altogether and to dissolve their own organisation.

Left-wing Zionism had been based on the assumption that the Jewish question was insoluble in capitalist society. The rise of Bolshevism created an entirely new situation. The new régime, internationalist in character, formally abolished all forms of discrimination against minorities, promised to change the social structure of the Jewish masses, to find productive work for them, and did not preclude some form of cultural-national autonomy. The end of antisemitism seemed in sight, and, if so, it must have appeared utterly pointless to leave a Socialist country for one which was as yet far from reaching this advanced stage in its political-social development. Discussing these problems, the Poale Zion parties split on the following lines: the Palestinian Poale Zion had long given up orthodox Borokhovism, and joining the Communist International was completely out of the question. The Russian Poale Zion, having shed its 'reformist ballast', entered into direct negotiations with the Comintern which lasted for a year and caused further dissension in its ranks. Some of its members (the JKP – *Jiddishe Kommunistische Partei*) were willing to jettison Zionism altogether, while others advocated a Communist-Zionist synthesis. JKP ultimately joined the Communist Party of the Soviet Union, via the Jewish section of the Communist Party (*Yevsektsia*), which had been established when Stalin was Commissar for Nationalities to deal with the specific problems of non-assimilated Jewish Communists. The Yevsektsia continued to exist for a number of years, but most of its leading figures disappeared in the purges of the 1930s.

That part of Poale Zion which preferred not to surrender its independence survived in the Soviet Union till 1928 when, a small and shrinking group which gave the authorities little concern, it was finally dissolved. Its leading members gradually emigrated to Palestine. Men such as Erem, Abramovich, Nir, Yitzhaki and Zerubavel, had been leaders of some influence in eastern Europe, but in Palestine they were generals without an army. Their doctrinaire approach both to ideological issues and to day-to-day political problems, their opposition to agricultural settlement, the fact that they preferred Yiddish to Hebrew, limited their political appeal from the start. There was something touching in their devotion to their party, their unceasing efforts to promote their old ideas in an inauspicious environment, their internal squabbles on abstruse points of Marxism-Borokhovism, their passionate debates on the 'correct approach' to events in far-away countries on which they could not possibly have any influence. They were forever discussing revolutionary strategy and proletarian unity, debating whether or not to establish a popular front at a time when their 'mass basis' numbered a few hundred. The views of Hashomer Hatzair were often equally abstruse, but it had a youth movement and its agricultural settlements to fall back on, and it became in a real sense part of the Palestinian scene, whereas Poale Zion, figuratively speaking, had left Russia but had never really arrived in Eretz Israel. Like the Mensheviks in exile, they gradually faded away, the vanishing remnant of a proud Socialist tradition.*

It would be unjust to interpret the surrender of the majority of the Russian Poale Zion as a manifestation of weakness, or a special ideological susceptibility to the appeal of Bolshevism. Other Jewish parties did not behave differently. The attraction of linking their future to that of a far bigger and more powerful movement must have been overwhelming to many Jewish Socialists, the alternative being total isolation, growing police repression, searches, economic and political sanctions, and ultimately arrest. For the Zionists, according to Soviet doctrine, were not just nationalist deviationists, but 'objectively' agents of British imperialism, even if they gave full support to Soviet foreign policy. The anti-Zionist Bund abdicated even earlier than Poale Zion; in April 1920

* The main sources for the history of Poale Zion after 1917 are *Yalkute Poale Zion*, Tel Aviv, 1947, Jerusalem 1954; the recollections of Z.Abramovich, *Besherut hatnua*, Tel Aviv, 1965; and of N.Nir, *Wanderungen*, Tel Aviv, 1965; the selection of Y.Yitzhaki's writings (Merhavia, 1957), and the second volume of A.Tartakover's *History of the Jewish workers' movement* (Hebrew edition), Warsaw, 1930.

it decided to change its name to Communist Bund, and to modify its ideological platform. In less than a year it took the last fateful step and joined the Yevsektsia. Even non-Marxist groups such as the zs (Zionists-Socialists) were strongly attracted by the dynamic character of the young Soviet régime: 'We were spellbound by the daring of the Bolsheviks who were resolved to translate their ideas into reality', one of them wrote many years later.*

The new immigrants who came to Palestine with the third immigration wave had the choice of two workers' organisations, Hapoel Hatzair and Poale Zion. But these parties had been founded by a previous generation of pioneers, and their continued existence did not now necessarily make much sense. Even some of the prewar immigrants, such as Berl Katznelson, had found it impossible to range themselves with one of these groups against the other. After the war, the move to establish a United Socialist Party received a fresh impetus, and it was towards this end that a new group, the Labour Union (Ahdut Ha'avoda), was set up at a meeting in Petah Tiqva in spring 1919. This new body was meant to be a trade union confederation into which the existing groups were to merge, but as Hapoel Hatzair refused to join, it soon turned into a political party. By that time the ideological differences between the two parties had dwindled into insignificance. Like its adversary, it advocated a pragmatic constructivism. The fact that it continued to belong to the Socialist International, whereas its rival refrained from joining any international organisation, was hardly an issue of decisive importance. Hapoel Hatzair, unlike the Labour Union, did not regard the Jewish workers as a proletariat with interests rigidly opposed to those of other classes, but as an active force in building the national home on the basis of social justice.

There certainly was a difference in personality and character if one compares the leadership of the two parties. The leading people in Ahdut Ha'avoda tended to be tougher, more aggressive and radical, in both their Socialism and their nationalism. Hapoel Hatzair was more inclined towards moderation, averse to pathos, less politically minded.† It was opposed to a merger because it was afraid that the prospective united movement would soon be dominated by the Labour Union, with its strong political ambitions. No one was more emphatic in his opposition

---

* Yehuda Eres (ed.), *Sefer Z. S.*, Tel Aviv, 1963, p. 44.

† Among leading members of Hapoel Hatzair who subsequently attained prominence in the Zionist movement and the state of Israel were Yosef Sprinzak, speaker of the Knesset; Levi Eshkol, prime minister after Ben Gurion; and Eliezer Kaplan.

than old A.D.Gordon. But Hapoel Hatzair had to pay a heavy price for preventing 'union at any cost'. To compete with its rivals in the struggle for influence, it had willy-nilly to become just another political party, to copy and to duplicate the activities of the other side, and to a large extent it lost its specific character. The two groups competed in establishing trade unions, with some seamstresses and shoemakers belonging to Hapoel Hatzair unions, others joining Ahdut Ha'avoda. Some frequented the canteen run by one group, others preferred the food (or the ideology) of the other. Previously, Hapoel Hatzair had not been interested in the organisation of urban workers, but the competition with Ahdut Ha'avoda drew it into this new sphere of activity.

Above all, they competed for the allegiance of the new arrivals from eastern Europe. Zeire Zion was the strongest youth movement in eastern Europe at the time. Previously it had been closely linked with Hapoel Hatzair, which hoped for their adherence after their arrival in Palestine. But these expectations were only partly fulfilled, many members of Zeire Zion joining Ahdut. The polemics between the two groups proceeded not only on a literary level: they competed for every newcomer, and there were unedifying scenes in Jaffa harbour. Whenever a new ship anchored, representatives of the rival factions tried to enlist new members on the spot, like porters quarrelling over the baggage of tourists. The young Zionists, newly arrived from eastern Europe, were baffled, and then shocked and dismayed. This state of affairs affected Hapoel Hatzair even more than its rivals, for it had regarded itself as the conscience of the labour movement, not as just another party engaging in political strife. It did not want to waste its time working out new programmes and platforms. Its aim and *raison d'être* was to be the guardian of the basic values of the movement, which were put in jeopardy at a time of mass immigration.

Hapoel Hatzair had been influential among the agricultural workers; in the town it had only a limited following. On the other hand, it was supported by numerous writers, teachers and other intellectuals. Politically, such backing was insignificant, but it enhanced the prestige of the movement. While Ahdut Ha'avoda attracted more members in Palestine, Hapoel Hatzair, together with its supporters abroad, had the stronger faction at the Zionist congresses. In 1921 one of its members, Yosef Sprinzak, was elected to the Zionist executive, the first time that a member of one of the labour groups entered the top rank of the world movement. As the bitter struggle between the two parties continued, it gradually dawned on their members that the duplication of effort in almost every field was wasteful and counter-productive. The establishment of rival trade unions, in particular, was clearly self-defeating. In July 1920 an all-party commission was set up to explore the possibility of establishing united trade unions to take over all non-political activities such as the consumers union, the sick fund and the employment exchanges. In December 1920, after much discussion, the General Federation of Jewish Labour (Histadrut) was founded. Of the 87 delegates elected by the votes of 4,433 members to the council, Ahdut Ha'avoda had 37, Hapoel Hatzair 26, Hashomer Hatzair 16, and the left Poale Zion 6.

The economic activities of the Jewish workers were from now on concentrated in a neutral, non-partisan organisation which was also to run an immigration office, a workers' bank, and a number of economic undertakings. Within the next three years the number of workers organised in the trade unions doubled, and by 1923 every other Jewish worker was a member of the Histadrut, although conditions had been anything but auspicious when it was established: one out of four workers was unemployed and the World Zionist Organisation had not the financial resources to cope with the sudden crisis. The Palestinian government was willing to provide employment in the public-works sector, but there were few Jewish building workers, the newcomers having to be given special training. The Histadrut was desperately poor in those early years. The seven members of its first executive (four from Ahdut Ha'avoda, three from Hapoel Hatzair), had to share a single room. The seat of the executive was first in Tel Aviv, but was transferred in 1922 to Jerusalem. It returned to Tel Aviv in 1925 when it became increasingly clear that in Jerusalem it was cut off from the main concentrations of Jewish labour. The leaders of the Histadrut needed all their enthusiasm to surmount the obstacles facing them: 'The Labour and Immigration Office (housed in one single room) was sheer hell', one eye-witness reported. 'There was a general feeling that the Histadrut would fail and go out of business unless the crisis was overcome soon. Every day we had to register hundreds of hungry comrades; there was no work, no reserve fund to give financial assistance to the unemployed.'*

Like previous and subsequent immigration waves, the third aliya went through a period of 'great despair'. For a while it seemed likely that a substantial part of the urban workers would desert Zionism and join the Communists, who appeared under the label of MOPS (*Mifleget Poalim Sozialistit*, Socialist Workers Party). Emigration from Palestine also

---

* Y. Kaner, quoted in Even Shoshan, *loc. cit.* vol. 2, p. 13.

became a real problem. True, the percentage of those who went back to Europe was not nearly so high as it had been before 1914; according to reliable estimates only about 25 per cent of the postwar immigrants left again within a few years. But in 1923, when immigration was already on the decline, re-emigration rose to 43 per cent. This trend continued to 1924, when the economic crisis gave way to a new era of prosperity and an unexpected influx of immigrants opened a new era of great economic activity.

The history of the Palestinian Jewish labour movement begins, properly speaking, only after the First World War. All that had happened before had been in retrospect a mere prelude, its pre-history. True, the second aliya had laid many a foundation stone, but without the third immigration wave the building would not have been erected. The number of Jewish workers in both town and countryside had been minimal before 1914. Even the kvutza, perhaps the main achievement of the second aliya, had been no more than the forerunner of the kibbutz, which after 1918 inaugurated the era of large-scale collective agriculture. When Degania, the mother of the kvutzot, was set up, it had a dozen members. Ten years later, Ein Harod, the first kibbutz, had 215 at the time of its foundation.

The emergence of the kibbutz for a long time overshadowed the development of another kind of agricultural settlement, also established after the First World War – the *moshav* (literally, settlement). This was an attempt to combine individual initiative and collective action: in the moshav every member worked his own holding, but there were strict rules of cooperative marketing and purchase. Success in the moshav depended on the hard work and experience of the individual. It appealed to those who disliked either the lack of personal incentive or the intensity of social life in the kibbutzim. The first moshavim, such as Nahalal and Kfar Yeheskel, were founded at about the same time as the first kibbutzim, but they developed only slowly because, unlike the kibbutzim, they had no great attraction for the Zionist youth organisations in the diaspora. The kibbutz constituted a new way of life. The moshav was, from the outside, seen as at best a step towards the normalisation of the Jewish social structure. In 1930 there were altogether nine moshavim, with a total membership of nine hundred. But with the big immigration waves of the 1930s, 1940s and 1950s the moshav underwent a period of rapid development. In 1963 there were more than three hundred of them, with 110,000 members, more than the total membership of the kibbutzim. The moshav has attracted less interest among outside observers because it lacks the glamour of the kibbutz, its social and economic structure being less revolutionary and original. Unlike the kibbutz it did not at any stage exert any notable political influence. Furthermore, as time went by, the collective element in the moshav movement declined, with a corresponding extension of the private sphere in its economic and social structure. It was in some ways the stepchild of the Zionist movement, but it played a not unimportant part in the absorption of new immigrants and the development of agriculture.

The Third Aliya

The third immigration wave constituted at the time by far the strongest element among Jewish labour in Palestine. About 65 per cent of all agricultural and urban workers had, by the middle 1920s, arrived since the war; only 16 per cent were native Palestinians. As for its composition, this new working class was still not a 'normal' community: about 60 per cent were young and unmarried, and there was a heavy preponderance of men (72:28). Although two-thirds of the newcomers originally wanted to settle in kvutzot or kibbutzim, only 20 per cent were actually employed in agriculture, with about 25 per cent working on building sites and public works. But many of the latter regarded this as temporary; about half the building workers in the cities wanted eventually to take up agriculture. The weight of labour in the councils of the Palestinian Jewish community increased. Before 1914 its influence had been negligible, but with the immigration of the early 1920s labour gradually became a major social and political factor and its representatives entered the executive bodies of Palestinian Jewry.

The meeting between the second and third aliya was not without tension and conflict. There were pronounced differences in background, attitudes and political orientation. The generation gap was reflected in the greater radicalism of the new arrivals. But the leaders of the second aliya, sure of themselves and their ideas, kept the reins of leadership firmly in their own hands. Experience, too, was on their side. The year the Histadrut was founded Golda Meir was only twenty-two years old, Meir Ya'ari and Mordehai Namir twenty-three, Bar Yehuda twenty-five, Aran and Chasan twenty-one, Aharon Zisling nineteen, and Eliezer Kaplan, one of the oldest of this group, twenty-nine, to mention but a few prominent members of the third aliya. All these men and women later rose to positions of eminence in the Zionist movement and the state of Israel, but most of them only after the leading members of the second aliya had begun, one by one, to retire from the political scene. There were a few exceptions: Chaim Arlosoroff became head of the political department of the Jewish Agency at an early age, and Eliezer Kaplan, like Arlosoroff a former member of Hapoel Hatzair (less rich than Ahdut Ha'avoda in public figures), became financial director of the Jewish Agency in the 1930s. But by and large leadership remained in the hands of the older group.

The leaders of the second aliya were more or less of the same age and came from remarkably similar backgrounds: Ben Zvi, David Bloch, Blumenfeld, Kaplanski and Javneeli were born in 1884, Sprinzak in 1885, Ben Gurion, Zerubavel, Israel Shochat and David Remes in 1886, Tabenkin, Berl Locker and Berl Katznelson in 1887.* While this list is not complete, it includes most of the men who represented labour for almost five decades. Most of them hailed from White Russia and the northern Ukraine. Sprinzak was born in Moscow and later worked in Warsaw, but he was almost the only one of that generation to come from a big town. There was hardly anyone from Poland or Galicia – Kaplanski, who worked in Vienna, had been born in Bialystok, and Yosef Ahronowitz, one of the founders of Hapoel Hatzair, who left for Palestine from Galicia, where he had taught for many years, was in fact born in the Ukraine. Within this general area in which labour Zionism flourished, there was a further concentration: the majority hailed from certain small towns. Both Syrkin and Witkin were born in Mohilev, where Remes and David Sakai later worked. Bobruisk, the birthplace of Berl Katznelson and Tabenkin, also produced many other leading members of the second aliya. A very small place like Plonsk produced David Ben Gurion, Shlomo Zemach and Shlomo Lavi, who played a decisive part in the settlement of the Yesreel valley and the establishment of the first kibbutzim. The Shochat clan came from the Velkovisk area, as did the Golomb family. On the other hand, one would look in vain for leading labour Zionists hailing from Warsaw or Odessa, Riga or Moscow, Lvov or Vilna.†

Almost all of them learned Hebrew in a traditional religious school (*cheder*) or, if the family was well off, from a private tutor. All of them rejected orthodox Judaism in their private life, but retained a strong

---

* Salman Shazar was born in 1889 and Levi Eshkol, one of the youngest members of the second aliya, who arrived only shortly before the First World War, in 1895.

† According to a study by Y.Gorni about the social structure of the second aliya, about 70 per cent of its members hailed from small towns. 42 per cent did not know Hebrew when they first arrived in Palestine (in D.Carpi (ed.), *Hazionut*, Tel Aviv, 1970, p. 210 *et seq.*)

positive sentiment towards Jewish traditions, none of them becoming virulently anti-religious, as did so many Bundists. One small group stands out among the leaders of the second aliya: these were the young Palestinians – Moshe Sharett, Dov Hos (born in 1894) and Eliyahu Golomb (born in 1893). They were too young to play an important role in the prewar period, but they rose to positions of eminence in defence (Golomb) and Zionist diplomacy (Sharett and Hos) in the 1920s and 1930s. They, too, had been born in Russia. Sharett's family came from the Kherson district, Hos from Orsha, and Golomb from Velkovisk. While still of school age they had been sent or taken by their families to Palestine, and finished their studies at the Herzl high school in Jaffa-Tel Aviv. In school they established a Zionist youth organisation and, after graduating, went to Kineret and Degania to work in an agricultural commune. They came from families which were comfortably off – Golomb's family, for instance, owned a flour mill – but, influenced by Socialist ideas, they decided to throw in their lot with the labour movement. They were eventually accepted by their seniors as equals despite marked psychological differences, for the fact that the younger ones had spent some of their formative years in Palestine, not in eastern Europe, put them in a category apart.

Among the leaders of the second aliya, the similarity in their backgrounds was reflected in common interests and purposes.* Almost all of them had pronounced cultural interests, most of them published books at one time or another, many were amateur philologists. Shazar (Rubashov) wrote essays and poetry, Berl Katznelson became an accomplished master of the language, Ben Gurion studied philosophy when he was in his sixties. Golomb, who was in charge of Hagana, the Jewish defence force, was also for a time editor of his party's weekly journal. All began their political career as agricultural labourers in Petah Tiqva or one of the nearby colonies. Remes worked at Kastina, and Eshkol in an agricultural settlement near Jerusalem, but not many remained in agriculture for more than a few years.† This seems a little surprising in view of the strong emphasis put by the Socialist-Zionist movement in east Europe on manual labour, and their disdain not just for higher education but for all specialised professional knowledge. The ideal type for them was the competent worker, an expert in irrigating orange groves, and with no professional ambitions beyond that. The

---

* They counted relatively few women, even though the full equality of the sexes was axiomatic among them.

† Golda Meir was for a short time after her arrival in Palestine a member of Merhavia.

circumstances of their life cut across these ideals. Aware that their education had been incomplete, Ben Gurion and Ben Zvi decided to study at the University of Constantinople, where they met David Remes. Later on, Sharett and Dov Hos also went to the Turkish capital. Shlomo Zemach went to Paris and Salman Shazar to Germany to study philosophy and history; both returned only after the end of the First World War. By the early 1920s, ten years after they had arrived in Palestine, almost all of them had become party or trade union officials. The iron law of elitism and bureaucratisation in political movements had again prevailed.

With all their traditional education, with the strong emphasis they put on their Jewishness, it was their east European small-town background which gave its specific character to the second aliya. Living in semi-isolation, east European Jewry had in fact always been strongly influenced, consciously and unconsciously, by its surroundings. These influences manifested themselves in its songs, its traditional attire, and even its language. The mental make-up, the habits, customs and interests of Russian and east European Jewish students were remarkably similar around the turn of the century. Many were not fully aware of this impact of their surroundings – those particularly proud of their specific Jewish heritage would have angrily rejected any imputation of alien influences. But the vitality, the idealism, the *shirokaia natura*, the eagerness for passionate debate, the fondness for long speeches, the predilection for pathos and well turned-out phrases – these and other traits of character were common to Russian and Russian-Jewish intellectuals.

The leaders of the second aliya were men and women of considerable intelligence, and most of them showed in later life an impressive capacity to grow with the increasing responsibilities imposed on them. Ben Gurion at forty-five was a trade union official with no more than a rudimentary knowledge of international politics and hardly any experience in statecraft. He was to reach his full stature only in his sixties. But even among the most gifted of them, only a few ever completely transcended the concepts, tastes and moral and cultural standards of the little towns of White Russia and the Ukraine: Pinsk and Mohilev in some ways always remained at the back of their minds. They revealed an astonishing ability to learn and to adjust themselves to new conditions, just as their cousins did who emigrated to America. But even the most adaptable could not totally overcome the narrowness of the Russian-Jewish shtetl. They were righteous men and women, absolutely convinced of their cause, and therefore quite unable to understand the point of view of their opponents. These very limitations made it easier for them to succeed in politics, for it was precisely this unshaken certainty which gave them their strength. Hamlet-like natures would hardly have managed to cope with the uphill tasks facing them in Palestine. In some ways they resembled their counterparts on the Russian political scene, the Mensheviks and the social revolutionaries, but as a group they were tougher and more determined.

The sense of *savoir vivre* in these men and women was underdeveloped. In private life they were modest; dandies and gourmets were not to be found among them. They could not understand how people could spend time and money on frivolities instead of concentrating on the really important things in life. The first American ambassador described the utterly primitive conditions in which Ben Gurion continued to live in Tel Aviv after he became prime minister. This egalitarianism was strongly rooted in the Russian-Jewish Socialist tradition. At the first Histadrut conventions, speakers insisted that white-collar workers should on no account earn more than manual workers and stressed that it would be unseemly for trade union and party leaders to have a higher standard of living than the workers they represented. Differences in income remained for decades much smaller in the Palestinian labour movement than in the Soviet Union or other Communist countries. Even in the 1940s, a doorman at the Histadrut main building, father of seven children, was likely to get a higher salary than the chief executive of that body.

The men and women of the second aliya were firm believers in democracy, and regarded any attempt to curtail it, whether emanating from the extreme Left or the far Right, not just as political deviation but as a criminal act. Even more fanatical was their Zionism: to be an enemy of Zion (*Ssone Zion*) was the worst epithet that could be flung at anyone. Neither the Communists nor the revisionists were ever forgiven their misdeeds. The terms *Yevsek* and *Fraktsioner*, denoting Jewish Communists, were always pronounced in such a way as to convey loathing and nausea, for these were not just renegades but moral degenerates, the scum of the earth. Nothing would anger and depress Berl Katznelson more than young Jews whoring after false gods – fighting the revolutionary struggles of all peoples but their own.* They were not liberals but Socialists, and democratic rights for the enemies of democracy was a luxury they could not afford. There was never any danger that an autocrat would establish himself as leader among them. They were far

* See, for instance, S.Shazar's obituary in *Or Ishim*, vol. 2, Jerusalem, 1963, pp. 130–1.

Moses Hess (1812–75)

Leo Pinsker (1821–91)

Theodor Herzl (1860–1904)

DER

JUDENSTAAT.

VERSUCH

EINER

MODERNEN LÖSUNG DER JUDENFRAGE

VON

THEODOR HERZL

DOCTOR DER RECHTE.

❦

LEIPZIG und WIEN 1896.
M. BREITENSTEIN'S VERLAGS-BUCHHANDLUNG
WIEN, IX., WÄHRINGERSTRASSE 5.

'Der Judenstaat'

The Basle Programme (1897): text of the official programme of the Zionist Organization as distributed druing the deliberations of the First Zionist Conference in Basle, 1897

Max Nordau (1849–1923)

Aḥad Ha'am (1856–1927)

David Wolffsohn (1856–1914)

Nahum Sokolow (1859–1936)

Leo Motzkin (1867–1933)

Martin Buber (1878–1965)

Louis Brandeis (1856–1941)

Stephen Wise (1874–1949)

Chaim Weizmann (1874–1952)

Arthur James Balfour
(1848–1930)

Allenby's entrance into
Jerusalem (1917)

Foreign Office,

November 2nd, 1917

Dear Lord Rothschild,

I have much pleasure in conveying to you, on behalf of His Majesty's Government, the following declaration of sympathy with Jewish Zionist aspirations which has been submitted to, and approved by, the Cabinet.

"His Majesty's Government view with favour the establishment in Palestine of a national home for the Jewish people, and will use their best endeavours to facilitate the achievement of this object, it being clearly understood that nothing shall be done which may prejudice the civil and religious rights of existing non-Jewish communities in Palestine, or the rights and political status enjoyed by Jews in any other country"

I should be grateful if you would bring this declaration to the knowledge of the Zionist Federation.

Y. ing

Arthur James Balfour

The Balfour Declaration (1917)

The foundation ceremony of Tel Aviv (1909)

Tel Aviv forty years later

Vladimir Ze'ev Jabotinsky (1880–1940)

Menahem Ussishkin (1863–1941)

Henrietta Szold (1860–1945)

Arthur Ruppin (1876–1943)

David Ben Gurion (1886–1973)

Chaim Victor Arlosoroff (1899–1933)

Moshe Sharett (1894–1965)

Prime Minister Ben Gurion reading the proclamation of the establishment of Israel.
Tel Aviv, 14 May 1948

too critical, and the party central committee presented an effective check to any would-be dictator. They were vulnerable in other ways: talkative and disputatious, there was always the danger of unending discussions which could drag on without leading to any decision or action.

For all this tendency towards collective leadership, there were two outstanding men among them who frequently imposed their views on the rest: David Ben Gurion and Berl Katznelson. Ben Gurion was less easy going than some of his contemporaries. He introduced an element of toughness, resolution and single-mindedness uncommon among the men and women of that generation, and he was a wholly political animal, sometimes suspected of Machiavellianism. In some respects more far-sighted than his colleagues, he could be incredibly stubborn and idio-syncratic in his decisions, traits of character which became more pro-nounced with the years. Berl Katznelson, who died at a comparatively early age in 1944, was the intellectual and moral preceptor of the move-ment, the keeper of the conscience of his generation. A self-made man of tremendous erudition, an accomplished speaker who carried his audience with him by the strength of his personality, the depth of his conviction (or fanaticism, as his critics said), and his transparent honesty, he was accepted as the teacher of his own generation and exerted great influence on the following one. Whereas Ben Gurion kept aloof, and had few friends or even close confidants, Berl Katznelson genuinely liked people and went out of his way to make new friends, especially among the young halutzim. He was the moving force behind Ahdut Ha'avoda during the 1920s, and in the early years the central figure of Mapai, indefatigable in his struggle to restore unity in the ranks of Jewish labour.

The second aliya ruled Palestinian labour, then the Zionist movement, and ultimately the state of Israel.* Its immediate impact came to an end with Ben Gurion's resignation as prime minister, though indirectly its influence continued well beyond that date. The third aliya, whose achievements as a group exceeded those of its predecessor, had to wait for the disappearance of the old guard, by which time its members were in their fifties and sixties. The third aliya produced leaders who in some respects differed sharply from their predecessors, such as Mordehai Namir and Abba Hushi, Eliezer Kaplan and Golda Meir, more compe-tent in the field of administration and economics, less accomplished

* According to Gorni, the second aliya was not *per se* an elite. But the author also notes that of the twenty members of the Mapai executive committee in 1930, sixteen had come to Palestine before 1914.

Hebraists, not so forceful as speakers and without the urge to write books. The future opposition within Mapai was led by the kibbutz element: Tabenkin belonged to the second aliya, Zisling and Galili had come to Palestine as children with their families just before the First World War.

The Hashomer Hatzair leadership was not of Russian-Jewish origin. Meir Ya'ari and Oren hailed from Galicia, Ya'akov Chasan from Lithuania, Bentov and Riftin from Poland. Most of them came from well-established families: Bentov's father was an old maskil, Ya'ari's a leading Lover of Zion. By putting themselves into deliberate opposition to the second aliya establishment almost from the day of their arrival, they were out of the running for the leadership of the Palestinian labour movement. Hashomer Hatzair produced a considerable number of gifted and attractive personalities, by no means inferior to their contemporaries in Mapai. But their doctrinaire approach condemned them to growing isolation, which in its turn exaggerated their peculiarities: the less responsibility they had outside their own faction, the more easily did they turn to radical solutions, the more divorced from realities did they become. In later years they identified themselves closely with Soviet foreign policies, and it took a long time and many painful blows to disabuse them of their illusions.

Like all generalisations, those about the common characteristics of the third aliya are at best incomplete. There were quite a few who did not fit into any category. With all the emphasis on collective life, there was a strong individualistic streak in these young Jewish Socialists who were preparing themselves unknowingly for the greater tasks ahead while they served as kibbutz secretaries and trade union officials, organising meetings and deliberating on strikes and sick funds, and as cultural commissars preparing speeches about that most favourite of all topics, 'On the present situation'. These were the future leaders of the Jewish state.

The Struggle for Power

The economic depression of 1923 was overcome the following year, which also marked the beginning of the fourth aliya: fourteen thousand Jews entered Palestine in 1924, thirty-four thousand in 1925, fourteen thousand in 1926. About half of the new arrivals came from Poland, immigration from that country having been triggered off by the anti-Jewish legislation enacted by the government of the day (Grabski), designed to squeeze the Jews out of many branches of the Polish economy.

Among those who had come to Palestine in the years immediately after the First World War the Russian element was the strongest, but the fourth aliya differed from the previous immigration wave also in its social composition. Only about one-third of those who came in the middle 1920s were halutzim who wanted to become manual labourers. The majority were small traders, middlemen, 'the proletariat of the lower middle class' as Arlosoroff called them, the overspill from the Jewish quarters of Warsaw and Lodz. Suddenly small shops mushroomed all over Tel Aviv; there was a new shop for every five families. The fourth aliya brought to Tel Aviv the latest Warsaw fashions, higher buildings and higher prices – it also initiated a fresh wave of optimism and initiative.* It was mainly an urban aliya. Most of its members settled in Tel Aviv and Haifa: between 1923 and 1926 the population of Tel Aviv rose from sixteen to forty thousand. Many hundreds of new houses were built, and many small and medium-sized enterprises came into being. For a time it seemed as if Borokhov's predictions about the 'stychic' influx of Jewish capital which would develop Palestine had come true.

The labour movement regarded the fourth aliya ('capitalists without capital') with great misgivings, considering that the transplantation of the unhealthy social structure of eastern Europe to Palestine was not likely to add to the strength of the Zionist enterprise.† Even those who came with some money often lacked the vision and the initiative to found industries from which the country as a whole would benefit. Instead, much of the capital went into land speculation and building, and only to a small extent into factories and the expansion of agriculture. By late 1926 the fears of labour had been realised: the boom collapsed and building came to a standstill. By 1927, eight thousand workers were unemployed and when Ben Gurion appeared at public meetings he was met with shouts of 'leader, give us bread'. The numbers leaving Palestine in 1927 were almost twice that of the new immigrants. Throughout the country, groups of Polish and Russian repatriates were organised. Some Zionists suggested that to avoid panic, emigration from Palestine should be planned by the official Jewish bodies. By 1927–8 the prospects of Zionism were dimmer and its adherents more despondent than ever before. Only a few optimists believed that the movement could recover within the foreseeable future. Yet on balance, beyond the speculation and

---

* Chaim Arlosoroff, in *Pirke Hapoel Hatzair*, vol. 2, Tel Aviv, 1938, p. 162.

† For a Socialist appraisal of the fourth aliya, see M.Braslavski; *Tnuat hapoalim ha'eretz israelit*, Tel Aviv, 1956, vol. 2, p. 16 *et seq.*

the other unhealthy phenomena, the contribution of the fourth aliya to the growth of Jewish Palestine was not negative, even though this aspect loomed so prominently at the time. After the collapse of the artificial building boom, capital streamed into more productive branches of the national economy. Citrus growing received a major fresh impetus, and the plain north and south of Tel Aviv developed quickly as new middle class settlements came into being. The labour movement, too, continued to grow, acquiring many new adherents. Membership of the Histadrut, the General Federation of Jewish Labour, had been 4,400 in 1920; by 1927 it had grown to more than 22,000. Many new economic enterprises (about which more below) were sponsored by the Histadrut during that period, and in the cultural field, too, it expanded its activities. *Davar*, the Histadrut daily, first appeared in 1925, and in the same year a workers' theatre was founded ('Ohel' – the Tent).

Politically, these were difficult years for the labour movement. The fourth aliya had given fresh confidence to the right-of-centre Zionist parties, representing the interests of the property-owning classes. They had all along been opposed to the growing influence of the Left. Among the first to open the offensive was Jabotinsky,* but Zionist federations in Europe (especially in Poland) and in America shared the view that the workers, their institutions and their enterprises, had been too long molly-coddled. The middle class had demonstrated in 1925–6 that it could contribute to the growth of the country and its economy without needing constant financial assistance from the Zionist executive, as labour did. According to this school of thought the workers had shown an inability to make ends meet in their agricultural settlements and even less aptitude in their building cooperatives and industrial enterprises. The Socialist leaders did not deny that there had been substantial deficits, but they argued that they had been engaged in pioneering work, building the foundations of a new economy, and that consequently profits could not be expected for a long time to come. Private enterprise would never have been ready to invest in projects which were of the greatest national importance but from which few if any immediate rewards could be expected.

These arguments were rejected by the fourteenth and fifteenth Zionist congresses. It was resolved that the movement was from now on to be run on normal business lines. Preference was to be given to immigrants with means of their own, and to urban over agricultural settlement.

* See his articles 'Basta' and 'Vrag Rabotchikh', in *Rassvet*, 28 June and 2 August 1925.

Unemployment was to be tackled by stopping relief, thus compelling the unemployed and other needy persons to emigrate.* 'Socialist experimentation' was to be discontinued. The workers' settlements would have to show that they could stand on their own feet, and if not they would have to face the consequences. The Zionist congress decided that after so many years of squandering money, the Palestinian economy was at long last to be put on a normal footing. The representatives of the Socialist parties were forced to resign from the executive in 1927, and the new line, the 'Sacher régime' (named after one of the leaders of British Zionism), became the official policy of the Zionist movement.

The right-wing critique of Socialist economics in Palestine was not totally unfounded. The leaders of the Jewish labour movement were not financial wizards or geniuses in business management. They lacked economic and organisational experience; errors were committed and money had on occasion been squandered. But this was mainly the result of deflation and the fall in farm prices. The mistakes were on a comparatively small scale, inevitable perhaps in the circumstances. On the other hand, the record of private enterprise, as practised by the fourth aliya, was not impressive either, and the 'Sacher régime', far from contributing to the recovery of the Palestinian Jewish economy, resulted in stagnation and decline. The Zionist Left reacted bitterly: 'Bourgeois Zionism is bankrupt', Ben Gurion declared; the working class was objectively identified with the interests of the country; it was more than a faction within Zionism, it was its main pillar. Other social groups pursued their own narrow class interests, only labour had the interests of the whole nation at heart.† Berl Katznelson concluded that labour now had no alternative but to conquer the Zionist movement from within.

This must have sounded more than somewhat Utopian at the time, for as the Socialists had been forced in 1927 to give up their position in the Zionist executive, the prospects of power seemed more distant than ever. But labour Zionism was no longer a negligible force. In the elections to the Zionist congress in 1927 it had received 22 per cent of the total vote, and its influence in the movement continued to increase. In the elections of 1931 its share rose to 29 per cent, and in 1933, with 44 per cent of the vote, it emerged as by far the largest faction, polling 71 per cent of the total in Palestine. In June 1929 two left-wing representatives had rejoined the executive: in 1931 Chaim Arlosoroff became the head of the political

* W. Preuss, op. cit., p. 78. Even Shoshan, loc. cit., vol. 2, p. 256 et seq.
† D. Ben Gurion, Mema'amad le'am, Tel Aviv, 1933, passim.

department of the Jewish Agency, and Berl Locker was made director of the organisation department. Again, two years later, Ben Gurion and Eliezer Kaplan also joined the Jewish Agency executive, and Moshe Shertok (Sharett) succeeded Arlosoroff, who had been killed earlier that year. Thus, only a few years after their defeat, hegemony in the Zionist camp passed into the hands of the Socialists.

In retrospect, many reasons can be adduced to explain the triumphant rise of labour Zionism. It was an important factor both in Palestine and in the diaspora, not only among the younger generation, and 'bourgeois Zionism' should have been aware that the movement could not be run for any length of time without, let alone against it. It should have been obvious that for many years to come the halutzim, the pioneers, almost all Socialists, would have to play a central part in the building of the country, and that they should not be antagonised. Labour had several capable leaders, whereas on the Right there were hardly any outstanding personalities except Jabotinsky and the aged Ussishkin. The left-wing factions joined forces during this period. Mapai was founded in 1930, and at the Zionist congresses labour Zionism appeared as one united group. The centre and the right-wing groups, on the other hand, were divided. The General Zionists split into one group tending to support right-wing policies, and a left-of-centre caucus which saw labour Zionism as a potential ally. To a certain extent the international constellation also favoured labour Zionism. The world economic crisis and its political repercussions strengthened the Left (and the extreme Right) all over Europe and weakened the centre groups.

In the Zionist camp labour benefited from this process of radicalisation, but so did the revisionists. In 1931 every fourth delegate at the Zionist congress represented Jabotinsky's movement. A bitter struggle developed between labour and the revisionists, whose influence was by no means restricted to the Polish-Jewish lower middle class, but who had fairly substantial working-class support and a strong youth movement. There were clashes in Tel Aviv between members of the Histadrut and the revisionists, and the fact that Jabotinsky's disciples had taken to wearing brown shirts reminiscent of the German S.A. did not endear them to the Left. The revisionists had meanwhile set up their own ('national') trade union, which enjoyed the patronage of some factory owners and leading orange growers eager to break the Histadrut monopoly of employment exchanges. In Petah Tiqva, Kfar Saba and elsewhere, they negotiated directly with the revisionists to get workers for their enterprises, bypassing the Histadrut. On some occasions, such as the strike in the Frumin biscuit factory, revisionists acted as strike-breakers.* They argued that they were fighting not the Jewish worker but merely the Histadrut which, far from being unpolitical in character, had become a tool of the Socialist parties and discriminated against revisionist workers. The labour leaders regarded this as a deliberate attempt to break the power of the trade unions on behalf of the 'class enemy', and ultimately to establish a semi-fascist dictatorship. The tension reached its height with the murder of Chaim Arlosoroff, the head of the political department of the Jewish Agency, the Zionist foreign minister so to speak. On the evening of 16 June 1933 he was shot while walking along the Tel Aviv sea-shore. The circumstances of the murder were never cleared up and the identity of the assassin has not been established to this day. But hardly anyone on the Left doubted for a moment that revisionists were behind the crime, even though the revisionists themselves emphatically denied responsibility. The murder had been preceded by a hate campaign against labour in the revisionist press. 'Traitors', and 'despicable lackeys of the British', were among the epithets hurled at Weizmann, Arlosoroff, and the other leaders of the Zionist movement. For a while it seemed as if Jewish Palestine was on the eve of civil war. Perhaps it was only the outside danger facing the community and the Jewish people in general which prevented general bloodshed, for these were the weeks after Hitler's rise to power. After that revisionism slowly declined. In the elections to the Zionist congress in 1933 Jabotinsky's party suffered a defeat, its share of the poll falling from 25 to 14 per cent. Following this setback Jabotinsky decided to leave the Zionist congress and to establish an independent world organisation. The struggle between revisionism and labour continued, but Jabotinsky had manœuvred himself into political isolation and was now confronting the opposition of the whole Zionist movement. An agreement reached between Ben Gurion and Jabotinsky concerning relations with the revisionist trade unions was rejected by a majority of Histadrut members in 1935. This had been merely an attempt to reduce demarcation disputes between rival trade unions; Ben Gurion was by no means more sympathetic to revisionism than his own party. In fact, to the very end of his political career he refused to cooperate with revisionists both in the Jewish Agency executive and in the government of the state of Israel.

* On the struggle between revisionism and labour Zionism, see D.Ben Gurion, *Tnuat hapoalim veharevisionismus*, Tel Aviv, 1933; Ch.Ben Meir, *Harevisionism, ssakana le'am*, Tel Aviv, 1938; Eliezer Liebenstein, *Wo steht der Revisionismus?*, Berlin, 1934.

The economic crisis in Palestine was overcome in 1929, the same year which saw the beginning of the world economic depression. The flow of immigration in 1929–31 was small, but increased in 1932, and in 1933, the year Hitler came to power, reached the unprecedented figure of 38,000, with further increases in 1934 and 1935. There was a larger influx of capital than ever before: £P 31 million in 1932–5, in comparison with £P 20 million during the eleven preceding years. The new immigration wave, the fifth, was not preponderantly pioneering in character; in 1935, the peak year, only 45 per cent of the new immigrants came on workers' permits. But it was essentially different, more productive than the preceding aliya. Those who came on 'capitalist' immigration certificates, i.e. those with £P 1,000 or more to their name, established new industrial enterprises and agricultural settlements. Most of them were not Socialists but their political orientation was on the whole left of centre. Organised labour greatly increased in strength during this period, 73,000 new members joining the Histadrut between 1932 and the outbreak of the Second World War. The fifth immigration wave also differed from the preceding one in respect of its origins: a sizeable part of the workers (about 37 per cent) came from central and western Europe, mainly from Germany and Austria. Many of the new immigrants had been members of Socialist Zionist youth movements in the diaspora, and they wanted to join existing kibbutzim or to establish new ones.

The kibbutz comes of age

The few hundred young men and women who had initiated the kibbutz movement in the early years had no clear concept of the future of their collectives. It was by no means certain that they were to stay in Degania and Kineret, or whether they wanted to expand the settlements. There was in fact no kibbutz network, only a number of settlements, loosely connected; technical cooperation between the seven hundred members of the kibbutzim hardly existed in 1922. Five years later the kibbutz population had risen to 4,000. Over the next decade it quadrupled, and by the outbreak of the Second World War it was almost 25,000, 5 per cent of the total Jewish population in Palestine. After two decades the kibbutz had come of age, outgrown its experimental stage. The collective way of life was constitutionally regulated even though there continued to be substantial differences between kibbutz and kibbutz, traceable in some cases to the social origin and cultural background of the settlers. There was no unanimity as to what collective life should be like in detail, and there were marked differences of opinion about the place of the kibbutz in Palestine-Jewish politics. The attempt to unite all kibbutzim in one overall organisational framework, undertaken in the late 1920s, was therefore bound to fail. Instead, three separate groups came into being: the United Kibbutz (*Kibbutz Hameuhad*) in 1927, the countrywide network of Hashomer Hatzair also founded *Kibbutz Artzi* in 1927, and lastly the *Chever Hakvutzot*, the Association of kvutzot, made up of the earliest collective settlements such as Degania and Kineret, which came into being in 1928.

The United Kibbutz was based at first on Ein Harod, the original 'big kibbutz' which had split from the Labour Legion and settled in the valley of Yesreel. From Ein Harod small groups went to other parts of the country to establish new collective settlements. At first, these regarded themselves as part of Ein Harod. Only gradually did they assume an identity and a name of their own. The Kibbutz Meuhad criticised its two rivals for the exclusivity of their settlements and believed in the principle of big collectives. Its statutes, adopted in 1927, emphasised the necessity of building 'large collective settlements' open to outsiders to join. The members of the settlements were to engage in agriculture, industry and handicrafts, and the kibbutzim were to expand as rapidly as possible in order to absorb new immigrants. This was to be achieved through more intensive working methods, the establishment of new enterprises, and through the increase of the area under cultivation. There was in the 1920s and 1930s a tendency towards economic self-sufficiency, which was later abandoned; kibbutzim used to bake their own bread, sew their own clothes, and even make their own shoes. But gradually it was realised that this was a wasteful system and that it would be far better to have a rational division of labour with other kibbutzim in the neighbourhood, regardless of their political outlook, or to buy the commodities needed in the nearby towns.

In the early days there were not a few quarrels about the respective rights of each kibbutz within the network to which it belonged; whether, for instance, a settlement could be compelled to unite with another collective. Gradually, by trial and error, a *modus vivendi* was worked out. As indicated, the Kibbutz Meuhad did not believe in élitism and was less selective than its rivals in accepting new members. As a rule, everyone willing to join, able to work and to share the kibbutz way of life was accepted after a short trial period, regardless of origin, cultural level or social compatibility: the larger the collective, the less these considerations mattered. The biggest kibbutzim, such as Yagur (near Haifa) and Givat

Brenner (south of Tel Aviv), had about 400–450 members by the late 1930s and the day did not seem far off when a thousand people would live in a kibbutz – a far cry from the vision of the founders of Degania.* The apocryphal story of the two people from Yagur who met in town and discovered by accident that they were members of the same kibbutz became a standard joke.

The kibbutzim of the Hashomer Hatzair quickly adapted themselves to the new conditions. There had been four of them in 1927, but when the Second World War broke out their number had risen to thirty-nine. With the big immigration wave of the 1930s thousands of members of European youth movements arrived from eastern and central Europe and established new settlements all over the country. The individual kibbutz also grew in size; in the early days the average settlement had numbered about sixty members, but as the kibbutz economy expanded, and more working hands were needed, it was believed that sixty families, that is about 120 members, would be the optimal number. Yet these estimates, which some took to be iron laws, proved far too low. Three decades later some settlements of the Hashomer Hatzair had three hundred members with a total population of six hundred or more.

The usual procedure for a group of halutzim newly arrived in the country was to take up temporary quarters – usually in tents, sometimes in barracks in the vicinity of a town or village. They would work on building sites and in neighbouring orange groves. After a few years of acclimatisation, acculturation and gaining experience, they would either join one of the existing older kibbutzim or, more frequently, establish a new settlement on land put at their disposal by the National Fund. Most male members of the kibbutzim were engaged in agricultural work. It was far more difficult to provide 'productive' employment for the women, who were heavily concentrated on work in the kitchen and laundry, and of course the children's house. While all favoured full equality of the sexes in every respect, it proved impossible to find a satisfactory solution while the kibbutzim derived almost their entire income from agriculture. This changed with the gradual spread of light industries in the late 1930s and especially during and after the Second World War. The first factories produced plywood, building materials, jams, and canned food. Later, industry expanded to a wide range of products, some requiring highly sophisticated processing. By the 1960s the kibbutzim derived about half their income from industry, while

* The first kibbutz to exceed this milestone was Yagur, with 1,007 inhabitants in 1941, but it was soon overtaken by Givat Brenner.

providing about one-third of the total agricultural produce of the state of Israel.

Mention has been made of the turn to the Left of Hashomer Hatzair in 1927. The initiative for moving closer to the orbit of Soviet policies came from Poland, but it spread to the Palestinian movement, and caused mounting dissension between Hashomer Hatzair and the other kibbutzim which did not accept the pro-Soviet orientation. After contesting the Histadrut elections with its own list of candidates, Hashomer Hatzair turned in 1930 to the idea of a political party of its own. In 1936 an organisation of sympathisers with the movement outside the kibbutzim was set up, the Socialist League. This body did not attain much political importance and was eventually dissolved, but it served as an interim stage on the road towards a fully fledged political party (Mapam) after the Second World War.

Kibbutz Meuhad, less elitist, more 'proletarian' in character, followed with growing misgivings the developments in Hashomer Hatzair. Its programme also explicitly stressed the Communist way of life as the social basis of the collective, and its members were obliged to belong to the Histadrut. These basic principles apart, every member was free to support the political party of his choice, in contrast to the Hashomer Hatzair for which 'ideological collectivism' was a *conditio sine qua non*; members of its kibbutzim had to share not just a way of life but also the same *Weltanschauung*. The politisation of the kibbutz movement, inevitable perhaps, had serious consequences. The case of Bet Alfa and Ramat Yohanan in the 1930s was the first in a long series of splits which shook the kibbutz movement to its foundations. Bet Alfa had been the first of the Hashomer Hatzair kibbutzim, but it included a substantial number of members who did not subscribe to Hashomer Hatzair ideology. The political conflict spilled over into the social sphere, poisoning personal relations until old friends and comrades found it impossible to live together any longer. After a long period of growing tension a population transfer was decided upon. Since a similar situation existed in Kibbutz Ramat Yohanan, it was resolved to concentrate all members of Hashomer Hatzair in Bet Alfa and to make Ramat Yohanan a Mapai kibbutz.

It was a painful operation, but no more so than the incredible situation which developed in the Kibbutz Meuhad after the split in Mapai in 1944, and in particular after the second split in 1951. Separate dining halls and kindergartens were established for members of the rival factions and their offspring, and when these palliatives did not help, old established and flourishing kibbutzim such as Givat Haim, Ashdot Ya'akov

and Ein Harod were divided, separate settlements being set up sometimes no more than a mile apart. Within a decade or two a new
generation had grown up, and the reasons which had caused these splits
were either totally forgotten or now seemed insignificant. But by that
time the new settlements had grown apart and reunion was no longer
possible.

The Chever Kvutzot consisted of the oldest collective settlements in
the country, but for many years it was the least dynamic branch of the
movement. While the other groups expanded, Degania and Kineret,
Geva and Ginegar stagnated. Gradually its members realised that by
continuing to adhere to the original type of settlement, the small kvutza,
they had cut themselves off from the mainstream of the kibbutz movement. They were not able to develop economically and to absorb new
immigrants. Their great fear was that by growing too fast the original,
intimate character of their collectives would be lost. They abhorred the
radical political phraseology of the Hashomer Hatzair and the impersonal
atmosphere prevailing in places like Yagur. These were certainly not the
new societies of which A.D.Gordon had dreamed. Yet with all their
reservations they would have been in favour of a policy of cautious
expansion if only there had been suitable candidates to join their settlements. Instead they lost members, mainly to the moshavim; of 57
members of Degania and 68 of Kineret in 1922, only 32 and 27 respectively were left eight years later.*

The Chever Kvutzot, unlike its competitors, had neglected its links
with the young generation of Socialist pioneers preparing themselves in
Europe for life in the kibbutz. The Hashomer Hatzair youth movement
spread from Poland to many other countries and had thousands of
members. The Kibbutz Meuhad could count on members of half a dozen
Jewish youth movements in Europe and on the Palestinian 'Working
Youth' (*Noar Oved*). In 1930 Naan, the first kibbutz of Palestinian youth,
was founded. But Degania and Kineret had no reserve army. Facing
internal crises and economic stagnation, there was a distinct danger that
they would disintegrate. Salvation came from unexpected quarters: the
youth movement *Gordonia* had developed in Poland in the 1920s without
the assistance of the Chever Hakvutzot and almost without its knowledge.
Its members shared the ideals of the founders of Degania, and after their
arrival in Palestine in the 1930s they joined the settlements belonging to
this movement, providing a much needed stimulus. Existing settlements
absorbed these new immigrants and new ones were founded. By the

* Viteles, *A History of the Co-operative Movement in Israel*, vol. 2, p. 50.

middle 1930s Degania had 130 working members, while by 1939 the Chever counted twenty-one settlements and a dozen groups located in temporary quarters while waiting for the allocation of land. It remained the smallest of the three movements, but the crisis which had threatened its existence was surmounted.

The trade unions

The General Federation of Trade Unions, the Histadrut, developed in conditions totally different from trade union movements elsewhere. The normal function of a trade union is to defend the interests of its members against the employers, and on occasion to provide certain social services not offered by the state. The problems facing Jewish workers in Palestine in the 1920s and 1930s were of a different character. Since industry was as yet hardly developed, and private enterprise showed little enthusiasm for pioneering work, the Histadrut had to take the initiative in creating work for its members and for those yet to come. The logic of events drove it into becoming the biggest employer in the country in addition to defending the interests of the employees. It was an anomalous situation to be sure. No one had planned it that way, and a great many problems grew from this duality. What, for instance, if the workers clashed with the management in a Histadrut enterprise?

The Histadrut came to act as an entrepreneur in agriculture (*Tnuva*, marketing the agricultural produce of all collective and cooperative settlements) and in the building industry (*Solel Boneh* built roads, houses and factories, and acquired stone quarries and brick-works). The Histadrut was the first to promote high-seas fishing, shipping, and even civil aviation in Palestine. It set up cooperative retail stores, urban housing offices, a workers' bank, a big insurance company (*Hasneh*), and countless medium-sized enterprises in industry, transport and agriculture. Solel Boneh expanded rapidly after the depression of 1926–7. From modest beginnings it grew into a major concern even by international standards, eventually building up to fifty thousand houses a year. *Koor*, its industrial branch, controlled steel rolling mills, chemical plants, cement and glass factories, and held subtantial interests in the timber and food-processing industries. Forty years after the foundation of the Histadrut, these enterprises accounted for no less than 35 per cent of the total gross national product (53 per cent in agriculture, 44 per cent in building, 39 per cent in transport, and 25 per cent in industry).

The share of the Socialist sector of the economy was most impressive, but to what extent was it still subject to democratic control? In theory, every member of the Histadrut was automatically a member of the Cooperative Association of Labour (*Chevrat Ovdim*), which functioned as the central organisation of all Histadrut enterprises and also as their owner. In theory, every member had a say in the management of Histadrut-owned enterprises. But in practice, as membership increased and economic activities multiplied, this right to share in decision-making became a dead letter. According to the original constitution there was to be no hired outside labour in the cooperatives and no outsiders were to be employed. But this golden rule, too, was disregarded almost from the outset, in producer and transport cooperatives alike, and later on also in many moshavim and even kibbutzim, for these enterprises were subject to marked seasonal fluctuation, needing additional working hands at certain times and only minimal labour at others. The dilemma was insoluble. Resolutions were passed from time to time to give workers and clerical staff seats on administrative committees and a share in management as well as in financial surpluses. But these demands, as in other countries, encountered opposition on the part of the management, which jealously guarded its prerogatives. Nor was there any particular desire among the workers to take on these responsibilities. In this respect, too, a wide divergence developed between Socialist theory and practice, with considerations of efficiency and profitability prevailing over time-honoured doctrine.

As Labour Zionism became the dominant factor in the Zionist movement, its history and that of the Jewish community in Palestine merge and are no longer clearly distinguishable. In the early 1930s the leaders of Mapai emerged as the central figures in Zionist policy, and an account of their ideas and actions can no longer be presented in isolation from the much wider issues of the period, such as relations with the Arabs and the mandatory power and the development of the yishuv in general. Yet it was precisely in this period that the labour movement enjoyed a phase of rapid growth. Many new initiatives were sponsored, and existing enterprises expanded beyond recognition. It is to some of these activities outside the traditional scope of party politics and trade unionism that we shall next turn.

The Pioneers

The history of Labour Zionism cannot be written without reference to the *Hehalutz*, the organisation of young Jewish pioneers which prepared a whole generation in the diaspora for a life of manual work in Palestine. The original idea had been Trumpeldor's, first formulated around 1908. His experiences in Palestine during the days of the second aliya had strengthened his belief that prospective immigrants should receive intensive training in their country of origin to prepare them for the new life in Palestine. They were to live together on a farm or, in rare cases, in an urban commune, to gain experience in agriculture as well as in other essential professions. In a conversation with Jabotinsky during the First World War, Trumpeldor described the Hehalutz as he envisaged it, as an army of anonymous servants of Zion, having neither private interests nor inclinations, nameless workers entirely devoted to the supreme challenge of building up Jewish Palestine, willing to do any work demanded of them. Similar ideas were developed by Ben Gurion and Ben Zvi during their stay in America in 1917–18.

The Hehalutz came into being towards the end of the First World War, its main strength being then in Russia. With the emigration to Palestine of many of its members, and its subsequent suppression by the Soviet régime,* the centre of the movement shifted to the west. Most Jewish youth movements in the diaspora decided to educate their members for a halutzic life in Palestine. The picture of the halutz in his blue shirt and khaki trousers working in an orange grove with spade or hoe appeared in thousands of Jewish homes, competing with photographs of Herzl and the panorama of Jerusalem, projecting the vision of a new society in the national home. All labour Zionist parties supported the Hehalutz and competed for the allegiance of its members, just as they had tried to win over the immigrants of the third aliya. Ben Gurion and a few others, however, had doubts about the efficacy of *hachshara* (preparation) outside Palestine. They thought the aim praiseworthy, but conditions in Europe were so dissimilar from those they would meet in Palestine that a useful apprenticeship there seemed well-nigh impossible.

The Hehalutz head office was located in Berlin in the early 1920s and later transferred to Warsaw. Its first world conference took place in Karlsbad in 1921. Membership rose from 5,400 in 1923 to 33,000 in 1925, but fell again to 8,000 in 1928, accurately reflecting the ups and downs in the fortunes of the Zionist movement as a whole. It was only during the 1930s that the Hehalutz became a real mass movement, membership rising to 83,000 in 1933. About one-quarter of them worked on farms in Poland and Germany. The movement spread to places as far afield as

* Described in detail in Dan Pines, *Hehalutz bekur hamahpecha*, Tel Aviv, 1938.

Cuba, Iraq and South Africa. Many a farmer in Europe and America was nonplussed by the spectacle of city-bred Jewish boys and girls trying desperately hard, if not always successfully, to milk cows, to shovel dung, and to cope with other strenuous and uncongenial jobs for which, all too obviously, they were not prepared. Altogether, some 34,000 halutzim arrived in Palestine during the 1930s, almost half of the total who came on workers entry permits. (Within the yearly immigration schedule the mandatory authorities made provision for various categories such as 'capitalists', workers, students, etc.)

In 1935, when immigration was drastically cut, the Hehalutz began again to decline. Its members were now forced to remain in training centres not just for a year or two, as had been the case previously. Among the eight thousand still in training centres on the eve of the Second World War, some had been waiting four years or longer for their turn to go to Palestine. Life in these centres was deliberately Spartan and primitive. There was a veritable cult of harshness and self-denial, and everything was subordinated to mastering heavy manual work, a severe challenge to young people who neither by background nor education had been prepared for it. This was done at the expense of ignoring other and seemingly insignificant aspects of life. Even the more common amenities were often lacking, and cleanliness and cultural activities were neglected. Such excess of zeal occasionally shocked even the emissaries from Palestine, themselves hardened veterans of the second and third aliyas.*

Defence

Some of the halutzim still stranded in Europe in 1938-9 eventually succeeded in reaching the shores of Palestine. They came as illegal immigrants, owing their lives to the systematic efforts undertaken to save as many as possible in contravention of the stringent immigration laws imposed by the mandatory authorities following the outbreak of the Arab riots. An earlier attempt, the voyage of the *Velos* in 1934, organised by a member of Degania, ended in failure. But after 1937, with tens of thousands of prospective immigrants impatiently waiting for their entry permits, with the clouds of war gathering on the European horizon, and with no change in sight in the attitude of the mandatory government, illegal immigration was resumed on a massive scale. Small, ancient, unseaworthy ships, hardly bigger than motor launches and designed to

---

* See Even Shoshan, *loc. cit.*, vol. 2, p. 143 *et seq.*; vol. 3, p. 21 *et seq.* for the activities of the Hehalutz.

carry a few dozen passengers only, arrived with many hundreds on board, in conditions the like of which had not been seen anywhere in modern times. Some of them successfully ran the blockade, others were detected and apprehended. About 11,000 illegal immigrants came in 1939, and even after the outbreak of war some ships continued to arrive; 3,900 men, women and children in 1940, and 2,135 in 1941. After that date immigration, both legal and illegal, dwindled to a mere trickle. Many of the organisers of this illegal traffic were labour Zionists, usually members of kibbutzim. Most of those who came in these ships were members of the Hehalutz and left-wing youth movements. The whole enterprise is another example of the unorthodox activities of the heirs of Borokhov and Syrkin, well outside the confines of the political and industrial struggle. But illegal immigration was merely one aspect of the activities of the Jewish defence organisation, the Hagana, which was dominated by men and women belonging to the labour movement, even though considerable efforts were made to induce non-Socialist groups to participate at every level of Hagana activities.

The beginnings of defence organisation date back to Hashomer, the Jewish watchmen's association founded before the First World War. After 1918, following the Arab attacks in Galilee and Jaffa, Hagana came into being. Illegal arms stores were established, as well as rudimentary training centres for young Jews of both sexes all over the country. These efforts were on a small scale and usually quite amateurish. Only with the outbreak of the Arab revolt of 1936 did Hagana perforce become a tightly organised and reasonably effective defence force, composed of thousands of part-time soldiers. While it was an unwritten rule that every young member of the community should do the job assigned to him by Hagana, both the command and the great majority of those serving in it belonged to the labour movement. It was to all intents and purposes a working-class militia, with all the advantages and drawbacks of an organisation of this kind. There was no militarist spirit in its ranks since it was composed entirely of volunteers. Discipline, on the other hand, was sometimes deficient, and as a fighting force it had its limitations. Its left-wing character was so pronounced that those opposed to labour Zionism opted for the IZL (*Irgun Zvai Leumi*-National Military Organisation) which, following Jabotinsky's lead, had split away from the Hagana in the early 1930s. The right-wing parties were apprehensive about the emergence of a working-class army, and their fears, while exaggerated, were not altogether without foundation. For a militia was bound to be dominated by the Left because it alone had a sufficiently broad mass basis, through its youth organisations and the kibbutzim, to undertake an illegal enterprise of this magnitude. The kibbutzim played a particularly significant part in Hagana, both as strategic strongpoints in times of crisis and as bases for military training and storing arms beyond the reach of the mandatory police.

Both the night squads initiated by Wingate and the *Palmach*, which was set up during the Second World War, had their bases in the kibbutzim. Since there was no money to finance the nucleus of a standing army, however small, such as the Palmach was intended to be, to cover expenses its members divided their time more or less equally between military training and agricultural work, no doubt a unique experiment in the history of modern warfare. The morale of these groups, too, was *sui generis*, differing from that of any other known fighting force. They exemplified the spirit of the pioneer youth movements. There were no uniforms and no insignia of rank. Indoctrination was left-wing Socialist in character, with members of the Kibbutz Meuhad in prominent positions of command (Israel Galili served as chief-of-staff of the Hagana, Yigal Allon as commander of the Palmach), and a veteran of the Russian civil war (Yitzhak Sade) acted as the father figure of the young generation of commanders. Ben Gurion was not far from the truth when in 1948 he called the Palmach a private army of the Kibbutz Meuhad. It was an elite corps, and had to be dissolved when a regular army was organised, but its traditions continued to have a powerful impact, while many of its junior commanders rose to the highest army positions in later years.

The members of the kibbutz movement were reluctant warriors. They came to take a leading part in defence organisations because their settlements were attacked in 1929 and again in 1936–9. The Arab rebellion of 1936 did not stop further Jewish settlement. New kibbutzim were founded during this period, which entered Palestinian history under the name of 'Wall and Watchtower' (*Homa vemigdal*), among them Hanita and Ein Gev, Sha'ar Hagolan and Revivim. Their establishment had to be planned like military operations, with clockwork precision, usually by night or in the early hours of the morning. A convoy would descend on land which belonged to Jews but which for security reasons had not been cultivated. Within a few hours a number of block houses and a watchtower would have been up, with defence posts and barbed wire to protect the settlement against attack. It was a far cry from the peaceful colonisation envisaged by the fathers of labour Zionism, more reminiscent of how the American west had been settled, or central Asia and the Caucasus.

The doctrine of proletarian internationalism clashed with the cruel facts of life as the young generation became aware of the vital importance of defence for which ideologically they had been quite unprepared.

This list of the extracurricular activities of the Palestinian labour parties, the kibbutzim and the trade unions, is by no means complete. Mention, however brief, ought to be made of their initiatives in the cultural field. The Histadrut had its own network of schools – nine hundred of them in 1953, when Israeli education was 'nationalised'. There were teachers' seminars, libraries and cultural clubs all over the country. The workers' councils in the cities and the kibbutzim ran impressive cultural programmes, sponsored sports clubs (*Hapoel*), and eventually established flourishing publishing houses. Under the auspices of the *Am Oved* and *Sifriat Poalim* publishing houses, set up by the Histadrut and Hashomer Hatzair respectively, more than two thousand books were brought out. In addition to *Davar*, the Histadrut newspaper, the main Socialist parties also published daily newspapers of their own (*Al Hamishmar*, the Hashomer Hatzair paper, first appeared during the Second World War. *Lamerhav* was sponsored by Ahdut Ha'avoda on the eve of the split in Mapam). These were no common achievements: bigger and more powerful Socialist parties, such as those in Britain and France, had failed to maintain their daily newspapers. It was another illustration of the determination and resourcefulness of the Jewish labour movement, which, moreover, provided a specific way of life for its members and sympathisers.

The kibbutz, a closed society, obviously constituted a unique way of life, but in the towns, too, a trade union member had no need to move far outside the compass of the Histadrut sector, even if he did not work in one of its enterprises. He could do his shopping in a cooperative store, deposit his money in a workers' bank, send his children to Histadrut-sponsored kindergartens and schools, and consult a doctor at the *Kupat Holim* (Histadrut Sick Fund), which was ultimately to provide medical services for 65 per cent of the total population, a semi-official national health service in fact. But for the fact that the Histadrut did not own cemeteries, it would have been true to say that the Histadrut provided the great majority with all amenities from the cradle to the grave. Critics were concerned about the danger of total domination, but there were in fact natural limits to Histadrut expansion; some of the functions it fulfilled under the mandate were no longer needed once the Jewish state came into being.

These achievements were all the more remarkable since Jewish labour was by no means united. Mention has been made of the division between various factions before and after the First World War. The two largest of them, Ahdut Ha'avoda and Hapoel Hatzair, merged in January 1930 to form Mapai. It was a turning point, but not the end of the splits. For many years to come Mapai was to be plagued by internal strife.

Towards labour unity

The Palestinian Labour Party was formed under the impact of the riots of 1929, when the Jewish community in Palestine and the Zionist cause were under attack. The need for unity had been realised well before. Since the abortive attempt in 1919 to unite the two main groups in Jewish Labour, many leading figures in both camps had continued to advocate a merger. As the movement came under attack from the right after 1925, Ahdut Ha'avoda and Hapoel Hatzair drew closer together. The continued division seemed an anachronism, for ideological differences had almost disappeared. A small left-wing Marxist minority in Ahdut Ha'avoda feared that its Socialist values and aims would be further compromised and watered down in the case of a merger with people who in principle opposed the class struggle, whose orientation was not towards the working class but towards the whole people, and especially the young generation. Equally, inside Hapoel Hatzair there was still a body of opinion which was concerned, as A.D. Gordon had been ten years earlier, lest the specific humanistic values of their movement should be submerged as the result of union with a group exclusively interested in party politics, even if the common ideological platform was so vaguely phrased as not to present a deterrent. But the majority in Hapoel Hatzair, headed by Arlosoroff, carried the day. They had cooperated with Ben Gurion, Berl Katznelson, and the other leaders of Ahdut Ha'avoda for years in the trade unions and the Zionist movement, and knew from experience how little in fact divided them. They all subscribed now to constructivism or 'reformism', as their Marxist critics defined it.* Eventually, 85 per cent of the members of Hapoel Hatzair and 82 per cent of Ahdut Ha'avoda voted for the merger, which was consummated on 5 January 1930, when the representatives of 5,650 members of the two groups assembled in Tel Aviv to found Mapai. Two years later, at a conference in Danzig, the supporters of the two factions outside Palestine, the world Poale Zion and the Hitachdut, also joined forces in a body to be called *Ihud Olami* (World Union).

* Cf. P. Merchav, *Toldot tnuat hapoalim be'eretz Israel*, Merhavia, 1967, p. 63 *et seq.*

It was an important step towards unity but it did not cover the whole labour community, for two smaller groups, Hashomer Hatzair and the left-wing Poale Zion, refused to join. Mapai membership doubled within the first five years of its existence. It dominated the trade unions and was the strongest party by far both in the world Zionist movement and in the elected bodies of Palestinian Jewry. But its leaders did not speak with one voice. The internal opposition, led by Kibbutz Meuhad, complained that on the road to power and respectability the new party was losing its radical impetus and that the pioneering spirit was fading away. Tabenkin, the leader of *Sia Bet* (the 'second faction'), found allies among urban members of Mapai, especially in the Tel Aviv branch. In the elections to the party executive of December 1938 the opposition attracted about one-third of the total vote. Among the issues involved in the growing conflict there were ideological questions such as the attitude towards the Soviet Union and world Communism. There was also an increasing feeling among members of the kibbutzim that their erstwhile comrades of Sejera and the Labour Legion, having transferred their activities to Jerusalem and Tel Aviv, no longer regarded the collective settlements with the same enthusiasm. There was some truth in this, for as Ben Gurion began to think and plan more and more in terms of a Jewish state, his concept of statehood (*mamlachtiut*), with all its theoretical and practical implications, conflicted on occasions with the specific interests of the working-class, and the kibbutz no longer enjoyed the same absolute priority. These considerations apart, there were also personal factors involved, rivalries and antagonisms dating back to the days of the second and third aliyas.

For several years it appeared as if the conflict could be contained within Mapai as the two chief factions were represented in all the main policy-making bodies according to their numerical strength. The outbreak of the Second World War and the dangers facing the Jewish community also inhibited for a while a deepening of the split. But the Mapai majority reached the conclusion that the state of internal division could not be permitted to continue, for it paralysed the party. Its members, and above all its elected representatives, had to be subject to party discipline. The Mapai conference of Kfar Vitkin in 1942 thus decided that it could no longer recognise the existence of factions. This in turn led to the exodus of Sia Bet, which in May 1944 established itself as an independent party under the name Ahdut Ha'avoda. In April 1946 it merged with the left-wing Poale Zion, which had rejoined the Zionist congress in 1937 after boycotting it for several decades. In January 1948, on the eve of the establishment of the state of Israel, a further step was taken towards unity on the Left, when Ahdut Ha'avoda and Hashomer Hatzair decided to set up Mapam (*Mifleget Poalim Meuhedet* – United Workers Party). The traditional differences between the advocates of a bi-national state (Hashomer Hatzair) and those who had stood for militant action against the mandatory power and favoured the establishment of a Jewish state over the whole of Palestine (Ahdut Ha'avoda) lost their meaning as the new state found itself fighting for its existence. Representatives of Mapam entered the government of Israel in which the two Socialist parties constituted the majority.

But Mapam seems not to have been born under a lucky star, and once the immediate external danger had passed, the party quickly fell apart. As Soviet policy became more and more anti-Israeli (and anti-Jewish) in Stalin's last days, as purge followed purge, Ahdut Ha'avoda found it increasingly difficult to accept the enthusiasm of Hashomer Hatzair for what some of its leaders called their 'second homeland'. As a result of the 1952 Prague trial, in which one of Hashomer Hatzair's leading figures, Mordehai Oren, was sentenced to a long term of imprisonment on the most preposterous charges, and several similar shocks, the party was plunged into a deep internal crisis, which after much wrangling led in 1954 to a final split. Ahdut Ha'avoda had never really embraced the specific brand of Marxism-Leninism which for Hashomer Hatzair had become an essential part of its doctrine. Such ideological issues had seemed of little importance in 1948 but assumed much greater significance five years later.

These events, however, took place after the establishment of the state of Israel, and thus lead us beyond the scope of the present survey. The same applies to the splits which took place within Mapai when Ben Gurion quarrelled with Lavon and later on with Eshkol, as a result of which *Rafi* was established in 1965. Paradoxically, all these splits led eventually to greater unity: Ahdut Ha'avoda merged with Mapai in 1965; in 1968 most members of Rafi rejoined Mapai; and in 1969 Hashomer Hatzair, after years of heart-searching, and not without some opposition from within its own ranks, also became part of the labour 'alignment' (*ma'arakh*). More ambitious than a mere coalition, less than a full merger, it was a milestone in the development of the Jewish labour movement. After more than sixty years the great aim had been achieved, when for the first time in its history the movement in its overwhelming majority was gathered under one roof, united on most essential political issues facing it.

Seen in wider perspective, the history of Labour Zionism shows parallels with Socialist movements in other parts of the world. Like other parties it was always divided into a left and right wing, or to be more precise, into a 'radical' and a 'reformist' branch. But objective conditions limited the scope for revolutionary action from the very beginning. A Jewish proletariat in Palestine did not exist but had to be created. The 'Left' no less than the 'reformists' adopted a policy of 'constructivism' even though this entailed basic changes in its ideological concepts. The main concentration of the Left was in the kibbutzim. It did not gain a strong foothold in the cities, and this, as well as its doctrinaire approach, limited its effectiveness as a political force. 'Reformism' was essentially pragmatic in its attitude. It wanted a reasonably just society in which political hegemony was exercised by labour Zionism. To this extent it was successful. The Jewish community in Palestine was highly egalitarian, so that when the state was established the income differential among wage earners was a mere 1:2·5. There was a great deal of upward mobility and steady deproletarianisation. Only a small proportion of the pioneers who had arrived with the second, third, or fourth aliya were still engaged in manual work twenty or thirty years later. The majority had moved on to form an establishment that held the leading positions in politics as well as in the economy and in social life. It was a natural process, and the lamentations about the disappearance of the pioneering spirit were out of place as the country outgrew the pioneering phase. For several decades the high priority given to agricultural settlements was a political and economic necessity, but as agricultural technology made rapid progress, and, as in other advanced countries, a relatively small farming population sufficed to provide the necessary produce, the relative importance of the kibbutz began to decline. 2·5 per cent of the Jewish population in Palestine lived in kibbutzim in 1930. By 1947 the figure had risen to 7·3, but twenty years later it had fallen to 3·9. The importance of the youth movements also declined. The Hehalutz ceased to exist and there were not many new candidates for life in the kibbutz. Agriculture would in any case not have been able to absorb the big immigration of the early 1950s.

As the old-timers moved up the social ladder, the newer immigrants took their place as, figuratively speaking, the hewers of wood and drawers of water. Jewish workers (as the number and intensity of strikes demonstrated) were no less militant in the defence of their interests than workers elsewhere. But at the same time many of them wanted to better themselves, to rise in the social scale, or at any rate to provide a better future for their children. Objective trends hastened the process of deproletarisation: the rise in productivity and the new technology resulted in a relative decrease in the size of the industrial working class. In its foreign political orientation the Left continued to differ from the reformists, despite the fact that the hostility of the Soviet Union and the world Communist movement to Zionism did not make this easy for them. Doctrinally the radicals subscribed to proletarian internationalism, regarding the Arab worker as an ally in the class struggle for a Socialist, bi-national Palestine. But, rejected by the Soviet Union, and unable to find allies among the Arabs, the freedom of action of the extreme Left in the Zionist camp was strictly limited. Once their settlements were attacked, they had to defend themselves regardless of the class origins of those firing the guns. Borokhov no longer provided guidance for the problems confronting them in the 1930s and after.

Nor was there anything in Syrkin's writings to serve as a compass for Mapai once it had become the leading party in the Zionist movement and the Palestinian Jewish community. The radical slogans of the leaders of Poale Zion were dropped one by one. Like the European Social Democratic parties, the main body of Jewish Socialists became less and less ideological as the years went by. Just as the dual character of the Histadrut, as both trade union and employer, created many problems, so the dual character of Mapai as state party (*the* party as it was frequently called) and as the representative of the working class created serious dilemmas. The membership of Mapai did not increase a hundredfold, as did the Histadrut between 1920 and 1960, but it too grew very rapidly and inevitably changed its character. There was a great deal of bureaucracy and patronage (though little outright corruption), and many joined the party simply to improve their chances in a professional career. But unlike the Social Democratic parties of France and Italy, Mapai had the inner resources and the dynamism to adjust itself to changing conditions. It managed to transform itself into a movement with a political appeal reaching well beyond the working class. It projected with some success the image of a modern party with both a mass basis and a capable leadership, worthy to be entrusted with the guidance of the affairs of the new nation.

Such a transformation, which necessarily meant discarding the spirit of the second and the third aliya, was bound to produce an internal crisis. What exactly was the *raison d'être* of Mapai? What was its orientation? In what ways did it differ from other political parties? Why should young men and women be attracted to it? However much opposed to doctrinaire Socialist attitudes, the members of Hapoel Hatzair, and leaders such as Berl Katznelson would have found it exceedingly difficult to accept the kind of society which came into being under the leadership of the party they had helped tó found. And they would have disapproved of much of it. This was not so much a question of political attitudes as of values, of a whole style of life. The attempts to create a society in conformity with youthful dreams had been at best only partly successful. But the same applies to Socialist movements everywhere. Given these limitations, it is remarkable to what extent the labour movement did succeed, for better or worse, in putting its imprint on Israeli society.

In the last resort, the erosion of ideology affected Mapai less than other Socialist parties simply because it had been more pragmatic from the beginning. The state of siege after 1948 did not provide a climate conducive to doctrinal introspection and revival. As in other democratic societies, the party has become a transmission belt in both directions, having acquired a momentum of its own regardless of political-theoretical considerations. Having achieved its original aims, it may well have outlived its historical function. But in the absence of other forces able to take its place it has continued to play a decisive role in Israeli politics.

IN BLOOD AND FIRE:
JABOTINSKY AND
REVISIONISM

Between the two world wars the existence of the Zionist movement was imperilled by bitter internal strife. Whatever its other qualities, the movement had never distinguished itself by a high degree of unity within its ranks. Even while the going was good there had been a great deal of dissension, and at a time of crisis Zionism, weakened by conflict, was torn in different directions. At the time of the Balfour Declaration and for some years thereafter a state of euphoria had prevailed. Few were the Zionists who did not believe that the messianic age was at hand, that within the near future a Jewish commonwealth would emerge in Palestine in which hundreds of thousands, if not millions of Jews would find their home. *Altneuland,* the idyllic modern society which Herzl had envisaged, seemed around the corner. Only a handful of far-sighted leaders knew that the real uphill struggle was about to begin. As for the rest, it took them a number of years to realise that progress would be agonisingly slow.

The British administration in Palestine was by no means totally sympathetic towards Zionism, and the Arabs were actively hostile. The Balfour Declaration was gradually whittled down. Immigrants were relatively few, and agricultural settlement and industrialisation expanded only slowly, the Zionist organisation having no reserves to finance large scale enterprises – the 200,000 Jews of Berlin gave more money for social welfare in their community than the whole Jewish people gave for building Palestine. The charter of which Herzl had dreamed had at last been won, but the future of the whole venture seemed almost as uncertain as before. There was stagnation and in some respects decline, while all over Europe ominous signs were appearing that the position of the Jewish communities was becoming ever more precarious. Anti-semitism was more virulent and more widespread than before the First World War, and the political storm clouds gathered darkly as the economic crisis of the 1930s struck one country after another. In these circumstances, dissatisfaction with official Zionist policy was bound to spread. The executive was accused of weakness and lack of initiative, and Weizmann personally was made responsible for the set-backs. He was charged with indecision, leaning excessively towards the British, opting for a new 'miniature Zionism', betraying the legacy of Herzl and Nordau. Poland, where the situation of the Jews was most critical, was the main breeding ground of this mood, but the demand for a more activist policy quickly spread and found vociferous supporters in other parts of the world. This opposition movement had a leader of genius; it was in fact dominated by Vladimir (Zeev) Jabotinsky to such an extent that it is impossible to write its history without constant reference to the personality of the man who shaped its destinies for two decades.

Jabotinsky, the *Wunderkind* of Russian Zionism, was already well known and widely admired in his early twenties as an accomplished essayist and brilliant speaker, probably the best in a movement which did not lack first-rate orators. Born in Odessa in 1880 into a middle class family which became impoverished with the death of the father, young Jabotinsky grew up in the lively atmosphere of his home town – a strong cultural centre, its inhabitants a mixture of peoples and religions, cosmo-politan, colourful, open to new trends and ideas. In his early days he had shown little interest in Judaism, nor did he join, as did so many of his contemporaries, the revolutionary movement.* Russian literature was his great love. He wrote poetry in that language and at the age of sixteen began to publish essays in the local newspapers. His first contribution was on a subject which remained topical for many years to come – a criticism of the use of grading marks in school. He studied first in Switzerland and for a longer period in Italy, which became his second spiritual home. There he devoured the writings of the leaders of the *risorgimento*. More recent authors such as Croce also profoundly influenced him, and he began to write poetry in Italian. His interest in Jewish affairs was only slowly awakened. The pogroms of 1904–5 were for him, as for many others of his generation, a rude awakening. Jabotinsky took an active

---

* The two main sources for Jabotinsky's early years are his *Autobiography* (in Hebrew), Jerusalem, 1947, and J.Schechtman's two-volume biography, *Rebel and Statesman*, New York, 1956, and *Fighter and Prophet*, New York, 1961.

part in the organisation of Jewish self-defence, translated Bialik's poem about the Kishinev massacre into Russian, and, at the age of twenty-two, went as a delegate to the sixth Zionist congress where (as he later wrote) Herzl made a colossal impression on him. Having embraced the new creed, no one was more enthusiastic in spreading the gospel. Within a few years he became a professional Zionist, a travelling agitator, very much in demand as a speaker all over Russia. According to Gorky, Kuprin and other leading writers of the day, this total absorption with Jewish affairs and Zionism was a great loss to Russian literature. Suddenly Jabotinsky had become aware not just of the fact that Jews had been depicted in a most unfavourable light in the works of his beloved Russian writers; he sensed that the position of a Jew who had ambitions to be a Russian writer was highly problematical.* There was something unnatural and undignified, he wrote, when Jews took a leading part in the celebration of the centenary of a writer like Gogol, whose stories were replete with antisemitic remarks.

Jabotinsky had become an enthusiastic Zionist but in his political orientation he was by no means more radical than his contemporaries. True, he opposed the Uganda project, but later on admitted that the issues were less clearcut than he had thought at the time. He helped to convene the Helsingfors meeting in November 1906 which adopted a resolution in favour of equal rights for Jews and all other nationalities of the Russian empire. This may sound innocent enough but it was in fact a major new departure from the Zionist point of view. Why should Jabotinsky have bothered to insist on full equality for the Jews if he was convinced, with Pinsker and Herzl, that antisemitism was endemic in Europe and that east European Jewry was doomed? He did not believe that a national revival was possible outside Palestine, but he was no longer determined to boycott Zionist work in the diaspora (*Gegenwartsarbeit*) altogether. Jabotinsky's work in Constantinople, where he assisted Jacobson, who represented the Zionist executive in the Turkish capital, was cut short because of a quarrel concerning a book, about the ultimate aims of Zionism, by Jacobus Kann, the Dutch Zionist leader, which it was feared would gravely compromise the position of Zionism in the Ottoman empire. Jabotinsky curiously enough opted for caution rather than 'maximalism'.

In 1914 he was at a loose end. 'What would I have done if the world had not broken out in flames?' Jabotinsky wrote in his autobiography,

* See, for instance, his essays 'Hayehudim ve hasafrut harussit', 1908, and 'Haletifa harussit', 1909, in Z. Jabotinsky, *Ktavim Nivcharim*, Tel Aviv, 1936, vol. 1.

in a rare attack of self-pity. 'I had wasted my youth and early middle age. Perhaps I would have gone to Eretz Israel, perhaps I would have escaped to Rome, perhaps I would have founded a political party.' Such fits of depression never lasted long, for he was almost incurably optimistic. The war uprooted Jabotinsky, his family and friends. It brought about the ruin of Russian Jewry, but it also provided the historical chance for the Zionist movement to realise its aim, and it catapulted Jabotinsky into its front ranks. The stormy petrel of 1914 emerged at the end of the war as an outstanding leader and statesman.

The idea of a Jewish legion, which from now on held a central place in Jabotinsky's thinking, was born when as a war correspondent in Egypt in late 1914 he heard that hundreds of young Jews had been deported by the Turkish authorities. He helped to found the Mule Corps, consisting of Jewish soldiers, which later on saw action at Gallipoli. But he envisaged a far more ambitious enterprise; it took several years of effort and suffered a great many setbacks before the establishment of a Jewish regiment (the Judaeans) was officially announced in London in August 1917. The legion reached Palestine the following March and played a certain, militarily not very significant, part during the last phase of the war.

In his struggle for the formation of a Jewish legion Jabotinsky was 'almost alone, discouraged and derided everywhere', to quote Weizmann, one of the few who followed his activities with some sympathy. That Jabotinsky faced opposition from non-Zionists goes without saying. Both the liberal assimilationist establishment and the left-wing pacifists were bitterly hostile.* But there was strong resistance among Jabotinsky's colleagues too. After all, Zionists were fighting in this war on both sides, and there was a real danger that the Turks would react severely. Was it worth while to endanger the very existence of the small Jewish community in Palestine for a project of doubtful military or political value? While Weizmann was certain that the Allies would win the war, many Russian Zionist leaders were much less sure; nor, as far as Russia, the bulwark of antisemitism, was concerned, did they think the perpetuation of tsarist rule, the likely outcome of an allied victory, desirable.

For Jabotinsky the establishment of a legion was more than a tactical move. He was not a born militarist; as a young man he had in fact written a pacifist play. True, he had a strong romantic, even adventurist streak,

* See V.Jabotinsky, *The Story of the Jewish Legion*, New York, 1945; J.H.P.Patterson, *With the Judaeans in the Palestine Campaign*, New York, 1922; J.Trumpeldor, *Tagebücher und Briefe*, Berlin, 1925; E.Golomb, *Chevion Oz* (2 vols.), Tel Aviv, 1953.

and he found a certain personal satisfaction in army life despite its disappointments and hardships. Perhaps he saw himself, a Jewish Garibaldi, liberating Palestine at the head of a Jewish army. But above all there were two basic considerations which made him so fanatically persistent in his struggle for the legion: he was absolutely convinced that a Jewish army, however small, was a historical necessity. However many agricultural settlements were established, they would be defenceless in the absence of Jewish military units. The legion came into being, despite much opposition. In later years Jabotinsky grossly exaggerated its political significance during the war. It was simply not true (as he argued) that half the credit for the Balfour Declaration should go to the legion.* Jabotinsky became a great believer in the value of military training and discipline, which he thought were of special importance for a people which for so many centuries had been unable to defend itself. Henceforth these ideals played a central part in Jabotinsky's thought. Of 'militarism' he wrote: 'We ought not to be deterred by a Latin word'. The early Zionists, after all, were not put off by the nationalist label. There were two kinds of militarism – the one aggressive, out for territorial conquest; the other the natural defence effort of a people which had no homeland and was faced by the threat of extinction: 'If this is militarism, we ought to be proud of it.'†

The legion in which Jabotinsky served as a lieutenant was demobilised soon after the end of the war, much to his chagrin. He had hoped that it would be the nucleus of a Jewish army – under British command, if necessary. Jabotinsky was made political officer of the Zionist commission which during the interval between the armistice and the beginning of the mandate acted as a liaison officer with the British military authorities. From the beginning he was apprehensive about the hostility of the local administration and criticised Weizmann for being too pliant in his dealings with the British government. Not a single day should be lost, he felt, in creating *faits accomplis*. He referred specifically to immediate large-scale immigration and a Jewish armed force but found little sympathy among the other Zionist leaders. Weizmann said that he had not the courage to come to the Jewish people and submit a large-scale programme when he knew beforehand that it was not practical: 'Zionism cannot be the answer to a catastrophe.' Ussishkin, not exactly an Anglophile, and much closer to Jabotinsky politically, commented that

---

* *Hamishmar*, August 1932.

† V. Jabotinsky, *Die Idee des Betar*, Lyck, 1935, p. 14; see also 'Al Hamilitarism' in *Baderech Lamedina*, Jerusalem, 1960.

the country could not be built up in a hurry, as in the exodus from Egypt, but by slow immigration, as after the Babylonian exile.*

At the time of the first Arab attacks in Jerusalem in April 1920, Jabotinsky was head of the Hagana in that city. As his *aide de camp* he had chosen Jeremiah Halpern, the son of Michael Halpern, who thirty years earlier had been the first proponent of a Jewish legion. After the riots subsided Jabotinsky was arrested and a few days later sentenced to fifteen years penal servitude. It was a scandalous trial, for Jabotinsky and his men had been acting in self-defence precisely because the British authorities had been unable to maintain public order and to safeguard the lives of the Jews in the city. Shortly after his arrival in Palestine, Herbert Samuel, the first high commissioner, granted an amnesty to Jabotinsky and the other Jewish prisoners sentenced at the same trial. Jabotinsky had been in prison for a few months only, and as a political prisoner had enjoyed preferential treatment. Upon his release he was given a hero's welcome, but he was full of bitterness, and most reluctant to be released under an amnesty which also gave freedom to Arabs who had taken part in the attacks on Jews. Later he took legal action and succeeded in having the sentence quashed by the commander-in-chief in Egypt. More strongly than ever before he felt the need for an army for the purposes of self-defence. Nor should it be clandestine; without it colonisation was just not practical.

On this issue he parted ways with the Labour Zionists, who otherwise endorsed much of his criticism regarding Weizmann's policy. Jabotinsky rejected the argument that a Jewish armed force would provoke the Arabs. On the contrary, he claimed, two thousand regular soldiers under British command would be less of a provocation than ten thousand illegally organised Jewish soldiers. Ben Gurion, Golomb, and the other Socialist leaders were not averse in principle to the idea of a legion, but they put two questions to which Jabotinsky had no convincing answers: how could they be sure that a Jewish legion would afford protection to the yishuv if it was not under Jewish command? And since, even if all went well, it would be some time before the legion was ready, who would protect the community during the interim period?

Jabotinsky joined the Zionist executive together with two political friends, Richard Lichtheim and Joseph Cowen, in March 1921. For almost two years he took a leading part in its activities – as political adviser, fund raiser and all-purpose Zionist propagandist. He spent several months in the United States, where he quarrelled with the local

* Schechtman, *Rebel and Statesman*, p. 304.

Zionist leaders (Brandeis and Mack), whose 'minimalism' was utterly opposed to his way of looking at things. Whereas they believed that the political phase of Zionism was more or less over, he was firmly convinced that the real struggle was just about to begin. Jabotinsky was greatly worried by events in Palestine, especially the open hostility to Zionism displayed in the Haycraft report of 1921, which put the responsibility for the Jaffa riots in May 1921 largely on the Jews. He wrote to the Zionist executive in November 1922 that the 'wobbling attitude' of the British government was the logical consequence of Herbert Samuel's policy 'and our own meekness in dealing with his administration'. 'Our own meekness' – this was the *leitmotif* of all his speeches and articles in the years to come.* He was most unhappy about the Churchill White Paper, which provided a restrictive interpretation of the Balfour Declaration. It was a lost battle, but, as he said at a subsequent Zionist congress, he could not desert his colleagues in a desperate emergency: 'I felt it my moral duty to share with my colleagues the shame of defeat.'†

His position on the executive was compromised by his talks with Slavinsky, a minister in Petliura's Ukranian exile government. Jabotinsky suggested the establishment of a Jewish gendarmerie within the framework of the Petliura régime to protect Ukrainian Jewry against pogroms. Slavinsky was a Ukrainian liberal intellectual with a fairly good record, but under Petliura's rule thousands of Jews had been murdered. The fact that Jabotinsky was willing to negotiate even indirectly with the man responsible for these massacres provoked a storm of indignation in the Jewish world. (Petliura was killed by a Jewish student in Paris a few years later.) Paraphrasing his old hero Mazzini, Jabotinsky said in his defence that he would ally himself with the devil on behalf of Palestine and the Jews. Whatever the desirability and efficacity of such alliances, in this particular case it was totally unnecessary. The 'pact' was not only a disastrous tactical move, it was of no practical importance, since the invasion of the Soviet Ukraine which had been planned from Poland never came off and the Ukrainian government-in-exile collapsed shortly after. The incident harmed Jabotinsky politically, giving him the reputation of an extreme reactionary and a collaborator with pogromists. This was unjust, but Jabotinsky had only himself to blame. His political judgment had been at fault, and he had engaged in political activity for activity's sake – a pattern that was to repeat itself in the years to come.

---

* Schechtman, *Rebel and Statesman*, p. 418.
† *Stenographisches Protokoll . . . XV Zionisten Kongress*, p. 229.

Jabotinsky resigned from the executive in January 1923 in protest against what he regarded as Weizmann's fatal policy of renunciation and compromise. 'Weizmann believes that mine is the way of a stubborn fantast', he told a friend after a conversation with Weizmann, 'while I feel that his line is the line of renunciation, of subconscious Marannism.' His own approach was a difficult, stormy one, but it was to lead to a Jewish state.* He believed that Britain and Zionism had common interests in the eastern Mediterranean and that no British government would dissociate itself from the Balfour Declaration. Hence he saw no danger in asking awkward questions in London and pressing the British to fulfil their obligations under the mandate. If, however, as some of his colleagues claimed, the community of interests was questionable, if the mandate had no solid foundation of interest, and the pledge might be broken at any time, if it had all been a misunderstanding – what, then, was the use of keeping up appearances for another few months? Jabotinsky maintained that, all other considerations apart, the continuation of an anti-Zionist policy in Palestine was ruining the movement financially. Who would be willing to contribute to a cause which could not show that it was making progress? The policy of the Palestine administration was effectively blocking any advance.

Jabotinsky's resignation from the executive was accepted without regrets. His colleagues had been irritated by his inclination to dramatise political issues, his frequent speeches and declarations in which he criticised their policies. They agreed with him that the British government and, *a fortiori*, the mandatory authorities, were not fulfilling their duties in accordance with the mandate, but did not believe that the alternative was as easy and clearcut as Jabotinsky contended. 'Either there is a community of interest, in which case they will ultimately do what we want, or there isn't, in which case we have nothing to lose, because the mandate will be repudiated anyway.' Weizmann, who understood the British better than Jabotinsky, knew that some British statesmen were more in favour of cooperation with Zionism than others; that Zionism was just one factor among many in British Middle Eastern policy. In other words, there was nothing Jabotinsky could have done which Weizmann did not do. He could have protested more often and more loudly, but what difference would it have made? The only real alternative would have been a fundamental reorientation – away from Britain, towards some other power, or group of powers. But Jabotinsky

* Schechtman, *Rebel and Statesman*, p. 424.

was not at all in favour of reorientation, though later on, in the 1930s, he played half-heartedly with the idea of an alliance with Warsaw which was not, however, a real alternative.

The fundamental weakness of Jabotinsky's policy clearly appeared from the moment he went into opposition to official Zionist policy. His analysis of the weaknesses of the line his colleagues were taking, especially in the foreign political field, was forceful if usually somewhat exaggerated. But he had no alternative to offer, other than the promise that if given the opportunity he would achieve better results. At the fourteenth Zionist congress he was challenged by his critics to say what he would use to bring pressure to bear on Britain. He replied that he was neither a friend nor an enemy of Britain but that he knew that force was not needed to persuade a civilised people like the British. He could not tell them in advance how he would convince them; nor would Herzl have been able to give such information to the congress. The main thing was that the demands of the Zionists were logical and consistent and should be pressed forcefully.*

The origins of Revisionism

When Jabotinsky left the executive he intended to withdraw from politics altogether for a time, but he was deluding himself. Temperamentally he was quite unsuited to a life outside politics. He felt constantly obliged to react in print and by word of mouth to current Zionist politics, needing immediate contact with his readers and listeners. He was invited to join the editorial board of *Rassvet*, for many the leading organ of Russian Zionism, which now became his mouthpiece. But the appeal of his articles, always hard hitting and well written, was limited. *Rassvet* was not the ideal platform for reaching the Jewish masses, certainly not the younger generation. The idea of setting up a political party and a youth movement occurred to him during a trip to Latvia and Lithuania in late 1923. The day after a speech in Riga on Zionist activism he was invited to speak to the local Jewish student association and was told that he had no right to preach such views and to stir up young people if he did not intend to call them to action: 'You either keep quiet or organise a party.'† On his return he wrote to a friend that he had met a generation of youth that was worth believing in and that he had made up his mind

* Z. Jabotinsky, *Neumim*, 1905–26, Tel Aviv, n.d., p. 286.
† *Rassvet*, 28 February, 7 March 1926. J.B.Schechtman and Y.Benari, *History of the Revisionist Movement*, Tel Aviv, 1970, vol. 1, p. 22.

to enlist them for the cause of Zionist activism. Riga, where a youth organisation (named after Trumpeldor) became the birthplace of *Betar*, the revisionist youth movement.

Jabotinsky now had to formulate the basic tenets of revisionism, as the new movement was to be called, following the suggestion of one of his lieutenants. It was not intended as a radical new departure. Not Zionism was to be revised, only its current policies. Revisionism saw itself as the only true heir of the Herzl-Nordau tradition of political Zionism, in contrast to the official Zionist leadership, which, by making concession after concession, had deviated from it. Jabotinsky and his followers were maximalists, claiming not only Palestine for the Jews but 'the gradual transformation of Palestine (including Transjordan) into a self-governing commonwealth under the auspices of an established Jewish majority'.* They regarded this as the only admissible interpretation of the term 'national home' in the Balfour Declaration and the mandate. Transjordan was an inseparable part of the territory of Palestine, to be included in the sphere of Jewish colonisation. The British White Paper which had restricted the interpretation of the Balfour Declaration in 1922 had been accepted by the Zionist movement under duress, in the hope that it would lead to the acceptance of the Declaration by the Palestinian Arabs. Since the Arabs had refused to recognise the Declaration, the 1922 White Paper was no longer valid.

Writing in 1926, Jabotinsky defined the creation of a Jewish majority in Palestine, west and east of the Jordan, as the first aim of Zionism. A normal political development on a democratic parliamentary basis could be envisaged only after this target had been achieved.† The final aim was the solution of the Jewish problem and the creation of a Jewish culture. Jabotinsky emphatically rejected the thesis that the Zionist aim should not be openly proclaimed. It was too late to preach minimalism, for the Arabs, too, were aware of Herzl's *Judenstaat*. To engage in conspiracies, to cover up their real aims, would confuse their friends, not their enemies. To achieve a majority Jabotinsky proposed immigration at the rate of forty thousand a year over a period of twenty-five years. If Transjordan were included, there would have to be fifty to sixty thousand immigrants a year. Transjordan, he claimed, had always been part of Jewish Palestine; it was also much less densely populated and therefore more promising for colonisation.

---

* *Basic Principles of Revisionism*, London, 1929, p. 3. The formulation was Sir Herbert Samuel's, made in a speech in London on 2 November 1919.

† V. Jabotinsky, *Was wollen die Zionisten-Revisionisten*, Paris, 1926, p. 3.

This position was revolutionary inasmuch as it demanded the establishment of a Jewish state at a time when it was not openly advocated by any other Zionist leader or movement. At this early stage Jabotinsky was perhaps not thinking of full independence. The concept state (he once said) had various meanings in political usage – France was a state, and so was Nebraska and Kentucky. State did not necessarily imply complete independence, but while the degree of self-government could be discussed, there was no room for manœuvring with regard to one basic factor: either there was a Jewish majority or there wasn't.* On this point there could be no meeting of minds with Weizmann, who at the time of the Zionist congress at which Jabotinsky launched the discussion about the *Endziel* (final aim), declared in an interview with a journalist: 'I have no understanding of or sympathy for a Jewish majority in Palestine.' This statement provoked much opposition and a few days later was one of the factors leading to Weizmann's defeat. But it did not make Jabotinsky's policy any more acceptable to the majority at the congress.

Jabotinsky did not shirk the Arab problem. He regarded Arab opposition to Zionism and Jewish settlement as natural and inevitable. But since the Jews in Europe were facing a catastrophe, whereas the situation of the Arabs was secure in the Middle East, he believed the moral case of the Jews to be infinitely stronger. Revisionism recognised that there would be a substantial Arab minority in Palestine even after Jews became the majority. Jabotinsky wrote in his programme that in the Jewish state there would be 'absolute equality' between Jews and Arabs, that if one part of the population were destitute, the whole country would suffer.† Meanwhile, the Arabs would continue to fight Zionism until an 'iron wall' was built. Then, and only then, would they understand that there was no hope of destroying Zionism, that they would have to accept it and live with it. If the transformation of Palestine into a Jewish state was morally justified, resistance to it was unjustified. Hence Jabotinsky's refusal to compromise with what he regarded as unjust demands from the Arab side, all the more so as on the question of the majority there was no room for manœuvre. 'Either – or' was the basic pattern of Jabotinsky's policy on the Arab question, as it was in his attitude towards the British or his demand for a Jewish army: either the Jews had a right to their state, in which case Arab resistance was immoral, or they had no such right, in which case the whole argument for Zionism collapsed. These dramatisations of complicated issues were always

---

* *Protokolle ... XVII. Zionisten Kongress*, pp. 164–78.
† *Was wollen die Zionisten-Revisionisten*, p. 22.

rhetorically effective, but the issues themselves were far too complicated, both morally and politically, to be illuminated, let alone solved, by categorical declarations of this kind.

Jabotinsky never swerved from his demand for a Jewish army, however small. Why should the British taxpayer be responsible for the defence of the Jews in Palestine? Sooner or later, he would no longer be willing to carry this burden, nor was Britain morally bound to provide such security. Zionism was obliged either to offer the men and the money needed, or to give up its political demands. A small Jewish legion, consisting of three battalions (approximately three thousand men) would cost no more than £120,000 a year. This would not be unproductive expenditure, as his critics asserted. On the contrary, it was the prerequisite for any colonisation scheme.

As relations with Britain deteriorated, Jabotinsky and his friends put most of the blame on the officials on the spot: Allenby had been against Zionism, Herbert Samuel too weak to assert himself. Instead of criticising the first high commissioner and his administration, he went on, the Jewish public had never openly attacked him. The setbacks to Zionist policies and the disappointments suffered were not inevitable, not the outcome of conditions over which no one had any control, but the result of human shortcomings, of the hostile policy of the local administration, and 'the consequence of the shortsightedness, the thoughtlessness, and the weakness of our leaders'.* Despite his own unfortunate experience, Jabotinsky did not reject the idea of an alliance with Britain, provided the mandatory power reaffirmed the original spirit of the mandate. When Sir Josiah Wedgwood, a pro-Zionist politician, promoted the idea of Palestine as a seventh dominion within the British Commonwealth, it received the blessing of the revisionists at their third world conference in Vienna in 1928, but after 1930 hopes began to fade. Jabotinsky said he wanted one 'last experiment' to reach a *rapprochement* with Britain. Schechtman, another revisionist leader, wrote in 1933 that a situation might arise in which the Jewish people would no longer be interested in the continuation of the mandate.†

In 1934 the revisionists began to advocate non-cooperation with the mandatory authorities, which provoked charges of inconsistency from their critics. How could they at one and the same time demand a Jewish legion under British command, and preach non-cooperation? How

---

* R.Lichtheim, *Revision der Zionistischen Politik*, Berlin, 1930, p. 25.

† J.Schechtman, *Judenstaatszionismus*, quoted in S.Schmitz and H.Brauner, *Die Wahrheit ueber den Revisionismus*, Moravska Ostrava, 1935, p. 8.

would noisy demonstrations persuade the British that Zionism was the surest pillar of British policy in the orient? Revisionism, with all its criticism of British policy, was in the last resort as pro-British at the time in its basic assumptions as Weizmann. It believed that fundamentally the British government was well disposed towards Zionism and that it would live up to its obligations, both for reasons of self-interest and as a moral duty. They were less aware than Weizmann that a new generation of British leaders increasingly regarded the Balfour Declaration as an unwelcome burden, if not an outright mistake, in view of their many interests and commitments in the Muslim world. In their eyes Zionism was an embarrassment, not a potential ally.

Much of the revisionist critique of the Zionist leadership had to do with economic and social policy. Jabotinsky had been interested in economics as a student, and under the influence of his Italian Socialist teachers had written in 1906 that class conflicts between employers and employed could not be reconciled, and that the nationalisation of the means of production was the only solution.* He had not belonged to a Socialist party but had certainly believed in Socialist ideals. Even twenty years later, when defining the revisionist programme, he wrote that the class struggle in Palestine was an inevitable, even healthy phenomenon. Revisionists would neither join the chorus of those who talked about the bankruptcy of the collective settlements nor would they attack the ('bourgeois') fourth aliya. Every form of settlement was legitimate and compatible with revisionism.† Richard Lichtheim on the other hand maintained that if revisionism wanted to create a Jewish majority in Palestine in the shortest possible time, the class struggle was clearly a luxury the country could ill afford. But the movement was not against the working class. Unlike (Italian) fascism, it did not seek an alliance with big capital; it was neither Socialist nor capitalist.‡

Gradually Jabotinsky retreated from his early views about Socialism and nationalisation: the class struggle was perhaps justified in other countries; however sharp the conflict between German workers and employers, it would not destroy the German economy, whereas the building of Palestine was only at the beginning and irreparable damage could be caused by major class conflicts.§ He saw no basic difference between Socialism and Communism, and wrote that nationalisation

---

* *Evreiskaia Mysl*, 12 October 1906, quoted in Schechtman, *Rebel and Statesman*.
† *Was Wollen die Zionisten-Revisionisten?* p. 23.
‡ Lichtheim, *Revision der Zionistischen Politik*, p. 52.
§ 'Ma'amad', in *Uma vechevra*, p. 246.

of the means of production, if realised, would result in a society where there was even less freedom and equality than in the present one. For some time he was influenced by the original theories on the ideal economic system developed by Josef Popper Lynkeus, a figure of some literary renown in Vienna who was in contact with Robert Stricker, Jabotinsky's chief aide in Austria. A more lasting impact was exerted by some of his followers in Palestine, ex-Socialists who later turned sharply against Labour Zionism. In Mapai and the Histadrut they saw the chief enemy, more dangerous than either the mandatory government or the Arabs.

While Jabotinsky was aware of the dangers of this openly anti-Socialist trend and privately rebuked the 'hotheads', he did not openly dissociate himself from them. As a result revisionism became more and more anti-Socialist in character. It had been its original aim to remain above the social struggle and to minimise its impact, to be neither of the Right nor of the Left. Now, through its involvement in the political fight, it became more and more identified with opposition to organised labour. The revisionists attacked the economic programme of the Zionist executive from opposite angles at one and the same time: it was too liberal, in the sense that it assumed that the building up of the country could be financed solely by voluntary contributions, and it was not liberal enough, for it discriminated against private initiative in agriculture and industry.

The revisionist programme demanded a 'systematic colonisation régime to be charged with the positive task of creating the conditions necessary for a Jewish mass colonisation'.* No other Zionist party would have disagreed with the demand that the entire complex of Jewish immigration should be entrusted to the sole competence of the Zionist Organisation. Another demand called for a thorough land reform to be carried out, with the object of establishing a land reserve for colonisation, to include all lands not under permanent cultivation both west and east of the Jordan, subject to satisfactory compensation being paid to the present owners. The revisionists proposed the floating of a big international loan to finance mass immigration and settlement. They charged the Zionist executive with having given hardly any help at all to middle class initiative in industry and agriculture.

Some of the criticism was well founded. Soskin, a veteran agricultural

---

* *Basic Principles of Revisionism*, p. 6; see also E. Soskin, *Das Kolonisationsproblem*, Paris, 1929, and *Kolonisations-Revisionismus*, Vienna, 1927; J. Schechtmann, *Judenstaats-Zionismus* Prague, 1933; Lichtheim, *Revision der Zionistischen Politik*.

expert, urged the promotion by all possible means of intensive agriculture, and opposed the tendency towards autarky prevailing at the time in some circles, according to which agricultural settlements were to produce more or less everything they needed. More often revisionist proposals exuded a spirit of well-meaning dilettantism: the advice extended to the Zionist executive to 'think big', to plan ahead, and to float a substantial loan was unlikely to be disputed. It reminds one of the old Jewish saying that to be young, healthy and rich is preferable to being old, sick and poor. Who would have provided the money for these projects? Independent countries offering more security and better economic prospects to investors failed to get loans during the 1920s, and after the onset of the great depression it was well-nigh impossible to borrow money on a large scale.

Jabotinsky's approach was reminiscent of Herzl's enthusiastic belief that somehow, something would turn up if one tried hard enough: Micawber in the role of the *grand seigneur*. But this was no longer 1897. When Herzl tried unsuccessfully to enlist the help of potential donors, when he made promises, hinting obscurely that enormous sums were at his disposal, the Zionist movement could afford to be irresponsible – it had neither assets nor obligations. Three decades later it carried the responsibility for the growing Jewish community in Palestine. If hard pressed, Jabotinsky would no doubt have admitted that he had no alternative suggestion, either in the economic or in the political field, but that once the movement received a powerful impetus there would be fresh enthusiasm and the dynamic energy generated would help to overcome all obstacles. There would be money and immigrants, as well as political support.

His main intention was to give new hope to the movement at a time when it was facing a steady loss of momentum which he feared would result in decline and ultimately disintegration. This support seemed all the more vital because the crisis in Zionism coincided with a deterioration in the situation of European Jewry and emigration was becoming a matter of urgent necessity. Not long before Hitler came to power, Jabotinsky said to a group of friends that he had no doubt that one, and probably only one point in the programme of the Nazi Party would be carried out in full – that which concerned the Jews. Being a politician, and the leader of a mass movement, he could not tell the Jewish masses that there were no easy solutions, no panaceas. He had to formulate slogans and demands which were clearcut, imaginative and easily intelligible, but which were bound to provoke charges of dilettantism

IN BLOOD AND FIRE

and demagogy because they were so obviously unrealistic. All too often he chose to play the role of the *terrible simplificateur*. After his tour of the Baltic countries in February 1924 he reduced his policy to a simple formula:

The programme is not complicated. The aim of Zionism is a Jewish state. The territory – both sides of the Jordan. The system – mass colonisation. The solution of the financial problem – a national loan. These four principles cannot be realised without international sanction. Hence the commandment of the hour – a new political campaign and the militarisation of Jewish youth in Eretz Israel and the diaspora.*

The new party

Within less than a year of his resignation from the executive in 1923 he was back in the thick of the political struggle. It was not just a matter of unfulfilled ambitions. Whatever his shortcomings, Jabotinsky never suffered from any major personal frustrations. There was at the time widespread discontent in the ranks of the Zionist movement, inchoate, but basically on the lines of Jabotinsky's thinking. Wherever he went he encountered enthusiastic support from local Zionist militants. His first backers were his old comrades, the Russian Zionists in exile. In Petrograd in May 1917 a group of active legionaries had been founded, among them some of Jabotinsky's future leading political supporters, Meir Grossman and Joseph Schechtman. Thus it did not come as a surprise when *Rassvet* was taken over in 1924 by Jabotinsky and some of his closest supporters (Julius Brutzkus, J.Klinov, J.Trivus). In March 1924 a small office was opened in Berlin to coordinate the activities of the local circles of his followers in various countries. In September 1924 Jabotinsky wrote to a friend that there were now fifty such groups, from Canada to Harbin in Manchuria. But they formed at most a loose association, still without an organisational centre.

Only in April 1925, with the first conference of the *Zohar* (Zionim-Revisionistim), was the first step taken towards the establishment of a party. The conference, which convened in the *Taverne du Panthéon* in the heart of the Quartier Latin, adopted the formula mentioned already, that there was only one permissable interpretation of the term national home, namely the gradual transformation of Palestine into a self-governing commonwealth under the auspices of an established Jewish

* *Sefer Betar*, Tel Aviv, 1969, vol. 1, p. 32.

majority. It emphatically rejected Weizmann's plan for a broadening of the Jewish Agency to include non-Zionists. All members of the Jewish Agency executive would have to be elected by the Zionist congress and to be responsible to the congress. The revisionists were not willing to give non-Zionists full rights to vote on vital political issues. They envisaged cooperation with non-Zionists only in the economic field. Lastly, the conference elected Vl.Tiomkin head of the United Zionists Revisionists (uzr).

The importance of this first convention lay not (as a historian of the movement later wrote) in the substance of the new programme, nor in the ideological discussions that took place, but in the whole atmosphere, the enthusiastic mood which attracted intellectuals and young people.* The movement was still numerically small. At the fourteenth Zionist congress it had only four delegates, including Jabotinsky himself. There were no well-known old Zionists among its leaders, with the exception of Meir Grossman, a Russian-Jewish journalist and agitator whom Jabotinsky had known since before the First World War. His friends in the Paris and Berlin Russian-Jewish emigration carried little weight in Zionist counsels and Schechtman, his future biographer, did not have the qualities of a political leader. A prominent supporter in the early days was Wolfgang von Weisl, an Australian journalist who toured the Middle East on behalf of a leading Berlin newspaper; he, too, was not a second Herzl. Among the early converts to revisionism was a young Viennese student of Hungarian descent, Arthur Koestler. He dropped out of the party and from the Zionist movement a few years later, but continued to be an admirer of Jabotinsky.

As the malaise in the Zionist movement and the discontent with Weizmann's policy deepened, Jabotinsky won the support of Richard Lichtheim and Robert Stricker, both respected figures in the central European Zionist movement. Lichtheim had represented the executive in Constantinople before the war. Together with Kurt Blumenfeld, he had been the most effective propagandist of German Zionism. A man of independent views (and independent means), he agreed with Jabotinsky that the time was ripe for a revision of Zionist policy. But neither he nor Stricker, a native of Vienna and an engineer by profession, was a popular leader likely to attract the masses. The revisionists tried hard, and not unsuccessfully, to gain influence among the Jews of Sefardi origin in the Mediterranean countries and especially in Palestine, who for a long time

---

* B.Lubotzki, *HaZohar uBetar*, Jerusalem, 1946, p. 12.

had been neglected by the Zionist movement. But not one Sefardi personality of stature emerged to take a leading place in their inner counsels.

More than any other Zionist party, revisionism always remained a movement identified with one man. Even though his colleagues were often opposed to Jabotinsky, they knew that without him the movement was nothing. When Grossman once disagreed with Jabotinsky he was told by another revisionist: 'With him you are Grossman [a big man], without him you are Kleinmann [a small man].' Jabotinsky's most faithful followers were the young people from Poland and Latvia whom he met during his tours in eastern Europe – Propes, Lubotzky and Dissenchik in Riga, Remba and Klarman in Poland, Weinshal who represented revisionism in Palestine. They and the thousands of nameless Betarim constituted the backbone of the movement, a new generation of Zionists, very different in character and mental make-up from the professionals who met at the Zionist congresses every year.

The years after the foundation of the Zohar, 1925–9, were devoted to the consolidation of the movement. Jabotinsky settled for a while in Palestine. He went on a propaganda campaign to South Africa, where he had considerable success, and to the United States, where he fared less well. The Palestine government, displeased by the 'extremist' activities of the revisionists, decided not to permit Jabotinsky to return as he 'endangered public safety'. He was compelled to settle again in Paris, subsequently in London, and during the last phase of his life in New York. The movement grew by leaps and bounds. From four representatives at the Zionist congress to nine, to twenty-one, to fifty-two within little more than six years. The UZR conventions (December 1926 and December 1928) were to a large extent devoted to the discussion of organisational questions, of the situation inside the Zionist movement, and to the elaboration of a socio-economic programme of revisionism. Whether the revisionists should act in future from within the Zionist movement or from without became one of the main bones of contention. Lichtheim, speaking at the third Zohar world conference, expressed the view of the majority when he said that the movement had no chance of succeeding outside the Zionist camp and that it ought therefore try to conquer it from within.* For the time being Zohar lacked influence; neither Britain nor anyone else would take it seriously. Even the Zionist movement under Herzl had needed many years to gain recognition,

---

* The proceedings of this conference are summarised in Schechtman and Benari, *History of the Revisionist Movement*, pp. 143–54.

and but for the war it would not have achieved it when it did.* The Palestinian revisionists, on the other hand, pressed for secession as early as 1928, and Jabotinsky was more than half-determined to support them. He did not want to force a decision at the third conference, saying that he was bowing to the majority while plainly hinting that he saw little hope of taking over the Zionist movement. He made no secret of his conviction that the logic of events would drive his movement towards secession and full independence.

Two years later, at the fourth conference in Prague (August 1930), he had reached the conclusion that the time was ripe. He argued in closed session that revisionism was not so much a political party or an ideology (*Weltanschauung*) as a 'psychological race', a definite inborn mentality which could not be communicated to those who did not inherently possess it. It was therefore the mission of the movement to look for people of its own 'race', to organise them and not waste its energies in attempts to 'conquer' a Zionist crowd with a very different outlook.† Jabotinsky insisted on secession despite the steady growth of the UZR, which at the seventeenth congress had become the third strongest faction in world Zionism. But he felt, probably rightly, that the old guard was too firmly entrenched, that the Zionist movement could not be revolutionised from within. Shortly before the congress, at a meeting of the Zionist Action Committee, Weizmann had declared that the Jewish state was never an aim in itself, only a means to an end: 'Nothing is said about the Jewish state in the Basle Programme, nor in the Balfour Declaration. The essence of Zionism is to create a number of important material foundations, upon which an autonomous, compact and productive community can be built.'

This statement, the exact antithesis of revisionism, strengthened Jabotinsky in his belief that the final showdown was at hand. In his speech at the congress, as usual one of the central events, he declared that he still believed in the honesty of the world and the power of a just cause: 'I believe that great problems are decided by the powerful influence of moral pressure and that the Jewish people is a tremendous factor of moral pressure.' If the elan of the Zionist movement had decreased, if Zionism had lost its spell over the Jewish soul, this was the result of 'our own errors'; the methods and the system had to be changed: 'It has become a political necessity to clean the atmosphere, and this can be done only by telling the truth. Why should we allow the term 'Jewish

---

* *Protokolle der III. Weltkonferenz der Union der Zionisten-Revisionisten*, Paris, 1929, pp. 35–6.
† Schechtman, *Fighter and Prophet*, p. 143.

state' to be called extremism? The Albanians have their state, the Bulgarians have their state. The state is, after all, the normal condition of a people. If the Jewish state were in existence today, nobody would say that it was abnormal. And if we want to normalise our existence, who dares to call it extremism – and are we ourselves expected to say so?'

The split

Jabotinsky failed in his attempt to compel the congress to adopt a clear, unequivocal stand on the 'final aim'. Weizmann was defeated at the congress but there was no substantial change in policy. The leadership was not offered to Jabotinsky, as some had expected, but to Sokolow. By a majority decision Jabotinsky's resolution was not even put to the vote, whereupon pandemonium broke loose. Grossman, who wanted to make a statement on behalf of the revisionists, was shouted down. Jabotinsky climbed on a chair, shouted 'This is no longer a Zionist congress', tore up his delegate card and attended no further sessions.

The scene was without precedent. Passions were running higher than ever, but there was still no majority in favour of secession among the revisionist leaders. True, it had been decided at a meeting in Boulogne shortly before the congress that the party would establish its own world organisation if the congress rejected its resolution in favour of a Jewish state. But even after the stormy scenes at the congress there was still hesitation at the head office in London about whether the last, fateful step should be taken. In protest, Jabotinsky withdrew for several months from active leadership and returned to his post only in September 1931. Meanwhile the debate about the advantages and drawbacks of secession continued in the revisionist press. At a meeting in Calais in late September 1931 a compromise solution was adopted: the revisionists were no longer part of the Zionist movement, but the question of a new, independent organisation was to be shelved for the time being. Individual revisionists were free to belong or not to belong to the Zionist movement, and at the fifth revisionist conference in August 1932 the Calais compromise was endorsed against the vote of the leader of the movement.

Jabotinsky's attitude to Britain hardened in 1931. 'The Balfour Declaration is degenerating into an anti-Zionist document,' he declared. 'In Jewish eyes, England's policy has deprived her of the right to continue as the mandatory power . . . some people still hope that England will be compelled to change her policy radically. Others are convinced that our alliance with England has come to an end.' Again, Jabotinsky took a 'centrist' position. Most members of the revisionist executive believed that the alliance with Britain had not come to an end, whereas among the Palestinians and the revisionist youth movement anti-British sentiment was rapidly spreading and there was growing impatience with Jabotinsky's shilly-shallying. Jabotinsky, however, wanted to prevent a split among his followers at almost any price. He had agreed that in the new executive of five, four of the seats should go to men (Grossman, Machover, Stricker and Soskin) who were not in sympathy with his policy. But since the disagreement concerned fundamental issues, party unity could not be patched up for long. By early 1933 a split had become unavoidable. Jabotinsky's colleagues did not share his view that revisionist party discipline took precedence over Zionist discipline. This was unacceptable to Jabotinsky. Bowing to Zionist discipline was tantamount to abstaining from independent action, which in his view was political suicide. A stalemate had been reached, and when the issue was submitted for decision to the party council in Kattowitz in March 1933, both sides were prepared for a break. Yet once again the meeting ended in utter confusion: the majority were opposed to Jabotinsky's views, but did not want to expel him.*

Jabotinsky needed a few more days to make up his mind to cross the Rubicon. On 23 March he announced that he had personally assumed the leadership of the movement, suspended its elected bodies, and established a new provisional executive. At the same time he called on all party members to participate in the elections to the eighteenth Zionist congress. This, in the words of his biographer, was a tactical masterstroke. He had defeated his opponents while taking the wind out of their sails by refraining for the moment from pressing for secession. There was great indignation among the deposed leaders about Jabotinsky's high-handed and undemocratic behaviour. Grossman compared him to an oriental belly dancer: 'It is hard for me to grasp how democratic principles can be reconciled with the dictatorship of a single person who turns his coat before the eyes of the world in the same way as a *Nackttänzerin* . . .'.† If the leadership was opposed, Jabotinsky had the enthusiastic support of the rank and file. There was no doubt whatever that the revisionist movement preferred him to

---

* The struggle is described in detail in *ibid.*, p. 158 *et seq.*, and in Jakob Perelman, *Rewizjonizm w Polsce*, Warsaw, 1937, p. 227 *et seq.*

† *Herut*, 26 March 1933, quoted in Schechtman, *Fighter and Prophet*, p. 175.

his colourless colleagues, not just in the election campaign but in the greater political struggles ahead. Jabotinsky's optimism was borne out by the results of the elections to the congress: his list gained forty-six seats, that of his opponents only seven. In Betar, the revisionist youth organisation, support for him was overwhelming: 93 per cent of the members expressed confidence in their leader. The rival faction, headed by Grossman, founded the Jewish State Party, but it lacked both a mass basis and a clear policy.* It went on vegetating for several years and after the Second World War, when the revisionists re-entered the World Zionist Organisation, the State Party rejoined them.

In 1933 Jabotinsky's position as a leader was unassailable. Now at long last he seemed to have complete political freedom. The new executive was staffed by his supporters. It was less clear what use he would make of the unlimited mandate given to him. Revisionism after the exit of its elder statesmen was not the same. The influence of new forces, the Betar and the Palestinians, was bound to increase. As younger leaders came to the fore the next years witnessed the gradual radicalisation of the movement, not always in a direction which Jabotinsky desired.

Betar

The cradle of the youth movement was in Riga. The local activist youth had defined itself as 'a part of the legion which will come into existence in Eretz Israel'.† It took the Betar a number of years to grow roots in Poland, where eventually its main strength was concentrated. Hashomer Hatzair, its chief rival, was firmly entrenched in Poland, but as it became politically committed, turning from scouting to the extreme Left, Betar, with its emphasis on 'monism' (unadulterated Zionism), gained in strength. Unlike Hashomer Hatzair, it was not elitist but always aspired to be a mass organisation, appealing not only to high school students but to young people in all walks of life.‡ From Poland it spread to many other European countries and also established branches overseas, and of course in Palestine.

Betar wholeheartedly subscribed to Jabotinsky's political doctrine. But it also wanted autonomy; there was little inclination to play second

---

* For the programme of the State Party, see R.Stricker, *Di Judenstaatspartei* (Yiddish), Warsaw, 1935, *passim*.

† Lubotzki, *HaZohar uBetar*, Jerusalem, 1946, p. 11.

‡ The main source for the history of the revisionist youth movement is Ch.Ben Yeruham (ed.), *Sefer Betar*, Tel Aviv, 1969. See also Perelman, *Rewizjonizm w Polsce*, p. 168 *et seq.*

fiddle to the Zohar and to accept party discipline blindly. It always maintained that its loyalty was to Jabotinsky, the head of Betar, and resisted attempts by other politicians to interfere in its internal affairs, let alone to dictate. In later years, after the Irgun had come into being, there were frequent disputes between these two organisations. Betar had thousands of followers in Palestine in the 1930s, but its main base was always in the east European diaspora, and with the destruction of east European Jewry it withered away in Palestine too. Despite its opposition to elitism, the educational values it wished to implant among its members were aristocratic, resembling in some respects the ideals of knighthood and chivalry prevalent in certain sections of the German *Buende* in the 1920s.* Like other Zionist youth movements, it prepared its members for life in Eretz Israel, maintained training farms, and put great emphasis on the study of Hebrew. It differed from them in its insistence on para-military education, with uniforms, solemn processions, military organisation, discipline, and training in the use of light arms.

Betar ideology was profoundly and unashamedly militaristic. Jabotinsky saw no contradiction between his old liberal ideals and an education which was anything but liberal. He wanted to give fresh hope to a generation which was near despair, and he believed that this could be done only by invoking myths – blood and iron and the kingdom of Israel (*malkut Israel*). A Sorelian who may have never read Sorel, he developed his ideas both in his writings for Betar and, most succinctly in his novel *Simson*: all great states fulfilling a civilisatory mission were founded by the sword. Simson the hero tells his people by way of an emissary that they must give everything to get iron: 'There is nothing more valuable in the world than iron.' Simson's people also needed a king to rule them, impose his discipline and make an effective fighting force out of an unruly mob.

One of the central features in Betar ideology was 'Hadar'. This educational ideal (to quote Jabotinsky) could only with difficulty be translated into other languages. It implied outward beauty, respect, self-esteem, politeness and loyalty; it covered cleanliness and tact and quiet speech; it meant, in brief, to be a gentleman.† The stress on military training, leadership, discipline, and the whole ideology of 'conquer or die', gave it a certain similarity to the fascist youth movements of the 1920s and 1930s. Such tendencies did exist, and Betar was frequently attacked on these grounds by its opponents. But it is only fair to add that Jabotinsky's

---

* W.Laqueur, *Young Germany*, London, 1962, p. 133 *et seq.*
† 'Rayon Betar', in *Kitve Z. Jabotinsky, Baderekh lamedina*, Jerusalem, 1941, p. 321.

ideal pattern was not the Italian *Ballila* but the Czech *Sokol*, a democratic mass movement of national liberation.* He was convinced that without systematically inculcating certain manly virtues sadly missing in Jewish life there could be no national revival.

More than other youth movements, Betar practised the cult of leadership. But this was a spontaneous development, not, as in fascism, part and parcel of the official ideology. Jabotinsky did not aspire to be a dictator and on various occasions rejected the 'epidemic dream of a dictator' with scorn and disgust. He told his Palestinian admirers, who wanted to make him *Fuehrer*, that he believed in the great ideas of the nineteenth century, the ideas of Garibaldi and Lincoln, Gladstone and Victor Hugo. The new ideology, according to which freedom led to perdition, that society needed leaders, orders, and a stick, was not for him: 'I don't want this kind of creed', he wrote. 'Better not to live at all than to live under such a system.'† Of the fifth world meeting of the Betar in Vienna he wrote that there was no room in the movement for people for whom the fascist dictatorship had become an integral part of their Weltanschauung.‡ He thought that only a handful of his followers had been infected by the epidemic, and that even with them it was more a matter of fashion and phraseology than of deep-seated belief.

Jewish Fascism?

This interpretation erred in the direction of charity and optimism, for among some of his Palestinian followers dangerous doctrines and practices had grown deeper roots than Jabotinsky wished to recognise. Aba Achimeir, the leading ideologist of Palestinian neo-revisionism, made no secret of the credo of his group: it wanted to break with the spirit of liberalism and democracy which, as he claimed, had ruined Zionism. The Palestinian trend of the revisionist movement which produced these aberrations was founded in 1924. Quite a few of its leaders and ideologists had previously belonged to Socialist parties: Achimeir, Yevin, U.Z.Grinberg, Altman, Weinstein and others had been members of Hapoel Hatzair or Ahdut Avoda. It was in all probability a revolt against their own early beliefs which produced such a violent reaction. The organ of the Palestinian extremists expressed the view that but for Hitler's antisemitism German National-Socialism

---

* *Ibid.*, p. 319.
† *Rassvet*, 18 September 1933.
‡ *Chasit Ha'am*, 7 October 1932, quoted in Schechtman.

would have been acceptable and that, anyway, Hitler had saved Germany.* Even before, in 1932, they had welcomed the great national movement which had saved Europe from impotent parliaments and, above all, from the dictatorship of the Soviet secret police and from civil war.† In Mussolini Achimeir saw the greatest political genius of the century. When Jabotinsky arrived in Palestine Achimeir appealed to him to be 'Duce' – not just the leader of a party.‡ Deeply embarrassed, Jabotinsky rejected the call in no uncertain terms.

The outstanding poet Uri Zvi Grinberg, another ideologist of this group, had begun his career with poems and essays (first in Yiddish, later in Hebrew) in praise of the pioneers; on occasions he had saluted Trotsky and Lenin. Later he came to see in the Socialist movement a most dangerous enemy, and became more and more convinced that a dictator was needed to lead the masses. He accepted the view that to influence public opinion truth alone would not do. He allegedly advised Yevin, a co-ideologist and editor of *Chasit Ha'am*, to accuse the leaders of the Histadrut of having embezzled money because this was likely to make an impression on Jews abroad. Yevin did not need much encouragement. In his novel *Jerusalem is waiting*, Baresha, a leader of the Palestinian labour movement, dreams of Soviet-style concentration camps and of having his enemies executed.§ Zionist leaders were described in this literature as secret agents, British spies, and accused of every possible crime.

It was not surprising that after such a campaign of character assassination suspicion for the murder of Arlosoroff fell on this group. Achimeir, as emerged during the trial, had written an ideological pamphlet for his group (*Megilat Hasikarikin*) which maintained that the judgment of a political crime was a subjective affair. Referring to the actions of the *Sikarikin* (a radical sect during the Jewish war against the Romans who carried a short sword, *sika*, under their clothes and used to kill their political enemies during mass meetings, often escaping in the disorder which ensued), Achimeir wrote that any new order established itself on the bones of its opponents. The *Sikarikin* as he described them were unknown heroes who chose as victims central figures of the established order. They were not murderers, since they were not out for personal

---

* *Ibid.*, 6 May 1932, quoted in Schechtman. On the early history of Palestinian revisionism (such as the *Amlanim* group), Schechtman and Benari, *History of the Revisionist Movement*, pp. 193–217.

† *Chasit Ha'am*, 29 March 1932, quoted in Schechtman.

‡ Y. Nedava, *Jabotinsky bechason hador*, Tel Aviv, 1950, p. 223.

§ *Yerushalayim mechaka*, Tel Aviv, 1932, pp. 9–10.

gain. What mattered was not the action itself but the purpose behind it. On another occasion he wrote that the amount of blood shed was the sole criterion of a revolution.* There were also the usual slogans about great things being achieved by fire and blood only, and about the dangers of moderation in times of supreme crisis.

Achimeir was the leader of a small group of activists called *Brit Habiryonim* (again a reference to an extremist sect in ancient Jewish history), whose exploits were of no great political significance though they attracted a great deal of publicity. The Biryonim interrupted the speeches of pacifist professors at the Hebrew university (such as Norman Bentwich) and organised a boycott against the population census being carried out at the time by the mandatory government.† Its activities and eccentric views are of interest mainly because they served as a source of inspiration to some of the leading figures of the Irgun and the Stern Group; in some ways the Biryonim were their predecessors. But there is no straight line from Achimeir to Raziel, Stern and Begin. Whereas the Biryonim saw the main enemy in the labour movement, and engaged simultaneously in a battle on three or four different fronts, the Irgun and Stern's followers wanted to fight only the outside enemy. The Stern group, moreover, very much in contrast to Achimeir, believed in a Socialism of sorts.

In Achimeir's political thought (as in Stern's), death and sacrifice are cardinal motifs, recurring with monotonous regularity. He was at his most effective in his attacks on 'Marxists', a term which he used to cover virtually everyone to the left of him. But he was essentially a *litterateur*, not a politician, and still less a military leader. He had a few admirers but his impact on the younger generation was strictly limited. In the world as he saw it there was little to hope and live for: men were evil, politics a jungle. It was a picture of almost unrelieved gloom, of crime, betrayal and destruction. Such perspectives were unlikely to capture the imagination of a young generation essentially romantic in inspiration. Achimeir had the courage of his convictions and spent long periods in mandatory prisons until, in the middle 1930s, he dropped out of the active political struggle for personal reasons. The other ideologists of the group were not by nature activists. They followed the political struggle from the sidelines. After Hitler's rise to power the Biryonim

---

* *Davar*, 23 August 1933.

† On the history of this group, see *Brit Habiryonim*, edited by the Jabotinsky Institute, Tel Aviv, 1956; David Nir, op. cit., vol. 1, p. 179 *et seq. Sefer Betar*, vol. 1, pp. 380–2; *Sefer Toldot Hahagana*, vol. 2, p. 493 *et seq.*

were involved in a few anti-Nazi demonstrations (such as tearing down the flag of the German consulate in Jerusalem).

Jabotinsky was ambivalent in his attitude towards the Palestinian zealots. Repeatedly he expressed admiration for their activist spirit and he even called Achimeir – albeit tongue in cheek – *rabenu vemorenu* (our spiritual guide and teacher). At other times the political and psychological differences seemed unbridgeable. Jabotinsky, the aristocrat, resented the style of the Palestinian *sansculottes*, their poisonous personal attacks. He too could write bitingly about 'Ben Bouillon', the boastful Mapai leader, but he was not vindictive by nature, whereas the Palestinians never forgot or forgave. In 1932 he had written to the leaders of the Biryonim that there was no room for them and him in the same movement and that he would leave if their views prevailed.* He deeply resented the attitude of Achimeir and his friends to Nazi Germany, and stated in a letter to one of the editors of their newspaper that the 'articles and notices on Hitler and the Hitlerite movement are to me, and all of us, like a knife thrust into our backs. I demand an unconditional stop to this outrage. To find in Hitlerism some feature of a "national liberation movement" is sheer ignorance. Moreover, and under present circumstances, all this babbling is discrediting and paralysing my work. . . . I demand that the paper joins, unconditionally and absolutely, not merely our campaign against Hitler Germany, but also our hunting down of Hitlerism in the fullest sense of the term.'†

The editors later argued that Jabotinsky had not read the paper regularly and had relied on second-hand reports. They had strong reservations about Jabotinsky's style and his policies, denouncing the 'General Zionist' mentality within the revisionist movement, deriding the petition initiative (on which more below), and referring disparingly to Jabotinsky's lack of decision, lack of courage, and even to his senility. On several occasions they were in open revolt and threatened to leave the revisionist movement. Later on the antagonism lessened, partly because Jabotinsky became personally involved in a running fight with left-wing Zionism during the 1930s, partly because he felt he could not dissociate himself from the Biryonim while these were under arrest on the charge of belonging to an illegal terrorist organisation. Achimeir had been arrested again in 1933 on suspicion of being the spiritual instigator of the plot to kill Arlosoroff. According to an official revisionist source, published many years later, Jabotinsky gave his blessing to all actions of the

---

* In an article on adventurism in *Chasit Ha'am*, 11 March 1932, quoted in Schechtman.
† Letter to Yevin, 14 May 1933, quoted in Schechtman.

Biryonim.* He was willing to find excuses for the 'hotheads'; 'impulsive maximalist tendencies in our movement are understandable and legitimate', he wrote in a private letter. He was opposed only to any organised opposition which would disrupt the party internally and also affect its status as a legal movement.†

In his attitude towards the fascist aberrations of some of his followers, the tendency to belittle what was unforgivable, Jabotinsky showed that he was not wholly free of opportunism. The tergiversations in his approach to religion point to a similar inclination. He had grown up in the liberal-rationalist tradition, a fervent believer in freedom of thought. The supreme value was always secular European civilisation, of which, as he once wrote, the Jews had been the co-authors. He bitterly criticised the baneful impact of organised religion in recent Jewish history which had impeded the pursuit of scientific study, detrimentally affected the position of women in society, and in general interfered far too much in daily life.‡ In 1931 he wrote to a colleague that the movement would never swallow the smallest dose of (religious) traditionalism.

But in 1935 he decided to introduce a quasi religious plank into the revisionist constitution. He had rediscovered, as it were, the sacred treasures of Jewish tradition. Indifferent tolerance was no longer enough; he even mentioned the necessity of a synthesis between nationalism and religion. His explanations for this sudden turnabout are unconvincing; this was not a case of sudden conversion. However vehemently he denied it, Jabotinsky's real intention was to gain the support of orthodox-religious circles in eastern Europe. Perhaps the stand taken by Rabbi Kook, the spiritual head of the Ashkenazi community in Palestine, in defence of the Biryonim, under attack at the time of the Arlosoroff crisis, influenced him. Perhaps, as his biographer says, Jabotinsky felt that secular impulses were insufficient to generate and maintain moral integrity in a nation.§ Be that as it may, basically it was a tactical move lacking inner conviction. The opening towards organised religion was quite popular within the revisionist movement, but it undermined its ideological basis, for Socialism could no longer be plausibly rejected in the name of 'monism' while the revisionists compromised with the religious establishment.

---

* *Brit Habiryonim*, p. 9.
† Schechtman, *Fighter and Prophet*, p. 441.
‡ His answer to J.Klausner in *Rassvet* 26 September 1926.
§ Schechtman, *Fighter and Prophet*, p. 290.

The Petition

When the revisionist movement split, Jabotinsky was committed to attend the eighteenth Zionist congress. He even seems to have expected that it would accept his political programme which had earlier been rejected. There was in fact little ground for such optimism. The congress was held shortly after the Arlosoroff murder. It was dominated by Labour Zionism and the revisionists found themselves ostracised. The Left refused to sit with them on the executive and their entire delegation walked out whenever a revisionist speaker appeared on the rostrum. It was a humiliating experience, on which Jabotinsky later commented with great bitterness: it showed that official Zionism was finished and that it could no longer be regenerated from within. But he did not immediately press for the establishment of an independent organisation. The year 1934 was devoted to the big signature campaign sponsored by the revisionist movement: some 600,000 signatures were collected for an appeal to the governments of all civilised states drawing attention to the plight of Jews in Europe and to the demand that the gates of Palestine should be opened to mass immigration. Those signing it declared that only by emigrating to Palestine could they rebuild their life and that of their families. The Zionist executive sharply denounced the petition campaign as yet another revisionist public relations stunt, devoid of any political significance, intended to increase their popularity in the Jewish communities of eastern Europe, and raising false hopes. Jabotinsky was charged, not for the first time, with a flagrant breach of Zionist discipline.

It was not, however, the petition campaign alone which triggered off the chain reaction that led to the final break and the establishment of the New Zionist Organisation. In October 1933 the leadership of Betar sent a new circular ('No. 60') to its members instructing those who wanted to emigrate not to do so in collaboration with the Jewish Agency, claiming that it had been discriminated against. Betar was to negotiate directly with employers in Palestine, who were entitled under the established immigration regulations to invite workers from abroad. The official explanation given by the revisionists was that this was a protest demonstration against the mandatory government, which in October 1933 had allocated to the Jewish Agency only 5,500 entry permits for six months, as against the 24,700 asked for. But when circular 'No. 60' became known, the Jewish Agency interpreted Betar policy in a very different light, namely as an act of sabotage and an attempt to break Zionist solidarity. In March 1934 instructions were sent out to all Jewish

Agency immigration offices to give no more permits to members of Betar under the labour schedule. The revisionists reacted by boycotting the Jewish National Fund, and launched instead a fund of their own, 'Tel Hai'.* Violent clashes were reported from many Jewish communities between members of Betar and the Socialist youth movements. There had been a major incident in Tel Aviv, on the last day of Passover 1933, when a Betar parade had been attacked. There were many more such clashes during the following years.

The situation was further aggravated when the revisionists decided, at their fifth world conference in August 1932, to establish their own National Labour Federation. In a widely quoted article ('Yes – to break!') Jabotinsky justified the decision.† He did not want to minimise the role of labour in Eretz Israel, nor did he have any quarrel with the Socialist ideal. But the monopoly of the Histadrut and its privileged status had to be broken. The class struggle, which Zionism could ill afford, was to be replaced by a national system of arbitration. The Revisionist Labour Federation was founded in spring 1934. Its activities were attacked by the Histadrut, which regarded them as systematic and dangerous strike-breaking on a massive scale which had to be fought tooth and nail. Jabotinsky's decision was not welcomed by some of his followers, who regarded the conflict which was bound to ensue as unnecessary, harmful both for the revisionist movement and for Zionism in general. They predicted, quite correctly, that as a result of establishing a separate trade union movement, revisionism would be identified in the public mind with the employers and their interests, and thus lose much of its popular appeal.

Jabotinsky was not impressed by these arguments. Whatever he might say publicly, he had no illusions about winning a substantial following among the Left. 'Don't delude yourself,' he told Schechtman in a private conversation. 'Though many workers are tempted to accept our programme, our true field is the middle class. We will never be able to come to terms with people who possess, in addition to Zionism, another ideal, namely Socialism.'‡ His views in this respect had undergone substantial change; he was now a bourgeois and proud to be one. Writing in 1927, he explained that 'we don't have to be ashamed, my bourgeois comrades'. The cult of the proletariat as the only carrier of progress was misplaced. The future was with the bourgeoisie, if it would but discard its spineless

* *Judenstaat*, 30 March 1934.
† *Haint*, 4 November 1932.
‡ Schechtman, *Fighter and Prophet*, p. 233.

behaviour and its inferiority complex. The lofty principles of liberty, equality, and fraternity, 'now upheld primarily by the classless intelligentsia', were first proclaimed by the bourgeoisie, which even at the present time was the main guarantor against the establishment of a super police state.*

While praising the virtues of the middle class, Jabotinsky asserted that the class struggle had no *raison d'être* in Zionism. The Left countered by calling him a Jewish fascist. This did not unduly bother Jabotinsky, who enjoyed a fight. Nor was he greatly worried when Ben Gurion called him Vladimir Hitler. Labels such as 'fascism' and 'Hitler' did not at that time have all the sinister connotations of later years. But in 1934, after the foundation of the Revisionist Labour Union, the conflict seemed to get out of hand. There were too many acts of violence for anyone's comfort. In October, on the initiative of Pinhas Rutenberg, founder and director of the Palestine Electric Corp., Jabotinsky met Ben Gurion in London. Despite the wide divergences in their political views, the two men had a certain admiration for each other. They came to understand and even to like each other as the result of these meetings. Ben Gurion addressed Jabotinsky in a letter as 'friend', and Jabotinsky in his reply said that he was deeply moved by these warm words, that perhaps it was his fault that he had long forgotten this kind of language.† An agreement was worked out and initialled providing for a *modus vivendi* between the sixty thousand members of the Histadrut and the seven thousand belonging to the Revisionist Union. Acts of violence as well as libels and insults were to be banned. The revisionists were to suspend their boycott of the national funds and the Betar was again to obtain immigration certificates through the Jewish Agency. Even more ambitiously, the understanding provided for the return of the revisionists to the Zionist organisation at a later stage, and their representation on the executive.

But though the two leaders had found a common language, their movements did not. There was strong resistance from the revisionists, especially, as expected, from the Palestinians and the Betar. At a meeting in Cracow in February 1935 the revisionists announced that they would insist on the right of independent political action whatever the Zionist Organisation decided. The Histadrut membership rejected the agreement in a referendum by a small majority in March 1935. The Zionist executive decided the same month on yet another step bound to antagonise the revisionists. Internal discipline was to be strengthened:

---

* 'We, the Bourgeois', in *Rassvet*, 17 April 1927.
† Schechtman, *Fighter and Prophet*, p. 249.

the yearly payment of the shekel and the acceptance of the Basle Programme would no longer suffice. Every Zionist would have to accept as binding the decisions of the leading bodies of the Zionist movement. After the failure of the talks between Jabotinsky and Ben Gurion, complete secession was a foregone conclusion, and it came almost as an anticlimax when in April 1935 the revisionist executive decided to form an independent world organisation. Among the leadership there was still some opposition, but in a plebiscite held in June of that year 167,000 revisionists voted in favour and only 3,000 against. Jabotinsky faced this decision with an untroubled conscience. For him the old Herzlian Zionist organisation was dead, and the Socialist-dominated Jewish Agency would have in future to negotiate with him and his movement as equals. The foundation congress of the New Zionist Organisation took place in September 1935; 713,000 voters in thirty-two countries dispatched delegates, more than had participated in the elections to the Zionist congress. True, there was no way of checking these figures, and Jabotinsky, moreover, had made it rather easy for his supporters to collect signatures; it was not even necessary to pay a nominal membership fee, such as the shekel, a short declaration of sympathy being sufficient. But even if the official figures were inflated – Jabotinsky originally aimed at a million – there could be no doubt that there was impressive support for him, especially in Poland and other east European countries, and not just among simple unsophisticated people willing to give their blessing to anyone promising them salvation; it was especially marked among the young generation and the intelligentsia.* For as the world situation deteriorated, there was growing impatience among all sections of the Jewish communities, and if Weizmann's backstage diplomacy had not worked, Jabotinsky ought to be given a chance.

Jabotinsky's foreign policy

Thus in 1935, at long last, Jabotinsky had his own New Zionist Organisation of which he was the undisputed leader. Headquarters were established in London. Jabotinsky travelled on behalf of his movement to many countries, addressed enthusiastic audiences, gave newspaper interviews, established contact with the mandates commission of the League of Nations. There were meetings with presidents, ministers, and members of parliament, and in some capitals, notably in eastern Europe, the

---

* On the support given to the revisionists in Poland, see I.Remba, 'Hatnua harevisionistit', in *Encyclopaedia shel galuyot*, Warsaw, Tel Aviv, 1959, vol. 6, p. 185 *et seq.*

revisionist movement encountered much goodwill, for reasons presently to be discussed. But it was not at all clear where these activities were leading. For years Jabotinsky had complained that his hands were tied. Now he had full freedom of action, and his movement was even gaining international recognition. While he had been the leader of the opposition it had been Jabotinsky's privilege to criticise the official Zionist leadership for its lack of ideas and success. Now, criticism was no longer enough. He was expected to provide a real alternative, to succeed where the official Zionist movement had failed. It was the hour of *hic Rhodus, hic salta* – the test of leadership.

These were the years of the royal commission and the partition plan. Jabotinsky was called to give evidence before the commission in February 1937 and he delivered a forceful statement of his policy. The position of east European Jewry, he said, was a disaster of historic magnitude. Millions, many millions of Jews had to be saved. They wanted a state because this was the normal condition for a people. Even the smallest and the humblest nations, who did not claim any merit, any role in humanity's development, had states of their own. Yet when Zionism asked for the same on behalf of the most unfortunate of all peoples, it was said that it was claiming too much. The Arabs, it was said, would become a minority in the Jewish state. But why should this be regarded as a hardship? The Arabs already had several national states:

One fraction, one branch of that race, and not a big one, will have to live in someone else's state. Well, that is the case with all the mightiest nations of the world. I could hardly mention one of the big nations, having their states, mighty and powerful, who had not one branch in someone else's state . . . it is quite understandable that the Arabs of Palestine would also prefer Palestine to be the Arab state No. 4, No. 5, or No. 6. . . . But when the Arab claim is confronted with our Jewish demand to be saved, it is like the claims of appetite versus the claim of starvation.*

Jabotinsky said that he believed in Britain, as he had done twenty years earlier. But if Britain could not live up to its obligations under the mandate, 'we will sit down together and think what can be done'. He claimed that the Jewish Agency represented neither the whole nor even the majority of Zionist Jewry, but he refrained from discussing internal Zionist differences until asked to do so by members of the commission. It was a powerful performance, but the case he made did not differ greatly from the views expressed by other Zionist leaders. He accused Weizmann

* *Evidence submitted to the Palestine Royal Commission by Mr V. Jabotinsky, 11 February, 1937.*

of willingness to sacrifice 'nine-tenths of the Jewish national territory'.
The majority resolution of the twentieth Zionist congress was in his eyes
a 'betrayal', though it did no more than empower the executive to enter
into negotiations with the British government to ascertain the precise
terms for the proposed establishment of a Jewish state. Jabotinsky was
confident that the partition scheme would come to naught, and its final
abandonment by the British government in November 1937 justified his
prediction. But little was gained in political terms by the revisionist
campaign against partition. They were not alone in their opposition.
Many members of other Zionist parties, including the extreme Left
(though for very different reasons) had also been against it and denounced
it no less vigorously. But the rejection of the scheme solved nothing. The
impasse with regard to the future of Palestine was not broken, while the
situation of east European Jewry further deteriorated as Nazi power
continued to expand.

Several years earlier, Jabotinsky had called for a 'change of orientation'
and for a time he seems to have played with the idea of establishing closer
links with other countries. But his main aim was, as he wrote in a letter,
'to make England apprehensive about Jewish allegiances'.* There is no
evidence that he intended to offer the mandate to Mussolini in 1932 or
that Mussolini would have shown any interest. Later, Italy became more
actively engaged in Mediterranean politics and there was not the slightest
hope that any advances on the part of revisionist circles would have
succeeded; in fact Jabotinsky advised strongly against contacts with
Rome, as suggested in 1937 by some of his followers. The year before, the
New Zionist Organisation had outlined a scheme for the settlement of
one and a half million Jews in Palestine over a period of ten years.† This
plan resembled Max Nordau's old project (of 1918–19) for the settlement
of six hundred thousand Jews in the shortest possible time. The revisionist
plan underwent several modifications. After the outbreak of the Second
World War Jabotinsky reformulated it as follows: the whole exodus was
to take about ten years; the first million settlers were to be transferred
within the first year or less; all planning was to be done during the war,
so that work could start on the morrow of the peace conference.‡

The reasoning in support of his scheme was briefly this: antisemitism
in eastern Europe was endemic and incurable. Quite apart from the
'antisemitism of men', there was the 'antisemitism of things'; objective

---

* Quoted in Schechtman, *Fighter and Prophet*, p. 295.
† *The Ten Year Plan for Palestine*, London, 1938.
‡ V. Jabotinsky, *The Jewish War Front*, London, 1940, p. 189.

realities in central and eastern Europe were inherently and organically hostile to a scattered minority. The policy of governments could affect this trend, i.e. increase the hardship to a certain extent, but basically the ghettoes of east-central Europe were doomed: 'No government, no régime, no angel or devil could have transformed it into anything even remotely approaching a normal homeland.'* He first advanced the idea of the evacuation scheme in 1935. It attracted some attention the following summer, after several newspaper articles and press conferences, and stirred up a major storm among the Jewish public. To some it gave fresh hope. In November 1936 a few hundred Polish Jews, without passports, visas or money, began to march on foot from Warsaw to Palestine. Their sole equipment for this pilgrimage was a commander-in-chief, uniforms, flags, and the rallying cry 'Israel Awake'. The march ended a few miles outside Warsaw.

Jabotinsky was accused of playing into the hands of the antisemites, of aiming at a bargain with the Polish government to help them get rid of their 'surplus Jews'.† He was charged with jeopardising the civic status of the Jews in eastern Europe, whitewashing antisemitic governments, without at the same time offering any real practical solution. For even if he were somehow miraculously to succeed in transplanting one million Jews from Poland, there would still be nearly three million left in Poland (allowing for natural increase over the ten years), compared with three and a half million in 1936, thus leaving the Jewish problem substantially unaffected. But Jabotinsky was not impressed by the charges levelled against him. Herzl, too, had been an advocate of evacuation and had been ridiculed for it. He compared the situation of the Jews to that of a village at the foot of a volcano menaced by an eruption. The lava was there, it was rapidly coming nearer, something had to be done immediately. It was not intended that the Jews should be forcibly expelled, they would leave of their own free will. To the editors of a Jewish newspaper in Warsaw which had published his articles for many years but now attacked his scheme editorially, he said in a farewell message: 'I regret that you do not see the dark clouds that are gathering over the heads of the Jews in Europe.'‡

Jabotinsky set energetically to work to promote his scheme. He was received by the prime minister of Poland, Slawoy-Skladkowsky, by

---

* *Ibid.*, pp. 55–7.
† *The Futility of Revisionism*, London, n.d., p. 9; *Revisionism a Destructive Force*, New York, 1940, p. 3 *et seq.*
‡ Schechtman, *Fighter and Prophet*, p. 340.

Colonel Beck, the foreign minister, by Marshal Rydz-Smigly, Poland's strong man. They all promised their support. King Carol of Rumania received him, so did Benes, the president of Czechoslovakia, Smetona, the president of Lithuania, Munters, the foreign minister of Latvia. He talked to de Valera, the Irish president, and to Francis Biddle, the American ambassador. All assured him of their goodwill, but unfortunately none of them had any influence as far as the future of Palestine was concerned. Despite all setbacks, Jabotinsky believed that the strategy of indirect approach would ultimately succeed. Elemental floods would soon break over the heads of all east European Jewry, so terribly powerful that even the German catastrophe would be eclipsed. As a result, a Jewish majority in Palestine would emerge overnight. The march of events was so ordained by God himself that it would end in a Jewish state 'independently of what we Jews do or do not do'.* Right up to September 1939, he was certain that there would be no war: the crisis would subside, the Italians would again make friends with Britain, and in five years there would be a Jewish state. When war did break out, Jabotinsky resumed his attempts to set up a Jewish army, but the scheme was doomed from the outset. East European Jewry, the one potential reservoir of manpower, was under Nazi occupation and, as he wrote, there was little to expect from the ghettoes of Mayfair and the Faubourg St Honoré.

Jabotinsky's last years were a period of tragic futility and defeat. The situation of European Jewry was steadily worsening, and he could do no more about it than any other Jewish leader. He had made great promises and it now appeared that he, too, had no effective alternative. There were desultory moves designed to bring about a reconciliation with the Zionist movement. Meetings took place with Weizmann, Berl Katznelson and Golomb, but nothing substantial came of them. Within the revisionist movement there were ominous signs of disintegration; as it failed to make progress internal dissension spread in its ranks. In January 1938 leading officers of Betar turned against the members of their own executive, claiming that these still believed in a pro-British orientation. At the revisionist congress in Prague in March 1938 there was a sharp conflict between the Palestinian delegation and those from abroad. Schechtman, who had been involved in negotiations with the Zionist movement, was not re-elected. Irgun, originally little more than a branch of revisionism, became increasingly independent in its actions and policy. Some of its leaders no longer felt bound by directives from the

* *Ibid.*, p. 352.

party leaders or even from Jabotinsky personally. Jabotinsky, for tactical reasons, had always stressed the independence of Irgun in talks with outsiders. As far as specific military actions were concerned he did not even want to be consulted; 'Don't ask father' (*Man fregt nit den Taten*), he once told Begin, when the future leader of Irgun wanted to receive instructions. The Irgun leaders began to take such advice literally: father was not to be bothered. By the late 1930s revisionism as a political movement had spent most of its force and lost much of its importance. Irgun, on the other hand, became a factor of some significance in the Palestinian Jewish community.

Armed struggle

Irgun (IZL – *Irgun Zvai Leumi*, National Military Organisation) had been founded in 1931 under the name Hagana B, when a majority of Jerusalem Hagana commanders and rank and file left the Jewish defence force and established an independent organisation. They were joined by branches in Safed, Haifa and Tel Aviv and there was an informal agreement with Betar and Maccabi (the countrywide sports club) for the recruitment of new members.* Political and personal differences played a role in this split but there were other causes as well. The Arab attacks of 1929 had revealed serious shortcomings in Jewish self-defence and this gave rise to bitter disputes. Hagana B was not part of the revisionist movement; on its executive various right of centre parties (including the non-Zionist Agudat Israel) were represented. But *de facto* power lay with the revisionists, who provided most of the officers as well as the rank and file. Its commander, Abraham Tehomi, was not however a party man and did not owe his appointment to Jabotinsky. During the first years of its existence, Irgun was small, had few weapons and hardly any money. In 1933–4, after the murder of Arlosoroff, the polarisation in the Palestinian Jewish community brought many new recruits to Irgun. Young men of middle class background joined, more branches were founded in rural settlements, and new immigrants swelled the ranks.

After the outbreak of the 1936 riots, Hagana advised against acts of retaliation. In Irgun, counsels were divided. Tehomi (and Jabotinsky) were also opposed to counter-terror, but many junior commanders disagreed and engaged in such actions without the permission of the central command.† Tehomi, moreover, had by that time reached the conclusion

---

* D.Nir, *Ma'arakhot hairgun hazvai haleumi*, Tel Aviv, 1965, vol. 1, p. 156, *et seq.*
† *Ibid.*, p. 268 *et seq.*; *Sefer Toldot hahagana*, Tel Aviv, 1964, vol. 2, p. 722 *et seq.*

that there was no room for two separate Jewish defence organisations at a time of national emergency. When Hagana suggested reunification, he agreed, and was supported by most of his non-revisionist backers. Jabotinsky and his disciples, on the other hand, opposed the scheme. In April 1937 the organisation split, following a vote on whether to rejoin Hagana. About one-half, or slightly less, of its three thousand members followed Tehomi back into Hagana, the rest continuing to exist as a separate para-military force under the command of Robert Bitker and later of Moshe Rosenberg and David Raziel. Irgun, in theory at least, put much greater stress on military discipline than the Hagana, which as befitting a militia was more loosely organised. But in fact there was an almost constant tug-of-war within Irgun and there was pressure and counter-pressure on the supreme command from the local branches. The issue came to a head as opposition to the official policy of non-reaction (*havlaga*) grew. Individual Irgun units, in response to the killing of Jews, began to attack Arabs passing through Jewish quarters. There was also indiscriminate bomb throwing in Arab markets and at bus stations. While such acts of retaliation were not too risky, they were quite ineffective. They did no harm to those who had been responsible for taking Jewish lives, and they failed to stop the Arab terror.

Jabotinsky was unhappy about the murder of Arab women and children and asked the Irgun leaders to warn the Arabs in time for them to evacuate the areas that were to be attacked. The Irgun commanders replied that such warnings could not be given without endangering the success of the attacks and the lives of those engaged in them.* After the execution of Ben Yosef, a young Irgun fighter who had been sentenced to death by a British military court, the number of Irgun attacks on Arab civilians rose. When Irgun ambushed and killed a Jew in Haifa whom they had mistaken for an Arab, the assailant was arrested by the Hagana. Irgun retaliated by kidnapping a Hagana member. Faced by the possibility of a Jewish civil war, emergency talks were held between the commanders of the rival bodies, but Ben Gurion refused to compromise. He maintained that there could be no partial agreement on defence so long as the revisionists did not accept Zionist discipline on major policy decisions. Negotiations were renewed after Jabotinsky's death but with no more success. Many Hagana members were strongly against any form of cooperation with Irgun, which they regarded as an adventurist and wholly destructive force; if so, they should have tried to bring Irgun

---

* Schechtman, *Fighter and Prophet*, p. 453.

under their control by either absorbing or breaking it. But the Hagana command, unwilling to compromise, and probably too weak for a full-scale showdown, continued its irresolute policy.*

When the Second World War broke out Raziel and other leading Irgun commanders, who had been arrested shortly before, were released following undertakings given by Jabotinsky. The revisionist leader had announced that for the duration of the conflict world Jewry would forget its grievances against the British administration and join the war effort against the Axis powers. This declaration precipitated a crisis which had been brewing in Irgun for some time. While most of its members accepted the Jabotinsky line, albeit with some reluctance, and enlisted in the British Army or at any rate abstained from acts of hostility against the British, a minority rejected it. This group was headed by Abraham Stern, for years one of the central figures in Irgun, who believed that Britain, not Germany and Italy, was the main enemy. Consequently he refused to stop the fight against the mandatory power.† Unlike Irgun, the 'Stern gang' did not regard the Arabs as a danger to Zionist aspirations, some even viewing them as potential allies in the struggle for national liberation.

The split in Irgun occurred in the first half of 1940. It did not come altogether as a surprise, for the attitude towards Britain was not the only issue at stake. For several years previously Stern had pursued a policy assigned to detach Irgun from revisionism. He had represented his organisation in Poland in 1938–9, organising the training of selected members with the help of the Polish Army. Stern had purchased arms for his group and helped to establish newspapers in Yiddish and Polish to promote his policy, irrespective of revisionist policy and party discipline. He also tried to take over the organisation of illegal immigration which had hitherto been in the hands of others. Stern made no secret of the fact that he thought little of Jabotinsky. At a press conference arranged by him and his group Jabotinsky was referred to as an 'ex-activist leader' who had become soft and complacent.‡ Stern and his friends had lost all faith in diplomatic action. Their radicalism stemmed from a burning belief in 'direct action' on the one hand and massive political ignorance on the other, a combination which led them to adopt a policy so obviously suicidal. In some ways Stern's attitude was like Achimeir's, but for Achimeir in 1939 the main enemy was still Mapai whereas for Stern it

* Y.Bauer, *Diplomatia vemahteret*, Merhavia, 1963, p. 115.
† See Y.S.Brenner, 'The "Stern gang" 1940–8', in *Middle Eastern Studies*, October 1965.
‡ Schechtman, *Fighter and Prophet*, p. 460.

IN BLOOD AND FIRE

was Britain.* In Stern's strategy, as in his poems, a strong death wish can be detected.

Jabotinsky was deeply disturbed by these developments. He regarded Stern's policy as fatally mistaken in its rejection of political action: it was 'Weizmannism in reverse'. A few days before his death in August 1940, Jabotinsky cabled Raziel to resume the leadership of Irgun, from which he had resigned under pressure from below. Stern refused to obey and seceded. With some followers he set up the National Military Organisation in Israel (the name was later changed into Israeli Freedom Fighters – *Lehi*). Irgun activities were suspended as from November 1940, and their activities ceased until early 1944 when they resumed their attacks on the British after Menahem Begin had taken command. Stern and his handful of followers, on the other hand, continued the armed struggle throughout the war. Their activities caused the British authorities little concern, since their targets were usually Jewish banks, and the victims in these and other incidents were mainly Jews. In February 1942 Stern was shot after having been arrested; according to his captors he had tried to escape. Most of his followers were also caught, and for two years Lehi was inactive. It again made the headlines with the murder in November 1944 of Lord Moyne, the British minister resident in Cairo.

A detailed review of the subsequent history of Irgun and Lehi after that date is beyond the scope of the present study, but certain ideological differences between the two groups emerging from revisionism should be mentioned in passing. While Irgun remained faithful to the Jabotinsky tradition, Lehi developed a doctrine of its own, highly original inasmuch as it tried to embrace elements that were mutually exclusive. It combined a mystical belief in a greater Israel with support for the Arab liberation struggle. In its foreign political orientation enmity towards Britain was the one consistent factor; after 1942 it displayed pro-Soviet sympathies. In contrast to Irgun, the Sternists regarded themselves as 'revolutionary Socialists', believing that the best way to gain the support of the Soviet Union was to take an active part in the liberation of the whole Middle East from the imperialist yoke.† They advocated a planned economy, opposed strike-breaking, and adopted the slogan of a Socialist Hebrew state.‡ This ideological transformation was not altogether unique. In neighbouring Arab countries, notably Egypt and Syria, groups of young

* On Stern, see Y.Weinshal, *Hadam asher basaf*, Tel Aviv, 1956, *passim*.

† *Lehi. Ktavim*, Tel Aviv, vol. 2., p. 714 and *passim*; on Lehi ideology, see also Eldad in *Sulam*, Tevet, 1962, p. 46.

‡ See Miriam Getter's unpublished M.A. dissertation, *The Ideology of 'Lehi'* (in Hebrew), Tel Aviv, 1967, p. 79 *et seq.*

intellectuals and officers, who up to 1942–3 had gravitated towards fascism and had believed in an Axis victory, later on transferred their political sympathies to the Soviet Union and subscribed to a Socialism of sorts.

Both Irgun and Lehi were dissolved after the establishment of the state of Israel. Most Irgun members found their way into the Revisionist Party, which had continued to exist even though it lost much of its momentum after Jabotinsky's death. The Revisionist Party became Herut which later merged with other right-wing groups, still 'activist' in its foreign political orientation, on the whole a conservative force, representing the interests of private enterprise as opposed to the Histadrut sector. The subsequent fate of the members of Lehi, the smaller of the two groups, was more checkered. Some veered for a while towards 'National Communism', others continued to propagate the idea of a 'Greater Israel'. A few reached the conclusion that a reconciliation with the Arabs was the most important political task, even if it meant giving up the tenets and aims of traditional Zionism.

The anarchist from Odessa

The history of revisionism ends, strictly speaking, with the death of the leader, for Jabotinsky, as his biographer says, *was* the revisionist movement. It had no one else of remotely comparable stature and Jabotinsky apparently never gave a thought to what would happen after his death. It is said that he could not suffer contradiction, especially in his later years, and that he was surrounded by a group of admiring mediocrities. Others have asserted that such an assessment is not altogether fair, for Jabotinsky valued most those qualities in his closest followers which he himself lacked: organisational talent and a capacity for fund raising. He preferred 'practical men' – there was no lack of speakers, propagandists, and 'all-round' politicians.

Weizmann has drawn a shrewd if unsympathetic and somewhat patronising portrait of Jabotinsky, whom he first met at the early Zionist congresses:

Jabotinsky, the passionate Zionist, was utterly un-Jewish in manner, approach and deportment. He came from Odessa, Ahad Ha'am's home town, but the inner life of Jewry had left no trace on him. When I became intimate with him in later years, I observed at closer hand what seemed to be a confirmation of this dual streak; he was rather ugly, immensely attractive, well spoken, warm-hearted, generous, always ready to help a comrade in distress; all of those qualities were however overlaid with a certain touch of the rather theatrically chivalresque, a certain queer and irrelevant knightliness, which was not at all Jewish.*

Ben Gurion, who fought many a bitter battle with Jabotinsky, was fascinated by the 'wholesomeness' of his antagonist's personality. 'There was in him complete internal spiritual freedom; he had nothing in him of the Galut Jew and he was never embarrassed in the presence of a Gentile.'†

There is no denying that Jabotinsky lacked certain qualities believed to be Jewish, and at the same time put great stress on others. The result must have appeared incongruous to those of his contemporaries who grew up in the Yiddish-speaking small town *milieu*. In this he resembled Herzl and Nordau, who also remained outsiders all their life in relation to east European Jewry. He lacked Herzl's stature and majestic bearing, but shared with him his great belief in outward form, manners, ceremony. Like Herzl, he was a strong individualist, a believer in aristocratic liberalism. Better than Herzl he understood the necessity of a mass movement; like him he believed in the importance of leadership, and of course in his own mission to lead the masses. Certain striking similarities between Herzl and Lassalle, the German Socialist leader of Jewish origin, have been noted. Jabotinsky, too, seems to have been fascinated by Lassalle. It cannot be mere coincidence that he knew Lasalle's literary writings by heart. These had never been thought to have great merit, and none but a few German experts in the history of Socialism knew of them. In a conversation in the 1930s with a Polish Foreign Ministry official the question came up whether reason or the sword ruled human destiny. Jabotinsky quoted Lassalle's *Franz von Sickingen*‡ to the effect that all that is great, owes, in the end, its triumph to the sword.

It was the flamboyant, romantic, sentimental element in Lassalle and in Jabotinsky that influenced their political style and led them beyond liberalism: the one towards Socialism, the other towards Zionist activism. At the same time both were deeply rooted in the traditions of liberalism and rationalism: Jabotinsky's Zionism was, in fact, anything but romantic. As a young man he had written that his belief in Palestine was not a blind, half-mystical sentiment, but the result of a dispassionate study of the essence of Jewish history and the Zionist movement. The link

---

* Weizmann, *Trial and Error*, p. 63.
† Quoted in Schechtman, *Fighter and Prophet*, p. 248.
‡ *Ibid.*, p. 477.

with Zion was based on more than a powerful instinct; it was the legitimate outcome of rational analysis. To that extent Jabotinsky's conversion to Zionism resembles that of Herzl and Nordau, who had come to the conclusion that the Jews needed a national movement not because they had suddenly heard the call of an inner voice previously suppressed, but because they were confronted with the situation of the Jews in the modern world and realised the need for an immediate solution. Nordau, in a speech in Paris in 1914, emphatically dissociated himself from Zionist mysticism: 'I cherish the hope of some day seeing in Palestine a new Jewish national life. Otherwise I would have only an archaeological interest in that country.'* Herzl showed at the time of the Uganda debate that in his view the solution of the social and political question, the normalisation of Jewish life in an independent state, had higher priority than Zionism *tout court*.

Facing a similar situation, there is little doubt that Jabotinsky would not have reacted in a different way. In this he would have found it as difficult as Herzl, had the dilemma arisen, to persuade his contemporaries. For most of them Zionism was not so much a logical conclusion as an emotional necessity. Like Herzl, Jabotinsky sensed that the masses of east European Jewry, downtrodden and persecuted, needed a message to sustain their faith. Hence his insistence on national symbols and heraldry. He must have thought of Garibaldi when in August 1939 according to one source he played with the idea of an illegal landing in Palestine. This, he imagined, may well turn out to be the signal for an armed revolt in the course of which Government House in Jerusalem would be seized. He anticipated that the revolt would be quickly suppressed, but the provisional government of the Jewish state proclaimed during its shortlived existence would continue to function in exile.

It has been the custom among his admirers and friends to compare Jabotinsky with Garibaldi.† His Zionism was influenced by what he knew about the *risorgimento*, a movement for national liberation which, while democratic and popular in character, did not reject armed force since it knew that it would not attain its aim by gradual, peaceful change. Garibaldi had various imitators, not all of them wholly admirable – it would have been interesting to know what Jabotinsky made of D'Annunzio and his exploits. But Jabotinsky's romanticism was by no means all pervasive; his policies, however mistaken, usually had a rational kernel, though he often erred in his appraisal of situations and

* *Die Welt*, 3 April 1914.
† Y.Nedava, *Jabotinsky bechason hador*, Tel Aviv, 1940, *passim*.

men. It is not at all clear in retrospect why he had to leave the Zionist Organisation if he believed that in the last resort diplomatic, not military action would be decisive. The fight against labour Zionism into which he was drawn appears with the benefit of hindsight unnecessary, even self-defeating. Was it inevitable that anti-Socialism should become part of his ideological platform? As a young man he was far more sympathetic towards Socialism than, for instance, Weizmann, who referred to it in the most contemptuous terms, with all the disdain of a young intellectual influenced by Nietzsche.

It is difficult to explain this break in his views without reference to his Russian background, in which he was rooted to a much greater extent than Weizmann, and to the impact of the revolution of 1917. Jabotinsky and his friends regarded the Soviet revolution as a great disaster and the source of most of the evils in the subsequent history of mankind, in particular with regard to the fate of the Jewish people. It was not just that they had been personally affected, for Jabotinsky, for one, had few earthly possessions, and leaving Russia in 1914 he may not have intended to return there anyway. But as a result of the revolution Russian Jewry had been severed from the main body of world Jewry and had ceased to play a part in the Zionist movement. Above all, Russian Bolshevism triggered off counter-movements all over Europe. To put it in the simplest terms: without Bolshevism there would have been no Hitler – and without Hitler no Second World War and no holocaust. The Russian cataclysm and the opposition to Bolshevism explain Jabotinsky's rejection of Socialism. Any form of Socialism if radically pursued would lead to a dictatorship and thus to results similar to those witnessed in Russia.

Sections of the revisionist movement were strongly influenced by the advent of authoritarian movements in the 1920s and 1930s. The fact that Jews were often victims of fascism did not necessarily make them immune to fascist influences. Revisionism believed in strength – in a sinful world only the strong were likely to get what was due to them. This manifested itself in the ideology of Betar, particularly the cult of militarism with all its antics – the parades, the stress on uniforms, banners, insignia. To a certain extent all political movements of the 1920s and 1930s were influenced by the *Zeitgeist*. This all too often led to moral relativism, to deriding democracy, to aggression and brutality, and belief in an omnipotent, omniscient leader. In the leader of the revisionist movement the similarities to fascism were more apparent than real. The basic tenet of fascism was the negation of liberalism, whereas Jabotinsky to the end of his life remained a confirmed liberal, or, to be precise, a liberal anarchist. One of his followers once told him to his face that the movement would never be in good shape so long as it was headed 'by an anarchist from Odessa'.* Jabotinsky had no use for the idea of the totalitarian state, dictatorship, suppression of political enemies, and though he was not free of vanity he did not believe in the leadership principle. True, he was at one and the same time head of Zohar and Betar, and, in theory at any rate, the supreme commander of Irgun. But he was expressing his genuine belief when he wrote about himself that 'I am just the opposite [of a fascist]: an instinctive hater of all kinds of *Polizei Staat*, utterly sceptical of the value of discipline and power and punishment, etc. down to a planned economy.' Far-fetched as the comparison may seem, he resembled the New Left, inasmuch as he was a liberal who had lost patience partly because he was innately an impatient man, partly because he sensed that the Jewish people faced a great catastrophe (though he too underrated its magnitude) and that no time was to be lost.

Jabotinsky, however much one may dislike some of his ideas and actions, was not a fascist, and since a fascist movement headed by a non-fascist is clearly an impossibility, the revisionist movement, for this reason if for no other, cannot be defined as fascist in character. Within the movement there were however sections, some of them influential, which were less deeply imbued than Jabotinsky with the old-fashioned principles of liberalism, or even actively opposed to them. Among them fascist ideas had made considerable headway and, but for the rise of Hitler and Nazism, would no doubt have become even more pronounced. The revisionist evacuation scheme in the 1930s was totally unrealistic and was attacked at the time as a blatant and irresponsible example of demagogy. Yet what seemed preposterous at the time appeared in a different perspective ten years later. No stone should have been left unturned in the effort to save European Jewry. No one is now likely to accuse Jabotinsky of overdramatising the issue. To that extent his policy should be judged less harshly by the historian than it was by many of his contemporaries. It was not farsightedness which made him press these demands so strongly. On similar reasoning he should not have opposed partition in 1937, for an independent Jewish state, however small, would have been able to save at least tens of thousands of Jews who eventually perished. But he was right in sensing instinctively that in the specific historical situation facing his people moderation was no virtue, that

* Schechtman, *Fighter and Prophet*, pp. 561-2.

every possible remedy, however desperate, had to be tried to save as many of them as possible.

It is not easy to pass final judgment on Jabotinsky and revisionism, with their many inherent contradictory elements. No other Zionist leader provoked such strong emotions. No one had such fanatical followers and such bitter enemies. The main impact of revisionism was not that of a political doctrine, for as an ideology it was weak and inconsistent. But it gave perfect expression to a mood widespread among many Zionists, especially among the younger generation. Perhaps because it was less sophisticated, it recognised certain basic facts earlier and more clearly than other Zionist parties: that without a majority, there would be no Jewish state, and that in view of Arab opposition to Jewish immigration and settlement even on a relatively small scale, there was no political solution but a Jewish state. The other Zionist leaders and parties preferred not to talk about these issues, which they considered premature: 'Let us cross these bridges when we come to them' was their attitude during the 1920s and 1930s.

Jabotinsky was almost the only one willing to face the problem squarely. He had the vision of a Jewish state, but when he died the goal seemed as distant as ever. But for the murder of millions of Jews and a unique international constellation after the end of the war, the Jewish state would not have come into existence. He was over-optimistic with regard to Arab acceptance of the Jewish presence. The 'iron wall' has existed for a long time but the Arabs have yet to become reconciled. The logic of events to which Jabotinsky referred from time to time led to the Jewish state, but in circumstances very different from those he had envisaged. After the state came into being, the movement which he had founded and inspired petered out, or, to be precise, underwent substantial change. Like Trotsky, who died in the same year, Jabotinsky left no clear message to be readily applied in the world of the 1970s. A quarter of a century after his death Jabotinsky's coffin was reinterred in Jerusalem, where he received a state funeral. With Herzl, Weizmann, and the leaders of labour Zionism, he was one of the architects of the movement which led to the establishment of the state which was his lodestar for so many years. What Schiller said of Wallenstein applies *a fortiori* to Jabotinsky: *Von der Parteien Hass and Gunst verworren schwankt sein Charakterbild in der Geschichte* (His place in history, entangled in partisan approval and hatred, fluctuates to and fro).

8

ZIONISM AND ITS CRITICS

The opposition to Zionism is as old as Zionism itself. It has come from many directions, Jewish and non-Jewish, left and right, religious and atheist. It has been asserted on the one hand that the Zionist goal was impossible to achieve, on the other hand that it was undesirable, and by some that it was both illusory and undesirable. Arab opposition is not surprising, but attacks came from other quarters too, including the Catholic Church, Asian nationalists suspicious of European intruders, Arabophile European politicians and orientalists, and the Communists. Pacifists condemned it as a violent movement. Gandhi wrote that as a spiritual ideal Zionism had his sympathy, but that by the use of force the Jews had vulgarised and debased their ideal. Tolstoy said that Zionism was not a progressive but basically a militarist movement; the Jewish idea would not find its fulfilment in a territorially limited fatherland. Did the Jews really want a state on the pattern of Serbia, Rumania, or Montenegro?*

Some antisemites welcomed Zionism, others denounced it in the sharpest terms; for both the Jews and Judaism represented a destructive element and their policy therefore was aimed at reducing Jewish influence and getting rid of as many Jews as possible. It might seem that they should have welcomed a movement which intended precisely that, namely to reduce the number of Jews in the various European countries, but in fact they have frequently turned against it. Palestine, it was felt, was too good or too important to be given to the Jews, who in any case had lost the capacity to build a state of their own. They were bound to remain parasites, and Zionism was therefore a sham. It was not a constructive effort, but on the contrary a mere ruse, part of the conspiracy to establish Jewish world rule. Mixing his metaphors and similes, Alfred Rosenberg, the Nazi ideologist, wrote in 1922:

* O.Pergament (ed.), *Graf Leo Tolstoi über die Juden*, Berlin n.d., pp. 18, 23.

Some of the locusts which have been sucking the marrow of Europe are returning to the promised land and are already looking for greener pastures. At its best Zionism is the impotent effort of an unfit people to achieve something constructive, but in the main it helps ambitious speculators as a new field in which to practise usury on a world-wide scale.*

Rosenberg demanded the outlawing of Zionism as an enemy of the German state, and the indictment of Zionists on the charge of high treason.

The present study does not intend to record all manifestations of hostility to Zionism throughout its history. Its scope is more limited, being confined to the opposition emanating from within the Jewish community. Broadly speaking, there have been, and still are, three basic anti-Zionist positions: the assimilationist, the orthodox-religious, and the left-wing revolutionary. All three have existed from the beginnings of Zionism to the present day. Other critics, such as the territorialists, who favoured a Jewish national revival outside Palestine, in the diaspora, have come and gone. It remains to be added that while opposition to Zionism from within the Jewish community was on the whole more intense sixty or seventy years ago than it is today, opposition from outside has become more vocal and much sharper in the same measure that Zionism has lost its Utopian character and become a political reality.

The Liberal Critique

The most plausible case against Zionism, and the one most frequently advanced up to the establishment of the state of Israel, was usually directed against its basically utopian character. Both those who welcomed the dispersion of the Jews, and those who deplored it, shared the belief that nothing could be done to undo this historical process. It was too late to concentrate millions of Jews in a part of the world that was already settled and which played an important role in world politics. Mankind was progressing towards assimilation, cosmopolitanism, a one-world culture. Everywhere, economic and social developments were reducing national distinctions. The attempt to arrest the movement of history, to resist this trend, was utopian and reactionary. Assimilation among the Jews of western Europe had proceeded too far to permit a return to Jewish nationalism. In eastern Europe, on the other hand, there was still both a Jewish national consciousness and a

* Alfred Rosenberg, *Der staatsfeindliche Zionismus*, Hamburg, 1922, pp. 62–3.

real social problem, but this was on such a massive scale that Zionism could not provide a cure. Before the First World War even leading Zionists thought that in the next twenty to thirty years between one hundred thousand and a million Jews at most would settle in Palestine (Lichtheim); Ruppin mentioned a figure of 120,000 families. But the 'Jewish problem' affected millions in eastern Europe, not hundreds of thousands. The critics of Zionism rejected the movement as Utopian 'not because something like this has never happened before or because some imagination is needed to envisage such a solution', but for the common sense reason that even the settlement of several hundreds of thousands, and cultural autonomy for the rest, would not be a solution. Landauer and Weil, who were among the most sober and best informed early critics of Zionism, maintained that the belief that west European Jewry could be preserved from assimilation was utopian, even if a Jewish state were to come into existence in Palestine. The Jewish question in the west would ultimately be solved by assimilation, but as for the situation in east Europe, no one had an answer.*

These were weighty arguments. The Zionists had nothing to offer but the hope that somehow a *deus ex machina* would provide the Jewish state; rational grounds for such a belief there were none, or virtually none. Meanwhile, assimilation made further progress. Herzl felt about it as Marx did about the feasibility of non-violent revolution, namely that it might be possible in a few countries but not in others. With certain notable exceptions (such as Jacob Klatzkin) the attitude of the next generation of Zionist leaders was more radical: they thought assimilation not only undesirable and undignified but also practically impossible. A few individuals could possibly 'pass', and ultimately be absorbed into gentile society, but the great majority could not. For beyond the wishes and aspirations of individuals, there was the 'objective Jewish question'.

This referred to sociological factors and also to the distinct character of the Jews as a race. Some western Zionists were influenced by the writings on race theory published during the two decades before the First World War, and a few (including Ruppin and Elias Auerbach) pursued their own studies in this field. The theory of racial constancy taught that certain distinctive qualities were inherited irrespective of social, cultural and geographical circumstances. These ideas were adopted, developed and 'modernised', especially in Germany (but not only there) by nationalist ideologists who on shaky scientific foundations erected imposing constructions proving the superiority of certain races

---

* Karl Landauer and Herbert Weil, *Die zionistische Utopie*, Munich, 1914, p. 80.

and the inferiority of others. They also claimed that racial purity was the greatest blessing and racial mixture the greatest misfortune for every people. These views were later absorbed by the Nazis and provided the justification for Hitler's racial policy, aimed at the extermination of Jews and the enslavement of other 'racially inferior elements'. As a result the whole field of race study fell into disrepute, for was it not bound to stress differences and thus to aggravate tensions? But the suppression of studies of the significance of racial differences, however well meaning, has not helped to resolve racial conflict. Differences between races do exist even if there are no pure races. There was the indisputable fact that in Germany and in Austria, in Poland and Russia, Jews were often easily recognisable. According to the Zionists, this, for better or worse, was a matter of some importance, whereas the liberals either belittled these differences or refused to attach any significance to them. They regarded racialist antisemitism as a major nuisance, but of no consequence historically, a rearguard action by the retreating forces of reaction. The liberal critics of Zionism could point to the undeniable fact that, despite warnings by antisemites, mixed marriages between Jews and non-Jews were on the increase all over central and western Europe and the United States. Given several generations of peaceful development, the Jewish question was likely to disappear. Zionists on the other hand, while not denying that assimilation was theoretically possible, claimed with Herzl: We shall not be left in peace.

They pointed to the sociological theory of antisemitism: experience had shown that wherever Jews lived in substantial concentrations there was antisemitism – largely no doubt as a result of their anomalous social structure. For historical reasons Jews rarely engaged in primary production such as agriculture and industry, but there were many of them in trade, in sundry marginal occupations, and of late in the free professions. As a result they were bound to be the first victims of any crisis, to suffer more than others from competition, likely to be squeezed out of their occupations without finding new ones. Since a normalisation of the Jewish social structure was most unlikely in the given conditions in eastern Europe, Zionism was the only remedy. Nor was there any certainty that the process of emancipation which had begun in central and western Europe after the French revolution would not be halted and reversed. The Jewish millionaires, Nordau said in a speech in Amsterdam, with all their snobbishness and arrogance had an atavistic fear: they might not know much history but they felt in their bones that their position in the world was perhaps not as secure as they would have liked to believe. Perhaps they had heard that there were Jewish millionaires too under Richard Coeur de Lion, under Philip the Handsome in France, under Philip and Isabella in Spain, but that one dreadful day, without any warning, many were killed, others became beggars overnight and their descendants were now starving in the ghettoes of Poland and Rumania.*

The liberals regarded this as a wilful misreading of the lessons of history, an irresponsible attempt to create panic. True, in the past Jewish emancipation had depended on the goodwill of the ruler, and what had been given could be taken away. True again that modern antisemitism could make assimilation more difficult by, for instance, closing certain professions to Jews. It could impede it, but it could not make it impossible. For the emancipation of the Jews was no longer based on subjective factors, but on world historical socio-economic trends and on the irresistible progress of civilisation. Liberals would explain antisemitism with reference to the backwardness of certain sections of the population, whereas Socialists would explain it as an attempt by the ruling classes to find a lightning conductor to protect themselves from the discontent of the masses. The Socialists also referred to an inclination on the part of the middle classes to make Jewish competition responsible for their economic and social problems. But as the labour movement gathered strength and became more class conscious, the workers would understand the real source of their misery: the lightning conductor would no longer function.†

Zionists saw no reason for such optimism. The lessons of the past were not encouraging: the Reformation had broken some chains, but not those of the Jews. The enlightenment had freed the spirit, but hatred of Jews had not abated. The principles of the French revolution had conquered the world, but the liberals had indicated to the Jews more or less politely that their cooperation in the struggle for political freedom was not desired:

Socialism will bring the same disappointments as did the Reformation, the Enlightenment, the movement for political freedom. If we should live to see Socialist theory become practice, you'll be surprised to meet again in the new order that old acquaintance, antisemitism. And it won't help

---

* Max Nordau, *Zionistische Schriften*, Cologne, 1909, p. 258.

† See Bernard Lazare, *Antisemitism*, New York, 1903, *passim*; Landauer and Weil, *Die zionistische Utopie*, p. 32. The French edition of Lazare's book appeared in 1894; by the time the American translation was published he had radically modified his views on the subject. There was no solution for antisemitism, he wrote in 1897, assimilation was no answer, the only solution of the Jewish question was Jewish nationalism, Zionism.

at all that Marx and Lassalle were Jews. . . . The founder of Christianity was a Jew too, but to the best of my knowledge Christianity does not think it owes a debt of gratitude to the Jews. I do not doubt that the ideologists of Socialism will always remain faithful to their doctrine, that they will never become racialists. But the men of action will have to take realities into account. In the foreseeable future the feelings of the masses will dictate to them an antisemitic policy.*

Such fears seem to have been fairly widespread at the time. Ehrenberg, the old businessman in Schnitzler's *Weg ins Freie*, tells his young acquaintance, a Jewish Socialist, that he will fare no better than the Jewish liberals and pan-Germans before him:

Who created the liberal movement in Austria? The Jews. . . . Who betrayed and deserted the Jews? The liberals. Who created the German national movement in Austria? The Jews. And who deserted them, who spat on them like dogs? . . . Exactly the same is bound to happen with Socialism and Communism. Once soup has been served, you'll be chased from the dinner table. It was always like this, and it always will be.†

Such dire predictions did not, however, in the least deter successive generations of young Jews in central and western Europe, who in their thousands continued to join the radical parties of the Left. For them the messianic appeal of Socialism was irresistible, incomparably more attractive than any political activity within the narrow confines of the Jewish community. They did not deny the existence of a Jewish problem, but they were firmly convinced that the solution would be found only when the ideals of humanism and internationalism prevailed, on the morning after the revolution. Nationalism, these Socialists maintained, was a thing of the past, and since they felt no special ties with the Jewish community, any appeal to their national consciousness and pride was bound to fall on deaf ears. At this point communication in the debate usually broke down and the most Zionists could hope for was that the anti-Zionist Jewish Socialists would learn by bitter experience that they were not wanted in the struggle for the social liberation of other peoples, and that by pushing themselves into positions of command and authority they would do more harm than good.

Nordau always returned to this theme of the rootless western Jew and his problems in a gentile society. In his address at the first Zionist congress he drew a sombre picture of Jewish spiritual misery in western

---

* Nordau: *Zionistische Schriften*, pp. 268–70.
† A. Schnitzler, *Gesammelte Werke*, Berlin, 1913, vol. 3, pp. 94–5.

Europe, more painful than physical suffering because it affected men of high station, men who were proud and sensitive. The western Jew was still allowed to vote, but he was excluded with varying degrees of politeness from the clubs and gatherings of his Christian fellow countrymen. He was allowed to go wherever he pleased, but everywhere he encountered the sign: No Jews admitted. He had abandoned his specifically Jewish character, yet the nations did not accept him as part of their national communities. He fled from his Jewish fellows, because antisemitism had taught him to be contemptuous of them, but his gentile compatriots repulsed him. He had lost his home in the ghetto yet the land of his birth was denied to him as his home. He had no ground under his feet, no community to which he belonged. He was insecure in his relations with his fellow man, timid with strangers, and suspicious even of the secret feelings of his friends. His best powers were dissipated in suppressing and destroying or at least concealing his true character and identity. He had become a cripple within and a counterfeit person without, ridiculous and hateful, like everything unreal, to all men of high standards. He was a new Marrano who no longer had a faith to sustain him. He had left Judaism in rage and bitterness, but in his innermost heart, even if he himself did not acknowledge it, he carried with him into Christianity his personal humiliation, his dishonesty, and whatever compelled him to live a lie.*

The theme of the uprooted cosmopolitan, the wanderer between two worlds with no home in either, appeared in many Zionist writings and speeches. It was a universal problem but no one was likely to feel it more acutely than the Jewish intellectuals. They were at one and the same time part of the intellectual establishment and yet in some vital respects total outsiders. In Germany they had made an enormous contribution to cultural life, felt confident of their place in society, and then suddenly were given to understand that, after all, they did not belong. Jakob Klatzkin sketched a sharp portrait of the 'typical' Jewish intellectual who seemed almost totally assimilated and yet found it so difficult to be accepted by the host people, precisely because he hailed from a spiritual aristocracy with its own specific and unassimilable features. He was highly developed intellectually, rich in creative and destructive faculties, dynamic, too active in his desire to be assimilated, and hence ultimately a nuisance. His strengths were ridicule and irony, barren intellectualism. He acted as mediator between various national cultures, but all too often he barely touched the surface of things, and had no real

* Quoted in A. Hertzberg, *The Zionist Idea*, New York, 1959, pp. 239–40.

390

feeling for the deeper roots of the national genius. He tried to mix things that were incompatible, being at home everywhere and nowhere. He was attempting to reinterpret the German spirit, discovering in it ideas of tolerance, justice, and even messianism, until it became half German, half Jewish. These intellectuals had a strong inclination towards radicalism, negation and destruction. Intellectual proletarians, they found no rest, since they had lost their own moorings in history. Lacking roots themselves, they were compelled to try to change the world, to preach the overthrow of the existing order.*

It was not a flattering picture, and it exaggerated certain features common to a relatively small group of *Literaten*. The great majority of the German Jewish intelligentsia was liberal – but not too liberal – in its politics; it was deeply rooted in German culture, and fairly content with its lot; it wanted change but certainly not anarchy and revolution. The soul-searching of the Jewish literary intelligentsia attracted so much attention because it affected the most vocal section of the community, the one most exposed to the limelight. Which is not to say that their problems were not real or significant.

The issues involved emerged most clearly when Moritz Goldstein published an article in March 1913 entitled 'German-Jewish Parnassus',† creating something of a minor scandal. It provoked some ninety letters to the editor and was discussed for years in the German press. Briefly, Goldstein argued that the Jews were dominating the culture of a people which denied them both the right and the capacity to do so. The newspapers in the capital were about to become a Jewish monopoly. Almost all directors of the Berlin theatres were Jews, as were many of the actors. German musical life without the Jews was almost unthinkable, and the study of German literature was also to a large extent in Jewish hands. Everyone knew it, only the Jews pretended it was not worthy of notice. For what mattered, they claimed, were their achievements, their cultural and humanistic activities. This, said Goldstein, was a dangerous fallacy, for 'the others do not feel that we are Germans'. They could show these others that they were not inferior, but was it not naïve to assume that this would in any way diminish their dislike and antipathy? There was a basic anomaly in the Jewish situation. The liberal Jewish intellectuals were good Europeans, but they were also split personalities, divorced from the people amidst whom they were living. They could make a great contribution to science, for science

* Jakob Klatzkin, *Krisis und Entscheidung*, Berlin, 1921, pp. 196–8.
† *Der Kunstwart*, March 1913.

knew no national borders. But in literature and the arts (and he might have added in political life) any major initiative had to be rooted in a popular and national framework. From Homer to Tolstoy all the really great works had their origins in the native soil, the homeland, the people. And this 'rootedness' the Jews lacked, despite all their intellectual and emotional efforts.

Among those who answered Goldstein was the poet Ernst Lissauer, who during the First World War achieved notoriety in connection with his 'Hate England' song. He bitterly opposed any attempt to restore a ghetto on German soil or a 'Palestinian enclave'. On the contrary, he felt that the process of assimilation must be carried to its successful conclusion. If so many Jewish intellectuals were radicals, and still had no feeling for the German national spirit, this was no doubt because they were still discriminated against in so many ways. But once these barriers had fallen, they too would be fully integrated into the mainstream of German life.

Lissauer's optimism seems almost incredibly naïve in retrospect, but it is not at all impossible that but for the First World War and its repercussions his predictions might have come true. Antisemitism did not at the time succeed in halting the progress of the Jews in central Europe. Paradoxical as it may sound after the Hitler period (Nahum Goldmann wrote), the history of the Jews in Germany from 1870 to 1930 represents the most spectacular advance any branch of Jewry has ever achieved.* The great majority of central European Jews did not write books or plays, did not own newspapers or manage theatres. There were strains and stresses and conflicts threatening their status in society. But these were regarded as the inevitable concomitants of the process of assimilation. The fact that assimilation was more difficult than anticipated did not mean that it was bound to fail. Zionism in western Europe was the reaction to these difficulties. All Jews were compelled to confront this challenge but only a few were impelled to embrace the new creed. The only ones who did not react at all were those who had already broken with Judaism. They had either left the Jewish community or were about to do so, and did not therefore bother to reflect about their special position as Jews. No ties bound them to the Jewish religion or any other form of national solidarity. They no longer felt Jewish and consequently the whole dispute between Zionism and its adversaries did not concern them. They would comment on Zionism as they did on other political or cultural curiosities: 'This time the Jews will not arrive

* Nahum Goldmann, *Memoirs*, London, 1970, pp. 58–9.

dry shod in the promised land; another Red Sea, social democracy, will bar their way'.* But more often they would simply ignore Zionism. The real debate was between the Zionists and the great majority which had not opted out of Judaism but interpreted it in a different way.

Central Europe, Germany and Austria in particular, had been the birthplace of modern Zionism. It was also the birthplace of liberal anti-Zionism. But the reaction in England, the United States and other western countries was not, as will be shown presently, essentially different. Herzl had invested much effort in winning over Moritz Guedemann, the Viennese chief rabbi, but without any lasting success. Herzl's *Judenstaat* was followed by Guedemann's *Nationaljudentum*, an outspoken anti-Zionist tract. Guedemann explained Zionism as a reaction to the rise of antisemitism, which had provoked indignation and defiance among many Jews. They had picked up the gauntlet: 'If they regard us as aliens, we ought to accept the challenge.' But this psychologically understandable reaction did not make Jewish nationalism any more acceptable in Guedemann's eyes; it was contrary to the essence of the Jewish religion. Quoting Grillparzer, the Austrian national writer ('from humanity through nationality to bestiality'), the rabbi concluded that Jews had to fight for their rights rather than give up the struggle.†

Similar views were aired by the executive of German rabbis soon after Herzl had issued his summons to the first Zionist congress. The declaration of the 'protest rabbis' (as the Zionists contemptuously called them) stated that the aspirations of the 'so-called Zionists, to establish a Jewish national state', contradicted the messianic promise of the Bible and the other sources of the Jewish religion. Judaism made it obligatory for those professing it to serve the country to which they belonged and wholeheartedly to promote its national interests. The 'protest rabbis' emphasised that their opposition was directed against political Zionism. They were not against Jewish agricultural settlement as such in Palestine, because these 'noble aspirations are not aimed at the foundation of a national state'.‡

Vogelstein, one of the most outspoken opponents of Zionism, rejected the new movement very much in the same spirit as Gabriel Riesser, the great advocate of Jewish emancipation in Germany: Germany is our

---

* Karl Kraus, *Eine Krone für Zion*, Vienna, 1898, p. 30.
† M.Güdemann, *Nationaljudentum*, Vienna, 1897, pp. 4, 5, 12.
‡ Quoted in H.Vogelstein, *Der Zionismus, eine Gefahr fuer die gedeihliche Entwicklung des Judentums*, Stettin, 1906, p. 11.

fatherland; we have and need no other. The German Jews for whom Vogelstein spoke were tied to Germany by many links. Ever since the emancipation they had been German patriots, and over the generations had developed a distinctly German national consciousness. A national revival in the Zionist sense was not compatible with the aims of Judaism as they envisaged it. According to the liberal version a nation-state might have been needed in ancient times to achieve and preserve pure monotheism. But once this had been attained, once these beliefs had been absorbed by the Israelites, a territorial centre was no longer needed. On the contrary, divine providence had sent the Jews into the dispersion to serve as witnesses everywhere to the omnipotence of the idea of God. Liberal Judaism agreed with the religious orthodoxy that it was Israel's mission to promote the realisation of the prophetic ideal in the diaspora.*

There were no substantial differences in approach between the advocates of liberal Judaism in the various countries of the west. According to Joseph Reinach, the leading French-Jewish politician, Zionism was a trap set by the antisemites for the naïve or thoughtless. If Dr Vogelstein stressed the attachment of the German Jews to Germany, his liberal contemporaries in London emphasised that since Judaism was a religion, British Jews could completely identify with the British. Isaac Wise, a leading American rabbi, speaking at the close of the first Zionist congress, said 'we denounce the whole question of a Jewish state as foreign to the spirit of the modern Jew of this land, who looks upon America as his Palestine and whose interests are centred here'.† 'Liberal Jews do not wish or pray for the restoration of Jews to Palestine', wrote Claude Montefiore, the spokesman of liberal Judaism in Britain. The establishment of a Jewish state would refurbish the anachronism of a Jewish God. Judaism was not a national religion; one part of it was universalist, for all mankind, the other specific. But there was nothing in the national part to prevent the Jews being perfect Englishmen. Abstention from the flesh of hares and rabbits did not, after all make them less English.‡ According to a like-minded contemporary, Laurie Magnus, the Zionists were partly responsible for the antisemitism which they proposed to destroy. He advocated their exclusion from parliament and public office since they wanted to change the status of Jews to that of foreign visitors. Magnus did not deny Jewish

---

* *Ibid.*, pp. 4–7.
† Quoted in E.Berger, *The Jewish Dilemma*, New York, 1945, p. 240.
‡ C.G.Montefiore, *Liberal Judaism and Jewish Nationalism*, London, 1917, pp. 6–7.

nationality altogether, but this, as an unkind critic paraphrased his views, was something so sublime that it could be realised only by being abandoned.*

If the American and British liberals were above all concerned with the political implications of Zionism, the Germans took it more seriously, trying to analyse and refute its philosophical roots. Felix Goldmann, an anti-Zionist rabbi, regarded Jewish nationalism as a child of the general chauvinist movement which had poisoned recent history but which would be swept away in the new era of universalism. Zionism wanted to sacrifice religion in order to establish some petty state.† The Zionists, few in number but aggressive and sure of their cause, answered every liberal argument and moved to the offensive whenever possible. Between 1900 and the end of the First World War the debate never ceased, about Zionism and religion, about liberalism as a halfway house between Judaism and total apostasy, about dual loyalties.‡

Since there was a limited number of arguments and counter-arguments, this literature is highly repetitive. Even the debate between Hermann Cohen, the neo-Kantian philosopher, and Martin Buber, less than half his age, was more significant as a reading of two personal documents than for any new philosophical insight. According to Cohen, Zionism rejected the messianic idea, but without this there was no Jewish religion. He and others of his generation had found in German thought the spirit of humanism and the real *Weltbuergertum* which was in full harmony with Jewish messianic religiosity: 'I do not read Faust just as a beautiful poem; I love it as a revelation of the German spirit. I feel in a similar way even about Luther, about Mozart and Beethoven, Stein and Bismarck.'§ Cohen argued that the Zionists were muddled about the national issue. The Jews were members of the German nation even if they belonged to a different nationality. When he wrote that a nation was created by a state he was thinking no doubt of the Jews and the absence of a Jewish state. But this was a dubious assertion, which

---

* L.Magnus, *Zionism and the neo-Zionist*, London, 1917, *passim*; *Religio Laici Judaici*, London, 1907, p. 140; and the reply by Leon Simon, *The Case of the Anti-Zionists*, London, 1917, *passim*.

† F.Goldman, *Zionismus oder Liberalismus*. Frankfurt a M., 1911, pp. 6, 71.

‡ For instance, Max Kollenscher, *Zionismus oder liberales Judentum*, Berlin, 1912; *Zionismus und Staatsbuergertum*, Berlin, 1910; Dr Joseph, *Das Judentum am Scheideweg*, Berlin, 1908; R.Breuer, *Nationaljudentum ein Wahnjudentum*, Mainz.

§ *Antwort an das offene Schreiben des Herrn Dr Martin Buber an Hermann Cohen*, Frankfurt a M., 1916, p. 13; see also Hermann Cohen, *Religion und Zionismus*, Crefeld, 1916; M.Buber, 'Begriffe und Wirklichkeit', *Der Jude*, August 1916.

prompted the Zionists to ask the obvious question: Had the German
nation been nonexistent before 1870?

While the liberal rabbis were on the whole moderate in their attacks
on Zionism, admitting for instance that it had done a great deal to
reawaken active interest in Judaism and the Hebrew language, some
laymen went much further in their opposition. Professor Ludwig
Geiger, the son of one of the founders of liberal Judaism, and one of its
representatives on the executive of the Berlin Jewish community,
suggested, as Magnus did in Britain, that Zionists should be deprived
of their civic rights, and denounced the 'blasphemous prayers' in the
Jewish ritual which reminded the faithful of Zion. 'Zionism is as
dangerous to the German spirit as are social democracy and ultra-
montanism,' he wrote on another occasion.* The future of the German
nation must remain the only one on which German Jews based their
hopes. Any desire to form, together with their co-religionists, a people
outside Germany was sheer ingratitude to the nation in whose midst
they were living. For German Jews were Germans in their national
peculiarities, and Zion for them was the land of the past, not of the
future.

Zionists in Germany and the United States complained that their
supporters were being systematically discriminated against, that Jewish
communities were refusing to employ Zionists as rabbis, teachers, or
even librarians. The anti-Zionists argued on the other hand that whoever criticised Zionism was immediately attacked in the most abusive
terms and his personal motives invariably made to appear suspect. The
Central Association of German citizens of the Jewish faith (*Zentralverein*),
the main body of non-orthodox German Jewry, was in two minds about
how to deal with the Zionists. On various occasions resolutions were
adopted according to which a Zionist could be a member only if his
Zionism implied helping to find a new home for the oppressed Jews of
eastern Europe or enhancing the pride of his co-religionists in their
history and religion. But there was no place for those who denied a
German consciousness, who felt themselves merely guests in their native
country. These declarations caused great indignation among Zionists.
But for the extreme adversaries, who believed that Zionism was the
greatest misfortune of German Jewry, since it played into the hands of
antisemites, they were by no means far-reaching enough. They
repeatedly accused the leadership of the Association of being 'soft on

* L.Schön (ed.), *Die Stimme der Wahrheit*, Würzburg, 1905, p. 163 *et seq.*

Zionism' for opportunist reasons.* After the First World War, opposition to Zionism on the whole decreased, with the exception of the shrill denunciations of a small group of ultra-nationalist German Jews. But even if the polemics diminished, the attitude of the *Zentralverein* towards the Palestinian venture remained sceptical and it continued to combat Zionism in so far as it regarded the German Jew as living in an alien land.†

In the debate with assimilationists, Zionist spokesmen did not find it difficult to score points against those advocates of liberal Judaism who based their argument on the messianic mission of the Jews, maintaining that a state had been a historical necessity two thousand years earlier but was no longer needed because Judaism was so deeply anchored in the hearts of its adherents. Such a claim was not borne out by the facts, for obviously there had been more apostasy from Judaism in recent decades than in past ages. Putting it more bluntly, the Zionists maintained that the talk about the Jewish spiritual world mission was just a pretext: in the modern world they had no such mission. If German, French and British Jews nevertheless chose to stay in their respective countries, it was because they longed for the fleshpots rather than the messiah. The Zionists were in a position of strength because it was already obvious before the First World War that the tide was running against liberalism. Mankind was not becoming more civilised, cosmopolitanism was not making striking advances, all over Europe nationalism and anti-liberal ideas were winning new adherents. But the anti-liberal tide was at the same time a mixed blessing. It strengthened the Zionist thesis about the precarious situation of European Jewry, but it also put Zionism into undesirable ideological proximity with right-wing and reactionary movements and ideas.

Nationalism and religion, and the relationship between these two concepts remained ticklish ideological issues for the Zionists. Many of them were not at all religious, and some did not in principle exclude the possibility of having members who did not belong to the Jewish religion. Zionist organisations coped with this problem in different ways: The Dutch Zionists decided at one stage not to accept members with non-Jewish spouses. Nordau, for instance, would not have qualified. On the other hand, Lewis (later Sir Lewis) Namier, the eminent British historian, who acted for several years as political secretary of the Jewish Agency in London, had been baptised. Some early German Zionists

---

* *Deutsche Israelitische Zeitung*, 15, 30 May 1913; *C.V.Zeitung*, February 1919.

† Alfred Wiener, *Kritische Reise durch Palaestina*, Berlin, 1927, p. 118.

took race theory too seriously, others drew their inspiration from the writings of the ideologists of German nationalism such as Fichte and even Lagarde. This made it easy for their opponents in western Europe before and during the First World War to attack Zionism as a movement dominated by Germany and serving German interests. 'The *Judenstaat* is a time bomb invented by the German national genius to destroy the world of Abraham; the state of Israel is Germany', wrote a French-Jewish author in 1969.* This was, to put it mildly, a distortion, for the ideas of Herder and Fichte served as the ideological basis of nationalism not just in Germany but in many other countries as well. However, in the light of the subsequent development of German nationalism, essays that were innocent enough when written appeared several decades later in a sinister light, with Martin Buber as an early protagonist of *Blut und Boden* and other Zionist ideologists as advocates of the *voelkische* idea. Torn out of their historical context they now make embarrassing reading and the critics of Zionism have not failed to make the most of them.

But the real weakness of the Zionist position was a practical one.† Having destroyed as it were the liberal position, having shown the inconsistency and falseness of assimilationism, what alternative could it offer in exchange? Emigration to Palestine before 1914 was rare. A few daring spirits visited Palestine as tourists but not more than a handful of German Zionists, and even fewer from Austria, decided to settle there. Even after 1918 the number of Jewish immigrants from central Europe was counted in hundreds, not thousands, and virtually no one came from western Europe or the United States. This was so despite all the solemn undertakings and promises, such as the resolution passed at the German Zionist Conference in Posen, that it was the duty of every Zionist to prepare himself for a life in Palestine. What, then, did it actually mean to be a Zionist in these circumstances? In most cases it implied no more than giving money to the national funds, reading Zionist literature, talking about Palestine, engaging in various political activities, and perhaps learning Hebrew. But 99 per cent of west and east European Zionists, both the rank and file and the leaders, while stressing that they were a people on the move, continued to live more or less happily in the countries of the diaspora, to practise medicine and the law, to engage in trade and industry, to publish books and articles.

* Emanuel Levyne, *Judaisme contre Sionisme*, Paris, 1969, pp. 20–1.
† See the *Schriften zur Aufklärung über den Zionismus*, published by the Antizionistisches Komittee, Berlin, n.d., (*ca.* 1910–13.)

The anti-Zionists, charged by their opponents with 'living a lie', could easily counter by pointing to the far more flagrant discrepancy between Zionist theory and practice.

A convincing case could be made from the Zionist point of view for insisting on full civic rights in their country of origin, despite the fact that their allegiance was to another nation. It was far more difficult to justify the active participation of Zionists in German, British or French politics. They were to be found in senior positions in the civil service in these countries as well as in the British and French parliaments and even as leaders of political parties. This was a contradiction that could not easily be resolved: either the Zionism of a public figure of this kind was not very deep or he was facing a permanent conflict of loyalties.

Nor was it easy to dismiss the assimilationist critics of the Zionist position in the cultural field. They maintained that Zionism was by no means a revival of Jewish tradition but had been inspired by the general nationalist trend in Europe. Those who stood for a national-cultural revival could not point without great difficulty to specific Jewish values outside religion. Having lived for so many centuries in the diaspora, what did the Jews still have of their own cultural substance? The religious holidays had been taken from other peoples, the languages of the Jewish masses both in Europe (Yiddish) and the Mediterranean area (Ladino) had been borrowed from German and Spanish respectively. There was no Jewish school of painting or music, of philosophy or history. There were many Jewish writers but no Jewish literature. Everywhere the Jews had entered into a cultural symbiosis with the host nations. Zionists might claim that the resulting 'cultural chaos' was sterile and undignified, but in the last resort they could not point to any clear alternative. Their songs and drawings, created with great gusto during the early years of the national revival, hardly amounted to the beginnings of a new culture. Most Zionists admitted that a cultural revival could take place only in Palestine, but this was tantamount to admitting that there was no specific Jewish life in the diaspora. If this was so, then diaspora Zionism was no more than a mood, a vague longing, a feeling of nostalgia. Orthodox Jews still had their traditional beliefs, but those advocating a secular nationalism had little to offer their followers. This was a source of concern to many western Zionists; in eastern Europe, where a Jewish folk culture still existed, the situation was quite different.

Elsewhere in western Europe opposition to Zionism was no less strong or vociferous than in Germany and Austria. The Lovers of Zion had a few sympathisers in England even before Herzl, and Weizmann in later years found friends who were a source of strength at the time of decision. But the representative bodies of Anglo-Jewry, above all the Board of Deputies and the Anglo-Jewish Association, regarded Zionism not merely as irrelevant but positively harmful, believing that it jeopardised the legal rights won by the Jews over many decades, and that Jewish patriotism was incompatible with their loyalties as British subjects. The main figure in the anti-Zionist campaign was Lucien Wolf, president of the Anglo-Jewish Association. Herzl's ideas, he wrote, were worse than satire, they were treason: 'Dr Herzl and those who think with him are traitors to the history of the Jews, which they misread and misinterpret.' The Zionists were provoking antisemitism, their scheme was foredoomed to failure, they had commercialised a spiritual idea, traded on the resources of prophecy. With ingenious effrontery, Herzl had represented his scheme of evading the mission of the exiles and their duty to the lands of the dispersion as a fulfilment of the ancient prophecy. Quoting another contemporary critic of Herzl, Wolf said that the Zionist programme was the most contemptible, if not the most grotesque, species of idealism ever laid before the remnant of the descendants of a great nation.* There was a Jewish problem, but Jews in each country had to fight for emancipation and religious liberty.

Even where persecuted, as in Rumania at the time he was writing, they were in duty bound to remain in order to help that country to become a civilised state. 'This is the mission of Israel in exile, the mission that British Israel has fulfilled.'† In the comparatively few years since their emancipation the Jews of Britain had identified themselves with the nation to which they belonged. There was no specific Jewish interest differentiating them from the rest of the king's subjects. Zionism could not be realised, for this 'travesty of Judaism' depended on the goodwill of a Mohammedan prince. The western governments, Wolf predicted, would not show the least disposition to invite an outburst of antisemitism by acknowledging their Jews as strangers, nor did they want to complicate the eastern question by planting another weak state in the uneasy and troublesome Near East. These views were shared by most leaders of Anglo-Jewry up to the First World War, and though after the Balfour Declaration they no longer argued that Zionism was utopian, they continued to regard Palestine as at best a refuge for their unfortunate co-religionists from eastern Europe. After the war the thesis of the

---

* L. Wolf, *Aspects of the Jewish Question*, London, 1902, pp. 18, 23.
† *Ibid.*, p. 58.

civilising mission of east European Jewry became untenable. But as assimilation in Britain did not suffer any major setback, and anti-semitism was relatively mild, the lack of enthusiasm for Zionism was not surprising. In Vienna, Prague and Berlin Zionism had a few intellectual supporters, whereas in France and Britain, before Hitler, there were almost none. Whatever backing there was came from other sections of the Jewish community, usually recent arrivals from eastern Europe. In France one of the few exceptions was Bernard Lazare, another was Edmond Fleg, but neither of these for a moment, considered settling in Palestine. After attending a Zionist congress, Fleg wrote that he felt himself very Jewish among all those strange faces, but also very French: the Jewish homeland was only for those who had no other.* Leon Blum, another distant sympathiser, expressed the same view in a message to a Zionist meeting: The Jewish homeland was a wonderful thing for all those who, unlike himself, did not have the good fortune to be free and equal citizens in their countries of birth.† Other French intellectuals were far less sympathetic and condemned Zionist 'racism'. Herzl had become a Zionist as a result of the Dreyfus affair but most French Jews reacted differently. The small groups of east European Jews in Paris who advocated Zionism were regarded with a certain *méfiance*; Zionist dreams were likened to the excitations of Communism and nihilism.‡ Julien Benda derided the *'adorateurs de leur sang'* who wanted to establish a semitic nationalism.§

Opposition to Zionism in Russia before 1917 was by no means limited to Jewish and non-Jewish Socialists. While assimilationist hopes received a blow from which they did not recover as a result of the pogroms, opposition to the Jewish national movement remained widespread and vocal in liberal circles, mainly for ideological reasons. But there were also practical objections: Yushakov (to give but one example) argued in 1897 that Palestine was unsafe – the Turks would kill the Jews.‖ One of the most interesting spokesmen of spiritual anti-Zionism was Mikhail Gershenson, a Russian emigré to western Europe who developed a highly personal, mystical philosophy of history concerning the destiny of the Jewish people. He was not an enemy of Zionism; on

* E.Fleg, *Pourquoi je suis juif*, Paris, 1928, p. 94.
† Andre Blumel, *Leon Blum, juif et zioniste*, Paris, 1952, p. 13.
‡ Michael R.Marrus, *The Politics of Assimilation*, Oxford, 1971, p. 277.
§ J.Benda, *Un regulier dans le siècle*, Paris, 1938, p. 220.
‖ See *Russkoe Bogatstvo*, 12, 1897, and M.Lilienblum, *Palestinofilstvo, Zionizm i ikh protivniki*, Odessa, 1899, *passim*.

the contrary Zionism touched him; it had, he wrote, a great psychological beauty. But it was based on the nation-state as the only normal form of human existence, a false nineteenth-century European concept. Repudiating the idea of election, Zionism rejected the whole of Jewish history, selling it for a nationalist mess of pottage. Having suffered so much from nationalism, in whose name the greatest crimes had been committed, it was perhaps inevitable that this bloodthirsty Moloch was now asking its due from Israel. Gershenson firmly believed that the Jews were bound to be eternal pilgrims, that their terrible apprenticeship was to continue, 'for the kingdom of Israel is not of this world'.* It was a glorious and terrible destiny, not an accident of history but deeply rooted in the national soul. He did not profess to know the purpose and meaning of the trials to which the Jewish people had to submit; these were well beyond human understanding. Gershenson's theory of suffering was nearer to Slavophilism then to Judaism, but in some respects it also resembled the views of the ultra-orthodox Jews who claimed that Israel was being punished by God for its sins. To the Zionists, needless to say, all this was anathema: if a few assimilated intellectuals wanted to suffer, the overwhelming majority of the Jews wanted to escape oppression and lead a normal life. Again and again the Zionists refused to accept theories about a Jewish spiritual mission in the diaspora at their face value. If intellectuals opposed Zionism this was no doubt because Palestine could not offer them the opportunities which they had in central and western Europe.

When Zionism first appeared on the American scene, the Jewish establishment reacted like their liberal co-religionists in western Europe. It was the 'momentary inebriation of morbid minds' (Isaac Wise), a movement arresting the march of progress and tolerance. For rabbis and laymen alike Zionism was a disturber of their peace of mind, an offence to their Americanism, an obstacle to Jewish adjustment in a democratic environment. It revived memories they wished to forget.† A decade before Herzl published his *Judenstaat* the convention of reform rabbis had declared from their Pittsburgh platform: 'We consider ourselves no longer a nation but a religious community. And therefore expect neither a return to Palestine . . . nor the restoration of any of the laws concerning the Jewish state.' After the first Zionist congress another resolution expressed disapproval of any attempt to establish a Jewish

---

* M. Gershenson, *Sudby evreiskovo naroda*, Berlin, 1922, *passim*. A French translation, *Les destins du peuple juif*, was published in Paris in 1946.

† L. Lipsky, *A Gallery of Jewish Profiles*, New York, 1956, p. 156.

state, which implied a total misunderstanding of Israel's mission. 'Ziomania', as the movement was called by its critics, was thought to be not merely reactionary in character but a menace to Jewish security. As in Germany, feelings ran high and the few early Zionists had a difficult time in the communal organisations. The purge of Zionist sympathisers from the Hebrew Union College was merely one instance of discrimination against them.

Opposition was by no means limited to the middle class and upper class Jewish establishment and its rabbis. Among the masses of recent arrivals from eastern Europe, too, Zionism had little support. In so far as they were interested in politics, they tended to gravitate towards various shades of Socialism. After the Balfour Declaration and the Russian revolution, opposition to Zionism decreased in America as in Europe. When in 1918 David Philipson tried to organise a conference to combat Zionism, some of the leading figures in Jewish life such as Oscar Strauss and Jacob Schiff refused to cooperate. Louis Marshall wrote in his answer that Zionism appealed to the imagination and to poetry and was an affirmative policy.* The American Jewish Committee in a resolution gave cautious approval to the Balfour Declaration while making it clear that only a part of the Jewish people would settle in Palestine. As for American Jewry, it was axiomatic that they owed unqualified allegiance to their country of which they were an integral part. The Reform rabbis passed another resolution to the effect that Israel was not a nation, Palestine not the homeland of the Jewish people – the whole world was its home.†

Nevertheless, throughout the 1920s and 1930s Zionism gained many new sympathisers. Reform Judaism (in the words of one of its critics) tacitly endorsed synthetic Zionism in 1937 in a resolution intended to supplant the Pittsburgh platform.‡This caused much dismay among diehard anti-Zionists who, at a meeting in Atlantic City in 1942, decided to work out a programme to reactivate their case. While conceding the contribution of 'Palestinian rehabilitation towards relieving the pressing problem of our distressed people', it asserted that the political emphasis in the Zionist programme was contrary to 'our universalistic interpretation of Jewish history and destiny'.§

* *Correspondence on the advisability of calling a conference for the purpose of combating Zionism.* New York, 1918, p. 10.
† Central Conference of American Rabbis, *Yearbook*, vol. 30, 1920, p. 142.
‡ E.Berger, *The Jewish Dilemma*, New York, 1945, p. 241.
§ See *The Flint Plan – a Program of Action for American Jews*, New York, 1942, *passim*; and Milton Steinberg, 'Zionism and the new Opposition', in *Zionism*, New York, 1943, *passim*.

The case against Zionism was very briefly that (a) as a secularist movement it was incompatible with the religious character of Judaism; (b) as a political movement it was inconsistent with the spiritual emphasis on Judaism; (c) as a nationalist movement it was out of keeping with the universalist character of Judaism; and (d) it was a threat to the welfare of Jews as it confused gentiles in their thinking about Jews and thus imperilled their status. In all essentials these arguments were identical with those formulated by the German liberals forty years earlier, although there were different nuances in approach: for example the radical anti-Zionists always referred to the 'myth of the Jewish people', whereas the more moderate elements (such as Rabbi Lazaron) referred on occasion to the Jewish people and its 'religio-cultural heritage', implying that Judaism was more than a religion. In 1943 the American Council for Judaism was established and announced in its statement of principles that 'we oppose the effort to establish a national Jewish state in Palestine or anywhere else as a philosophy of defeatism. . . . We dissent from all these related doctrines that stress the racialism, the national and the theoretical homelessness of the Jews. We oppose such doctrines as inimical to the welfare of Jews in Palestine, in America, or wherever Jews may dwell.'* The council had only a few thousand members, but some of them were influential in public life. It continued its activities after the establishment of the state of Israel, and some of its more extreme spokesmen, such as Alfred Lilienthal and Elmer Berger, supported the Arab case against Zionism. There was also opposition of a more moderate kind, expressed in articles published in *The Menorah Journal*, the most prestigious periodical of the period. The American Jewish Labor Committee, under Bundist inspiration, continued to reject political Zionism. Hannah Arendt, writing shortly before the establishment of the state of Israel, declared that Herzl's concept of the place of the Jews in the world had become even more dangerous than before: 'The parallels with the Shabtai Zvi episode have become terribly close.'† There were similar objections in the writings of Solow, Hans Kohn, William Zukerman, Koppel Pinson and others, but the majority of American Jews (90 per cent, according to a Roper poll in 1945), favoured the establishment of a Jewish state without necessarily joining the Zionist movement.

The debate did not end with the establishment of the state. The critics accepted Israel as a *fait accompli* but not without considerable mis-

* Quoted in Berger: *The Jewish Dilemma*, p. 246.
† *Commentary*, May 1946.

givings and reservations. The work of the Zionist politicians had been crowned with success, Ignaz Maybaum wrote, but history was not eternity, and the state of Israel was by no means the safest part of the Jewish diaspora. In the post-Zionist era it was merely part of the diaspora; it was not to be burdened with the Utopian task of ending Jewish life in the diaspora.* A systematic critique of Zionist ambitions was provided by Rabbi Jacob Petuchovski. It was sheer deception, he wrote, to argue that Israel was or would be the spiritual centre of world Jewry. At best it would be one spiritual centre among several;† the establishment of the state was not the fulfilment of the millennial aspirations of Judaism. Jewish culture was wider than Israel, and it was not true that only there was a full Jewish life possible. The Jewish tradition, Judaism itself, was shot through with assimilation – the Jewish holidays such as Passover, Shavuot and Succot had been taken over from the Canaanites, the legal concepts embodied in the Mishnah, the Midrash and the Talmud had been borrowed from a non-Jewish environment, and so it had been throughout the ages. There was no reason to assume that Israeli culture would be specifically Jewish in any meaningful sense or superior to Jewish culture elsewhere.

The controversy between Zionists and their liberal critics has continued for a long time and the end is not in sight. The essential arguments on both sides have changed little over the years. The optimistic assumptions of the liberals were not borne out by the turn European history took after the First World War. The reality of the holocaust surpassed by far the direct predictions of the Zionists. But as one anti-Zionist commented after the Second World War, that tragedy was not the result of the lack of a Jewish state. The annihilation could also have happened in Israel had Hitler not been stopped at El Alamein. Twice in their history Jews had suffered a national disaster when they had their own state.‡

The liberals' critique of Zionism was not all wrong. They were on weak ground in stressing Israel's universal, spiritual mission in the diaspora, but they were right in pointing out that assimilation had made great strides in central and western Europe, and that despite discrimination the majority of Jews in these countries felt rooted in their respective homelands. They had more in common with their non-Jewish compatriots than with east European Jews, let alone those in Morocco or

---

* I. Maybaum, *The Faith of the Jew in the Diaspora*, London, 1956, pp. 118, 132.

† Jacob J. Petuchovski, *Zion Reconsidered*, New York, 1966, p. 78.

‡ Emanual Scherer, in F. Gross and B. Vlavianos, *Struggle for Tomorrow*, New York, 1965, p. 153.

Yemen. They were right in insisting that Zionism, in the given political conditions, had no answer for the masses of east European Jewry. As for the spiritual problems, the quest for identity faced by the Jews of western and central Europe, described in such lurid colours by Nordau, was regarded by the liberals, not altogether wrongly, as unduly pessimistic and overdramatised. True, there were dangerous anomalies, such as the predominant position of Jewish intellectuals in Germany and Austria, but in France and England the situation was different. In certain professions they were fully exposed to the limelight, and were bound to attract particular attention and provoke enmity, but even among the intellectuals the majority were gradually moving into fields such as science or medicine which were much less vulnerable 'ideologically' and where ethnic origin did not greatly matter.

Assimilation was a natural process. There was nothing shameful about it, despite the questionable behaviour of individual Jews over-eager to forget their past and to dissociate themselves from their people. It was not the first time in their history that whole communities had become assimilated and disappeared; the fact that assimilation was not likely to function in some countries did not imply that it would not be a success in others. If the majority of Jews of central and western Europe did not feel an inner need for a national existence and a national culture, there was nothing Zionism could do about it. It was not a question of 'good' Jews and 'bad' Jews, of patriots and renegades. Since a territorial centre had not existed for many centuries, and since the need for one was no longer a generally accepted article of faith, it was up to the individual to make his choice. As the links uniting the Jews had grown so much weaker since the days of the emancipation, it was not a matter for surprise that the great majority in central and western Europe chose to remain in the existing fatherland rather than face the uncertainties of a national home.

This, briefly, is the case that can be made in retrospect for liberalism and assimilation. Despite Nazism and the murder of millions of Jews, it is not easy to refute. It was only a catastrophe of unprecedented extent which enabled Zionism to achieve its aim of a Jewish state. It could not have saved east European Jewry. It had a blueprint for a solution but the conditions for the transfer of millions of Jews simply did not exist. The debate between Zionism and assimilationism is, in a sense, over; few now advocate assimilation as the liberals and the protest rabbis did at the turn of the century. But as the majority of Jews have not chosen to become citizens of the Jewish state the dilemma persists and Zionism has not won the battle. Since a national or even a cultural revival in the diaspora is unlikely, assimilation is bound to take its course in the years to come with or without the benefit of ideological justification.

Zionism and Jewish Orthodoxy

While Zionism was ridiculed from the start by the liberals, it was taken far more seriously by the orthodox, who with some notable exceptions regarded it as their mortal enemy. If the liberals found, however reluctantly, some redeeming features in Zionism, the leading east European rabbis regarded it as an unmitigated disaster, a poisonous weed, more dangerous even than Reform Judaism, hitherto regarded as the main menace.* A few orthodox rabbis such as Raines gave it their blessing and established a religious faction within the Zionist movement. But orthodoxy in Germany, Hungary and the countries of eastern Europe rallied in order to be able to fight the national movement more effectively. To promote this aim *Agudat Israel* was founded in 1912, uniting leading rabbis and orthodox laymen from various countries. The doctrinal position of the orthodox was complicated, for the Torah stated unequivocally that it was the duty of every faithful believer to settle in the Holy Land (*Mitzvat Yishuv Eretz Israel*). Some of the ultra-orthodox argued that this was merely one out of 248 religious duties which could conceivably clash with others no less important. But this was hardly a tenable position, as other orthodox leaders pointed out. 'Thou shall not kill', was also only one out of many obligations, but it was unqualified. How then was opposition to Zionism to be justified?

Samson Raphael Hirsch, the spiritual leader of German Jewish orthodoxy in the nineteenth century, had stated well before the advent of Zionism that Jews had to hope and pray for their return to Zion, but actively to accelerate the redemption was a sin and strictly prohibited. Accordingly Zionism was interpreted as the most recent and the most dangerous phase in the continuing Satanic conspiracy against the House of Israel, the most recent and the least reputable of a long series of catastrophic pseudo-messianic attempts to forestall the redemption by human action.† The religious sages of eastern Europe joined in a chorus of condemnation. Zadok of Lublin wrote that he hoped unto the Lord

---

* For a collection of the sayings of leading rabbis against Zionism, see M.Blach (ed.), *Dovev sifte yeshenim* (3 vols.), New York, 1959.

† Emil Marmorstein, *Heaven at Bay*, London, 1968, p. 71.

that the Day of Redemption would come. But he was not willing to settle in Jerusalem lest such a step would be interpreted as giving accursed Zionism the stamp of approval. Or, as a representative of ultra-orthodox thought in Britain argued more recently, Zionism was a heresy consisting of a complete and essential denial of the whole content of Judaism: 'We are in Golus [the diaspora] for our sins. We have been elected by Divine Providence and must lovingly accept our sentence.'* (It may be noted in passing that this interpretation of Jewish tradition resembles the views of a liberal critic such as Gershenson who was an apostate from Judaism.)

Yet when all was said and done, there was still the obligation in the Bible to settle in Palestine, and the issue continued to trouble the orthodox camp. According to their spokesmen there was a difference between the obligation to live in Eretz Israel and the duty to settle there. Orthodox Jews were exempt for a variety of reasons, such as physical danger, economic obstacles, the difficulty of giving an orthodox religious education to their children, or the impossibility of studying the Torah in Eretz Israel.† Zionism, moreover, was not regarded as a movement to rebuild Palestine but on the contrary as a heretical attempt to establish a state, a Jewish kingdom, which according to tradition was the privilege of the Messiah. The ideologists of the ultra-orthodox wing, such as Isaac Breuer, regarded the Jews as a *religious nation*, i.e. a nation different from all others inasmuch as religion was its only content. Zionism wanted to leave religion out of the national revival and as a result the nation would become an empty shell. For without religion the whole of Jewish history over thousands of years lacked any purpose. The Jewish nation had refused to perish because it wanted to save its religion and, conversely, religion had saved the Jewish nation. Having suffered so greatly for two thousand years, would it not be madness now to aim at transforming the Jews into a nation like all others, to politicise them, to establish a state which was neutral towards religion.‡ According to this doctrine, Zionism was depriving the Jewish nation of its real cultural content by borrowing modern nationalism from western Europe. Thus it had embarked on the worst kind of assimilationism. To the argument that if the Jewish nation had produced geniuses like Spinoza and Marx, if it had made an enormous contribution to western civilisation even in the diaspora, it would reveal even greater capacities once the anomaly

* I.Domb, *The Transformation*, London, 1958, pp. 138, 192, 195.
† J.Rosenheim, *Kol Ya'akov*, Tel Aviv, 1954, p. 68.
‡ I.Breuer, *Judenproblem*, Halle, 1918, pp. 64–5.

and one-sidedness of the diaspora was replaced by a Jewish state, Breuer replied that these speculations were no longer based on historical experience, nor would they give legitimacy to Jewish national claims. A people could press its demands only on the basis of what it had achieved, not on what it was likely to achieve in the future.*

This, in brief and in its most sophisticated form, was the line taken by the anti-Zionist orthodox. In its propaganda and education Agudat Israel bitterly denounced Zionism. In east European communal politics it cooperated even with the assimilationists, for Zionism was the more dangerous enemy. On the other hand, for a long time Agudat Israel refused to collaborate with religious Zionist parties (such as the Mizrahi) because they were part of the world Zionist movement which had declared its neutrality in religious affairs. Occasionally concessions were made. At a meeting in Vienna in 1923 it was decided that the settlement of Eretz Israel in the spirit of orthodox religious tradition was one of the aims of Agudat Israel. But it was one aim out of many and not among the most important. After the Balfour Declaration orthodox opposition became in fact more intense as the Zionists used the opportunity not to promote the economic development of the country but to build it up on a secular basis, without taking into account the religious feelings of the orthodox.† The orthodox were thinking particularly of such abominations as giving women the right to vote and rejecting the advice of the orthodox rabbis concerning the observance of religious laws in daily life.

The extreme orthodox element in Palestine, mainly concentrated in Jerusalem, found an ally in the Aguda in its struggle against Zionism. Their leaders regularly protested to the British government and the League of Nations against Zionist oppression and against its endeavour to make the national home a Zionist home. On occasion they also tried to enlist the help of Arab leaders against 'Zionist domination'. The conflict came to a head with the murder of a member of the executive of the Aguda. De Han, a Dutch Jew by origin, was a gifted poet and a tormented soul. ('For whom am I waiting in this night, sitting at the wall of the temple – for God or for Muhammed the stable boy?' he asked in one of his poems.)‡ On other occasions he called himself a 'hater of God' or the 'pig of God'. At one time a Socialist and a free-thinker, and married to a Christian wife whom he would not divorce,

---

* *Ibid.*, pp. 66–7.

† I.Breuer, *Das Jüdische Nationalheim*, Frankfurt a. M., 1925, p. 23.

‡ J.De Han, *Quatrinen*, Amsterdam, 1924, pp. 77, 138.

he felt himself under the strongest compulsion to make amends after his conversion. He violently denounced Zionism in cables to British newspapers, and attacked the Balfour Declaration as well as the high commissioner and other British officials for their allegedly pro-Zionist policy.

Some of his writings were plainly antisemitic: the Jews stood for world revolution and a Jewish world government. Everywhere they constituted an element of destruction and decomposition. They had overthrown tsarism in Russia and were responsible for the defeat of Germany and Austria in the First World War.* If Russia and Poland could not absorb the Jews, Palestine could stand them even less. He dressed like an Arab and used to address Jews in Arabic though he knew that they had not mastered the language. De Han was assassinated in the streets of Jerusalem on 30 June 1924. Many years later it became known that he had been killed by members of Hagana without the knowledge of the high command. For the extreme orthodox Jews of Jerusalem he became a hero who had died like a medieval martyr for the greater glory of God. De Han was by no means a typical Aguda leader, but the whole affair revealed the depths of hatred that had accumulated. Rabbi Sonnenfeld habitually referred to Zionists as 'evil men and ruffians'; hell had entered Eretz Israel with Herzl. Rosenheim, the political head of central European orthodoxy, who was accustomed to using far more moderate language, nevertheless warned the religious Zionists against the 'mortal danger' they risked by collaborating with those who did not accept the divine law.†

The new realities created in Palestine gradually forced the leaders of anti-Zionist orthodoxy to modify their approach. They did not accept Zionism, but they slowly moved towards taking a more active part in settlement in Palestine. The main agents of change were the youth organisations of the Aguda and the workers section founded in Poland in 1922. Some of the latter's members migrated during the 1920s and 1930s and established settlements in various parts of the country. There was also a change in their attitude to the Hebrew language, which previously had been taboo; only the extremist fringe persisted in using Yiddish exclusively. The murder of orthodox, anti-Zionist Jews in Hebron, Safed and Jerusalem during the riots of 1929 came as a shock to members of the Aguda and made them more inclined to cooperate in some fields with the Zionists, even though they refused as a matter of

---

* *Kadosh De Han, Hayav vemoto*, Jerusalem, 1925, p. 39.
† Rosenheim, *Agudistische Schriften*, p. 58.

principle to join the National Council of Palestinian Jewry (*Va'ad Leumi*) which had been set up in the 1920s. They had pressed demands which were wholly unacceptable to the non-religious majority, namely that the National Council should acknowledge the authority of the Torah, that no open desecrator of the Sabbath should be eligible for membership, that women should not have the vote, and that the council should not subsidise institutions, such as the workers' kitchens, which served forbidden food.*

Above all, Nazi rule and the holocaust caused confusion and eventually a deep split in the ranks of the Aguda. Isaac Breuer accused his own movement of having neglected Palestine, though in theory 'constructive work in Palestine' had been part of its programme for a long time: 'Do not leave Jewish history to the Zionists', Breuer said in a speech in 1934; if Aguda really wanted to combat Zionism it had again to become part of Jewish history, to prepare the Jewish homeland and the Jewish people for their reunion under the rule of the Torah. This was the will of divine providence which orthodox Jewry could afford to ignore only at the risk of its own existence.† If the Zionists had sacrificed meta-history for history, i.e. the wish to be like all other nations, orthodoxy had been so involved in its struggle against Zionism that it had fallen down in its duty towards the Holy Land. It had not been aware that the Balfour Declaration and the resettlement of Palestine was a historical-metahistorical miracle, an encounter between these two strands in religion such as had occurred once before with the Revelation at Sinai.‡

In 1937 Breuer asked the Grand Assembly of the Aguda to make up its mind whether the Balfour Declaration constituted a divinely imposed task or a Satanic contrivance, but received no answer. Some of the Palestinian spiritual leaders of orthodoxy sympathised with him, whereas Rosenheim and other leading members expressed doubts. Was the Aguda strong enough to counteract Zionist influence in Palestine since the Zionists had such a headstart? Building up Palestine was meritorious, but only if the law of the Torah was observed; if not, the whole effort was in vain. Which meant that in Rosenheim's view (in 1934) it was not at all certain whether orthodox Jewry was right to link its fate to that of a secular Eretz Israel. He and his anti-Zionist friends

---

* Quoted in Marmorstein, *Heaven at Bay*, p. 82; see also Breuer, *Das jüdische Nationalheim*, *passim*.

† I.Breuer and J.Rosenheim, *Eretz Israel und die Orthodoxen*, Frankfurt a. M., 1934, *passim*.

‡ I.Breuer, *Moriah*, Jerusalem, 1944, p. 210.

did not essentially modify their views even after the holocaust. They argued that the Zionist slogan of evacuating Europe, of the ingathering of the exiles, was wrong, for who could know in what part of the diaspora the mysterious fate of the house of Jacob was yet to unfold itself before the coming of the Messiah?* The orthodox remnants of European Jewry thus received conflicting advice: emissaries from Palestine tried to persuade them to come to Eretz Israel to strengthen the orthodox forces there, whereas Agudist spokesmen from the west advised them to emigrate to America.

In Palestine in the years between the end of the war and the establishment of the state of Israel there was a small but highly active and vociferous ultra-extreme group which accused the Aguda of succumbing to Zionist influence. These were the 'Guardians of the City' (*Neturei Karta*) in Jerusalem, headed by Amram Blau and Aharon Katzenellenbogen. They had the support of the followers of the rabbis of Brisk (Poland) and Szatmar (Hungary), who had found their way to America and other western countries, and the blessing of several talmudic sages such as Hazon Ish.† According to their teachings, everyone who accepted the state of Israel was an apostate, for it was the purpose of the state to lead the Jews away from religion. In their eyes there was no longer any substantial difference between the Aguda, which was compromising with the Zionists, and the Mizrahi, which had been pro-Zionist from the start. The rabbis who supported the Aguda were charged by the ultra-extremists with responsibility for poisoning the new generation, and for the blasphemies committed daily and openly in the state of Israel.‡ The Guardians refused to take part in the war of independence of 1948, and demanded the internationalisation of Jerusalem under the supervision of the United Nations. They refused to accept Israeli identity cards, for they believed that any concession to secularism and modern life, however small, would sooner or later spell doom for traditional Judaism as they understood it. In their stubborn struggle to preserve their specific character they were willing to recognise every state in the world but the one established by their own co-religionists. Their attacks on the Aguda were justified in so far as this party had indeed, after the end of the Second World War, moved towards a compromise with Zionism. The bastions of religious orthodoxy

* *Eretz Israel und die Orthodoxen*, p. 19; also *Knesia mekhina fun Agudas Jisroel in London*, n.d., p. 4.
† Marmorstein, *Heaven at Bay*, p. 89.
‡ *Lifkoah Enayim*, Jerusalem, 1954, p. 15.

in eastern Europe having been destroyed, its leaders realised that the future of Judaism in Eretz Israel depended on Agudist support for the Jewish community in that country and the extraction of maximal advantages for the faith in exchange for displays of solidarity.* About one year before the establishment of the state, an understanding was reached between them and the Palestinian Zionist leaders on certain issues of special importance, such as observance of the Sabbath and of the dietary laws, and the laws on education and marriage. Thus the ground was paved for participation by the Aguda in Israeli politics as part of the United Religious Front. Later on, in 1961, the workers section of Agudat Israel, which had split away from the main body, was represented for the first time in the Israeli cabinet.

The conflicts within the orthodox camp after the establishment of the state and its disputes with the non-religious majority are beyond the scope of the present study. It may be unfair to describe the change in the Aguda attitude towards Zionism solely in terms of practical politics. The reorientation had started, after all, well before 1948. Addressing fellow members of the Aguda in 1936 from Jerusalem, where he had settled, Breuer stated that there could be no doubt of the continuity of the link between the Jewish people and Eretz Israel throughout the centuries. The Jewish people had no reason therefore to fear the judgment of the god of history in its dispute with the Arabs.† Ten years later Aguda representatives defended, albeit on religious grounds, the Jewish claim to Eretz Israel in their testimony to the Anglo-American Committee of Inquiry. In the coming of the state they saw the finger of God, heaven's gift to the martyred Jews. The establishment of the state was not the redemption, but it was the beginning of the redemption. Thus after almost a century of opposition the majority of the orthodox rallied to the Jewish state. Israel had come into being, as they saw it, not as a result of the efforts of the Zionists but as a gift from heaven. It was a 'sacred opportunity and challenge' and did not necessarily involve them in recognising Zionism.‡ With all their doctrinal extremism, the majority had always shown great realism in their policies. Following the injunctions of S.R.Hirsch and other sages, they had done nothing to help in the founding of the state. But once it had come into being it was a *fait accompli* which they could not ignore.

---

* Marmorstein, *Heaven at Bay*, p. 86.
† I.Breuer, *Eretz Jsrael Briefe*, Frankfurt a. M., 1936, p. 22.
‡ Marmorstein, *Heaven at Bay*, pp. 88–9.

Territorialism

Although in a modified form, the critique of Zionism from the liberal-assimilationist and the religious-orthodox points of view persists to this day, whereas the opposition of the Bundists and the Territorialists is now largely a matter for the historical record. The Territorialists split away from the Zionist movement after the plan to settle in Uganda had been rejected. In 1905 the Jewish Territorial Organisation (JTO) was founded in London under the leadership of Israel Zangwill and some Anglo-Jewish friends, and with the support of various left-wing ex-Zionist groups in eastern Europe. They maintained that the vital interests of the Jewish people were not in Palestine: 'We do not attach any real value to our supposed "historical rights" to that country.' Nor did they acknowledge any organic connection between Zionism and Palestine.* JTO organised an expedition to Angola and investigated the possibility of settlement in Tripolitania, Texas, Mexico, Australia and Canada. Nothing, however, came of all these schemes, and in 1925 JTO was disbanded. Ten years later the Freeland League, a neo-territorial movement, came into being. It did not insist on political independence but was ready to accept autonomy in cultural and religious affairs. It drew up plans for mass settlement in western Australia, Surinam, and other parts of the globe, but these were no more successful than the JTO schemes. The Freeland League welcomed the establishment of the state of Israel but declared that in view of its limited area the country could not solve the problem of Jewish homelessness. With the liquidation of the displaced persons camps after the Second World War and the absorption of these people in various parts of the world, the league faded away.

Far more substantial was the influence of the Bund, the strongest Jewish party in Poland during the interwar years. As a militant Socialist party, it was equally opposed to cooperating with the Jewish bourgeoisie, the orthodox, and the Communists. Unlike Lenin, its leaders believed that the Jews were a nation, even though they were dispersed over many countries. Their slogan was 'Nationhood without statehood', and they emphatically rejected the idea that the Jews had no fatherland, that they were strangers everywhere but in Palestine.† They claimed that the establishment of a Jewish state would perpetuate the conflict between Jews and Arabs and that in any case Palestine was too small

---

* Quoted in F.Gross and B.Vlavianos, *Struggle for Tomorrow*, New York, 1954, p. 115.
† *Ibid.*, p. 165.

to solve the Jewish problem. They criticised labour Zionism for its willingness to collaborate with capitalists and the orthodox, on the ground of their incompatibility with Socialist principles.

The Bund ceased to exist after the extermination of Polish Jewry and the establishment of a Communist régime in that country. Some of its leaders succeeded in making their way to America, where they continued to maintain in their publications that their opposition to Zionism had been fully justified. Israel would never contain more than a minority of the Jewish people. Moreover, its very existence was dependent on the well-being and prosperity of western Jewry. If American Jews were compelled to leave their native country, Israel could not escape ruin and disaster. What Zionism had fought for and what it had achieved were two different things. It had striven for the liberation of all Jews. It had accomplished, at best, the risky liberation of a minority. It had split the Jewish people into two different nationalities.*

The Bund had been a specifically east European phenomenon; its ideology could not be transplanted to the western hemisphere. It made a certain impact on the American Jewish labour movement during the years before and after the First World War, but as this movement became more and more Americanised, and as the social structure of American Jewry changed, this influence, too, faded away. The sons and daughters of the Bundist workers became physicians, lawyers and teachers, fully absorbed into American cultural and political life.

S.M.Dubnow, the greatest Jewish historian of his time, took a position somewhere between the Bund and Zionism. No one could have accused him of preaching assimilationism; he denounced it as treason and moral defeat. But in contrast to the early Zionists he saw the Jews as a 'spiritual-historical nation'. This did not necessarily conflict with their civic duties in their native countries. Unlike the Zionists, he did not regard the Jews as an abnormal nationality. Zionism was in his eyes a renewed form of Messianism, an ecstatic idolatry of the national idea. There was much idealism in it, but from the practical point of view it seemed to him a web of fantasy. The Lovers of Zion had assisted 3,600 Jews to settle in Palestine in seventeen years – 212 per year! Even if the Zionists succeeded in settling half a million within the next century, this would be no more than those living at present in the Kiev district. For this reason he thought it irresponsible of Lilienblum and Ahad Ha'am to talk about the rejection of the diaspora. Unlike the Bundists, he did not rejoice in the prospect of diaspora nationalism: 'If we had the

---

* *Ibid.*, p. 170, *et seq.*

power to transfer the entire diaspora to a Jewish state we would do so with the greatest joy. We acquiesce in the diaspora only because of historical necessity and we strive to preserve and develop the national existence of the greater part of the nation which will remain!' On another occasion (in 1901) he wondered whether it might be possible after all to effect the gradual colonisation of Palestine in such a way that there would eventually be a Jewish population of about one million. In that case the conditions would exist for achieving national autonomy as he envisaged it. Dubnow emigrated from his native Russia after 1917, settled in Berlin and was killed, well in his eighties, in the Riga ghetto in 1941. Not long before his death he noted in one of his books that Jewish Palestine had grown more quickly than he had anticipated in the 'days of his little faith' when he had accused the Zionists of lack of realism.*

Marxism and the Jewish Question

While Socialism had many followers among the Zionists, Socialist theory, especially the Marxist variety, was hostile to the Jewish national movement. Marx, Engels, and their immediate disciples were pre-occupied with the problems of class and class struggle. A systematic study of national movements was undertaken only later on, towards the turn of the century, especially in countries where these issues were of particular importance and urgency, as in prewar Austria. Marx and Engels shared the view of their liberal contemporaries that cultural, economic and social progress was gradually overcoming national exclusivity and that the world (or Europe at any rate) was moving towards internationalism. Unlike the liberals, they did not believe that all national movements were equal; some were downright reactionary. It all depended on whether a particular national movement served or impeded the cause of revolution. About east European Jewry they were ignorant, and as for the Jews in the west they again shared the liberal belief that assimilation would solve that problem. The young Marx did publish an essay on the Jewish question but it is of greater interest to the student of metaphysics than of history. Not for a moment did he believe in the existence of a Jewish people; for Moses Hess' Zionism he had nothing but contempt. The idea that Judaism and the Jews as a

---

* See his essays published in *Voskhod*, November 1897, January-April 1898, December 1901, *et seq*. German edition, *Die Grundlagen des Nationaljudentums*, Berlin, n.d.; and K.S. Pinson, *Nationalism and History*, Philadelphia, 1958, pp. 163, 185.

collective had a future must have appeared to him as an aberration typical of the loose thinking of someone too stupid to understand the implications of his own doctrine. Judaism for Marx was a totally negative phenomenon, something to be got rid of as quickly and as radically as possible. As far as he personally was concerned, his Jewish origin must have appeared an unfortunate accident of birth and a matter of considerable embarrassment. But this was by no means an original or specifically 'Marxist' attitude. Many of his anti-Socialist contemporaries reacted in exactly the same way. They were assimilationists who thought that a man's national origin was not of great importance. They were first and foremost citizens of the world and only secondarily German, Austrian or Russian nationals. Socialists of a later day held the same view, and in this respect there was no substantial difference between revolutionaries and reformists. Leon Blum and Eduard Bernstein, Rosa Luxemburg and Leon Trotsky thought of themselves above all as members of the international Socialist movement.

Only towards the end of the nineteenth century did the Jewish issue assume greater importance in Socialist thought and policy, partly as the result of the spread of antisemitism. There were many Jews in the leadership of the European and American Socialist parties; in fact some delegations at the meetings of the socialist International before 1914 were almost exclusively Jewish. But with the rise of nationalist and antisemitic currents their position became more difficult and they grew more conscious (and self-conscious) of their Jewish origin. This did not, however, affect their basic conviction, that the coming Socialist revolution would solve the Jewish question wherever it existed, and that meanwhile everyone had to participate actively in the struggle for the liberation of the working class in his country of origin. In western Europe early Zionism was regarded by Socialists as a romantic, Utopian, reactionary aberration. Bernard Lazare was almost alone in sympathising with the new movement. In eastern Europe, too, not only Zionism but even less ambitious forms of Jewish nationalism such as Bundism, with its demand for cultural-national autonomy, were emphatically rejected by the leading Socialists. For Plekhanov and the men of his generation the Bundists were merely 'Zionists suffering from seasickness'. The ideological rationale for Socialist anti-Zionism was provided by Karl Kautsky, for many years the most respected interpreter of Marxist doctrine for west and east European Socialists alike.

According to Kautsky, the traits derived from the primitive races of man tended to disappear as economic evolution progressed; the Jews were a mixed race, but so were the non-Jews.* In the past the Jews had been an exclusive, hereditary caste of urban merchants, financiers, intellectuals, and a small number of artisans, who from generation to generation bequeathed certain traits peculiar to these strata. But with the advance of industrial capitalism, the barriers were gradually broken down, the Jews obtained equal rights, and many of them were absorbed by the peoples among whom they lived. Antisemitism, or 'the Jewish peril', was given a new lease of life by the reaction of the petty bourgeoisie against liberalism. There were two forms of defence against this pressure: proletarian solidarity and Jewish solidarity. Among the Jews of eastern Europe, for specific economic and social reasons the call for national solidarity, i.e. Zionism, had found a considerable echo, but it had no future. Where could space be found for a Jewish state, since all regions in the civilised world had been pre-empted? How were the Jews to be induced to work in agriculture? How was a powerful industry to be developed in Palestine? All theoretical considerations apart, Kautsky thus saw in 1914 insurmountable obstacles on the road to the realisation of the Zionist aim.

His views had not basically changed when he returned to the subject after the war. He was impressed by the idealism of the Jewish pioneers in Palestine and their achievements, which, he thought, must convince anyone who had doubted Jewish energy and resolution.† But Zionist enthusiasm was not likely to persist. He predicted that Jewish *Luft-menschen* and intellectuals would again congregate in the cities and the Palestinian proletariat would become more class conscious. As a result, Jewish capitalists would lose interest, and without capital the process of rebuilding would come to a halt. At best, Jews in Palestine would come to outnumber the Arabs, and the new Jewish state, although not embracing the great mass of world Jewry, would nevertheless be predominantly Jewish in character. But this was not at all likely, for the political conditions were rapidly becoming worse: 'Whatever Zionism does not attain within the next few years, it will never attain at all.'‡ Zionism, to summarise Kautsky's view, was not a progressive but a reactionary movement. It aimed not at following the line of necessary evolution but at putting a spoke in the wheel of progress. It denied the

---

* K.Kautsky, *Rasse und Judentum*, Berlin, 1914; quoted here from the revised English translation, *Are the Jews a Race?* London, 1926, p. 89 *et seq.*
† *Ibid.*, p. 202.
‡ *Ibid.*, p. 207.

right of self-determination of nations and proclaimed instead the doctrine of historical rights.

At this point Kautsky deviated from the views of Marx and Engels, who attached little importance to national self-determination; they frequently referred with contempt to 'lousy little peoples' whose interests were to be ignored in the higher interest of history. Thus America's war against Mexico was progressive because it had been waged in the interest of history, and Germany's annexation of Schleswig was justified in the name of civilisation against barbarism, of progress against the *status quo*. The fact that Herzl and Nordau intended to carry western civilisation to the east would not necessarily have shocked Marx and Engels as it shocked liberals of a later day. They would have rejected Zionism for reasons of *Realpolitik*, because it appeared too late on the international scene and was not strong enough to accomplish its self-proclaimed task.

Kautsky was sure that the Palestinian adventure would end in tragedy. The Jews would not become more numerous than the Arabs, nor would they succeed in convincing the Arabs that Jewish rule could be to their advantage. 'Jewish colonisation in Palestine must collapse as soon as the Anglo-French hegemony over Asia Minor (including Egypt) collapses, and this is merely a question of time, perhaps of the very near future.'* There was no longer any doubt about the final victory of the Arabian [*sic*] people. The only question was whether they would reach it by peaceful concessions or by a period of savage guerrilla warfare and bloody insurrections. The poor, weak Jewish settlers in Palestine would be the chief sufferers in this battle, 'the least able to defend themselves, as well as least capable of escaping'.† All one could hope for, therefore, was that the number of victims would not be great: 'But the dangers to the Jews who are lured to Palestine by a messianic aspiration do not exhaust all the baleful effects of Zionism. It is perhaps far worse that Zionism is wasting the fortunes and resources of the Jews in a wrong direction, at a moment when their true destinies are being decided on an entirely different arena, for which decision it would be necessary for them to concentrate all their forces.'‡ Kautsky was referring to eastern Europe, where the fate of eight to ten million Jews was to be decided, and since emigration could not help them their destiny was intimately linked with the prospects of revolution. Zionism

* *Ibid.*, p. 211.
† *Ibid.*, p. 212.
‡ *Ibid.*, p. 213.

weakened them in this effort by encouraging ambitions which amounted to desertion of the colours.

What of the more distant prospect? Not liberalism, but only the victorious proletariat could bring complete emancipation. Then the Jews would be absorbed, would cease to exist as such. This was not to be deplored. The disappearance of the ghetto would not give rise to melancholy longings. Being city dwellers the Jews had the qualities most required for the progress of humanity. In western Europe, though few in number, they had produced Spinoza, Heine, Lassalle, Marx. But these spiritual giants had become effective only after they had burst the fetters of Judaism. Their work lay outside the sphere of Judaism, within the realm of modern culture, often in conscious opposition to Judaism. 'The Jews have become an eminently revolutionary factor [Kautsky wrote], while Judaism has become a reactionary factor. It is like a weight of lead attached to the feet of the Jews who eagerly seek to progress . . . the sooner [this social ghetto] disappears, the better it will be not only for society, but also for the Jews themselves.'* The disappearance of the Jews would not be a tragedy, like the disappearance of the American Indians or the Tasmanians. For it would not be a decline into degradation but an ascent to an immense field of activity, making possible the creation of a new and higher type of man. 'The Wandering Jew will thus at last find a haven of rest. He will continue to live in the memory of man as man's greatest sufferer, as he who has been dealt with most severely by mankind, to whom he has given most.'

Kautsky's views have been given at some length because they were the most consistent and systematic in their exposition of the Marxist arguments against Zionism. The critics of a later day, Communist, Trotskyite, or New Left, base their arguments in all essentials on his, occasionally with differences of detail and emphasis. The Zionist response to the Marxist critique can be summarised as follows: Marxism has been mistaken in underrating the importance of nationalism in recent history. National antagonisms have not declined in importance, even in countries in which Communism has prevailed. The Marxist analysis (like the liberal analysis) may be correct *sub specie aeternatis*, history may move in the direction of one world, with equality for all races, nations, and peoples. But Zionism is not concerned with these distant prospects. It emerged precisely because, in contrast to the liberal and Marxist analysis, it assumed that the Jewish question would not disappear in the foreseeable future. On the contrary, it was likely

* *Ibid.*, p. 246.

to become much more acute. The appeal to the Jews to participate in the revolutionary struggle in their homeland was no doubt well meant, but even on the assumption that the interests of the Jews and the revolution were identical, it was not practical politics. The Polish, German or Austrian working-class neither needed nor wanted the Jews as allies. They wanted to get rid of them, or at best regarded them as an embarrassment in their political struggle. Jews had played a leading part in the early phases of all Socialist and Communist parties, but since then they had everywhere been squeezed out. Among the founders and early leaders of the German Communist Party there were a great many Jews. The year before Hitler came to power there was not a single one among the hundred Communist deputies in the Reichstag. Events took a similar course in the Soviet Union. This was not necessarily a disaster in Zionist eyes, but it certainly underlined the argument that the position of the Jews in the revolutionary movement was highly problematical. A New Left critic of Zionism wrote in 1970 that subsequent events had shown that Trotsky and Zinoviev, Kamenev and Radek had been right, not the Zionists. But since all these Bolshevik leaders fell victims to Stalinism, the argument is not exactly convincing.* With antisemitism on the rise, the Jews in Europe were condemned to be passive onlookers, not active participants in the revolutionary struggle.

The Marxist critics did not foresee the victory of fascism and the extermination of the majority of European Jewry. It had been argued that the temporary victory of the counter-revolution, despite its appalling consequences, did not necessarily refute the Socialist thesis about the ultimate absorption and assimilation of the Jews in their native countries. But since Marxist analysis and prediction had been belied by recent history, there was no assurance that it would be borne out by future developments. The Marxist-Leninist thesis was based on the assumption that Communist régimes would successfully tackle the Jewish problem and that as a result the Jews as a group would disappear. But if there were no Jews left in Communist Poland in 1970 this happened not as the result of the emergence of a 'new and higher type of man', as Kautsky predicted, but in a manner reminiscent of the exodus of Jews from Spain in the fifteenth century. The Jews had been difficult to absorb for capitalist and Communist societies alike. Was it the 'reactionary character of Judaism' that was responsible for this, or the fact that the Jews were an 'eminently revolutionary factor' and thus

* *Zur Kritik der zionistischen Theorie und Praxis. Resistentia*, Frankfurt, 1970, p. 39.

likely to disturb the peace of post-revolutionary régimes? The possibility of Jewish assimilation in a truly internationalist society such as Lenin envisaged could not be excluded, but such a society had never existed and developments in the Soviet Union and the other Communist countries had moved steadily away from the internationalist ideal towards a new form of national socialism. In these conditions total assimilation had become difficult if not impossible.

Present difficulties quite apart, Zionists claim that recent history has shown that the Marxist concept of nationalism, of the nation-state in general and of antisemitism in particular, is at best grossly oversimplified. According to Marx and his disciples, such as Kautsky, the Jew was the representative of modern capitalism, or to be precise, commercial capitalism, and having lost this function was bound to disappear. But this concept never made much sense in eastern Europe, where the majority of Jews was concentrated, nor does it provide an explanation for pre- and post-capitalist antisemitism.

The Austrian Marxists, who faced the nationality problem in an acute form, were aware of the weakness of this aspect of Marxist theory, and provided in the works of Otto Bauer and Karl Renner a more sophisticated analysis. Whereas Kautsky had originally regarded a common language as the decisive criterion for the existence of a nation (later he added a second criterion: territory), Otto Bauer defined a nation as a community of fate, culture and character: 'An aggregate of people bound into a community of character by a community of fate.'*
The Jews were still a nation, especially those in eastern Europe, but everywhere they were in the process of ceasing to be one. As an 'absolute minority', one lacking a common territory, they were, unlike the Czechs, doomed as a nation, bound to be absorbed into the cultural community of the European nations.† While not rejecting Jewish national culture, and opposing compulsory assimilation, Bauer thought it would be wrong for the Jews to insist on national autonomy because this would retard the inevitable historical process.

This remained the attitude of the Jewish leaders and theoreticians of Austro-Marxism, and the advent of fascism did not make them change their mind. Friedrich Adler wrote in 1949 that he and his father (one of the founders of the party) had always considered the complete assimilation of the Jews both desirable and possible. Even the bestialities of Hitler had not shaken him in his belief that Jewish nationalism was

* O.Bauer, *Die Nationalitaetenfrage und die Sozialdemokratie*, Vienna, 1907, p. 135.
† *Ibid.*, p. 366 *et seq.*

bound to generate reactionary tendencies, namely the resurrection of a language which had been dead for almost two thousand years and the rebirth of an antiquated religion.* The non-Jewish leaders of Austro-Marxism took on occasion a more lenient view of Zionism. Karl Renner developed a highly complicated concept of non-territorial autonomy as the only feasible way to safeguard the interests of minorities in a multinational state. He did not include the Jews in this scheme, but, unlike Bauer, did not *expressis verbis* exclude them. Both Bundists and Zionists welcomed Renner's scheme and adapted it for their own purposes. According to Pernerstorfer, another Austrian Socialist leader, it was up to the Jews to decide whether they were a nation or not. There was no doubt that they had the right to national existence, but whether the practical difficulties on the road to national autonomy could be overcome was another question. Pernerstorfer thought that the Jews in eastern Europe would survive in the long run only if they got an independent state.†

Such individual voices apart, the attitude of International Social Democracy towards Zionism remained hostile until the First World War. *Neue Zeit*, the theoretical organ of the German Socialists, dismissed Herzl's *Judenstaat* as Utopian and unworthy of serious consideration, a beautiful cloak in which a nation no longer alive was to appear on the historical stage for the last time, to disappear after that forever.‡ A few years later another (Jewish) contributor explained Zionism as the reaction of the Jewish bourgeoisie to modern antisemitism. Social democracy was not against Zionism in principle, he argued, but since the (bourgeois) Zionists were trying to achieve their aim not by a liberation struggle but by bargaining with Turkey, and since they were moreover preaching class solidarity and national separatism and did not reject religion, International Socialism could not support them.§ In English Socialist circles Zionism was condemned as reactionary through and through, with Russian-Jewish emigrés such as Theodore Rothstein taking a leading part in denouncing the movement.‖ On occasion, more sympathetic voices were heard. An English Socialist journal promised that once the class struggle was won, the Jews too would find

---

* Quoted in *Leo Baeck Year Book*, 10, London 1965, p. 275.

† Rudolf Springer [Karl Renner], *Der Kampf der oesterreichischen Nation um den Staat*, Leipzig, 1902, *passim*. E. Pernerstorfer, 'Zur Judenfrage', in *Der Jude*, 1916–17, p. 308.

‡ *Neue Zeit*, vol. 15, 1896–7, p. 186; vol. 16 1897–8, p. 600.

§ *Neue Zeit*, vol. 19, 1900–1, p. 324 *et seq.*

‖ *Justice*, 21 October 1899; quoted in E. Silberner, *Sozialisten zur Judenfrage*, Berlin, 1962, p. 262.

a place in the sun to shape their own national destiny. But on the whole English Socialists did not pay much attention to the issue. French Socialists were even less interested, but certainly not favourably inclined. After the publication in *Revue Socialiste* of a pro-Zionist article commenting on the Kishinev massacre, an editorial note dismissed the belief in Palestine as the home of all Jews as a myth. Zionism was psychologically understandable as a reaction to cruel persecution, but was born of despair and based on a myth. It was, like all other forms of nationalism, reactionary and reprehensible.* Before 1914 the only major exception to this wholesale rejection of Zionism on the part of the Left was the circle of the *Sozialistische Monatshefte*, a revisionist journal edited by Josef Bloch in Berlin, which pursued an independent line on this as on many other issues.

After the First World War many Socialists modified their attitude. Kautsky and the Marxist fundamentalists remained opposed, and the attacks emanating from these circles were harsh in both form and content. Zionism, according to a pamphlet by Alexander Szanto (to provide a fairly typical example), was a harmful illusion, the sooner it was liquidated the better for the Jews. There was no earthly chance that they would ever become a majority in Palestine. Zionism was reactionary and chauvinistic; far from contributing to the solution of the Jewish problem it was trying to sabotage the absorption of the Jews in their native countries. In central and western Europe assimilation was about to be completed, Szanto wrote in 1930: 'Antisemitism is merely engaged in rearguard actions'.† Time was working against Zionism, but while it did its mischief it was the duty of every Socialist to combat it, and not to be neutral. For Zionism was not a marginal phenomenon, it was a cancerous disease. 'Whoever is not against it is for it.'

There was, however, no longer a censensus on these lines in Socialist ranks. Vandervelde, one of the most respected figures of the Second International, and for many years its chairman, visited Palestine in the 1920s. Subsequently he wrote with sympathy about the work of the labour Zionists. Other leading social democrats, including Louis de Brouckère, Vincent Auriol, Camille Huysmans, George Lansbury, Arthur Henderson and Rudolf Breitscheid joined, in 1928, a Socialist Committee for Working Palestine. The right of the Jewish people to a national home in Palestine was recognised in various resolutions of international Socialist congresses between 1917 and 1920. Jean Longuet

---

⁀ʋoted in *ibid.*, pp. 89–90.

⁀to, *Der Zionismus – eine nationalistische und reaktionaere Utopie*, Berlin, 1930, pp. 52–3.

(Karl Marx's grandson), one of the leaders of French Socialism, declared in 1918 that the idea of a Jewish national home in Palestine deserved the support of international social democracy. His colleague Leon Blum even became one of the non-Zionist members of the Jewish Agency in 1929.

Of interest also were the changes in the attitude of leading Socialists of the older generation, such as Axelrod and Eduard Bernstein, who had earlier sharply opposed Zionism. Axelrod declared in 1917 that he was now in favour of the realisation of the aims of Zionism. Bernstein, father of the reformist trend in German social democracy, also joined the pro-Palestine Socialist committee in 1928. Before 1914 he, too, had favoured the denationalisation of the Jews who, he said, no longer had any specific mission. He conceded that east European Jews might have to emigrate, but a rescue action on their behalf was not to be coupled with the idea of a Jewish state, which in any case would face insurmountable obstacles. That assimilation was desirable was axiomatic for Bernstein, as it was for Kautsky, his chief antagonist. There was in their view no justification for any specific Jewish solidarity or national separatism. Zionism was obnoxious and reactionary because it impeded assimilation.* After the war Bernstein admitted that he had underrated the importance and persistence of antisemitism. He declared that he felt too much a German to become a Zionist, but added that he followed their activities with sympathy; Zionism had inspired its followers to great creative achievements. Poale Zion was an active member of the Second International, much to the dismay of anti-Zionists like Szanto. By and large Zionism remained a marginal issue for European social democracy. Most of its leaders did not believe in the success of the Palestinian experiment, for both ideological and practical reasons, but after 1918 their tone was on the whole sorrowful rather than angry. Those who had any first-hand knowledge of the Jewish problem were now more aware than previously that the issues involved were much more intricate than they had originally believed. By the late 1920s most Socialists had realised that even if Zionism was mistaken, the Second International and its affiliated parties had no ready alternative answer to the Jewish problem.

Lenin, Stalin, Trotsky

Communism was not beset by such doubts, claiming that it did have a

---

* *Neue Zeit*, vol. II, 1891–2, pp. 236–7; J.Moses (ed.), *Die Lösung der Judenfrage*, Berlin, 1907, passim; *Neue Zeit*, vol. 32, 1913–14.

solution. Lenin's rejection of Jewish nationalism was based on the writings of Kautsky and Otto Bauer, whom he frequently quoted. In some respects he went beyond them, asserting that nationalism, even in its most justified and innocuous form, was incompatible with Marxism. Even the demand for national cultural autonomy ('the most refined and therefore the most pernicious kind of nationalism') was thoroughly harmful; it satisfied the ideals of the nationalist petty-bourgeois and was in absolute contradiction to the internationalism of the proletariat.* Marxists had to fight against any form of national oppression, but it did not follow that the proletariat had to support the national development of every nation. On the contrary, it had to warn the masses against any nationalist illusions and to welcome every type of assimilation unless based on coercion. The Jews of the west had already achieved the highest degree of assimilation in the civilised countries. In Galicia and Russia they were not a nation either, but had remained a caste, through no fault of their own but because of the antisemites.† Jewish national culture was the slogan of rabbis and the bourgeois, and its advocates were therefore enemies of the proletariat.

Stalin, writing in 1913, elaborated Lenin's view, defining a nation as a historically evolved, stable community of language, territory, economic life and mental constitution expressed in a community of culture. According to this definition the Jews were, of course, not a nation. They had no continuous territory of their own which served as a political framework and a national market. Only 3 or 4 per cent of them were connected with agriculture, the remainder were city dwellers, scattered all over Russia, not constituting a majority in any single province. What kind of a nation was this, Stalin asked, that consisted of Georgian, Dagestani, Russian, American Jews, and so on? What kind of race, whose members lived in different parts of the world, spoke different languages, never saw each other and never acted in concert? This was not a real living nation; it was something mystical, amorphous, nebulous, out of this world. The demand for national cultural autonomy was therefore ridiculous. Autonomy was demanded on behalf of a nation whose existence was yet to be proven and whose future had not been recognised. All the Jews had in common was their religion, their common origin, and a few remaining national characteristics. But no one could seriously maintain that petrified religious rites and vanishing psychological traits were stronger than their socio-economic and

* Lenin, *Sochineniya* (second Russian edition), vol. 17, p. 118.
† *Ibid.*, p. 141.

cultural surroundings, which were inevitably leading to assimilation.* The Bolsheviks sincerely intended to solve the Jewish question in Russia by giving full freedom to all Jews; assimilation was to be actively furthered. The oppressed Jews of Russia and Galicia were to become equal citizens of the new Socialist society.

A detailed survey of the Jewish policy of the Communist Party of the Soviet Union lies outside the range of the present study. In brief, after the revolution a 'Jewish Commissariat' was established to deal with the specific problem of the Jewish population. Dimanshtein, its head, promised that a Palestine would be built in Moscow by making the masses productive, and by organising Jewish agricultural communes. Later, greater emphasis was put on the industrialisation of the Jewish population. They could maintain their own cultural institutions, such as schools, clubs, newspapers and theatres. Hebrew was banned but Yiddish could be freely used during the 1920s and 1930s. In the Ukraine and the Crimea, predominantly Jewish areas even received regional autonomy, and in March 1928 it was decided to set aside a special area in the Far East, Biro Bidzhan, for Jewish settlement. It was announced that by 1937 at least 150,000 Jews would be living there. There was tremendous enthusiasm among Jewish Communists abroad: 'The Jews have gone into the Siberian forests', Otto Heller wrote. 'If you ask them about Palestine, they laugh. The Palestine dream will long have receded into history when in Biro Bidzhan there will be motor cars, railways and steamers, huge factories belching forth their smoke. . . . These settlers are founding a home in the taigas of Siberia not only for themselves but for millions of their people.'† Kalinin, president of the Soviet Union, predicted that in ten years Biro Bidzhan would be the cultural centre of the Jewish masses. Even staunch anti-Communists like Chaim Zhitlovsky, one of the theoreticians of Jewish Socialism, and Lestschinsky, the sociologist, were deeply impressed; Biro Bidzhan would be a Jewish republic, a centre of genuine Jewish Socialist culture.

The dream of a Siberian Palestine did not last. Only a few thousand Jews came, and most of them turned back within a few months. Forty years after its foundation, Biro Bidzhan was a drab provincial region with about 25,000 Jewish inhabitants, a small percentage of the total population. No one, least of all the Soviet authorities and the Jewish Communists, wanted to be reminded of the affair. Partly it was the result of insufficient and incompetent planning, but basically it was not

---

* J.V.Stalin, *Marxism and the National Question*, New York, n.d., p. 6 *et seq.*

† Quoted in J.Leftwich, *What Will Happen to the Jews?* London, 1936, pp. 137, 149.

the fault of the authorities: Soviet Jews had no desire to build a second Zion on the shores of the Amur.

Despite the failure of Biro Bidzhan there was much sympathy in the west for the Soviet Union, the only country in which Jews were believed to be secure and in which the Jewish question was said to have been solved. These were the years of the world economic crisis, of the rise of fascist and antisemitic movements all over Europe. What, in comparison, had Zionism to offer? Its bankruptcy 'was final and irrevocable', Otto Heller wrote in 1931 in a much discussed book. In western Europe the assimilation of the Jewish bourgeoisie, as well as of the lower middle class and the workers, was an irresistible process. In the east, under Socialism, the Jewish question had been solved once and for all: 'Next year in Jerusalem? This question was answered by history long ago. The Jewish proletarians and the starving artisans of eastern Europe pose a very different question: next year in a Socialist society! What is Jerusalem to the Jewish proletarian? Next year in Jerusalem? Next year in the Crimea! Next year in Biro Bidzhan!'*

Heller's *Downfall of Judaism* presented the Stalinist case. Its argument was borrowed by and large from Kautsky, though the 'renegade' Kautsky was, for different reasons, by that time no longer in the good books of the Bolsheviks. It differed from Kautsky in adopting a more virulent tone: Zionism was a phenomenon frequently observed among a dying people; shortly before their demise they suddenly feel a new lease of life, only to expire the more quickly. Zionism was a product of the petty bourgeois stratum in European Jewry, a counter-revolutionary movement. It was an historical mistake, an impossibility, since it tried to detach the Jewish question from the problem of commodity production with which the fate of Jewry was indissolubly connected. It was an anachronism, contradicting not just the laws of historical development but of common sense.† Heller freely used Kautsky's similes without acknowledging their origin: Zionism was the last appearance of Ahasuerus, the eternal Jew on the historical scene. He had reached the end of the road. Judaism was doomed because it had lost its privileged, monopolistic position in capitalist society. At the same time the social conditions for a revival of antisemitism had disappeared. 'Zionism, the last, most desperate and most wretched kind of nationalism, was thus breathing its last.'

It was a persuasive theme, and, if its ideological premises were

---

* Otto Heller, *Der Untergang des Judentums*, Vienna, 1931, pp. 173–4.
† *Ibid.*, pp. 21–2.

accepted, logical and consistent despite its shrillness and arrogance. But the book had one major flaw: it ignored the writing on the wall. When it appeared in the bookshops Hitler's brownshirts were already marching through the cities of Germany. Two years later antisemitism in its most rabid form had seized Germany and continued to expand all over Europe despite the confident announcement that antisemitism had lost its 'social foundations'. A few years later Heller and many other Jewish Communists lost their lives in Nazi extermination camps or in one of the Soviet prisons from which there was no return.

The case of Otto Heller is of interest; the views he expressed were shared by thousands of young Jewish Communists all over Europe who were firmly convinced that Communism and no other movement was capable of solving the Jewish question. Nor was this belief limited to committed party members; a growing number of fellow travellers were influenced by it and Hitler's seizure of power only strengthened them in their conviction.

When Heller's book appeared in 1931 Europe was still relatively quiet, the situation of European Jewry seemingly secure. Six years later, when William Zukerman published *The Jew in Revolt*, there could no longer be any doubt about the impending catastrophe. *The Jew in Revolt* is an ambitious analysis of the Jewish situation at a time of crisis which suggests remedies. In the sharpest terms the author condemns the schemes for emigration from Nazi Germany, for the German Jews were deeply rooted in German soil and bound to their country by a thousand spiritual ties:

It is a gross slander on the German Jews whose love for the fatherland is proverbial, to represent them all as being ready to rush in panicky haste from it in a mass exodus at the first approach of misfortune. . . . After all, the Jews are not the only victims of persecution in Germany today. Why not a wholesale exodus of German Communists, Socialists, Pacifists, Liberals and Catholics? . . . The Jewish acceptance of the Jewish exodus plan from Germany is at the same time the voluntary acceptance of the entire Nazi point of view with regard to the Jews. It is a complete Jewish capitulation to the racial theory of Hitlerism. . . . It is playing the Nazi game in a manner which Hitler himself probably never dared to hope that the Jews would do.*

Zukerman believed that the main responsibility for the contemptible plan for emigration fell on the Zionist bourgeoisie:

Fanatical Zionist theoreticians have been even more busy than the Nazis in preparing schemes and plans. . . . Zionist financiers have actually raised

* W. Zukerman, *The Jew in Revolt*, London, 1937, pp. 121–3.

huge sums of money for its organisation and have started it on the road to success. The fact is that, inasmuch as the exodus plan has now become a popular solution for the Jewish problem, it is due more to a number of Zionist zealots and to a few big Zionist financiers than to the fascists. Of all the paradoxes of our time, this one will probably go down into history as the most curious of all.*

But the author had no doubt that the plot for mass emigration would fail:

In spite of the brutal Nazi persecution the bulk of German Jews will remain in Germany, and they will be there long, long after Hitler is gone, when even his name is a mere legend in German history. . . . They bear the cross of their suffering with dignity and fortitude, as behoves an ancient people which has seen martyrdom and knows that tyranny, no matter how powerful temporarily, cannot forever turn back the wheels of history. . . . They know that even if Hitler be all-powerful now and his régime successfully established for years to come, this is no reason why Jews should willingly accept his gospel of the ghetto and exile.

The picture as Zukerman saw it was not all black, for there was one country where the Jewish problem had been solved and it was showing the road to salvation to Jews everywhere. What struck him most forcibly in Russia was both the economic transformation of Russian Jewry and the mental change that had come with it:

Gone is the almost pathological desire of every Jewish parent to bring up his offspring as doctors or lawyers. Although the universities and higher schools of learning are open to the Jews as in no other country, there is no rush of a disorderly mob of Jewish youth into them . . . Jews are positively the best factory workers in Russia and are sought after in every great plant.

The Soviet Union had been virtually freed of the scourge of Jew-hatred, the very meaning of the word antisemitism was being rapidly forgotten. The Soviet Union had solved the Jewish problem 'economically, politically, and even psychologically. Whatever larger successes the Soviet régime may or may not have to its credit, it has certainly evolved a perfect solution of the Jewish problem.'† Zukerman concluded this eloquent account by proclaiming that the golden age of liberalism was at an end, that there was only one road open to the Jews, whether he approved of everything going on in the Soviet Union or not: as a Jew he could do nothing but follow the road shown by Moscow for the

* *Ibid.*, pp. 112–13.
† *Ibid.*, pp. 131, 236.

solution of the Jewish problem. This was a moral necessity. The great revolt of the Jews not only against capitalism but also against themselves was morally cleansing: 'Whatever its social or political danger to the Jews may be, morally it atones for everything. Spiritually, the social-revolutionary movement is saving the Jews for the world.'*

These extensive quotations are necessary to convey the full flavour of Zukerman's case, and again it should be said that such views were by no means the monopoly of an outsider. They were shared by liberals who had succumbed to despair, even by some Jewish communal leaders and rabbis. For this was the time when belief in the Soviet Union was at its height: Stalin had stamped out unemployment and illiteracy, he had liquidated neurosis, crime, juvenile delinquency and alcoholism. He had produced a new type of man and in the process antisemitism was rapidly disappearing. The appeal to the Jew of Germany not to be seduced by the siren song of the Zionists but to stay in their native country was not exclusively Communist either. It was shared, for instance, by the Bundists from whom Zukerman may have received some of his original inspiration.

The Communist critique of Zionism had its heyday in the 1930s but later lost much of its appeal, and not just because Biro Bidzhan had failed to offer a serious alternative to Palestine. It was above all the growing discrepancy between Bolshevik theory and practice which made the Communist case unconvincing. Lenin had no doubt been sincere in his belief that mankind was inexorably moving towards internationalism. It could have been argued that however much the Jews resented the demand to give up their national identity, the price asked was not too high if in return they received complete equality before the law, and if eventually all nations were to undergo cultural assimilation. But events in the Soviet Union were taking a very different course from that which Lenin had anticipated. In the 1930s patriotism returned with a vengeance, the national heroes of Russian history were restored to a place of honour, and generally nationalism became a factor of growing importance in Soviet domestic policy. This left the Jews in a vulnerable position: they were still expected to give up their national identity and to become assimilated, but it was no longer clear whether they should try to become Russians, Ukrainians, or Turkmen, or whether to be Soviet citizens *tout court*. If so, they would be the first and only Soviet citizens, in the same sense that the German Jews had been almost the only liberals and republicans in the Weimar period, a position both

* *Ibid.*, p. 255.

431

unenviable and, in the long run, untenable. Assimilation might have worked within several generations as a result of intermarriage and the absence of Jewish education, if the Jews had been left in peace. But they were singled out for attack in Stalin's last years, and again later on under his successors, and their fate in Czechoslovakia and Poland was no happier. They were denounced as cosmopolitans and nationalists at one and the same time. Such attacks, far from solving the Jewish problem, helped to perpetuate it. The Soviet attitude towards Zionism has remained consistently hostile. Originally it was rejected as a tool of British imperialism. Later, Moscow's alliance with the Arabs made a firm anti-Israeli policy imperative. But there is every reason to assume that the Soviet attitude would have been negative even if considerations of foreign policy had not been involved. It would have been unthinkable to permit several millions of Soviet Jews to emigrate to Palestine, as this would have been tantamount to an open admission of the failure of the Soviet nationalities policy. Thus the Jewish problem in the Soviet Union has remained unsolved. While assimilation is still the aim, the conditions for making this policy a success do not exist. Consequently, the appeal of Soviet Communism has declined among Jews both within Russia and outside. Of the many Jewish Communists in the west who gave enthusiastic support to the Soviet cause in the 1920s and 1930s, few were those who did not leave the party in disappointment. The official Communist case against Zionism, once advocated with so much ardour and conviction, no longer presents a serious ideological challenge.

Whatever Trotsky's quarrel with the old guard Bolsheviks, he did not disagree with their policy towards the Jews. Like them, he regarded Zionism as a wholly reactionary phenomenon. He showed little interest in the problem, and while he commented on a great many issues in world politics at one time or another he hardly ever dealt with Jewish affairs. One of the few exceptions was an article in *Iskra* in 1904 in which he called Herzl a shameless adventurer and referred to the 'hysterical sobbings' of Zionism. Towards the end of his life he slightly modified his position. Recent experience had taught him, he said in an interview in 1937, that his old hopes for assimilation had been over-optimistic. Perhaps the Jews did need a territory of their own after all, even under Socialism. But it would probably not be Palestine, and in any case the whole problem would hardly find a solution under capitalism.*

* *Forward* (Yiddish), 28 January 1937; see also 'On the Jewish Question', *Fourth International*, December 1945.

Some of Trotsky's disciples took a greater interest, and while they made no significant theoretical contribution (for their views, too, were based on Kautsky), their opinions have a certain historical relevance, for they later influenced the New Left in its anti-Zionist outlook.* The chief Trotskyite ideologist on Zionism and the Jewish question was the Belgian Leon, a former member of a Socialist-Zionist youth movement. Unlike most other Marxists who dealt with the problem, he was familiar with the writings of the theoreticians of labour Zionism. Having reached the conclusion that Zionism, not excluding its extreme left wing, was incurably reactionary in character, Leon invested considerable efforts in refuting it: other national movements in Europe had been closely linked with the ascending phase of capitalism, whereas the Jewish national movement appeared on the scene only after the process of the formation of nations was approaching its end. Far from being a result of the development of productive forces, Zionism reflected the petrifaction of capitalism. Capitalist decay was the basis for the growth of Zionism, but at the same time it was the reason for the impossibility of its realisation.† Judaism had been indispensable in pre-capitalist society but capitalism had destroyed the social bases on which Jews had for centuries maintained themselves.

There is little in this that could not be found in earlier Marxist writers, not even the far-fetched thesis that economic developments in Europe compelled the Jewish bourgeoisie to create a national state in order to develop its productive forces. For this is more or less what Borokhov had predicted, but in contrast to Borokhov, Leon regarded this as a regressive development, for the Jewish question could be solved only after the victory of world revolution. Once world revolution had prevailed, once capitalism had been overthrown, the national problem would lose its acuteness. For national-cultural and linguistic antagonisms were only manifestations of the economic antagonisms created by capitalism. Leon seems not to have been particularly concerned about the advent of fascism, for the 'very exacerbation of antisemitism prepared the road for its disappearance'. Fascism, he predicted, would accelerate the proletarianisation of the middle classes.‡ Leon was arrested by the Germans a year or two after these lines were written and died, like millions of other Jews, in a Nazi extermination camp.

* See, for instance, N.Weinstock, *Le Sionisme contre Israel*, Paris, 1968.
† A.Leon, *Conception materialiste de la question Juive*, Paris, 1946. Quotations are from the English edition, *The Jewish Question. A Marxist Interpretation*, Mexico, 1950, p. 210 *et seq.*
‡ *Ibid.*, pp. 222, 228.

Zionists paid little attention to the views of Leon and other Trotskyite ideologists, for wherever they differed from Kautsky and the Bolsheviks they offered no startling new insights. Even in West Germany, where the New Left devoted much time to the study and critique of Zionism, it did not go much beyond the traditional arguments of anti-Zionism such as those voiced before the First World War by the ('bourgeois') Anti-Zionist Committee.* Shorn of the ideological underpinnings (Kautsky, Lenin, Horkheimer-Adorno) it always amounted to proving that Arab nationalism was progressive whereas Jewish nationalism was evil. More attention was devoted by the Zionists to the strictures of Isaac Deutscher, perhaps because, unlike the Trotskyite and New Left writers, he was a well-known literary figure who reached a wide public and who, because of his background, was bound to know more about the subject than they did. Deutscher too regarded Zionism as a profoundly reactionary movement, but he admitted that the Bolsheviks had taken an over-optimistic view of the chances of solving the Jewish problem. At one stage in his career he engaged in public heart-searching, writing in 1954 that he had abandoned his anti-Zionism, which had been based on his confidence in the European labour movement: 'If instead of arguing against Zionism in the 1920s and 1930s I had urged European Jews to go to Palestine I might have helped to save some of the lives that were later extinguished in Hitler's gas chambers.'† The Jewish state, he wrote in this moment of weakness, had become an 'historical necessity and a living reality'. But he still believed that basically Zionism was a reactionary force and it did not therefore come as a surprise when, after the Six Day War and shortly before his own death, Deutscher made a bitter attack on Israel in which he argued (as he had done forty years earlier) that Arab nationalism was progressive while Jewish nationalism was reactionary, that Israel represented neo-imperialism in the Middle East, preached chauvinism, etc.‡ Zionism had worked from the outset for a purely Jewish state. Marxists should not allow their emotions and the memories of Auschwitz to drive them to support the wrong cause.

Deutscher's instinctive rejection of the Jewish national movement went deeper and was in a way quite unconnected with the conflict between Israel and the Arabs. All the Jewish geniuses throughout recent centuries, he wrote in his credo, the great revolutionaries of

---

* *Zur Kritik der Zionistischen Theorie und Praxis*, p. 7.

† I.Deutscher, *The Non-Jewish Jew*, London, 1968, pp. 111–12.

‡ *Ibid.*, p. 126 *et seq.*

modern thought such as Spinoza, Heine, Marx, Rosa Luxemburg, Trotsky, and Freud, had been heretics. They had all found Jewry too narrow, too archaic and too constricting. It is interesting to compare this list of non-Jewish Jews with Kautsky's (Spinoza, Heine, Lassalle, Marx), and with Otto Bauer's (Spinoza, Ricardo, Disraeli, Marx, Lassalle, Heine). They all looked for ideals and fulfilment beyond Judaism. They had in common their rootlessness and their vulnerability. They were the natural protagonists of cosmopolitanism, the advocates not of nation-states but of internationalism. It was the paradoxical consummation of the Jewish tragedy that the decay of bourgeois Europe had compelled the Jew to embrace the nation state.*

The composition of Deutscher's hall of fame is open to dispute, and it does seem a little far-fetched to equate Freud's and Heine's attitude towards their fellow Jews with Trotsky's and Rosa Luxemburg's. These two failed precisely because they were 'rootless Jews' and did not realise the depth of national feeling in Germany and Russia which made it quite illusory to pursue an internationalist policy. Trotsky wrote in his autobiography that nationalist passions and prejudices were incomprehensible to him from his earliest childhood, that they produced in him a feeling of loathing and moral nausea. Rosa Luxemburg complained to a friend (Mathilde Wurm) in 1917: 'Why do you come with your special Jewish sorrows? I feel just as sorry for the wretched Indian victim in Putamayo, the Negroes in Africa . . . I cannot find a special corner in my heart for the ghetto.' This in a way was an understatement of her position, because like some other Jewish revolutionaries she showed symptoms of that familiar phenomenon, Jewish self-hatred. It is difficult to imagine that Lenin, an internationalist second to none, would have referred with such dismay to 'special Russian sorrows'. Deutscher, theoretically at least, was aware of the dilemma; after all he does mention the vulnerability of the cosmopolitan Jew. But he had no clear answer for the perplexed Jewish revolutionaries of his own time. Deutscher's opposition to Zionism was based in the last resort on the liberal critique of the Jewish national movement. The erstwhile follower of the Galician Rabbi of Ger emerges as a modern, Socialist, protest rabbi unshaken in his belief that the world is moving away from national sovereignty and the nation-state towards internationalism, and that the message of the world of tomorrow, the message of universal human emancipation, is the one which Jews should retrieve, not their misplaced enthusiasm for parochial nationalism. The belief in a specific Jewish

* *Ibid.*, p. 26.

spiritual mission is replaced by a purely secular credo. But the message of internationalism is not pronounced with the same measure of conviction as in the works of the Socialists before 1914. It was easier then to be optimistic in this respect than after 1945. Deutscher must have felt that his strictures against the evils of nationalism might conceivably influence some Jews, but he cannot have been confident about their effect on the Russians, the Chinese, or other nations, 'Socialist' or non-Socialist. It was easier to denounce Zionism than point to an alternative, for the prospects of the non-Jewish Jew acting as pioneer and apostle of internationalism in an intensely nationalist world were clearly not very promising.

What has been said of the liberal-assimilationist critique of Zionism applies *a fortiori* to the Socialist-Communist view. Marxists put great emphasis on economic factors in explaining antisemitism, but they agreed with liberalism in regarding assimilation as desirable, and rejected Zionism for trying to impede this inevitable process. Such a vision did not lack consistency; it certainly entailed fewer complications than the Zionist endeavour. Its main weakness was that it was a hopeful vision of the distant future which did not provide clear answers for the present. The Marxist appeal to Jewish toilers and intellectuals to share in the class struggle in their native countries was not practical politics in Germany in 1933, and it has encountered obstacles to a greater or a lesser degree everywhere. Zionists share the regret of Marxists and liberals that the emancipation of the Jews has encountered so many unforeseen difficulties. They might further concede that it was a historical misfortune that the Jewish national movement appeared so late on the historical scene; the emergence of a Jewish state in the nineteenth century would have faced fewer problems. They will accept the view that the nation-state is not the final goal of human history but only a transitional stage. But while it lasted, what were the Jews to do in those countries in which assimilation was just not possible?

To this vital question there has been no convincing answer by the left-wing critics of Zionism. They could argue, as some did, that the problems of individual nations have to be subordinated to the higher interests of the world revolution, and that seen from this vantage point, the Jewish problem was not the most important. The Jews were expendable. Other nations too had come and gone in history. Persecution, the slaughter of millions of Jews, was a regrettable episode, but the revolutionary Socialist is concerned with the future of all mankind. What does the future of a small people matter in the global context?

Zionists are unlikely to be impressed by this argument, for more than one reason. Those advocating abstract internationalist principles are usually influenced by the interests of the nations to which they belong. Furthermore, Zionism rejects as unreasonable the demand that the Jews should subordinate their national aspirations to the higher interest of the future ideal world state – which may (or may not) come into existence one day, and may (or may not) be superior to the present order. Zionism can be subjected to trenchant criticism from different points of view. But as a national movement and a *Weltanschauung* its validity can neither be proved nor refuted. As far as antisemitism is concerned Zionism has a strong case. Its analysis has been more fully confirmed by recent history than the predictions of the anti-Zionists. History will in due time provide an answer to the question whether Zionism has been a success or failure in political terms. But *Weltgeschichte* is not the *Weltgericht*. The survival and prosperity of the state will not by itself demonstrate the justice of the Zionist cause, just as its failure would not prove its injustice.

PART THREE

9

THE WEIZMANN ERA

The First World War had disastrous consequences for millions of Jews living in eastern Europe. The Russian civil war and the troubles elsewhere in eastern Europe were accompanied by pogroms in which many thousands found their death. By 1921 there was peace again, but whatever other benefits the new order in Poland and Rumania offered, it brought no improvement to the political, social and economic situation of Jews. The anomaly of their life did not lessen. On the contrary, it became more acute, since emigration now was far more difficult than before the war. The strong appeal of Zionism in eastern Europe in the 1920s and 1930s can be understood only against the background of pauperisation, of persecution both officially inspired and spontaneous, of general deterioration and growing despair.

The worst pogroms occurred in the Ukraine and in White Russia between 1918 and 1920. The main culprits were the nationalist Ukrainian forces under Petliura, but prominently involved were also Denikin's volunteer army and certain Cossack regiments such as the one under Ataman Grigoriev who joined the Whites after having served with the Reds. Other private armies did their share, some of them right wing, others 'populist' in character. The first major pogroms took place in Zhitomir and Berdichev, old Jewish centres, whence they spread to Proskurov (where fifteen hundred Jews were killed) and neighbouring places. Altogether about fifteen thousand were killed in these attacks and many more wounded. Much Jewish property was destroyed. The number of deaths was far higher than in the prewar pogroms. Human life had become very cheap after 1914, and whereas the death of a few dozen victims in Kishinev had aroused a storm of protest in the civilised world, the murder of thousands in 1919–20 caused hardly a ripple.

With the establishment of the Soviet régime the pogroms ceased. Jews throughout the Soviet Union obtained equal rights, and antisemitism was outlawed. Among the Bolshevik leaders there were many

441

Jews, a fact which was exploited by the propagandists of the extreme Right. That these Bolsheviks of Jewish extraction had not the slightest interest in the fate of the community into which they had been born, by accident so to speak, that they regarded themselves as the representatives of the Russian proletariat and not of the Jewish working class, was of course ignored. Jews were prominently represented in both camps: their part among the emigrés was also much higher than in the country at large. Of those who stayed, many lost their livelihood as a result of economic and social changes, but they were helped by the Soviet government to find other, more productive employment. While Soviet Jews did not receive full recognition as a national minority, they were given their own schools, theatres, publishing houses, and, here and there, even low-level regional autonomy. Religion was persecuted, Zionism outlawed, but the physical safety of individual Jews was more or less guaranteed.

If the Soviet leaders had a long-term perspective as to the future of Russian Jewry (a problem that did not figure high among their priorities) it was based on the assumption that they would gradually become completely assimilated, lose their specific character, and generally become indistinguishable from the rest of the population. This was the tacit understanding during the early, internationalist phase of Soviet rule. Later, with Stalin's rise to power and the gradual upsurge of (Russian) nationalism, Jews were deprived of cultural autonomy. Many leading Jewish Communists lost their positions. Once again the Jewish question became acute.*

The situation of Jews in Poland was precarious from the very beginning of the establishment of the Polish state. In spontaneous pogroms in Lvov, Vilna and other cities hundreds were killed during the interregnum of 1918–19. While they enjoyed minority protection by law, Polish nationalists had always insisted on a national state rather than a state of minorities and they were, as a rule, antisemitic. Jews were accused of being either pro-Russian or pro-German. Dignitaries of the Catholic Church maintained that Jews were fighting the Church and in general exerting an 'evil influence'. It was the declared policy of the *Endeks*, and later on of *Ozon*, to promote Polonisation and to reduce Jewish influence in economic and political life. Jewish merchants and

---

* For a brief general survey of the situation of eastern European Jewry, see O. Janowsky, *People at Bay*, London, 1938, and the writings of J. Lestschinsky on the economic and social aspects. On the history of Soviet Jewry, Solomon Schwarz' study is still the standard work, but the symposium edited by Lionel Kochan is a valuable addition (see bibliography).

professional people were boycotted, a *numerus clausus* was introduced in the universities, and the number of Jewish lawyers and physicians was systematically reduced. There were frequent small-scale pogroms, spreading a climate of fear. The introduction of state monopolies in commodities such as tobacco deprived thousands of Jewish families of their livelihood and the institution of licence fees for hawking hit many others who could not afford to pay. As a result of these and other measures, and of the effects of the world economic crisis, Polish Jewry, never very affluent, were rapidly becoming pauperised. By the early 1930s most were no longer able to pay the (nominal) community tax. More than one-third were destitute, living on the verge of starvation and dependent on communal aid.

There were no major pogroms in Rumania, where before 1914 anti-Jewish persecution had been more blatant than in any other European country. In 1920 the Jews of Rumania too received full rights of citizenship. But, the legal position quite apart, there existed in Rumania what Zionist ideologists sometimes called an 'objective Jewish question'. Few lived in the countryside, wheras in cities such as Czernowitz, Jassy, Radaut, Oradea-Mare, they were in the majority. To an even greater degree than in Poland they constituted the middle class, the intellectual elite. Leading banking houses, insurance companies, transport enterprises were in their hands. Many journalists and a high percentage of lawyers and physicians were Jewish. Few Rumanians considered this a natural state of affairs, and with the emergence of a native middle class the Jews were bound to suffer. At the same time the Jewish artisans of Moldavia and Bessarabia (where they constituted a majority) were facing growing competition.

A strong anti-Jewish movement, The National Christian Defence League, emerged with the declared aim of driving the Jews out of Greater Rumania. Even more extreme was the Iron Guard, a fascist organisation which saw in the Jews the main enemy of the Rumanian people. Even the more moderate Rumanian parties regarded them as unassimilable. Before the First World War, Rumanian Liberals like Bratianu, pupils of Mazzini and Garibaldi, had not hesitated to promulgate anti-Jewish laws.

There was in Rumania, as in Poland, an element of solid hatred of the Jews. While some of the governments used them as scapegoats for their own failures, antisemitism was a popular sentiment. To put the whole blame for its spread on the ruling classes would be a gross oversimplification. The social structure of the Jewish population in Poland

and Rumania was such that it was bound to create tension and conflict between the minority and the host people. A substantial part of Polish Jewry was not gainfully employed and the Warsaw government felt under no obligation to provide training and work, while the Jewish communities were too poor to help. An objectively dangerous situation was further aggravated by the intense nationalism of the newly independent nations, their intolerance of minorities, and by the effects of the economic depression. Instead of improving with time, the problem became steadily more acute. Each new government seemed that bit more antisemitic than its predecessor.

The anti-Jewish measures which were adopted did not, on occasion, lack a certain originality. In Rumania, Jewish students of medicine were required to do their research only on Jewish corpses. In Lithuania, truck drivers and servants had to pass a difficult language examination to get a labour permit. In the city of Plotsk, Rabbi Shapira, the local *Zadik*, was sentenced to death by a Polish court and executed in 1919 for having, it was alleged, given secret light signals to the advancing Red army. The cardinal sin of the Jews was that there were too many of them. As an editor of the semi-official *Gazeta Polska* once wrote: 'I like the Danes very much but if there were three million of them I would pray to God to take them away. Perhaps we would like the Jews very much if there were only fifty thousand of them in Poland.'* Forty years later there were forty thousand Jews left, but the Poles still did not like them.

The situation elsewhere in eastern Europe was less critical. In Lithuania immediately after the war the position of the Jewish minority was better than at any time before or since. They enjoyed full minority rights and there was a minister for Jewish affairs. But subsequently in Lithuania, as in Latvia, the tendency towards reducing the part of the Jews in the main branches of the national economy and in cultural life became stronger and caused great hardship. The economic situation of Hungarian and Czechoslovak Jewry was not bad on the whole, with the exception of some major islands of stark poverty (such as the Subcarpathian region). But the political status of Hungarian Jewry was in a state of uneasy balance. Some of them had taken a prominent part in the short-lived Communist régime of 1918–19. After the victory of the anti-Communist forces the community as a whole was made responsible for the actions of Bela Kun, Tibor Szamuely and their comrades.

---

* Quoted in Harry M. Rabinowicz, *The Legacy of Polish Jewry 1919–39*, New York, 1965, p. 74.

In Austria and Germany there was no official discrimination against Jews after the First World War. Victor Adler and Julius Deutsch became cabinet ministers. In Germany, the republican constitution was written by a Jew (Hugo Preüss) and Jewish social democrats such as Hilferding and Landsberg served as members of the central government. Jews rose to prominence in almost every field and in some, such as the press and cinema, they wielded considerable influence. But if the opportunities increased, so did antisemitism. The fate of Walther Rathenau, German foreign minister in 1921-2, and a German patriot second to none, was in many ways symbolic: he was shot in a Berlin street by youthful members of a right-wing extremist group. Antisemitism, latent in Germany and Austria, received a fresh impetus during the First World War. After the economic crisis of 1921-3 had been overcome, it seemed to decline. But this eclipse was temporary and in any case more apparent than real. The writing on the wall was seen by some far-sighted observers, even in the midst of prosperity, as antisemitism spread to western Europe.

What were the reasons underlying this new outburst? After many years of peace and prosperity the general optimism of Europe had been severely shaken. To many, the war came like a bolt from the blue. Millions had died in senseless slaughter and there had been unprecedented material destruction. Many Europeans found themselves at the end of the war without means and without much hope for the future. The war was followed almost everywhere by unrest, revolution, civil war, inflation and mass unemployment. In these circumstances many looked for a clear and easily intelligible answer to their questions about the causes of these catastrophes and of the unrest in the world in general. They found an answer in documents such as the *Protocols of the Elders of Zion*, the new Bible of the antisemites, a web of fantastic fabrications which, originally published in Russia well before the war, reached central and western Europe in 1919-20. Following this and similar publications, writings about a Jewish world conspiracy attracted many avid readers in England and the United States, even among politicians and otherwise sane public figures. In Britain and America the impact of the 'hidden hand' bogey was short-lived, but elsewhere in Europe it fell on more fertile ground and became part of the ideology underlying popular antisemitic movements. This, in briefest outline, was the situation facing European Jewry after 1918. It was in the general context of pauperisation, social unrest and growing political persecution that the Zionist movement had to re-examine its policy for the future.

Palestine during the war

The small Jewish community in Palestine suffered severely during the war. When Turkey became a belligerent Jewish leaders were subjected to systematic harassment by local Turkish officials pursuing a policy of thorough Ottomanisation. The Anglo-Palestine Bank was closed, and leading Zionists were put on trial, one of the main accusations being that they had authorised the use of National Fund stamps seven years earlier. The American Relief Committee, providing vital help to thousands of destitute persons, was dissolved by order of the local Turkish commander. All young Jews were made liable to conscription, though for the most part they were not put on active service but assigned to various labour battalions, the pariahs of the army. Many of them never returned, falling victim to disease or starvation.*

A new wave of spy trials started after the detection of a pro-allied organisation in Zikhron Ya'akov (NILI), headed by members of the Aaronson family, which gathered intelligence and transmitted it to Egypt. But for the intervention of the German government through its representatives in the Turkish capital and the local commander, General Kress von Kressenstein, the fate of Palestinian Jewry might have resembled that of the Armenians. The Turkish currency collapsed in winter 1916–17, and during the next spring, to top it all, immense swarms of locusts appeared. The entire population was enlisted to save the crops. Schools were closed and, equipped with tin vessels and sticks, the children chased the locusts away. But much damage had already been done: the year's vegetable crop was lost, and many orange groves, too, were affected. Shortly before the arrival of the British troops, Jaffa was evacuated by order of the Turkish authorities and mass searches were carried out to apprehend deserters from the army, numbering tens of thousands, most of them Turks and Arabs but including also a certain number of Jews.

When British units entered Jerusalem on the first day of Hanukkah 1917 they were welcomed by a depleted and impoverished Jewish community. From eighty-five thousand in 1914 its numbers had fallen to fifty-six thousand, a mere 8 per cent of the total population of Palestine. Only in Jerusalem and Tiberias were they in the majority. These cities were the centres of the old, non-Zionist yishuv. The new arrivals, the Zionists, were concentrated in Tel Aviv with its six thousand

---

* *Palestine during the War*, being a record of the preservation of the Jewish settlements in Palestine. Zionist Organisation, London, 1921, p. 31.

inhabitants, and in Haifa, which counted then only 2,500 Jews. The biggest agricultural colonies were Petah Tiqva with three thousand inhabitants, Rishon Lezion (fifteen hundred) and Rehovot (one thousand). The other Jewish rural settlements, fifty-seven altogether, were much smaller, numbering in all about twelve thousand souls, little islands among the eight hundred-odd Arab villages.

The Jewish community recovered only slowly from the ravages of the war. By 1920 it had grown to sixty-four thousand and only in 1922 was it back to its prewar size.* It would not have been able to defend itself against any outside attack, and the arrival in 1918 of the legionnaires, the 4,500 Jewish volunteers from England and America, was a momentous event. But of these thousands of volunteers only 260 chose to settle in the country. It was only with the beginning of the immigration wave in December 1918 that a transfusion of fresh blood took place and Zionist activities showed fresh life.

The British troops entering Palestine were received by a jubilant Jewish population. The beginning of liberation, the days of the Messiah seemed at hand. But the return to normal conditions took much longer than anticipated. There was no news from the Zionist executive in London and no money. Galilee, the northern part of the country, remained in the hands of the Turks almost to the end of the war. Immediately after the arrival of the British a Provisional Committee (*Va'ad Zemani*) had been set up to pave the way for the establishment of a representative council of Palestinian Jewry (*Asefat Hanivharim*). But this body, in which there was no outstanding personality, had little authority, and even if there had been leadership little could have been achieved without financial resources. Meetings were convened, blueprints prepared, resolutions passed, but all as it were in a vacuum. The orthodox Jews, opposing women's right to vote and the creation of a joint rabbinate, rejected the very idea of a common Jewish representative body. It was, in the words of a contemporary observer, the era of *Tohu vabohu*, utter confusion and anarchy.†

Palestine was administered from December 1917 to July 1920 by OETA (Occupied Enemy Territory Administration), a section of the British army. The officers established a system of direct rule, subject to the orders of the C-in-C, General Allenby. From the start there was friction between the Jewish population and the military administration. While the Zionists expected that the new masters would be above all

---

* *Sefer toldot hahagana*, part 2, p. 550.
† Medzini, *loc. cit.*, p. 61 *et seq.*

concerned with the implementation of the Balfour Declaration, most of the British officers, in so far as they were at all aware of the obligations entered into by Whitehall, were by no means in sympathy with official policy. A few, such as Wyndham Deedes, were pro-Zionist, but most preferred the Arabs to the Jews, whose insistent demands they regarded as at best a nuisance. In their eyes their main task was to preserve the *status quo*, to maintain public services with the least disturbance of the existing order. Even if they had been more sympathetically inclined towards the Zionist cause it is doubtful whether they would have been able to do much to promote it. For the war continued for another year after the occupation of Jerusalem, and during that time military requirements took precedence over all other considerations. Furthermore, they had little if any experience in administrative work, and when they first encountered Arab opposition to Zionism their instinctive reaction was to refrain from any step which might further antagonise the Arabs, who after all constituted the overwhelming majority of the population.

The Balfour Declaration had expressed a general intention to facilitate the establishment of a national home for the Jewish people but it was by no means clear at first what this would mean in practical terms. When the Zionists demanded the establishment of their own military defence force, this was rejected by the local command as premature. This in turn created much bitterness among the Jews, since the British forces (as was soon to appear) proved unable or, as some asserted, unwilling to protect the Jewish population against Arab attacks. Thus disillusion set in within only a few months after the arrival of the British forces. Small incidents poisoned the atmosphere, such as the case of the senior officers who remained seated when the *Hatiqva*, the Jewish anthem was played at a concert. OETA refused to use Hebrew together with Arabic and English as an official language on railway tickets, tax forms, and other official documents. The Red Cross received privileges which *Hadassa* was denied. The Land Registry Office remained closed and there was no legal possibility of acquiring land; even private transactions in land were not permitted.

Thus Palestinian Jewry became embittered and suspicious: 'the angels became devils in their eyes. They saw themselves the victims of a conspiracy.'* Rumours were rife that certain OETA advisers were not merely in sympathy with the Arab claim that the Balfour Declaration implied

---

* Sykes, *Crossroads to Israel*, p. 38. On OETA, see also Storrs *Orientations*; Horace B. Samuel, *Unholy Memoirs of the Holy Land*; Redcliffe N. Salaman, *Palestine Reclaimed*; Ashbee, *Palestine Notebook*; Graves, *Palestine, the Land of Three Faiths*.

the denial of the right of self-determination, but actively encouraged the Arab protest movement. These suspicions were perhaps exaggerated, but there is no denying that most British oriental experts were in fact convinced that their government had been mistaken in allying itself with the Zionists rather than the Arabs. As for the rest, probably the majority, they simply did not want to be bothered. There was a tendency (as one observer put it) 'to look down on the people in their care as a tiresome gaggle of Yids and Wogs', and since the Yids were clamouring even louder than the Wogs, insisting on their rights, demanding to be treated as equals, forever complaining about British arrogance if not downright antisemitism, they got the worst of the deal. Thus an unfortunate pattern for Zionist-British relations was established even before the mandate came into force. There was little Weizmann and other British Zionists could do to smooth things over.

Weizmann left for Palestine in March 1918 and stayed there for five months. He was a member of a Zionist commission (*Va'ad Hazirim*) which had been dispatched on the initiative of the British government to survey the situation and prepare plans for the future. The commission included a French Jew, Professor Sylvain Levi (an anti-Zionist) and an Italian (Levi Bianchini), but the majority consisted of Weizmann's friends and collaborators (David Eder, Joseph Cowen, Leon Simon and Israel Sieff). Weizmann had an introductory letter from Lloyd George, which, however, made little impression on Allenby, who immediately informed his guest that nothing could be done at present. Weizmann ruefully wrote that 'the messianic hopes which we had read into the Balfour Declaration suffered a perceptible diminution when we came into contact with the hard realities of GHQ'.* Subsequently he got on reasonably well with Allenby, though the commander-in-chief probably never changed his basic view that there was no future for the Jews in Palestine.

During his stay Weizmann met Emir Faisal; details of this inconclusive meeting are given elsewhere in the present study. And, in July 1918, while the war was still in progress, he laid the cornerstone of the Hebrew university on Mount Scopus which was to be opened six years later. Since there was little else that could be done for the time being, Weizmann decided to return to London to pursue the political work in the European capitals, which had by no means been completed. The Zionist commission took over the Palestine Office in Jaffa which had been established before the war by the World Zionist Organisation.

* Weizmann, *Trial and Error*, p. 218.

This body was in charge of all political work and served as liaison between the Jewish population and the British administration. Departments for agricultural affairs, engineering and education were established, but the commission suffered from successive changes in leadership. David Eder replaced Weizmann after his departure, and was in turn replaced by Lewin-Epstein, who was himself succeeded by two American Zionists, Friedenwald and Robert Szold. They were followed again by Eder, who was succeeded by Ussishkin, the Russian Zionist leader, who was succeeded by Kisch – all this within about three years.

Such frequent changes prevented any consistent effort, though it is doubtful whether in the uncertainties of 1918–20 much could have been achieved anyway. Relations with the British authorities deteriorated: Ronald Storrs, governor of Jerusalem district, wrote about 'Tsar Menahem (Ussishkin)': 'When he was announced for an interview I braced myself to take my punishment like a man, praying only that my subordinates would keep an equal control over their tempers.'* Storrs was clearly exasperated by the Zionists, to whom he applied Dryden's couplet: 'God's pampered people whom, debauch'd with ease, No King could govern and no God could please.' In their milder moments, the Zionists would say that God had not pampered them and that Storrs, at any rate, had not tried very hard to please. It was Storrs who in 1920 had his friend Ernest Richmond appointed political secretary of the Palestine government. Richmond, as it soon appeared, was a fanatical opponent of the idea of a Jewish national home in Palestine.†

The Struggle for the Mandate

The diplomatic battle in the capitals of the world for a Jewish Palestine entered a new stage on the morning after the Balfour Declaration and lasted until the San Remo Conference (spring 1920) which decided to include the Declaration in the peace treaty with Turkey. Strictly speaking it was not until August 1924 that the Treaty of Lausanne came into force, legalising the status of Palestine as a League of Nations mandate.‡ But *de facto* the mandate came into force in July 1920 when Herbert Samuel assumed office as the first high commissioner. Many

---

* Storrs, *Orientations*, p. 489.

† E.Kedourie, 'Sir Herbert Samuel and the Government of Palestine', *Middle Eastern Studies*, January 1969, p. 53.

‡ Paul L.Hanna, *British Policy in Palestine*, Washington, 1942, p. 60.

difficulties had to be overcome by the Zionist leaders: American policy hesitated between active participation in world affairs and isolationism. This introduced yet another uncertain factor into the situation, for the Balfour Declaration had not provided a clear answer with regard to the identity of the protecting power. The American King-Crane commission in 1919 reported that the Arab Muslims, the great majority of the population, were in favour of Syrian independence, and that a mandate over a united Syria, including Palestine, should be assigned to the Americans or as a second choice to Britain. This recommendation was not acted upon, but in London too there was no wholehearted support for a British mandate and the idea of an American mandate or a mandate under combined sponsorship was revived by influential circles. After lengthy deliberations the eastern committee of the war cabinet decided that a single power should be selected to administer Palestine and that it should be neither Italy nor France. Consequently the choice lay between the United States and Britain, the conclusion being that 'while we would not object to the selection of the United States of America, yet, if the offer was made to Great Britain we ought not to decline'. This decision was based largely on considerations of imperial defence; Zionism and the Balfour Declaration played little part in it.*

The scene next moved to Paris where the peace conference opened in January 1919. On 18 January the conference approved the creation of a League of Nations under which a mandatory system was to be established. The great powers were to act as trustees for the new states which were emerging in Europe and the Near East. There was, however, an obvious contradiction between the high-minded wartime declarations against imperialist annexations and the secret treaties about the division of spheres of influence. On the whole, the eastern question figured less prominently at the peace conference than generally expected; European affairs had top priority. Decisions concerning the Near East were postponed time and time again, one important reason being British-French rivalry. London informed Paris that it wanted Palestine and Mesopotamia 'and a good connection between them', and that it had no designs on Syria and Lebanon. But at the same time the British supported Emir Faisal's ambitions for an independent, united Syrian state, a scheme which was of course unacceptable to the French. Agreement between London and Paris became possible only after the British decided to drop Faisal. President Wilson demanded that the wishes of the population

* L.Stein, *The Balfour Declaration*, p. 610.

should be taken into account, whereas the Zionists, in the early drafts of their programmes for the peace conference, demanded majority rights for the existing Jewish community in Palestine irrespective of present numbers. The official Zionist memorandum eventually submitted was somewhat more cautious in approach.

When a Zionist delegation appeared on 27 February 1919 before the Supreme Allied Council, Weizmann was asked by Lansing, the American secretary of state what exactly was meant by the phrase 'a Jewish national home'. Weizmann replied that for the moment an autonomous Jewish government was not wanted, but that he expected that seventy to eighty thousand Jews would emigrate to Palestine annually. Gradually a nation would emerge which would be as Jewish as the French nation was French and the British nation British. Later, when the Jews formed the large majority, they would establish such a government as would answer to the state of the development of the country and to their ideals. Sylvain Levi used the opportunity to make an anti-Zionist speech which profoundly embarrassed Weizmann and Sokolow, who had stressed all along the attachment of the Jewish people since time immemorial to Eretz Israel. But Levi's appearance made no lasting impression on those present, nor did the Zionist cause suffer as the result of the fact that the negotiations between Faisal and Weizmann led nowhere.

Other attempts were made to torpedo Zionist policy: a cable from General Money, head of the British military administration in Palestine, advised London to drop the Balfour Declaration. The people of Palestine were opposed to the Zionist programme, he wrote, and if Britain wanted the mandate it was necessary 'to make an authoritative announcement that the Zionist programme will not be enforced in opposition to the wishes of the majority'.* On several occasions OETA demanded that the Zionist commission should be dissolved, but Balfour and Lloyd George were not inclined to accept this advice and Generals Money and Bols were instructed to make known to all concerned that the policy of the British government had not changed. This they did, but in a half-hearted way and with so many reservations that the impression was created among the Arabs (to quote a contemporary observer, Horace Samuel) that the administration favoured a pro-Arab policy and that the cabinet in London could be deflected from its policy by the requisite amount of energy and determination.

Whatever had been decided in London, the army command in Cairo and Jerusalem was in no mood to suffer gladly any civilian intrusion.

* *Ibid.*, p. 645.

When Weizmann arrived on his second visit in 1919, General Congreve, deputising for Allenby, did not even want to permit him to land, for he had been informed that the Zionist leader was likely 'to cause trouble'. He had never heard of Weizmann, he knew nothing about Zionism, and he cared less. The general changed his mind only when the War Office and the Foreign Office intervened.

This incident highlighted the precarious nature of the whole Zionist enterprise one year after the end of the war. There was no recognition in Jerusalem and no progress in Paris. Once the peace treaty with Germany had been signed, in June 1919, the heads of governments no longer concerned themselves with the details of the negotiations. The hardening of isolationism in America, and Anglo-French rivalry, delayed the peace settlement with Turkey. It was only towards the end of 1919 that some progress was made with regard to the future of Syria and Palestine. The French were no longer opposed in principle to the idea of a British mandate for Palestine but they did not want to be excluded altogether. They demanded a say in the arrangements for the Holy Places and opposed the incorporation of the Balfour Declaration in the terms of the mandate. Eventually, at the San Remo conference in April 1920, the French dropped their more extreme claims. A compromise formula was found which, while accepting in substance the British view, made it possible for the French to retreat without loss of face. Thus Great Britain at last became the mandatory power.

The task of drawing up the charter of the mandate was left to the mandatory power. The first draft was disappointing from the Zionist point of view because, among other things, it made no mention at all of a Jewish commonwealth. After some lobbying another draft was prepared which, while not meeting all Zionist wishes, seemed more in the spirit of the Balfour Declaration. It defined Britain's responsibility towards building a Jewish national home but did not define what kind of national home was envisaged; nor was a Jewish commonwealth promised in so many words. On the other hand, there was no specific safeguard for the political rights of the Arabs. In fact the term 'Arab' did not appear in the document.

From the Arab point of view this was of course altogether unsatisfactory and it was resisted, unsuccessfully, by the Arab spokesmen. They claimed that whereas Syria and Iraq, the other mandated territories, were temporarily placed under the tutelage of the powers, to become fully independent in due course, the Palestine administration (in which the Arabs would have no say) was pledged to carry out a policy abhorrent to the majority of the population.* Of particular importance to the Zionists was article four of the mandate which stated that an 'appropriate Jewish Agency' should be recognised as a public body 'for the purposes of advising and cooperating with the Administration of Palestine in such economic, social and other matters as may affect the establishment of the Jewish national home and the interests of the Jewish population in Palestine, and, subject always to the control of the Administration, to assist and take part in the development of the country.'

The mandate was said to have been 'framed in the Jewish interest', its primary purpose being to promote the establishment of a Jewish national home.† The Zionist leaders received it therefore with great satisfaction, as they did the appointment of Herbert Samuel, whereas the Arabs considered it a major defeat. It seemed only fitting that a Jew should be the first governor of the Holy Land and it was taken as an affirmation of the promise previously given to the Jewish people in the Balfour Declaration. But not many months were to pass before it was realised that the mandate had left some of the most important questions unanswered and that Samuel, in his attempt to be just and fair to all sections of the population, was leaning over backwards to win the confidence of the Arabs, to the detriment of the Zionist aspirations.

An indication of this trend was the publication of a White Paper in July 1922, defining the term 'national home'. Winston Churchill, then colonial secretary, had been to Palestine and, after meeting both Arab and Jewish leaders, issued a statement which was mistakenly interpreted by some observers at the time as yet another victory for Zionism. Churchill had told Arab representatives that the British government did not intend to halt immigration, as they demanded, and that the establishment of a Jewish national centre was a good thing – good not only for the Jews, but for the British and Arabs as well.

But there was another aspect to the 1922 White Paper. While not explicitly opposing the idea of a Jewish state, it 'redeemed the Balfour promise in depreciated currency', to quote a contemporary British source. Its aim was to appease both the Arabs and the opposition in Westminster, made up largely of right-wing Tories. It stated that His Majesty's government had no intention of Palestine becoming 'as Jewish

---

* Hanna, *British Policy in Palestine*, p. 59; on the development of the mandate, see also J.Stoyanovsky, *The Mandate for Palestine*, New York, 1928: F.Friedmann, *Das Palaestinamandat*, Prague, 1936; Quincy Wright, *Mandates under the League of Nation*, Chicago, 1930; N.Bentwich, *The Mandates System*, London, 1930.

† *Loc. cit.*, p. 67.

as England is English' and that the special position of the Zionist executive did not entitle it to share in any degree in the government of the country. Immigration, moreover, was not to exceed the economic capacity of the country at the time to absorb new arrivals. Churchill promised that the mandatory government would move towards representative institutions and self-government. A legislative council with a majority of elected members was to be set up immediately, but full self-government was a long way off; 'Our children's children will have passed away before this is completed.' Lastly, and almost unnoticed at the time, Transjordan was separated from Palestine and became a semi-independent state under Emir Abdullah.

The White Paper placated the opposition at home, but the Arabs were not appeased, and continued to refuse to cooperate with the mandatory authorities. A year later London went one step further and proposed the establishment of an Arab Agency analogous to the Jewish Agency. But the Arab aim was independence, an Arab state in which the Jews would be a minority without any special rights, and they therefore rejected the offer out of hand. The Zionists very reluctantly, and under considerable pressure, accepted the new policy as a basis of cooperation with the British government. Even Jabotinsky, who was a member of the Zionist executive at the time, did not dissent.

Some Zionist leaders were violently critical of Samuel as immigration was temporarily stopped in May 1921 following the Arab riots. The fact that Jews engaging in self-defence had been arrested, whereas the Arab attackers were quickly released from prison, provoked a storm of indignation. Later, the Zionists came to think more highly of the first high commissioner. After 1921 there was no major unrest, and 'peace and order and good government' were brought to Palestine, to quote an official Zionist statement. The first and most difficult stage in the Jewish national home was successfully completed, and the high commissioner acquitted himself 'by common consent with dignity and distinction, carrying with him in his retirement the enduring gratitude of the Zionist Organisation'.* Samuel had had the good fortune to retire at the right moment; for Zionism, 1925 was an excellent year, a year of unprecedented immigration and of a major economic boom.

With British acceptance of the mandate and the establishment of a mandatory administration, a new chapter opens in the annals of Zionist history. Between 1918 and 1921 the future of Palestine was still wide

---

* Report of the Executive to the XIV Zionist Congress, quoted in *Palestine* (Esco Foundation), New Haven, 1947, I, p. 291.

open, decisions were not yet final. A general statement of policy had been made in 1917, but it was by no means certain how, if at all, it would be implemented. By 1921 the pattern had been set for many years to come. The process of whittling down the mandate began early on but proceeded slowly. It was still believed in London that the national aspirations of Jews and Arabs were not incompatible. The Arabs adopted a policy of non-cooperation, occasionally with some effect, but in the long run with results detrimental to their cause. The Zionist movement did reasonably well, following up its earlier political successes. It did not commit any major mistakes and it is doubtful even in retrospect whether it could have obtained any better results. The Zionists were over-optimistic about their own long-term prospects. At the time most of them believed that a long period of peaceful construction was ahead as a result of which a Jewish commonwealth would gradually come into being. They assumed that there was no particular urgency and they also overrated British willingness to stick to the terms of the mandate in face of growing Arab opposition. But the hundreds of thousands of immigrants who had figured prominently in many speeches did not materialise and this was the great source of Zionist weakness during the years to come. Could they have come if they had wanted to? In the immediate postwar period frontiers had not yet been finally drawn and the political future of the Middle East was still in the balance. There is no certainty that the Arabs would have accepted mass immigration and settlement during that interregnum. But in fact only a few thousand immigrants came, not enough to affect the balance of power inside Palestine, but more than sufficient to irritate the Arabs and arouse their fears. A massive transfer of Jews to Palestine within two or three years of the Balfour Declaration might well have failed in view of the enormous practical difficulties that would have faced such an enterprise. But there was such a chance, however small, and it was not to recur.

New tasks for Zionism

With the end of the war the world Zionist movement resumed its political work within the Jewish community. During the war its activities had largely ceased, either because they had been illegal (as in the Russian empire before the overthrow of the tsar) or because so many of its members were on military service. First off the mark were the German Zionists, who in a conference less than two months after the war discussed at great length, and in considerable if somewhat abstract detail, the future of immigration and settlement in Palestine, including even such issues as the nationalisation of the land.*

Among the main topics of discussion was the form and rate of settlement. Ruppin envisaged a yearly immigration of twenty thousand families, half of whom were to be employed in agriculture. This was the lowest of the estimates at the time and, as subsequently emerged, the most realistic. Ruppin's main antagonist was Davis Trietsch, who had developed various highly original, sometimes splenetic colonisation schemes at the prewar Zionist congresses. For many years he continued to submit detailed programmes for mass immigration, all of them ignored by the experts or treated with disdain. In retrospect, however, Trietsch's arguments seem weightier than most of his contemporaries were ready to acknowledge: he advocated intensive agriculture in contrast to the advice given by most other experts at the time. Moreover, in view of the lack of agricultural experience among the Jews as well as other obstacles, he insisted on the paramount importance of developing industry for the absorption of mass immigration. Whereas Ruppin and the other experts thought that an investment of £1,000–£1,500 was needed for the absorption of one family, Trietsch argued that since funds of such magnitude would never be available, they should develop cheaper methods of settlement. The weakness of Trietsch's argument was, of course, that while industry would no doubt have absorbed more immigrants, it also involved substantial investment, and he was no more able than anyone else to point to potential donors.†

After 1918 German Zionism was no longer the force it had been in the world movement. The Berlin central office and the Copenhagen bureau ceased to function with the end of the war and the Constantinople agency also stopped its work in October 1918. In December 1917 a provisional London bureau was established under Sokolow and Chlenov, who was later replaced by Weizmann. While London thus became the centre of power, the constitutional situation was confused. It was the London office which convened the first meeting of the Action Committee in February 1919. This was followed by several other meetings and, also in London, the annual conference in July 1920 (also called 'the little congress'). All this may not have been strictly constitutional, but someone had to take the initiative and no one seriously disputed the authority of these meetings.

---

* *Protokoll des XV Delegiertentages*, Berlin, 1919, p. 53.

† See Trietsch's periodical *Volk und Land*, 1920, and his programmatic article against the official settlement policy in *Jüdische Rundschau*, 30 August 1921.

The post war executive consisted at first of Weizmann, Sokolow, Jacobson, S.Levin (all in London), and Warburg and Hantke of Berlin. In 1920 Ussishkin, Julius Simon and de Lieme were appointed to the executive. Weizmann, who was elected president of the organisation, also headed the political department together with Sokolow, who was named chairman of the executive. They were later joined for a time by Jabotinsky. The organisation department was managed first by Jacobson, later by Hantke and subsequently by Lichtheim; the Palestine department (also called the Palestine office) was headed by Julius Simon. The composition of the executive fluctuated widely in these early postwar years but it remained the supreme decision-making body, for the Action Committee, on which all local groups and parties were represented, counted more than eighty members and was much too unwieldy to be an effective instrument of policy.*

The 1920 London conference was not fully representative of the federations and trends which made up the world movement. The right-wing and religious parties were much more strongly represented than the Left. American and German Zionism had only relatively small delegations. Since it was the first major Zionist meeting for seven years it became almost automatically the battleground between the main contenders for leadership, American Zionism under Brandeis and the Europeans under Weizmann. As far as Brandeis was concerned it was not a contest for personal power, for, as a Supreme Court Justice of the United States, he was unwilling to accept any position other than that of honorary president.

It was a clash between two different concepts regarding the future of the Zionist movement, but there were also divergences in style and approach. The slogan of 'Washington against Pinsk' under which the battle was fought was a distortion of a highly complex situation, but there certainly was a grain of truth in it. The American Zionists, who had carried the major financial burden from the beginning of the war and who had played a central part in the political struggle before and after the Balfour Declaration, were extremely critical of the political leadership in London in which, incidentally, they were not represented. Brandeis believed that with the Balfour Declaration, or at the very latest with Samuel's appointment as high commissioner, the main political tasks of the movement had been accomplished, and that from now on energies had to be devoted to the building of Palestine.

* On the organisational reshuffles, see *Reports of the Executive of the Zionist Organisation to the XII Zionist Congress*, III, London, 1921.

The American Zionists opposed the establishment of a big executive office in London, feeling that the work for Palestine had to be done from Jerusalem. They favoured decentralisation and the introduction of modern business methods. American Jews, it was claimed, had greater administrative expertise than their European brethren. The Americans were critical of Ussishkin's colonisation methods. He had introduced a new Halukka system instead of appealing to private enterprise and initiative. They were willing to exert themselves on behalf of the Zionist cause but they demanded that their contributions should be devoted only to Palestinian projects. They found it scandalous that the rich Jews of Europe, of whom there were many, were unwilling to take upon themselves a similar burden, and they thought that the Ma'aser project, according to which rich Jews were to give one-tenth of their property to the Zionist funds, was totally unrealistic. They wanted a clear division between commercial investments in Palestine and voluntary donations. They were not in favour of diaspora nationalism and refused to pay for Zionist activities outside Palestine. Brandeis, moreover, was put off by Weizmann's behaviour; having reached agreement with him, Weizmann had acted behind his back to torpedo the agreement.* He was irritated by the proceedings of the London conference, the lack of preparation, order and purpose, the absence of any real authority, the constant speech-making. Brandeis, in brief, did not like what he saw of world Zionism. Weizmann and the European Zionists branded Brandeis' policy 'Zionism without Zion'. The American Zionists lacked a 'Jewish heart'. They had never understood the basic character of political Zionism, the demand for a revolution in Jewish life. Instead, they proposed an *ersatz* Zionism. The Europeans argued that Palestine could not be colonised in the same way as America had been built, by private enterprise, but that a central national effort was needed. Criteria of efficiency and business management were not the only ones applicable to a movement idealistic in character. This referred, *inter alia*, to the American opposition to collective agricultural settlements, which they predicted would only cause further deficits in the Zionist budget.

While the London conference marked the break between Brandeis and Weizmann and their respective backers, the struggle for control of the American Zionist organisation lasted for another year and ended with the defeat of Brandeis and Mack at the Cleveland convention in

---

* A pro-Brandeis account of the disputes is J. de Haas, *Louis Brandeis*, New York, 1929; see also Brandeis' interview with *Der Tog*, 10 January 1921.

June 1921. Brandeis resigned as honorary president, and together with his leading supporters, Felix Frankfurter, Stephen Wise, Nathan Strauss, Abba Hillel Silver and Julian Mack, withdrew from active work in the organisation. While Brandeis' decision was final, most of his followers rejoined the organisation in later years.*

The Brandeis crisis had its repercussions in Europe when two members of the executive, Julius Simon and Nehemia de Lieme, resigned in January 1921 for reasons very similar to those which had led to the withdrawal of the Americans. One of the main issues at stake was the character of the *Keren Hayesod* (Foundation Fund) which was initiated in 1920 at the suggestion of two Russian Zionist leaders. It was to raise £25 million for colonising work. The debates about the character of this fund (whether or not the political leadership was to have a say in its management) preoccupied Zionist conferences for several years and the amount of time spent on these heated debates was often in inverse ratio to the volume of money that was actually collected. Simon and de Lieme, like the Brandeis group, believed that it would be possible to build up Palestine while keeping investment in economically unproductive expenditure (i.e. education, social assistance, etc.) to a minimum.† They wanted the money to be used mainly to promote immigration and settlement. Only 10 per cent was used at the time for immigration, whereas 30 per cent went to supporting the Jewish educational system in Palestine. Simon and de Lieme believed in a strict division of labour between the Zionist executive and the Palestinian Jewish organisations, the latter to be responsible for specific local and municipal matters, including education. Many of the suggestions they made were quite realistic and were in fact adopted in later years. At the time they were thought to be premature and were rejected by the majority. The two therefore resigned from the executive.

Much of the Brandeis faction's criticism of the London Zionist leadership was only too justified. The east European leaders were still committed to the tradition of unending sentimental speech-making and the belief that a speech was by itself a political act. In organisational and financial matters they were amateurs, able perhaps to manage the affairs of a small-town community in Poland but quite incapable of building up a new country by modern methods. The main weakness of the Brandeis doctrine was that it would have transformed the executive into an economic committee located in Palestine with a branch in

---

* Louis Lipsky, *Thirty Years of American Zionism*, New York, 1929, p. 78.
† See *XII Zionistenkongress . . .* , vol. 2, p. 215 *et seq.*

London to deal with political affairs. The Americans overrated the willingness of the British mandatory authorities to help the Zionist movement and they underestimated the extent to which Zionism in eastern Europe, a popular movement aiming at the transformation of every aspect of Jewish life, needed organisation and leadership. By de-ideologising Zionism they would have deprived it of its soul, by neglecting the Zionist organisation they would have cut down the flow of immigrants. For the east European leaders Zionism was their whole life. For Brandeis and Mack it was just one of several preoccupations, albeit an important one. For this reason, if for no other, the Brandeis faction was bound to lose the struggle for the character and future policy of the movement.

Weizmann's victory was, however, by no means complete. Immediately after the Balfour Declaration he had been hailed as the leader of his people, a new Messiah. But at the London conference and at subsequent Zionist congresses there was growing criticism. All his mistakes, all his errors of commission and omission, were held against him, whereas his achievements were belittled, as Weizmann's colleagues became more and more impatient with his gradualism. Weizmann argued that he was indeed a *cunctator*, as Jabotinsky had said, as this was the only policy that could be pursued.* He tried to induce his colleagues to be less nervous and excitable about the ups and down of British policy. He tried to explain to them, not always successfully, that without money little could be achieved (the Palestine budget of the executive in 1923 amounted to less than £400,000). Sokolow echoed him; there was not much to be done in the political field at present, the centre of gravity had moved to economics. But these admonitions were not very effective. As early as 1920 Weizmann had to threaten to resign. This, in Ussishkin's view, would not have been a major calamity; in 1923 he declared that the whole Weizmann system had failed. The attack ended with Ussishkin's defeat, but a substantial (and growing) segment of the Zionist movement remained in opposition to Weizmann, and only its inability to agree on an alternative leadership prevented a major crisis.

The twelfth Zionist congress, the first after the war, opened in Karlsbad on 1 September 1921, with the delegates from Poland for the first time constituting the strongest group. Mizrahi, the religious party, was the largest single faction, since the centre group, the General Zionists, had no real internal cohesion. Much of the debate was devoted

* *Jüdische Rundschau*, 2 February 1923.

to financial problems. The Brandeis group boycotted the congress but Simon and de Lieme appeared and defended their position against the majority. The congress elected a new executive, half of whose members were to reside in Israel (Ruppin, Eder, Ussishkin, Pick, Sprinzak, Rosenblatt). It ended with a stirring speech by Bialik, the greatest Hebrew poet of his generation, who said the hour of action had come, that 'we have had too many dreams and fantasies – we want to see action'.* Once practical work got under way, Bialik predicted, the unending quarrels and theoretical disputations which had plagued Zionism would die away.

Bialik was over-optimistic, as the next congress (Karlsbad, 1923) proved. There were many complaints about the executive and many dire predictions. The Mizrahi and several General Zionists would have gladly ousted Weizmann. It was in many ways a typical congress : almost everyone argued that he and his group had been discriminated against. Blumenfeld claimed that Zionism had lost its militant character, a process which had begun before the war but had gathered momentum after 1918. Young Arlosoroff, emerging as one of the major figures in the movement, went even further, referring to the danger that Zionism would be ruined and disappear altogether.† One speaker, commenting on the announcement that 70,000 dunam had been acquired since the last congress, said that this was about the size of the estate of a single Polish landlord, and not even one of the biggest.

Yitzak Gruenbaum, the Polish Zionist leader and one of Weizmann's main antagonists throughout the 1920s, claimed that the Jewish people could wait if conditions in Palestine were too difficult for practical work. Like Nahum Goldmann and some other 'radical' Zionists, he upbraided Weizmann for neglecting the movement and concentrating on Palestine. Above all, the 'radicals' opposed the idea of making non-Zionists members of the Jewish Agency, the constitution of which had been discussed the year before for the first time.

This issue was to bedevil quite unnecessarily the Zionist movement for seven more years. Weizmann was the main protagonist of coopera-tion with non-Zionists, not only (and not mainly) because the establishment of the Agency was mentioned in the mandate, but because he realised earlier and more acutely than most of his colleagues that the means for building up Palestine could not be raised by the Zionists alone. He anticipated that non-Zionists would hardly be willing to join

---

* *Protokoll des XII Zionisten Kongresses*, Berlin, 1922, p. 735.
† *Protokoll des XIII Zionisten Kongresses*, London, 1924, pp. 249–93.

in the enterprise unless they were given some representation on the leading bodies of the movement. The 'radicals' claimed that this was watering down Zionist ideology, depriving the movement of its specific national character, altogether a catastrophe. These discussions generated a good deal of heat but they were, as subsequently appeared, quite irrelevant. For the enlarged Jewish Agency, as set up in 1929, did not play the role that had been envisaged, and the primacy of the Zionist movement and its character were not in the least affected.

The role of the Agency was not the only bone of contention between Weizmann and his critics. The east European Zionists viewed with deep suspicion the activities of the English Jews with whom Weizmann had surrounded himself – Kisch, Eder, Leonard Stein – and who, during his absence from London, were in charge of the political work of the executive. These men laboured under the misfortune of not having been born in eastern Europe. They spoke no Yiddish and little if any Hebrew. They had not participated in the prewar congresses and they had not served their apprenticeship in the movement. They were, in other words, unfamiliar types. How far could they be trusted? Weizmann was attacked for his 'dictatorial tendencies'. He had not bothered, for instance, to bring a resolution adopted (unnecessarily, as he thought) by the Action Committee against the establishment of an Arab Agency to the attention of the British government. He was constantly criticised for not presenting Zionist demands to the British government with sufficient emphasis. When he asked what Ussishkin and his friends would have done in his place (Weizmann later wrote) the reply was: 'Protest! Demand! Insist! And that seemed the ultimate wisdom to be gleaned from our critics. They seemed quite unaware that the constant repetition of protests, demands and insistence defeats its own ends, being both futile and undignified.'*

At the thirteenth congress Ruppin presented a sombre picture of the state of constructive work in Palestine: some of his colleagues had talked about one hundred thousand immigrants a year, whereas he had thought thirty thousand would be a more realistic figure. In fact a mere eight to ten thousand had come. The congress had envisaged a budget of £1,500,000, but in reality only one-third of this sum had come in and the Palestine budget had dropped to £300,000, quite insufficient to cover the expense of school and health services, let alone immigration and settlement.

At this congress three of Weizmann's supporters (Kisch, Lipsky and

* Weizmann, *Trial and Error*, p. 327.

van Vriesland) joined the executive. But he still bore the main burden, and in his desperate attempts to obtain money in America and elsewhere he had little help from either friend or foe. The world situation in 1923 was not conducive to obtaining loans or donations. Shortly after the congress Weizmann said in Baltimore: another such year and we are lost. There was a real danger that the Zionist congress was about to become a parliament in which endless ritual speeches were made by professional small-town dignitaries whose words bore no relation to the real situation of the Jewish people. There were no financial resources, nor was there any expansion of economic activities, and without these all the speeches about great future prospects sounded very hollow.

Parliament fell into disrepute in the 1920s in many European countries and the Zionist movement was no exception. Its congresses aroused passion and produced some oratorical highlights, but on the whole they were exercises in futility, for they were concerned largely with events and developments over which the Zionists had no control. The opposition to Weizmann was divided into Palestine-Firsters, who wanted a more radical approach by the executive *vis-à-vis* the British (Jabotinsky, Ussishkin), and the followers of Gruenbaum, who were mainly interested in work in the diaspora (*Gegenwartsarbeit*).

More and more impatience was displayed both by the leadership and the opposition as the financial plight thwarted activities everywhere. When Keren Hayesod had been founded, it was announced the £25 million would be collected in five years. In fact it took six years to collect a mere £3 million. Little could be achieved with such paltry sums. The Zionist organisation had been over-spending for years and by 1927 its deficit was £30–£40,000. This could not be called a staggering sum in absolute terms, for a movement trying to build a new country. But by Zionist standards the debt was enormous and it proved impossible for a long time to find anyone to cover this deficit; countless sessions had to be devoted to meeting this emergency. To provide another example: Hadassa, the American Women's Zionist Organisation, was very active in raising money on condition that it could retain annually for its own projects £110,000, about 20 per cent of the total Zionist budget at the time. This issue, too, was debated countless times by the American Zionist Federation and the World Zionist Congress.

The Zionists had been unable to enlist the help of wealthy Jews before the war and Professor Weizmann was not much more successful than Dr Herzl in bringing about a radical change. It was all the more galling since other institutions seemed more successful in getting the money they needed. When in the middle 1920s the Soviet government approached American Jewry to contribute to its Crimean settlement scheme, it got a friendlier reception than the Zionists. And when, in the 1930s, the Nazi government imposed a 'fine' of £80 million on German Jewry, it collected the money in no time. A fraction of this sum would have sufficed to build Palestine in the 1920s.

The fourteenth Zionist congress (Vienna 1925) was in many ways a repeat performance of the previous ones. The right-wing General Zionists attacked the Socialist settlers for leading a semi-parasitic existence, being supported by the movement. Ben Gurion and his comrades maintained on the other hand that since there was only one Jewish farmer for every forty-two Jewish residents of Palestine, the agricultural sector had clearly to be strengthened. Gruenbaum again charged Weizmann with destroying the Zionist movement, whereupon Weizmann angrily answered: 'I have never retreated from full-blooded Zionism. I am a Jewish statesman and you are an assimilatory Jew.' In a long and brilliantly delivered speech Jabotinsky attacked the executive for having failed all along the line. Weizmann in his answer paid tribute to Jabotinsky's rhetorical skill, but claimed that his arguments were based on the assumption that twice two makes five; Jabotinsky's whole colonisation philosophy rested on the belief that instead of paying for the purchase of land, the Zionist movement should insist on getting it free from the mandatory government. Such a policy might work, Weizmann said, in an empty country like Rhodesia but it was unrealistic when applied to Palestine.

Two years later, at the fifteenth congress in Basle, Jabotinsky made another long and closely reasoned speech, fairly moderate in tone, in which he referred to the Greek precedent: why was it that the Greek government had succeeded in resettling one and a half million Greeks from Turkey with an investment of a mere £15 million? Why did the Zionist executive claim it needed much more money for a considerably smaller number of immigrants? Weizmann had no difficulty in refuting the argument: the settlers had received land free of charge and the Greek government had also put at their disposal seventy thousand houses – Greece and Palestine simply could not be compared.* There was no great highroad leading to the building of Palestine, no miracles were likely to happen. Only patient work would develop the country. The Basle congress witnessed another clash between Right and Left, another Gruenbaum attack on Weizmann. Weizmann somewhat

* *Protokoll des XV Zionisten Kongresses*, London, 1927, p. 206 *et seq.*

unkindly suggested that Gruenbaum could have saved time by asking the delegates to reread the speech he had made two years earlier. The only major change concerned the composition of the executive:

1925	1927	1929
Weizmann	Weizmann	Weizmann
Sokolow	Sokolow	Sokolow
Cowen	Rosenblüth	Barth
Lipsky	Lipsky	Brodetsky
Kisch	Kisch	Kaplanski
Ruppin	Sacher	Rosenblüth
Pick	Szold	Sacher
Sprinzak	Eder	Meir Berlin
van Vriesland		Kisch
		Ruppin
		Sprinzak
		Szold
		Lipsky

But these changes did not greatly affect the policy of the executive. Of the members of the 1925 executive Lipsky had to be in the United States throughout most of the year in his capacity as head of the American Zionist Organisation. The members residing in Palestine were associated with specific functions (Ruppin was in charge of colonisation, Sprinzak of labour relations, etc.). The political work was done by Weizmann and Sokolow and their assistants in London. Leonard Stein acted as secretary of the political department. He was replaced in 1929 by Professor Lewis Namier.

It would be tedious to provide a detailed account of the proceedings of the Zionist congresses in 1925, 1927 and 1929. The basic issues were few, the freedom of manoeuvre of the movement limited, the speeches usually variations on the same theme. The executive was constantly admonished by its critics to take a tougher line with the British, to collect more money, not to squander its funds, and not to discriminate against anyone. The executive on its part issued slogans which were no less platitudinous, such as 'Consolidation' or 'Concentration of all forces'. The establishment of a Zionist office in Geneva was one of the few innovations. It was headed by Victor Jacobson, who was to maintain liaison with the League of Nations mandates commission to which the Palestinian government had to present yearly reports. While Jacobson and his assistants did some useful lobbying, they could not, as some Zionists fondly imagined, play off Geneva against Jerusalem and London, or vice versa. The Zionist Organisation was not acting from a position of strength. Moreover, some members of the mandates commission, such as its president, the Italian Marquis Theodoli, were bitterly anti-Zionist. The executive was represented in Jerusalem by Colonel Kisch, who was replaced by Arlosoroff in 1931. When Arlosoroff was murdered in 1933, his former assistant Moshe Shertok took over.

The Jewish Agency

The constituent meeting of the council of the Jewish Agency opened on 11 August 1929, after years of effort against stubborn resistance from various quarters. When Weizmann was given the floor, the entire audience rose in tumultuous acclaim. He had achieved the seemingly impossible: 'By his patience, foresight, persuasiveness and skill he had created an unprecedented unity in Israel. It was the hour of his triumph.'*

Since the early 1920s Weizmann had systematically tried to enlist the help of non-Zionists, especially in the United States. His main partner in this enterprise was Louis Marshall, head of the American Jewish Committee, whom he had first met at the Paris Peace Conference in 1919. Weizmann was greatly impressed by Marshall's forceful personality, his devotion to Jewish matters, and his wisdom. Marshall, an assimilated Jew born in upstate New York, had studied Yiddish in order to be able to follow Jewish affairs. Among Zionists the main objection to cooperation with men like Marshall (or Felix Warburg, the banker) was that they had not been democratically elected and did not represent American Jewry, only its upper crust. They feared that the millionaires would gain a decisive influence on the policy of the movement. If they wanted to cooperate, Weizmann's critics argued, the doors of the Zionist organisation were open to them.† But this was precisely what they refused to do, for with all their sympathy for the work done in Palestine, they regarded the Zionists as doctrinaires, more interested in Jewish nationalism than in saving Jewish lives. Moreover, it had always been Weizmann's intention to establish a Jewish Agency as a representative of the entire Jewish people; a resolution to this effect had been passed by the Action Committee in 1922.

Weizmann and Marshall convened their first conference in February 1924, bringing together American Jews outside the Zionist movement

* Morris Rothenberg, in M. Weisgal (ed.), *Chaim Weizmann*, New York, 1944, p. 223.
† Weizmann, *Trial and Error*, p. 306.

who were willing to help work in Palestine. There were further conferences in 1925 and 1928: a Palestine Economic Corporation was established and a commission of economic experts set up to prepare a report on development. It was agreed in principle that the non-Zionists should get half of the seats on the council of the Jewish Agency. The 1925 Zionist congress accepted this stipulation but insisted that all land acquired must be held as public property, that colonisation must be based on Jewish labour, and that the Hebrew language and culture must be promoted. It took three more years before the Action Committee in December 1928 endorsed the agreement by a vote of thirty-nine against five (two revisionists, two radical General Zionists and Stephen Wise). The sixteenth congress, the year after, gave its approval by a majority of 231 to 30.

The tug of war continued, however, with leading figures in the movement, such as Ussishkin, among the doubters. But there was also resistance from non-Zionist bodies. In Britain, for instance, the leading Jewish organisations refused to cooperate with the Zionists. But once the American Jewish leaders had given their blessing to the enterprise the road was clear. Together with Leon Blum, Albert Einstein and Herbert Samuel, Louis Marshall, Felix Warburg, Cyrus Adler and Lee K. Frankel, Weizmann appeared on the platform of the foundation meeting of the Jewish Agency. The president of the Zionist movement was to be *ex officio* president of the Jewish Agency; its main office was to be in Jerusalem, with a branch in London. Its constitution provided for a general council of about two hundred members, an administrative committee of forty, and an executive of eight.

It was a memorable occasion, Weizmann's most important achievement since the Balfour Declaration. After the meeting he had a long talk with Marshall and Warburg, who assured him that his financial troubles were over and that he would no longer have to travel up and down the United States to make emergency appeals to save his movement from bankruptcy. At long last it had been put on a broad and solid foundation. A few days after the conference Louis Marshall died. With the Wall Street crash the great depression set in, and from Palestine there came news of the most serious riots in the history of the mandate. The disturbances caused a change for the worse in British policy towards Zionism, and this in turn brought about Weizmann's resignation from the presidency. Within a few weeks of the establishment of the Jewish Agency the Zionist movement faced one of the most serious crises in its history.

Chaim Weizmann

At this turn in its fortunes it is useful to identify the leading trend within Zionism during the 1920s and the men who acted as their spokesmen. Weizmann, of course, dominated the scene, as no other leader had done since Herzl. Before the First World War he was virtually unknown outside the ranks of Russian Zionism. Born in 1874 in Motol, near the border between White Russia, Lithuania and Poland, the son of a small timber merchant, he studied chemistry in Berlin and Switzerland and settled in England in 1904. He had attended a number of Zionist congresses, but though he played a certain role in the opposition to the Uganda scheme and later on in the drive to overthrow Wolffsohn, he was certainly not among the leading figures of the movement. An observer at the Vienna congress (1913) described him as a 'listless young man'. It was a mistaken impression, for boundless energy in the service of Zionism was certainly one of Weizmann's outstanding characteristics. In contrast to most of his colleagues he was a great admirer of Britain, convinced of the identity of British and Zionist interests in the Near East, and from his early days in England he tried to make converts to his idea. He was not uncritical of English life. Soon after he had settled in Manchester he wrote to a friend about the social contradictions in the life around him, the stupidity in all walks of life, the terrible and cruel materialism, the outward glamour covering the ugliness within. But nothing shook his confidence in Britain as the one big power willing and able to help the Zionist dream come true. Weizmann played the most important part in paving the way for the Balfour Declaration and in the subsequent negotiations over the mandate. True, he tended to belittle the part played by others in these events (Aron Aaronson's was by no means inconsiderable), but there is no doubt that he was the main architect of what has been called 'the greatest act of diplomatic statesmanship of the First World War': 'If there was Jewish unity in the critical years between 1917 and 1920 it was mainly the result of Weizmann's energy, patience, psychological insight and complete knowledge of all the various aspects of European Jewry.'*

Recognition inside the Jewish camp came only slowly. The Russian Zionists thought him a lightweight and the Americans were critical from the very beginning of what they regarded as a one-sided orientation towards Britain. Weizmann's most faithful supporters came from the younger generation of British Zionists and later on also from the

* Charles Webster, *The Art and Practice of Diplomacy*, London, 1961, p. 114.

Germans. His own colleagues, the east Europeans, always regarded him with more than a little suspicion. Accustomed to collective leadership, they frequently charged him with dictatorial ambitions. It has been said that he was indifferent to praise and blame,* but this judgment was not shared by some of his closest confidants. Harry Sacher, writing to Leon Simon in January 1919, complained about Weizmann's vanity, that he, Weizmann, was absolutely certain in his own judgment and Ahad Ha'am was the only one whom he was willing to consult from time to time.†

Weizmann had negotiated with the British and the Americans during the war without formal authorisation by the Zionist organisation. He was co-opted on to the executive only in 1918 following Chlenov's death. But even after that, much to his chagrin, he had to share responsibility with Sokolow, and he was elected president of the World Zionist Organisation only at the London conference in 1920.‡ From the beginning there were strong misgivings about his leadership among some of those who elected him. When he concluded his survey of activities in 1920 with the cry: 'This is what we have done, Jewish people. What have you done?' it struck some of his listeners as both unjust and pretentious. Weizmann was certain that there was no short cut to a Jewish Palestine, that he had 'daily to convince the British that the implementation of the Balfour Declaration was both in the British interest and a moral necessity'.§ In his report to the Karlsbad congress in 1923 he said: 'I am not ashamed to say I have no success to produce. After the mandate there will be no political successes for years. Those political successes which you want you will have to gain by your own work in the Emeq, in the marshes and the hills, not in the offices of Downing Street.' Convinced that the most the Zionists could gain was freedom of action for their practical work, he became increasingly impatient with those who accused him of minimalism (if not defeatism), who thought that vociferous appeals and loud protests would induce the British government to mend its ways. Weizmann always ridiculed this approach. At the 1931 congress he noted that the walls of Jericho had fallen at the blowing of trumpets, 'but I have never heard of walls having been erected by such means'.

The ambivalence of the Zionist movement towards Weizmann's

---

* Isaiah Berlin, *Chaim Weizmann*, London, 1958, p. 27.
† Quoted in Israel Kolatt, *Manhiguto shel Chaim Weizmann*, Jerusalem, 1970, pp. 26–7.
‡ *Ibid.*
§ R.Weltsch, in M.W.Weisgal and Joel Carmichael (eds.), *Chaim Weizmann*, London, 1962, p. 188.

leadership became even more pronounced as relations with Britain worsened. He was, as Robert Weltsch wrote (and as Weizmann's critics reluctantly admitted) the only Zionist leader who could meet British ministers on an equal footing. There was no one who could speak so courageously and effectively on behalf of the Jewish cause. 'His extraordinary powers of mind and his ready wit made him a formidable controversalist; the moral weight and the magic power of his personality made him succeed where lesser men could not even get a hearing.'* But his Zionist patriotism was increasingly doubted and he was even accused of treason when he refused to act as spokesman for the extremist demands which were gaining ground in the Zionist movement. This widening gulf eventually led to his downfall in 1931. He returned to the leadership only four years later at a time of supreme crisis.

About the tremendous impact of Weizmann's personality there is general agreement. A non-Jewish observer once wrote that his persuasiveness was irresistible, even frightening. He was always more successful with the Jewish masses (and incidentally with non-Jews) than with his own colleagues among the Zionist leadership. The strength of his personality has been described in a moving tribute by Isaiah Berlin:

He was one of those human beings who . . . stood near the consciousness of his people and not on its periphery; his ideas and his feelings were, as it were, naturally attuned to the often unspoken, but always central hopes, fears, modes of feeling of the vast majority of the Jewish masses with which he felt himself all his life in deep and complete natural sympathy. His genius largely consisted in making articulate and finding avenues for the realisation of these aspirations and longings. . . . He was a man of immense natural authority, dignity and strength. He was calm, paternal, imperturbable, certain of himself. He never drifted with the current. He was always in control. He accepted full responsibility. He was indifferent to praise and blame. He possessed tact and charm to a degree exceeded by no statesman of modern days. But what held the Jewish masses to him until the very last phase of his long life, was not the possession of these qualities alone, dazzling as they were, but the fact that although outwardly he had become an eminent western scientist (which made him financially and therefore politically independent), and mingled easily with the remote and unapproachable masters of the western world, his fundamental personality and outlook remained unchanged. His language, his images, his turns of phrase were rooted in Jewish tradition and piety and learning. His tastes, his physical movements, the manner in which he walked and stood, got up and sat down, his gestures, the features of his exceedingly expressive face and

* R. Weltsch, in *Jewish Social Studies*, vol. 13, no. 3, p. 127.

above all his tone of voice, the accent, the inflexion, the extraordinary variety of his humour, were identical with theirs – were their own.*

Yet the picture of the greatest Jewish statesman of his age would be incomplete without mentioning, at least in passing, some of his shortcomings and weaknesses. His political views were those of a democratic nationalist, not unlike Masaryk's. He had absorbed them instinctively and remained always, first and foremost, an empiricist. Once shaped, his political views changed little if at all over the years. He read few books and had few interests outside Zionist politics and chemistry. Like Herzl he was no original political thinker. He was at least partly unaware of the great and mostly negative changes that were taking place in the 1920s and 1930s. He had easily found a common language, with Balfour and Lloyd George and men of their generation, but communication with their successors became increasingly difficult. His democratic humanism was out of tune with the new *Zeitgeist* and the new *Realpolitik*, out of tune with an increasingly violent world in which humanism and moral necessities counted for little and physical power was almost the only criterion. In these changed conditions Weizmann's effectiveness as a political leader was bound to diminish.

His attitude to his own people, to the Zionist movement, even to his closest collaborators, was highly contradictory and often ambivalent. He never failed to stress that he was a man of the people: 'If I have achieved anything, it is precisely because I am not a diplomat. If you want to hurt me, call me a diplomat.'† 'Herzl came from the west,' he said on another occasion, 'and used western concepts and ideas. I unfortunately hail from Lithuania. I know the Jewish people only too well, and it knows me even better. And therefore I lack the wings which were given to Herzl. . . . Had Herzl been to a *cheder*, the Jewish people would never have followed him.'‡ But the common touch was blended with elements of a Nietzschean contempt for the masses. He was fully aware of the weaknesses of the Jewish people, the unwillingness of the rich Jews of Europe and America to contribute financially and of the Jewish masses to emigrate to Palestine. The lack of gratitude often shown him only strengthened such feelings. On occasion he seems to have despaired of ever convincing his movement that an all-out effort of the whole people was needed to make the Zionist dream come true.

* Berlin, *Chaim Weizmann*, pp. 25–8.
† *Ha'aretz*, 15 December 1919; quoted in Kolatt, *Manhiguto shel Chaim Weizmann*.
‡ Speech in Czernowitz, December 1927, quoted in Chaim Weizmann, *Reden und Aufsaetze*, Tel Aviv, 1937, p. 185.

His attitude to his contemporaries in the Zionist leadership was, with a few exceptions, one of barely veiled contempt. Like Ben Gurion after him, he got along well with the younger generation, which looked up to him, but he found it exceedingly difficult to work with others as equals. 'He was never happy as a colleague,' Harry Sacher wrote. 'He disliked seeking counsel and he had no gift for reporting.'* He was a moody man and could turn his great charm on and off abruptly. More than once he used people only to discard them when he no longer needed them and was guilty of acts of gross disloyalty to some of his closest confidants. He hardly ever expected gratitude from others and only infrequently showed it himself. But the qualities which make a popular leader and a great statesman (one, to quote Berlin again, whose active intervention makes what seemed highly improbable in fact happen) are not exactly those of a saint. For someone active in politics throughout his life, his weaknesses were surprisingly few and his sins venial.

Other Zionist leaders

One of the earliest challenges to Weizmann's rule was made by Menahem Ussishkin, who had been a leader in Russian Zionism when Weizmann was still a student. Born near Mohilev in 1863, the son of a wealthy Hassidic merchant, he got his training as an engineer (a profession he never practised) in Moscow. A central figure among the Lovers of Zion, he spent his honeymoon in Palestine at a time (1891) when it was unfashionable, to put it mildly, to do so.† A heavy-set man with massive shoulders and blue eyes, he had the reputation of being unbending and hard as nails. There was indeed such a streak in his character, but there is reason to believe that he deliberately cultivated the image of the tough, forbidding man, and that behind this façade there was a romantic, dreaming of the redemption of the soil of Palestine. His political ambitions were bound to remain unfulfilled. He had his enthusiastic followers among the Russians but was temperamentally quite unsuited to lead the Zionist movement, which wanted not a dictator at the helm but a master in the art of gentle persuasion. He had the nature of a tsar (one contemporary wrote), his opinions were issued in the form of edicts. He was dead sure that he was always right and no one could be as right as he. It was not only his lack of linguistic ability which debarred him from the heights of Zionist diplomacy.

* Sacher, *Zionist Portraits*, p. 10.
† For further biographical details, see J.Klausner, *Menahem Ussishkin*, Jerusalem, 1942.

After having settled in Palestine, Ussishkin was made director of the Keren Hayesod. He was instrumental in buying lands which later became key areas in Jewish agricultural settlement (Yesreel valley, the Beisan valley, Emeq Hefer). While a man of the Right in his political philosophy, he warmly supported the Socialist pioneers in their endeavours even when these ran counter to his own beliefs, for settling on the land remained for him the ultimate test of commitment to the Zionist idea. He had absorbed the Russian Populists' belief in the unity of theory and action and had nothing but contempt for the diaspora Zionists who saw their own future in Europe rather than in Palestine. Ussishkin died in Jerusalem, the city he loved most, during the Second World War, his prejudices and passions and intellect undimmed; with all his foibles, a man widely respected, a pillar of strength of the Zionist movement.

Nahum Sokolow shared the leadership of the Zionist movement with Weizmann after 1917. He too had played a notable part in the events leading up to the Balfour Declaration. Sokolow was more widely educated than Weizmann but lacked the popular touch, the charisma and the toughness of the born leader. He was perhaps the most accomplished Zionist diplomat but he did not have the vision, the grand design of the great statesman. He was tolerant, sympathetic and generous in his appreciation of others, and modest in his appreciation of himself,* though he did not lack political ambition, as appeared at the Zionist congress of 1931 which deposed Weizmann and made him the leader of the movement. He was a handsome man, distinguished in manner, eloquent, witty and remarkably well read. But he lacked the demonic streak and the passion which was part of Weizmann's character. He was too much the intellectual to become the man of action, too courteous, too indecisive on important political issues. He was not a strong man and did not even try to give the impression of being one. Sokolow was reluctant to make enemies; he was not hard enough to be the leader of a popular dynamic movement. He became an elder statesman comparatively early in life, and was very much in demand as chairman and mediator. But he was not the man to provide leadership at a time of crisis.

Leo Motzkin, born in Lithuania, played an important role in the early period of the Zionist movement. He had been Weizmann's mentor in

* Sacher, *Zionist Portraits*, p. 36.

the Berlin days and later on presided over many Zionist congresses. Like Sokolow, he was a man of the centre, an excellent chairman, but he did not carry much weight in the inner councils of the movement. He lacked discipline and purpose and there was, again in the words of a contemporary, something unfinished about most of Motzkin's actions. He was said to be a gifted mathematician, but unlike Weizmann he did not finish his studies. He became an expert on the situation of Jews in Russia, and later on in other parts of the world. The compilation of documents he published on these topics was of considerable value, but there is little of his own writing.* In later years his main interest was diaspora politics – the World Jewish Congress was his brainchild, though he did not live to see it born (he died in 1934). He lacked the single-mindedness of Ussishkin or Weizmann. Perhaps he enjoyed life more than they did. He certainly came to love Paris, its boulevards, restaurants and cafés:

There he could meet Jews of all lands. If you sat at the Café de la Paix any afternoon, you would see a panorama of Jewish life pass by. . . . He spent more time drinking tea than at his desk. He loved good company and was a good listener. He read heavy literature and nothing light or easy ever crossed his eyes. He never seemed to have time for home life and could be relied on to pack a grip and at a moment's notice go to London or Vienna or New York – wherever a Jewish cause beckoned. He disliked quarrels and partnerships.†

He was knowledgeable and decent, but not cut out to be a leader of men.

Of all the leading figures in the movement Jabotinsky was the most colourful, but he was in opposition from the early 1920s onward and had little influence on official Zionist policy. His political career has been described elsewhere in the present study. The members of Weizmann's entourage were specialists, not all-round men like himself; they did not play a central role in internal Zionist politics even when they were members of the executive. Kisch, Eder, Harry Sacher, even Professor Brodetsky were half Jews, half Englishmen in the eyes of the east Europeans; their speeches were not always understood. As they did not share the east European cultural tradition they never felt themselves completely at home in the folksy atmosphere of the Zionist congresses.

* Some of his writings were published posthumously: A.Bein (ed.), *Sefer Motzkin*, Jerusalem, 1938.

† Louis Lipsky, *A Gallery of Zionist Profiles*, pp. 90–1.

Jabotinsky apart, the revisionists had no outstanding personality. Robert Stricker, who supported him in the 1920s, had no following and influence outside Vienna. Like Lichtheim he did not stay long with the revisionists.

The labour movement was represented in the leadership by Kaplanski, who was not well known in Palestine, for he settled in Haifa only in later years when he became head of the technical university there. Ben Gurion, Sprinzak, Remes, Ben Zvi, Katznelson made their appearance at the Zionist congresses in the 1920s but their speeches caused barely a ripple. They were still largely preoccupied with their own specific problems, and even the rhetoric of Berl Katznelson did not go down too well. The great prodigy of the Left was Victor (Chaim) Arlosoroff, born in Romny in the Ukraine, educated in Berlin, who entered Zionist politics at the twelfth congress and, in 1924, at the age of twenty-five, became a member of the Action Committee.

Arlosoroff was a man of remarkable gifts, combining Weizmann's tact, political instinct and intuition with outstanding organisational and oratorical talent. He was the best speaker in the movement, less flamboyant but more persuasive than Jabotinsky. He understood more about economics and sociology than any other Zionist leader, and was in fact a rare combination of the intellectual and the man of action. Politically he belonged to the Hapoel Hatzair and was one of the main architects of the merger with Ahdut Avoda out of which Mapai was born in 1930. He developed his own brand of Socialist doctrine (*Volkssozialismus*) but was the least doctrinaire of men, always ready to modify his views in the light of new developments and experiences.*
Early on he was asked to take on diplomatic missions on behalf of the executive – to Geneva, London and the United States. It was more than somewhat ironical that after Weizmann's fall he, a self-confessed extreme Weizmannite, was elected to be his successor as the foreign minister of the movement.

The political constellation when Arlosoroff took over was anything but auspicious: the movement faced financial bankruptcy. Sir John Chancellor, the high commissioner in Palestine, was not exactly a supporter of the Zionist cause. The London government was moving further away from the spirit and letter of the Balfour Declaration. The differences within the movement were steadily growing. Even some

---

* His writings and speeches were published posthumously in six volumes in Tel Aviv in 1934. There is a one-volume German selection of his writings: Chaim Arlosoroff, *Leben und Werk*, Berlin, 1936.

among the newly elected executive would not have been unduly distressed had Arlosoroff failed in his efforts. In this difficult situation he showed an enormous capacity for work, infinite patience, and a desire to make friends with Englishmen and Arabs alike despite constant discouragement from all sides. Above all he wanted to give a fresh impetus to Zionist work. As the year 1932 drew to a close there were signs of a slow improvement, but Arlosoroff did not live to see the turn of the tide. On the evening of 16 June 1933, he was shot while walking on the Tel Aviv beach. The identity of his killers has not been established to this day and the exact circumstances have remained a matter of controversy ever since. Members of a group of extreme revisionists were widely suspected of the crime, but there was insufficient proof and they were acquitted after a trial which caused a deep split in the Jewish community.

Among Weizmann's supporters in Germany Kurt Blumenfeld was one of the most influential. A most effective speaker, he was even more persuasive in a small circle and succeeded in gaining the support or many leading non-Zionists, Jewish and non-Jewish alike, for the colonising work in Palestine. Robert Weltsch, born in Prague, was the editor of the most influential Zionist organ of the period in any language, the *Jüdische Rundschau*, and, incidentally, wrote many of Weizmann's speeches. The *Rundschau* was often criticised for its ultra-Weizmannism (on the Arab problem, the question of the Jewish state) but no one disputed its high cultural level. It enjoyed great authority and had a marked educational impact far beyond the borders of Germany. Nahum Goldmann, born in eastern Europe, and educated in Germany, began to take a leading part in Zionist politics at an early age. He belonged to the radical Zionists who opposed Weizmann, but his main interest, like Motzkin's and Gruenbaum's, was diaspora politics rather than Palestine. Not quite of Arlosoroff's calibre, he was an excellent speaker and an accomplished diplomat. He attained a leading position in the movement only in the 1930s.

Among Weizmann's supporters in America Louis Lipsky was the most gifted and prominent. A man of considerable intellectual and artistic talents, he was at the same time an excellent organiser and the educator of two generations of American Zionists. He became general secretary of the American Zionist Federation early on and assumed its leadership after the defeat of the Brandeis-Mack faction. American Zionism had other outstanding leaders, such as Rabbi Stephen Wise, a formidable orator, who had, however, many interests outside Zionism: every humanitarian cause found a warm supporter in this radical democrat. There was Abba Hillel Silver, another fiery orator, also a rabbi and an early Zionist, who assumed a leading role in the 1940s. Jacob de Haas, born in England, who had won over Brandeis for the Zionist cause, was prominent at one time but dropped out after Brandeis' resignation. Few American Zionist leaders except Henrietta Szold made Zionism their only cause, and none of them with the exception of Henrietta Szold, Magnes and, in later years, Israel Goldstein, made Jerusalem their home.

This list of prominent Zionists is not only incomplete; it is to a certain extent misleading. The most accomplished orators, the leaders most in the limelight, were not necessarily those who constituted the backbone of the movement. Some of the leading ideologists of the earlier period, such as Idelson, Jacob Klatzkin or Pasmanik, now forgotten, exerted considerable influence at the time even if their ideas were often disputed. Arthur Ruppin, whose place in the history of Zionism has been mentioned, was for many years the executive's expert on all questions concerned with Jewish settlement. In the accounts of the dramatic debates and the memorable decisions his name does not often appear. He was the protagonist of practical work, doing his job inconspicuously with rare devotion, never in the limelight if he could help it. Yet in retrospect the importance of his work has no equal in the annals of Zionism. There were other such men, the unsung heroes of the movement, without whom Zionism would have remained a debating society, a parliament without a country, intriguing no doubt but of no practical consequence.

Zionist Parties

The World Zionist Organisation was composed both of separate unions (such as Mizrahi and labour Zionism), and of national federations, whose members subscribed to the Basle programme but were not bound by party discipline. Before the Second World War there were fifty such freelance federations and their members were by definition General Zionists. Thus General Zionism was the first party to exist but the last to get organised. It was the main stream, the movement itself was general Zionist. The term 'General Zionism' was adopted only in 1907 after the appearance on the scene of other parties within the movement.*

* I.Schwarzbart, in F.Gross and B.J.Vlavianos (eds.), *Struggle for Tomorrow*, New York, 1954, p. 27.

General Zionism was amorphous, 'a compound of many views, but not an ideological identity'.* As there were no permanent ties between the national federations they came to the congresses strong in numbers but divided and without a clear programme of action. At the twelfth (Karlsbad) congress they represented 73 per cent of the total, but suffered a decline when both the Right and the Left became much stronger. In 1923–5 their share was 50–60 per cent; in 1931 they were reduced to a mere 36 per cent, split, moreover, three different ways. Attempts to bring the three factions together at the first World General Zionist Conference (Basle, 1931) were only partly successful. Nor was the attempt to provide a specific General Zionist philosophy very convincing. Robert Weltsch claimed that General Zionism was not just equidistant between Left and Right, between capitalism and Socialism, between religious orthodoxy and atheism, between militarism and pacifism, between an aggressive and a sober realistic policy; it was not just a policy of passive compromise, the desire to choose the line of least resistance, but a positive, deliberate, conscious decision in favour of the centre and the unity of the movement.† Such motives may have induced Robert Weltsch and some of his intellectual friends to back General Zionism, but most of its leaders and supporters were attracted to it precisely because it was not a movement of extremes.

General Zionism was plagued by internal dissension. In 1923 the 'Democratic Zionists' broke away and established a faction in opposition to Weizmann. They rejected, *inter alia*, the idea of an enlarged Jewish Agency and they also claimed that Weizmann did not pay sufficient attention to the necessity of strengthening Zionist organisations in the diaspora. Moreover, he was said to be too pro-British in his foreign policy.‡ The main spokesman of this faction was Y. Gruenbaum, whose Polish group (*Al Hamishmar*) constituted the nucleus of the opposition. It was supported by Nahum Goldmann and some of his Berlin friends, a Rumanian group (*Renasterea*), and several small factions in Austria and Czechoslovakia. In 1927 the opposition was renamed 'Radical Zionism'. In its programme it tried to outflank the Weizmannites from both the Left and the Right. In contrast to Weizmann, it emphasised the importance of attaining a Jewish majority in Palestine and a Jewish

* *Ibid.*, p. 28. See also N. Goldenberg, *General Zionism*, London, 1937; I. Goldstein, *General Zionist Program*, New York, 1947; Moshe Kleinman, *Hazionim Haklalim*, Jerusalem, 1945.

† Felix Weltsch, in *Parteien im Zionismus*, Prague, 1936, pp. 10–12.

‡ *Zu den Hauptfragen des 14 Zionistenkongresses* (Flugschrift Nr. I der Konferenzgemeinschaft radikaler Zionisten), n.p., n.d., *passim*; and *Probleme des 14 Zionistenkongresses*, n.p., n.d., *passim*.

state as the final aim of Zionism. At the same time it stressed the need of democratic Jewish life in the diaspora, a reference, presumably, to Weizmann's 'dictatorship'. While most Jews were sympathetic to the idea of building up Palestine, they had not yet been won over to Zionism, and to achieve this was, according to the Radicals, one of the most urgent assignments of the movement. In brief, they asked for a more militant and dynamic policy without, however, always being able to specify in detail what policies they would have pursued that differed essentially from Weizmann's. Some of their demands, moreover, were mutually exclusive.*

Radical Zionism, like General Zionism, was a trend rather than a political party. Its early manifestos were signed not only by Gruenbaum and Goldmann but also by Jabotinsky, Schechtman, Stricker and other revisionists who soon established their own organisation. The Radical Zionists had at no stage the support of a sizable section of the movement. They polled 6 per cent of the total at the elections in 1927 but two years later their share dropped to 4 per cent. Subsequently Gruenbaum, Goldmann and most of their supporters returned to the fold of General Zionism, constituting, together with German, British and American leaders, the 'A' stream, in contrast to the rival 'B' faction headed by Ussishkin, Mossinson, Bograshow, Schwarzbart, Rottenstreich, Schmorak, Suprasky and F.Bernstein. At the 1935 congress, the former had eighty-one representatives, the latter forty-seven.

All General Zionists agreed that the national interest should always take precedence over party interests. But since the two wings differed both in their definition of national interest and in their attitude towards Weizmann's foreign policy, as well as in their approach to social and economic issues, such verbal agreement was not sufficient to restore unity for any length of time. The 'A' faction favoured fairly close collaboration with labour Zionism and advocated the inclusion of General Zionist workers in the Histadrut framework, whereas the 'B' faction (the 'World Union') gravitated towards the Right, preferring the establishment of a separate union outside the Socialist-dominated Histadrut. The 'B' faction came out in favour of a Jewish state as early as 1931, whereas the Weizmannites opposed it as premature at the time. The former wanted to transform General Zionism into a political party whose decisions were binding on all its members, whereas the latter preferred a loose confederation. After the split of 1935 most General Zionists joined group 'A', which had 143 delegates at the last prewar

* *Das Programm der Vereinigten Radikalen Zionisten*, n.p., n.d.

Zionist congress, whereas 'B' was represented by only twenty-eight members. After the war, in December 1946, a new world confederation of General Zionists came into being, but the rivalry continued and in the first parliamentary elections in the state of Israel the General Zionists split into no fewer than seven lists. Eventually most of the members of the 'A' faction joined the Progressive Party, whereas the members of 'B' established a General Zionist Party which eventually united with the revisionists (Herut). Outside Israel, American leaders such as Abba Hillel Silver, and later Israel Goldstein, were prominent in General Zionism, as far as it continued to exist.

Religious Zionism

The emergence of labour Zionism and of revisionism, and their subsequent fortunes, are discussed elsewhere in the present study. Religious Zionism, as represented by the Mizrahi, was less important, but no survey of the Zionist movement would be complete which ignored the part played by this, one of the oldest factions within the Jewish national movement.

Orthodox Zionists trace their roots to Ramban, the medieval sage, who according to tradition found only two Jews in Jerusalem when he arrived there some 650 years ago, and thereupon decided to work for the strengthening of Jewish settlement in Palestine. They see their precursors in Rabbi Israel Baal Shem Tov in the eighteenth century, and in Rabbis Kalischer and Gutmacher (a leading Kabbalist) in the nineteenth, in whose thought the rebuilding of Palestine figured very prominently. Among the Lovers of Zion there were several distinguished rabbis, such as Eliasberg and Mohilever, but the organisation of orthodox Jewry, Mizrahi, came into being only some years after Herzl had given fresh impetus to Zionism. The moving spirit behind the Vilna convention (1902) and the founder of Mizrahi was Isaac Jacob Raines, rabbi of Lida, a 'Litvak' who in the words of his biographer knew no language but Hebrew, had no general education, but 'was a man of much wisdom and knowledge, a Talmudic sage, a genius, a preacher of the rarest type, who blazed a trail in Aggadic literature'.* Raines had sympathised with the Lovers of Zion, but decided after much reflection to join Herzlian Zionism. Having pondered and rejected the arguments against Zionism by the ultra-orthodox rabbis, he reached the conclusion that whoever concluded that the Zionist ideal had any connection with

* Rabbi Judah L. Fishman, *The History of the Mizrahi Movement*, New York, 1928, p. 49.

free thought was liable to suspicion himself as a desecrator of things holy.*

At the Vilna conference, and at a subsequent meeting in Minsk, there was no agreement between those who argued that the Mizrahi should act as a watchdog within the Zionist movement, i.e. prevent it from falling into the hands of the 'freethinkers', and those who maintained that a purely negative approach would be ineffective in the long run and that Mizrahi should therefore engage in constructive work as well, such as education and settlement. These were differences of tactics rather than principle. Mizrahi members have always agreed that the basic aim of the organisation was to 'capture the Zionist institutions' and create a religious majority among the Jews of Palestine.† The constructivists gained the upper hand and it was decided that Mizrahi should collect the funds needed to establish a modern yeshiva in Lida, a school in Tel Aviv and a teachers' seminary in Jerusalem. The seat of the Mizrahi executive was transferred from Lida to Frankfurt and later to Hamburg-Altona, in view of the difficulties facing the movement in tsarist Russia.

At first little was done. Mizrahi was then a loose federation of local groups united in their religious and national beliefs and in their wish to act as a pressure group against the 'democratic faction' (Sokolow, Weizmann, Motzkin) which wanted the movement to engage in cultural and educational activities as well as in political and colonising work. Since educational work by the non-orthodox was *a priori* unacceptable to Mizrahi, a crisis occurred when it was finally decided at the tenth Zionist congress to accept the programme of the 'democratic faction'. The more rigid orthodox elements, especially those in Germany and Hungary, decided to leave the Zionist movement, but the great majority stayed within it.‡

Throughout its history Mizrahi has been plagued by dissension between those who regard themselves first and foremost as Zionists and the others who put orthodoxy above Zionism. Mizrahi ideology is a compromise between two extremes: it rejects Zionism as a purely secular movement, claiming that the spiritual and moral values of Europe have only limited value, that the Jewish nation without religion is a body without a soul, that religion and nation constitute an indis-

---

* Quoted in *Sefer Mizrahi*, Jerusalem, 1946, p. 53.

† Sh.Z.Shragai, *Chason Vehagshama*, London, 1945, p. 17.

‡ Meir Berlin, *Mevolozhin ad Yerushalayim*, Tel Aviv, 1940, vol. 2, p. 55; on the history of the Mizrahi, see also S.B.Feldman, *Brief Survey of the Mizrahi Movement*, London.

soluble unity.* Religion, in other words, must be the core of Zionism, and the religious tradition has again to become the law of the Land of Israel. Yet, in contrast to Agudat Israel, Mizrahi has always argued that religious faith without the national spirit was only 'half Judaism', and has insisted, again in contrast to the ultra-orthodox, that the Hebrew language must be the language of both spiritual and daily life. The Antwerp congress (1926) put the ideology into one brief formula: 'The Mizrahi is a Zionist, national and religious federation striving to build the national home of the Jewish people in Palestine in accordance with the written and traditional laws.'

Two of the younger and most active leaders, Rabbis Meir Berlin and Y.L.Fishman, were in America during the First World War and helped to build up the organisation there. 1922 was a milestone in the history of the movement: the seat of the executive was transferred to Jerusalem and *Hapoel Hamizrahi*, the workers section, was founded. During its early phase the movement had been dominated by rabbis, but gradually lay members gained a larger share in the leadership. One of them, Professor Hermann Pick, became the first Mizrahi representative on the Zionist executive. Special emphasis was put during the 1920s and 1930s on educational activities both in Palestine and in eastern Europe. A women's group was started and its youth section gained many adherents. In Palestine the Mizrahi established its own bank as well as a building workers cooperative. Later, with the arrival of the first members of Hapoel Hamizrahi, several kibbutzim and suburban settlements, such as Sanhedria in Jerusalem, were founded. The ten kibbutzim of Hapoel Hamizrahi had in 1967 about four thousand members.

In Zionist politics the Mizrahi at first supported Weizmann but later turned against him to join the right-wing opposition against the labour parties. It was basically a middle class party and therefore opposed the takeover of the Zionist executive in 1931 by the Left. These policies caused dissension. The orthodox workers' section, which subsequently joined the Histadrut, opposed this turn to the Right. It advocated 'Jewish Socialism', claiming that Socialism need not necessarily be materialist and atheist in character; that, on the contrary, Socialism based on the concepts of social justice as presented in the Bible was both legitimate and desirable. The Mizrahi leadership was not at first greatly impressed by these dissenting voices. On the contrary, its failure

---

* Berthold Lewkowitz, *Der Weg des Misrachi*, Vienna, 1936, p. 9.

to influence Palestinian and Zionist politics in the spirit of Jewish orthodoxy caused a further hardening of its attitude.

At the Cracow conference in 1933 Mizrahi decided to intensify its struggle against the non-orthodox, both in the Zionist movement and in the elected institutions of Palestinian Jewry.* This caused further friction in its ranks. The German Mizrahi left the world federation in 1931 (partly in protest against the anti-Weizmann line), and there was resistance to the new course in Britain, Austria and Switzerland as well as in Palestine. Hapoel Hamizrahi claimed, not without good reason, that by pursuing narrow class interests the movement would cut itself off from the very masses it wanted to influence in the spirit of Jewish traditions. Unity was restored after several years of dispute, but the Hapoel Hamizrahi emerged from the conflict greatly strengthened and more independent in its outlook and policy.

Youth Movements

Zionism was a movement supported predominantly by the young generation when it first appeared on the European scene, and youth movements have played an important role in its history ever since. The *Bilu* consisted of boys and girls in their late teens and early twenties, and those who came to Palestine with the second and third immigration wave were mostly of this age. The early supporters of Zionism in central and western Europe were students who met in corporations such as *Kadima* in Vienna; another *Kadima* was founded in London in 1887, well before Herzl's time. Similar groups were founded in Breslau in 1886, in Heidelberg (*Badenia*) in 1890, in Berlin in 1892 (*Jung Israel*), in Czernowitz (*Hasmonea*) and in several other universities. It was one form taken by the reaction against the emerging antisemitic movement which had its bastions in the universities. Some of these groups saw their main task in cultural work among their members, others put the stress on physical prowess. It was not uncommon for them to provoke duels with antisemitic students in order to demonstrate to themselves and and others that Jews were not cowards. These student corporations accepted political Zionism only gradually, but once they did so they became the backbone of the movement in Germany and Austria and in later years provided its leadership.

In 1913–14 Zionist students in Germany organised group excursions to Palestine. On the very eve of the First World War the local associations merged into the KJV, the central organisation (*Kartell Jüdischer*

* Moshe Ostrovski, *Toldot Hamizrahi beeretz Israel*, Jerusalem, 1943, pp. 132 *et seq.*

Verbindungen) which was to play an important part in central European Zionism after 1918. While the students movement pre-dated political Zionism, the idea of promoting physical education was first mooted at the second Zionist congress by Max Nordau and Professor Mandelstam. It was given further impetus at the fifth congress, when Nordau coined the phrase *Muskel Judentum* (muscle Jewry). *Bar Kochba*, the first big Jewish sports club, was founded in 1898 in Berlin. The movement rapidly spread to other countries and at the sixth congress it was decided to form an international federation of Zionist sports clubs. In 1921, at the Karlsbad congress, this became the Maccabi World Organisation, which in 1930 had about forty thousand members in twenty-four countries. In 1932 the first Jewish Olympic Games (the Maccabia) took place in Tel Aviv. Some of these clubs attained a considerable reputation particularly in athletics and boxing (Germany), and swimming, skiing and athletics (Austria and Czechoslovakia). Many boys and girls came to Zionism through these clubs. It would be a mistake to assume that the whole Zionist movement graduated from intense ideological discussions, and the study of Borokhov and Buber. The great emphasis put on physical education, traditionally neglected among the Jewish communities, was part of the Zionist campaign to normalise Jewish life, and it may have been influenced by the Czech Sokols.

An independent Jewish youth movement, free from control by adults, developing its own specific youth culture, came into being in 1912–13 with the establishment of the *Blau Weiss* in Breslau and Berlin. The impact of the German youth movement, the *Wandervogel*, was considerable: Blau Weiss adopted the same organisational forms. Its members sang the same songs and went on hiking and camping trips. It was permeated by the same neo-romantic mood, the protest against vulgar materialism and the artificial conventions of society, by the desire to return to a more natural, sincere, spontaneous life. What prevented the integration of young Jews in the German Wandervogel was partly the emergence of antisemitic tendencies in a movement which originally had been non-political: some German groups introduced a *numerus clausus*, other refused to accept Jews altogether, and in 1913 there was a country-wide discussion on whether Jews could and should be members.* Moreover, assimilated as most German Jews were, many of them felt they could have no place in a movement which drew so much of its inspiration from the mystic folk spirit so frequently

---

* Walter Laqueur, 'The German Youth Movement and the Jewish Question', *Leo Baeck Year Book*, 1961, p. 199.

invoked, in which elements of Teutomania and Christianity were so deeply ingrained. When war broke out, the members of the Jewish youth movements in Germany and Austria volunteered for the army. But if the experience of the war drove so many of their German contemporaries towards an exalted German patriotism, many young Jews discovered that whatever their legal status they were not regarded as fully fledged Germans by their fellow soldiers and officers. Some rediscovered their Jewish identity as a result of their first contact with east European Jewry. Blau Weiss, which had sympathised with Zionism from the beginning, was fully converted to it during the war, even though the internal disputes about 'what is Jewish' continued. With all its Zionist commitment, the movement was deeply immersed in German culture. One of its leaders confessed that his 'dreams ripened under northern firs', not under oriental palms. Others admitted that the good old German songs appealed to them more than the artificial Hebrew ones, whose meaning they did not understand. At a youth meeting in Berlin in October 1918 one of the spokesmen of the Blau Weiss declared that Zionism had to be liberated from the dead weight of tradition, and that a national revival did not necessarily entail the indiscriminate adoption of outworn religious dogmas and cultural beliefs.*

Such heretical views aroused a storm of indignation, but indignation alone did not answer the questions about the Jewish content: the German youth movement continued to serve as the organisational pattern and the ideological inspiration for Zionist youth. In one decisive respect, however, Zionist youth went far beyond the Wandervogel: at the Prünn meeting of the Blau Weiss in 1922 a resolution was adopted committing its members to emigrate to Palestine and to work and live there together. It had been the great weakness of the German youth movement that despite all the solemn declarations of personal commitment it had always been a transit camp: most of its members dropped out once they graduated from high school.

The Jewish youth movement wanted to succeed where its German contemporary had failed, to establish a *Lebensbund*, not a summer camp but a life community. The first Blau Weiss members went to Palestine in 1921–2, others followed in 1923 and 1924 and established a small

* For the history of the *Blau Weiss* and other Zionist Youth movements, see Hermann Meier-Cronemeyer, 'Jüdische Jugendbewegung', in *Germania Judaica* (2 vols.), 1969. See also the unpublished doctoral dissertation by Haim Shatzker, *Tnuat Hanoar hayehudit beGermania beshanim 1900–33*, Jerusalem, 1969. On the difficulties facing the historian of youth movements, W. Laqueur, 'The Archaeology of Youth', in *Out of the Ruins of Europe*, New York, 1971.

agricultural settlement and also a workshop in the city. These attempts failed, partly because the members had been insufficiently prepared for working life in Palestine and partly because of the economic crisis of 1925–6. Blau Weiss ceased to exist in 1927, but this was by no means the end of the Zionist youth movement in Germany; many of its members eventually found their way to Palestine.

During the 1920s and the early 1930s several more Zionist youth movements came into being (*JJWB*, *Brit Haolim*, *Kadima*, *Habonim*, *Werkleute*). Some of them subsequently established their own kibbutzim in Palestine (the *Werkleute* in Hazorea) while members of others (such as the religious *Bachad*) joined either collective or cooperative settlements. From an ideological point of view these groups, with their unending disputes about cultural and political issues, were a fascinating, ever-changing amalgam of Socialist or, at any rate, anti-capitalist elements (with Marx and Gustav Landauer as the strongest influences), cultural Zionism (Buber), the German youth movement, and to a growing degree *haluziut*, the idea of commitment to a working life in Palestine. Not all of those who committed themselves to a life in a kibbutz joined one in the end, and of those who did join, not all remained. Eventually, however, a higher percentage of German Jews went into agriculture than of immigrants from any other country.

The victory of Nazism gave a fresh impetus to the Zionist youth movement. The membership of *Hehalutz*, founded in Germany in the early 1920s on the initiative of, among others, Arlosoroff, rose to fifteen thousand after 1933, of whom seven thousand went to Palestine within the next three years, most of them joining existing kibbutzim. Of the younger members, those aged sixteen or less, several thousand reached Palestine with Youth Aliya, an enterprise directed by Henrietta Szold, the veteran American Zionist leader. They were absorbed in children's villages (such as Ben Shemen) and kibbutzim, where in a two-year training course they were taught the essentials of agriculture, learnt Hebrew, and received a general education of sorts.

The impact of the German youth movement was not limited to the German-speaking countries of central Europe. It exerted a powerful influence on eastern Europe as well. Hashomer Hatzair, of which mention has already been made, came into being as a youth movement subscribing to the principles of scouting.* Its cradle was in Galicia. During the war years some of its leaders came into contact with members of the German and Austrian Jewish youth movements and the

---

* *Sefer Hashomer Hatzair*, Merhavia, 1956, vol. 1, p. 24 *et seq.*

pioneers of a new, free education (S.Bernfeld). Their vanguard reached Palestine in 1920–1. Like the Blau Weiss, they were not yet by any means convinced Zionists. Nietzschean ideas about the fulfilment of the individual played a central role in their *Weltanschauung*. Later, the movement spread from Galicia to Poland, Rumania, Lithuania and many other countries.

By 1930 Hashomer Hatzair counted thirty-four thousand members and was by far the strongest youth movement. It had also become unequivocally Zionist and radically Socialist in character and subscribed to the idea of kibbutz life. Not all its members stood the test: many dropped out for personal reasons, others because they no longer accepted the ideological orientation of the movement. Left-wing critics claimed that there could be no synthesis between the aims of Zionism and revolutionary Socialism. They saw a 'tragic conflict' between the two, and in view of the overriding importance of world revolution they opted for Communism, or in some cases for Trotskyism. The right wing (mainly in Latvia and Czechoslovakia), on the other hand, maintained that there was already too much politics in their movement. The secession took place at the third world conference of Hashomer Hatzair in 1930. Most members of this group found their way into Mapai.

On the eve of the Second World War the Hashomer Hatzair world movement counted about seventy thousand members. During the war, those in the occupied countries of east Europe, like members of other Zionist youth movements, played a leading part in the resistance to Nazism. Many died. Of the few who survived most went to Israel after the war. The main Jewish communities in Europe had ceased to exist, and with them their youth movements, but branches of Hashomer Hatzair (like Habonim and the religious youth movements) continued operating in western Europe and the Americas, as well as in North and South Africa, Australia and, in fact, in most Jewish communities throughout the world.

Hashomer Hatzair was for many years the strongest youth movement, but it did not have the field to itself, even on the Left, not to speak of the revisionist Betar, of which mention has been made already. In 1923–4 *Gordonia* was founded in Poland, a youth movement inclined broadly speaking towards the Zionist Left. It was strongly influenced by the thought of A.D.Gordon and by the German youth movement, but in contrast to Hashomer Hatzair it subscribed to humanitarian Socialism rather than Marxism.* It orientated itself towards life in the

* Pinhas Lubianiker, *Yesodot*, Tel Aviv, 1941, p. 10.

kvutza, though in its early days it did not preclude other forms of agricultural settlement in Palestine. In the 1930s Gordonia merged with Makkabi Hatzair; it had its main bases in eastern Europe. In 1929 the first members of Gordonia arrived in Palestine and started a collective settlement.

In addition to those mentioned, dozens of Zionist youth movements came into being between the two world wars, and a few of them continued to exist after 1945. In Poland there was *Dror-Freihait*; in the United States *Young Judaea*, and later on *Avuka*, a student association with branches in more than twenty universities. *Habonim* developed in the early 1930s in London's East End and spread to other English-speaking countries, Sweden and Holland. Over the years its members helped to establish four kibbutzim (Kfar Blum, Kfar Hanassi, Amiad and Beth Ha'emeq). In 1951 a world federation of Habonim was established with its headquarters in Tel Aviv.

Some of these movements were shortlived. Their ideological discussions, like those of other youth groups, make in retrospect curious reading. But, like other youth movements, they should not be measured by the degree of their political sophistication. The issue that really mattered was the common experience and identity shared by the members, and seen in this context these movements played an important role in the history of Zionism. Among the present leaders of the state of Israel there are few, if any, who did not at one time belong to one of them.

At a time when family ties were loosening, when protest against school and other forms of authority was spreading, these youth movements provided new ideals and values, the promise of both national revival and a new and better way of life. In common activities, such as discussions, seminars, sports meetings, camping and excursions, a spirit of community was developed. The members were taught Hebrew and the essentials of Jewish history and culture. They regarded life in Palestine, and specifically in the collective settlements, not just as part of the solution of the Jewish question, long overdue, but as the most desirable way of life for idealistic young men and women. In this respect the Zionist youth movement differed from all other youth movements of the day, which in the European dictatorships simply served as a reserve army to replenish the ranks of the state party, or, as in the democracies, failed to carry the idea of a live community beyond the dreams of adolescence.

Years of crisis

The 1920s were on the whole an uneventful period in the history of mandatory Palestine. The over-optimistic expectations of the Zionists had been buried and there was resentment about the lack of assistance given by the British administration. But was it really the fault of the British, as Weizmann asked the Zionist congress, if the Zionists had bought only one million dunams of land rather than two, and if consequently their position was relatively weak? It was not, after all, surprising if the mandatory authorities were reluctant to aid the Zionists in building their national home as envisaged in the Balfour Declaration: the officials felt that there was an inherent contradiction in the task imposed on them. They realised that whatever they did they were bound to provoke either Arab or Jewish protest, and they therefore drew the conclusion, not unnaturally, that the less they did the better.

Samuel, the first high commissioner, was replaced by Field Marshall Plumer, after whom Chancellor was appointed. The Zionists were suspicious of Plumer. They had hoped that a Jew would again be made high commissioner, and feared that a professional soldier would have little understanding, let alone sympathy, for the Zionist cause. These fears were somewhat exaggerated. Plumer declared that he had no policy of his own but was simply following instructions from London.* The Jewish leaders were impressed by his firmness in dealing with Arab threats. When leaders of an Arab delegation told him that unless some Jewish parade was banned they could not be responsible for the maintenance of public order in Jerusalem, the high commissioner told his visitors that he did not expect them to do anything of the kind, since the preservation of law and order was his job. Relations between the Zionists and Chancellor were much cooler. In fact Chancellor was cordially disliked. He enjoyed neither the reputation of a statesman nor the prestige of a military leader. It was, moreover, during his term of office that the riots of 1929 took place, which were to put Anglo-Zionist relations to a severe test.

The chain of events in which 133 Jews were killed and several hundred wounded is described elsewhere in the present study. Soon after the end of the disturbances Lord Passfield (Sidney Webb), colonial secretary in the Labour government, appointed a commission of enquiry to investigate the immediate causes of the riots. The commission went to Palestine at the end of October, stayed there until late

* Christopher Sykes, *Crossroads to Israel*, p. 105 *et seq.*

December, and published its findings, known as the Shaw Report, in March 1930.* While putting the responsibility for the bloodshed squarely on the Arabs, it stressed that the fundamental cause was Arab animosity towards the Jews, consequent upon the disappointment of their national aspirations and the fears for their economic future. Specifically, the report mentioned Arab fears that as a result of Jewish immigration and land purchase they would be deprived of their livelihood and in time pass under the domination of the Jews. Arabs had been evicted from their holdings and as a result a landless and discontented class had been created. The crisis of 1927–8, the report claimed, was due to the fact that during the previous years immigration had exceeded the country's absorptive capacity, a mistake that should not be repeated.

The Shaw Commission noted that the Arabs were disappointed because no progress had been made towards self-government and resented the fact that unlike the Jews (who had the Jewish Agency), they had no direct channel to the government. Above all, the commission suggested that His Majesty's government should issue a clear statement of the policy it intended to pursue. These guidelines were to contain a definition, in clear and positive terms, of the meaning attached to the passages in the mandate providing safeguards for the rights of the Arabs. While the Zionists argued that the Palestine government had shown lack of sympathy towards the Jewish national home, and thus created conditions favourable to an Arab attack, the commission absolved the government of guilt, stressing that the Jews failed to appreciate the dual nature of its responsibility and that they had shown (like the Arabs) 'little capacity for compromise'.

The Shaw Report was received by the Arabs with jubilation, whereas the Jews were outraged.† The Zionists had suspected from the outset that the commission would exceed its assignment to deal with the immediate causes of the disturbances, and their worst fears had come true. Their reaction was summarised by Sokolow, in his speech at the Zionist congress in 1931, when he quoted the Jew in Kishinev who had said: 'God protect me from commissions – from pogroms I can protect myself.'

The Jewish Agency answered the report in a detailed memorandum. Lord Passfield, presumably to gain time for working out his own policy, countered by appointing Sir John Hope Simpson, a retired Indian civil

* Great Britain, Parliamentary Papers, 1930, Cmd. 3530.
† Hanna, *British Policy in Palestine*, p. 53.

servant, to prepare a further report on economic conditions in Palestine. This was delivered in August 1930 and dealt a further blow to Zionist hopes, for it stated that with the given methods of cultivation no land was available for agricultural settlement by new immigrants, with the exception of the undeveloped land already held by the Jewish Agency.* Regarding future immigration, the report stated that with comprehensive development there would be room for not less than twenty thousand families of settlers from outside. Hope Simpson was doubtful about the prospects of industrialisation. His report was attacked by the Zionists as based on insufficient evidence. He certainly greatly underestimated the cultivable land area available, as the spectacular agricultural development of Palestine since 1930 has shown.

The report was published in London on 20 October 1930, at the same time as the British government issued its statement of policy, the Passfield White Paper. This stated at some length that Britain's obligations to Jews and Arabs were of equal weight and that the Jewish Agency had no special political position.† While it was not said in so many words, the general impression created by the White Paper was that the building of the Jewish national home had more or less ended as far as Britain was concerned; its continued growth was to depend on Arab consent. The Zionist executive, with rare understatement, said the White Paper was a reinterpretation of the mandate in a manner highly prejudicial to Jewish interests, that it retreated not only from the Churchill statement of 1922 (which had itself been a retreat from the mandate), but that it did not even accept the positive recommendations for economic development contained in the Hope Simpson Report.‡ The White Paper, as Weizmann later wrote, was intended 'to make our work in Palestine impossible'.

The publication of Lord Passfield's statement of policy provoked intense indignation throughout the Jewish world. Weizmann tendered his resignation from the Jewish Agency, as did Felix Warburg and Lord Melchett. For the first time the Jewish leaders had not been kept informed of London's plans, and while it was known that Passfield was totally out of sympathy with Zionism, they had thought that there was at least a certain measure of goodwill among some of his colleagues. The one member of the Shaw Commission to make strong reservations as to its conclusions had been Henry Snell, a Labour MP, but there were also

* Great Britain, Parliamentary Papers, 1930, Cmd. 3686, p. 141.
† Great Britain, Parliamentary Papers, 1930, Cmd. 3692.
‡ Leonard Stein, *The Palestine White Paper of October 1930*, London, 1930, p. 31 *et seq.*

protests from many other quarters. When the White Paper was discussed in Parliament on 18 November, Passfield found the going rough. Conservative and Liberal spokesmen attacked it as a breach of trust and contract. Inside the Labour Party too there was a good deal of uneasiness about its provisions. Passfield beat a tactical retreat, admitting to doubts about certain passages. He assured Weizmann that the Zionists had misunderstood the Paper, but at the same time he continued to resist their essential demands (e.g. mass immigration); he was the 'head and fount of the opposition to our demands' (Weizmann). Under pressure from all sides, the government decided to modify its policy. It could not, for obvious reasons, withdraw the White Paper but the bureaucrats knew a way out of the dilemma: just as the White Paper had been an interpretation of the Churchill declaration of 1922, it was decided to issue a new document to serve as an authoritative interpretation of the Passfield White Paper. A committee composed of members of the government and representatives of the Jewish Agency, after lengthy deliberations, reached agreement on essential points, and made the outcome public in the form of a letter from Ramsay MacDonald to Weizmann. Disavowing any injurious allegations against the Jewish people, the prime minister reaffirmed the intention of his government to fulfil the terms of the mandate and acknowledged that it had made an undertaking not only to the Jews living in Palestine but to the Jewish people as a whole. There was no intention to freeze existing conditions. As far as immigration was concerned there was no desire to depart from the Churchill White Paper. The criteria applied to establish the absorptive capacity of the country were to be purely economic, not political in character.

The Passfield White Paper was an unsuccessful attempt to reverse the policy initiated by Balfour and Lloyd George. It failed, and the positive change in the attitude of the British government enabled the Zionists, to quote Weizmann again, to make the magnificent gains of the 1930s. But it was a warning sign inasmuch as it showed the Arabs that there were forces in Britain only too willing to yield to Arab pressure. If they had failed for the time being to press home their case, perhaps a renewal of violence on a bigger scale at some future date would be more successful? The restrictions on immigration and land purchase proposed by Passfield were embodied in the White Paper of 1939 which finally repudiated the policy of Balfour and Lloyd George.*

The MacDonald letter provided a respite of seven years, but this at a

---

* Esco Foundation, *Palestine*, vol. 2, p. 660.

critical period in Jewish history, and it enabled hundreds of thousands of refugees to find a new home. Many Zionist leaders rebuked Weizmann for having accepted a mere letter from the prime minister instead of a formal reversal of policy, and wanted to reject it as a basis for continued collaboration with Britain. But it was not the form of the answer that mattered but its substance, and Weizmann, the pragmatist, was absolutely right when he concentrated on the essential achievement and ignored the form.

The MacDonald letter was to remain Weizmann's last major political success for years. His position inside the Zionist movements had progressively weakened. Having resigned from the executive in October 1930, he was asked by his colleagues to carry on as its chairman to the next congress. But even some of his friends advised him not to put forward his candidature again. He was too strongly identified with the collaboration-with-Britain-at-any-price school, and as the difficulties with the mandatory power increased he became the chief target of the opposition. Even among the General Zionists, support for him fell to some twenty-five out of eighty-four delegates at the 1931 congress – the British, German, Czech and a few Americans of the Lipsky-Fishman faction. Weizmann, however, had the support of Palestinian labour. In a speech in Nahalal in March 1931 he declared 'my fate is connected with yours'. He complained bitterly about the mounting wave of attacks, the speeches and articles which referred to him as a traitor.* He did not really want to resign, but his fighting spirit was petering out a little after more than twelve years of serving as chief ambassador, propagandist and tax collector.

It was in this atmosphere of mounting tension and mutual recriminations that the seventeenth Zionist congress opened in Basle on 30 June 1931. The revisionists had decided to use the opportunity to press for a definition of the final aim, the *Endziel*, of Zionism. They claimed that there had been too much loose talk about parity between Jews and Arabs, even about a bi-national Palestine, that this defeatist line was clearly incompatible with political Zionism as preached by Herzl and Nordau. They insisted that the time had come for a showdown, a radical reorientation of policy.

The meeting was opened by Sokolow, who called it 'a congress of realism'. He apparently saw no contradiction between this statement and the declaration later on in his speech that there was no connection between the Arab riots of 1929 and the Balfour Declaration: the disturb-

* *Jüdische Rundschau*, 27 March 1931.

ances had been caused by religious fantacism. Weizmann, speaking after him, retraced the recent history of Zionism: he discussed the origins and motives of the Balfour Declaration and the various interpretations that had been put on it since.* He referred to the exaggerated expectations prevalent at the time and then surveyed the factors which had impeded the building of the national home – the greater influence of pro-Arab circles on the one hand, and on the other the impoverishment of east European Jewry and the loss to the Zionist movement of Russian Jewry. His own policy had been to steer a middle course between those who believed that after the Balfour Declaration there was no longer any need for political activity, and the other extreme which wanted to engage only in politics. Critics had talked with contempt about the old Lovers of Zion approach: yet another dunam, yet another few trees, another cow, another goat, and two more houses in Hadera. But 'if there is another way of building a house, save brick by brick, I don't know it,' Weizmann said. 'If there is another way of building a country save dunam by dunam, man by man, and farmstead by farmstead – again I do not know it. One man may follow another, one dunam may be added to another, after a long interval or after a short one – that is a question of degree and determined not by politics alone.'

It was an impressive speech, but it left many of his critics unconvinced. They had heard it too often and they wanted a change of leadership. Jabotinsky argued that economic achievements were not sufficient to create political positions of strength. The MacDonald letter was not satisfactory as a basis of cooperation with the mandatory power because it accorded the Arabs the right of veto against any measure in carrying out the mandate. It was not enough to aim at Jewish preponderance in Palestine at some unspecified future date. To clarify its position the movement had to declare that it aimed at a Jewish majority on both sides of the Jordan, a Jewish state. It was not Britain's fault alone if there had been a retreat from the spirit of the Balfour Declaration. It was the fault of the Zionist movement, or at any rate of its leadership, which had assured the British that the political situation was satisfactory.

Jabotinsky put the worst possible interpretation on the MacDonald letter, but on the whole his speech was statesmanlike, free of personal attacks. Other speakers were less restrained: Gruenbaum, while praising Weizmann's social and economic policies, sharply denounced his

---

* *Stenographisches Protokoll der Verhandlungen des XVII Zionisten Kongresses*, London, 1931, p. 55 *et seq.*

conduct of foreign affairs. His minimalism had been justified in the early years after the Declaration, when it had been necessary to avoid conflicts. But now his system had outlived its usefulness, it had died in 1929. There was no longer any confidence in England. Farbstein (representing Mizrahi) demanded Weizmann's resignation because in a speech at the Action Committee meeting the year before he had abandoned the demand for a Jewish majority.

The sharpest attack came from Rabbi Stephen Wise, who had many sterling qualities but lacked political instinct and foresight: you have sat too long at English feasts, Wise called out, apostrophising Weizmann.* Only men who believed in their cause could talk to the British, but not a leadership which said in fact: you are big and we are small, you are omnipotent and we are nothing. There were more bitter attacks from revisionists: U.Z.Grinberg, the poet, announced that life in Palestine had become 'hell', and Stricker said that the Zionist movement had to be guided either by the spirit of Herzl or the spirit of Weizmann – there could be no compromise.

Ben Gurion and Arlosoroff led the counter-attack. The former criticised the revisionists for their 'easy Zionism', the slogan-mongering and the demagogy, making the leadership responsible for each and every setback. The revisionists had declared in effect that 'we shall create a Jewish majority on both sides of the Jordan, if you give us a majority at the congress'. Naïve young men in Poland might be taken in by such words, but not anyone familiar with Palestinian realities. Arlosoroff charged Weizmann's critics with lack of political realism. They were apparently not aware that Zionism had been for several years in a not-too-splendid isolation, that the world political situation had deteriorated sharply. At the end of the debate, the most dramatic since the days of the Uganda controversy, it appeared that the movement was more or less evenly divided into supporters and opponents of Weizmann's policy.

In this precarious situation Weizmann unwisely decided to give an interview to a correspondent of the Jewish Telegraphic Agency in which he said that he had no sympathy and understanding for the slogan of a Jewish majority in Palestine, which would only be interpreted by the outside world as the wish to expel the Arabs. Even Arlosoroff called this interview politically harmful. A personal statement by Weizmann was of no great help. The damage had been done. Nahum Goldmann, who

* *Ibid.*, p. 230.

as a radical Zionist leader had long been among those aiming at Weizmann's overthrow, acted as spokesman of the political commission and decided to make the most of Weizmann's mistake. He said he regarded Weizmann's interview as a 'declaration of war' against the Zionist movement and demanded a vote of confidence, which Weizmann lost by 106 against 123 votes.

It was a well-timed manœuvre, the only way in effect to defeat Weizmann, for as it soon appeared, the majority which had rejected the old leader was sharply divided about his successor. The revisionist proposal to define once and for all the final aim of Zionism was heavily defeated and the new executive, elected against revisionist opposition (Sokolow, Arlosoroff, Brodetsky, Farbstein, Locker, Neumann), represented in its majority Weizmannism without Weizmann. It may have been the feeling of Weizmann's opponents (as he later wrote) that Sokolow's pliability would make it easier for them to give the movement the direction they had in mind. If so, they were mistaken, for Jabotinsky was not given his chance. Nahum Goldmann, ironically enough, who had helped to bring down Weizmann, many years later found himself in a position not dissimilar to that of Weizmann in 1931: he was removed from the leadership of the movement because of his advocacy of 'gradualism' and 'minimalism'.

The 1931 congress seemed to most participants a great turning point in Zionist history. This was a misjudgment, for its policy underwent no substantial change, and Weizmann returned to the leadership four years later. To attribute decisive historical importance to conflicts within Zionism betrayed a lack of perspective. The real turning point was of course 1933, and it came as a result of events over which the movement had not the slightest control.

The new executive took over at an inauspicious moment. True, relations with the mandatory power had somewhat improved following the publication of the MacDonald letter, and this was the prerequisite for any constructive work in Palestine. But the Zionist world organisation was financially weaker than ever before. The head of the political department complained that facing tremendous tasks, there was less money for his work than there had been ten years earlier. From America he received, like Weizmann before him, much advice but little money. The number of new immigrants in 1931 totalled 4,075, less than in any year after the First World War except 1927–8. The new high commissioner, General Sir Arthur Wauchope, was well-disposed towards Zionism but firm in his belief that the gradual introduction of a parliamentary system, a Constituent Assembly, was overdue. This would have been a catastrophe for the Zionists since it would have made immigration and settlement dependent on the goodwill of the Arab majority. The danger was averted only because of the stubborn demands of the Arab leaders, who insisted on a total ban on immigration and land sales as a condition for their collaboration in any political scheme.

The executive in London carried on very much as before. Sokolow was received that year by King Fuad of Egypt, President Lebrun of France, Mussolini, de Valera, the vice president of the United States, and even Mahatma Gandhi, from whom he received 'a satisfactory declaration'.* (Seven years later, after the November pogroms in Germany, Gandhi wrote to Martin Buber that the German Jews were in duty bound to stay in Germany and practise *satyagraha*, passive resistance, rather than emigrate to Palestine.) What was the outcome of these and other diplomatic activities? The more far-sighted Zionist leaders such as Arlosoroff, now in charge of the political department, were near despair. Arlosoroff met Arab leaders on various occasions, but soon realised that there was no real hope for agreement. He had long personal exchanges with the high commissioner, whom he persuaded to read Pinsker's *Autoemanzipation*. (Sir Arthur was impressed but said that there was no antisemitism in Britain.) Arlosoroff bitterly denounced the 'empty phrases' of the revisionists about a colonisatory régime to be introduced in Palestine. They wanted the British to pull the chestnuts out of the fire for them while looking for political support in Paris, Rome and Warsaw.† At the same time, scanning the political horizon, he reached conclusions which were not that dissimilar from the revisionist conception. He wrote to Weizmann in June 1932 that it might well appear one day that the Zionist analysis of the Jewish question had been correct but that it was unable to achieve its aim. Everywhere there was a return to the time-honoured Jewish fatalism, to Micawberish expectations that something would turn up. But evolutionary Zionism was of limited use only: it could neither excite enthusiasm nor raise money. Arlosoroff was anything but optimistic. He anticipated a new world war 'within the next five to ten years'. The question of relations with the Arabs was no nearer a solution: 'Perhaps we have to stumble along the road without knowing exactly where we are heading.' He did not rule out the possibility of a (temporary) revolutionary dictatorship to prevent

---

* *Bericht der Executive an den XVIII Zionisten Kongress*, London, 1933, p. 206.
† C.Arlosoroff, *Yoman Yerushalayim*, Tel Aviv, 1948, p. 342.

Arab domination, even if this was 'dangerously close to certain popular notions'.*

In 1932 the economic situation in Palestine improved, the number of immigrants being twice that of the year before. In 1933 thirty thousand came, the highest figure ever, and their arrival stimulated a minor boom. But while the Jewish position in Palestine became stronger, it deteriorated dramatically in central Europe. Zionists had always warned their co-religionists against any facile belief in the allegedly inevitable progress of tolerance and liberalism. But even the most pessimistic among them were not prepared for what was to come. When Weizmann said in November 1932 that Palestine would have to be built up on the ruins of diaspora Jewry,† he no doubt envisaged economic ruin, not physical destruction.

In Frankfurt in December 1932, the German Zionist Federation convened for its last meeting before Hitler came to power. Its chairman, Kurt Blumenfeld, had played Cassandra for a long time. By 1932 he had reached the conclusion that the German Jews would soon be reduced to second-class citizenship. Weizmann warned him not to jeopardise the situation of German Jews by such dire predictions, and it was decided that there should be two political addresses at Frankfurt, the second to counter-balance Blumenfeld's 'ultra-pessimistic' views. Nahum Goldmann, hot-foot from Geneva and familiar with the mood of the world's governments and statesmen, assured his listeners that France and England would never permit a government headed by Hitler to come to power, that Russia regarded the Nazis as their mortal enemy and would not look on passively, that, in other words, there was no cause for alarm.‡ Three months later Hitler was chancellor and after a few more weeks Germany had become a fully fledged dictatorship.

Jewish reaction was at first one of concern, but there was not yet any feeling of real urgency. It was believed that Hitler, after all, would not antagonise the outside world by carrying out his insane political programme. It was one thing to be the leader of an extremist political movement, another to be head of a government. Surely his newly acquired responsibilities would compel him to curb the more fanatical antisemites among his followers? By April, after the anti-Jewish boycott and the establishment of the first concentration camps, there was no

* *Ibid.*, p. 333.
† *Jüdische Rundschau*, 29 November 1932.
‡ Blumenfeld, *Erlebte Judenfrage*, p. 196.

longer room for illusions. The era of emancipation and equal rights was over for the Jews, the central organ of German Zionism wrote.* Zionists had always been a relatively small minority within the Jewish community in Germany. After Hitler's rise to power their influence among German Jewry grew by leaps and bounds. Suddenly there was great interest in all things Palestinian. Many hundreds came to Zionist meetings which had been attended in the past by a few dozen, the circulation of Zionist newspapers rose, Hebrew classes opened everywhere.† The process, to be sure, was not confined to Germany and, strictly speaking, it had begun even before January 1933. In late 1932 the Zionists had emerged for the first time as the strongest party in the Vienna Jewish community elections. The German crisis had its repercussions all over Europe; Jewish communities everywhere sensed the danger.

The spread of Zionism annoyed its Jewish critics, some of whom went so far as to assert that Nazism and Zionism were working hand in glove. Was it not true that Zionist slogans about the unity of the Jewish people, their insistence on the naturalness and inevitability of antisemitism, was grist to the mill of Nazi propaganda, and that the Nazi leaders in their speeches and writings quoted Zionist sources from time to time to prove that Jews were different, that they could not be assimilated? One of these critics wrote many years later: 'Did the Zionist programme and philosophy contribute decisively to the enormous catastrophe of the extermination of six million Jews by the Nazis, by popularising the judgment that the Jews were forever aliens in Europe? With the knowledge presently at our disposal, it is impossible to answer this question.'‡

Some Zionists used the opportunity to remind their liberal, orthodox and Communist critics how wrong they had been in their assessment of the situation of German Jewry. There was occasionally too much we-told-you-so talk about the bankruptcy of liberalism, but the imputation of cooperation or collusion with the Nazis is pernicious nonsense. No Jewish Molotov was ever dined and wined in Berlin. If the Nazis in their propaganda sometimes quoted Zionist spokesmen, they quoted equally often Jews of different political persuasion to prove whatever point they wanted to make.

Zionists did not enjoy a special relationship in Nazi Germany. Their

* *Jüdische Rundschau*, 13 April 1933.
† *Ibid.*, 28 March 1933.
‡ J.B.Agus, *The Meaning of Jewish History*, New York, 1963, vol. 2, p. 447.

leaders and press were subject to the same restrictions and persecution as the others. German Zionists were not permitted, for instance, to appear at the Zionist congress of 1933. The Nazis did on occasion encourage efforts to expedite emigration to Palestine, but similar facilities were given to non-Zionist institutions aiding emigration to other parts of the world. Zionism, as far as the Nazis were concerned, was part of the Jewish world conspiracy against the Aryans, different from but not preferable to liberalism or Bolshevism, a sworn enemy of the German people. There was in fact among the Nazi leaders one school of thought – Hitler seems at times to have leaned towards it – arguing that it was preferable to retain the German Jews as hostages rather than let them emigrate.

The World Zionist Organisation, like other Jewish bodies outside Germany, faced great difficulties in their relations with the Third Reich. They protested, of course, against the deprivation of rights of German Jews. Sokolow in his opening speech at the eighteenth Zionist congress in Prague (21 August–4 September 1933) said: 'It is dangerous to talk, but even more dangerous to be silent.'* A resolution passed by the congress appealed to the civilised world to help the Jewish people in its struggle to regain human rights in Germany. But these and similar proclamations hardly ever called for specific action. Individual Zionist leaders such as Rabbi Wise were in the forefront of the organisation of the boycott of German goods in 1933 and other anti-Nazi initiatives. Yet the movement as such had to act with restraint, for more than half a million German Jews were hostages in the hands of the Nazis, who could immediately retaliate against any hostile move by Jewish bodies outside Germany. Furthermore, there had to be some contact with the German authorities in connection with emigration. All this limited the freedom of speech and action of world Jewry in the struggle against Nazi Germany.

'Never have we felt so clearly and so cruelly the precariousness of our diaspora existence,' Sokolow said in his opening speech at the Prague congress. It would have been impossible to envisage such a development twenty, even five years earlier. Never had Zionism been proved so necessary. There was applause from the galleries at this point but Sokolow brushed it aside: 'I wish you had applauded thirty years ago.' Following him, Ruppin talked about the emergency plans to help Germany Jewry. The best protest against the anti-Jewish policy of the Nazis, he said, was to save the Jews. He predicted that about two hundred thousand, almost half the total, would lose their economic

* *Stenographisches Protokoll der Verhandlungen des XVIII Zionisten Kongresses in Prag*, 1934, p.20.

employment. Palestine would be able to absorb between one-quarter and one-half of that number within the next five to ten years. This prediction was to come true: half the Jews of Germany succeeded in leaving the country up to the outbreak of war and many of them went to Palestine. But there were only six years left, not ten, before the doors closed, and by 1938–9, after the annexation of Austria and Czechoslovakia, hundred of thousands more were in mortal danger.

Ruppin referred briefly to the activities of Sam Cohen, the manager of a Palestinian citrus company who had in 1933 signed an agreement with the German Ministry of Economics providing for the transfer to Palestine of one million marks of agricultural equipment to be purchased in Germany and sold in Palestine.* This was the forerunner of a much more ambitious transfer (Ha'avara) agreement, between the Zionist movement (acting through a Palestinian bank) and the Germans. This agreement was bitterly attacked by Jewish circles, both within the movement and outside, which regarded it as a betrayal, sabotaging the efforts to boycott German exports. The accusation was true to the extent that the Nazi government agreed to the transfer precisely in order 'to make a breach in the wall of the anti-German boycott', as one of its minor officials wrote at the time.†

Those who favoured the agreement assumed, however, that the boycott, lacking support outside Jewish circles, would in any case be short-lived. Neither the western powers nor the Soviet Union considered for a moment reducing or breaking off trade relations with Germany. On the other hand, there was a chance that the agreement would make the settlement of thousands of Jews possible, and would strengthen the Jewish position in Palestine and thus its absorptive capacity. The Nazis subsequently realised that the transfer agreement was helping to develop Jewish industry in Palestine and thus fostering the aspirations towards a Jewish state (the words were Eichmann's in an inter-office memo). This, needless to say, was highly undesirable, for it was Nazi policy to keep the Jews dispersed all over the world rather than promote the establishment of even a minute state.‡ Accordingly Berlin decided to phase out the transfer agreement. The sum involved had been thirty-seven million marks in 1937; it was reduced to nineteen million in 1938 and to eight million in 1939.

---

* David Yisraeli, 'The Third Reich and the Transfer Agreement', *Journal of Contemporary History*, April 1971.
† *Ibid.*
‡ *Documents on German Foreign Policy*, series C, vol 5, no. 664.

Hitler's seizure of power was the moment of truth for the Zionist movement. How little had they achieved in more than three decades! The *leitmotif* of failure, even impotence, recurred frequently in the speeches at the Prague congress: we have failed among the Jews, we have not taken the lead in getting help for German Jewry, we have not won over the Jewish masses to the Zionist idea.* The movement was still weak by any standards: of four million American Jews, a mere eighty-eight thousand had voted in the elections for the Prague congress and the membership of the American Zionist Federation had in fact declined since the late 1920s. In Rumania a mere forty thousand had voted, in Hungary only five thousand out of a Jewish community of half a million.

The movement was not only small, it was internally divided. The revisionists were about to secede and the other parties were also at loggerheads. The congress was a faithful picture of internal disunity. The Mizrahi spokesman complained of the desecration of the Sabbath in Palestine and elsewhere and also that it was not represented in the Zionist apparatus. Ussishkin reported that in the last twenty months a mere 44,000 dunam had been bought, an area insufficient even for the settlement of a tiny part of the new immigrants. But the Zionist Organisation had no money; the Palestine budget adopted by the congress – £175,000 – was the lowest ever. Gluska, speaking for the Yemenites, complained that the members of his community were still second-class citizens in Palestine, like non-Aryans in Germany (a somewhat far-fetched comparison). The Right argued that discrimination against private enterprise continued. The labour speakers countered by drawing attention to the abysmally low wages of Jewish workers in Tel Aviv and Haifa. Even Motzkin in his closing address admitted that the eighteenth congress had not been a success.

The congress decided to set up a central office for the settlement of German Jews in Palestine under the direction of Weizmann, who at the time was out of office and had not even attended the congress. Weizmann recalled how, as a young man studying in Berlin, he had gone to the central railway station to see the Russian emigrants, to exchange a few words with them in their language. He remembered how they were received kindly, but somewhat patronisingly, by the committees of German Jewry, guided from the frontier to the ports, and given a send off: 'I did not think then that a similar fate would befall the solid and

---

* *Stenographisches Protokoll*, speeches by Rubashov (Shazar), p. 258; Goldmann, p. 272.

powerful German Jewry, that they in turn would be driven from their homes.'*

The Zionist movement was weak and disunited, and yet it was bound to become the leader in the struggle to help the ever-growing number of European Jews facing persecution, economic ruin, and ultimately physical destruction. The extent of the catastrophe exceeded their worst fears, while the readiness of others to help was most disappointing. When Ruppin spoke of Jewish emigration from Germany, he took it for granted that the countries of western Europe as well as the United States would be willing to absorb tens of thousands. The number involved was after all small by absolute standards and it seemed obvious that the newcomers with their many skills and talents would make a notable contribution wherever they were allowed to settle.

He could not have been more mistaken. Not a single country, great or small, showed any enthusiasm to receive Jews. There were, to be sure, many arguments against extending shelter to Jewish refugees. There was still high unemployment everywhere, the effects of the depression had not yet been overcome. There were political and psychological obstacles. But the Jews from central Europe unfortunately could not wait until the economic situation improved and the less enlightened members of non-Jewish society had overcome their fear of competition or their prejudices. It was in this emergency that Palestine, however small and undeveloped, became the haven for more Jews than were admitted to all other countries.

* Weizmann, *Trial and Error*, p. 359.

EUROPEAN CATASTROPHE

The situation of European Jewry continued to deteriorate throughout the 1930s. In 1935 the Nuremberg laws codified and extended anti-Jewish legislation in Germany. One year later official antisemitism was slightly relaxed; the Olympic Games were to be held in Berlin and the German government wanted to represent a respectable front. But the interlude was brief and repression became more intense once the foreign visitors had departed. In February 1938 an editorial appeared in the *Schwarze Korps*, mouthpiece of the SS, entitled: 'What should be done with the Jews?' The writer complained that emigration fever had obviously not yet infected the Jews. They were not behaving as if they were sitting on their luggage, ready to leave the country at any moment. To encourage them new draconian measures were adopted, culminating in the '*Kristallnacht*' in November 1938, the burning of the synagogues, mass arrests, and a huge collective fine.

If during the first five years of Nazi power Jews had merely lost their livelihood and were reduced to second-class citizenship, they virtually became outlaws after November 1938. Yet Nazi policy in Germany was a model of restraint in comparison with their behaviour in Austria and Czechoslovakia. The process of eliminating Jews from German society and economic life which had taken five years in Germany was telescoped into as many weeks in Vienna and Prague. The stage of systematic extermination was reached only after the occupation of Poland and the invasion of Russia. Up to 1939 thousands of Jews were able to emigrate, but as the war spread the trap closed. At a high level meeting on 20 January 1942, at Grosser Wannsee in Berlin, it was decided to carry out the 'final solution', the extermination of European Jewry.

The rise of Nazism, at first limited to Germany, proved infectious. Fascist and antisemitic movements mushroomed all over the Continent. Even Italy, which had always proudly insisted that it was pursuing its own, the only genuine road to fascism, and had rejected antisemitism as alien to the Italian spirit, under German influence promulgated anti-Jewish laws in 1938. In Bucharest the Goga-Cuza government announced in January 1938 that the national status of all Rumanian Jews would be revised and that half of them would have to leave. Whether they would emigrate or drown in the Black Sea, was, as a government spokesman put it, a question of personal preference. According to the Teleki bill, introduced in the Hungarian parliament in 1938, three hundred thousand of Hungary's Jews were to lose their jobs within the next few years. They were no longer to hold any position in the state or the municipalities, in the trade unions or on public bodies, and all trade licences were to be withdrawn. A *numerus clausus* of 6 per cent was to be introduced in all professions except in commerce where it was to be 12 per cent. The position of Polish Jews also continued to deteriorate during the 1930s. There were three million of them, about 10 per cent of the total population, concentrated in the five largest towns where they constituted 30 per cent of the total. Pogroms took place in several Polish cities, and small- and large-scale boycotts. Jewish students were under constant pressure. It was the declared policy of successive Polish governments to make the position of Polish Jewry intolerable and compel them to emigrate.

For those who did not live through that period it is difficult to realise the depths of despair reached during those black years. The western democracies were suffering from a paralysis of will. They tried to ignore Hitler, and when faced with open aggression attempted to buy him off. Appeasement was costly, humiliating, and ultimately, of course, ineffective. By 1938 it seemed as if Hitler would gradually conquer the whole of Europe without even encountering resistance. If the policy of the western democracies was shortsighted and dishonourable, the less said about Stalin's and Russia's part the better. America was immersed in its own problems and had no intention of intervening in European affairs.

The Jews of central and eastern Europe, under growing pressure to leave their countries of origin, had nowhere to turn. In a more tolerant age nations and governments had been willing to extend help to the homeless stranger. Britain had taken in 120,000 French Protestants in 1685 after the revocation of the edict of Nantes. By March 1939, in contrast, Britain had given entry permits to barely nineteen thousand Jewish refugees from the Continent. It could be argued that the country was no longer capable of absorbing immigrants on a massive scale. But what of the less densely populated countries overseas? 'Give me your tired, your poor, your huddled masses, yearning to breathe free'; but since Emma Lazarus's poem had been inscribed on the Statue of Liberty attitudes had changed. The United States in 1935 accepted 6,252 Jewish immigrants, Argentine 3,159, Brazil 1,758, South Africa 1,078, Canada 624. In the same year the number of legal Jewish immigrants into Palestine was 61,854.

These figures speak for themselves: the European countries, however reluctantly, gave shelter to more refugees than those overseas with the exception of Palestine, which absorbed more than all the others put together. By the time the war broke out thirty-five thousand had found temporary shelter in France, twenty-five thousand in Belgium and twenty thousand in Holland. But there was no real security for Jews in Europe, for many of those who had escaped were overtaken by the advancing German armies. In October 1938 twenty-eight thousand Jews of Polish nationality living in Germany were rounded up and dumped by the Nazis at various points on the German-Polish border. A few months later thousands of Jews of Hungarian origin were expelled from Slovakia.* Big new Jewish communities came into being in places such as Zbonszyn, of which no one had ever heard before. They were located in a no man's land, without shelter or food, suffering from cold and disease, exposure and starvation. There were floating Jewish communities such as those on *S.S.Königstein, Caribia,* or *St Louis.* These had left Hamburg in 1938 for Latin America with many hundreds of passengers on board, but were not permitted to land in their countries of destination. The Nazis were willing to take them back – into concentration camps. And so these ghost ships continued their macabre voyage between Europe and Latin America, between the Balkans and Palestine, treated as if they were carriers of the plague.

To bring some element of order into an utterly confused situation, and to coordinate help for German refugees, President Roosevelt invited representatives of thirty-two governments to a conference in Evian, in France in July 1938. The British insisted that Palestine, the most important country for Jewish immigration, should not be discussed. When Weizmann asked permission to appear before the conference his request was turned down flat by the American presiding over the conference.† The outcome was predictable. One speaker after another went to the rostrum and reported that there was no territory suitable for Jewish settlers. Some did so with expressions of regret. Others, such as

---

* M.Wischnitzer, *To Dwell in Safety,* Philadelphia, 1948, p. 196 *et seq.*

† A.D.Morse, *While Six Millions Died,* London, 1968, p. 211; H.L.Feingold, *The Politics of Rescue,* New Brunswick, 1970, pp. 22–44.

the Australian delegate, said that they had no racial problem and were not desirous of importing one. The one surprise was the statement by the Dominican delegate that his country was willing to accept refugees. It was a generous gesture, even though it was not clear whether the area set aside for the refugees was suitable for any known form of settlement. The conference resulted in the establishment of a permanent Inter-Governmental Committee on Refugees headed by Lord Winterton, a leading British anti-Zionist. The delegates were not callous men. They were carrying out the instructions of their respective governments, and the position taken by the governments reflected the state of public opinion. On the eve of the Evian conference the American Veterans of Foreign Wars passed a resolution calling for the suspension of all immigration for ten years. In London the Socialist Medical Association at their annual reunion complained of the 'dilution of our industry with non-Union, non-Socialist labour'; the Conservative *Sunday Express* proclaimed editorially that 'just now there is a big influx of foreign Jews into Britain. They are overrunning the country'.*

The outcome of the Evian conference was nil. Once the gates of Palestine had been all but closed, Jews from central Europe, unless they had close relations or special skills, could move without any restriction to only one place on the entire globe – the International Settlement in Shanghai. But the Japanese authorities, too, clamped down on Jewish immigration in August 1939. As the London *Times* in its 'Review of the Year' for 1938 succinctly put it, 'the great surplus Jewish population remained an acute problem'. There were, in other words, too many Jews.

When Herzl had first thought of a Jewish state he had envisaged a gradual migration to Palestine; he had not imagined a catastrophe. Neither he nor any other Jewish leader after him, not even Jabotinsky, had claimed that Palestine could absorb all Jews. But the foundations had been laid in Palestine in the 1920s for the settlement of hundreds of thousands. In the middle 1930s, when 'it was no longer a question whether Zionism was a good idea or a bad idea, whether it was desirable or not', the community had grown to four hundred thousand; it was no longer a political theory but a fact.† British experts, who only a few years earlier had been concerned about the absorptive capacity of the country, now conceded that the big immigration wave of 1933–5 (134,000 legal immigrants) far from reducing that capacity had actually increased it:

---

* E.Hearst, in *Wiener Library Bulletin*, April 1965; on Evian conference, *ibid.*, March 1961: *Sunday Express*, 19 June 1938.

† A.Koestler, *Promise and Fulfilment*, London, 1949, p. 21.

the more immigrants, the more work they created for local industry.* Palestinian imports and exports rose by more than 50 per cent between 1933 and 1935. The consumption of electric energy, always an accurate index of economic growth, almost trebled during that period. While other governments at the time had deficits amounting to billions of dollars, the government of Palestine had a mounting surplus. Thirteen hundred firms were represented at the 1932 Levant Fair at Tel Aviv, a rapidly growing city. In 1935 it had 135,000 inhabitants. There were 160 Jewish agricultural settlements in that year and more were being established every month.

Immigration would have risen even more quickly but for the restrictions imposed by the mandatory government. Under an ordinance issued in 1933 different categories of immigrants had been established, the two most important being Category A ('capitalists') and the 'labour schedule'. A capitalist, according to the standards of those days, was a person who had £500 to his name; later, the figure was raised to £1,000. The labour schedule became the main bone of contention between the Palestine government and the Jewish Agency. In 1934 the Agency asked for 20,000 certificates for labour immigrants and received 5,600. For the year starting in April 1935 it asked for 30,000 and obtained 11,200. In 1936, after the outbreak of the Arab riots, the government severely restricted immigration. Of the 22,000 certificates requested by the Agency, little more than 10 per cent, 2,500, were granted. The upshot was that in the years when European Jewry needed Palestine most its gates were gradually closed.

Year	New immigrants
1935	61,800
1936	29,700
1937	10,500
1938	12,800
1939	16,400

Eventually, in the White Paper of 1939, it was announced that five years later Jewish immigration was to stop altogether. The reasons were political, not economic in character. They had nothing to do with absorptive capacity. The Arab national movement was growing in strength. After the abortive general strike of October 1933 there were two years of peace, but April 1936 saw the outbreak of a rebellion which petered out only in 1939. No one doubted that the Arabs had benefited

* *Palestine Royal Commission Report*, Cmd. 5479, London, 1937, para. 82.

from Jewish immigration. Their numbers had almost doubled between 1917 and 1940, wages had gone up, the standard of living had risen more than anywhere else in the Middle East. The Jews had certainly not dispossessed the Arabs. 'Much of the land now carrying orange groves was sand dunes or swamp and uncultivated when it was purchased', the Peel Commission reported. Malcolm MacDonald, the colonial secretary, and no friend of Zionism, wrote that 'if not a single Jew had come to Palestine after 1918, I believe the Arab population today would still be round the 600,000 figure, at which it had been stable under Turkish rule'. But the Jewish immigrants had come, and they had been instrumental in generating a Palestine Arab national movement.

The Arabs were afraid of becoming a minority in Palestine, and while they were divided into half a dozen political parties, all of them agreed on opposing Zionism. The Arab character of Palestine had to be retained, the establishment of a Jewish national home resisted. The militants among them resorted to violence and carried the more moderate forces with them. The movement drew encouragement from the successes of Nazism and Italian fascism, and from the impotence shown by the western powers in their attempts to stop the aggressors. The ineffectiveness of the League of Nations' sanctions against Mussolini's invasion of Abyssinia had a notable impact in the Middle East. Egypt had made a big step towards independence following the Anglo-Egyptian treaty of 1936, and the Syrians and the Iraqis, too, had made a marked advance. The Palestinian Arabs did not want to lag behind their Arab brethren.

Britain was in no mood to resist. The riots had, of course, to be put down, but at the same time a decision was taken to liquidate the Zionist experiment, or, to be precise, to freeze it at the existing level. These were the years of appeasement in Europe. As the clouds of war thickened, Britain needed Arab friendship more than the goodwill of the Jews, which was assured anyway. For, unlike the Arabs, the Jews could not opt for Hitler and Mussolini, nor for Stalin. The majority of the generation of British statesmen which had sponsored the Balfour Declaration had disappeared from the political scene; those few who still survived had more urgent preoccupations.

Winston Churchill, one of these survivors, certainly did not approve of the turn in British policy: 'I cannot understand why this course has been taken', he said in his speech in the parliamentary debate (23 May 1939) on the White Paper. 'I search around for the answer. . . . Is our condition so parlous and our state so poor that we must, in our weakness, make this sacrifice of our declared purpose? Can we strengthen ourselves by repudiation? Never was the need for fidelity and firmness more urgent than now.' He turned to the government front bench and said: 'By committing ourselves to this lamentable act of default, we will cast our country, and all it stands for, one more step downwards in its fortunes. It is twenty years now that my Rt Honourable friend [Neville Chamberlain] used these stirring words: "A great responsibility will rest on the Zionists, who before long will be proceeding with joy in their hearts to the ancient seat of their people. Theirs will be the task of building up a new prosperity and a new civilisation in old Palestine, so long neglected and misruled." Well,' Churchill continued, 'they have answered the call. They have followed his hopes. How can we find it in our heart to strike them this mortal blow?' These were strong words, but they did not entail political action. Churchill was a back bencher at the time, in opposition to government policy. One year later he was back in power but did little to reverse British policy in Palestine. The international constellation could not have been worse for the Zionists. Never had the movement counted for less.

The Palestinian scene 1933–7

The years of prosperity in Palestine (1933–5) were politically uneventful. The Jewish Agency executive did not receive much help from the British government but it had, within limits, freedom of action. Weizmann, Ben Gurion and Shertok conferred from time to time with the colonial secretary and with the high commissioner, but these meetings had a routine character. There were occasional protests against searches and arrests of illegal immigrants by the police, but on the whole the Agency executive had little reason to complain. At a session of the Action Committee in March 1934 in Jerusalem, Ussishkin, as so often before, complained that not enough was being done to buy land. Forty thousand new immigrants had arrived but only sixteen thousand dunam had been bought. The occasion was memorable mainly because the proceedings were for the first time conducted in Hebrew.

There were no major surprises at the 1935 Zionist congress. Over the years a certain routine had developed: long reports were delivered by members of the executive on political developments, organisational problems, and the economic situation. These were followed by a general debate opened by the spokesmen of the various parties, with the second and third rankers filling in after them. The time at the disposal of the speakers was allocated according to an elaborate system and the main task of the chairman was to keep them within the allotted schedule. At the end of the meeting resolutions on many topics were read out and voted upon. The system was highly unsatisfactory, and since much of the important work was in any case done in committee, it was proposed to do away with the 'general debate'. It seemed altogether pointless to try to cover all the important subjects in a parliament which met for a fortnight every other year. But the system, however defective, had grown roots. An entire generation of Zionist politicians had come to accept it and attempts to change it encountered strong resistance.

In his opening address at the congress Sokolow said that the movement had advanced all along the line. This claim was not altogether unjustified for, quite apart from the progress made in Palestine, Zionism had won many new adherents. Almost one million Jews had bought the shekel that year and thus acquired the right to vote. This despite the revisionist secession and the establishment of the New Zionist Organisation by Jabotinsky's followers. Even so, Zionists were only a minority within world Jewry. Their most dangerous enemy, as Ben Gurion pointed out at the time, was the indifference of the Jewish communities.* In Palestine about one-third of the community had acquired the shekel, and in Lithuania, West Galicia, and Latvia the Zionist position was also relatively strong, with between 20 and 30 per cent of the local community adhering. More had expressed sympathy without taking the trouble to register. But the situation in the two largest communities was much less rosy: in Poland only one Jew out of ten had brought the shekel, and in the United States only one out of thirty.

To return to the proceedings of the Lucerne congress: Weizmann was elected president, Ben Gurion, in his keynote speech (given in Yiddish), said that while the present generation could not complete the work of Zionism it had an urgent and easily definable task: to settle one million families in Palestine.† Ruppin, surveying twenty-five years of colonising work, defended the collective settlements against their detractors and said that agriculture was still lagging behind the general development of the country. Grossman, who with a few friends had split away from Jabotinsky, accused Mapai of strangling private

* D.Ben Gurion, 'The Zionist Organisation and its Tasks', *Zionist Review*, April 1936.
† *Stenographisches Protokoll der Verhandlungen des XIX Zionisten Kongresses*, Vienna, 1937, p. 84.

initiative in Palestine and condemned the transfer agreement with Germany. The general debate was mainly between Mapai and the General Zionists. Mizrahi boycotted it since their demand to give the movement (and, above all, life in Palestine) a greater religious content had not been accepted. They were somewhat mollified when one of their leaders, Rabbi Fishmann, was elected to the new executive, the other members being Weizmann (Sokolow became honorary president of the world organisation), Ben Gurion, Brodetsky, Gruenbaum, Kaplan, Rottenstreich and Shertok – a coalition representing all the main trends in the movement.

Weizmann's return after four years in the wilderness was the most important event. He wrote later that he was a little reluctant to accept the call because there had been no real change of heart in the movement. Many had simply reached the conclusion 'that they had nobody who could do much better'. The American Zionists who had voted against him on past occasions now became his strongest supporters. The world situation had deteriorated and inside the movement there was growing impatience and less and less desire to face realities: 'This impatience, that lack of faith, was constantly pulling the movement towards the abyss.' Weizmann who, unlike the leaders of Mapai, lacked an organised power base inside the movement, had to rely on the alliance (the 'unwritten covenant') between a small group of faithful supporters among the General Zionist group and the 'great mass of workers in the settlements and factories in Palestine which formed the core of the Zionist movement. This was the guarantee of our political sanity.'*

Less than a year after the nineteenth congress Zionism found itself in a mortal struggle against overwhelming pressure on three different fronts: the wave of antisemitism in Europe, the Arab attacks on Jewish settlements, and the decision of the British that Zionist work had to be suspended.

The riots began with armed attacks on individual Jews, probably uncorrelated. Unrest quickly spread and within a few days there was a whole series of murderous assaults. As the Arab Higher Committee, under the leadership of the mufti, declared a six months' general strike, armed bands took up guerrilla warfare in various parts of Palestine. The evidence points to a secret understanding between the Arab political leadership and Fawzi Kaukji, who headed the largest private army, and that there was some coordination with other bands.† The Zionists

---

* Weizmann, *Trial and Error*, pp. 361, 363.
† *Sefer Toldot Hahagana*, vol. 2, part 2, p. 654 *et seq*; Sykes, *Crossroads to Palestine*, p. 184.

were inclined to belittle the whole affair, to accuse the government of lack of firmness, and to regard it as the work of a few professional demagogues who had mobilised the flotsam and jetsam of Arab society. But such explanations presented only part of the picture: true, the mandatory government appeared indecisive, and there certainly was a criminal element in the uprising; more Arabs than Jews were killed by the insurgents, either because they refused to collaborate or because they resisted the extortionists. But all the same it was a national movement with a broad popular basis in both the towns and the countryside. Moreover, it had not only the sympathy but the active assistance of other Arab countries, which in the past had shown no direct concern about the future of Palestine.

The high commissioner asked for reinforcements, and when some twenty thousand British troops were finally concentrated in Palestine, the Arab Higher Committee felt the need for a breathing space. In October 1936 it followed the recommendation of the heads of the Arab states to rely on the good intentions of the British and to end the general strike, but refused to give evidence before the royal commission, whose appointment had just been announced in London, so long as there was no total stoppage of Jewish immigration. The commission was headed by Lord Peel, a grandson of Robert Peel, a lawyer by training and an experienced colonial administrator. Unknown to most, he was already very ill at the time and died shortly after of cancer. His deputy was Horace Rumbold, who as ambassador to Berlin had seen Nazism at first hand, and was familiar with its ideas, practices and aims. The commission arrived in Palestine on 11 November 1936 and stayed for two months, in the course of which it held sixty-six meetings. Towards the end of its stay the Arabs changed their mind and decided to give evidence. The commission also held meetings in London and some of its members met Emir Abdulla in Amman.

It was the most high-powered of the various commissions of enquiry which had visited Palestine, and its report, published in July 1937, was a model of insight, precision and lucidity.* Seldom, if ever, has an intricate political problem been so clearly and comprehensively presented and analysed by men who had little previous knowledge of the issues. The Zionist position, as outlined in the memorandum submitted to the commission as well as in the oral evidence given by Weizmann and Ben Gurion, was that notwithstanding the riots, Jews

---

* *Palestine Royal Commission Report*, Cmd. 5479, London, 1937.

and Arabs could reach a *modus vivendi*.* It reiterated the basic principle that, regardless of numerical strength, neither of the two peoples should dominate or be dominated by the other. Weizmann repeated that the Zionist movement was perfectly willing to accept the principle of parity: if a legislative council was established, the Jews would never claim more than an equal number, whatever the future ratio between the Arab and Jewish population.† Ben Gurion in his evidence also emphasised that it was not the Zionist aim to make Palestine a Jewish state. Palestine was not an empty country. There were other inhabitants and these did not want to be at the mercy of the Jews just as the Jews did not want to be at their mercy: 'It may be the Jews would behave better, but they are not bound to believe in our goodwill. A state may imply . . . domination of others, the domination by the Jewish majority of the minority, but that is not our aim. It was not our aim at that time [of the Balfour Declaration] and it is not our aim now.'‡

The position of the mufti, who appeared as the main Arab spokesman, was that the experiment of a Jewish national home should be discontinued, and immigration and land sales stopped. Hebrew should no longer be recognised as an official language, and Palestine should become an independent Arab state. There were some antisemitic undertones: Auni Abdul Hadi, a leader of the left-of-centre Istiqlal, said that the Jews were a more usurious people than any other, and if sixty million Germans, who were cultured and civilised, could not bear the presence of six hundred thousand Jews, how could the Arabs be expected to put up with the presence of four hundred thousand in a much smaller country? When the mufti was asked whether Palestine could digest and assimilate the four hundred thousand already there, he said flatly 'No'.§ Were these Jews to be expelled or 'somehow to be removed'? 'We must all leave this to the future,' said the mufti. 'That is not a question which can be decided here,' said Auni Abdul Hadi.

Weizmann gave a masterly presentation of the Jewish case on 25 November. It was one of the highlights of his career. He later described his feelings as he made his way to the speaker's table between the rows of spectators in the dining-room of the Palace Hotel in Jerusalem:

I felt that I not only carried the burden of these well-wishers, and of countless others in other lands, but that I would be speaking for generations

---

* Jewish Agency for Palestine, *Memorandum to the Palestine Royal Commission*, p. 5.
† Cmd. 5479, p. 143.
‡ Quoted in ESCO, vol. 2, p. 802.
§ *Palestine Royal Commission*, Minutes of Evidence, London, 1937, p. 297 (mufti), pp. 310–15 (Auni Abdul Hadi).

long since dead, for those who lay buried in the ancient and thickly populated cemeteries on Mount Scopus, and those whose last resting places were
scattered all over the world. And I knew that any mis-step of mine, any
error however involuntary, would be not mine alone, but would rebound
to the discredit of my people. I was aware, as on few occasions before or
since, of a crushing sense of responsibility.*

Weizmann surveyed Jewish history in modern times, and the development of Zionism as an answer to Jewish homelessness. He spoke of the
spread of antisemitism all over Europe and how one by one all the gates
had been closed to them. There were six million Jews in east and central
Europe, 'doomed to be pent up in places where they are not wanted and
for whom the world is divided into places where they cannot live and
places into which they cannot enter'. Seven years earlier Lord Passfield
had told him that there was no room to swing a cat in Palestine, but
many a cat had been swung since then; the Jewish population had in
fact doubled. At the end of his speech he said the commission had come
at a time when the Jewish position 'has never been darker than it is
now, and I pray it may be given to you to find a way out'.

In early January Weizmann appeared again before the commission,
this time in closed session. Having listened to the spokesmen of the two
sides, its members were inclining towards the idea of cantonisation. The
Arabs were uncompromising, totally ruling out any idea of further
Jewish immigration. One member of the commission, Professor
Coupland of Oxford, a veteran student of Indian history, eventually
reached the conclusion that cantonisation did not go far enough and
that a more radical approach was needed. It appeared unlikely that
harmony between Jews and Arabs could be restored in the near future.
If so there was no other way to peace than the termination of the
mandate by agreement. This meant the splitting of Palestine into two,
and consequently the emergence of an independent Jewish and an
Arab state.

Partition schemes

Weizmann reports that this was the first time the idea of partition was
broached to him. As a good diplomat he did not reply immediately, but
asked for time for reflection and to consult his colleagues. The more he
thought about the idea, the more he liked it. A private meeting with
Professor Coupland was arranged. To keep it secret, it was held in a

* Weizmann, *Trial and Error*, p. 383.

hut belonging to the girls' agricultural training farm in Nahalal.* Coupland was firmly convinced that no two peoples who had developed national consciousness could live together as equal partners in a single state. From this rule he was willing to except only the British who had established reasonably happy relations with the Afrikaners in South Africa.† He told Weizmann that it was quite unrealistic in the given world situation to expect any decisive help from Britain for the future development of the Jewish national home. There had to be surgery; no honest doctor could recommend aspirin and a water bottle as a cure.‡ Nine years later, in conversation with Abba Eban, the future Israeli foreign minister, Coupland said that his decision had been the right one, that it was the only solution compatible with justice and logic or, at any rate, the one involving least injustice. Coupland took it upon himself to persuade his colleagues that cantonisation, favoured by the mandatory administration, would not work, and that partition was the only way out. Weizmann was more than satisfied. When he left the hut in the evening he told the farmers assembled outside: '*Hevra* [comrades], today we laid the foundation for the Jewish state!'

The Peel Report was published in July 1937. Since its main recommendations were not accepted by the British government a very brief summary should suffice. In contrast to previous commissions, the Peel Commission realised that an irrepressible conflict had arisen between the two communities and that there was no common ground between them. The British people would have little heart to continue ruling the country without the consent of its inhabitants, nor could the problem be solved by giving either side all it wanted. After dismissing cantonisation, the commission recommended the termination of the mandate on the basis of a partition scheme which would have to fulfil three essential conditions: it would have to be practical, it would have to conform to British obligations, and it would have to do justice to both Arabs and Jews. The commission presented a plan (and a map) according to which Palestine was to be divided into three zones: a Jewish state, including the coastal region from south of Tel Aviv to north of Acre, the Valley of Esdraelon and Galilee; an Arab state, including the rest of Palestine as well as Transjordan; and a British enclave under permanent mandate,

* J.L.Meltzer, 'Towards the Precipice', in M.W.Weisgal (ed.), *Chaim Weizmann*, London, 1962, p. 240. Meltzer and C.Sykes, who quotes him, give the date as an 'early Saturday in February'. But the meeting must have taken place earlier for the commission was back in London on 30 January 1937.
† Sykes, *Crossroads to Palestine*, p. 202.
‡ Meltzer, 'Towards the Precipice'.

including Jerusalem, Bethlehem and a narrow corridor to the Mediterranean including Lydda and Ramle.

Some of the provisions made this plan very difficult for any Zionist to accept, quite apart from the question of Jerusalem: Haifa, Acre, Safed and Tiberias, though within the borders of the proposed Jewish state, were to remain temporarily under British mandate, Nazareth was to be part of the British enclave, and Jaffa part of the Arab state. British official reactions were at first favourable: the White Paper accompanying the report stated that the government adopted its recommendations since partition on the general lines suggested represented the most hopeful solution of the deadlock.* Pending completion of the details of the plans, immigration was to be drastically restricted. Only eight thousand certificates were to be granted for the next seven months.

The partition scheme was contemptuously rejected by the Arabs, and sharply criticised by most Zionists, while in Britain itself second thoughts produced grave doubts. In an impressive speech in the House of Lords, Viscount Samuel, the first high commissioner, pointed to the many contradictions of the new plan: there were to be 225,000 Arabs against 258,000 Jews in the proposed Jewish state. He ruled out a population transfer as entailing too much hardship. The scheme would have the effect of creating a Saar, a Polish Corridor, and half a dozen Danzigs and Memels in a country the size of Wales.

On 3 August 1937, less than a month after the publication of the report, the twentieth Zionist congress opened in Zurich. The delegates had barely enough time to study the bulky document and to ponder its implications, but passions were running high, for everyone believed, wrongly as it soon appeared, that the Zionist movement was facing a decision as momentous as at the time of the Uganda debate. Weizmann was the chief protagonist of the partition plan, or to be precise, of the principle of partition, even though his enthusiasm too had waned after studying the commission's map. But he regarded partition as the lesser evil. Of the six million Jews waiting in Europe, two million, he thought, could be saved if there were a state to give them shelter. Through intensive cultivation of the fertile areas it would be possible to bring in one hundred thousand immigrants annually. It was easy to criticise the scheme, but what was the alternative? The restriction of immigration, with the Jews a permanent minority. Never had the Zionist movement faced a heavier responsibility.†

* Cmd. 5513, London, 1937.
† *Kongress Zeitung*, 5 August 1937.

Weizmann was opposed by many of his General Zionist colleagues, by Ussishkin and his followers, the Mizrahi, Grossman's Jewish State Party, and the left-wing Hashomer Hatzair. Ussishkin, like most other opponents, attacked the scheme both in principle and on practical grounds: the proposed Jewish state would simply not be viable. Without Jerusalem it would be a body without a head, said Berl Katznelson, one of the Mapai opponents of partition (together with Golda Meirson). The Mizrahi opposed it because the basis of the Jewish claim to Palestine was the Bible, a covenant which could not be changed at will. Hashomer Hatzair, on the other hand, rejected the scheme because it had not abandoned the idea of a bi-national state. But what was the alternative to partition, a young Polish Zionist, Moshe Kleinbaum (Sneh) asked. The opponents answered that if the Zionist movement offered determined resistance to the British attempt to repudiate the mandate, Britain would be compelled to adhere to its original provisions. Rabbi Wise in a dramatic speech proclaimed his 'non possumus'; there were some things which a people simply could not do. One delegate read out a letter from Field Marshal Smuts in which he, one of the architects of the Balfour Declaration, expressed his opposition. Even Brodetsky, usually one of Weizmann's faithful followers, was doubtful: the absorption of two million immigrants was an illusion. Weizmann interjected that sooner or later things would in any case move towards partition, 'even if we had sixty thousand immigrants annually over a period of ten to twelve years and if we had attained majority status'.

Those who supported partition, like Ben Gurion, emphasised that time, the most important factor, was working against the Jews. The international situation was deteriorating, so was the position of the Jews in Europe. The other 'A' mandates had been abolished. The only question was when it would be Palestine's turn. A Jewish state, however small, would generate new faith, and at the same time create the possibility of saving many hundreds of thousands of Jews. It was not an end but a new beginning.* Gruenbaum, who on so many past occasions had been in the camp opposing Weizmann, now agreed with him. The alternative to a Jewish majority in a Jewish state was a Jewish minority in Arab Palestine. Shertok admitted that partition would be a cruel operation, but should they forgo an historical opportunity because, as someone had argued, Modi'in and Massada, those two symbols of resistance in Jewish history, would not be within the borders of the state? They had to make the greatest possible use of historical

* *Ibid.*, 10, 11 August 1937.

519

opportunities.* Partition was risky, Goldmann admitted, but there were no other solutions. He recalled that some Zionist leaders, such as Victor Jacobson, had envisaged it years before.

Ussishkin, in his final speech, reiterated his view that a state without land could not exist in the long run: the experience of Carthage and Venice should serve as a warning. Or would they be compelled to build skyscrapers in Tel Aviv for want of land? 'We have to make the best of it,' Weizmann replied. They had eight thousand certificates for seven months. How could the critics claim that the prospect of two million immigrants should count as nothing? Gruenbaum believed that Arab-Jewish relations would improve as the result of partition; the alternative was 'permanent terror'. There was a struggle within the soul of each delegate, as Rubashov (Shazar) said. Old friends found themselves in opposed camps; even Hagana in Palestine was divided, with Eliahu Golomb favouring partition and Shaul Meirov (Avigur) opposing it.

Eventually 300 delegates voted in favour of the Weizmann resolution and 158 against. The majority was substantial but only because the resolution adopted was fairly vague, evading a clear stand on most of the critical issues. It rejected the assertion of the royal commission that the mandate had proved unworkable and demanded its fulfilment. It refused to accept the conclusion that the national aspirations of Jews and Arabs were irreconcilable, and condemned the 'palliative proposals' put forward by the commission. The strongest protest was directed against the decision of the British government to fix a political maximum for Jewish immigration. Thus the scheme of partition as put forward by the commission was rejected as unacceptable, but at the same time the Zionist executive was empowered to enter into negotiations with a view to ascertaining London's precise terms for the establishment of a Jewish state.

The congress was followed, as usual, by a session of the Jewish Agency Council. There, too, strong opposition to partition was voiced, albeit for different reasons. The non-Zionist representatives were no supporters of the idea of a Jewish state. The point which had received most attention at the congress – that the state as envisaged would be too small – was not their chief concern. They suggested that an Arab-Jewish conference should be convened by the British government to seek a solution within the terms of the mandate.

What had started as a promising venture ended in a flurry of recrimination, and Weizmann's patience was wearing thin. His British

* *Ibid.*, 11 August 1937.

friends had not even troubled to send him an advance copy of the Peel Report. After some sharp words to Ormsby Gore, the colonial secretary and a friend, he was told 'not to burn his boats and to go off at the deep end'. He replied bitterly:

I have no boats to burn. I have borne most things in silence; I have defended the British administration before my own people, from public platforms, at congresses, in all parts of the world, often against my own better knowledge, and almost invariably to my own detriment. Why did I do so? Because to me close cooperation with Great Britain was the cornerstone of our policy in Palestine. But this cooperation remained unilateral – it was unrequited love.*

Parliament, the League of Nations, and the Zionist congress had, albeit with great reservations, accepted the principle of partition, but the Palestinian Arabs mobilised the heads of Arab states against the scheme. At a pan-Arab congress in Bludan (Syria) in September 1937 it was resolved that the preservation of Palestine as an Arab country was the sacred duty of every Arab. Meanwhile riots broke out again in Palestine and became more intense. In October the British district commissioner for Galilee and his escort were shot in front of a Nazareth church. The British arrested five members of the Arab Higher Committee, while the mufti succeeded in escaping. The Arab attacks continued, and it took the authorities eighteen more months before the rebellion was suppressed. This failure has baffled many observers, and it has been said that it was due to lack of will rather than lack of resources. Fawzi Kaukji, the guerrilla leader, who in 1936–8 pinned down many thousand British soldiers, was routed within a few days by the small, badly trained and ill-equipped forces of the Hagana ten years later. But it is only fair to add that at the time both the British and the Jews lacked experience in guerrilla fighting. Armoured cars and planes were quite unsuitable for coping with irregular forces supported by the local population.

To recommend new boundaries for the Arab and Jewish states yet another commission was appointed in February 1938. This group was headed by Sir Charles Woodhead; most of his colleagues were, like its chairman, distinguished ex-Indian civil servants. According to its terms of reference, the commission was at full liberty to suggest modifications. It stayed in Palestine from late April to July 1938 but was boycotted by the Arabs. Moreover, its members must have been aware

* Weizmann, *Trial and Error*, p. 393.

that London was already retreating from the idea of partition. The appointment of yet another commission may well have been an attempt to gain time while a new policy was worked out.

The commission's report was published in November, but in the words of one commentator it is not easy to say precisely what it did, or did not, recommend.* It discussed three different projects. Plan A envisaged a Jewish state more or less within the boundaries suggested by the Peel Commission, in which, it was noted, 49 per cent of the population would be Arabs who would own about 75 per cent of the land. Under Plan B Galilee, mainly populated by Arabs, would be detached as well as some other areas from the Jewish state. Plan C envisaged a still smaller Jewish state, consisting of the coastal plain from Rehovot in the south to Zikhron Ya'akov in the north, four hundred square miles with a total of 280,000 inhabitants. It was essentially a Jewish Vatican, Tel Aviv and its suburbs. But even this mini-state was subdivided into two parts by the Jaffa-Jerusalem corridor. The four members of the Woodhead Commission failed to agree among themselves: one of them preferred Plan B, two had strong reservations about Plan C, and all rejected Plan A.

In essence the commission reached the conclusion that no Jewish state could be devised which, while including only a small number of Arabs, would be large enough to allow for new immigration.† Instead of openly admitting failure, the commission felt under an obligation to produce a scheme of its own, however half-hearted and confused. Several weeks after the publication the British government, in yet another White Paper, turned partition down as impractical in view of the political, administrative and financial difficulties it raised, claiming that peace and prosperity in Palestine could be restored only if there was an understanding between Jews and Arabs.‡ It was also announced that a conference would soon be held in London to which representatives of the Jewish Agency as well as Arabs from Palestine and the neighbouring states, would be invited. If no agreement was reached within a reasonable period, the government would be obliged to impose a settlement.

Various peace-makers volunteered their services to mediate between Arabs and Jews. Among the well-meaning individuals who took a hand in the search for a solution were A.H.Hyamson, the former head of the

* Cmd. 5634, London, 1938; Sykes, *Crossroads to Palestine*, p. 229.
† ESCO, vol. 2, p. 873.
‡ Cmd. 5893, November 1938.

immigration department of the mandatory government; Colonel Newcombe, a well-known advocate of the Arab cause; Dr Magnes, chancellor of the Hebrew university; and Nuri Said, the Iraqi foreign minister. Some of the blueprints produced were based on the cantonisation scheme, others on the concept of one sovereign Palestinian state in which the maximum Jewish population should be less than half – thus providing a Jewish national home but not a state. But these schemes aroused no interest among either Jews or Arabs: the Zionists had been unhappy about Lord Peel's state and they rejected *a fortiori* the idea of permanent minority status. The Arabs, on the other hand, rejected not only partition but also a bi-national state based on parity. Nor were they willing to consider further Jewish immigration.

The London Round Table Conference opened on 7 February 1939 with a speech by the prime minister, Neville Chamberlain. The feeling among the Jews was one of unrelieved gloom. The previous October Hitler had invaded Czechoslovakia and on the very day that parliament was debating the Woodhead Report, the big pogrom in Germany (the *Kristallnacht*) took place. Hitler and Mussolini openly supported the Arabs: fascist Italy had always regarded a Jewish Palestine as a danger to the Italian empire because it was bound to become a British imperial base, another Malta or Gibraltar. Zionism could expect no help from France or the United States. In so far as they were at all interested in Middle Eastern politics, the Soviet Union, and the Communist parties following its line, supported the Arab rebellion.

Zionism was thus totally isolated, completely dependent on British goodwill. Moving appeals reached London from German Jewry: 'It is a question of life and death, it is inconceivable that Britain will sacrifice the German Jews.'* But the fear, grief and agony of a persecuted people counted for little in world politics. As Namier wrote at the time: 'All the sacrifices were demanded from us, and all the gains were offered to the Arabs.'†

Three years earlier Namier had vainly tried to persuade the British that their interests and those of the Jews were inseparable, that the Jews, while numerous enough to be an irritant, were not at the moment sufficiently strong to serve as a defensive shield, that in a coming world conflict the Arabs would be against Britain anyway, and that it was therefore in the British interest to get the Jews to the other shore as quickly as possible. This was not how the British policy-makers saw it,

* *Jüdische Weltrundschau*, 20 March 1939.
† 'Palestine and the British Empire', in *In the Margin of History*.

and even after the appeasement policy in Europe was seen to have failed, the attitude towards Zionism did not change. The Arabs were many and the Jews were few. Precisely in view of the coming war, Arab goodwill had to be won.

The question whether British policy was effective as *Realpolitik* will no doubt be debated for a long time to come. It has been argued that if the pro-Axis elements in the Arab world failed in their bid for power in 1941, as in Rashid Ali's revolt in Iraq, if Egypt was quiet even when Rommel reached El Alamein, this was the result of the far-reaching concessions made by London to the Palestinian Arabs. It seems, however, more probable that the revolt in Iraq would have been suppressed anyway, and that (like General Franco) the Arab rulers, whatever their sentiments *vis-à-vis* Britain, were not willing to come out openly for the Axis until Hitler and Mussolini were sure of victory.

In his opening statement at the London conference Weizmann reiterated world Jewry's belief in British good faith. Cooperation with the British government had always been the cornerstone of Zionist policy, and the movement was approaching its present task in the same spirit. The Jewish delegation was the most representative which had ever taken part in an international conference. All leading Zionists were present as well as some of the best known non-Zionist Jewish leaders. The Palestinian Arab delegation included Jamal Hussaini, its acting chairman, but not the mufti. Among the delegates from other Arab countries there were leading figures like Ali Maher, Nuri Said, the Jordanian prime minister, and Emir Faisal, Ibn Saud's son. The Arabs refused to sit at one table with the Jews and arrangements were made for them to reach the conference hall in St James's Palace by a different entrance. There were, in fact, two separate conferences. Only on two occasions did informal meetings take place between Jewish leaders and the representatives of Egypt, Iraq and Saudi Arabia. The Palestinian Arabs refusing any contact with the Jews.

The Zionists had gone to the conference with great misgivings. At the Inner Zionist Council meeting in December 1938 eleven members had voted in favour of participation and eleven against. It had been decided to leave the final decision to the executive, which agreed on participation because, as Ben Gurion wrote, they had been assured by Malcolm MacDonald, the colonial secretary, that the British were still bound by the Balfour Declaration and the mandate, that they rejected the idea of an Arab state, and that Jewish immigration would not be stopped.*

* Quoted in Y.Bauer, *Diplomatia vemakhteret*, Merhavia, 1963, p. 31.

Both Weizmann and Ben Gurion believed that London would not wash its hands entirely of the Jewish cause. They wanted, moreover, to use the opportunity to have direct talks with Arab leaders. Ben Gurion is reported to have said on one occasion that from the Arabs he would be willing to accept less favourable terms than from the British. He predicted at the time two historically inevitable processes: one making for an Arab federation, the other for a Jewish state. If the Arabs were willing to accept the Jewish right to immigration there would be room for fruitful negotiation, perhaps agreement on a Jewish state within an Arab federation.*

The meetings soon showed that Zionist hopes, modest as they were, had been exaggerated. The British had more or less accepted the Arab demand to terminate the mandate and to establish a Palestinian state allied to Britain. Under this plan the British would continue to administer the country for several years and the special rights of the Jews as a minority in an Arab state would be discussed during this transition period. The Egyptians, Iraqis and Jordanians showed a more conciliatory attitude than the Palestinian Arabs. They were willing to tolerate the existence of a Jewish community of four hundred thousand. But, like the Palestinian Arabs, they emphasised that they regarded Palestine as an Arab country with which the Jews had no special connection. What Weizmann said about the principle of non-domination was of no interest to them, since they stood for Arab rule, not for a bi-national state, however constructed.

The meetings between the Jewish delegation and the colonial secretary took place in a tense and unfriendly atmosphere. Much of the discussion concerned the situation likely to arise in the event of war. The Zionists stressed repeatedly that they constituted a military element that could not be ignored, whereas the British could not count on Arab help in a war against Hitler. But the British representatives were not impressed: the danger of an Arab revolt loomed much larger in their calculations than any benefit they could derive from Jewish support. Occasional veiled threats that there would be trouble if illegal immigrants were turned away did not impress the British: what alternative did the Jews have to support for Britain? As MacDonald told them, if they would not cooperate, it was a fair certainty that His Majesty's government would leave them to their fate, and the results of that could easily be foreseen.† To the Arabs this attitude was most welcome. They

* Ben Gurion, 12 February 1938, *ibid.*, p. 28.
† Bauer, *Diplomatia vemakhteret*, p. 32.

had told MacDonald that the Jews would not present a problem if Britain were to withdraw. But the British had no intention of doing so on the eve of a world war in which Palestine would be an important strategic base. They had accepted the Arab demand that the Jews should be reduced to permanent minority status, but insisted on their being given certain rights and on the continuation of limited immigration. At one meeting Weizmann announced that he was willing to accept restrictions on immigration if this would help to bring nearer an agreement with the Arabs. The other Zionist leaders were not happy about this concession but nothing came of it, since the Arabs did not take it up. MacDonald stressed time and again that the Jews would have to obtain Arab consent to immigration, which provoked Weizmann's observation that the British, too, were not in Palestine by Arab consent.*

The Jewish delegates were most unhappy about the total repudiation of the Balfour Declaration. They felt that the British attitude worsened almost daily: at first parity had been suggested and the negotiations proceeded on the basis of the mandate. Later it was said that the number of Jews should eventually reach 40 per cent at most, a figure subsequently reduced to 35 per cent and then to 33⅓ per cent. The renunciation of the mandate was also proposed at a later stage of the conference. In their counter-proposals in early March, Weizmann and Ben Gurion mentioned various possibilities: the establishment of a Jewish state in part of Palestine, or the establishment of a federal Arab-Jewish administration on the basis of parity, with the proviso that immigration would not be stopped. As a last resort they suggested a freezing of the situation: the immigration quota was to be fixed for the next five years, during which time all other outstanding problems were to be discussed.

MacDonald was dissatisfied with the Zionist reaction. Originally he had, he said, been opposed to the idea of an Arab veto on immigration but the intransigent attitude of some members of the Jewish delegation had made him realise that so long as the Jews had the British government behind them, they would never meet the Arabs halfway.† The final British suggestions, made on 15 March, envisaged the establishment of a Palestinian state after a transitional period of about ten years, during which time self-governing institutions would gradually be established, a national assembly convened, and a constitution drafted.

* *Ibid.*, p. 30.
† *Ibid.*, pp. 31, 37.

There would be guarantees for the Jewish minority and possibly even a federal structure of Arab and Jewish cantons. During the coming five years a maximum of 75,000 Jews were to be permitted to enter Palestine, so that the Jewish population would be one-third of the total.

The scheme was turned down by the Jewish delegation, and the Arabs, too, found it unacceptable. They had hoped for independence in the immediate future, were opposed to another ten years of British rule, and, above all, insisted on the total cessation of Jewish immigration. There was nothing more to discuss, and on 17 March the conference came to an end. Two months later, on 17 May, the British government, as it had intimated previously, announced that in view of the inability of the two sides to reach any agreement it would impose its own plan. It seems that London had all along assumed that the conference would end in failure but went through the motions of a full-scale conference in order to gain time to work out its plan.

The Zionist leaders without exception regarded this turn in British policy as an unmitigated disaster, a 'death sentence', as Weizmann, the most moderate among them, called it. Even the confirmed pessimists among them had believed that British behaviour was part of the general pattern of appeasement. Since it had been demonstrated beyond any shadow of doubt that appeasement did not work in Europe, was there not a chance that with a turn in the policies of the western democracies the British attitude towards Zionism too, would improve? This optimism, as events were soon to show, was misplaced, for Zionism had become a liability to Britain irrespective of events in Europe.

Various last minute attempts were made by the Zionist leaders to prevent the publication of the White Paper. Weizmann asked for an interview with Neville Chamberlain, but accomplished nothing: 'The prime minister of England sat before me like a marble statue, his expressionless eyes were fixed on me, but he never said a word . . . I got no response.'* Weizmann went to Cairo and met the Egyptian prime minister without, of course, expecting any immediate outcome. A Jewish delegation met President Roosevelt in early April and was warmly received. The British were in a terrible state, Roosevelt said. The Balfour Declaration and the yishuv were to be sacrificed on the altar of appeasement.† He promised to press for the postponement of the White Paper. In fact he did nothing of the sort.

---

* Weizmann, *Trial and Error*, p. 410.

† N. Goldmann to Ben Gurion, quoted in J.B. Schechtman, *The United States and the Jewish State Movement*, New York, 1966, p. 22.

The White Paper

The White Paper, published on 17 May 1939, consisted of a preface and three main sections dealing with constitutional issues, immigration and land respectively.* It repeated that it was the objective of H.M. government that an independent state should come into being within the next ten years. Some 75,000 immigrants were to be admitted over the next five years. After that, from 1 March 1944, immigration was to be permitted only with the consent of the Arabs. Moreover, Jewish settlement was to be prohibited altogether in certain parts of Palestine and to be restricted in others. In all essential points the White Paper thus followed the British plan communicated to the Zionist leaders during the St James conference. Reacting immediately, the Jewish Agency said that the White Paper was a denial of the right of the Jewish people to rebuild their national home in their ancestral country, a breach of faith, a surrender to Arab nationalism. But this blow, coming at the darkest hour of Jewish history, would not subdue the Jewish people: they would never accept the closing to them of the gates of Palestine, nor let their national home be converted into a ghetto. Weizmann, in a letter to the high commissioner, and Ben Gurion, in an analysis of the White Paper, were no less forceful.† Weizmann registered the 'strongest possible protest' against the repudiation of the mandate. Ben Gurion wrote that 'the greatest betrayal perpetrated by the government of a civilised people in our generation has been formulated and explained with the artistry of experts at the game of trickery and pretended righteousness.'

The Zionists were deeply angered by the sophistry of the British interlocutors: if they had been bluntly told that H.M. government had realised that the Balfour Declaration had been a mistake, not in the best interests of Britain, and that, in any case, the present British government was no longer strong enough to carry out this policy, it would, of course still have been a cruel blow. But such an open admission of failure would have caused less resentment than the cynicism of the White Paper. As Namier wrote of MacDonald's performance on another occasion: 'He soothed uneasy consciences. He earned gratitude, the atmosphere was reminiscent of the days of Godesberg and Munich.'‡

---

* Cmd. 6019, 1939.
† These two documents, as well as other relevant ones, have been published several times. They are quoted here from the special White Paper issue of *Jewish Frontier*, October 1943.
‡ *Manchester Guardian*, 15 March 1940.

British opponents of the White Paper took a similar view. Herbert Morrison, later a minister in Churchill's cabinet, said in the parliamentary debate on 23 May: 'I should have had more respect for the Right Hon. Gentleman's speech [Malcolm MacDonald] if he had frankly admitted that the Jews were to be sacrificed to the incompetence of the government.' Morrison called the White Paper 'dishonourable to our good name', a 'cynical breach of pledges'. There were other strong speeches in a similar vein: Leopold Amery said that he could never hold up his head again to either Jew or Arab if the British government were to go back on its pledge. Noel-Baker called the White Paper cowardly and wrong and said that the British people would not agree to it. Archibald Sinclair, a Liberal leader, said several months later in the debate on the land regulations: 'What a moment to choose to inflict fresh wrong on the tortured, humiliated, suffering Jewish people, who are exerting themselves to help us in this war.' But the Chamberlain government had a safe majority in both houses, and though its majority on this occasion was a hundred less than usual, it was not unduly worried. The British press, with one exception (the *Manchester Guardian*) either approved the government decision or gave it minimum coverage. There was a marked feeling of unease about the whole affair.

Nor was the British government greatly concerned about the reaction of the Permanent Mandates Commission of the League of Nations. All the seven members present when the issue was debated expressed the view that the White Paper was not in accordance with the interpretation which the commission had always placed on the mandate. Three of them (including the British delegate) argued, however, that circumstances might justify a change in policy if the League council did not oppose it. The four other representatives simply registered their view that the White Paper was not in accordance with the mandate. After the outbreak of war the League council no longer met. Thus the White Paper was not ratified and it did not, strictly speaking, acquire international sanction. But after 1 September 1939 no one bothered any longer about legal niceties.

The Zionist leaders faced an impossible problem: to find an effective policy to combat the new British policy. Various suggestions were discussed at closed meetings. There was support for a campaign of civil disobedience in the Indian style, including the systematic violation of those laws designed to prevent the further development of the national home. Illegal immigration was to be intensified, new settlements founded, and stronger emphasis placed on military training for young people. For the first time Hagana carried out several acts of sabotage directed against the mandatory authorities, including the destruction of a patrol boat used to combat illegal immigration. But these activities were uncoordinated and on a small scale and were discontinued even before the outbreak of war. There was no unanimity as to the strategy to be adopted. Ben Gurion maintained that the White Paper had created a vacuum which should be filled by the Jewish community: they were to behave as though they were the state of Palestine and should so act until there was a Jewish state. At another meeting he said they should no longer talk about the mandate as a possible and desirable solution but demand the establishment of a Jewish state. But with all this, it seems that at the time he still wanted to bring about a change in British policy rather than expel the British from Palestine.

Much has been made of the political differences between Ben Gurion and Weizmann in 1939 and later. Unlike Weizmann, Ben Gurion did not exclude the possibility of armed conflict in Palestine. In a cable to Chamberlain in April 1939 he said that the Jews were determined to make the supreme sacrifice rather than submit to the White Paper régime. If London's object was pacification, it would surely be defeated, for the government would be compelled to use force against the Jews.* Weizmann, on the other hand, still favoured cooperation with Britain. As he saw it, the Jewish community in Palestine needed the help of a great power, and however inadequate British goodwill, they could rely even less on any other power. Ben Gurion seems to have reached the conclusion that there was no chance of making the British modify their policy unless Zionism demonstrated its nuisance value. If Arab resistance had inconvenienced the authorities, the yishuv could make things at least equally difficult.

One of the main issues at stake was illegal immigration. Between 1936 and 1939 the number of illegal immigrants had risen sharply: they came mostly in small ships from the Balkans hired either by the Hagana or by political parties, or, in a few cases, by private entrepreneurs. It was the policy of the authorities to arrest the 'illegals', some of them being kept in detention camps in Palestine, others being turned back. Ben Gurion at one stage in 1939 favoured open landings which would inevitably have led to armed clashes between the Hagana and the British. He thought that such a demonstration would have an impact on world public opinion and thus perhaps force the British to modify their

* Quoted in Bauer, *Diplomatia vemakhteret*, p. 41.

policy. But most members of the Jewish Agency executive in Palestine opposed this course of action. They argued that the overriding aim was to save as many Jews as possible and that illegal immigration should therefore proceed in such a way as to ensure maximum numbers rather than maximum publicity.* Illegal immigration was quite openly discussed at Zionist meetings: Rabbi A.H. Silver, subsequently a leading activist, opposed it at the congress in 1939, whereas Berl Katznelson, the Palestine labour leader, vehemently defended it.†

The Geneva congress of August 1939 was the shortest on record and the most subdued. For the first time German was not the official language. 'We met under the shadow of the White Paper, which threatened the destruction of the national home', Weizmann wrote later, 'and under the shadow of a war which threatened the destruction of all human liberties, perhaps of humanity itself.'‡ Up to 22 August, when the Nazi-Soviet pact was signed, there was still a faint hope that the general catastrophe could be averted, but on that date, with the congress still in session, the Jewish calamity, again in Weizmann's words 'merged with, was engulfed by, the world calamity'. The usual petty intrigues, warnings and manoeuvres seemed out of place. The right-wing faction of the General Zionists threatened to walk out and join the revisionists if the general debate, as had been suggested, were to be omitted.

But the world situation was too serious for the usual party jockeying for position. Weizmann said in his opening speech that bitter injustice had been done to the Jewish people: 'We have not failed, we believed in Britain.' He reviewed the events of the past year, and said that it was again the almost impossible task of the Zionist movement to find the Archimedal point in a confused world. In spite of the White Paper the Jews would support British democracy in its present dark hour. Constructive work in Palestine would continue whatever the circumstances. Even in the straitjacket of the White Paper there were certain possibilities.§ This was challenged by other speakers: 'For us the White Paper does not exist,' Ben Gurion declared. Weizmann said in explanation that he was thinking, *inter alia*, of immigration. Surely no one would turn down the entry permits provided for by the White Paper?

* *Ibid.*, pp. 57–8.
† *Eton Hakongress*, 24 August 1939.
‡ Weizmann, *Trial and Error*, p. 413.
§ *Eton Hakongress*, 21 August 1939: *Jüdische Weltrundschau*, 18 August 1939.

The opposition speeches did not point to a real alternative: Grossman argued that Weizmann's loyalty to Britain had suffered bankruptcy, so had his policy of evading conflict with the Arabs at any price. Zerubavel, representing the Poale Zion, appearing again for the first time in thirty years at a Zionist congress, told the delegates that they should never have tied their fate to an imperialist power. But how could they have built Palestine if not on the basis of the Balfour Declaration and the mandate? They should have relied on the Socialist revolution instead. Rabbi Berlin (on behalf of the Mizrahi) said they should trust in God. Such well-meaning exhortations apart, there was no practical advice. Even an outspoken critic of Weizmann such as Rabbi Silver admitted that much: not Weizmann but Britain had failed, and there was still hope that the White Paper policy would be nullified. Therefore extremist measures should not be adopted. It was risky to provoke an open conflict with Britain. Zionism in its despair should not put weapons into the hands of its enemies. It was dangerous to act as though the yishuv was the state, when it was not.*

There were delegations from Germany as well as from Nazi-occupied Czechoslovakia and from Austria. The short speech of Dr Franz Kahn, from Czechoslovakia, was the most moving of all: 'Palestine is our only anchor in these days of adversity. If the gates of Palestine are closed there is no hope left.' In his political survey Shertok sharply condemned the revisionist terror which, he said, was without purpose, suicidal, damaging from the military point of view and morally reprehensible. The congress ended, earlier than originally envisaged, with a short speech by Weizmann whose *leitmotif* was 'there is darkness around us'. He said that it was with a heavy heart that he took leave:

If as I hope we are spared in life and our work continues, who knows – perhaps a new light will shine upon us from the thick, bleak gloom. . . . There are some things which cannot fail to come to pass, things without which the world cannot be imagined. The remnant shall work on, fight on, live on until the dawn of better days. Towards that dawn I greet you. May we meet again in peace.

The annals of Zionist congresses always registered at this late stage in the proceedings joyful scenes and prolonged applause. The protocols of the twenty-first congress tell a different story: 'Deep emotion grips the congress, Dr Weizmann embraces his colleagues on the platform. There are tears in many eyes. Hundreds of hands are stretched out towards

---

* *Eton Hakongress*, 24 August 1939.

Dr Weizmann as he leaves the hall.' Old rivalries were forgotten for the moment at least. Weizmann's heart was overflowing, he embraced Ben Gurion and Ussishkin as though he would never let them go, Blanche Dugdale, Balfour's niece, noted in her diary.

Less than a week later the German armies invaded Poland. Most delegates had great difficulty in making their way home through a continent which within a few days had become an armed camp. By the time the Palestinians had returned, war had in fact been declared. In a letter to Chamberlain dated 29 August 1939, Weizmann had promised full support for Britain in the war against Germany and offered to make immediate arrangements for utilising Jewish manpower, technical ability and resources. The Agency executive in Jerusalem in its declaration a few days later said that 'the war is also our battle'. Ben Gurion declared at a press conference 'that we have no right to weaken our resistance to the White Paper', but Shertok added that Jewish Palestine was in a state of armistice with Britain, and the Jewish offer of assistance was not necessarily confined to action within the boundaries of Palestine.*

On 11 September the IZL announced in circulars distributed in the streets of Tel Aviv that it was suspending its terror campaign in order to join Britain in the fight against Hitlerism. But the conditions were inauspicious; two Jewish illegal immigrants on board SS Tigerhill were killed on 4 September when a coastguard cutter opened fire. The ship had won fame during the Spanish civil war as a blockade runner. It was discovered south of Jaffa while discharging its passengers, and fled on the approach of the coastguard cutter with about two hundred immigrants still on board. Those who had already embarked were taken to the Sarafend detention camp.

Within two weeks of the outbreak of war most of Poland was occupied by the Wehrmacht: it was the beginning of the end of the largest European Jewish community. Every Jewish community in Europe, and eventually in Palestine too, faced the danger of extinction. The First World War had given the Zionist movement its great chance, the charter for which it had striven for so long. As the Second World War broke, what was at stake was not further expansion but survival.

The Second World War

The thunder of the battle in Europe sounded only faintly in Palestine during the first year of the war. The Arab rebellion had slowly died

* Daily News Bulletin, *Jewish Telegraphic Agency*, 9 September 1939.

down, and after September 1939 ceased altogether. Jews and Arabs again lived in peace side by side even though the conflict between the national aspirations of the two peoples remained unresolved. But the repercussions of the fall of France were soon felt: 1941 and 1942 were years of crisis. The German armies in a giant pincer movement reached the western desert and advanced to the Caucasus. In Syria the Vichy administration had taken over and the pro-Axis Rashid Ali coup endangered British bases in Iraq. The tide turned as 1942 drew to its close. With the German armies in full retreat both in the Soviet Union and in North Africa, the danger of invasion was averted. Apart from a few isolated air attacks, Palestine was not directly affected by Axis military activities. The country became an important base for the allied forces in the Middle East, and its economic development received a powerful impetus.

During the early part of the war the yishuv suffered severely from economic dislocation. Citrus exports ceased, all but paralysing the most important branch of the national economy. According to government estimates, the number of unemployed in the Jewish sector was fifty thousand in 1939–40, a staggering figure in a community of little more than half a million. But industrial activity and public works expanded at a rapid rate. Some thirty thousand men and women had been employed in 1936 in industry and manufacture; their numbers had more than doubled by 1943. The newly established Haifa refinery played an important part in the fuel supply for the allied war effort, a new diamond industry came into being, and the textile industry underwent rapid expansion.

Relations between the Jewish community and the mandatory authorities did not improve. The high commissioner and his assistants continued to carry out the White Paper policy, showing no willingness to adjust it in the light of the tragic fate of European Jewry. During the first six months after the outbreak of war, when immigration became a matter of greater urgency than ever, no permits at all were granted. The Land Transfer regulation of 1940 virtually confined the Jews to a new pale of settlement, 5 per cent of the total area of western Palestine. Not even land officially classified as 'uncultivable' was exempt from these prohibitions. It was a clear case of discrimination on grounds of race and religion, the Jewish Agency claimed, 'such discrimination being explicitly forbidden by the mandate'.*

Violent anti-government demonstrations took place throughout

* Quoted in *Jewish Frontier*, October 1943, p. 29.

Palestine and the tension was further exacerbated by the government's unrelenting struggle against illegal immigration. Little ships packed with refugees succeeded in making their way to the shores of Palestine even after the outbreak of war in Europe. Thus in November 1940, 1,770 Jews arrived in Haifa on two vessels, but whereas British policy in the past had been to detain illegal immigrants in Palestine, it was now decided to deport these new arrivals to the island of Mauritius in the Indian Ocean. There were bloody clashes and eventually Hagana decided to carry out an act of sabotage on the *Patria*, which was to take the refugees to Mauritius. Because of an error in calculating the amount of explosive used, and an insufficient number of lifeboats aboard, more than 250 immigrants were killed.* The British government intervened at this stage and announced that those saved from the *Patria* would be permitted to stay after all, but the refugees from the *Atlantic*, about seventeen hundred in number, who had arrived at the same time, were to be exiled, 'never be allowed to return to Palestine'.

This was not the last in this chain of tragedies. The *Salvador* sank in early 1941 in the Sea of Marmora with a loss of two hundred lives. There was the tragic case of the *Struma*, which left the Black Sea port of Constanza in October 1941 and reached Istanbul in December. But since the British authorities announced that the 769 passengers would not be permitted to land in Palestine, the Turkish government decided to turn the ship back. It was torpedoed in the Black Sea and sunk with the loss of all but one or two of its passengers. Such was the unwillingness of the mandatory authority to admit any further immigrants that when the transitional period specified by the White Paper ended in 1944, only about two-thirds of the 75,000 permits which had been set aside had been utilised. Nor was any encouragement given to the Jewish war effort, even though 136,000 young Jews had volunteered shortly after the outbreak of war to place their services at the disposal of the British military authorities. On the other hand, Hagana, the Jewish defence organisation, came under attack. In late 1939, forty-three officers were arrested (among them Moshe Dayan) and given long prison sentences. Searches and arrests were carried out in agricultural settlements, including Ben Shemen, the children's village. All arms found were seized, despite protests that they were needed for self-defence. The searches and arrests continued, albeit with interruptions, throughout the war. In July 1943 Saharov, who had acted as Weizmann's bodyguard, received a seven-year sentence for illegal possession of two rifle

* Y.Bauer, *From Diplomacy to Resistance*, Philadelphia, 1970, p. 108.

bullets. In November of that year a member of Kibbutz Ramat Hakovesh was killed during a search at the settlement.

The mandatory government claimed that it was dangerous to permit aliens from Nazi-occupied Europe to land, for how could they be certain that there were no spies and saboteurs among them? (The same argument, incidentally, was used in the United States by those who opposed the admission of Jewish refugees, such as Breckinridge Long.)* As for the searches and arrests in the Jewish settlements, the authorities argued that the Jewish Agency was arrogating to itself the powers of an independent government, thus openly defying the government. This argument was unanswerable, unless the desire of the Jewish community to defend itself in the event of a German invasion was regarded as legitimate, overriding laws that had not provided for such an emergency. The mental response of the mandatory government, in the words of a British historian, was dull and flat-footed, turning people who had no other wish but to serve the allied war effort into enemies.† Such resentment, which gradually turned into hatred, found little open expression while the war was in its critical phase, but it provided the background to the anti-British terror in the later stages of the war.

Zionism during the war

The subject of the present study is the history of the Zionist movement, not of Palestine, and it is to the activities of its leaders that we have to turn next. Weizmann, who had been re-elected president, was also in charge of the London office and, together with Professor Selig Brodetsky, headed its political department. David Ben Gurion was head of the Jerusalem office of the Jewish Agency, and with Moshe Shertok shared the responsibility for the political department there. Isaac Gruenbaum directed the labour department, Rabbi Fishman the department for artisans and small traders, and Emil Schmorak the section for commerce and industry. Ussishkin and Ruppin, both of whom died during the war, were attached to the Jerusalem executive in an advisory capacity, while Lipsky, later joined by Nahum Goldmann, represented the Jewish Agency in America with a seat on the executive, also in an advisory capacity. On the Jewish Agency there were also four representatives of non-Zionist bodies (Senator, Hexter, Karpf and Rose Jacobs), but three of them lived in New York and none played a leading part in wartime policies.

* Henry L. Feingold, *The Politics of Rescue*, New Brunswick, 1970, pp. 145, 159–66.
† Sykes, *Crossroads to Palestine*, p. 258.

The 1939 Zionist congress had elected a General Council of seventy-two members, of whom twenty died or were killed during the war. This council met for the first and only time the day after the congress ended, on 25 August 1939. It elected ('for the purpose of carrying out special and urgent tasks') an inner council of twenty-eight, not counting the chairman of the general council and two representatives of the Va'ad Leumi (Ben Zvi and E.Berligne), the central organisation of Palestinian Jewry. Thirteen of its members belonged to Mapai, eleven to the General Zionists, the rest to the smaller parties. The inner council met more than fifty times during the war and, together with the executive, became the central decision-making body of the movement. It discussed and voted on all important political issues, carried out legislative duties, engaged in various organisational activities, and confirmed the budgets of the Jewish Agency. It should be noted in passing that the budget of the Agency rose almost tenfold during the war, from £P 720,000 in 1939–40 to £P 6,500,000 in 1945–6. The two largest items of expenditure were immigration and agricultural settlement, accounting for 53 per cent over the period. The share of the political department was only 20 per cent, and this despite the fact that it included provisions for such special purposes as recruitment and soldiers welfare.*

Early in the war the centre of activities shifted from London to Jerusalem. In December 1939 Churchill had told Weizmann that he agreed with his view that after the war a Jewish state should be built with three or four million inhabitants.† But Weizmann had few illusions: while the war was still undecided neither the British government nor public opinion was prepared to consider questions of major policy or to re-open negotiations on the future of Palestine.‡

Communication between New York, London and Jerusalem was difficult and hazardous, but the Zionist leaders continued to travel a good deal between these main centres of activity. Weizmann went to America in 1940 and again in March 1942, when he stayed for more than a year. On both occasions he met President Roosevelt. In 1940 Ben Gurion went to London and on to America, where he stayed till the early summer of 1941. He also spent most of 1942 in the United States. There was growing tension between the leading members of the executive, which cannot be explained entirely by reference to the

---

* The Zionist Organisation and the Jewish Agency for Palestine, *Reports of the Executive submitted to the 22nd Zionist Congress at Basle*, Jerusalem, 1946, vol. 2, p. 13.

† Weizmann, *Trial and Error*, pp. 418–19.

‡ *Political Report of the London Office of the Jewish Agency submitted to the 22nd Zionist Congress*, London, 1946, p. 13.

difficulties in communication. Weizmann complained on many occasions that Ben Gurion did not keep him informed of important political moves and developments in Palestine and elsewhere. Ben Gurion took issue no less bitterly with the style of work of the president of the world movement. Weizmann had never been accustomed to take anyone into his confidence except for his closest colleagues in London, and he was not among Ben Gurion's admirers. It is perhaps significant that the first time the name of the leader of Palestinian labour appears in his autobiography is toward the end of the book, when at the 1946 congress Ben Gurion demanded his resignation. Weizmann was moody, given to sudden changes of temper, to feverish activity followed by periods of indolence. As he grew older and suffered personal bereavement (his elder son was killed in action while serving in the RAF) he was certainly not an easy man to deal with.

The distrust between the two leaders was mutual. Ben Gurion's style of work was no less idiosyncratic. If his moods changed less often, his political assessment of the situation was by no means consistent. Before 1939 he had had little experience of international affairs, and lacked Weizmann's finesse in dealing with non-Jews. He was to show in later years the qualities of a statesman, but in 1941 he was still a beginner on the world scene, growing in stature, but unaccustomed to sharing power and responsibility and ill at ease on committees. He had one decisive advantage over Weizmann, a power base in Palestine. The longer Weizmann stayed away from Jerusalem (his first visit after the outbreak of the war was in 1944), the weaker his position became. Weizmann no doubt had Ben Gurion in mind when he complained in a letter to Stephen Wise of the constant heckling and badgering he had to endure from some of his colleagues in other lands, who thought that a 'mere affirmation of our aims constituted an action towards the achievement of our objective'.* He had once made similar charges of 'maximalist demagogy', not without justice, against Ussishkin and Gruenbaum, and Ben Gurion, in his single-mindedness, must have reminded him of past quarrels in the movement. When Weizmann returned to Palestine after the war he noted certain phenomena which caused him grave concern: a relaxation of the old, traditional Zionist purity of ethics, a touch of militarisation, and a weakness for its trappings, a 'tragic, futile, un-Jewish resort to terrorism' and, worst of all, in certain circles, a readiness to play politics with terrorism.† He must have sensed even earlier that

---

* Eban, 'Tragedy and Triumph', p. 267.
† Weizmann, *Trial and Error*, p. 439.

he was losing touch with the yishuv, and may well have made Ben Gurion responsible for this estrangement.

Ben Gurion's quarrels with Weizmann and some of his other colleagues led twice to his resignation, in February 1940 and again in October 1943. But each time Ben Gurion returned to office, the second time only after five months. The quarrels are not easy to retrace, for the issues were by no means clearcut. It is not that the two held at all times diametrically opposed views. In May 1940, for instance, Ben Gurion wrote from London that 'the distance between us is far smaller than that between myself and some of the Zionists in Jerusalem and Tel Aviv'.* It is not the case, as was once widely believed, that Ben Gurion early reached the conclusion that the Zionist movement had to strive for a Jewish state whereas Weizmann continued to believe in other solutions. On the contrary, early in the war Weizmann began to refer more and more frequently to the pressing need for a Jewish state in western Palestine which would have involved the resettlement of at least part of the Arabs elsewhere. Ben Gurion at the time considered both partition and bi-nationalism, with complete equality for Jews and Arabs, as possible solutions. Even in July 1940 he doubted whether the time was right for making final plans. The differences between the two leaders were not unbridgeable, but they seldom reached similar conclusions at one and the same time.

During the early months of the war they failed to reach agreement on Zionist policy *vis-à-vis* Britain. Despite all disappointments and frustrations, Weizmann continued to believe that all hope was not lost, whereas Ben Gurion was pessimistic. He wanted the struggle against the White Paper to take precedence over everything else, envisaging 'activism' leading up to serious and protracted unrest. Several meetings of the executive between February and May 1940 were devoted to a consideration of proposals for intensifying resistance to the White Paper, but Ben Gurion, supported only by Ussishkin and Rabbi Fishman, was outvoted. This was the period of the 'phony war'. The Nazi invasion of Holland and Belgium, the defeat of France, and the battle of Britain put an end to these schemes. The appointment of Churchill as prime minister was a source of encouragement to Weizmann, and Ben Gurion, too, became for a while more optimistic. He reported from London that three of the five members of the new war cabinet were friendly to the Zionist cause. In a letter to Lord Lloyd ('a known pro-Arab but nevertheless an honest and sympathetic man') he wrote that he was a

* Quoted in Bauer, *From Diplomacy to Resistance*, p. 74.

convinced believer in the spiritual mission of the British empire, that it stood for something much greater than itself, for a cause wider than its own frontiers. But this interlude did not last. Two years later Ben Gurion bitterly attacked Weizmann for his one-sided pro-British stand which, he claimed, disqualified him from being the leader of the Zionist movement.

Ben Gurion's growing disappointment was no doubt connected with the failure to obtain British support for the formation of a Jewish fighting force in the framework of the British army. The negotiations were protracted, with frequent ups and downs. General Sir Edmund Ironside, Chief of the Imperial General Staff, wrote to Weizmann in late December 1939 that he agreed in principle to the raising of a Jewish division, but there was no further progress until after Churchill had become prime minister, when Weizmann was told by Lord Lloyd that Jewish units would be established in the British army. 'A great day,' Mrs Blanche Dugdale, Balfour's niece and an ardent Zionist, wrote in her diary. 'The walls of Jericho have fallen. Chaim just back from this interview elated and solemn. He said: 'It is almost as great a day as the Balfour Declaration.'

The War Office appointed a brigadier as liaison officer with the Jewish Agency and another to command the Jewish division. Methods of recruitment, rates of pay and allowances had already been discussed, when Weizmann was suddenly informed by Lord Moyne, who had succeeded Lord Lloyd, that Churchill had decided that owing to the shortage of equipment the project was to be put off for six months. But the real obstacle was the opposition of the mandatory officials as well as of General Wavell, C-in-C Cairo. After six months had passed, Weizmann was informed that new technical difficulties had arisen which made it necessary to keep the project in cold storage for the time being. On 23 October 1941 there was a further communication from Lord Moyne: since the government had to give all possible help to Russia, shipping space could not be spared and it would not be possible to form a Jewish division.

There was no progress at all during 1942 and 1943. But in November 1943 Weizmann and Namier saw Grigg, secretary for war, who submitted the proposal for the creation of a Jewish fighting force to the cabinet. In August 1944 Weizmann was told by Churchill that the War Office would soon be in a position to discuss concrete proposals. A few days later a positive decision was reached and Palestinian Jewry were asked to help in mobilising 3,500 men and 150 officers for a Jewish unit.

The brigade came into being and saw action in Italy towards the end of the war. A statement of the Jewish Agency executive, while noting the delay in the formation of the brigade, interpreted it as an acknowledgment of services rendered and of the Jewish desire for national recognition.

The creation of the brigade has been called an important achievement, the 'greatest political accomplishment' of Zionist diplomacy during the war.* But it was a modest achievement, and it came much too late. Nor did the existence of a Jewish fighting force have great political significance; it was by no means a guarantee that the Zionist movement would be represented at the postwar deliberations on the future of the Middle East. Even the more modest hope that the brigade would one day form the nucleus of a Jewish army was only partly fulfilled. For meanwhile Palmach had come into existence, the strategic reserve of the Hagana, which based on the kibbutzim, was to play the central role in the war of independence.

Although the war cabinet included a majority of sympathisers with the Zionist cause, the issue was not important enough to warrant a major effort in the middle of the war to overcome administrative routine and the anxiety of the local authorities to keep Palestine quiet. This consideration was given greater weight than the possible benefits of a course of action which might 'upset the whole situation either by conscription or by favouring the nationalistic ambitions of one of the rival races'.† This is not to say that the decision to form a Jewish fighting force, precisely because it was of marginal importance, might not have gone the other way in 1940 after Churchill came to power. But it is unlikely that it would have made much difference in Zionist postwar politics.

The overall picture of Anglo-Zionist relations was not, however, one of unrelieved gloom. When Weizmann lunched with the prime minister and Attlee, the deputy prime minister, in October 1943, Churchill, in one of his famous monologues, announced that the Jews would have to be established, after Hitler had been crushed, 'where they belong . . . I have had an inheritance left to me by Balfour and I am not going to change'.‡ Partition and the formation of a Jewish state seem to have been on Churchill's mind, together with many other second-rank

* *Ibid.*, p. 350.
† *The Times*, 30 May 1942; quoted in G.Kirk, *The Middle East in the War*, London, 1952, p. 246.
‡ Eban, 'Tragedy and Triumph', p. 267.

problems. In July 1943 a cabinet subcommittee was set up to consider the future of Palestine. In its report to the cabinet in December of that year it suggested partition on lines more favourable to the Jews than any previous British scheme.

Whatever British policy was going to be after the war, it seemed to be a foregone conclusion that there was to be no return to the White Paper. As Churchill wrote in a memorandum to Lord Ismay in January 1944: 'There cannot be any great danger in our joining with the Jews to enforce the kind of proposals which are set forth in the Ministerial paper. . . . Obviously, we shall not proceed with any plan of partition which the Jews do not support.' In April 1944 the national executive of the Labour Party, a partner in the wartime coalition government, recommended measures for the establishment of a Jewish state which went further than the demands of the Zionist leaders themselves. If there had been a strong case for a Jewish majority in Palestine before the war, it said, the case had become irresistible after the unspeakable Nazi atrocities: 'Let the Arabs be encouraged to move out as the Jews move in. Let them be compensated handsomely for their land, and their settlement elsewhere be carefully organised and generously financed.'* The resolution was pushed through – as usual on such occasions – by a small, active minority, but significantly it met no opposition.

Again, when Weizmann saw Churchill on 4 November 1944 the prime minister seemed very willing to discuss Palestine and said that he was in favour of the inclusion of the Negev in the Jewish state: 'If you could get the whole of Palestine it would be a good thing, but I feel that if it comes to a choice between the White Paper and partition – you should take partition.'† Churchill stressed that active American participation was needed, whereas Weizmann was disturbed by rumours concerning a partition scheme which would result in a state too small to be viable. To reassure him, Churchill revealed that a government committee was dealing with the question and hinted that Lord Moyne, the minister resident in the Middle East, had moved to a position which the Zionists would find acceptable. Unknown to Weizmann, Moyne, who had been thought to be an enemy of the Zionist cause, had in effect recommended partition to the cabinet some time before.

Two days after this interview Moyne was assassinated in a Cairo street by two members of the Stern gang. All further discussions between the Zionist executive and the British government were suspended. The

---

* *The International Post-War Settlement*, London, 1944, p. 7.
† Eban, 'Tragedy and Triumph', p. 274.

detailed memorandum submitted by the Jewish Agency at about this time was ignored, as was the appeal to inaugurate a 'new era' by drawing the logical conclusion from the Balfour Declaration and the demand for the quickest possible increase of the Jewish population as a prerequisite for Jewish statehood. Weizmann sent Churchill a long memorandum asking for an immediate decision to establish Palestine as a Jewish state, and for giving the Jewish Agency the necessary authority to bring to Palestine as many Jews as it might be found necessary and possible to settle. In June 1945 he received a brief and almost hostile reply: 'There can, I fear, be no possibility of the question being effectively considered until the victorious Allies are definitely seated at the peace table.' There was no mention of a commitment, of the many promises made before and during the war. It seemed the final failure of all Weizmann's efforts and he intended to resign in protest. The victory of the Labour Party in the elections shortly thereafter induced him to change his mind.

The demand for a Jewish state, generally accepted by most Jews by the end of the war, had only gradually gathered momentum. Weizmann had been the first though not the most consistent advocate of a state that was to comprise less than the whole of western Palestine ever since he had voted in favour of partition in 1937. 'We shall have on our hands [at the end of the war] a problem of at least three million people,' he had written in 1941. 'Even on purely financial grounds a Jewish state is essential in order to carry out a policy of such magnitude.'* In a long programmatic article in *Foreign Affairs* in 1942 he wrote that a Jewish state was more than the necessary means of securing further immigration and development, it was a 'moral need and postulate, a decisive step towards normality and true emancipation'. As for the Arabs, 'they must be clearly told that the Jews will be encouraged to settle in Palestine and control their own immigration'.† Lewis Namier, Weizmann's faithful supporter and collaborator in London, echoed his demand with reference to the situation likely to arise in Europe after the war. Most of the remaining Jews would want to emigrate, and in the Moslem countries, too, they were endangered by virulent nationalism. The transfer of two or three million was a formidable task but it was manageable if the refugees had a commonwealth of their own to go to.‡

Weizmann did not, however, envisage the emergence of a Jewish

* *Zionist Review*, 12 September 1941.
† 'Palestine's Role in the Solution of the Jewish Problem', *Foreign Affairs*, January 1942.
‡ *Zionist Review*, 19 November 1943.

state as something isolated from other developments in the Middle East. Like Ben Gurion, he repeatedly predicted that at the end of the war an Arab federation and a Jewish commonwealth would emerge, and he stressed the desirability of close cooperation between them. Nor did he regard a state as an end in itself: 'I do not think that any of us want a Jewish state for the sake of the paraphernalia which are bound up with a state,' he declared at the 1944 annual conference of the British Zionist Federation. 'We ask for the state because we believe that through the state we shall be able to do the maximum of good to the maximum number of people.'*

Ben Gurion's conversion was more gradual, but once he had adopted the concept of Jewish statehood there was no more radical advocate. He too had been in favour of partition in 1937, but during the early phase of the war, as already mentioned, he thought that conditions were not opportune for discussing the *Endziel*. Only after his first wartime visit to America did he tell his colleagues that Palestine ought to be turned into a Jewish state, 'not as a final goal, but as a means of moving millions of Jews to Palestine after the war, at the fastest possible rate'. In his view it was the only possible remedy for postwar Jewish misery, 'and we are determined to achieve it'.†

In their speeches Ben Gurion and his colleagues usually referred to a Jewish commonwealth or a Jewish authority in Palestine, but they clearly meant a state. As to ways and means, Ben Gurion was not dogmatic. At one time he considered dominion status in the British commonwealth, and at another advocated armed struggle if they failed to gain British support for Jewish statehood. He seems to have anticipated Arab opposition and favoured a voluntary exchange of population. But he promised that Arabs who did not want to leave would be assured of full civic, political and national equality. The Jews would make an effort to bring their standard of living up to the Jewish level in every respect.‡

On two vital issues Ben Gurion's views differed from Weizmann's; he emphasised more and more America's growing importance for the future of Zionism. Weizmann had not been encouraged by his visits to the United States: he had found real sympathy with Zionism among the political leaders, but the State Department was hostile: 'Our difficulties were not concerned with the first rank statesmen. . . . It was always

---

* *Zionist Review*, 4 February 1944.
† Bauer, *From Diplomacy to Resistance*, p. 231; *Zionist Review*, 2 January 1942.
‡ Bauer, *From Diplomacy to Resistance*, p. 231.

behind the scenes, and on the lower levels, that we encountered an obstinate, devious and secretive opposition which set at nought the public declarations of American statesmen. And in our efforts to counteract the influence of these behind-the-scenes forces we were greatly handicapped because we had no foothold there.'* President Roosevelt had been friendly but non-committal, and Weizmann was too old a hand in the diplomatic game to give much weight to sweeping but vague professions of sympathy. Ben Gurion, on the other hand, was deeply impressed by America's growing strength and confidence. He was convinced that at the end of the war the United States would be in a very strong position and that American Jewry, in view of its numbers and influence, would be able to play a decisive role in shaping the future of Zionism if only its energies were channelled in the right direction. Gradually he reached the conclusion that a change in British policy in Palestine could be brought about only as a result of American pressure.

The other point on which he disagreed with Weizmann was one of approach and emphasis rather than of substance. In his *Foreign Affairs* article Weizmann had written that two million Jews would have to be transferred to Palestine at the end of the war, and on another occasion he mentioned a figure of five million.† But whereas Weizmann seems to have used these figures as a political slogan, Ben Gurion believed in the possibility of an immediate transfer to Palestine of millions of Jews. This in Weizmann's eyes was sheer fantasy; Palestine was not capable of absorbing more than about one hundred thousand new immigrants a year. He thought that to use such enormous figures would antagonise potential supporters. It seems in retrospect that Ben Gurion might have understood American psychology better than Weizmann, whose way of thinking was more attuned to Britain. Ben Gurion instinctively felt that they would not make an impact on American public opinion unless there was a great vision, unless the Zionists were willing to 'think big'.

Biltmore

Ben Gurion's new programme was formulated between 6 and 11 May 1942, at the Biltmore conference, a gathering of some six hundred delegates representing the main Zionist groups in New York, who met to discuss and reformulate, *inter alia*, the aims of their movement. The

---

* Weizmann, *Trial and Error*, pp. 431–2.
† In a letter to Leon Simon in November 1941, quoted in Bauer, *From Diplomacy to Resistance*, p. 234.

eight-point programme adopted reflected the new militant thinking of American Zionism. Its demands were considerably more radical than those previously voiced outside the ranks of revisionism, and it was to play a central role in Zionist debates for years to come. The programme called for the fulfilment of the 'original purpose' of the Balfour Declaration and the mandate, and reaffirmed the Zionists' unalterable rejection of the White Paper. It demanded recognition of the right of the Jews of Palestine to play their full part in the war effort and the defence of their country through a Jewish military force fighting under its own flag. The most important part was the last paragraph:

The conference declares that the new world order that will follow victory cannot be established on foundations of peace, justice and equality, unless the problem of Jewish homelessness is fully solved. The conference urges that the gates of Palestine be opened; that the Jewish Agency be vested with control of immigration into Palestine and with the necessary authority for upbuilding the country, including the development of its unoccupied and uncultivated lands; and that Palestine be established as a Jewish commonwealth integrated in the structure of the new democratic world.*

Such outspoken language appealed not only to American Zionists; it fired the imagination of American Jewry in general. The majority of American Zionists had favoured the idea of a Jewish state since 1937; the three leading Yiddish-language papers had advocated it before the outbreak of war. It has been argued that Biltmore was a major defeat for Weizmann, who regarded the sudden conversion of American Zionists to revisionism as a setback to his policy. In the words of one historian, his seemed to the delegates a voice out of the past, 'uttering unacceptable homilies more appropriate to a State Department man than to the president of the World Zionist Organisation'. Weizmann is said to have thought that nothing should be done to antagonise the Arabs any further and thus to damage the British war effort.† That the Biltmore formula was almost identical with the sovereignty long demanded by the revisionists did not escape the attention of the British Embassy in Washington, which in an *aide mémoire* to the State Department noted with some concern that Zionist policy had become maximalist and that a *rapprochement* with the revisionists was taking place.‡

* Full text in ESCO, vol. 2, pp. 1084–5.
† R.Silverberg, *If I Forget Thee, O Jerusalem*, New York, 1970, p. 194.
‡ B.Halpern, *The Idea of the Jewish State*, Cambridge, 1961, p. 39; *Foreign Relations of the United States*, 1942, vol. 4, Washington, 1963, p. 552.

In fact, the background of Biltmore was far more complex. The record shows that the Biltmore formula was prepared by Meyer Weisgal, one of Weizmann's closest political aides, and that Weizmann was by no means unduly worried by either British or Arab reactions. In a speech in December 1942 he reaffirmed his full agreement with the programme, calling for a 'reinvigoration of Zionist purpose' in support of its demands. The resolution was sufficiently vague to allow for many different interpretations. For Weizmann it was not a matter of immediate practical politics, since it left wide open the question of implementation. It was no more than the statement of a maximum demand. Ben Gurion, on the other hand, regarded the formula as the new platform of the Zionist movement. Biltmore was not a defeat for Weizmann: when Ben Gurion wanted to overthrow the president of the World Zionist Organisation soon after this meeting, charging him with being excessively pro-British, weak and unreliable, the American Zionist leaders rejected these accusations as baseless.*

In Jerusalem Ben Gurion was more successful in the struggle for his interpretation of the new programme; there his colleagues proved more receptive. The programme was not just an emotional response to the need for Jewish liberation and independence, as Yehuda Bauer has noted. It also seemed to point the way out of the confusion that had reigned in Zionist ranks since the beginning of the war. Several members of the Jerusalem executive had their doubts about its feasibility. Kaplan regarded it as no more than a slogan, and Shertok also thought it utopian. But all agreed that the Jewish people should not be silent while other nations were putting forward their claims. In these circumstances it was no doubt better to ask for too much than for too little. If the whole of western Palestine could become a Jewish state, well and good; if not, they would have to think again. They agreed with Ben Gurion that the Zionist maximum had now become the Zionist minimum, and that even if Biltmore was only a political slogan, it was certainly a topical and powerful one.

The Zionist Action Committee adopted the Biltmore programme, at its meeting on 19 November 1942, by twenty-one votes against three, with three abstentions. The opposition came mainly from Hashomer Hatzair, on the ground that the new policy was likely to be interpreted by the powers as releasing them from their responsibility, and that in any case the mandatory government would not give real independence to the yishuv. This was a valid argument, for if Britain had been

* Bauer, *From Diplomacy to Resistance*, p. 242.

unwilling to carry out the mandate it seemed altogether unthinkable that it would help to establish a Jewish state. Hashomer Hatzair also argued that Biltmore was based on the assumption that no satisfactory solution was possible to the Arab question, a view with which it emphatically disagreed, suggesting a bi-national state as an alternative. But since it insisted at the same time that control over Jewish immigration should not depend on Arab goodwill, and since such goodwill was nonexistent, the Hashomer Hatzair proposal, however attractive in theory, was yet another exercise in political futility.

The debate continued well after 1942, but became more and more unreal in view of the destruction of European Jewry. At Biltmore Weizmann had estimated that 25 per cent of central European Jewry would be physically destroyed under German rule.* In November 1942 news reached Palestine that sporadic pogroms and expulsions had given way to the systematic physical extermination of European Jewry. In December of that year the State Department confirmed that two million had already perished and that another five million were in danger of extermination. The Biltmore programme was based on the assumption that there would be millions of refugees at the end of the war. After November 1942 it became clear that millions of refugees would not be left at the end of the war. 'But at the same time the emotional underpinning to the plan grew all the stronger. It was out of the question that justice should not be done to the Jewish people, that it should lack a home, a state. . . . Just at the moment when the politico-diplomatic value of the Biltmore programme crumbled, the heart-touching summons, on which the programme rested, grew stronger.'†

Both adherents and opponents of the Biltmore programme were mistaken in believing that it was a decisive turning point in the history of Zionism. It failed to materialise because it was based on premises that were not realistic. Nor did it do much harm, as its critics at the time believed. Churchill, for instance, seems not to have been deterred by it. In April 1943 he wrote to the colonial secretary that he had always regarded the White Paper as a gross breach of faith and that the majority of the war cabinet would never agree to any positive endorsement of this policy. The Arabs in any case believed the worst as far as Zionist intentions were concerned, and did not need the Biltmore programme to confirm their suspicions. In the last resort Biltmore was not a policy but a symbol, a slogan, reflecting the radicalisation of the Zionist

* *Zionist Review*, 15 May 1942.
† Bauer, *From Diplomacy to Resistance*, p. 243.

movement as the result of the war and of the losses suffered by the Jewish people. It foreshadowed the bitter postwar conflict with the British government.

The progress of American Zionism

Shortly after Biltmore Ben Gurion noted in one of his speeches in Jerusalem that whereas until recently the American Zionist movement had concentrated on providing financial assistance to Israel, the situation had been radically transformed by the war. A review of Zionist policy during the war that was limited to London and Jerusalem would be quite incomplete, for with the destruction of European Jewry American Zionism had become the single most important factor in the world movement. With the steady growth of American influence in international affairs, Washington had become the most important centre in world politics, and consequently in Jewish politics.

American Zionism, it will be recalled, had undergone a severe crisis in the late 1920s, and it was not until 1932 that its fortunes picked up again. Membership of the Zionist organisation of America (ZOA) rose from 8,400 in 1932 to 43,000 in 1939. By the end of the war it had topped the 200,000 mark. Funds remitted to Palestine by the United Palestine appeal increased almost sevenfold between 1932 and 1939.* The income of the United Jewish Appeal rose from $3·5 million in 1940 to about $50 million in 1947. Critics of Zionism have always attributed enormous strength and unlimited financial resources to American Zionism through its alleged connections with Wall Street. Its task would have been much easier had this been true. In fact the multi-millionaires cared little, if at all, about Palestine. Nor was public response encouraging: when ZOA tried in 1935 to carry out a national roll call to get the signatures and one dollar from each of its 250,000 registered sympathisers, the results were deplorable; less than one-tenth, about twenty thousand, responded.

The real upsurge in American Zionism came only after 1936, when prominent Jewish organisations such as the Bnai Brith and some of the leading Reform synagogues began to show an interest in Palestine. There was a marked shift towards Zionism as a result of the Nazi persecution of German Jews. The events in Europe after the outbreak of war and American reluctance to admit Jewish immigrants to the United States gave further momentum to this process. Sympathies for Zionism and Palestine increased even more quickly and more extensively than is reflected in the growth of ZOA membership. American Jewry

* S. Halpern, *The Political World of American Zionism*, Detroit, 1961, p. 27.

became overwhelmingly pro-Zionist, whereas in the past the majority had been indifferent or even actively hostile.

During the first years of the war this goodwill did not amount to a political force. Eliyahu Golomb, the chief of Hagana, wrote to Ben Gurion: 'When I tell you all I saw in Jewish and Zionist circles in America I would paint a rather dismal picture. . . . A force can be crystallised from among American Jews for political action and practical aid for our cause. But so far it does not actually exist – it is only a potential force.'*

At the time of the Geneva congress, shortly before the outbreak of war, a Zionist emergency council had been set up to fight the White Paper, with Rabbis Stephen Wise and Abba Hillel Silver as co-chairmen. But during the first eighteen months of its existence it did little. In fact, until late 1940 it did not even have a full time secretary or a New York office of its own.† The circumstances were not favourable; the United States was not yet at war and there was a strong isolationist current in American public opinion. The country was, as Weizmann put it after a visit in 1940, 'violently neutral' and making an extraordinary effort to live as though nothing unusual was happening. Mention of the Jewish tragedy was associated with war-mongering: 'It was like a nightmare which was all the more oppressive because one had to maintain silence; to speak of such things [the danger to European Jewry] in public was "propaganda".'‡

The turning point came in early 1941. More Americans became reconciled to the idea that their country would not be able to remain neutral indefinitely. Rabbi Silver, the stormy petrel of American Zionism, decided to speak out at a fund-raising dinner in New York in January 1941: only by the large-scale settlement of displaced Jews in Palestine, with the aim of its reconstruction as a Jewish commonwealth, could the Jewish problem be permanently solved. He ended his fiery speech by quoting Daniel O'Connell, the hero of the Irish struggle for national liberation: 'Agitate! Agitate! Agitate!', and Danton's 'L'audace, encore l'audace, toujours l'audace!'

The same month Emanuel Neumann took over the department of public relations and political action of the emergency committee and gave fresh impetus to its work. It revived the American Palestine committee, a group of pro-Zionist Christian public figures which was

---

* Quoted in Silverberg, *If I Forget Thee, O Jerusalem*, p. 184.
† Halpern, *The Political World of American Zionism*, p. 269.
‡ Weizmann, *Trial and Error*, p. 420.

instrumental in gaining support for the Zionist cause. A statement published on 2 November 1942, the anniversary of the Balfour Declaration, calling for the establishment of a Jewish national home, received the signature of 68 senators and 194 congressmen as well as hundreds of other communal leaders and public figures.* These and other initiatives were a cause of much concern to the State Department, and even more to British diplomats: if before Pearl Harbour the Zionists had been under attack for trying to draw America into the war against Hitler, after December 1941 they were accused of harming the allied war effort by their partisan activities.

As news was received through unofficial channels of the fate of European Jewry, and as both government and the mass media seemed to draw a curtain of silence over the subject, a mood of impatience and bitterness prevailed among American Jewry. Weizmann, not given to overstatement or excessive emotionalism, said in a speech at Madison Square Garden on 1 March 1943:

When the historian of the future assembles the bleak record of our days, he will find two things unbelievable; first the crime itself, second the reaction of the world to that crime. . . . He will be puzzled by the apathy of the civilised world in the face of this immense, systematic carnage of human beings. . . . He will not be able to understand why the conscience of the world had to be stirred. Above all, he will not be able to understand why the free nations, in arms against a resurgent, organised barbarism, required appeals to give sanctuary to the first and chief victim of that barbarism. Two million Jews have already been exterminated. The world can no longer plead that the ghastly facts are unknown or unconfirmed.

There was in Jewish circles much resentment against an indifferent world which ignored the holocaust. There was also mounting anger against Jewish leaders who refused to speak out, apparently in fear of having their American patriotism questioned. These moods were exploited by a young Palestinian revisionist leader named Peter Bergson (Hillel Kook), who found a valuable ally in Ben Hecht, a successful playwright and Hollywood figure, with connections on Broadway and in Hollywood, as well as Madison Avenue. With the help of several devoted colleagues these two, initially operating on a small budget, organised a public relations campaign for the immediate establishment of a Jewish army which all but overshadowed the activities of the official Zionist movement. Bergson and Hecht received the support of the

* Silverberg, *If I Forget Thee, O Jerusalem*, pp. 187–9.

secretaries of the army and the navy, the chief justice, many congressmen. They put on mammoth pageants ('We will never die – A memorial to the two million Jewish dead of Europe'), and in general created a great deal of commotion. The direct political results of these activities were nil, but, for all its self-dramatisation, shrill language, and distortions, the Palestine Liberation Committee (which at various times also called itself 'Committee for a Jewish Army' and 'Emergency Committee to save the Jewish people of Europe') helped at this stage to stir up American-Jewish awareness of the extent of the catastrophe.

There was the risk that the Zionist organisation would be outflanked by the revisionists, but a much more formidable danger facing American Zionism was the lack of unity among the various Jewish bodies. The Zionists had agreed among themselves on the Biltmore formula, but they understood – and none better than Weizmann and Ben Gurion – that they would be able to exert real political influence in Washington only if they succeeded in gaining allies. It was not too difficult to win over the powerful Bnai Brith, headed at the time by Henry Monsky, a Zionist; the American Jewish Committee, on the other hand, was much less willing to give political support. Ben Gurion had reached agreement with Maurice Wertheim, then president of the American Jewish Committee, to act in common for maintaining Jewish rights in Palestine. But the AJC was in no circumstances willing to subscribe to the Biltmore formula, and Judge Proskauer, Wertheim's successor, showed no enthusiasm for any common action.

After much bickering and protracted negotiations, the various Jewish bodies agreed to convene a representative American Jewish conference in New York in 1943. Among the 502 delegates at this meeting the Zionists had a large majority, but they had agreed beforehand on a moderate approach, with the stress on the elements common to all Jewish groups rather than the divisive features. For that reason it was decided not to raise the issue of Jewish statehood but to concentrate instead on rescue operations. This gentlemen's agreement was broken by Rabbi Silver, who was not scheduled to speak but who decided nevertheless to make the most of the occasion. In a fiery speech he asserted that to refrain from expressing their convictions was to show neither statesmanship nor vision, neither courage nor faith: 'We cannot truly rescue the Jews of Europe unless we have free immigration into Palestine. We cannot have free immigration into Palestine unless our political rights are recognised there. Our political rights cannot be recognised unless our historic connection with the country is acknowledged and our right to rebuild our national home is reaffirmed. These are inseparable links in the chain. The whole chain breaks if one of the links is missing.'*

With this speech Rabbi Silver staked his claim to the leadership of American Zionism. It was received with thunderous cheers. Many wept, and at the end of the conference a resolution submitted by Silver was adopted by 497 votes against four. The political effect of the performance was problematical, for as a result the AJC withdrew from the united front and much effort had to be spent in later years to restore unity of action.

Rabbi Silver's militant tactics caused division even within the Zionist ranks. He did not get along well with the Washington office of the Jewish Agency, headed by Nahum Goldmann and Louis Lipsky, which had been established in May 1943. There were constant disputes about prerogatives and the division of labour. He quarrelled with Stephen Wise in 1944 and was forced to resign in late 1944 for having by his impetuosity brought a major diplomatic defeat on the Zionist cause. Silver was a Republican, whereas Wise, a lifelong Democrat, had advised the Zionist movement to put its trust in Roosevelt's goodwill. Silver believed in a bi-partisan approach, distrusted 'quiet diplomacy', and was firmly convinced of the wisdom of the maxim: 'Put not your trust in princes'. Silver pressed for bringing a pro-Zionist resolution to Congress without the approval of the president and the State Department. The resolution was defeated and Silver had to resign, but since he had such strong support among the Zionist rank and file he was back in office by July 1945.

Despite the many activities of American Zionism, despite the sound and fury of Bergson and Hecht, the results achieved during the war years were meagre. Roosevelt and his administration had the confidence and the warm support of the overwhelming majority of American Jewry. He was the champion of the common man; a good many Jews were appointed to public office during his presidency. After his death a poem appeared in the Zionist *New Palestine*:

> He was our friend when friends were few indeed
> He raised his voice – when few his voice would heed
> To stir the conscience of the world, to plead
> That ancient wrongs be righted and our people freed.†

* Quoted in *ibid.*, p. 228; Yeshayahu Vinograd, *Abba Hillel Silver*, Tel Aviv, 1957, p. 140 *et seq.*

† Quoted in Schechtman, *The United States and the Jewish State Movement*, p. 94.

Yet on the two most vital issues, on Palestine and the admission of refugees, Roosevelt said little and did less. His conduct was anything but unequivocal. By comparison with American policy on Palestine, the British record was, as one historian has put it, one of almost Buchmanite honesty and straightforwardness. David Niles, who was assistant to Roosevelt and later on to Truman, wrote that he seriously doubted whether Israel would have come into existence if Roosevelt had lived. Roosevelt was a consummate politician. He knew that a determined effort on behalf of the Jews would have reaped few tangible rewards, for the Jewish vote was in any case his. At the same time it would have caused a great many difficulties and complications both at home and abroad. Roosevelt's attitude towards the Jews was certainly not unfriendly, he was simply unwilling to go out of his way to help them. There was in him nothing like the vision and the moral conviction which had motivated men like Balfour or Lloyd George. If even a confirmed Zionist like Churchill claimed that nothing could be done for Zionism during the war there was no reason to expect support from an American president who had no firm convictions on the subject.

Roosevelt was at his most charming when he saw Weizmann in June 1943 and proposed a Jewish-Arab conference at some future date, possibly in his and Churchill's presence – as if such a meeting would have served any useful purpose. He authorised Wise and Silver in March 1944 to announce that the American government had never given its approval to the White Paper. He declared that when a decision was reached in the future, justice would be done to those who sought a Jewish national home, for which the American government and people had always had the deepest sympathy. Yet in his communications with Arab rulers at the same time, assurances were given that the president did not really mean what he said. When Sir John Singleton, a member of the Anglo-American Commission of Inquiry of 1946, saw the State Department files, he commented that Britain had not been the only power to promise the same thing to two different groups.*

A good deal of effort was put into a bi-partisan resolution to be submitted to Congress expressing clear support for Zionist aims. It was tabled by representatives Wright and Compton, and Senators Wagner and Taft. It proposed that the doors of Palestine should be opened and full opportunity be given for colonisation 'so that the Jewish people may ultimately reconstitute Palestine as a free and democratic Jewish

---

* *Ibid.*, p. 242.

commonwealth'. But the initiative soon ran into trouble: anti-Zionist Jewish groups opposed it, as did Arab representatives. Above all, the State Department and the army registered their objections. General Marshall, the chief of staff, announced that he could not be responsible for the military complications in the Moslem world if the resolution were passed. Cordell Hull, secretary of state, said that it might disrupt negotiations with Saudi Arabia concerning the building of an oil pipeline. Hull suggested that the president himself should intervene if there was a real danger that the resolution would be adopted.*

The legislative decided to postpone hearings on the resolution for reasons of military expediency. Seven months later, the secretary of war informed Senator Taft that the military considerations which had led to his department's veto were no longer so strong as before and that the issue should now be judged on its political merits. But the president and the State Department were still opposed, and Rabbi Silver's attempt to circumvent them ended in failure. A third attempt to push the resolution through was made in October 1945 and succeeded (for what it was worth). President Truman, who had initially favoured it, withdrew his support when the Anglo-American Commission of Inquiry was set up and it was feared that the resolution might interfere with its work.

In 1944 the Zionists succeeded in having pro-Zionist planks inserted in the electoral platform of the two big parties. It made little impression on President Roosevelt: when Senator Wagner suggested to him that Jewish displaced persons should not be returned to their countries of origin but allowed to proceed to Palestine, the president replied that about a million Jews were willing to go to Palestine, but that seventy million Moslems were eager to cut their throats, and he wanted to prevent such a massacre.

Roosevelt's opposition was reinforced by his meeting with King Ibn Saud after the Yalta conference. He declared that he had learned more about the Jewish and Moslem problem in talking to the desert king for five minutes than in long exchanges of letters. Stephen Wise, as agitated as the other Jewish leaders about the absence of any reference to the Jewish tragedy in the president's attitude, registered a protest. Whereupon the president assured him that he still favoured unrestricted immigration into Palestine. But again messages went out to Arab leaders that the United States would not countenance any change in the status of Palestine which would be objectionable to the Arabs.

* *Ibid.*, p. 239 *et seq*; Schechtman, *The United States and the Jewish State Movement*, p. 74 *et seq.*

The Zionists clearly were not very successful in their attempts to win Roosevelt for their cause, and it is tempting to speculate how the president, had he lived longer, would have retained the friendship of both Jews and Arabs. The Zionists managed to create a climate of opinion favourable to Zionism among legislators, church dignitaries, journalists and the public in general. The fate of European Jewry aroused sympathy among non-Jews, the efforts of a pioneering community in Palestine appealed to many Americans. But once the Zionists came up against the State Department, the Pentagon, and the White House, they faced interests and forces superior to their own, and references to the tragedy of the Jewish people did not cut much ice. The president himself, a curious mixture of patrician and popular tribune, of naïvety and sophistication, of honesty and duplicity, clearly regarded the whole issue as a minor nuisance.

The last stage

In Palestine during the latter part of the war things were going from bad to worse. Twenty members of the Stern gang escaped from Latrun prison camp, their leader having been shot by British police in a raid in February 1942. They carried out bank robberies and other acts of terror on a small scale. The highlights of their activities were the attempt to kill the high commissioner, Sir Harold MacMichael, in the course of which his *aide-de-camp* was seriously injured, and the murder of Lord Moyne in Cairo by two of their members. The Zionist authorities cooperated with the British police in rounding up the terrorists, whom they regarded as a menace not so much to British rule as to the Jewish community. The ultra-patriotism of the Stern gang had manifested itself even earlier in totally indefensible actions, such as their attempts in 1941 to contact German emissaries in Beirut in order to establish a common anti-British liberation front.

IZL, which decided in winter 1943–4 to renew its anti-British activities, was a problem of a different order. During the early part of the war it had participated in the war effort. Several of its leading members had been killed in special operations undertaken on behalf of the British army command. By late 1943 the new leadership of IZL thought the time was ripe for resuming its attacks on the British. The danger of a German invasion had faded, and the British authorities continued to carry out the White Paper policy. IZL attacked the Palestine broadcasting station at Ramalla and various police stations in the Tel Aviv and Haifa area during 1944. More than two hundred of its members were arrested and exiled to Eritrea. The British authorities demanded the full support of the Jewish Agency in stamping out terrorism. Such assistance was given, albeit with some reluctance. The IZL had the support not only of the revisionists, but also, to a certain extent, of members of the religious parties and the right-wing General Zionists. Even sections of the Zionist Left were so exasperated by the lack of any effective help for European Jewry on the part of the British that the terrorist acts were sometimes understood if not condoned in these circles. What induced the Zionist leaders to turn against the terrorists was the overriding political consideration: the dissidents were doing grave, perhaps irreparable harm to Zionist policy. How could a Zionist foreign policy be formulated and carried out if the terrorists refused to accept internal discipline, trying to dictate their own line to the elected leadership of the yishuv?

The acts of terror were defended by some as desperate attempts to draw attention to the plight of the Jewish people. The world had ignored countless Zionist memoranda and declarations. Perhaps it would be more responsive to bullets and bombs? It was a mistaken assumption: while the war was on no one was likely to be favourably impressed by the assassination of a few British policemen.

It was not, however, only among some hot-headed youngsters that frustration and despair was spreading. When Weizmann came to Palestine in November 1944 he sensed the prevailing bitterness of the yishuv, reflected in official policy statements: Ben Gurion declared that in contrast to Weizmann and the Hashomer Hatzair he was firmly convinced that a political solution could not wait and that the speedy transfer of the displaced persons to Palestine was a most urgent necessity.* Weizmann found it necessary to reiterate his belief in the coming of a Jewish state: 'I don't know when the Jewish state will come,' he said in Tel Aviv on 30 November, 'but it will not be long delayed.' A few days later he was uttering words of warning against forcing the issue; a time of transition was needed; five or six years were nothing in a period such as the world was then going through. But this was exactly what the yishuv no longer wanted to hear. To a people not very patient at the best of times, five or six years now seemed an eternity. Weizmann again argued that he did not believe in sudden 'jumps'. But how, the critics asked, was a basic change to be made if not by a sudden jump?

* *Jewish Telegraphic Agency Bulletin*, 3 December 1944.

Did he really believe that a Jewish state would somehow emerge as the result of patient negotiations, backstage diplomacy, hard work, persuasion and political pressure?

The psychological background to this mood was the profound horror caused by the murder of millions of Jews in Europe, and the absence of any effective reaction on the part of the civilised world. The liberal element in Zionism, the faith in humanity, suffered a blow from which it was not fully to recover. The appeals to fraternal help, to human solidarity, to which a former generation of Zionists was accustomed, no longer found a ready response. In the hour of their deepest peril few had stood by them, there had been pious platitudes and much hand-wringing but little real help. They had learned their lesson: no one could be trusted, it was everyone for himself.

The story of the holocaust has been told in great and dreadful detail. The first reliable reports of the mass murder were received in late 1942 from the representatives of the Jewish Agency in Switzerland. The State Department reacted by banning the transmission of such news through diplomatic channels from Switzerland. A conference in Bermuda in early 1943 called to deal with the refugee problem was a total failure. Even in July 1944, when the tide of war had finally turned and there seemed to be a real chance to save many thousands of Hungarian Jews, there was no willingness in the west to come to their help. Himmler and Eichmann had suggested that the dispatch of Jews to Auschwitz would be stopped in exchange for ten thousand trucks. But when Weizmann and Shertok saw Anthony Eden, the British foreign secretary, they were told that there must be no negotiation with the enemy. All they got from Churchill was a promise that those involved in the mass murder would be put to death after the war.

The Jewish Agency asked that the death camps at Auschwitz should be bombed if only, as Weizmann said, 'to give the lie to the oft-repeated assertions of Nazi spokesmen that the Allies are not really so displeased with the action of the Nazis in ridding Europe of the Jews'.* But the answer was again that this was impossible. On 1 September 1944 Weizmann was told by Eden that the Royal Air Force had rejected the request for technical reasons. Similar attempts by Dr Goldmann in Washington, and by American officials such as John Pehle of the War Refugee Board, were equally unsuccessful. The answer of John McCloy, assistant secretary of the army, deserves to be quoted:

---

* Quoted in Eban, 'Tragedy and Triumph', p. 273.

After a study it became apparent that such an operation could be executed only by diversion of considerable air support essential to the success of our forces now engaged in decisive operations elsewhere and would in any case be of such doubtful efficacy that it would not warrant the use of our resources. There has been considerable opinion to the effect that such an effort, even if practicable, might provoke more vindictive action by the Germans.

It remained the secret of the War Department what more vindictive action than Auschwitz could have been expected.*

What shocked the Jews so much was not that the rescue operations were ineffective. It might have been possible to save more Hungarian Jews and to delay the process of extermination by direct air attacks. The oilfields of Ploesti in Rumania, equally distant from London, had been bombed despite technical difficulties. Whether these measures would have served their purpose is not at all certain. Once Hitler had set his mind on exterminating European Jewry, once the Nazi machinery was set in motion, rescue efforts could not radically affect the situation. The only effective way to rescue Jews was to defeat Nazism as quickly as possible. But for the allied victory Palestinian Jewry too would have been doomed. Zionism had no panacea for a threat of this magnitude. All this is true, but it does not explain, let alone justify, the absence of any serious attempt to help the Jews in their hour of mortal danger. There was a wall of indifference which shut off even the narrowest path of escape. The feeling among the survivors was that in their own country, in the case of a Nazi victory, they would have gone down fighting, not been led to the slaughter like cattle. It was this widespread mood which gave Zionism a tremendous impetus at the end of the war.

The extent of the Jewish catastrophe became fully known during 1944. But it was only in the last months of the war, when the first extermination camps fell into allied hands, that the full significance of the disaster was realised. Up to that time there had been a lingering belief that the news about genocide had perhaps been exaggerated, that more Jews had survived than originally assumed. By April 1945 there were no longer any doubts. Of more than three million Jews in Poland, fewer than a hundred thousand had survived; of 500,000 German Jews – 12,000. Czechoslovakia once had a Jewish community of more than 300,000, of whom about 40,000 were still alive. Of 130,000 Dutch Jews some 20,000 still existed, of 90,000 Belgian Jews – 25,000; of 75,000 Greek Jews – 10,000. The only countries where the losses were relatively lighter were Rumania (320,000) and Hungary (200,000), but there too

* Feingold, *The Politics of Rescue*, p. 257.

the Jewish community had been more than twice those sizes before the war. It is estimated, though exact figures could not be obtained, that the Jewish population of the Soviet Union was halved as the result of Nazi mass killings. In a few countries, in Bulgaria, Italy and Denmark, the majority had survived, either because the local authorities had protected them or because of certain fortunate local circumstances. But these were countries with small Jewish communities; the big concentrations had disappeared. Roughly speaking, out of every seven Jews living in Europe, six had been killed during the war.

In the 1920s there had been widely read novels describing the exodus of Jews from Vienna and Berlin. The authors of these works of political science fiction had independently reached the conclusion that these two great capitals were not able to manage without the Jews and that eventually they had to implore them to return. The first part of the prediction had come true. In Vienna, once a community of 180,000, two hundred Jews had survived with the knowledge of the Nazis; eight hundred, as it later appeared, had been in hiding and lived to see the day of deliverance; 2,500 elderly people returned from the Terezin show camp. This was the total that remained of a community that had once helped to make Vienna one of the great capitals of the world. Hitler had lived in Vienna as a young man. It was there that he had become an antisemite, and the Viennese Jews were persecuted with special ferocity. Nor was it a matter of surprise that hardly a Jew survived in the capital of the Reich. But the Nazi bureaucratic machinery worked relentlessly everywhere: Hitler had never been to Greece and had no particular grudge against the Jews of Salonika. Nevertheless, of the 56,000 in that city, only 2,000 were alive when the war ended.

Of the remnant of European Jewry many were refugees from their native lands. Tens of thousands of Polish Jews had found temporary shelter in the Soviet Union but did not want to remain there, nor did they intend to settle in Poland. Switzerland had given refuge to 26,000, Sweden to 13,000, Belgium to 8,000. Britain had absorbed some 50,000 altogether and many had found shelter in France. The smaller European countries were eager to get rid of the aliens, but where were they to go? Few of them were ready to start life afresh in Germany, or indeed anywhere on a continent which had become the slaughterhouse of their families and their people.

As a result of the holocaust, the idea of the Jewish state seemed to have lost its historical *raison d'être*. Herzl and Nordau had thought of the Jewish state as a haven for the persecuted European Jews; Jabotinsky had written about the 'objective' Jewish question; the Biltmore programme had been based on the assumption that millions of Jews would survive the war. The prophets of Zionism had anticipated persecution and expulsion but not the solution of the Jewish question by mass murder. As the war ended Zionism seemed to be at the end of its tether.

There were victory celebrations on VE day in Jerusalem, Tel Aviv and Haifa, as in most European cities. The shops had sold out all flags and no material for banners could be had. A flag with black borders was flown in Tel Aviv in memory of those who had been killed. Chief Rabbis Herzog and Uziel declared a day of thanksgiving, on which psalms 100 and 118 were to be read, as well as a special prayer – that wisdom, strength and courage might be given to the rulers of the world to restore the chosen people to their freedom, and peace in the Holy Land. A hundred thousand people converged on the streets of Tel Aviv and shouted 'Open the gates of Palestine'. In the night of this rejoicing and thanksgiving Ben Gurion noted in his diary: 'Rejoice not, o Israel, for joy, like other peoples' (Hosea 9, 1).*

The war in Europe was over, the world had been liberated from Nazi terror and oppression, peace had returned. For the Jewish people it was the peace of the graveyard. Yet paradoxically, at the very time when the 'objective Jewish question' had all but disappeared, the issue of a Jewish state became more topical than ever before. The countries around Palestine were all well advanced on the road to independence. The Jewish community in Palestine had come of age during the war; it was now to all intents and purposes a state within a state, with its own schools and public services, even an army of its own. The victors in the war had an uneasy conscience, as the stark tragedy of the Jewish people unfolded before their eyes. It was only now that the question was asked whether enough had been done to help them and what could be done for the survivors.

Before the war Zionism had been a minority movement – sometimes a small minority – in the Jewish community. But in 1945 even its former enemies rallied to the blue and white flag. Typical of this conversion was the May Day 1945 speech in Manchester, by the new chairman of the British Labour Party, Harold Laski. He felt like the prodigal son coming home, Professor Laski said; he did not believe in the Jewish religion and was still a Marxist; before the war he had been an advocate

---

* D. Ben Gurion, *Medinat Israel hamekhudeshet*, vol. 1, Tel Aviv, 1969, p. 65.

of assimilation and had thought that to lose their identity was the best service which the Jews could do for mankind. But now he was firmly and utterly convinced of the necessity of the rebirth of the Jewish nation in Palestine. They were all Zionists now.

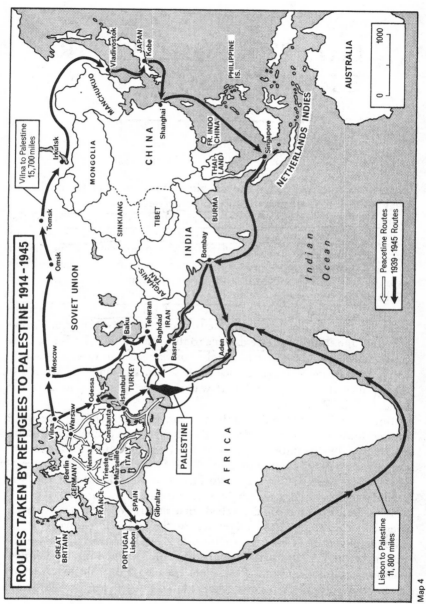

ROUTES TAKEN BY REFUGEES TO PALESTINE 1914–1945

Vilna to Palestine 15,700 miles

Lisbon to Palestine 11,800 miles

PALESTINE

Peacetime Routes
1939 · 1945 Routes

0   1000

GREAT BRITAIN
GERMANY
Berlin
Vienna
FRANCE
Trieste
ITALY
Marseille
SPAIN
Gibraltar
PORTUGAL
Lisbon
Warsaw
Vilna
Odessa
Constanta
Istanbul
TURKEY

SOVIET UNION
Moscow
Baku
Omsk
Tomsk
Irkutsk
MONGOLIA
MANCHUKUO
Vladivostok
JAPAN
Kobe

SINKIANG
TIBET
CHINA
Shanghai

AFGHANIS.
IRAN
Teheran
Baghdad
Basra
Aden
Baku

BURMA
THAI-LAND
FR. INDO CHINA
INDIA
Bombay

PHILIPPINE IS.

NETHERLANDS INDIES
Singapore

AUSTRALIA

AFRICA

Indian Ocean

Map 4

THE STRUGGLE FOR
THE JEWISH STATE

Three years after the end of the war the state of Israel came into being. They were years of mounting tension between the Palestine Jewish community and the British government, which eventually reached the conclusion that abandoning the mandate was the only course of action open to it. In the interval there were further commissions of enquiry, of complex blueprints for a solution, of arrests and acts of terror, ending with the British withdrawal and bitter fighting between Jews and Arabs. The birth of the Jewish state was the fulfilment of the Zionist dream. But it had taken the destruction of European Jewry to realise this aim. Zionism had not been able to prevent the catastrophe. On the contrary, the state owed its existence to the disaster. The Jewish Agency continued to exist, there were Zionist conferences and even a full-scale congress. But the real significance of these years is that they witnessed the birth of the state of Israel. It was the most critical period in the history of the Zionist movement.

Immediately after the end of the war, on 27 May 1945, the executive of the Jewish Agency petitioned the British government to declare Palestine a Jewish state. It also submitted a programme for a free and democratic Jewish commonwealth to the San Francisco conference of the United Nations. The appeal to Britain was no doubt made for the record; there was not the slightest chance of a favourable response. Anglo-Zionist relations had reached their nadir. Weizmann, as already mentioned, contemplated resignation at the time. The advent of the Labour government was hailed by one Zionist journal as an epoch-making event of world-wide significance which opened up hopeful new perspectives for Zionism.* Past experience with British governments should have taught the Zionist leaders to be cautious; there was always

---

* *Jewish Frontier*, August 1945.

a lag between promise and performance. With Labour in power the distance between the two was particularly striking, simply because the Tories promised less in the first place.

The outlook in Washington was equally uncertain: Rabbi Wise saw Harry Truman on 20 April 1945, in his second week as the new president. Truman had been forewarned by Stettinius, the secretary of state, that the Zionists would try to get some commitment from him. With unconscious irony Truman assured Wise that he would carry out Roosevelt's policy. He was totally unaware of the bundle of incoherent and contradictory promises he had inherited. Truman was by no means a Zionist. In early August he said at a press conference that he had no desire to send half a million American soldiers to Palestine to make peace in that country. A few weeks later he received the report of Earl Harrison, whom he had sent to Europe on a fact-finding tour, concerning the refugee situation. The report said that the situation was intolerable and that the Jewish refugees in the camps wanted to be evacuated to Palestine. One week later Truman sent a copy of the report to Prime Minister Attlee with the suggestion that one hundred thousand immigration certificates should be granted forthwith.

This move aroused a great deal of indignation among some leading members of the Labour government, and in none more than in Ernest Bevin, the new foreign secretary. Bevin, like his chief Attlee, was neither pro- nor anti-Jewish. He simply believed that the Jews, unlike the Arabs, were not a nation and did not therefore need a state of their own. The Jews, as he and Attlee saw it – and as the Foreign Office had told him – were ungrateful, devious and cantankerous. The Arabs, on the other hand, were a simple, straightforward people with a deep liking for Britain.* When Weizmann went to see Bevin on 10 October 1945, he had a frosty reception, and in a statement on 13 November the foreign secretary announced that the White Paper policy would be continued. He had not the slightest intention of carrying out the Labour Party plank on Palestine; even the demand for the hundred thousand certificates was resented. He implied that Truman had been impelled by electoral considerations (the New York Jewish vote) to support the Zionist demand. Bevin's stubbornness, his unwillingness to make any compromise even with regard to the displaced persons, put him on a collision course, not only with the Jewish community of Palestine, but with Americans and others to whom such behaviour seemed unreasonable.

* R.H.S.Crossman, *A Nation Reborn*, London, 1960, p. 70.

Such are the ironies of history that, as far as the birth of the state of Israel is concerned, Bevin's obstinate adherence to the policy recommended by his Foreign Office aides (such as Harold Beeley) played an important, probably essential role. It is quite likely that had the Foreign Office gone to Hugh Dalton or someone else less stubborn, the demand for the hundred thousand certificates (as well as some other urgent Zionist demands) might have been met. The problem might then have lost its acute character and the unendurable tension and thus the need for the state of Israel would have lessened.* The Middle East policy of Bevin and his advisers was based on the assumption that the Arab states were essentially pro-western and, if properly handled, factors of stability in the area, whereas Zionism meant the intrusion of an alien and disruptive element which was bound to weaken the western position.

Palestinian Jewry, naturally, was not interested in calculations of imperial interest and global strategy. They had heard the arguments too often and felt that it was always at their expense. The war effort had always been invoked to explain the impossibility of diverting resources to save Jewish lives. But the war was now over, and even before Bevin's statement in November there had been talk in Jerusalem, and not only talk, about armed resistance. At a meeting of the Inner Zionist Council in October, Dr Sneh (formerly Kleinbaum), then commander-in-chief of the Hagana, said that the Zionist movement had never faced a more serious crisis; it had to show the British that they would have to pay a high price for pursuing the White Paper policy. At the same meeting Rabbi Berlin said: 'Soon perhaps we may all have to go underground.'† It is difficult to imagine such a conspicuous figure as Rabbi Berlin in illegal conditions. In October also, the Palmach, the Hagana elite corps created during the war, sank three small naval craft which had been operating against ships carrying illegal immigrants, and blew up railway lines in fifty different places. In the same month a clandestine radio station, 'Voice of Israel', began broadcasting.

There had been hints concerning armed resistance even earlier, at the World Zionist Conference in London in September, the first international Zionist meeting after the war. While Weizmann again predicted that the road ahead would be long and arduous, the Americans claimed that it was a question of 'now or never'. 'If our rights are denied to us', Rabbi Silver said, 'we shall fight for them with

* Eban, 'Tragedy and Triumph', p. 280.
† Central Zionist Archives. File S 5/351. Meeting of 7 October 1945.

whatever weapons are at our disposal.' He told Weizmann to demand not certificates but a Jewish state, and suggested that on occasion it might be the height of statesmanship to be unstatesmanlike. Ben Gurion, too, advocated more intense pressure to bring a Jewish state into being. There was the usual wrangling in committee – Mizrahi once again wanted more power and announced that it would resign, but at the last moment withdrew the threat. The plenary meetings showed that there was a broad consensus, and resolutions were passed endorsing the demand for a Jewish state which 'will be based upon full equality of rights of all inhabitants without distinction of religion or race in the political, civic, religious and national domains and without domination or subjection.'*

The constitutional status of the conference and the legal validity of its resolutions were doubtful, but since there had been no time to call a congress, it simply assumed the prerogatives of a congress. A new executive was elected, consisting of Weizmann, Ben Gurion, Shertok, Kaplan, Berl Locker, Dobkin, Nahum Goldmann, Lipsky; Rabbis Wise, Silver, and Goldstein; Rose Halprin, Chaim Greenberg; and Rabbi Fishman and Moshe Shapira of the Mizrahi.

The new executive immediately began to negotiate with the British, but the results were disappointing. They were offered a monthly immigration schedule of fifteen hundred from which, however, illegal immigration was to be deducted. As a result of these restrictions, immigration to Palestine in 1945 was in fact slightly less (13,100) than in the previous year (14,500). This, of course, was totally unacceptable to the Zionists. When Bevin charged the Jews with trying too hard to get to the head of the queue, Weizmann asked whether it was too much if, after the slaughter of six million, those who remained sought the shelter of a Jewish homeland and asked for a hundred thousand certificates.†

If the British were refusing immigration certificates, the Jews had made up their minds to come anyway. There were tens of thousands of them in the camps. At the end of the war some fifty thousand, both displaced persons and local residents, found themselves in Germany and Austria. But the stream from the east, mainly from Poland, continued. There were ups and downs in this steady migration. After the pogrom in Kielce (Poland) in which forty-one Jews were killed, the influx increased considerably. It is estimated that altogether some

* *The World Zionist Conference*, London, 1945, p. 6.
† Speech in Atlantic City, *JTA Bulletin*, 23 November 1945.

300,000 Jews passed at one time or another through the camps of Austria, Germany and Italy.*

The initial impetus for immigration to Palestine was spontaneous, or, to be precise, originated among those former members of Zionist youth movements from eastern Europe who had survived and were now the main organisers in the DP camps. They were joined later by emissaries from Palestine and the Jewish brigade. The British government claimed that the wish to go to Israel was the result of the work of Zionist propagandists. Richard Crossman, the Labour MP who had visited the camps as a member of the Anglo-American commission in early 1946, wrote that the Jews would have opted for Palestine even if not a single foreign emissary or a trace of Zionist propaganda had reached the camps. This, no doubt, was a correct account of the situation during the first year or two. Later the mood began to change, partly as a result of the demoralisation which was the inevitable result of the enforced stay in the camps. But it is also a fact that many survivors wanted above all a quiet life after all they had been through, and Palestine in 1947 hardly promised this. An American Jewish adviser to the military government wrote in late 1947 that the emergence of the Jewish state was not substantially affecting the *Drang nach Amerika*. Given equal opportunity to go to Palestine or to the States, 50 per cent would join the unfortunate *Galut* Jews in America.†

Illegal immigration had never ceased altogether and Hagana began to organise it after the end of the war on a much bigger scale than before. Refugee ships appeared regularly off the shores of Palestine. A few succeeded in breaking the blockade, but most were apprehended and their passengers detained – first in Palestine, and from summer 1946 on in camps in Cyprus. The story of illegal immigration culminated in the case of the *President Garfield*, an old 4,000-ton Chesepeake Bay steamer which, acquired by Hagana and renamed *Exodus 1947*, carried some 4,200 illegal immigrants. To discourage any further exploits London decided to turn the ship back to Port de Bove near Marseilles. After the passengers refused to disembark there, they were forcibly disembarked at Hamburg. There were violent scenes and some casualties on this as on previous similar occasions. The British government claimed, correctly no doubt, that in organising illegal immigration into Palestine the Jews had defied the law of Palestine and of other countries from which the traffic had been carried on: 'It is no answer to this to

---

* Yehuda Bauer, *Flight and Rescue: Brichah*, New York, 1970, p. 320.
† *Ibid.*, pp. 317–18.

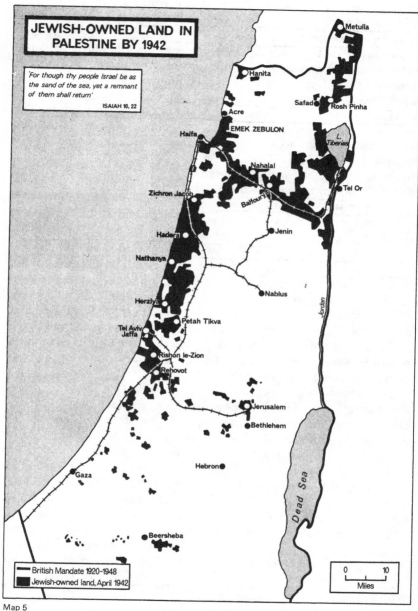

JEWISH-OWNED LAND IN PALESTINE BY 1942

'For though thy people Israel be as the sand of the sea, yet a remnant of them shall return'

ISAIAH 10, 22

Metulla

Hanita

Safad ● Rosh Pinha

Acre

EMEK ZEBULON

Haifa

L. Tiberias

Nahalal

Tel Or

Zichron Jacob

Balfour

Jenin

Hadera

Nathanya

Nablus

Herzlya

Petah Tikva

Tel Aviv
Jaffa

Rishon le-Zion

Rehovot

Jerusalem

Bethlehem

Hebron ●

Gaza

Dead Sea

Jordan

Beersheba

—— British Mandate 1920-1948
■ Jewish-owned land, April 1942

0 ——— 10
Miles

Map 5

say that the law is unacceptable or that it is illegal, when it is not.'*
Legal arguments were not, however, likely to persuade those who felt
that it was an outrage to compel Jewish refugees to return to Germany.
In answer to Truman's repeated demands for a hundred thousand
certificates, and also, no doubt, to gain time, the Labour government
proposed on 19 October 1945 the establishment of an Anglo-American
committee to investigate the wider issue of Jewish refugees and to make
recommendations for both an interim and a permanent solution. The
offer was received with less than enthusiasm by Jews and Arabs, who
agreed that they had seen enough commissions and that the issues were
already clear enough. Truman, on the other hand, accepted the
proposal after he had succeeded in more strictly defining its scope and
timetable: it was to examine the suitability of Palestine as a shelter for
the refugees and to have its report ready within four months.

Truman had grown weary of the constant pressure exerted by the
American Zionists. Palestine is not ours to dispose of, he wrote at the
time; to impose a political structure on the Middle East could only
result in conflict. On the eve of the final approval by Congress of the
Taft-Wagner act, Truman announced that he no longer believed in
resolutions aiming at the creation of a Jewish state. This was a severe
blow to the American Zionists, who believed they had at long last
achieved a decisive breakthrough. Bevin, on the other hand, was elated
and promised the committee that, provided it turned in a unanimous
report, he would do everything in his power to put it into effect. He was
soon to regret this rash promise.

The members of the committee went first to the German camps, then
to the Middle East. They listened to many witnesses, the most impressive
of whom was, as usual, Weizmann, both for his eloquence and his
candour. There is no absolute justice, he said, only rough human
justice. Injustice there was bound to be. But the Arabs had already two
kingdoms and four republics. What was the number of their casualties
in the Second World War? They had, moreover, a foolproof guarantee
with regard to the fate of their fellow Palestinians in the Jewish state,
for Israel was bound to remain an island in the Arab sea.†

The committee's report was published on 1 May 1946: it made ten
recommendations, and gave a brief survey of the situation of the Jews
in Europe and a note on the state of affairs in Palestine. It suggested

* *Supplementary Memorandum by the Government of Palestine including Notes on Evidence Given to
UNSCOP up to July 12, 1947*, p. 34.
† Ch.Weizmann, *The Right to Survive*, Jerusalem, 1946.

that since the attempt to establish either one Palestinian state, or Arab and Jewish states in Palestine, would result in civil strife which might threaten the peace of the world, the only practical solution was the continuation of the mandate, for the time being by the British and ultimately under the United Nations. The Jews were to get their hundred thousand certificates, and the White Paper and land transfer regulations were to be rescinded.*

The Arabs flatly rejected the report and declared a general strike. The Jews were happy with some of its provisions, bitterly opposed to others. Ben Gurion regarded it as a thinly disguised, more cleverly compiled edition of the White Paper, and the American Zionist leaders rejected it for its denial of Jewish rights and aspirations.† Other Zionist leaders took a more conciliatory line, believing that with all its weaknesses the report could serve as a basis for discussion and negotiations. Truman said, *inter alia*, that he was happy that the request for the hundred thousand certificates had been endorsed and the abrogation of the White Paper suggested.

The British government, however, was most unhappy about the outcome. Crossman was told by the leaders of his party that he had let them down. In a statement on 1 May 1946 Attlee said that 'the report must be considered as a whole in all its implications', which meant in less diplomatic language that he did not like any part of it. Its execution would entail very heavy immediate and long-term commitments. When pressed for details Bevin said, a few weeks later, that it would involve the dispatch of another division and £200 million to implement the admission of the hundred thousand. And he returned to his favoured theme: the Americans were putting so much pressure on London because they did not want too many Jews in New York. If Truman was annoyed by Zionist pressure, Bevin's constant innuendoes did not improve his mood, especially since he was working at this very time for a liberalisation of American immigration laws. The president continued to ask the British for action on the hundred thousand certificates, and the Labour government continued to stall.

In Jerusalem, counsels were divided. Weizmann said at a meeting of the Inner Zionist Council that it had perhaps been a mistake to ask for a Jewish state: 'We are always trying to push too hard.'‡ But the

---

* Cmd. 6808, London, 1946, p. 11.

† David Horowitz, *State in the Making*, New York, 1953, p. 94; Silverberg, *If I Forget Thee, O Jerusalem*, p. 307.

‡ Central Zionist Archives, Meeting of 21 May 1946, File S 25/1804.

activists had the upper hand; on 16 June 1946 there was another large-scale Hagana action in which nine bridges (including the Allenby bridge across the Jordan) were blown up and the Haifa railway workshops damaged. The British retaliated on 29 June by ordering the arrest of the members of the Zionist executive in Palestine as well as many other public figures. The Jewish Agency offices were sealed off and public buildings and settlements were searched.

British-Zionist relations were reaching their lowest ebb when the Irgun blew up the King David Hotel in Jerusalem, with the loss of almost one hundred lives, British, Jews and Arabs. The British imposed a three-day curfew on Tel Aviv, during which 787 men and women were arrested. The terrorist leaders were not among them. General Barker, commanding the British forces, issued an order to his officers which said that he would punish the Jews in a way this race disliked most of all, 'by striking at their pocket and showing our contempt for them'. This declaration in its turn provoked a great outcry and there were further acts of violence.

The British were charged by the Zionists with using Nazi methods and trying to destroy the Jewish national home. There were acts of torture and even murder, but on the whole the British troops behaved with considerable restraint in the face of frequent physical attacks and much abuse. It is not difficult to imagine how American or Russian or most other troops would have reacted in a similar situation. It was not the fault of the individual British officer or private if he had to carry out the conflicting orders of a government which, facing an impossible task, no longer had a policy. There was only a vague hope that by procrastinating, hanging on to Palestine, the problem might become more tractable. While a campaign for non-cooperation got under way in Palestine, Weizmann appealed to London on 9 July to act quickly. Shortly after, the Jewish Agency building was handed back, and several hundred detainees, including the aged Rabbi Fishman of the Jewish Agency executive, were released. But Shertok and the other members of the executive remained in detention for several more months.

Ben Gurion and Sneh, who had evaded arrest, convened an executive meeting in Paris on 1 August 1946. Weizmann was ill at the time and could not be present; nor did Rabbi Silver attend. The mood was one of almost unmitigated gloom. Rabbis Wise and Fishman had second thoughts about Biltmore and partition. Perhaps they should have accepted the Peel Report at the time after all? Even the irrepressible Rabbi Silver wrote that it was a terrible situation, with the Americans inactive and 'all the cards stacked against us'.* In a vote taken on 5 August, with Ben Gurion and Sneh abstaining, a resolution was adopted which marked a clear retreat from Biltmore: the Jewish Agency was willing to negotiate on the basis of a viable Jewish state in an adequate area of Palestine, rather than in the whole of western Palestine. Goldmann immediately returned to Washington and began to negotiate with the administration on the basis of this resolution.

Meanwhile a new project had appeared on the scene; it was discussed and rejected in record time. Details of the Morrison-Grady scheme were revealed in a debate in the House of Commons on 31 July and 1 August 1946. Less than two weeks later Attlee had word from Truman that the plan was unacceptable. It was essentially a Foreign Office document to which Herbert Morrison, one of the central figures in the Labour cabinet, had given his name. It had been discussed in London with a small American working party headed by Ambassador Grady. The scheme envisaged a division of Palestine into four areas (Arab and Jewish provinces, a district of Jerusalem, and a district of the Negev), with the central government (British) having exclusive authority on defence and foreign affairs, and with the high commissioner as the supreme arbiter of, *inter alia*, the extent of immigration. The scheme was not new; it had been submitted to the members of the Anglo-American committee who had been to Palestine earlier that year and had been rejected by most of them.

The concept of partition as defined by the Zionists at their Paris meeting seems to have appealed to the American administration, but there was no marked advance in Goldmann's talks in Washington. Nor did Weizmann make much headway when he resumed his contacts with Bevin in Paris. On the eve of the Day of Atonement (shortly before the New York elections) President Truman in a public statement reiterated his request for the hundred thousand certificates, for the liberalisation of America's immigration laws, and, for the first time, mentioned the idea of a 'viable Jewish state in an adequate area of Palestine' (the Paris formula) as something to which the American government could give its support.

This announcement was generally interpreted as the most pro-Zionist ever made by an American president. It angered Bevin, who found his pet theory about the influence of the New York Jews confirmed, outraged the Arabs, and provoked anger among the anti-Zionists in the American administration. Nor did the Zionists display

* Quoted in Bauer, *Flight and Rescue*, p. 256.

much enthusiasm either, since the statement was open to conflicting interpretations. The president did not define 'viable', but he probably meant a very small Jewish state, which would be unacceptable to the Zionists. Rabbi Silver probably had this danger in mind when, at the ZOA convention of 26 October, he attacked his old political enemies, Weizmann and Goldmann. He argued that the executive had no right to negotiate on partition without the approval of the Zionist congress.* A resolution was passed, stressing again the claim to the whole of mandatory Palestine.

These declarations had no practical results, and the next stage in this struggle for the future of Palestine opened at the twenty-second Zionist congress in Basle on 9 December 1946. The number of voters who had participated in the elections – 2,159,850 – was far larger than ever before.† It differed radically in its constitution from its predecessors; it was, as Tabenkin sadly noted, an 'English' not a 'Jewish' congress. More than 40 per cent of the votes had come from the United States, and the Americans had by far the largest delegation. The three left-wing parties – not united at the time – had 125 mandates; the General Zionists, equally torn by internal strife, 106; the Mizrahi 48; and the revisionists 36. The congress should have met in Palestine; Weizmann had been one of the few to express doubts whether this was feasible in the given political circumstances. Events, as so often, proved him right, but this did not make him any more popular. He was under fire from the very start in view of the failure of his 'pro-British orientation', but was determined to fight back. In his opening address he said that Zionism was a modern expression of the liberal ideal. Divorced from it, it lost all purpose and hope. He, too, was in favour of the immediate establishment of a Jewish state. But the acts of terrorism were abhorrent and barren of all advantage. Against the heroics of suicidal violence he urged the 'courage of endurance and the heroism of superhuman restraint'.‡ Massada, for all its heroism, had been a great disaster in Jewish history.

The counter-attack was led by Emanuel Neumann, a ZOA vice-president, who said that the conciliatory line was a costly experiment that had already failed. He opposed Zionist participation in the new London conference which the British government was about to initiate.

---

* Quoted in Silverberg, *If I Forget Thee, O Jerusalem*, p. 318.
† Some of the figures, such as 112,000 for Germany and 100,000 for Poland, look somewhat suspect.
‡ *HaKongress Hazioni ha 22. Din vekheshbon stenografi*, Jerusalem, n.d., p. 7 *et seq.*

(It should be noted in parenthesis that some of the bitterest conflicts in Zionist history concerned conferences or schemes which either never went beyond the planning stage or were doomed to fail soon after.) Neumann called for a more active struggle against the mandatory power. Diplomacy, he said, could succeed only if backed by force, by a resistance movement.* Goldmann, defending the policy of which he had been one of the main architects, said that if the deadlock had not been broken by the Paris initiative, America would have washed her hands of the whole affair and things would have further deteriorated: 'What we attained with our proposals was to bring America back into the picture.'†

The confrontation between 'activists' and 'moderates' reached its climax with Weizmann's answer to his critics. Speaking in Yiddish at the seventeenth session, he again condemned in the sharpest terms the terror, that 'cancer in the body politic of the yishuv', which would destroy it if it was not stamped out. He criticised Dr Sneh, who had advocated both armed struggle and a political reorientation. 'Sneh's arguments frighten me', Weizmann cried, and, pointing to Herzl's picture on the wall, he quoted Ahad Ha'am's old slogan: 'This is not the road'.‡ The American Zionists were the main target of Weizmann's speech: the eleven new settlements recently established in the Negev had a far greater weight than a hundred speeches about resistance, especially if these speeches were made in Washington and New York, whereas the resistance would be put up in Jerusalem and Tel Aviv. Neumann interrupted him and shouted 'Demagogue!', whereupon Weizmann, deeply offended, gave free rein to his fury:

I – a demagogue! I who have borne all the ills and travails of this movement. The person who flung this word in my face should know that in every house and every stable in Nahalal, in every workshop in Tel Aviv or Haifa, there is a drop of my blood. [Most delegates rose to their feet.] You know that I am telling you the truth. Some people don't like to hear it – but you will hear me. I warn you against bogus palliatives, against short-cuts, against false prophets, against facile generalisations, against distortion of historic facts. . . . If you think of bringing the redemption nearer by un-Jewish methods, if you lose faith in hard work and better days, then you commit idolatry and endanger what we have built. Would I had a tongue

* Ibid., p. 87.
† Ibid., p. 142 et seq.
‡ Ibid., p. 344. Sneh left the Zionist movement not long after and became a member of the Communist Party; his break with Moscow came only many years later and after countless disappointments.

of flame, the strength of prophets, to warn you against the paths of Babylon and Egypt. Zion shall be redeemed in Judgment – and not by any other means.*

It was one of the most dramatic scenes at a Zionist congress, but in political terms Weizmann's moving appeal was ineffectual. He received great applause, but the vote went against him. By a small majority (171–154) the congress rejected the proposal to attend the London talks, which was tantamount to a vote of no-confidence. Weizmann was not re-elected as president, and though out of respect to him the post was left vacant, this was the end of his career in the Zionist movement which he had served for more than fifty years. In his autobiography Weizmann bitterly notes that, as in the past, he had become the scapegoat for the sins of the British government, and since his critics knew that their assault on Westminster was bound to be ineffective, they turned their shafts against him.

It is easy to take issue with his critics for inconsistency and indeed demagogy. The crowning irony was that four weeks later the Zionist leaders went to the London talks after all, and that nothing of any consequence came of these negotiations. But Weizmann's position had become untenable irrespective of the vote of no-confidence. More and more Zionists had reached the conclusion that their cause could be advanced only against, not with Britain, and that Weizmann was no longer the right man to lead the movement in this new phase. The recourse to armed resistance was dangerous in both its foreign political and domestic implications, but in retrospect it may be seen as an essential element in the struggle for independence. The powers dealt with the Palestine problem as a matter of urgency not because of speeches made or resolutions adopted, but because it constituted a danger to peace. Armed resistance and illegal immigration helped to dramatise the state of emergency much more effectively than the patient, constructive work ('another settlement, another shed, another cow in Hadera') which for so many years under Weizmann's leadership had been Zionist policy.

The congress marks the midway passage between the end of the Second World War and the establishment of the state. In political terms it had been a failure. An English newspaper noted that Weizmann had been overthrown by a 'coalition of incompatibles' which included the revisionists and Mizrahi on the one hand, and left-wing labour on

* *Ibid.*, pp. 344–5.

the other.* The yishuv was disappointed: fifty-three long speeches and countless shorter interventions had not resulted in any clear and concrete policy decisions. American Zionism was deeply split as a result. Stephen Wise withdrew from office in the ZOA, which in his words had become a 'collection of personal hatreds, rancours and private ambitions'.

But for Weizmann's departure, the newly elected executive of the Jewish Agency and of the Zionist movement hardly differed from the previous one. The General Zionists received somewhat stronger representation; Eliahu Dobkin of Mapai became head of the organisation department; Moshe Shapira was made director of the department of immigration; and Fritz Bernstein, an old Dutch Zionist, was coopted as a full member. There was no change in the direction of political affairs.

The conference called by Bevin early in 1947 was a repeat performance for those who had been to St James' Palace eight years before. There were no new proposals to be discussed, nor, as in 1939, were there any direct meetings between Jews and Arabs. The latter expressed the view both privately and on occasion in public, that historical conflicts are always settled by force of arms and that one might as well have the struggle right away and get it over. The Zionist plan (partition) was unacceptable to the British, and of course to the Arabs. Bevin's attempt to save the conference through a modified version of the Morrison-Grady scheme was rejected by both sides. The main purpose of the London meeting was apparently to give Bevin a last opportunity to find some compromise solution. When it appeared that the Arab delegation was not only opposed to the idea of a Jewish state in principle, but rejected Jewish immigration and land sales under any circumstances, Bevin and his advisers lost interest in the proceedings. On 18 February 1947 it was announced in the House of Commons that the only course open to Britain was to submit the problem to the judgment of the United Nations, since it had no power under the terms of the mandate to award the country either to Jews or Arabs or to partition it between them. On 2 April the secretary-general of the United Nations was asked to arrange for a special session of the General Assembly on Palestine; it was held later that month.

The possibility that the Palestine issue might be referred to the United Nations had been considered by the Zionist leaders on various occasions. In a speech on 1 August 1946 Churchill had said that the 'one rightful, reasonable, simple and compulsive lever which we held was and is a

* *The Times*, 8 January 1947.

sincere readiness to lay our mandate at the feet of the UNO and thereafter to evacuate the country'. Nevertheless, when the decision was
announced, the Zionist reaction was one of 'scepticism and distaste'.*
Scepticism, because they suspected that Britain, banking on the east-
west stalemate in the United Nations, expected that no decision would
be reached in New York and that therefore the mandate would
continue. Such calculations may have influenced some British advisers,
but it is unlikely that this was the decisive factor. Both the British
government and public opinion were fed up with Palestine and ready
to accept almost any solution to relieve them of the burden. The
Zionists viewed the move to the UN with not a little apprehension
because they feared that their cause would not fare any better, and most
probably much worse, in Flushing Meadows and Lake Success than in
Whitehall.

Thus the centre of the political scene again shifted to New York, and
the Zionist executive, working against time, set out to win the support
of the nations, big and small, which were soon to decide the fate of
Palestine. It was an uphill task, above all because the American position
at this stage was not helpful. President Truman and his advisers were
firmly resolved not to give any lead to the United Nations but to wait
for the emergence of a consensus. Much to the surprise of the Zionists,
the Soviet attitude was much more positive. This first became evident
when the Jewish Agency asked to be permitted ('as a matter of simple
justice') to appear at the UN on behalf of the Jewish people, since the
Arabs were already represented there. They had the immediate support
of the Soviet delegation, and, on 15 May, Gromyko spoke not without
sympathy about the 'aspirations towards Palestine of a considerable
part of the Jewish people', of the calamities and sufferings they had
undergone during the last war ('which defy description'), and the grave
conditions in which the masses of the Jewish population found themselves after the war. He mentioned partition as one of several possible
solutions.†

This unexpected support continued throughout 1947 and led later
that year to the Soviet decision to vote for partition. Traditionally, the
Soviet attitude to Zionism had been extremely hostile, and since
Moscow reverted to its earlier position not long after the state of Israel
came into being, one can only conclude that the short-lived *rapproche-*

---

* Eban, 'Tragedy and Triumph', p. 295.
† The English text of the speech was distributed by the press department of the Soviet
Embassy in London; see *Zionist Review*, 23 May 1947.

ment came exactly at the right moment for the Zionists. Without it they would not have stood a chance. What then were the Soviet motives? It was the Soviet aim to diminish western influence in the eastern Mediterranean and, if possible, advance its own interests in the power vacuum that was bound to follow the western withdrawal. Ten years later Stalin's heirs were to pursue this policy in close collaboration with the radical forces which had come to power in the Arab world. But in 1947 Egypt was still ruled by King Faruq, and Iraq and Jordan by the Hashemites, régimes linked to Britain by many ties. In the circumstances a vote for the partition of Palestine must have seemed to most Soviet policy-makers a reasonable course of action.

On 15 May 1947 the General Assembly approved the establishment of a committee of eleven to investigate the Palestine question, to make proposals for a settlement, and to report back by September. None of the big powers was represented on this committee, which entered history under the name of UNSCOP. It consisted of delegates from Australia, Canada, Czechoslovakia, Guatemala, India, The Netherlands, Persia, Uruguay and Yugoslavia. Its chairman was Judge Sandstrom, a Swede, with Ralph Bunche representing the UN.

UNSCOP heard witnesses for three and a half months in America, Europe and Palestine, and toured DP camps and Arab and Jewish cities and rural settlements. Among the Zionist representatives the most effective was again Weizmann, appearing for once in an unofficial capacity. The committee was given a brief lecture on the nature of antisemitism: what are Poles? What are Frenchmen? The answer is obvious, Weizmann said; but if one asks who is a Jew, lengthy explanations are necessary, and these are always suspect. Why did the Jews insist so stubbornly on Palestine rather than some other country? It was no doubt the responsibility of Moses who had taken them to Palestine. Instead of the Jordan they might have had the Mississippi: 'But he chose to stop here. We are an ancient people with a long history and you cannot deny your history and begin afresh.'

When asked about the prospects of bi-nationalism, Moshe Shertok made the point that willingness to work together was the prerequisite for the existence of a bi-national state, but unfortunately it did not exist. A Jewish state was needed because Palestinian Jewry had come of age, to save the remnant of European Jewry, and to ensure the future of the Jewish people.* Questioned by Sandstrom, Ben Gurion said that

* *The Jewish Evidence before the United Nations Special Commission on Palestine*, Jerusalem, 1947, pp. 25–6.

he foresaw the settlement of the first million Jews in a Jewish state in the shortest possible time – three to four years. In the period of transition he envisaged a régime of diarchy with the mandatory power, as in India. Ben Gurion rejected the idea of parity, which would result in permanent deadlock on all vital issues such as immigration. Instead of an Arab-Jewish federation he proposed a confederation of states.

As the members of UNSCOP came to grasp the complexity of the situation, two opposed views emerged: India, Iran and Yugoslavia favoured a federation, not altogether dissimilar to the Morrison-Grady plan. There was to be common citizenship, and a federal authority controlling foreign policy, national defence, immigration and most economic activities. During the transitional period, which was to last for three years, the administration was to be conducted by an authority appointed by the United Nations.

The UNSCOP majority came out in favour of partition, but recommended at the same time economic union, without which they believed the proposed Arab state would not be viable. All members of the commission agreed that the transitional period should be as short as possible. There was also a consensus on keeping the Holy Places accessible to all, and there was an appeal to Arabs and Jews to refrain from acts of violence. But on matters of political substance no common denominator could be found to reconcile the majority and minority views, and consequently there were two separate reports.

The UNSCOP findings were published on 31 August 1947. Both the majority and the minority reports had been drawn up by the same man – Dr Ralph Bunche. The majority plan envisaged a Jewish state and an Arab state (both of which were to come into being by September 1949), with the city of Jerusalem remaining under international trusteeship. The Jewish state was to consist of three sections: upper Galilee and the Jordan and Beisan valleys; the coastal plain from a point south of Acre to a point north of Isdud, including the city of Jaffa and most of the Valley of Esdraelon; and lastly, most of the Negev. The Arab state was to include western Galilee, most of the West Bank down to and including Lydda, and the Gaza Strip, from the Egyptian border to a point some twenty miles south of Tel Aviv.

The Zionist leaders had fought very hard throughout the UNSCOP hearings for the inclusion of western Galilee and the Negev in the Jewish state, so as to have at their disposal sparsely populated areas for future development. They failed as far as western Galilee was concerned, and the fate of the Negev was uncertain, for when the UNSCOP majority plan came to the vote later that year, the American delegation wanted the Negev to be assigned to the Arabs, to make the scheme more palatable to them. Weizmann went to see a most reluctant President Truman to prevent any change in the proposed borders. The minority report was rejected without further ado by the Zionists. On the majority report counsels were divided. While abstaining from the vote on partition in Paris a year earlier, Ben Gurion had clearly retreated from Biltmore. In a letter to Weizmann of October 1946 he had said that 'we should be ready for an enlightened compromise even if it gives us less in practice than we have a right to in theory, but only as long as what is granted to us is really in our hands'.* Rabbi Silver said that the boundaries as drawn by UNSCOP were a great blow and had to be fought.† But after this initial negative reaction Silver, too, retreated, having realised that the majority report was the maximum the Zionists could possibly hope for. He understood that the commandment of the hour was not to press for more, which was unrealistic, but to work for acceptance of the report by the United Nations.

The prospects were by no means rosy: Britain was clearly opposed to partition, so were the Arab countries and most of the Asian nations. As the views of the rest were not at all clear, the American position was likely to be a factor of paramount importance. In Washington the State Department (General Marshall, Dean Acheson, Robert Lovett, Loy Henderson) was clearly against a Jewish state, as was Forrestal, the secretary of defence. Truman wrote in his diary that the nation's military leaders were primarily concerned about Middle East oil and, in long-range terms, about the danger that the Arabs, antagonised by western action in Palestine, would make common cause with Russia. These were weighty arguments and they were pressed home with immense concern by Forrestal and others. Forrestal argued that the failure to go along with the Zionists might lose the Democrats the states of New York and California. But was it not high time to consider whether giving in to Jewish pressure 'might not lose the United States'? Since the Soviet Union was a co-sponsor of partition, and since Forrestal could not have foreseen the switch in the Soviet position, his anxiety was exaggerated. Since the west was the only major market for Arab oil, there was no reason to fear that the Arabs would try to boycott their best customers.

Subsequent developments seem to have partly justified Forrestal's

---

* Quoted in Eban, 'Tragedy and Triumph', p. 288.
† *Der Tog*, 5 September 1947. Quoted in Silverberg, *If I Forget Thee, O Jerusalem*, p. 343.

warnings, for Palestine was no doubt one of the main issues as the radical Arab countries moved to a position hostile to the United States. However, the evidence is by no means conclusive. Similar processes took place all over the Third World, with the exception of a few countries directly threatened by the Soviet Union. King Faruq may have lasted a few more years but for the emergence of a Jewish state, but there is little doubt that political and social change sprang from indigenous conditions in the Nile Valley. On the other hand, it could be argued that but for the existence of Israel, serving as a lightning conductor, the 'moderates' would have been overthrown by the 'radicals' everywhere, or that in the absence of a common enemy the Arab world would have fallen into a state of anarchy. All this, of course, is highly speculative; no one can say what might have happened but for the emergence of the state of Israel.

A hesitating President Truman gave his assent to the partition scheme on 9 October 1947. He faced considerable opposition within his administration, and the strident tone of American Zionist propaganda and the pressure constantly brought on him, had antagonised him. Nevertheless, he seems to have given instructions in November to give assistance to the Zionist representatives in New York who were trying hard to gain the necessary majority for the UNSCOP report. There were delays and it was not certain up to the last moment whether the motion would succeed. The vote was taken on Saturday, 29 November, and the motion carried by thirty-three to thirteen. Among those against were the Arab and some Asian states as well as Greece and Cuba. Among those who abstained were Argentina, Chile, China, Ethiopia, Britain, Yugoslavia and several South American republics.

There were celebrations that day in New York, in Palestine, and wherever Jews lived. Traffic stopped in Tel Aviv and Jerusalem as people danced in the streets until the early hours of the morning. The decision imposed heavy responsibility on the yishuv and the entire Jewish people, Ben Gurion said in an interview. 'After a darkness of two thousand years the dawn of redemption has broken', declared Isaac Herzog, the chief rabbi. 'It looks like trouble', said Dr Magnes, who for many years had fought valiantly and vainly for a bi-national state.*

The next morning the Palestinian Arabs called a three-day protest strike, and Jews in all parts of the country were attacked. On that first day of rioting seven were killed and more injured; the fighting continued to the end of the mandate. The next months, as chaos engulfed Palestine,

* *New York Times*, 30 November 1947.

were a time of crisis for the Jewish community. Britain announced that it would leave the country by 16 May 1948, but the administration made no preparations to transfer power to Jews and Arabs, nor indeed to the Committee of Five which had been appointed by the UN to administer Jerusalem. The most pressing task facing the Jewish population was to strengthen its defences, since the Arab countries had already announced that their armies would enter the country as soon as the British left. Syria was not willing to wait that long: an 'Arab Liberation Army' inside Palestine was established in February with the help of Syrian officers as well as irregulars.

Hagana was by no means as well equipped and trained a fighting detachment as was commonly believed. Its forces and equipment were sufficient to cope with a civil war, but they seemed inadequate to defend the yishuv against regular armies. While Britain continued to supply arms to the neighbouring Arab countries, and America had declared a general arms embargo, the Jewish forces had great difficulty in obtaining supplies. By February the Arab forces were on the offensive throughout the country. While they did not succeed in capturing Jewish settlements, they all but paralysed the traffic among them, and even Jerusalem was about to become a besieged city. The Jewish relief force sent to the help of the Ezion settlements had been wiped out to the last man, a terrible loss by the standards of those days.

At the UN the Palestine Commission reported despairingly that nothing could be done before the end of the mandate. They could not demarcate the frontiers or set up a provisional government in the Arab state, and this would prevent economic union, and jeopardise the Jewish state and the international régime for Jerusalem.* The British announced that they could not support the UN resolution because it committed the Security Council to carrying out the partition scheme or giving guidance to the Palestine Commission. Palestine sterling holdings in London were blocked and the country expelled from the sterling bloc. It seemed as if London was determined to wreck whatever chances remained for an orderly and peaceful handover. Perhaps it wanted to demonstrate that the Palestinian problem was intractable and that where Britain had failed, no one else could succeed.

As events in Palestine took a turn for the worse, as far as Jewish interests were concerned, the resolve of the United States to support partition, never very strong, was further weakened. Senator Austin, telling the Security Council on 24 February that his country was not

* Quoted in H. Sacher, *Israel: The Establishment of a State*, London, 1952, p. 105.

really bound by the recommendation of the General Assembly, prepared the way for the retreat. On 18 March he formally declared that since the partition plan could not be put into effect peacefully, the attempt to implement it should be discontinued and a temporary trusteeship established by the UN. Only a day before this announcement Truman had assured Weizmann that the United States was in favour of partition and would stick to this policy.

The shift in the American position was not apparently the result of a carefully thought-out political line; it simply reflected the drift, the lack of resolution and coordination in the American capital and the conflicting views within the administration. The trusteeship proposals were unrealistic, for if the UN had no authority to send a police force to supervise partition, who was going to enforce trusteeship? But events in Palestine had their own momentum, and the country was moving towards partition. In April Truman informed Weizmann that there would be no change in the long-term policy of the United States. If partition was not reversed in the General Assembly, and if after 15 May a Jewish state came into being, Washington would recognise it.

During March and April the military situation in Palestine suddenly improved for the Jews. It was still doubtful whether Hagana would be able to withstand the attack of Arab regular armies, but the main Arab guerrilla forces near Jerusalem and Haifa were routed. Fighting became more intense and savage, as acts of reprisal followed one another. On 8 April, most of the inhabitants of the Arab village of Dir Yassin on the outskirts of Jerusalem, 254 in number, were killed by a combined IZL-Sternist force. Three days later, a Jewish medical convoy on its way to the Hadassa hospital on Mount Scopus was ambushed in the streets of Jerusalem with the loss of seventy-nine doctors, nurses and students. A British force stationed two hundred yards away did not intervene.

As the armed struggle became more bitter, the Jews were fighting with their backs to the wall, whereas the Arabs could take refuge in neighbouring countries. By the end of April, about 15,000 Arabs had left Palestine. What impelled them to do so has been debated ever since. The Arabs claim that the Jews, by massacres and threats of massacre, forced them out and that this was part of a systematic policy. The Jews asserted that the Palestinian Arabs followed the call of their leaders, believing they would soon return in the wake of victorious Arab armies.

As the end of the mandate drew nearer, the Jewish organisations prepared for the establishment of the state. Manpower was mobilised, emergency loans floated; the name of the new state, its constitution, flag, emblem, the seat of government were discussed, and there were hundreds of other questions to be decided. In reply to Washington's trusteeship proposal, the Jewish Agency executive resolved on 23 March 1948 that immediately after the end of the mandate a Jewish government would take over. The Jewish Agency (at its meeting of 30 March) and the Zionist Council (on 6–12 April) decided on the establishment of a provisional government to be called *Minhelet Ha'am* (National Administration) and a provisional parliament, *Moezet Ha'am* (National Council).* On 20 April, these terms were first used in the Palestinian press. The new government was to consist of thirteen members and the council of thirty-seven; they were to be located for the time being in the Tel Aviv area. Thus the era of the Zionist institutions in the history of Palestine came to an end.

The mandate was due to end at midnight, 14 May, but the new Jewish administration began to function several weeks earlier. The blue and white flag was hoisted on public buildings in Tel Aviv, new stamps were issued, the taxation services reorganised. (One of the main problems facing the new administration was to find a sufficient number of Hebrew typewriters.)† Meanwhile in New York and Washington the Americans and the UN went through the motions of establishing a caretaker commission as zero hour approached. But a report from the Consular Truce commission in Jerusalem announced that partition in the capital was already a fact. Officials in Washington thought that the chances that the Jewish state, if proclaimed, would survive, were not very good. Moshe Shertok was warned by General Marshall, the secretary of state, that if the Jewish state was attacked it should not count on American military help. There were suggestions by Dean Rusk and others that the proclamation of the state should be postponed for ten days, perhaps longer, and that meanwhile the truce should be restored.

Shertok arrived in Tel Aviv on 12 May, just in time for the session of the provisional government which was to decide on the proclamation of the state. He supported the proposal that a truce should be declared and that, while a government should be appointed at the end of the British mandate, the proclamation of the state should be delayed. But Ben Gurion was not willing to budge. The motion was defeated by a

* Zeev Sharef, *Three Days*, London, 1962, p. 44 *et seq*; A.N. Poliak, *Bekum Medinat Israel*, Tel Aviv, 1956, p. 175.
† Sharef, *Three Days*, p. 167.

vote of six to four, as, with a small minority, was the suggestion that the proclamation of the state should mention its borders as defined by the United Nations.*

The state of Israel came into being at a meeting of the National Council at 4 p.m. on Friday, 14 May 1948 (*Iyar 5*, 5708), at the Tel Aviv Museum, Rothschild Boulevard. The *Hatiqva* was sung first, and then David Ben Gurion read out the declaration of independence: 'By virtue of the natural and historical right of the Jewish people and of the resolution of the General Assembly of the United Nations we hereby proclaim the establishment of the Jewish state in Palestine to be called Israel.' This took little more than fifteen minutes, after which the members of the council signed the document in alphabetical order. Rabbi Fishman pronounced *Shehekheyanu*, the traditional benediction (. . . that we lived to see this day . . .). The first decree adopted by the National Council as the supreme legislative authority was the retroactive annulment of the White Paper. The ceremony was over well before the Sabbath set in. Ben Gurion said to one of his aides: 'I feel no gaiety in me, only deep anxiety as on 29 November, when I was like a mourner at the feast.' Half an hour before midnight the last British high commissioner left Haifa, and the following Sunday Dr Weizmann was elected president of the new state.

The first country to recognise the new state was the United States. President Truman made a brief statement to that effect on Friday, shortly after 6 p.m. Washington time. Within the next few days the Soviet Union, Poland, Czechoslovakia, Guatemala, Uruguay and other countries followed. A cable was received by the chairman of the Security Council from the Egyptian foreign minister: the Egyptian army was crossing the borders of Palestine with the object of putting an end to the massacres raging there, and upholding the law and the principles recognised among the United Nations; military operations were directed not against the Palestinian Jew but only against the terrorist Zionist gangs. During Friday night, the invasion of Palestine began. On Saturday morning Tel Aviv's power station and Aqir airport were attacked from the air. It was the beginning of a series of wars which was not to end for many years.

---

* *Ibid.*, pp. 122–3; Ben Gurion, *The Peel Report and the Jewish State*, p. 86.

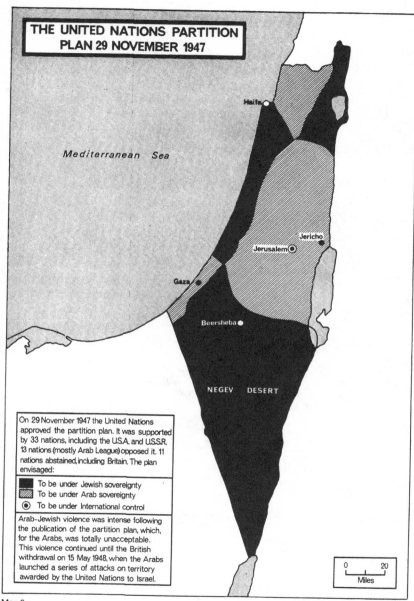

THE UNITED NATIONS PARTITION PLAN 29 NOVEMBER 1947

Mediterranean Sea

Haifa

Jericho

Jerusalem

Gaza

Beersheba

NEGEV DESERT

On 29 November 1947 the United Nations approved the partition plan. It was supported by 33 nations, including the U.S.A. and U.S.S.R. 13 nations (mostly Arab League) opposed it. 11 nations abstained, including Britain. The plan envisaged:

- ▮ To be under Jewish sovereignty
- ▨ To be under Arab sovereignty
- ◉ To be under International control

Arab-Jewish violence was intense following the publication of the partition plan, which, for the Arabs, was totally unacceptable. This violence continued until the British withdrawal on 15 May 1948, when the Arabs launched a series of attacks on territory awarded by the United Nations to Israel.

0   20
Miles

Map 6

CONCLUSION:
THIRTEEN THESES ON ZIONISM

Political Zionism appeared on the European scene more than three-quarters of a century ago. Its intellectual origins go back to the French revolution and the romantic wave of national revival which followed it. As a political movement it was part of the liberal-humanist tradition of the *risorgimento*, of Kossuth and Masaryk. It differed from other contemporary national movements because the Jews were a landless people who to a certain extent had lost their own specific character. At the time the idea of a national revival among the Jews appeared only as a chimera. But if the forces of cohesion were weak, the persecution of both individual Jews and the community at large helped to fan and to consolidate the waning national consciousness.

Zionism is the belief in the existence of a common past and a common future for the Jewish people. Such faith can be accepted or rejected, it can be a matter of rational argument only to a very limited extent. Like other national and social movements Zionism has developed an ideology but its 'scientific' claims are bound to be inconclusive. The Zionist analysis of antisemitism and its solution could have been right, but Zionism would still have been a failure if its call had passed unheard and if its solution could not have been applied by it because of lack of support among the Jews or because of adverse international conditions. Equally, the success of Zionism would not necessarily prove that it is based on a correct analysis of the 'Jewish problem'. As far as national movements are concerned, myths are always more powerful motives than rational arguments.

It is too early to assess Zionism in terms of success and failure. Nor is it altogether certain what success and failure mean in this context. A military victory may be an episode in the history of a nation. To a certain degree Zionism is bound to be a disappointment; only political movements whose histories do not extend beyond the utopian stage retain their pristine virtue and cause no disappointment. All others, sooner or later, clash with reality and the result cannot possibly live up to expectations. The syndrome of *comme la République était belle sous l'Empire* applies to all secular movements. Zionism faced gigantic obstacles, it had to fight for the realisation of its aims in the most adverse conditions and this was bound to affect the ultimate outcome. The origins of Zionism and its subsequent fortunes are full of paradoxes; some of them appear a little less inexplicable in the light of the unique character of Jewish history and the position of the Jews in nineteenth century European society.

1. Zionism is a response to antisemitism. To note this is not to disparage the original impulses and the character of the movement. All national movements have come into existence and developed their specific character in opposition to and usually in the fight against outside forces. Jewish religion, Zion as a symbol, the nostalgia for the lost homeland and other mystical factors played a role in the development of Zionism. But political Zionism as distinct from mystical longings would not have come into existence but for the precarious situation of central and east European Jewry in the second half of the nineteenth century. It became a psychological necessity for central European intellectuals, who realised that the emancipation of Jews had triggered off a powerful reaction and who then found the road to full emancipation barred by strong hostile forces. For the Jewish masses in eastern Europe Zionism was the dream of redemption from their misery. But it could then be no more than a dream. While the Ottoman empire existed, mass immigration to Palestine was ruled out. Up to the Balfour Declaration Zionism's main function was cultural-psychological: it sustained the faith of its believers but was of no political importance. After the First World War the trend towards Zionism was strengthened by the growth of antisemitic movements which culminated in the rise of Nazism. Had it not been for this increase in tension and anti-Jewish persecution, Zionism might still have existed as a small literary-philosophical sect of idealistic reformers. It became a political force as the result of outside pressure, not because eccentric Jewish *littérateurs* published stirring appeals. Persecution *per se*, needless to say, would not have resulted in a national revival. But one cannot stress too strongly the force of circumstances: in a world without antisemitism Zionism would not have flourished. Critics of Zionism have, however, often drawn the wrong conclusion from this indisputable fact. Political movements never develop in a vacuum.

Without the *ancien régime* there would have been no French revolution, without tsarism, no 1917.

2. Antisemitism in its most rabid and murderous form did not prevail in eastern Europe, where the 'objective' Jewish question existed in its most acute form. It came to power in central Europe, where the relatively small Jewish communities had progressed far on the road to assimilation and where the Jewish question was no longer a major socio-economic problem. It is one of the many paradoxical features of modern Jewish history which makes nonsense of the attempt to explain antisemitism simply in socio-economic terms. It came as a complete surprise to the Jewish critics of Zionism, but the Zionists, too, were unprepared for a catastrophe of this magnitude.

While the rise of Nazism and the Jewish catastrophe in Europe were not inevitable, there would have been a Jewish problem anyway, since nowhere in Europe were the Jews generally accepted as fully belonging to the community. They were and are tolerated within the liberal order of western Europe. Elsewhere they could at most strive for national minority status. Throughout their history the Jews have become (or remained) a group on the whole identifiable, with certain specific characteristics. For historical reasons, and in view of the possibility for individuals to opt out of the community, many Jews have been only partly aware of the peculiar character of their social existence, and this has caused some confusion among them. They have tended to forget that for all practical purposes their status in society does not depend on an act of will but is decided upon by non-Jews. This decision depends by no means only on the degree of their assimilation, their loyalty as citizens, or the contributions they have made in various fields to the prosperity, the culture and the defence of their native country. The Zionists believed with Mazzini that without a country they were bound to remain the bastards of humanity. Others did not accept the idea of a national state as a historical necessity.

3. Zionism has always regarded assimilation as its main enemy, without clearly distinguishing between emancipation and assimilation. It has decried life in the diaspora as physically unsafe and morally degrading, intolerable for proud, self-respecting Jews. Zionism has preached the more or less inevitable 'ingathering of the exiles'. This is to ignore the background of emancipation and to regard assimilation as a weakness of character rather than a historical process with a logic and a momentum

of its own. For Zionism, the secular form of religious mystique, is a child of assimilation; but for the deep and prolonged exposure to European civilisation there would have been no national revival among the Jews. Zionism, in brief, is the product of Europe, not of the ghetto. Given the general situation and the position of the Jews in European society, assimilation was inevitable in central and western Europe and to a lesser extent elsewhere. While it was probably bound to fail in Poland and Rumania, it has made great strides in other countries. Jewish history does not prove the impossibility of assimilation, nor did Herzl rule it out ('If they let us be for just two generations . . .'). He also wrote: 'Whole branches of Jewry may wither and fall away. The tree lives on.' But the main branch – east European Jewry – disappeared in the holocaust. Assimilation in the western world was retarded by the antisemitic wave of the 1930s and the holocaust, which strengthened Jewish consciousness. But it seems to have been only a temporary setback, and as the shock passed, assimilation again came into its own. Antisemitism has appeared in one form or another in all countries where Jews have lived (and in some where they did not). But low-level antisemitism has not made assimilation impossible, and it has certainly not acted as an agent of Zionism. History has always shown that substantial numbers of men and women have chosen to leave their native country only when facing intolerable pressure. Zionist doctrine has rejected assimilation as morally reprehensible: Nordau often dwelt on the rootless cosmopolitans without ground under their feet, suffering personal humiliation, forced to suppress and falsify their personalities. The image of the new Marranos and their spiritual misery was overdramatised even with regard to the world before 1914. It bears little relation to the present-day world. Jews as individuals and groups have faced difficulties, but it is certainly not true that 'all the better Jews of western Europe (or America) groan under this misery and seek for salvation'. Nordau, who wrote this, never set foot on Palestinian soil, but continued to write from Paris for his European public. Yet Nordau was only half a generation removed from Jewish tradition. Subsequent generations grew up in an environment more remote from Judaism. Many are no longer religious and the Jewish tradition is largely meaningless to them. The new assimilationists are not conscious traitors to their people, nor are their personalities necessarily warped or permeated with self-hate. The ties have loosened; they have grown away from Jewish tradition and become indifferent to it. A catastrophe would be needed to stop this process. Assimilation involved a conscious effort in the nineteenth century, when society was imbued with tradition and had generally shared values and rigid standards. To be fully accepted, the assimilationist Jew had to conform to the standards and values of this society and to give up what set him apart from it. Present-day pluralistic western society is different in character: not only have the Jews much less of their own substance, but society itself has lost its moorings. Traditional values have been jettisoned; like the Jew, society is becoming rootless. This cultural crisis, which may be protracted, may be conducive to assimilation while it lasts. But while it helps to break down some of the barriers between Jews and non-Jews, it also undermines the spirit of liberal tolerance on which Jewish existence in the western world is based.

4. Like the Poles and the Czechs, Zionists had their historical opportunity only after the First World War. Moreover, they were bound to clash with another people since the Jews had no homeland. A mass influx of Jews into Palestine in the early part of the nineteenth century (provided the Ottoman government had agreed to it) might have proceeded without much resistance on the part of the native population, because the idea of nationalism had not yet grown roots outside Europe. But there was no national movement at the time among the Jews either: east European Jewry had not yet left the ghetto; central and west European Jews had not yet experienced the new antisemitism.

5. Being a latecomer among the national movements, Zionism from the very beginning was a movement in a hurry, forever racing against time. Both the Balfour Declaration and the UN resolution of November 1947 came at the last possible moment. A few years later the decision would, in all probability, have gone against Zionism. Herzl had written that the success of the idea depended on the number of its adherents and that 'the Jews who will it shall achieve their state'. But most Jews were indifferent, and success did not depend on them alone, even if there had been more who wanted it. The four years after the Balfour Declaration were perhaps the last opportunity to transplant hundreds of thousands of Jews to Palestine and to create *faits accomplis* without causing a major political upheaval. This opportunity was not to recur.

Throughout its history Zionism failed to mobilise substantial financial support. Despite all his efforts Herzl did not get the help of the Jewish millionaires who he thought would underwrite a major loan to Turkey and thus enable him to get a charter. Up to the late 1930s the budget of the World Zionist Organisation was considerably smaller than that of any major Jewish local community in Europe or America. The freedom of action of the Zionist movement was severely circumscribed by its extreme poverty: land could not be bought, sufficient support could not be given to new immigrants, and funds for political work in Palestine and in the diaspora were altogether inadequate.

6. Zionism had neither money, nor military power, nor even much political nuisance value. It could rely only on moral persuasion, not one of the most powerful levers in world politics before 1918, and almost totally ineffective thereafter. While others had done important spadework, the Balfour Declaration was essentially the work of one man – Chaim Weizmann. Without his leadership and persistent lobbying the Zionist movement would not have received the charter on which its subsequent activities were based. It was the 'greatest act of political statesmanship of the First World War '(Charles Webster). There were certain political considerations which facilitated Weizmann's task. But Britain needed the Jews at the time much less than the Jews needed Britain. The overall benefits which Britain could derive from the declaration were small, the risks considerable. Lloyd George and Balfour were persuaded by Weizmann to issue the declaration, in the last resort, not because it was advantageous or expedient from the British point of view, but because they accepted that it was the right thing to do. That Weizmann and his supporters could be of considerable help to the allied war effort was a contributing factor, but not the decisive consideration. It was on the whole a selfless act, perhaps the last time that an individual succeeded almost single-handedly in inducing the government of a major power to take a decision irrespective of national interest. That Palestine was not an issue of paramount importance made the decision easier. Nor did the statesmen expect the complications which later occurred and which made subsequent British governments gradually relinquish the Balfour Declaration.

7. The Jewish state came into being at the very time when Zionism had lost its erstwhile *raison d'être*: to provide an answer to the plight of east European Jewry. The United Nations decision of November 1947 was in all probability the last opportunity for the Zionist movement to achieve a breakthrough. Public opinion in many countries felt uneasy about the Jewish tragedy and, above all, about the fact that not more had been done to rescue Jews. The United States and Russia, the former with great reservations, reached the conclusion that the partition of

Palestine was the only workable solution. One or two years later the world situation would no longer have been conducive to a resolution giving the Zionists what they wanted. The British government would probably have pulled out of Palestine anyway, and a civil war would have ensued. The Jewish state might nevertheless have come into existence – but without United Nations sanction and international recognition and, generally speaking, under very inauspicious circumstances.

8. Up to the 1930s the Zionist movement had no clear idea about its final aim. Herzl proclaimed that a Jewish state was a world necessity. But later he and his successors mentioned the state only infrequently, partly for tactical reasons, mainly because they had no clear concept as to how a state would come into being. Two generations of Zionist leaders, from Herzl to Weizmann, believed that Palestine would at some fairly distant date become Jewish without the use of violence or guile, as the result of steady immigration and settlement, of quiet and patient work. The idea that a state was the normal form of existence for a people and that it was an immediate necessity was preached by Jabotinsky in the 1930s. But he was at the time almost alone in voicing this demand. It took the advent of Nazism, the holocaust and total Arab rejection of the national home to convert the Zionist movement to the belief in statehood. The bi-national solution (parity), advocated by the Zionist movement in a half-hearted way in the 1920s and, with more enthusiasm, by some minority groups, would have been in every respect a better solution for the Palestine problem. It would have been a guarantee for the peaceful development of the country. But it was based on the unrealistic assumption that Arab agreement could be obtained. Bi-nationalism and parity were utterly rejected by the Arabs, who saw no good reason for any compromise as far as the Arab character of Palestine was concerned. They were not willing to accept the yishuv as it existed in the 1920s and 1930s, let alone permit more Jewish immigration and settlement. They feared that a further influx of Jews would eventually reduce the Arabs to minority status in Palestine.

9. The Arab-Jewish conflict was inevitable, given the fact that Zionism wanted to build more than a cultural centre in Palestine. Nor is it certain that a cultural centre would not have encountered Arab resistance. Zionism, the transplantation of hundreds of thousands of Jews, was bound to effect a radical change in Palestine, as a result of

which the Palestinian Arabs were bound to suffer. It was not the Arabs' fault that the Jews were persecuted in Europe, that they had awakened to the fact that they wanted again to be a nation and therefore needed a state in the country in which they had lived two thousand years before.

The effects of Zionism on the Arabs should not be belittled. The fact that they derived economic and other benefits from Jewish immigration is immaterial in this context. This is not to say that Zionism was bound to result in the evacuation or expulsion of many Palestinian Arabs from Palestine. Had the Arabs accepted the Peel Plan in 1937, the Jewish state would have been restricted to the coastal plain between Tel Aviv and Haifa. Had they not rejected the UN partition of 1947, most of Palestine would still have remained in their hands. The Arab thesis of inevitable Zionist expansion is a case of self-fulfilling prophecy: the Arabs did everything in their power to make their prophecy come true, by choosing the road of armed resistance – and losing. The Zionist movement and the yishuv matured in the struggle against the Arab national movement. Eventually it reached the conclusion that it was pointless to seek Arab agreement and that it could achieve its aims only against the Arabs.

Arab intransigence was the natural reaction of a people unwilling to share its country with another. For European Jewry the issue was not an abstract one of preserving a historical connection, religious and national ties. With the rise of Hitler it became a question of life or death, and they felt no pangs of conscience: the danger facing the Jews was physical extinction. The worst fate that could befall the Arabs was the partition of Palestine and minority status for some Arabs in the Jewish state. Zionism is guilty no doubt of many sins of commission and omission in its policy on the Arab question. But whichever way one looks at it, the conflict on immigration and settlement could not have been evaded since the basis for a compromise did not exist. Zionism could and should have paid more attention to Arab grievances and aspirations. But despite all concessions in the cultural or economic field, the Arabs would still have opposed immigration with an eye to the inevitable consequences of mass immigration.

10. Seen from the Arab point of view, Zionism was an aggressive movement, Jewish immigration an invasion. Zionists are guilty of having behaved like other peoples – only with some delay due to historical circumstances. Throughout history nation-states have not come into existence as the result of peaceful development and legal contracts.

They developed from invasions, colonisation, violence and armed struggle. It was the historical tragedy of Zionism that it appeared on the international scene when there were no longer empty spaces on the world map. Wherever the Jews would have chosen to settle, they would have sooner or later come into conflict with the native population. The creation of nation-states meant the perpetration of acts of injustice. The native population was either absorbed and assimilated or it was decimated or expelled. The expulsion of ten million Germans from eastern Europe was almost immediately accepted as an established fact by the outside world and those unwilling to put up with it were denounced as revanchists and war-mongers. Given the realities of Soviet power, it was clear that the new order in eastern Europe could not be challenged except through a new world war. But Zionism was not in a position of such strength, nor was there a danger of world war. Hence the fact that the territorial changes in eastern Europe have been accepted as irreversible, while those in the Middle East continue to be challenged by many.

Zionism has been challenged on the level of abstract justice: it has been argued that the Jews had no right to a state of their own, because they staked their claim too late and because it was bound to affect the fate of another people. It has been maintained that in these circumstances the Jews had no right to survive as a group. But arguments concerning the *raison d'être* of nations and states are double-edged, quite apart from the fact that the Jews faced extermination not only as a group but as individuals. Equally, on the level of abstract justice, the fact that a nation or a state has existed for a long time is not by itself a valid argument for its continued survival, unless it has made a substantial contribution to the advance of mankind. Few nations and states can make such claims. If a case can be made for a just distribution of property among individuals, the same applies (again on the level of abstract justice) to peoples and nations.

11. Arab opposition apart, Zionism has been rejected from various angles. The opposition of the ultra-orthodox Jews is based on a totally different system of beliefs and values, and there is no room for any debate between them and Zionists. The non-religious critique of Zionism appears in different variants, but it is based in the last resort on the same ideological assumptions. The critiques of the extreme Left and the liberal-assimilationist doctrine rest on the argument that Zionism is an anachronistic movement, that assimilation is an inevitable historical

process and that it has proceeded too far to be undone. Hence the conclusion that the desire of the Jews to survive as a national group runs against the course of world history. Since social and economic developments cause the gradual disappearance of national peculiarities, any effort to reverse this process is bound to be reactionary in character. While nation-states have played a progressive role in earlier ages, nationalism has turned into an obstacle on the road to further progress. The Jews were the first to be denationalised, but the other nations will gradually follow. Instead of reverting to the nation-state, the Jews should try to fulfil the role into which they were cast by history: that of an *avant-garde* of a new world order. According to the liberals, antisemitism is bound to disappear as civilisation and enlightenment spread. According to the radical Left, it will wither away with the overthrow of capitalism.

To a large extent the early Zionist leaders shared this belief in human progress. But they did not expect that the new world order would soon come into being, and they feared that meanwhile persecution and oppression would continue. The course of world history has not confirmed the predictions of the optimists. If civilisation has made progress, it is agonisingly slow. National movements and nation-states are nowhere on the decline. International working-class solidarity is invoked less and less – even as a slogan. Antisemitism has antedated capitalism and still exists in post-capitalist societies. As Communism has moved from proletarian internationalism to a nationalist brand of Socialism the position of Jews under these régimes and in Communist movements will remain precarious for a long time; the demand for internationalists is strictly limited. On the contrary, the conspicuous participication of Jews in radical political movements has resulted in an upsurge of antisemitism, regardless of whether these movements attained power or not. The non-Jewish Jew is thus acting indirectly as an agent of resurgent Jewish nationalism.

12. The main source of Zionist weakness has been the fact that conditions for the realisation of the Zionist dream were never favourable. It never quite overcame the inertia of the Jews, it always lacked resources. The establishment of a national home in one of the world's main danger zones, against the opposition of the Arabs and without any powerful allies, meant that the future of the state would inevitably remain uncertain for a long time to come. From the very beginning the smallness of the territory limited its absorptive capacity: it has served as a

national home for less than one-fifth of world Jewry. Even of those in sympathy with Zionism only a few went to Palestine. Only an infinitesimal portion of American, British, French or German (before 1933) Jewry has settled in the Jewish national home. There is no 'objective' socio-economic Jewish question in these countries, even though the concentration of Jews in certain professions may still create tensions and occasionally even constitute a political problem. But the process of assimilation interrupted by Nazism has gathered fresh momentum. The percentage of mixed marriages has increased substantially. In these circumstances political and economic motives are unlikely to be decisive in making individual Jews opt for Zionism. They are more likely to be attracted by the Israeli way of life, idealism and the extent to which Israel is spared some of the afflictions occurring elsewhere in the western world.

13. The basic aim of Zionism was twofold: to regain Jewish self-respect and dignity in the eyes of non-Jews; and to rebuild a Jewish national home, for Jews to 'live as free men on their own soil, to die peacefully in their own homes' (Herzl). The Zionist movement has certainly succeeded in carrying out part of its assignment. The establishment of the Jewish state has been the greatest turning point in two thousand years of Jewish history and has had a profound effect on Jewish life all over the world. But whereas the national home has attracted much sympathy, its potential as a cultural centre is limited. As normalisation proceeds, the more fanciful claims (Zion as a new spiritual lodestar, a model for the redemption of mankind, a centre of humanity) are receding into the background. While esteem for Jewish determination and prowess has increased as the result of the creation of the state, the position of Jews – contrary to widespread hopes – has not become more secure. If there has been a certain decline in antisemitism in the diaspora, a reaction to the horrors of Hitlerism as much as a consequence of the birth of Israel, hostility towards the new state on the part of its neighbours has increased. The state created by Zionism thus faces an uphill struggle in its endeavour to make its neighbours recognise its right of existence. While this struggle continues, the existence of the state and its independence is no more assured than that of other small countries whose geopolitical location exposes them to the expansive designs of a superpower.

BIBLIOGRAPHY

There are many thousands of books and pamphlets on Zionism. The most useful annotated bibliographies are *Bibliografia Zionit* (ed. A.Lewinson), Jerusalem, and the appendices (by Kressel and Klausner) to Y.Gruenbaum's *Hatnua hazionit behitpatchuta* (4 vols). The most important general works are Nahum Sokolow's *History of Zionism* (*1600–1918*) (2 vols), London, 1919, and Adolf Böhm's *Die zionistische Bewegung* (2 vols), Berlin, 1937. The stenographic reports of the Zionist congresses are an invaluable source, as are Herzl's diaries, Alex Bein's Herzl biography, Leonard Stein's study of the Balfour Declaration, Weizmann's autobiography, and Schechtman's biography of Jabotinsky – to mention only some of the most important primary and secondary sources. Of the periodicals published by the Zionist movement, *Die Welt* (Vienna), *Ha'olam*, *Jüdische Rundschau* (Berlin), and *New Judaea* (London) are among the most important. The Central Zionist Archives were founded in Berlin in 1919; its collections were transferred to Jerusalem in 1933–4. Other important archives are those of the labour movement in Tel Aviv, the revisionist party (Mezudat Ze'ev) also in Tel Aviv, the Zionist Archives in New York, and the Weizmann Institute in Rehovot.

Chapter 2 : The Forerunners

Alex Bein, *The Return to the Soil*, Jerusalem, 1952.

Eliezer Ben Yehuda, *Kol Kitve* . . . , Jerusalem, 1941.

S.Ben Zion, *Die Bilu auf dem Weg. Die Bilu am Ziel*, Tel Aviv, 1935.

Nathan Birnbaum, *Ausgewählte Schriften zur jüdischen Frage* (2 vols), Czernowitz, 1910.

H.H.Bodenheimer (ed.), *So wurde Israel. Erinnerungen von Dr. M.I.Bodenheimer*, Frankfurt, 1958.

R.Brainin, *Peretz Smolenskin*, Warsaw, 1896.

S.L.Citron, *Toldot Hibat Zion*, Odessa, 1914.

B.Dinaburg, *Hibat Zion*, Tel Aviv, 1922–4.

B.Dinaburg (ed.), *Sefer Hazionut*, vol. 1, Tel Aviv, 1938.

A.Droyanov, *Ketavim letoldot Hibat Zion* . . ., Odessa, 1919; 'Pinsker vesemano' (*Hatekufa*, vols 12, 13, 27).

S.M.Dubnow, *Toldot hehassidut*, Tel Aviv, 1930.

Leo Errera, *Die russischen Juden*, Leipzig, 1903.

Harold Frederic, *The New Exodus*, London, 1892.

N.M.Gelber (ed.), *Die Kattowitzer Konferenz*, Brno, 1919.

N.M.Gelber, *Vorgeschichte des Zionismus*, Vienna, 1927; *Aus zwei Jahrhunderten* Vienna, 1924.

J.Gessen, *Istoriya evreiskovo naroda v Rossii* (2 vols), Leningrad, 1925; *Gallereya evreiskikh deiatelei*, St Petersburg, 1898.

Y.L.Gordon, *Iggarot*, (2 vols), Warsaw, 1894.

Richard J.Gottheil, *Zionism*, Philadelphia, 1914.

Louis Greenberg, *The Jews in Russia* (2 vols), New Haven, 1951.

Y.Gur Arie, *Harav Y.H.Alkalay*, Tel Aviv, 1929; *Harav Zvi Kalisher*, Jerusalem, n.d.

Leo Herrmann, *Nathan Birnbaum. Sein Werk und seine Wandlung*, Berlin, 1914.

Moses Hess, *Rom und Jerusalem*, Leipzig, 1862.

M.Joeli, *Y.L.Pinsker: Mevaser hatekhiya haleumit*, Tel Aviv, 1942.

Hirsch Kalischer, *Drischat Zion*, Berlin, 1905.

I.Klausner, *Hibat Zion beRomania*, Jerusalem, 1948; *Hatnua lezion beRussia*, Jerusalem, 1962.

Joseph Klausner, *Sefer Pinsker*, Jerusalem, 1921.

Hans Kohn (ed.), *Nationalism and the Jewish Ethic: Basic Writings of Ahad Ha'am*, New York, 1962.

G.Kressel, *Hesione Medina*, Tel Aviv, 1954.

F.Lachover, *Toldot hasafrut haivrit hehadasha* (4 vols), Tel Aviv, 1927–33.

Ernest Laharanne, *La Nouvelle Question d'Orient*, Paris, 1860.

Richard Lichtheim, *Die Geschichte des deutschen Zionismus*, Jerusalem, 1954.

M.L.Lilienblum, *Hattat Neurim*, Vienna, 1876; *Kol Kitve M.L.Lilienblum*, Odessa, 1913.

P.Marek, *Ocherki po istorii prosveshcheniya evreev v Rossii*, Moscow, 1909.

Michael R.Marrus, *The Politics of Assimilation*, Oxford, 1971.

Josef Meisl, *Haskalah*, Berlin, 1919.

Leo Motzkin (ed.), *Die Judenpogrome in Russland* (2 vols), Cologne, 1909–10.

Leo Pinsker (ed. B.Natanyahu), *Road to Freedom*, New York, 1944.

Jacob S.Raisin, *The Haskalah Movement in Russia*, Philadelphia, 1913.

A.Robinsohn, *David Wolffsohn*, Berlin, 1921.

J.Salvador, *Paris, Rome, Jerusalem, ou la Question Réligieuse au XIXe Siècle*, Paris, 1860.

Edmund Silberner, *Moses Hess, Geschichte seines Lebens*, Leiden, 1966; *Moses Hess Briefwechsel*, The Hague, 1959.

Edmund Silberner (ed.), *The Works of Moses Hess*, Leiden, 1958.

Leon Simon, *Ahad Ha'am*, Philadelphia, 1960.

Peretz Smolenskin, *Hatoe bedarke hehayim* (4 vols), Vienna, 1876; *Ma'amarim* (3 vols), Jerusalem, 1925–6.

BIBLIOGRAPHY

Nahum Sokolow, *Hibat Zion,* Jerusalem, 1935; *Ishim* (3 vols), Jerusalem, 1935.
Meyer Waxman, *A History of Jewish Literature,* vols 3 and 4, New York, 1960.
Jehuda L. Weinberg, *Heinrich Löwe. Aus der Frühzeit des Zionismus,* Jerusalem, 1946.
Paula Wengeroff, *Memoiren einer Grossmutter,* Berlin, 1908.
Israel Zinberg, *Di Geshikhte fun Literatur bei Yiden,* vol. 9, *Die Bli Tekufa fun der Haskala,* New York, 1966.
Theodor Zlocisti, *Moses Hess,* Berlin, 1921.

Chapter 3: Theodor Herzl

Alex Bein, *Theodor Herzl,* Philadelphia, 1945.
Hannah Bodenheimer, *Toldot Tokhnit Basel,* Jerusalem, 1947.
Adolf Böhm, *Die zionistische Bewegung,* vol. 1, Berlin, 1935.
Ruben Brainin, *Haye Herzl,* vol. 1, New York, 1919.
Andre Chouraqui, *Theodor Herzl,* Paris, 1960.
Ben Zion Dinaburg and others, *Sefer Hazionut,* Tel Aviv, 1938.
Jacob de Haas, *Theodor Herzl: A Biographical Study* (2 vols), New York, 1927.
Theodor Herzl (ed. L. Kellner), *Zionistische Schriften* (2 vols), Berlin, 1920; *Feuilletons* (2 vols), Berlin, 1911; *Philosophische Erzählungen,* Berlin, 1900; (ed. R. Patai), *The Complete Diaries* (5 vols), New York, 1960; *Neumim ve ma'amarim,* Tel Aviv, 1937; ed. M. Lowenthal), *The Diaries of Theodor Herzl,* New York, 1956.
Leon Kellner, *Theodor Herzls Lehrjahre,* Vienna, 1920.
Israel Klausner, *Oppositzia leHerzl,* Tel Aviv, 1959; *Me Katowitz ad Basel,* Jerusalem, n.d.
Saul Raphael Landau, *Sturm und Drang im Zionismus,* Vienna, 1937.
Ludwig Lewisohn, *Theodor Herzl,* Cleveland, 1955.
Richard Lichtheim, *Die Geschichte des deutschen Zionismus,* Jerusalem, 1954.
Moshe Medzini, *Hamediniut hazionit mereshita ve'ad moto shel Herzl,* Jerusalem, 1934.
Anne and Maxa Nordau, *Max Nordau,* New York, 1943.
Max Nordau, *Zionistische Schriften,* Berlin, 1923.
Mordehai Nurok, *Weidat Zione Russia beMinsk,* Jerusalem, n.d.
Thilo Nussenblatt (ed.), *Herzl Jahrbuch,* vol. 1, Vienna, 1937; *Zeitgenossen über Herzl,* Brünn, 1929.
Raphael Patai (ed.) *Herzl Year Book* (6 vols), New York, 1958–65.
Oskar K. Rabinowicz, *Herzl, Architect of the Balfour Declaration,* New York, 1958; *Fifty Years of Zionism,* London, 1957.
Nahum Sokolow, *History of Zionism,* London, 1919.
Stenographische Protokolle der Verhandlungen des Zionisten Kongresses: I, Vienna, 1898; II, Vienna, 1898; III, Vienna; 1899; IV, Vienna, 1900; V, Vienna, 1901; VI, Vienna, 1903.

A HISTORY OF ZIONISM

Meyer W.Weisgal (ed.), *Theodor Herzl. A Memorial*, New York, 1929.
Chaim Weizmann, *Trial and Error*, New York, 1949.

Chapter 4: The Interregnum

Ahad Ha'am (ed. L.Simon), *Essays, Letters, Memoirs*, London, 1946; (ed. H.Kohn), *Nationalism and the Jewish Ethic*, New York, 1962; *Ten Essays on Zionism and Judaism*, London, 1922; *Kol Kitve . . .*, Tel Aviv, 1937.
American Jewish Committee, *The Jews in the Eastern War Zone*, New York, 1916.
L.S.Amery, *My Political Life*, London, 1953.
H.H.Asquith, *Memoirs and Reflections*, London, 1928.
A.J.Balfour, *Speeches on Zionism*, London, 1928.
Bericht über die Tätigkeit des Kopenhagener Büros der Zionistischen Organisation von Februar 1915 bis Dezember 1918, Copenhagen, 1919.
H.Bergmann, *Jawne und Jerusalem*, Berlin, 1919.
R.Blake, *The Unknown Prime Minister*, London, 1955.
K.Blumenfeld, *Erlebte Judenfrage*, Stuttgart, 1962.
Y.Bodenheimer, *Darki Lezion*, Jerusalem, 1953.
A.Böhm, *Die Zionistische Bewegung*, vol. 1, Berlin, 1935.
M.Brod and F.Weltsch, *Zionismus als Weltanschauung*, M.Ostrau, 1925.
M.Buber, *Reden über das Judentum*, Berlin, 1932; *Israel and the World*, New York, 1948; *Die jüdische Bewegung* (2 vols), Berlin, 1920.
L.Chasanowitsch and L.Motzkin, *Die Judenfrage der Gegenwart*, Stockholm, 1919.
Y.Chlenov, *Pirke Khayav vepeulato*, Tel Aviv, 1937.
E.B.Cohn, *David Wolffsohn*, Amsterdam, 1939.
J.De Haas, *Louis D.Brandeis*, New York, 1929.
A.Djemal Pascha, *Erinnerungen eines türkischen Staatsmannes*, Munich, 1922.
B.Dugdale, *Arthur James Balfour*, London, 1926.
L.Evans, *United States Policy and the Division of Turkey*, Baltimore, 1965.
N.Gelber, *Hazharat Balfour vetoldoteha*, Jerusalem, 1939.
D.Gillon, 'The Antecedents of the Balfour Declaration', *Middle Eastern Studies*, May 1969.
P.Goodman, *Zionism in England 1899–1949*, London, 1949.
P.Goodman and A.D.Lewis, *Zionism: Problems and Views*, London, 1916.
Y.Gruenbaum, *Hatnua hazionit*, vols 3 and 4, Jerusalem, 1949, 1954; *Havle Geula*, Warsaw, 1929.
A.Hertzberg (ed.), *The Zionist Idea*, New York, 1966.
G.Holdheim and W.Preuss, *Die theoretischen Grundlagen des Zionismus*, Berlin, 1919.
The Intimate Papers of Colonel House, London, 1928.
Im Kampf um die hebräische Sprache, Berlin, 1914.

BIBLIOGRAPHY

E. Kedourie, *England and the Middle East*, London, 1956.

J. Klatzkin, *Krisis und Entscheidung im Judentum*, Berlin, 1921; *Techumim*, Berlin, 1925.

R. Learsi, *Fulfilment : The Epic History of Zionism*, Cleveland, 1951.

Sh. Leslie, *Mark Sykes: His Life and Letters*, London, 1923.

Sh. Levin, *Mezikhronot Khayai*, vol. 4, Tel Aviv, 1942.

R. Lichtheim, *Geschichte des deutschen Zionismus*, Jerusalem, 1954; *Rückkehr*, Stuttgart, 1970.

L. Lipsky, *A Gallery of Zionist Profiles*, New York, 1960; *Thirty Years of American Zionism* (2 vols), New York, 1927.

D. Lloyd George, *The Truth about the Peace Treaties*, London, 1938; *War Memoirs*, London, 1933–6.

M. Lowenthal, *Henrietta Szold: Life and Letters*, New York, 1942.

F. E. Manuel, *The Realities of American-Palestine Relations*, Washington, 1949.

I. S. Meyer (ed.), *Early History of Zionism in America*, New York, 1958.

G. Mosse, *Germans and Jews*, New York, 1969.

P. Nathan, *Palästina und Palästinischer Zionismus*, Berlin, 1914.

J. Nevakivi, *Britain, France and the Arab Middle East*, London, 1968.

A. Robinsohn, *David Wolffsohn*, Berlin, 1921.

Royal Institute of International Affairs, *Great Britain and Palestine 1915–1945*, London, 1948.

A. Ruppin, *Pirke Khayai* (3 vols), Tel Aviv, 1968; *Building Israel*, New York, 1949.

H. Sacher, *Zionist Portraits and Other Essays*, London, 1959.

H. Samuel, *Memoirs*, London, 1945.

L. Schön (ed.), *Die Stimme der Wahrheit*, Würzburg, 1905.

Sefer Warburg, Jerusalem, 1948.

L. Shpizman: *Geshihte fun der Tsiyonistisher Arbeter Bavegung* (2 vols), New York, 1955.

H. Sidebotham, *England and Palestine*, London, 1918.

L. Simon, *Ahad Ha'am*, Philadelphia, 1960.

N. Sokolow, *History of Zionism* (2 vols), London, 1919.

L. Stein, *The Balfour Declaration*, London, 1961.

C. Sykes, *Two Studies in Virtue*, London, 1953.

Vom Judentum (Bar Kochba Prag), Leipzig, 1913.

Ch. Weizmann, *Trial and Error*, New York, 1950.

E. Zechlin, *Die deutsche Politik und die Juden im Ersten Weltkrieg*, Göttingen, 1969.

Zionisten-Kongress, *Stenographische Protokolle der Verhandlungen: 7 Kongress*, Cologne, 1905; *8 Kongress*, Cologne, 1907; *9 Kongress*, Cologne, 1910; *10 Kongress*, Berlin, 1911; *11 Kongress*, Berlin, 1914; *Bericht des Aktions-Komitees*, Haag, 1907; Hamburg, 1909; Basel, 1911; Vienna, 1913.

Chapter 5: The Unseen Question

Ahad Ha'am, *Nationalism and the Jewish Ethic*, New York, 1962.
P.A.Alsberg, 'Hashe'ela ha'aravit . . .', *Shivat Zion*, Jerusalem, 1956.
G.Antonius, *The Arab Awakening*, London, 1938.
A.C.Arlosoroff, *Yoman Yerushalayim*, Jerusalem, 1949.
M.Assaf, *Hatnua ha'aravit be'eretz Israel vemekoroteha*, Tel Aviv, 1947.
Beayot Hayom, Jerusalem, 1944–8.
M.Beilinson, *Bime Masa*, Tel Aviv, 1930.
D.Ben Gurion, *Anakhnu veshekhnenu*, Tel Aviv, 1931; *Sichot im manhigim aravim*, Tel Aviv, 1967.
Y.Ben Zvi, *Hatnua ha'aravit*, Jaffa, 1921.
M.Bentov (ed.), *The Case for a Bi-national Palestine*, New York, 1946.
N.Bentwich, *For Zion's Sake*, Philadelphia, 1954.
R.Binyamin (ed.), *Al Parashat Darkenu*, Jerusalem, 1939.
M.Buber and others (ed.), *Towards Union in Palestine*, Jerusalem, 1947.
A.Cohen, *Israel vehaolam ha'aravi*, Merhavia, 1964.
Disturbances in May 1921, Report of the Commission of Enquiry, London, 1921.
ESCO, *A Study of Jewish, Arab and British Policies* (2 vols), New Haven, 1947.
J.B.Hobman, *David Eder*, London, 1945.
Z.Jabotinsky, *Ktavim*, vols 4 and 7, Jerusalem, 1947, 1953.
J.M.N.Jeffries, *Palestine the Reality*, London, 1939.
F.H.Kisch, *Palestine Diary*, London, 1938.
J.Klatzkin (ed.), *Die Araberfrage in Palästina*, Heidelberg, 1921.
S.D.Levontin, *Le'aretz Avotenu*, Tel Aviv, 1924–8.
R.Lichtheim, *Rückkehr*, Stuttgart, 1970.
J.L.Magnes (ed.), *Arab-Jewish Unity*, Jerusalem, 1946; *Like All Nations?* Jerusalem, 1930; (ed.), *Palestine – Divided or United?* Jerusalem, 1947.
N.Mandel, 'Turks, Arabs and Jewish Immigration . . .', *Middle Eastern Affairs*, London 1965; 'Attempts at an Arab-Zionist Entente, 1913–14', *Middle Eastern Studies*, April 1965.
J.Marlowe, *Rebellion in Palestine*, London, 1946.
M.Medzini, *Esser Shanim Shel Mediniut Eretz Yisraelit*, Jerusalem, 1928.
M.Orenstein, *A Plea for Arab-Jewish Unity*, London, 1946.
Palestine: *Correspondence with the Palestine Arab Delegation . . .*, Cmd. 1700, London, 1922.
Palestine Royal Commission (Peel Report), Cmd. 5479, London, 1937.
Palestine Royal Commission (Peel Report), *Minutes*, London, 1937.
M.Perlman, 'Chapters of Arab-Jewish Diplomacy 1918–22', *Jewish Social Studies*, 1944.
Report of the Commission on the Palestine Disturbances of August 1929, London, 1930.
Y.Ro'i, 'Attempts of the Zionist Organisation . . .', *Zion*, 3–4, 1967; 'The Zionist Attitude . . .', *Middle Eastern Studies*, 1968.

A.Ruppin, *Pirke Khayai* (3 vols), Tel Aviv, 1968.

H.Samuel, *Memoirs*, London, 1945.

A.Saphir, *Unity or Partition*, Jerusalem, 1937.

Sefer Toldot Hahagana (2 vols), Tel Aviv, 1954–9.

E.Sereni (ed.), *Jews and Arabs in Palestine*, New York, 1936.

M.Sharett, *Yoman Medini*, Tel Aviv, 1968.

She'ifotenu, Jerusalem, 1930–3.

Y.Shimoni, *Arvie Eretz Israel*, Tel Aviv, 1947.

M.Smilansky, *Prakim betoldot hayishuv*, Tel Aviv, 1954.

L.Stein, *The Balfour Declaration*, London, 1961; *Memorandum on the Report of the Commission on the Palestine Disturbances*, London, 1930.

Stenographisches Protokoll 2–17, Zionisten Kongress.

R.Storrs, *Orientations*, London, 1937.

Y.Washitz, *Ha'aravim be'eretz Israel*, Merhavia, 1946.

Ch.Weizmann, *Trial and Error*, New York, 1950.

A.Wiener, *Juden und Araber in Palästina*, Berlin, 1930.

I.Zangwill, *Speeches, Articles and Letters*, London, 1937.

Zum Jüdisch-Arabischen Problem (ed. Hechaluz), Berlin, 1933.

Chapter 6: *Building a New Society: The Progress of Left-Wing Zionism*

Z.Abramovitz, *Besherut hatnua*, Merhavia, 1965.

Y.Ahronowitz, *Ktavim*, Tel Aviv, 1941.

Ch.Arlosoroff, *Ktavim*, Tel Aviv, 1934; *Yoman Yerushalayim*, Tel Aviv, 1949.

A.Bein, *The Return to the Soil*, Jerusalem, 1952.

N.Benari, *Prakim Letoldot tnuat hapoalim be'eretz Israel*, Warsaw, 1936; *Zun Geschichte der Kvutza und des Kibbutz*, Berlin, 1934.

D.Ben Gurion, *Mema'amad leam*, Tel Aviv, 1933; *Tnuat hapoalim veharevisionismus*, Tel Aviv, 1933.

Y.Ben Zvi, *Kitve . . .*, Tel Aviv, 1936.

B.Borokhov, *Ktavim* (3 vols), Tel Aviv, 1955–66; *Sozialismus und Zionismus*, Vienna, 1932.

M.Braslavsky, *Tnuat hapoalim haeretz-israelit* (4 vols), Tel Aviv, 1946–63.

Y.Ch.Brenner, *Kol Ktavav . . .* (9 vols), Tel Aviv, 1924–30.

H.Darin Drabkin, *The Other Society*, London, 1962.

Sh.Eisenshtat, *Prakim betoldot tnuat hapoalim hayehudit* (2 vols), Merhavia, 1944.

Z.Even Shoshan, *Toldot tnuat hapoalim be'eretz Israel* (3 vols), Tel Aviv, 1963–6.

Gdud Ha'avoda, Tel Aviv, 1932.

A.D.Gordon, *Ktavim* (5 vols), Tel Aviv, 1925–9.

N.Kantorowicz, *Di Tsiyonistishe Arbeter Bawegung in Poilen (1918–39)*, New York, 1969.

B.Katznelson, Kitvei . . . (12 vols), Tel Aviv, 1946–9; *Roshe Prakim letoldot tnuat hapoalim be'eretz Israel*, Ktavim, vol. 11, Tel Aviv, 1948; (ed.), *Hakibbutz vehakvutza*, Tel Aviv, 1940.

Kehiliatenu, Haifa-Gedda, 1922.

D.Leon, *The Kibbutz*, Oxford, 1969.

P.Lubianiker, *Yesodot*, Tel Aviv, 1941.

H.Meier-Cronemeier, *Kibbutzim*, vol. 1, Hanover, 1969.

Perez Merhav, *Toldot tnuat hapoalim be'eretz Israel*, Merhavia, 1967.

Naftole Dor ('Zeire Zion'), Tel Aviv, 1947.

Netive Hakvutza vehakibbutz, vol. 1, Tel Aviv, 1958.

Pirke Hapoel Hatzair, Tel Aviv, 1935.

W.Preuss, *The Labour Movement in Israel*, Jerusalem, 1965.

M.Rafes, *Ocherki istoriya evreiskovo rabochevo dvizheniya*, Moscow, 1929.

Sh.Rehav, *Mivhar Ktavim*, Merhavia, 1966.

A.Ruppin, *Three Decades of Palestine*, Jerusalem, 1936; *Pirke Chayai* (3 vols), Tel Aviv, 1968.

Sefer ha'aliya hashlishit (2 vols), Tel Aviv, 1964.

Sefer ha'aliya hashniya, Tel Aviv, 1947.

Sefer Hashomer, Tel Aviv, 1957.

Sefer Hashomer Hatzair (3 vols), Merhavia, 1956–64.

Sefer Hehaluz, Tel Aviv, 1940.

Sefer Idelson, Tel Aviv, 1946.

Sefer Toldot Hahagana, Tel Aviv, 1954–9.

Sefer Z.S., Tel Aviv, 1963.

M.Shmueli, *Prakim betoldot hazionut vetnuat ha'avoda* (4 vols), Tel Aviv, 1938–46.

M.Singer, *Bereshit hazionut hasozialistit*, Haifa, 1958.

M.Syrkin, *Nachman Syrkin*, New York, 1961.

N.Syrkin, *Ktavim*, Tel Aviv, 1939.

A.Tartakover, *Toldot tnuat haovdim hayehudit*, Warsaw, 1929.

H.Viteles, *A History of the Cooperative Movement in Israel*, vols 2 and 3, London, 1967–8.

M.Yaari, *Befetakh Tekufa*, Merhavia, 1942; *Bederekh Aruka*, Merhavia, 1947.

Yalkut Poale Zion (2 vols), Jerusalem, 1947, 1954.

G.S.Yisraeli, *MPS-PKP-Maki*, Tel Aviv, 1953.

Ch.Zhitlovsky, *Ktavim*, Merhavia, 1960; 'Sotsializm i natsionalny vopros', *Serp*, 1906.

Chapter 7: In Blood and Fire: Jabotinsky and Revisionism

A.Achimeir, *Reportazha shel bachur yeshiva*, Tel Aviv, 1937; *Im kriat hagever*, Tel Aviv, 1940; *Hazionut hamahpechanit*, Tel Aviv, 1966.

Y.Banai, *Hayalim Almonim*, Tel Aviv, 1958.

BIBLIOGRAPHY

Basic Principles of Revisionism, London, 1929.

M.Begin, *Bemachteret* (2 vols), Tel Aviv, 1959.

D.Ben Gurion, *Tnuat hapoalim veharevisionismus*, Tel Aviv, 1933.

Ch.Ben Meir, *Harevisionism ssakana leam*, Tel Aviv, 1938.

Ch.Ben Yeruham, *Sefer Betar,*, vol. 1, Tel Aviv, 1969.

Betar, *This is Betar*, New York, 1946.

S.Gepstein, *Zeev Jabotinsky*, Tel Aviv, 1941.

U.Z.Grinberg, *Sefer Hakitrug vehaemuna*, Jerusalem, 1937.

Machon Jabotinsky (ed.), *Brit Habiryonim*, Tel Aviv, 1953.

V.Jabotinsky, *The Jewish War Front*, London, 1940.

Z.Jabotinsky (ed. Y.Klausner), *Ktavim nivcharim* (2 vols), Jerusalem, 1943; *Works* (Hebrew, 18 vols), Tel Aviv and Jerusalem, 1940 (of special interest: vol. 1, Jabotinsky's autobiography; vols 4 and 5, Speeches 1905–40; vol. 8, first Zionist writings; vol. 9, Nation and Society; vol. 11, On the Road to the State; vol. 12, In the Storm).

S.Katz, *Yom Ha'esh*, Tel Aviv, 1966.

K.Katznelson, *Shkiat hatnua hajabotinskait*, Tel Aviv, 1961.

R.Lichtheim, *Revision der zionistischen Politik*, Berlin, 1930; *Revisionisten*, Prag, 1930.

E.Liebenstein, *Wo steht der Revisionismus?* Berlin, 1934.

Lochme Herut Israel, *Ktavim*, vol. 1, Tel Aviv, 1959.

B.Lubotzki, *Hazohar uBetar*, Jerusalem, 1946.

Y.Nedava, *Jabotinsky bechason hador*, Tel Aviv, 1950.

D.Niv, *Maarakhot hairgun hazvai haleumi* (2 vols), Tel Aviv, 1965.

J.H.Patterson, *With the Judaeans in the Palestine Campaign*, New York, 1922.

J.Perelman, *Rewizjonizm w Polsce*, Warsaw, 1937.

David Raziel (ed. Jabotinsky Institute), Tel Aviv, 1956.

Rassvet.

I.Remba, *Jabotinsky's Teg un Necht*, Paris, 1951; *Kefi shehikartem*, Ramat Gan, 1959.

Sh.Salzman, *Min heavar*, Tel Aviv, 1943.

J.B.Schechtman, *The Jabotinsky Story*: vol. 1, *Rebel and Statesman*, New York, 1956; vol. 2, *Fighter and Prophet*, New York, 1961; *Judenstaats-Zionismus*, Prague, 1933.

J.B.Schechtman and Y.Benari, *History of the Revisionist Movement*, vol. I, Tel Aviv, 1970.

S.Schmitz and H.Brauner, *Die Wahrheit über den Revisionismus*, Moravska, Ostrava, 1935.

S.Shwartz, *Jabotinsky – lochem hauma*, Jerusalem, 1942.

Sefer Toldot Hahagana (2 vols), Tel Aviv, 1954–9.

E.Soskin, *Das Kolonisationsproblem*, Paris, 1929; *Kolonisation-Revisionismus*, Vienna, 1927.

R.Stricker, *Di Judenstaatspartei*, Warsaw, 1935.

Union der Zionisten-Revisionisten, *Protokolle der II. Weltkonferenz*, Paris, 1929.

Y.H.Yevin, *Yerushalayim mechaka*, Tel Aviv, 1932.

Y.Weinshal, *Hadam asher besaf*, Tel Aviv, 1956.

Zionist Congresses, Minutes of Proceedings (Congresses 12–18).

Chapter 8: Zionism and its Critics

D.Balakan, *Die Sozialdemokratie und das jüdische Proletariat*, Czernowitz, 1905.

O.Bauer, *Die Nationalitätenfrage und die Sozialdemokratie*, Vienna, 1907.

Ben Ehud, *Zionismus oder Sozialismus*, Warsaw, 1899.

E.Berger, *The Jewish Dilemma*, New York, 1945.

M.Blach (ed.), *Dovev Sifte Yeshenim*, New York, 1959.

I.Breuer, *Messiasspuren*, Frankfurt M., 1918; *Moriah*, Jerusalem, 1944; *Das jüdische Nationalheim*, Frankfurt M., 1925.

I.Breuer and J.Rosenheim, *Eretz Israel und die Orthodoxie*, Frankfurt M., 1934.

J.Breuer, *Judenproblem*, Halle, 1918.

R.Breuer, *Nationaljudentum, ein Wahnjudentum*, Mainz, 1903.

H.Cohen, *Religion und Zionismus*, Krefeld, 1916.

Correspondence on the Advisability of Calling a Conference on Combatting Zionism, New York, 1918.

I.Deutscher, *The Non-Jewish Jew*, London, 1968.

I.Domb, *The Transformation*, London, 1958.

S.M.Dubnow, *Die Grundlagen des Nationaljudentums*, Berlin, n.d.

L.Ernst, *Kein Judenstaat sondern Gewissensfreiheit*, Vienna, 1896.

M.Gershenson, *Sudby evreiskovo naroda*, Berlin, 1922.

F.Goldmann, *Zionismus oder Liberalismus*, Frankfurt M., 1911.

F.Gross and B.Vlavianos (eds), *Struggle for Tomorrow*, New York, 1954.

M.Güdemann, *Nationaljudentum*, Leipzig, 1897.

'HaKadosh de Han', *Khayav vemoto*, Jerusalem, 1925.

O.Heller, *Das Ende des Judentums*, Berlin, 1931.

JTO Pamphlet, no. 1, London, 1905.

K.Kautsky, *Are the Jews a Race?* London, 1926.

M.Kollenscher, *Zionismus oder liberales Judentum*, Berlin, 1912; *Zionismus und Staatsbürgertum*, Berlin, 1910.

K.Kraus, *Eine Krone für Zion*, Vienna, 1898.

S.Z.Lande and J.Rabinovitz, *Or Layesharim*, Warsaw, 1900.

K.Landauer and H.Weil, *Die zionistische Utopie*, Munich, 1914.

M.Lazaron, *Homeland or State*, Baltimore, 1942.

Lenin on the Jewish Question, New York, n.d.

A.Léon, *Conception Matérialiste de la Question Juive*, Paris, 1946.

E.Levyne, *Judaisme contre Sionisme*, Paris, 1969.

E.Liebenstein, *The New Territorialism*, Jerusalem, 1944.

M.Lilienblum, *Palestinofilstvo, Zionism i ikh protivniki*, Odessa, 1899.

J.Mack, *Americanism and Zionism*, New York, 1944.

L.Magnus, *Zionism and the Neo-Zionists*, London, 1917; *Religio Laici Judaici*, London, 1907.

E.Marmorstein, *Heaven at Bay*, London, 1969.

M.E.Marrus, *The Politics of Assimilation*, Oxford, 1971.

I.Maybaum, *The Faith of the Jew in the Diaspora*, London, 1956.

C.G.Montefiore, *Liberal Judaism and Jewish Nationalism*, London, 1917.

J.Petuchowski, *Zion Reconsidered*, New York, 1966.

K.S.Pinson (ed.), *Nationalism and History*, Philadelphia, 1958.

Resistentia Schriften, *Zur Kritik der zionistischen Theorie und Praxis*, Frankfurt, 1970.

J.Rosenheim, *Kol Ya'akov*, Tel Aviv, 1954.

Schriften zur Aufklärung über den Zionismus, I and II, *Antizionistisches Komittee*, Berlin, n.d.

S.M.Schwarz, *The Jews in the Soviet Union*, New York, 1951.

M.Shenfeld (ed.), *MeKatowitz ad Yerushalayim*, Tel Aviv, 1954.

E.Silberner, *Sozialisten zur Judenfrage*, Berlin, 1962.

L.Simon, *The Case of the Anti-Zionists*, London, 1917.

J.Stalin, *Marxism and the National Question*, London, n.d.

A.Szanto, *Der Zionismus: eine nationalistische und reaktionäre Utopie*, Berlin, 1930.

H.Vogelstein, *Der Zionismus, eine Gefahr . . .*, Stettin, 1906.

S.Wallach, *Jews Must Choose*, Philadelphia, n.d.

N.Weinstock, *Le Sionisme contre Israel*, Paris, 1969.

A.Wiener, *Kritische Reise durch Palästina*, Berlin, 1927.

L.Wolf, *Aspects of the Jewish Question*, London, 1902.

W.Zukerman, *The Jew in Revolt*, London, 1937; *Voice of Dissent*, New York, 1964.

Chapter 9: The Weizmann Era

F.F.Andrews, *The Holy Land under Mandate* (2 vols), Boston, 1931.

C.R.Ashbee, *A Palestine Notebook 1918–23*, London, 1923.

C.Arlosoroff, *Leben und Werk*, Berlin, 1936.

N.Bentwich, *England in Palestine*, London, 1932.

I.Berlin, *Chaim Weizmann*, London, 1958.

M.Berlin, *MeVolozhin ad Yerushalayim* (2 vols), Tel Aviv, 1940.

K.Blumenfeld, *Erlebte Judenfrage*, Stuttgart, 1962.

A.Böhm, *Die zionistische Bewegung*, vol. 2, Berlin, 1937.

I.Cohen, *The Zionist Movement*, London, 1945.

J.Cohn, *England und Palästina*, Berlin, 1931.

ESCO, *Palestine* (2 vols), New Haven, 1947.

S.B.Feldman, *Brief Survey of the Mizrahi Movement*, London, n.d.

J.L.Fishman, *The History of the Mizrahi Movement*, New York, 1928.

F.Friedmann, *Das Palästina Mandat*, Prague, 1936.

N.Goldenberg, *General Zionism*, London, 1937.

S.Goldman (ed.), *Brandeis on Zionism*, Washington, 1942.

Y.Gruenbaum, *Chavle Geula*, Warsaw, 1929.

J.de Haas, *Louis Brandeis*, New York, 1929.

P.Hanna, *British Policy in Palestine*, Washington, 1942.

A.Hyamson, *Palestine Old and New*, New York, 1938.

O.Janowsky, *People at Bay*, London, 1938.

F.H.Kisch, *Palestine Diary*, London, 1938.

J.Klausner, *Menahem Ussishkin*, Jerusalem, 1942.

M.Kleinmann, *Hazionim Haklalim*, Jerusalem, 1945.

J.Lestschinsky, *Das jüdische Volk im neuen Europa*, Prague, 1934.

J.Lestschinsky, *Der Wirtschaftliche Zusammenbruch der Juden in Deutschland und Polen*, Geneva, 1936.

B.Lewkowitz, *Der Weg des Misrachi*, Vienna, 1936.

L.Lipsky, *A Gallery of Zionist Profiles*, New York, 1941.

P.Lubianiker, *Yesodot*, Tel Aviv, 1941.

R.Mahler, *Yehude Polin bein shte milhamot olam*, Tel Aviv, 1968.

M.Medzini, *Esser shanim shel mediniut eretz Israelit*, Tel Aviv, 1928

H.Meier-Cronemeyer, 'Jüdische Jugendbewegung', *Germania Judaica*, 1969.

M.Ostrowski, *Toldot hamizrahi beEretz Israel*, Jerusalem, 1943.

A.M.Rabinowicz, *The Legacy of Polish Jewry 1919–1939*, New York, 1965.

O.K.Rabinowicz, *Fifty Years of Zionism*, London, 1952.

Royal Institute of International Affairs, *Great Britain and Palestine 1915–45*, London, 1946.

A.Ruppin, *The Jews in the Modern World*, London, 1934.

H.Sacher, *Zionist Portraits and Other Essays*, London, 1959.

H.B.Samuel, *Unholy Memoirs of the Holy Land*, London, 1936.

Sefer Hashomer Hatzair, vol. I, Merhavia, 1956.

Sefer Mizrahi, Jerusalem, 1946.

S.Z.Shragai, *Hazon vehagshama*, London, 1945.

L.Stein, *The Palestine White Paper of October 1930*, London, 1930.

L.Stein, *The Balfour Declaration*, London, 1961.

J.Stojanovski, *The Mandate for Palestine*, London, 1928.

R.Storrs, *Orientations*, London, 1936.

C.Sykes, *Crossroads to Israel*, London, 1965.

M.W.Weisgal and J.Carmichael (eds), *Chaim Weizmann*, London, 1962.

M.W.Weisgal (ed.), *Chaim Weizmann*, New York, 1944.

C.Weizmann, *Israel und sein Land*, Berlin, 1924.

M.Wischnitzer, *Die Juden in der Welt*, Berlin, 1924.

S.S.Wise and J.de Haas, *The Great Betrayal*, New York, 1930.

Zionist Organisation, *Palestine during the War*, London, 1921.

Great Britain, Cmd. 1700 (Churchill Statement), London, 1922.

Great Britain, Cmd. 3530 (Report of the Commission on the Palestine Disturbances of 1929 – the Shaw Report), London, 1930.

Great Britain, Cmd. 3692, *Statement of Policy* (The Passfield White Paper), London, 1930.

Great Britain, *Palestine. Report on Immigration, Land Settlement and Development* (Hope Simpson Report), London, 1930.

Stenographisches Protokoll der Verhandlungen des XII. Zionisten Kongresses in Karlsbad, Berlin, 1922.

Also the Protocols of the thirteenth congress (London, 1924); fourteenth congress (London, 1926); fifteenth congress (London, 1927); sixteenth congress (London, 1929); seventeenth congress (London, 1931); eighteenth congress (London, 1934).

Chapter 10: European Catastrophe

Neville Barbour, *Nisi Dominus*, London, 1946.

Yehuda Bauer, *From Diplomacy to Resistance*, Philadelphia, 1970.

Menachem Begin, *The Revolt*, London, 1951.

D.Ben Gurion, *The Peel Report and the Jewish State*, London, 1938.

Abba Eban, 'Tragedy and Triumph', in Weisgal and Carmichael (eds), *Chaim Weizmann*, London, 1962.

ESCO, *Palestine*, vol. 2, New Haven, 1947.

Eton HaKongres (Twenty-first Zionist Congress), Daily, August 1939.

Henry L.Feingold, *The Politics of Rescue. The Roosevelt Administration and the Holocaust*, New Brunswick, 1970.

T.R.Feiwel, *No Ease in Zion*, London, 1939.

Great Britain. Parliamentary Debates, Commons, vol. 347 (1939) and vol. 350 (1939).

HaKongress Hazioni haesrim, Jerusalem, 1937.

HaKongress hazioni haesrim ve'echad, Jerusalem, 1939.

Samuel Halperin, *The Political World of American Zionism*, Detroit, 1961.

Ben Halpern, *The Idea of the Jewish State*, Cambridge, 1961.

Paul L.Hanna, *British Policy in Palestine*, Washington, 1942.

Raul Hilberg, *The Destruction of the European Jews*, Chicago, 1961.

Ira A.Hirschman, *Lifeline to a Promised Land*, New York, 1946.

J.C.Hurewitz, *Struggle for Palestine*, New York, 1950.

Jewish Agency for Palestine, *Memorandum to the Royal Commission*, Jerusalem, 1936.

Jewish Agency for Palestine, *Political Report of the Executive to the XX Zionist Congress*, Jerusalem, 1937.

Jewish Agency for Palestine, *Political Report of the Executive to the XXI Zionist Congress*, Jerusalem, 1939.

Jewish Agency for Palestine, *Report to the XIX Zionist Congress*, Jerusalem, 1935.

Jewish Agency for Palestine, *Documents and Correspondence Relating to Palestine, August 1939 to March 1940*, London, 1940.

Jon Kimche, *Seven Fallen Pillars*, London, 1950.

George Kirk, *The Middle East in the War*, London, 1952.

Kongress Zeitung (Twentieth Zionist Congress), Daily, August 1937.

Frank E. Manuel, *The Realities of American-Palestine Relations*, Washington, 1942.

John Marlowe, *The Seat of Pilate*, London, 1959.

J.L. Meltzer, 'Towards the Precipice', in M.W. Weisgal (ed.), *Chaim Weizmann*, London, 1962.

Arthur D. Morse, *While Six Millions Died*, New York, 1967.

Palestine Land Transfer Regulations, Cmd. 6180, London, 1940.

Palestine Partition Commission Report (Woodhead Report), Cmd. 5854, London, 1938.

Palestine Royal Commission Report (Peel Report), Cmd. 5479, London, 1937.

Palestine Royal Commission: Minutes of Evidence, London, 1937.

Palestine. Statement of Policy by H.M.Government in the U.K. (White Paper on Partition), Cmd. 5513, London, 1937.

Palestine. Statement of Policy (White Paper), Cmd. 6019, London, 1939.

Gerald Reitlinger, *The Final Solution*, New York, 1961.

A. Revusky, *Partition or Zionism*, New York, 1938.

Royal Institute of International Affairs, *Great Britain and Palestine 1915–1939*, London, 1946.

A. Ruppin, *Jewish Fate and Future*, London, 1940.

M. Samuel, *Harvest in the Desert*, Philadelphia, 1944.

Joseph B. Schechtman, *The United States and the Jewish State Movement*, New York, 1966.

A.H. Silver, *Vision and Victory*, New York, 1949.

Yehuda Slutsky and others (eds), *Sefer Toldot Hahagana*, vol. 2, Tel Aviv, 1959.

Stenographisches Protokoll der Verhandlungen des XIX. Zionisten Kongresses, Vienna, 1937.

Survey of International Affairs, vol. 1, London, 1938.

C. Sykes, *Crossroads to Palestine*, London, 1965.

Daphne Trevor, *Under the White Paper*, Jerusalem, 1948.

H.L. Weisman, *The Future of Palestine*, New York, 1937.

Chaim Weizmann, *Devarim* (4 vols), Tel Aviv, 1937.

Mark Wischnitzer, *To Dwell in Safety*, Philadelphia, 1948.

Stephen S. Wise, *Challenging Years*, New York, 1949.

Chapter 11: The Struggle for the Jewish State

Anglo-American Committee of Enquiry, *Report,* Cmd. 6808, London, 1946.

Y.Bauer, *Flight and Rescue: Brichah,* New York, 1970.

M.Begin, *Bamakhteret,* Tel Aviv, 1959–62.

D.Ben Gurion, *Rebirth and Destiny,* New York, 1954; *Bama'arakha,* Tel Aviv, 1957; *Medinat Israel Hamekhudeshet,* vol. 1, Tel Aviv, 1969.

R.Crossman, *Palestine Mission,* London, 1946.

B.C.Crum, *Behind the Silken Curtain,* New York, 1947.

ESCO, *Palestine,* vol. 2, New Haven, 1947.

J.G.Granados, *The Birth of Israel,* New York, 1948.

B.Halperin, *The Idea of the Jewish State,* Cambridge, Mass., 1961.

S.Halpern, *The Political World of American Zionism,* Detroit, 1961.

D.Horowitz, *State in the Making,* New York, 1953.

J.C.Hurewitz, *Struggle for Palestine,* New York, 1950.

Jon and David Kimche, *Both Sides of the Hill,* London, 1960.

A.Koestler, *Promise and Fulfilment,* London, 1949.

HaKongress Hazioni ha 22, Din veheshbon stenografi, Jerusalem, n.d.

Kovetz Lehi, Tel Aviv, 1959.

J. Marlowe, *Seat of Pilate,* London, 1959.

A.N.Poliak, *Bekum Medinat Israel,* Tel Aviv, 1956.

Proposals for the Future of Palestine, HMSO, Cmd. 7044, London, 1947.

Harry Sacher, *Israel: The Establishment of a State,* London, 1959.

J.Schechtman, *The United States and the Jewish State Movement,* New York, 1966.

Zeev Sharef, *Three Days,* London, 1962.

A.H.Silver, *Vision and Victory,* New York, 1949.

R.Silverberg, *If I Forget Thee, O Jerusalem,* New York, 1970.

C.Sykes, *Crossroads to Israel,* London, 1965.

D.Trevor, *Under the White Paper,* Jerusalem, 1948.

Harry S.Truman, *Memoirs,* London, 1956.

United Nations: *Ad Hoc Committee on Palestine, Summary Record of Meetings,* New York, 1947.

Chaim Weizmann, *Trial and Error,* New York, 1949.

World Zionist Conference, London, 1945.

Zionist Organisation and the Jewish Agency for Palestine: *Reports of the Executive . . .,* 23rd Zionist Congress at Basle, Jerusalem, 1946.

INDEX

INDEX

628